Egypt

The World of the Pharaohs

Egypt
The World of the Pharaohs

Edited by
Regine Schulz and Matthias Seidel

Contributing authors are
Hartwig Altenmüller, Dorothea Arnold, Edith Bernhauer, Günter Burkard,
Albrecht Endruweit, Rita E. Freed, Renate Germer, Manfred Görg, Manfred Gutgesell,
Friederike Kampp-Seyfried, Dieter Kessler, Rosemarie Klemm, Dieter Kurth, Ulrich Luft,
Eva Pardey, Daniel Polz, Wafaa el Saddik, Helmut Satzinger, Thomas Schneider,
Marcel Schoch, Regine Schulz, Matthias Seidel, Stephan Seidlmayer,
Abdel Ghaffar Shedid, Elisabeth Siebert, Hourig Sourouzian, Rainer Stadelmann,
Christine Strauss-Seeber, Martina Ullmann, Ursula Verhoeven,
Gabriele Wenzel, Joachim Willeitner, Stefan Wimmer, Susanne Wohlfarth

Contents

Introduction

Ancient Egyptian Art Today

"I want to see the Egyptian art first!" The writer has heard these words again and again from visitors entering The Metropolitan Museum of Art in New York for the first time. And indeed the Egyptian works of art – after the famous Impressionists – are the most popular in the museum. This has been the case for decades and still is, not just in New York but in museums all over the world.

What draws people in our computer age so irresistibly to the sculptures, reliefs, paintings, and small artifacts from the valley of the Nile in northeast Africa, objects that are now thousands of years old? Cyril Aldred, the great historian of Egyptian art, attributes their fascination to a simple but immediately compelling common denominator: "The overwhelming impression [of Egyptian art] is of its humanity." Irrespective of all the monumental temples and the many huge sculptures, the dimensions of most ancient Egyptian works of art can be surveyed at a glance, and their content is directly comprehensible. Men, women, and children stand before us in simple clothing, with a few readily understood symbolic attributes. They look straight ahead of them with eyes usually wide open to the world, and their bearing and gestures display self-confidence. Individuality is expressed not only through the precise depiction of physical features but by integration into such generally human categories as the "perfect woman," the "old man," the "corpulent dignitary," the "father of fine children," the "scribe," the "experienced, responsible official," and so on.

An awareness of connections is characteristic of all humanity and its actions. It is expressed in the three-dimensional stone sculptures of Egypt by lingering traces of the cubic form of the original block of stone: in the slabs and pillars that serve as background to the figures and in the "shadow areas" between one standing and one striding leg, between a leg and the pillar behind it, between torso, arms, and hands. The human figure, bound to the stone, is also secured and supported by it. If wooden and metal figures do not display these qualities but show the human body freestanding in space, it is not simply for technical reasons; the fact also emphasizes the special feeling of ancient Egyptian culture for stone as the noblest of materials and a pledge of eternity.

The existence of freestanding figures of wood and metal as well as stone statues is an impressive indication of the experimental creativity of Egyptian artists. The ancient Egyptians themselves thought that artists were directly linked to the divine creative power, as Cyril Aldred again has cogently put it.

All the figures in Egyptian reliefs and paintings are part of a firmly established fundamental system of order. The ordered structure of the world is expressed in the grid pattern into which all the walls are organized. The base lines of each rectangle in the grid may be understood as base lines in the literal sense, lines upon which humans and animals stand and act. Figures standing free in space almost always symbolize the dissolution of order in the Egyptian state. The arrangement of animals and human beings in registers, on the other hand, indicates a structural organization that was of the utmost importance, even in prehistoric times: an act turning the ambient chaos into a civilized world capable of being surveyed and controlled.

Within this system of order reclaimed from chaos, the rich world of life in the Nile oasis can develop freely and be made present in artistic depiction. These works of art show people not only plowing, sowing, harvesting, drawing up lists, storing and distributing food, but building ships and making furniture and other items for everyday use. We see them at celebrations with their families and friends, dancing, making music, and caring for the welfare of the dead in their tombs. As a priest, pharaoh mediates with the gods on behalf of humanity, and as a warrior he wards off the ever-present threat of chaos.

Order as experienced in this world also offers succor in the face of fears of death, for the sun – regarded by the Egyptians as the most important manifestation of the creator god – visits the underworld by night in a life-giving rhythm. Again, the sun generates and maintains life on this side of the tomb. Its light enables the artist to observe the finest of nuances in the faces and bodies of men and beasts, and to depict them on the surface area of sculptures with matchless realism, yet without abandoning the ordered structural system of Egyptian art as it had been created. The linking of that structural order with precise natural observation made the ancient Egyptians perhaps the most creative inventors of "signs" of all time, for their scribes devised and refined thousands of written characters. In hieroglyphic script, word and image were always one, and interpretive art was both writing and symbol.

Despite the great and varied powers of attraction exerted by Egyptian works of art on people of our own time, remarkably few books are devoted specifically to this aspect of the culture of the Nile Valley. The present volume represents an outstanding exception.

Dorothea Arnold

Foreword

Roman emperors, Arab scholars, early travelers, and millions of modern tourists coming year after year have been captivated, and still are, by the extraordinary and powerful fascination of the high civilization of ancient Egypt. The pyramids of Giza, the temple city of Karnak, and the Valley of the Kings, with the tomb of Tutankhamun, represent the unique values of a cultural achievement that will claim its place in the history of mankind for ever. It has a number of characteristic peculiarities that often baffle those from other cultural backgrounds, and to this day many of its real or presumed mysteries are the focus of enduring interest.

The search for ancient wisdom, mystical experiences and hidden treasures has led many who feel the fascination of Egypt to turn repeatedly to the same subjects, for instance the Sphinx and the Pyramid of Cheops, the mummies, the curse of the pharaohs, and powerfully "efficacious" symbols and rites. The chief reason for this may be the impressive size and quality of many pharaonic monuments and their durability in apparent defiance of time, an impressive contrast to the fast-moving world of modern man.

Such notions, born of wishful thinking, constantly come to the fore, and the really sensational aspects of ancient Egypt are often insufficiently appreciated. They include not only the astonishing technical and administrative achievements of the ancient Egyptians, the high standards of their script and their literature, their architecture and pictorial art, but also a concept of the world as a whole that was based on very exact observation of nature, and in which science and religion were an indissoluble unity. However, that concept of the world can easily tempt us to see ancient Egyptian society and its ideas as static, and thus to adopt far too superficial a way of studying them. In view of the countless monuments, the huge quantity of inscriptions and the almost inconceivable wealth of archaeological finds discovered and studied daily by thousands of scholars, we have a constantly changing picture of ancient Egypt to which we can do justice only by formulating a very wide variety of questions.

The present volume therefore hopes to convey an idea of ancient Egypt that is sufficiently differentiated to indicate the wide variety of development within the state, but it does not dispense with general statements that illustrate particular features of Egyptian culture. It is designed to provide a mixture of the familiar and the new, of basic and detailed information, with an extensive account of the various historic situations, social backgrounds, and religious systems of ancient Egypt. It also attempts to trace the view of the world as a whole that was adopted by the Egyptians themselves.

We would like to express our thanks to the staff of the Seminar für Ägyptologie of Cologne University, the Institut für Ägyptologie of Munich University and the Pelizaeus-Museum in Hildesheim for all their help with the work on this publication, and for making their facilities available to us.

We also offer our grateful thanks to all the authors and our colleagues who have contributed to this project in spite of their many other duties, and who have also been ready and willing to help us overcome a series of unforeseen difficulties. Finally, our thanks go to the editorial team for working with enthusiasm and commitment, in circumstances that were not always easy, on the production of this book, particularly unusual as it is for its wide range and its wealth of illustrations.

Regine Schulz
Matthias Seidel

Egypt's Path to Advanced Civilization

Stephan Seidlmayer

Culture and Natural Surroundings

Cultural development is very closely linked to geographical and ecological conditions, and Egypt provides a perfect example of that link. The valley of the Nile is a river oasis lying between two deserts: the wide expanses of the Sahara to the west, and the rugged mountain ranges separating Egypt from the Red Sea to the east. Only in the northeast does a narrow passage over the north coast of the Sinai give access to Palestine and the Near East. The river valley itself, protected and cut off from the outer world, spreads out into an increasingly broad alluvial plain north of the first cataract at Aswan, until the river divides into many distributaries to the north of Cairo, creating the broad fan of the Nile Delta. The country has low rainfall, but the annual flooding of the Nile in late summer provided the conditions for stable agrarian prosperity. These fundamental ecological factors have always, correctly, been recognized as the basis of the pharaonic culture that made such a deep impression on all succeeding generations.

However, these conditions were not always present. In seeking the prehistoric roots of Egyptian culture, we must also examine the changes in its geographical setting. The climate was subject to great variation. Two factors should be taken into consideration: rainfall and the inundation of the Nile. While the latter influenced living conditions in the valley itself, the former decided whether the bordering desert regions were habitable or not, thus determining the relationship of the Nile Valley to its surroundings, and the relations of its inhabitants with their neighbors.

The Beginnings

Finds of stone tools provide evidence of human life in the Nile Valley going back to the Early Paleolithic. However, it is impossible to discern any characteristics specific to Egypt as a cultural area at this time. Those characteristics emerge only in the Late Paleolithic, somewhere between 25,000 and 10,000 BC. During this period a phase of extreme drought drove the early human groups out of the savannas of the Sahara, where they had led a nomadic life as hunter-gatherers, and into the valley of the Nile. The Nile was still a small river at this time,

1 Head of a human idol
Merimda, the most recent settlement level; ca. the middle of the fifth millennium BC; clay; H. 11 cm; Cairo, Egyptian Museum, JE 97472. Materials representing hair and beard were originally threaded through the holes around the face. A cylindrical hole at the bottom of the head enabled the object to be mounted on a stick.

2 Hand axes
Theban area; early Paleolithic, pre-100,000 BC; flint; L. 16 cm; London, The British Museum, EA 41496–7.
Heavy hand axes trimmed to shape from flints are a characteristic and universal tool of the earlier Paleolithic. Many such tools are found in the gravel terraces running beside the course of the Nile in Upper Egypt.

3 Polished pottery with herringbone pattern
Merimda, the oldest settlement level; ca. the end of the sixth to the beginning of the fifth millennium BC; Cairo, Egyptian Museum. The pottery of the oldest settlement level at Merimda is of high quality. Bowls and deep dishes of fine clay were polished smooth with a hard object on the outside, and on the inside so far as could be reached. The process gave the surface a dark red-to-purple tone. In many items, a decorative band with a herringbone pattern was incised over the shoulder of the vessel below the rim.

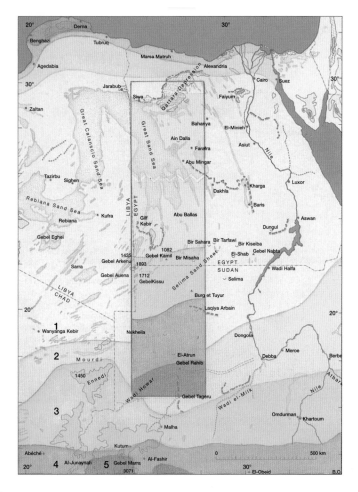

4 Diagram: the eastern Sahara
The climate of northeast Africa was subject to considerable fluctuations until the beginning of historical times. These variations sometimes caused shifts in the belt of vegetation, as shown in the diagram for the early fifth millennium BC. The zones are divided as follows: 1. Desert; 2. Desert with rain-dependent vegetation; 3. Semi-desert; 4. Thorn savanna; 5. Savanna with foliage plants (according to K. Naumann).

The Neolithic in Egypt

A far-reaching climatic change from about 10,000 BC, with a general increase in rainfall, led to high (sometimes extremely high) inundations of the Nile Valley, and the rise in precipitation made the bordering desert areas habitable once more. They became savannas well provided with watering holes and oases. There were settlements in the Sahara again, and innovations of great significance are evident here in the eighth and seventh millennia BC. The technological features of the Neolithic period make their appearance in early pottery and polished stone axes. People still lived a semi-nomadic life as hunters, and were not yet cultivating crops, but collecting the seeds of wild grasses. However, these groups seem to have domesticated cattle. The Near East, the Levant and Palestine, on the other hand, saw the building of fortified settlements, the beginnings of farming and the domestication of sheep and goats during the eighth millennium. The technological, economic and social features that, taken as a whole, were to be characteristic of a new era in the history of mankind, emerged and interacted over the entire extended area of northeast Africa and southwest Asia.

The Nile Valley in Egypt seems to have played no part in this process at first. The archaeological evidence is scanty, and a series of very high inundations may have destroyed entire levels of sites. The well-known sites at Elkab, in the Faiyum and at Helwan, however, show that the Egyptian way of life that developed at the end of the Paleolithic, in adaptation to conditions in the Nilotic area, continued into the sixth millennium BC. The unusual wealth of the area where they lived allowed the people to maintain a primitive lifestyle, and there was no change in these conditions until another period of drought, in the seventh and sixth millennium BC, forced the inhabitants of the border regions back into the Nile Valley. At this time, the end of the sixth millennium and the fifth millennium BC, the first Neolithic cultural groups appear in Egypt. The quantity of archaeological finds does not yet allow us to trace the merging of the Epipaleolithic traditions of the Nile Valley with the cultures of immigrant groups. However, the originally heterogeneous character of the Egyptian Neolithic can be accounted for only if it arose in this way.

A progressive increase in aridity, leading to the modern climatic situation in the middle of the third millennium BC, made the Nile Valley more clearly a strictly delimited area. In a process of internal colonization and the fusion of cultural factors, an independent form of culture appeared that can now be called genuinely Egyptian. Although it was late in coming by comparison with the cultures of neighboring areas, it developed all the more powerfully in the fourth millennium BC, and at the turn from the fourth to the third millennium it led to the creation of the pharaonic state and the advanced civilization of Egypt.

The Prehistoric Cultures of Lower Egypt

Merimda Beni Salama, probably the oldest truly Neolithic Egyptian site, is situated in Lower Egypt on the western border of the Nile Delta and, at its southern extremity, about 50 km northwest of Cairo. Recent excavations of this extensive site have identified five archaeological phases, the oldest of which probably goes back to the sixth millennium BC, while the later phases cover most of the fifth millennium BC.

The oldest cultural level of Merimda clearly shows independent features. In the excavator's opinion, the fishbone patterns incised into plates, dishes, and deep bowls of beautiful, fine, polished or burnished pottery indicate contact with the Near East, as do the arrowheads. On the second cultural level, however, there is also evidence of contact with

probably containing water in its bed only seasonally, but it offered subsistence. Sites where stone tools and traces of food have been found prove that a number of small groups had adapted to life in the conditions then prevailing here. Instead of traveling over large areas, they probably moved relatively short distances between seasonal campsites and ate the foods naturally available, depending on the time of year. Next to hunting and gathering, fishing in particular played a key role in the economy of these people.

Within this context, developments of great significance began to occur. The stone tools, predominantly small blades and geometrical microliths, do not look impressive at first sight. However, they were used to give a sharp edge or point to composite tools – knives, arrowheads, spears, fishhooks and harpoons – and they actually represent enormous technical progress. The remnants of food found show that provisions such as fish were already being dried and stored to tide people over the months of scarcity. The first step to economic foresight and the storing of surpluses had been taken. Finally, the increasing number of such sites over the course of time also shows that a semi-settled way of life made population growth possible.

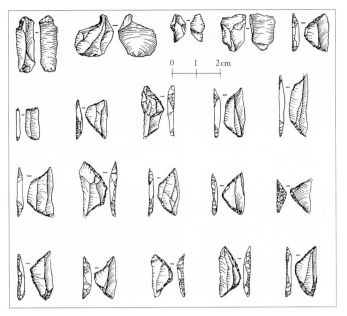

5 *Microlithic stone tools*
Esna region; Late Paleolithic, ca. 11,000 BC; flint.
Microliths are small blades and geometrically shaped flakes, often no larger than a fingernail, used as cutting edges and points in tools whose other parts were made of wood, reeds, and bone. Many kinds of different lightweight tools for hunting and fishing were made in this way, as well as weapons far more functional than those made of heavy stone. The intellectual progress shown by the manufacture of such complex implements out of a variety of coordinated materials is remarkable.

6 *Types of pottery from the Khartoum Mesolithic period*
Ca. seventh millennium BC.
Recent excavations have made the Central Sudan increasingly known as the cradle of a dynamic cultural development. At the end of the Paleolithic (the Mesolithic), ceramics with heavily decorated "combed" and imprinted undulating lines were manufactured there. Ceramic production in the Sudan can now be traced to the ninth millennium BC.

the south, in the shape of bone harpoons and axes of Nubian stone: a warning that the background of the Delta's prehistoric cultures should not be sought exclusively in the Near East.

In the settlement area, remains of oval huts have been found. Some of them were set a little way into the ground and had reed screens to protect them from the wind. Large baskets sunk into the ground acted as silos to store grain and similar produce. The people kept sheep, goats, and pigs. Most of the later pottery of this period contains a large admixture of straw and chaff. Consequently, it is of coarser appearance, but the process facilitated the making of larger vessels and narrower shapes: pots and bottles as well as dishes and bowls.

The making of stone implements was obviously very important in the Merimda settlement. Plenty of the requisite large flints were available here on the edge of the desert, and since the inhabitants of settlements in the central Delta had no access to this raw material, there was a wide market outlet for early barter transactions. Another particularly interesting feature is the first evidence of artistic activity in small terracotta figures of livestock, and a remarkably impressive head of a human figure.

A number of graves were also found in the Merimda settlement. The dead lay on their sides in shallow pits, in the fetal position. Grave goods are rare, and indicate no social distinctions between the dead. It used to be thought that they had been buried within the settlement, but new excavations show that over the long period during which it was inhabited the settlement zones extended further and further, so that at a later date there were dwellings above the old burial grounds. Finds corresponding chronologically more or less to those of Merimda are known to us from the Faiyum and el-Omari, near Helwan, southeast of Cairo. However, the later phase of the prehistoric culture of Lower Egypt, dating from the first two-thirds of the fourth millennium BC, is represented by the archaeological finds from the settlement of Maadi. The Maadi site also lies southeast of Cairo. An extensive settlement site and two associated burial grounds offer a broad cross section through its culture. The pottery is of a very specific kind here. Most important of all, at this period, copper tools, needles, fishhooks, and axes are represented in great quantity (or their existence can be deduced), and they were beginning to displace similar tools made of bone and stone. Copper ore, probably for use as a dye in cosmetics, has also been found in Maadi.

This material suggests intensive trade relations and contacts with the south of Palestine and the Near East. However, connections with the contemporaneous culture of Upper Egypt can also be traced, for instance in imported Upper Egyptian pottery and local copies of it, and imported slate. Taken as a whole, these items shows that the site was a commercial trading station between the Near East and the Nile Valley, also enabling the early cultures of Upper Egypt to gain access to those areas for the first time. New excavations in Buto, in the northwest of the Delta, have revealed an archaeological level corresponding to the Maadian culture, thus providing evidence that this form had quite wide geographical distribution. Important indications of contact with the Near East have also been found here, for instance terracotta pins resembling the clay studs used to ornament the temple buildings of Mesopotamia in the Uruk Period.

Several cemeteries illustrate the burial customs of the Maadian culture; as at Merimda, they were on a rather modest scale. The dead lay in shallow, oval pits, wrapped in matting and accompanied by a few grave goods such as clay vessels, and sometimes shells of the kind found in the burials of the Merimda culture. Other items, for instance combs or hairpins, are rare. There were great differences between the fourth millennium BC cultures of Lower and Upper Egypt, not only in the equipment they left but also in their customs and therefore, probably, in the social structures reflected in those customs.

Although recent fieldwork has placed our knowledge of the prehistoric cultures of the Nile Delta on a new foundation, the problems are as great as ever. The reason lies in the Delta's geographical situation. Unlike the sites of the Upper Egyptian valley, with its long bordering desert regions, the Delta sites are within the river's immediate area of contact, and in many cases they are now buried under thick layers of sediment.

Crucial questions, therefore, remain open. In the later tradition of pharaonic culture, Delta towns like Buto and Sais play an important part beside the great royal cities of Upper Egypt. What prehistoric realities lie behind this phenomenon? Were there rich trading towns in the Delta making contact by sea with the Near East, as one theory suggests? Were the buildings in such towns, their temples or palaces, in fact the predecessors of architectural forms such as the niche facades, undoubtedly inspired by the Near East, that suddenly appeared fully developed in the funerary architecture of the Early Dynastic Period? And what was the social and political organization of the Nile Delta in the fourth millennium BC? Did it consist of city states, or an extensive kingdom? These are all questions of critical import for our understanding of the rise of the pharaonic state.

The Archaeological Cultures of Upper Egypt

The northern part of Central Egypt is also poor in archaeological sites. Sites at both ends of this section of the valley, near the Faiyum and at Deir Tasa, south of Asiut, indicate that groups whose culture was of the Lower Egyptian tradition originally extended beyond the Delta and far to the south. We are on sure ground, archaeologically speaking, only on coming to the southern part of Central Egypt and the Upper Egyptian Nile Valley, where there is plenty of evidence, based on a wealth of finds, for the settlement of the country in the fourth millennium BC. The development of pharaonic culture rises primarily from this Upper Egyptian cultural tradition, and it also forms the chronological backbone of Egyptian prehistory.

The oldest truly Neolithic cultural group of Upper Egypt is represented by a series of settlement sites and cemeteries on the east bank of the Nile, near the village of Badari, south of Asiut. Chronologically, the early stages of this culture overlap the end of the Merimda culture in the north, about 4400 BC, and it coincides with the beginning of the Naqada culture in the early fourth millennium, around 3800 BC.

The settlement sites provide evidence of a series of small villages in the strips of flat desert bordering on the fertile country. Remains of huts, silos sunk in the ground, and vessels to hold provisions, as well as strata containing refuse from the settlements, show that the economic

7 A burial of the Maadi culture
Wadi Digla cemetery; fourth millennium BC. The body lies on its right side, legs drawn up, hands in front of the face. The head was probably originally resting on a stone to support it. Three vessels of the rounded shape typical of the Maadian culture are placed behind the back of the dead. There are no other grave goods.

8 Footed vessel
Near Heliopolis, cemetery of the Maadi culture; fourth millennium BC; pottery; H. 18 cm; Cairo, Egyptian Museum.
The characteristic pots of the Maadi culture are flat-bottomed, barrel-shaped vessels with a rim that narrows and then flares outward. Sometimes a conical foot is joined to the pots, as in the item shown. Round bottles and short-necked rounded containers were also made.

9 Ribbed and burnished dish
Matmar region; Badarian culture, end of the fifth millennium BC; pottery; Diam. 21 cm; Berlin, SMPK, Ägyptisches Museum, 23668.
The special technique producing ribbed and burnished surfaces is typical of the pottery of the Badarian culture. The same technique is found in several other cultural groups of the Nubian and Sudanese area, and therefore, like a preference for pots with rounded bases, constitutes evidence of contact with the south. In both these features the Badarian culture differs from the early Naqada culture, which existed side by side with it in Upper Egypt, at least for a time.

activities of these people covered a broad spectrum, including farming, the rearing of livestock, hunting, and fishing. Early forms of farming here did not involve too much hard labor. The river itself had created a system of natural dams and basins in the valley plain, and the principle of irrigation from a reservoir that was to be the basis of Egyptian agriculture, later perfected by the addition of artificial dikes and canals, was already provided naturally.

The dead were buried in small burial grounds on the outskirts of the villages, most of them lying on their left sides in the fetal position, eyes turned to the west. As a rule they were wrapped in matting and were often accompanied by a wealth of grave goods. While large clay vessels of coarse ware predominate in the settlement area itself, fine ceramics of great beauty are often found in the graves. Plates, bowls, and dishes were usually made of red or brown polished clay. The blackened rim produced by a special firing technique is characteristic. The surface of the vessel was often "combed" before polishing, giving an attractive ribbed effect.

The graves also contained a broad range of items chiefly relating to cosmetics and the adornment of the body. The carvings on bone and ivory are particularly striking. These utensils are often decorated with figures. They include stone cosmetic palettes, carved spoons for ointments, hairpins, decorative combs and bracelets of bone and ebony, and necklaces of turquoise beads, glazed steatite (soapstone), shells, and various stones. Copper is also occasionally found, made into pins and beads.

These finds in the Badarian cemeteries are the first manifestation on Egyptian soil of the highly developed funerary cult that was to have so much influence on ancient Egyptian culture in the future. Since the dead were buried with their most personal possessions and in their own clothes, the funerary cult also provided a medium for social display and the expression of social distinctions.

Features of the items found indicate the origin and external contacts of the Badarian culture. The technique of its pottery points

10 Ointment container in the shape of a hippopotamus
Mostagedda; Badarian culture, end of the fifth millennium BC; ivory; H. 6.3 cm; London, The British Museum, EA 63057.
The earliest emergence of the visual arts may be seen in the shapes given to everyday objects. Painting, decoration with figures, and finally the figurative structure of the entire item, as in this unusual piece, distinguish certain particularly expensive objects from the mass of ordinary utensils. However, a quantity of unexpected, imaginative shapes is found in prehistory and on into the Early Dynastic Period. With the development of the artistic genres of wall painting and monumental sculpture, everyday utensils were superseded as a medium for artistic expression.

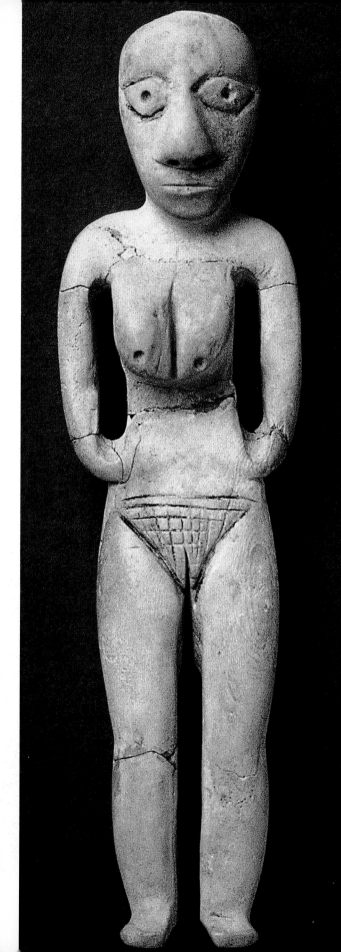

to Nubia, while the use of glazed beads, turquoise, and copper is of Near Eastern origin, like the domestication of certain species of animals.

The Early Naqada Culture

The Badarian culture was succeeded by the Naqada culture, the most important prehistoric culture of Upper Egypt. Its development can be traced without a break to the founding of the Egyptian state. Divided into three main phases (Naqada I–III), each with several subdivisions, it provides a line along which the technological, social, and political progress of the Predynastic Period can be clearly traced.

At the beginning of the fourth millennium the oldest phase, Naqada I (also known as Amratian) initially ran parallel to the Badarian culture, which was geographically next door to it, gradually superimposing itself and finally replacing it. However, the area of origin of the Naqada culture lies south of the known area of distribution of the Badarian culture, in the region between Luxor and Abydos, that part of the Nile Valley where the great routes running east and west crossed the river, linking the Red Sea and the oases.

In its ecological and tehnological character and its basic material features, the early Naqada culture resembles the Badarian culture. However, its unmistakable feature appears in the typology of its craftsmanship, particularly clearly illustrated once again by the finds from the cemeteries. In the Naqada I culture fine ceramic ware predominates: red-polished pottery, either plain or with a black rim. Besides plates and dishes, the main items are tall, flat-bottomed pots of a wide conical shape. Only in the course of time did the upper parts of such vessels become progressively narrower, so that bottles and voluminous pots could be made.

Red-polished pottery painted with cream line decoration is a special feature of the Naqada I culture. At first the patterns were geometrical, but they can sometimes be interpreted as stylized floral motifs. In the later Naqada I period, however, they have figure decoration most frequently showing animals, particularly those of the Nile Valley such as hippopotamuses and crocodiles. Now and then the decoration consists of scenic compositions with human figures, and these are clearly pictures of hunts, or sometimes perhaps scenes of worship or of battle. The first depictions of boats also appear. Along with painted decoration, small sculptural figures are sometimes set on the rims of vessels. The amount of figurative depiction in other artistic areas was also increasing. Female idols, only three specimens of which are known from the Badarian culture, now appear in greater numbers. Bearded male figures feature on pendants (perhaps amulets) and ivory sticks (known as "magic wands"). We can only speculate on the true function and significance of these items, but it is obvious that it must have lain in the symbolic or imaginative and not the practical sphere.

Characteristic rhomboid slate palettes and disk-shaped, stone maceheads are other common forms in the Naqada I culture. Maceheads appear as grave goods in high-ranking male burials, until finally, in historic times, the mace, now useless as a weapon, became a part of pharaonic regalia.

A crucial feature of the Naqada culture is its geographical dynamic. Setting out from its core area on the loop of the Nile at Qena,

11 Female idol
Badari; Badarian culture, end of the fifth millennium BC; ivory; H. 14.3 cm; London, The British Museum, EA 58648.
Three female idols from the Badarian culture are known, early examples of a genre that would grow and flourish slightly later; there are also many examples in the pharaonic period. Unfortunately, we have no information enabling us to interpret the symbolic significance of this piece with any certainty.

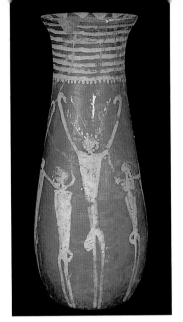

12 Tall vase with figurative scene
Naqada I period, first half of the fourth millennium BC; pottery; H. 28.6 cm; Brussels, Musées Royaux d'Art et d'Histoire, E 3002.
Depictions of scenes with figures are still rare in the Naqada I Period, and unfortunately it is often difficult to identify and interpret their highly stylized themes. The design running around the body of this slender vase shows two tall male figures wearing phallus sheaths, with arms raised and twigs in their hair, and a tall plant motif that cannot be more closely identified. Each of the spaces between these figures contains two smaller male figures, two of the pairs joined at the neck. The design can probably be regarded as a festive or ritual scene or tradition.

it spread north to the Asiut region even in its first phase (and perhaps as far as the area between Asiut and the Faiyum, where there have been no archaeological finds), and south to the far side of the first cataract. The colonization of hitherto uninhabited regions is not the only possible reason for this process. In the same context, the cultural adaptation of groups of people already living in the area must also be considered; they may still have led the life of hunter-gatherers and fishermen, presenting a less clear archaeological picture.

In any case, we should not be too ready to identify the spread of an archaeologically defined culture with the dispersal of a people or even a political structure. In studying the surface development of the Naqada culture in Egypt, we are primarily tracing the way in which a new lifestyle and economic strategy, a new complex of technological knowledge, a new kind of social organization and its forms of expression became established on a broad basis.

13 Bowl with image of two crocodiles and plant motifs
Naqada I Period, first half of the fourth millennium BC; pottery; L. 20 cm; Lyon, Musée Guimet, 90000045.
The pictorial motifs of the Naqada I Period concentrate primarily on the animals of the Nile Valley, showing how closely these people's ideas and way of life were connected with the valley itself. The image on this bowl is of two crocodiles in their natural habitat, indicated by fronds of vegetation. The painting style of the Naqada I Period, which favors filling in spaces with cross-hatching, here depicts the pattern of scales on the crocodiles' armor very precisely, and the fronds of vegetation have already moved away from the geometric style.

14 Black-rimmed pottery
Naqada I Period, first half of the fourth millennium BC; H. of largest pot 13.2 cm; Cairo, Egyptian Museum, JE 421247, JE 26530 (CG 2008), JE 41251.
The most characteristic kind of pottery in the early Naqada Period consists of red-polished vessels fired with a black rim. At first flat-based beaker shapes widening into a cone were the most usual; gradually, more enclosed, broad-shouldered cask-shaped vessels developed, along with a number of other shapes suitable for a wide range of functions. Quite often, pots of complex and ornate forms are found, for instance vessels with two tubular mouths. All these pieces were modeled freely by hand without the aid of the potter's wheel, and consequently most of them are more beautiful and regular than the factory-made products of the Old Kingdom.

The Material Evidence of the Naqada II Period

The archaeological finds provide records of the further material development of the Naqada culture. If several characteristics are considered as a whole, the Naqada II phase (also known as Gerzean) can be discerned from about the middle of the fourth millennium.

The black-rimmed pottery so predominant in the earlier period becomes less and less common. Two new technical developments were to acquire increasing importance. One was the use of Nile silt coarsely mixed with chaff for the production of ceramics. Such material appeared in the earlier finds at settlement sites, in the shape of rough and ready tableware, vessels and storage containers, but now it was used for a broad range of pottery utensils.

However, the most important innovation was undoubtedly the introduction of a kind of ceramic ware made from clay of different geological origin, principally found embedded in the limestone formations of the mountain ranges bordering the valley and known as "marl clay." Technically, this material is much more difficult to work, but it produces hard, dense ceramic ware of high quality, extremely suitable for containers intended for the storage of fluids, milk products, honey, and similar foodstuffs over a fairly long period.

Marl clay ware was used to make a new kind of decorated pot that superseded the white-painted vases of the Naqada I period. These pots

15 Female idol

Late Naqada I Period, mid-fourth millennium BC; unfired clay; H. 25 cm; Turin, Museo Egizio, Suppl. 1146.
Female idols are among the oldest and most widespread subjects of the early visual arts, and were still being made in great numbers in pharaonic times, side by side with the canon- ical art forms. This photograph shows an example that is one of the most impressive of its kind. Physical shapes are reduced to a basic schematic pattern of great expressive power. The eyes are emphasized with streaks of green cosmetic, and the body is painted with tattoos and (on the back) images of plants and animals.

16 Bearded male idol

Gebelein; Naqada I Period, first half of the fourth millennium BC; breccia; H. 50 cm; Lyon, Musée Guimet, 90000171.
The male idols of the Naqada Period are even more mysterious than their female counter- parts. The long, pointed beard regularly shown could be a precursor of the artificial beards later worn by gods and kings.

17 Narrow footed vessel with bored lug handles

Naqada; Naqada I Period, first half of the fourth millennium BC; basalt; H. 24.5 cm; Berlin, SMPK, Ägyptisches Museum, 12928.
Vessels such as this regularly feature in grave goods of the Naqada I culture; however, their shape is basically different from the other pottery of this culture. The narrow shape and the foot greatly resemble the forms found in the pottery of the Maadi culture in Lower Egypt. These pots were therefore probably imported from the north, while conversely such items as Upper Egyptian cosmetic palettes were known in Maadi.

are mainly small or medium-sized vessels, barrel-shaped or broad and globular, often with handles pierced by holes. The decoration, now applied on a cream ground in dark reddish-brown paint, tends to be limited to geometrical shapes, dots, and spirals. The idea was obviously to imitate the play of color of stone vessels, just as the shapes of the pots themselves resemble those of containers made of stone. Such vessels, especially containers for ointment, were very skillfully made of colorful, expensive hard stone and breccia. They were extremely popular at this period, and were to become a favorite sphere of crafts- manship in pharaonic culture.

Other pots had figurative decoration. A basically very limited range of motifs was assembled to form friezes running around the bodies of the pots. Stylized chains of triangular hills and zigzag lines suggesting water represent the landscape of the Nile Valley. There are also depictions of animals, flamingo-like birds and gazelles, and plants. The most prominent pictorial subjects, however, are ships: large,

18 Painted marl clay vessels
Naqada II Period, second half of the fourth millennium BC; H. 12.3 cm, 15.4 cm, 19 cm; Turin, Museo Egizio, Suppl. 4689, Suppl. 413, Suppl. 383.
Round and cask-shaped vessels with broad, bored handles imitate the expensive vessels made of colored hard stone that are also frequently found, and the painted spirals and dots on the ceramics seek to imitate the patterns of the stone. The depiction of a ship on the central pot, on the other hand, derives from the Naqada II repertory of figurative painting, in particular on large, rounded containers for provisions.

19 Stone vessels in animal shapes
Naqada II Period, second half of the fourth millennium BC; red breccia and graywacke; H. of ibis vessel 13 cm; Berlin, SMPK, Ägyptisches Museum, 24100 (ibis), 19738 (turtle), 16025 (fish).
These containers in the shape of an ibis, a turtle, and a fish illustrate the imaginative wealth and technical sophistication of the figurative working of vessels from hard stone. The colored effect of breccia was especially popular. The pots were used to hold cosmetic oils and pigments, and it is noticeable that the animal shapes chosen correspond in every way to those on the figurative cosmetic palettes of the Naqada II Period.

sickle-shaped boats with cabins made of woven matting and a great many oars. Emblematic standards reminiscent of the divine standards of later times repeatedly appear, planted upright in the boats.

Interpretation of the significance of these boats, and of the scenes as a whole, remains merely hypothetical. The ship later became a key motif of pharaonic culture. Ships featured in funerary rites, and were also used symbolically in divine worship and celebrations of royal magnificence.

The cultural atmosphere of the Naqada Period itself was marked by expansive dynamism, trade, and wide-ranging contacts. As an emblem of mobility, the ship suggests this momentum, and it may be that it developed into the symbol of dominance it later became within this cultural and historical context. Human forms are only subsidiary figures, most of them broad-hipped women with their arms raised. Sculptural versions of such figures also occur as idols.

The other main kinds of marl clay pots are high-shouldered vessels, barrel-shaped or at first sometimes bulbous, flat-bottomed and with undulating handles; they are known as wavy-handled pots. They derive directly from imported Palestinian models that are also found at the same sites. In the Egyptian version, where handles were very unusual, the shape went through a degenerative process, eventually producing the slender cylindrical vases of the Early Dynastic period, with a single narrow band of decoration. This morphological procedure is of importance to Egyptology. W. M. Flinders Petrie, founder of the scientific study of Egyptian archaeology, thought the chronology of Egyptian prehistory could be anchored to it. In principle, he was correct, but in view of the stock of archaeological material as a whole, his theory cannot be strictly applied today.

New characteristic shapes also emerge in other categories of objects in the Naqada II Period. Particularly striking is the variety of animal-shaped palettes used to mix cosmetics. A type of shield-shaped cosmetic palette with two heads of birds in the upper corners was the ancestor of the decorated ceremonial palettes of the Early Dynastic Period.

Large flint knives worked on both sides (or "retouched") and technically similar knives of a special fishtail shape (a form that continued in use as a ritual knife into the pharaonic period) provide evidence of a high degree of skill in working flint. Their shapes could hardly have been designed without the influence of copper knives of the same period.

In fact, the importance of metalworking continued to increase. Carved decorative pins and combs, amulets, beads of many different materials – in short a whole range of items belonging to the sphere of personal adornment – are represented in increasing quantity and variety.

The Cultural Dynamics

The Naqada II Period may be regarded as an era of rapid cultural change in the development of its material goods. An understanding of the way different clays react to firing, the smoothing and drilling of stone vessels, the manufacture of fine flint knives, and of course metalworking and the making of glazes all called for knowledge, training, and tools far beyond the level of domestic production. These objects

were made by specialists who could devote themselves entirely or very largely to their trade, and practiced it in professional workshops.

Such developments in craftsmanship had to be based on a corresponding development in agriculture to provide a material basis. Surpluses originally stored only as a cushion against occasional lean years had to be accumulated more and more systematically. Unfortunately the archaeological material at our disposal does not allow us to trace this process so directly. Here and there, however, we can see how the center of settlement was shifted from the desert borderland area into the plain of the valley itself. This suggests that cultivation of the inundated area was more and more dominant, while exploitation of the biotope of the outskirts of the desert, a region that was probably becoming impoverished anyway by the increasingly arid climate, became less important. Technically, it was a question of making the best possible use of the natural situation, by building small dikes and branch canals to improve the flow of water into and out of the natural basins. Large systems of dikes and canals were not necessary, and would have been pointless, since there was no need as yet to enlarge the cultivated area. In a situation where everything ultimately depended on the rising and falling of the river, which was not subject to human control, the exercise of social power could not hinge on the water supply, and it is a

20 Animal-shaped cosmetic palettes
Naqada II Period, second half of the fourth millennium BC; graywacke; L. of largest item 20.5 cm; Berlin, SMPK, Ägyptisches Museum, 14423 (elephant), 11341 (hippopotamus), 10595 (turtle).
Cosmetic palettes were a flourishing art form in the Naqada II Period. Previously, they had been simple rhomboid shapes; palettes

were now made in the shape of animals. Fish and birds are particularly frequent, but there are also palettes shaped like elephants, hippopotamuses, rams, turtles, and many other species. Sometimes the depiction goes into more detail than a mere outline. There are patterns of lines, relief work, and inlaid material, for instance for the eyes.

21 Painted marl clay pot
Naqada II Period, second half of the fourth millennium BC; H. 24 cm; Berlin, SMPK, Ägyptisches Museum, 20304.
The painting of this ovoid vessel shows the characteristic motifs of the Naqada II Period. Under a frieze of large triangles running around the rim, probably intended to show the range of desert mountains marching along the

valley, a large curved boat with oars and two cabins occupies the pictorial area. A standard with two streamers and a double arrow symbol, reminiscent of the emblem of the god Min, is planted in the middle of the boat. The bows are ornamented with two palm fronds. Above the boat are depictions of animals, a bird and several gazelles, a plant motif, and the figure of a woman with her arms raised.

22 Double-sided retouched knife

Naqada II period, second half of fourth millennium BC; flint; L. 26.6 cm; Brussels, Musées Royaux d'Art et d'Histoire, E 1236.
Valuable knives such as this, not meant for everyday use, are found in only a small number of tombs. However, we cannot tell for certain what kind of people were distinguished by having them as grave goods.

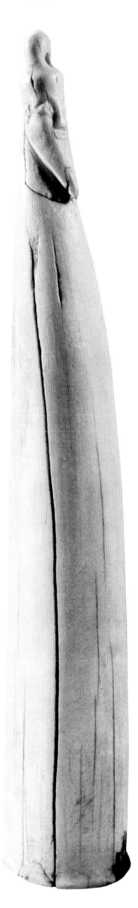

23 Female idol

Ma'mariya; Naqada II Period, second half of the fourth millennium BC; fired clay; H. 33.8 cm; New York, The Brooklyn Museum, 07.447.502.
Female idols with heads shaped like the heads of birds, broad hips and raised arms give sculptural expression to a pictorial theme current in painting of the Naqada II Period.

24 Staff with carved head of a bearded man

Naqada II period, second half of fourth millennium BC; ivory; H. 24 cm; Turin, Museo Egizio, 1068.
This ivory staff, with its end carved in the shape of a bearded male head, is hollow inside and has a groove running around the lower end. It was probably a closable case to hold ritual instruments, for the carved head raises this artifact above the level of ordinary everyday objects.

mistake to present the organization of the irrigation system as a prime factor in the evolution of structures of dominance in Egypt.

Crucial factors for an understanding of cultural development in the Naqada period are the territorial dynamic of that culture and its external relations. The appearance of wavy-handled pots in Egypt has provided important proof of intensive trading contacts in the Palestinian area. Egyptian imports in Palestine itself symmetrically complement that evidence. It is particularly easy to trace the foreign contacts of the Naqada culture in Nubia, to the south. There was an independent Neolithic culture in the Nubian Nile Valley, the so-called Nubian A group, and its sites were almost inundated with Egyptian imports. They are mainly pottery, vessels that originally arrived as packaging for agricultural produce exported by Egypt to the less fertile neighboring area, and were of such high quality that they continued in use. Nubian pots, on the other hand, have seldom been found in Egypt. We must suppose that the flow of trade the other way was in raw materials, as indeed the records show at a later date. Ivory, copper, precious stones, fine woods, and skins were among these imports. Some of the goods came from Lower Nubia itself, but some were brought north from Central Africa.

The further expansion of the Naqada culture in Egypt itself should be seen in this wide context. With the Naqada II phase, the cemeteries of the Naqada culture reached north into the Faiyum, no doubt the northern frontier of a region that had been continuously inhabited for a long time. Recent excavations in the Delta, however, have produced evidence that the Naqada culture was already emerging here towards the end of its Phase II, at least sporadically. The details of this process, like the extinction of the Lower Egyptian culture of Buto and Maadi that accompanied it, need further clarification of a kind that can be acquired only from archaeological fieldwork.

However, the finds we have do show that the spread of the Naqada culture in the Nile Delta, and the merging of the traditions of Upper and Lower Egypt to form a single countrywide cultural area, were not the result of political unification but the reason for it. Trade means more than the mere exchange of material goods. Intensive trade relations bring both sides together in an interactive framework; it may not be represented by any central institution, but it implies agreement on values, the mutual adaptation of social and organizational structures, cooperation, and competition.

The Rise of Urban Centers

A determining factor in the social evolution of the Predynastic Period was the rise of a number of different kinds of settlements. Beside the country regions where people lived in villages, towns began to form, early urban centers. Hierakonpolis, a town south of Luxor on the west

25/26 Wall painting in Tomb 100 at Hierakonpolis
Naqada II-c Period, ca. 3300 BC; painting on plaster; L. 497 cm.
This is the only known example of wall painting in tombs of the Naqada Period. However, painted fabrics of the same period are known, and it is possible that the decoration of a wall hanging was painted on the wall itself in this case, and has thus been preserved. In any case, there must have been some artistic medium in which the repertory of motifs illustrated here was developed and handed on.

bank of the river, provides an illustration of this development, and with its cult of Horus of Hierakonpolis it was regarded in pharaonic times as one of the kingdom's places of origin. Moreover, the extensive prehistoric legacy of the town has been relatively well studied in recent fieldwork.

There is evidence that a settlement had existed in the area since the beginning of the Naqada period, covering a length of 3 km and a breadth of about 400 m, and situated on the strips of desert land bordering the fertile country. The early settlement also extended for up to 2 km into a large desert wadi entering the Nile Valley at Hierakonpolis. We should not, of course, picture this large area entirely covered with buildings. Instead, it consisted of scattered (but relatively close) villages and farms and their burial grounds. However, these finds do prove that there was an increase in population density. There are traces of rectangular houses here even in the Naqada I period, in contrast to the simple round huts found elsewhere.

During the Naqada II Period and up to Early Dynastic times there was progressive concentration of the population in the region of the town itself, situated on a broad height of sedimentary soil near the mouth of the wadi in the fertile area. It can also be shown to have had temple precincts and fortifications since the Early Dynastic Period. Traces of specialized crafts occur repeatedly in the extended settlement area.

The furnaces, obviously designed with great skill, are particularly striking. Some of them are built into the wind channels of the sides of the wadi, so that very high firing temperatures, necessary for manufacturing ceramic ware of the highest quality, could be achieved by natural ventilation. There are also workshops where stone vessels were hollowed out and polished, and for working flint and boring holes in decorative beads. Kilns for drying grain also indicate the development of techniques for the preserving and storing of foodstuffs.

Such finds illustrate one important function of these urban centers. Specialized crafts were concentrated here as the pivot on which the exchange of craft goods and agricultural produce turned. However, trade beyond the immediate vicinity must also have been linked with the network of the regional economy. This was a place where supply and demand met, practical and organizational skills were concentrated, and information was exchanged: in fact the emphasis was on all the classic functions of a city as a form of settlement and a way of life. As it happened, Ancient Egypt did not take the path leading to the city state, but towns played a major part in its own development into a state.

27 Plan of excavations of the Naqada II palace and ritual precinct in Hierakonpolis
In the center, the floor of the oval courtyard area is shown. Around it, the places where buildings stood can be identified by the postholes. The dimension of the posts, some of which were entire tree trunks, gives an idea of the monumental character of the complex.

28 Hypothetical reconstruction of the complex
Architectural structures built solely of timber and matting can be only theoretically reconstructed from the postholes, all that is left for archaeological excavation. Here, there are traces of the locations of four gigantic posts on the southern side of the oval court, which may be interpreted as the facade of a monumental building. On the opposite side of the court, two large posts mark the location of a gateway with smaller rectangular buildings on both sides. Those features of the complex that can be deduced with certainty from the site as excavated allow comparison with the buildings in Djoser's pyramid complex, where such buildings made of posts and matting were imitated in stone.

It was here that an elite social class formed and institutional dominance was established, an aspect tangibly presented by the burial grounds linked to the settlements. In fact the development of the lavish funerary cult sketched out even in the earliest phases of prehistoric Upper Egyptian culture was now accelerating. The pits dug for interment become larger and rectangular, their walls were partially lined with masonry or reinforced with wooden planks, and side chambers to hold grave goods began to be made. The grave goods themselves became more and more extensive: a concentration of particularly fine objects is found in the tombs, in contrast to people's ordinary everyday utensils. Naturally not all the tombs were lavish to the same degree. Indeed, the increasingly long and varied scale of grave goods expresses an ever-extending range of social distinctions.

Very large tombs of this period now stood in their own small burial grounds. The type of the elite cemetery was emerging. Hierakonpolis has two such areas, taking over from each other throughout the period from the end of the Naqada I culture to Early Dynastic times. The combination of rich tombs with small, exclusive cemeteries in use over a long period shows that these were not individual cases of high-ranking persons: instead, they are the burial grounds of a whole social class, never comprising a large number of people, and deliberately set apart from the rest of society.

The expense these people could lavish on their tombs shows in itself that they must have occupied a key position in the economic network of the urban centers. In fact one can easily imagine the courts of the elite as centers for interaction between agriculture and craftsmanship, the local economy and external trade, in just the same way as the organizational structure of the palace economy functioned at the king's court in the early Old Kingdom.

A lucky discovery provides us with more detailed information about the role of the predynastic elite: that of the famous Painted Tomb of Hierakonpolis. To the south of the settlement, it was probably part of a Naqada II elite cemetery that, unfortunately, has never been systematically excavated. Architecturally, the tomb is conventional if very large: a rectangular pit 5 m long, over 2 m wide and about 1.5 m deep. The walls are lined with masonry and the room is divided by a partition projecting into it to create a side chamber for grave goods. Judging by the remains of the grave goods themselves, there can be no doubt that the tomb dates from the second half of the Naqada II Period (Phase II-c). However, it is the wall painting on the plaster of the burial chamber that makes it so spectacular, and unique among the finds here.

The main picture runs around three adjacent walls in a great frieze. The pictorial motifs are depicted separately on the background. The main line consists of six ships, five painted white and with curved hulls, the sixth distinguished by its black color and high bows. The ships are surrounded by depictions of hunting: huntsmen and hounds pursuing gazelles and ibex, and animals caught in traps. However, the scene does not remain in this everyday sphere. At one point a hero approaches two lions swinging his mace; elsewhere he is taming two lions in the character of "Master of the Beasts." Finally, there are pictures of men fighting, and underneath, in a perfunctorily added vignette, a depiction of the victor using his mace to smash the skulls of three enemies he has seized. This motif, the "Smiting of the Foes," became the great emblem of the power of the Egyptian king, endlessly reiterating and elaborating his claim to dominion until the end of pharaonic culture. A very recent discovery takes us a step further: on the outskirts of the desert, near the settlement area of Hierakonpolis, a palace and a ritual precinct of the same period have been identified. The reconstruction produced by the excavators shows a large oval courtyard surrounded by impressive buildings made of posts and matting. The design and the style of the buildings clearly anticipate the royal ritual precincts of the Early Dynastic Period, in particular the *sed* festival complex in the tomb of Djoser in Saqqara.

Approaching the Unification of the Two Lands

The elite class of the sophisticated Naqada II Period brings us to the roots of Egyptian kingship, and the beginnings of the construction of the unified state can also be deduced from the distribution in space and time of the archaeological evidence.

Early elite cemeteries exist not only in Hierakonpolis but also in Naqada, perhaps also in Diospolis Parva on the river loop at Qena, where evidence of at least one large tomb of a member of the elite has been found, and above all in the town of This (or Thinis) with its funerary site at Abydos, whose early history, going far back in time, has become known only from recent excavations. The neighboring Nubian culture was caught up in the surge of Egyptian developments too, although only rather later. Elite cemeteries are also known to have existed at Sayala on the loop of the Nile at Korosko, and at Qustul near the second cataract.

Furthermore, the distribution of the early elite cemeteries shows that the Naqada culture did not represent a homogeneous political structure. In the south of Upper Egypt alone, which has been archaeologically well investigated, there were at least three and perhaps four centers of similar standing. These areas were at the heart of chiefdoms or proto-states that existed side by side, and from whose amalgamation the pharaonic state of the Early Dynastic Period finally emerged.

The territorial aspect of the process can also be deduced from the distribution of elite cemeteries. In Phase III of the Naqada culture, around the time of the "unification of the two lands," there is evidence of outstanding princely tombs at only two places, Hierakonpolis and Abydos. And only in Abydos does the series of tombs of chieftains, beginning in the Naqada I Period, continue without a break to the tombs of the first kings who ruled a united Egypt.

The Rise of the State to the Second Dynasty

Stephan Seidlmayer

Early Historical Times

Archaeological research enables us to trace the origins of the pharaonic kingdom to the prehistoric past, and ancient Egyptian culture itself was aware of the great depths of time lying behind it. In the annals of the Old Kingdom, historical tradition already gave a long list of names of prehistoric rulers before the kings of the dynastic period. This list, based on oral tradition, may perhaps mention the names of some genuine prehistoric chieftains and petty kings, but it is impossible to check today. The later historical traditions of ancient Egypt, as they have come down to us in New Kingdom documents, transferred the prehistory of the pharaonic kingdom to the realms of mythology, deriving the origin of the kings' dominion over Egypt from the sun god's control over his creation. The kingship is ascribed to its first human bearer only after generations of gods and ancestral spirits have been mentioned. The King Lists give the name of Menes to this ruler, who was supposed to head the list of historical holders of the office. His image appears in the ornamental relief of the funerary temple of Ramesses II, in a procession of statues of royal ancestors, after Mentuhotep II, founder of the Middle Kingdom, and Ahmose, founder of the New Kingdom. The writers of classical antiquity, headed by the Greek historian Herodotus, relied on this tradition, and constructed an image of the first king of the First Dynasty as originator and cultural founder of the realm.

The search for this King Menes – so prominent in later tradition – in the contemporary sources of the Early Dynastic Period proves to be unexpectedly difficult. Judging by its form, the name Menes is the king's birth name. However, the oldest monuments call the rulers exclusively by their "Horus name," the name they took only on accession to the throne and bore by virtue of their royal role. Consequently it is only inference from a number of clues (although a fairly safe infer-

ence) that makes us believe that King Menes was the "Horus Aha" (the name means "warrior") whose tomb lies in the necropolis of the First Dynasty kings in Abydos, and who is named in many contemporary documentary records.

Why did the ancient Egyptian view of history present this king's emergence as such a turning point? Modern research, preferring to emphasize continuity and demonstrate slow, smooth developments by detailed analysis, does not find it easy to relate to this clear-cut, epochal line. Is it simply coincidence, the incidental result of some development in bureaucratic accounting techniques – or is it pure fiction? Can any definite meaning be found in it?

29 Fragment of the annals stone
Old Kingdom, Fifth Dynasty, ca. 2470 BC; olivine basalt; H. 43 cm, W. 25 cm; Palermo, Museo Archeologico, no number.
The Palermo Stone is the best-preserved fragment of a large rectangular slab on the back and front of which were recorded the annals of the kingdom of Egypt during the Fifth Dynasty, from its inception up to that time. In the upper register, an extract from the list of Predynastic rulers has been preserved. The kings from the First Dynasty onward are listed in the lines below. At this point information was available for each year of a reign, so the kings' names were written in the narrow horizontal lines, while a rectangular box for each year was placed in the broader areas beneath them. The years are named by important events, usually of a ritual nature. The height of the Nile inundation is noted at the bottom.

30 The great founders of the kingdom
Western Thebes, funerary temple of Ramesses II; New Kingdom, Nineteenth Dynasty, ca. 1250 BC.
The celebrations of the festival of Min are represented in the funerary temple of Ramesses II on the west bank at Thebes. A procession of royal statues carried by priests appears in this context. The series, showing the predecessors and ancestors of Ramesses II, begins on the left, with the founders of the three great periods of Egyptian history, the Old, Middle and New Kingdoms, as they are still accepted historically today: Menes (1), Mentuhotep (2) and Ahmose (3). They are followed, individually, by the kings of the New Kingdom as the immediate predecessors of Ramesses II.

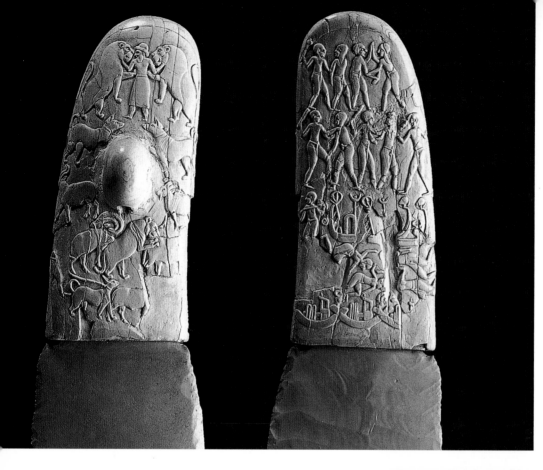

31 The Gebel el-Arak knife handle
Late Predynastic Period, ca. 3150 BC; hippopotamus ivory; H. 9.5 cm, W. 4.2 cm; Paris,
Musée du Louvre, E 11517.
At the top of the pommel side, this piece
shows the motif of the "Master of the Beasts"
taming two lions, a subject encountered
earlier in the Painted Tomb of Hierakonpolis.
In this case the figure is wearing Mesopotamian costume. The area below shows
hunting scenes. On the back, there is a frieze
of battle scenes; below them, two rows of
ships with dead men drifting among them in
the water.

32 Comb
Late Predynastic Period, ca. 3150 BC; ivory;
H. 5.7 cm, W. 4.0 cm; New York, The Metropolitan Museum of Art, 30.8.224.
Animal friezes are a frequent motif of Predynastic and Protodynastic artistic reliefs.
However, the composition of the rows here is
very unusual, and the same curious design
occurs in several other pieces.

The Unification of the Two Lands

Any discussion of this issue must revolve around the term "unification." It too is ultimately a concept of ancient Egyptian culture. The
land of Egypt was regarded as made up of two linked halves, Upper
and Lower Egypt, and the pharaonic kingship as a double institution:
the Pharaoh ruled both parts of the country. Every ruler had to perform
anew the ritual of the "unification of the two lands" on ascending the
throne. This pattern of geographical dualism permeates Egyptian thinking. Crowns, architectural forms, emblematic plants and divinities
were symmetrically allotted to the two parts of the country. It made no
difference to this state of affairs that the crown of Lower Egypt, the Red
Crown, for instance, is pictorially represented for the first time (in the
mid-fourth millennium BC) in the middle of Upper Egypt, in fact in
Naqada itself, and cannot possibly have been of genuinely Lower
Egyptian origin. Such cases make the conventional and historically
very dubious character of this schematic approach clear. Consequently,
only an unprejudiced study of sources from the period just before the
First Dynasty can show how far the key to understanding of the foundation of the ancient Egyptian state is to be discovered there. Archaeological finds help us to trace the rise of kingship through the
development of elite cemeteries and the tombs of rulers, a development
continuing into the Protodynastic period (in archaeological terms, the
Naqada III Period).

A remarkable example of this group of finds has recently been
discovered in excavations of the elite cemetery at Abydos, later the royal
cemetery. This tomb, consisting of bricks lining a rectangular pit, is
unexpectedly differentiated in structure. The burial chamber itself,
where the ruler to whom the tomb belonged was once laid to rest in a
wooden coffin, adjoins a complex of several other rooms, possibly

representing a palace building or a work of ritual architecture. By good fortune, large quantities of the grave goods have been preserved, including hundreds of imported clay vessels from Palestine that probably once held wine, and labels and ink inscriptions providing evidence of an administrative labeling system at quite a sophisticated level. Such material gives us some idea of the splendor and the political and economic resources of the courts of Predynastic rulers.

A few generations before Menes, the first inscriptions recording kings' names in the style of the later royal titulary appear. They show the Horus falcon on a stylized palace facade with the king's name inscribed in it. It has become usual to describe the series of rulers recorded like this as "Dynasty 0." It is not easy to form any detailed idea of the role of these kings and the areas over which they reigned; sometimes only local evidence is available. Only the last king of this group, Narmer, the predecessor and (if the records are correct) the father of Horus Aha or Menes, is mentioned throughout the country, from Hierakonpolis in the south to the northeast of the Delta; it was by Narmer at the latest that the political unification of the country was finally achieved.

Objects with relief ornamentation, particularly cosmetic palettes, ivory knife handles and maceheads, constitute an important source of information on this period and its culture, and contemporary historical events. In these items Egyptian art expresses itself for the first time in large-scale compositions on a high aesthetic level. There is clear Mesopotamian influence, stylistically and in the repertory of motifs; sometimes, as in the Gebel el-Arak knife handle, it is so strong that we may even assume the reliefs on this obviously Egyptian piece were executed for an Egyptian patron by a Mesopotamian artist living in Egypt. Animals are a major subject of this kind of art: both in compo-

33 Tomb of a ruler
Abydos, late Predynastic elite cemetery; Naqada III period; ca. 3200 BC.
The burial chamber of this complex (U-j) is the rectangular area top right in the picture. A complex of nine further chambers adjoins its broader side. They are linked to each other and the burial chamber by slits, thought to symbolize doors. Two more rectangular storage chambers were added to the longer side of this complex at a later date.

The frequent mention of the name 'Skorpion' (I.) under the inscriptions on the vessels makes it probable that this ruler was the owner of the tomb. The discovery of a single so-called Heka scepter of ivory which, together with the frond, formed the classic insignia of the pharaohs in ancient times, emphasizes the doubtless royal character of the structure.

34 Ceremonial palette
Hierakonpolis; late Predynastic Period, ca. 3150 BC; graywacke; H. 42 cm, W. 22 cm; Oxford, Ashmolean Museum, E 3294.
The decorated palettes of the late Predynastic Period derive from a basic type of shield-shaped palette already found in the Naqada II Period. Even then, the two upper corners bore animal heads, originally the heads of birds. In this example, from the votive offerings in the temple of Hierakonpolis, the outline of the palette is framed by two hyenas. A fundamental feature of palettes is a round bowl-shaped depression on one side, in which cosmetics were mixed. If monumental palettes were not simply for display, it is possible that they were used in religious ritual to anoint the image of a god.

35/36 "Cities Palette"

Late Predynastic period, ca. 3150 BC; slate;
H. 19 cm, W. 22 cm; Cairo, Egyptian
Museum, JE 27434 (CG 14238).
The fragment preserved consists of only the
lower third of a palette very similar in design
to the Narmer Palette. On one side, animal
forces are destroying seven cities, each of
which is shown as a fortified walled area.

Inside, a hieroglyphic symbol gives the city's
name. Above are remnants of the upper part
of the scene, showing the feet of people who
must have been part of a battle scene. The
animal friezes on the back are reminiscent of
the emblematic animal frieze ornamentation
of older ivory carvings, but here domestic
animals replace the rows of wild beasts.

site friezes of curious design, but chiefly in pictures of animals fighting, for instance dogs and predatory wild cats bringing down antelopes. Occasional fabulous creatures such as griffins and snake-necked panthers show that an imaginary world is being depicted. Other subjects are hunting, and above all war. These depictions show emblematic standards, personified as part of the king's retinue by the addition of arms, leading away bound enemies while the dead are torn to pieces by birds of prey on the battlefield. Lions and bulls triumphing over a human opponent are often shown in such contexts. They are symbolically exaggerated representations of the king, and the lion and bull were still the most common symbols of the pharaoh at a later date. The political content of the scene is thus clear, and can be identified even more precisely once there are accompanying inscriptions. For instance, one side of a palette preserved in fragmentary condition shows the destruction of fortified settlements by animals representing the protective powers of the king. The design on the back of the palette probably shows the loot being taken away: a herd of three rows of animals above an orchard with the inscription "Libya." It is clear that the battles to which the pictures relate went beyond Egyptian territory. However, the ceremonial palette of King Narmer, probably the best known item of this genre, is concerned with the political union of Egypt. On one side, it shows the king standing, striking down an enemy whose name (or that of the territory he represents) is inscribed next to him. The depiction on the right repeats the same information, partly in writing, partly in pictures. A falcon holds an oval of land on a leash; the land, personified by the addition of a human head, is identified by the papyrus reeds growing from it. The top part of the other side shows the king with his retinue, inspecting two rows of decapitated enemies. These scenes have always been thought to depict the conquest of an area in Lower Egypt, and a label from the time of Narmer recently found in Abydos, identifying a year by the "smiting" of a land identified by papyrus reeds, confirms this interpretation. The picture of the two captive snake-necked panthers in the lower part of the palette, with the depression to take ointment set in it, has been compared to the symbolic representation at a later date of the "unification of the two lands" in which the two emblematic plants of Upper and Lower Egypt are intertwined in a similarly symmetrical composition. Although it is impossible to give even an approximate account of the historical events this palette records, it may be regarded as referring to the final stage in the political unification of the country.

Stylistically, the Narmer palette shows the basic features of the canonical art of pharaonic Egypt in its clear-cut (one might almost say rigid) construction. By comparison with the drama of older pieces, the tendency toward a stiffly emblematic design is unmistakable. The whole concept of the representation also shifts from procedure to structure: from violence and war as deeds and events in themselves to the political order they have imposed. Consequently the picture of the king striking down his enemies represents not just a single moment and a single event, but the state's claim to dominion in general and its monopoly of power.

In most cases, it is not known in exactly what circumstances such pieces were found. The Narmer palette, however, and several ornamented maceheads, come from the temple of Hierakonpolis, where they had been dedicated to the god Horus. In this connection their format is interesting. More than twice the size of the everyday items from which their shapes derive, they are not only masterpieces of craftsmanship but already show art striving toward monumentality. Remains of monumental pieces have also been found in the temple of the town of Coptos, on the east bank of the Nile opposite Naqada, a little way north of Thebes. The finest among them are the torsos of at least three statues of the god Min, which must once have stood some

37 *"Battlefield Palette"*
Late Predynastic Period, ca. 3150 BC; gray-wacke; H. of main fragment, 32.8 cm; London, The British Museum, EA 20791.
Such ceremonial palettes with ornamental relief work are particularly valuable as records of political and historical events. The style links realistic motifs with elements of a script-like and emblematic nature, thus increasing its expressive force. The symbolic elements here are the lion, representing the king, and the emblematic standards depicting falcons personified by the addition of arms and leading bound enemies away. This theme in particular shows that the subject was a scene of war. However, the back of the palette (not shown) bears a purely emblematic design of two giraffes symmetrically placed by a palm tree; it is difficult to interpret its meaning.

38/39 *The Narmer Palette*
Hierakonpolis; Dynasty 0, ca. 3100 BC; gray-wacke; H. 64 cm, W. 42 cm; Cairo, Egyptian Museum, JE 32169 (CG 14716).
This palette, fortunately preserved complete, is both the finest and the last of the monumental palettes with relief ornamentation. Heads of the sky goddess Hathor, half-cow and half-human, adorn the upper rim, with the king's name between them written inside a palace facade motif. Below, horizontal lines divide each side into a number of pictorial registers showing several scenes of victory over a Lower Egyptian territory. As on the "Battlefield Palette," an emblematic animal represents the figure of the king at the bottom on the side with the bowl-shaped depression. In this case he is shown as a bull breaking through the fortifications of a town and trampling an enemy.

4 m high. These finds illustrate the importance and magnificence of the temples of the gods in the central towns of Upper Egypt. They also provide evidence of the part played by the practice of their cults as a platform for the ruler while the institution of the monarchy was emerging.

Seen as a whole, the period of the unification of the two lands has a character very much its own, and the unification itself proves to have been a long process rather than a sudden event. King Menes, therefore, does not figure as the creator of the country's political unity but as heir to it, and matters remained more or less the same. What had once been at dispute was now secured: unopposed, a unified political system covered the entire territory of Egypt within its natural boundaries, a state of such dimensions as the world had never seen before. The consequences of this new situation became the history of the Early Dynastic Period.

The Royal Cemetery of Abydos

With the founding of the unified Egyptian state, the monarchy had also acquired a new dimension, and a new character in its socio-political role. These are most closely reflected in the development of royal tomb architecture, which can be traced in the Abydos cemetery until the end of the First Dynasty. The necropolis lies in the desert area, some 1.5 km away from the strip of fertile land. Its tombs are rectangular chambers sunk into the desert soil and shored up on the outside by brick walls. The first stage of development came with Horus Aha.

His tomb, instead of having two chambers sunk side by side, as in the case of three previous tombs from "Dynasty 0," comprised three considerably larger chambers. In addition, his tomb shows the first evidence of a custom that flourished intensively for a short time, and then fell into disuse at the end of the First Dynasty: the custom of burying members of the royal household in neighboring tombs. The finds on the site as a whole make it hard to avoid concluding that the people buried here were in fact killed on the occasion of the royal funeral. Stelae referring to such tombs mention servants, including people of small stature ("dwarfs"), who were popular as part of a royal household, and women and dogs. In the case of Aha, thirty-six secondary tombs were laid out in three parallel rows. Investigation of bones cast aside by earlier excavators as worthless recently produced some results as surprising as they were revealing. King Aha had also taken a group of young lions into the next world with him as a symbol of royalty. Judging by the state of their bones, the animals had lived and were probably even born in captivity; in other words, the royal court kept lions.

In the next large tomb complex, that of King Djer, the new structural organization is completed and was the point of departure for gradual further development in following generations. Instead of several small chambers, there is only one rectangular burial chamber laid out in a deep pit in the desert sand, but it is a very much larger one. The traces still show that a wooden coffin was set against its back wall, and the king was buried in this coffin. The burial chamber was covered by a massive timber ceiling, above which, still within the top of the pit, a low tumulus of sand was piled up and enclosed by brick walls. It is not at all certain what these tombs looked like from the outside: new excavations have left no room for illusion on that topic. Since there are no remains of buildings, and indeed architectural factors would categorically prohibit it, the tombs can have had no monumental superstructures. The most that can be assumed is the presence of a low heap of sand contained within brick walls above the tomb. The pairs of stelae sometimes found in front of the tombs would have indicated a

40 Statue of the god Min
Coptos; late Predynastic Period, ca. 3150 BC; limestone; H. 177 cm; Oxford, Ashmolean Museum, 1894.105e.
The fragment of this colossal statue is from the temple of the fertility god Min at Coptos, where it stood with at least two other similar statues. These early examples of monumental temple sculpture already show the divinity with an erect phallus, as he appears in the later pictorial canon.

41 Tomb complex of King Qa'a
Abydos, the royal cemetery; First Dynasty, ca. 2870 BC.
In the middle is the royal burial chamber, with remains of the wooden coffin; it is surrounded by storage rooms and subsidiary tombs. The burial chamber could be reached from the stairway even after construction of the entire complex had been completed. After the burial this access was closed off by a stone slab, shown in place in the photograph.

42 Plan of the royal cemetery of Abydos
To the right of the plan are the relatively small double chamber tombs of Dynasty 0, and the tomb complex of Aha, with three large chambers and a series of sets of three subordinate tombs. Above and to the left are the adjoining group of First Dynasty tombs, each surrounded by subordinate burials. The gallery tomb of Khasekhemui is visible at the extreme left, dating from the late Second Dynasty.

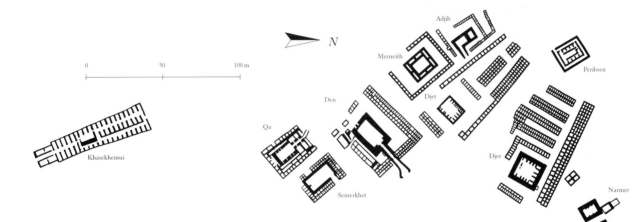

place of sacrifice; their inscriptions give the names of the kings and thus identify the owners of the tombs.

While at first the roofing of the pit and the erection of the burial mound could have been carried out only after the funeral rites were completed, later on, from the time of King Den in the middle of the First Dynasty, a stairway closed by stone slabs led down to the burial chamber.

The subsidiary tombs were arranged in a rectangle around the royal tombs themselves, first in large and then in swiftly dwindling numbers. Access was regularly left free to the southwest. In the tomb of Den, a stairway led from this opening down to an underground statue chapel adjoining the outside of the royal burial chamber: a place where the king could be ritually addressed, and where he could be imagined stepping out of his tomb.

The royal tombs of the First Dynasty thus acquired a new complexity, and were rich in symbolism, but they cannot be described as monumental even in the context of contemporary comparisons. However, there was yet another component to the royal tomb complex from the time of King Djer at the latest. Additional huge, rectangular precincts were laid out some 1.5 km north of the cemetery, on the borders of the fertile land near the town and the temple of the local god

43 Funerary stela of Queen Merneith
Abydos, the royal cemetery; First Dynasty, ca. 2940 BC; limestone; H. 157 cm; Cairo, Egyptian Museum, JE 34550
Beside the kings of the First Dynasty, a woman was buried in the necropolis of Abydos: Merneith, mother of King Den. She had probably acted as regent for her son until he came of age. Her tomb is typologically similar to the tombs of the kings, and like them was marked by a pair of stelae.

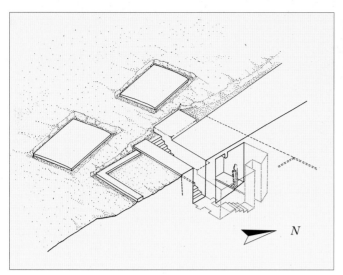

44/45 Back of the statue cult area in the tomb of King Den; reconstruction (above)
Abydos, the royal cemetery; First Dynasty, ca. 2910 BC.

The stairway leads down to a roofed chapel. Only one royal statue can be reconstructed, standing on the limestone plinth at the center of the back wall. Unfortunately, the statue that once stood here is lost.

Khontamenti, who was also god of the necropolis. Djer's precinct consists of a rectangle 100 x 55 m in size, surrounded by a brick wall over 3 m broad and at one time about 8 m high, ornamented on the outside by a regular niche pattern. Access to the precinct was through monumental gates at the southeast and northeast corners.

As yet we have very little idea of any buildings inside the precinct. Remains of a number of structures have been identified in later complexes, but it is to be supposed that the only ones erected at this date for certain ritual celebrations consisted of light materials (wood and matting) and have left no traces. These "valley precincts" are also surrounded by rows of subsidiary tombs. There is no doubt that such precincts are connected with the royal tomb complex: a direct line leads from their design to the entire pyramid complex of King Djoser at the beginning of the Third Dynasty at Saqqara. In its turn, this connection enables us to conclude with great probability that the valley precincts of Abydos served for the ritual of great festivals, celebrating the sacred role of kingship and the renewal of the king's dominion in the next world on the occasion of his funeral.

Memphis

The kings of the first two dynasties gave high priority to the traditions of the past by having themselves interred in the ancient cemetery at Abydos, in the territory of their town of origin This (the name of the town is the reason that the two first dynasties are described in classical antiquity as Thinite, from This).

However, it had been clear for some time that the true cultural center of the country was moving farther and farther north, to the area between the beginning of the Faiyum and the southern extremity of the Delta. This was a central location between the large cultivated areas of Middle Egypt and the Delta, and closer to the routes communicating with the culturally very important Near Eastern areas. Once the kingdom had been unified, Memphis was laid out here as the new

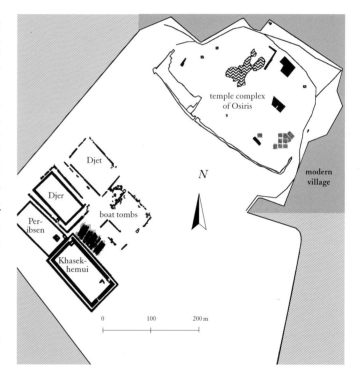

46 The ritual precincts of Abydos
The ritual precincts of the kings of the First and Second Dynasties lie in a concentrated group on the outskirts of the fertile land, near the town and temple of Abydos. Like the royal tombs themselves, the large, walled rectangles were surrounded by rows of subordinate tombs during the First Dynasty. New excava-tions have recently revealed a series of boat pits reminiscent of the later ship burials near the pyramids of the Old Kingdom. So far, however, the dating of this spectacular find remains uncertain; it may be of the First Dynasty or perhaps as late as the end of the Second Dynasty.

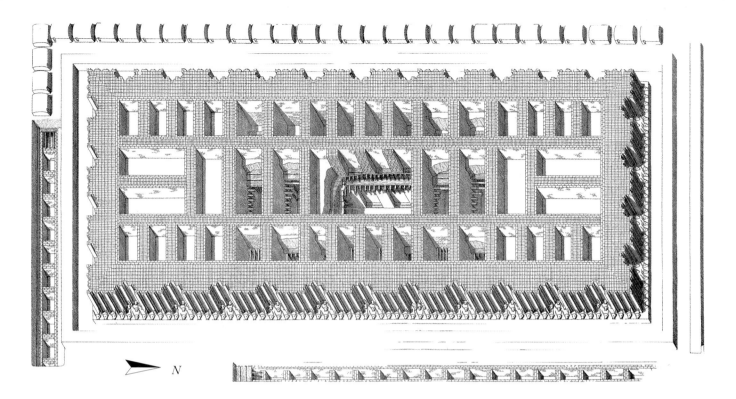

N

capital and the king's royal residence, and archaeological evidence
confirms the information provided by the later tradition of classical
antiquity, naming King Menes as its founder. Only recently have traces
of the early settlement been found under later strata of fertile land. Once
again, however, it is principally the evidence of the burial grounds that
allows us to draw conclusions about the importance of the site: these
burial grounds comprise the extended cemetery of Helwan and the
necropolis of the kingdom's elite in Saqqara.

The Great Niche Mastaba Tombs at Saqqara

The largest of the tombs standing here in a long line on the desert
plateau that rose above the old settlement are of truly royal dimensions,
but in design they are very different from the complexes of Abydos.
These monuments are large, rectangular buildings, known as mastaba
tombs, their exteriors decorated with a complex niche pattern that was
even more striking in its original condition because of the colored paint
on the plaster. Such niche tombs are found not only in Saqqara but
also at certain burial sites between Tarkhan, north of the exit route
from the Faiyum, and Abu Roash at the southern end of the Delta.
Only a single example of this genre is known in Upper Egypt, but it is
one of the oldest.

It cannot be supposed that such a complex type of building,
appearing here so suddenly during the rule of King Aha, had no
models. In Egypt, one would expect to find these models in urban
temple and palace architecture, and indeed there is such an example in
the Early Dynastic complex of Hierakonpolis, although unfortunately
the function of the building concerned is not clear. In terms of architectural history, however, the trail leads to the Near East, where the development of niche architecture from the pilasters required for structural
reasons to the complex type of decoration for official buildings found in
Egypt can be followed step by step. The niche facades in the tombs at
Saqqara were mostly built on a low base course, where the heads of

*47 Isometric reconstruction of a large niche
mastaba*
North Saqqara, tomb 3504, First Dynasty, ca.
3000 BC.
The rectangular body of the mastaba is
decorated on all sides with a complex niche
pattern and surrounded by an enclosure
wall, as well as a series of subordinate tombs.
The subterranean burial chamber inside the
tomb is covered by a timber ceiling and a
tumulus surmounted by the mastaba itself.

cattle modeled in clay were frequently placed. A slab stela was found
outside one niche at the southern end of the east wall of one particular
mastaba, showing the occupant of the tomb seated, and giving his title
in an inscription. It was probably originally set at the back of the niche,
as frequently seen later in the false doors of the early Old Kingdom.

Inside the tombs, the burial chambers were dug out of the desert
ground and, like the complexes of Abydos, were roofed with timber and
covered with a tumulus above which stood the superstructure. Here
again a stairway was introduced during the First Dynasty, giving access
to the burial chamber and allowing construction on the tomb to be
completed before the funeral.

Since the discovery of the great niche mastabas in Saqqara, there
has been dispute as to whether these were the real tombs of the First
Dynasty kings, in which case the complexes of Abydos would be cenotaphs or "false tombs," merely a remnant of tradition. In view of the
number of tombs at Saqqara, which exceeds the number of kings of the
First Dynasty, only some of the largest complexes could in fact be royal.
Nonetheless, it would be surprising to find the tombs of kings and officials promiscuously mingled and only gradually coming to differ in
terms of size. Later on, the royal burial place was always distinct in
quality from the tombs of even the highest administrative officials, just
as Pharaoh himself was not *primus inter pares*, but by virtue of his royal
office stood closer to the divine creator himself than to humanity.

However this difficult question may finally be decided, for all
their differences the close connection between the large niche tombs
and the royal tombs at Abydos must not be overlooked. They are linked
by the development of the shape of the burial chamber and the covered
tumulus above its roof. At Saqqara the tumulus is even sometimes

48 *Heads of cattle on the base course of the niche facade of one of the large mastaba tombs at Saqqara*
First Dynasty, ca. 3000 BC.
The animal heads themselves are modeled from Nile mud, but the horns of sacrificed beasts were added. The number of cattle heads surrounding the mastaba on all four sides illustrates the extraordinary expense lavished on funerary ritual.

49 *Stone vessel in the shape of a basket*
North Saqqara; First Dynasty, ca. 2900 BC; graywacke; L. 22.7 cm, W. 13.8 cm; Cairo, Egyptian Museum, JE 71298.
A specialty of the early art of stoneworking was the making of vessels in unusual shapes. They imitated containers made in soft, organic materials, as in this copy of a basket with its woven pattern carefully reproduced. Other vessels are shaped like leaves, palm trees, and so forth. Early architecture provides a parallel: timber and matting buildings were copied in stone, with all the constructional details peculiar to those building materials.

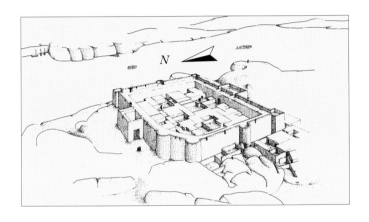

50 *Label from the time of King Den*
Abydos; First Dynasty, ca. 2900 BC; ivory; H. 4.5 cm; London, The British Museum, EA 55586.
The rectangular label has a hole in the top right corner, for a string to tie it to the labeled item. The front side names the year as the "First Conquest in the East." This incident is illustrated by the emblematic pattern of the "smiting of the foe" beside it.

51 *First Dynasty fortifications*
Elephantine; ca. 3000 BC.
The reconstruction shows the fortified complex, amounting to about 50 sq. m. and lying on the highest point of the island of Elephantine, to control river traffic. The masonry was built in several circuits, reinforced by towers at regular intervals.

found with a stepped exterior, which naturally calls the later Step Pyramid to mind. Subordinate tombs surrounding the main tomb were built at Saqqara too. Moreover, elements of later royal funerary architecture are anticipated in the large niche tombs.

This is particularly clear where a funerary temple actually adjoins the mastaba tomb on its north side, just as a temple does later in King Djoser's funerary precinct at the beginning of the Third Dynasty. This site is not an isolated find. One of the oldest mastabas had a complex of enclosed courtyards, with walled benches probably used for sacrificial purposes, on the north of the tomb precinct. A cult area north of the tomb therefore seems typical of the design of such precincts. Boats as grave goods, known from the pyramid complexes of the Old Kingdom, also seem to appear for the first time in the great niche tombs of the First Dynasty.

The royal tomb architecture of the Old Kingdom, then, is certainly based on a synthesis of elements from the entire spectrum of the funerary architecture of the elite. Nor is this surprising, for although the kings set great ideological store by their exclusive status, in sociological terms they were also members of the kingdom's elite. Their family members and the highest functionaries of their courts may be sought in the niche mastaba complexes of other cemeteries too.

From the beginning of the First Dynasty, these tombs provide us with our first view of not just the kings but the other leading figures of the kingdom, a clearly defined sociological group concentrated in the region of the capital, and this is almost the most distinctive cultural contrast between the period of the unification of the two lands and the Predynastic Period.

The Culture of the Elite at the Capital

The lavish nature of the grave goods preserved at Saqqara casts light on this group's lifestyle, a way of life very different indeed from that of the majority of Egyptians. They include furnishings and utensils of ivory and fine woods, ornamented with delicate carving, stone vessels in ornate forms, items sometimes elaborately constructed from parts consisting of various different materials. Large numbers of ceramic storage vessels to hold food suggest a life of luxury. These items bring to light for the first time the living conditions of the elite at the capital, and it was from those conditions that the culture of the Old Kingdom would spring.

Even more important in the context of funerary architecture is the development of major art forms. The thematic patterns and iconographic conventions of canonical art had already taken broad shape in the period of the unification of the two lands. At the time, as in the prehistoric period, pictorial design featured on everyday utensils, although some works already approached monumental form. The temple statues of Coptos pointed the way to the major artistic genres of a later date, and the process was greatly accelerated in the Early Dynastic period. Freestanding tomb stelae and stelae on false doors, as well as funerary statues, not only gave rise to important genres in the visual arts but defined their function and the situations in which they would be employed.

The Internal Structure of the State

The social structure of the early period, first perceptible in the tombs of the elite, and the elite culture expressing itself in those tombs, was based on an advanced state organization evident chiefly in the activities of the administration.

The first factor to be mentioned here is the development of the hieroglyphic script. We now know that markings incised and inscribed in ink on vessels go back at least to the Naqada III Period, and related labeling systems would continue in dynastic times side by side with hieroglyphic script. Independent in its origin, the form of its signs, and its systematic structure, Egyptian hieroglyphic script must be recognized as standing apart from other early scripts. The oldest sphere in which it and its earlier forms were used was the administration. Names of goods, information about their quality, dimensions, and quantity, names of institutions, the names and titles of officials, and so on could all be set down in writing, creating documentary records of economic circumstances and institutional structures. Through the new medium, information could be stored and passed on, so that economic transactions were no longer restricted by the limitations of personal memory and direct communication.

At about the same time, however, the possibilities of the script were also being employed in art. Here it was used to identify people, places and situations, and again, consequently, only a few nouns were noted down, the great majority of them names. Consecutive narrative texts describing events or complex circumstances were not written down until the time of the Old Kingdom.

The oldest papyrus roll dates from the First Dynasty, so even then there was nothing to prevent the composition of long documents. Unfortunately no one wrote on this roll. All we have are notes made by the officials themselves on labels, inscriptions, and seal impressions. A description of the nature and origin of the goods was inadequate for labeling foodstuffs: the date had to be recorded as well, and it is here that we find the first evidence of dating years. At first they were not

52 Lion-shaped playing pieces
Abu Roash, Tomb M. VIII; First Dynasty, ca. 3000 BC; ivory; H. 3.5 cm, L. 6.5 cm; Cairo, Egyptian Museum, JE 44918 A–F. Beautifully made luxury items are found in the tombs of the elite who lived in the capital.

Carving in wood, bone, and ivory, an art form extending far back to Prehistoric times, reaches its finest flowering here. Everyday items became little treasures, and were all part of the refined lifestyle of the upper class in the new state.

53 *Rock carving from Gebel Sheikh Suleiman*
First Dynasty, ca. 3000 BC; sandstone; Khartoum, National Museum.
The rock relief shows a ship, bound prisoners, and dead men drifting in the water. To the left is a stylized palace facade, with a falcon sitting on it in the manner of the Horus names of Egyptian kings. The name of the king himself, however, is not entered, a situation also found in some inscriptions on pots.

exchanges with neighboring countries, particularly Nubia and Palestine, can be traced far back into prehistory, when contact areas were created in border regions where Egyptian and non-Egyptian settlements overlapped. We can conclude that there was an open trading system from the distribution of imported and exported goods, particularly as it can be studied in the Nubian area.

The First Dynasty brought with it fundamental change. Monuments dating from the unification of the two lands already record warlike confrontations with neighboring peoples, and the year names of the First Dynasty, as they have come down to us in the annals and on labels, repeatedly mention such conflicts. A First Dynasty Egyptian rock carving far to the south, near the second cataract, shows that they were more than merely border disputes. The issue was not the conquest of foreign territory, but the assertion of Egypt's economic interests and trade, and the plundering of the resources of neighboring countries.

The formation of the state had given Egypt new opportunities and a new radius of political action. The Egyptians could equip expeditions in the grand style, could engage in expensive intermediary trade, and could promote their interests within a wide geographical area. They were in a position to assert themselves in armed conflict against attacks by local groups. In addition, Egyptian policies now emanated from an area within clearly defined territorial boundaries. The addition of a fortress to Elephantine, the island settlement at Aswan by the first cataract, made it Egypt's southernmost border town.

These developments had unwelcome consequences for the peoples of the neighboring countries. In Lower Nubia, exchange with Egypt had been an important factor of cultural ecology. The native settlement system of Lower Nubia collapsed with the advent of the First Dynasty, and the local population was forced into a nomadic existence. As a result, the development of Nubian chieftainships, which had run parallel to the rise of the Egyptian state up to this time, was nipped in the bud.

Egypt had thus risen to a unique position of dominance above the peoples surrounding it. As a great power surrounded by tribes, it was always easily able to claim unrestricted preeminence, and there is no doubt that this is where the roots of the calm self-assurance of pharaonic culture lay.

The Second Dynasty

The First Dynasty lasted about 175 years. Almost another 150 years were to pass before the Old Kingdom began. This Second Dynasty period saw the far-reaching transition from the oldest form of the archaic state to the structures of the first flowering of the pharaonic kingdom. Unfortunately, we have very little clear knowledge about these processes.

The tombs of the first three kings of the Second Dynasty were built in Saqqara. The first ruler, Hetepsekhemui, founded a royal cemetery there south of the later pyramid complex of Djoser, and therefore also some distance south of the necropolis containing the great niche tombs of the First Dynasty. The shortage of space in the necropolis made such a move essential.

Only the subterranean portion of Hetepsekhemui's tomb complex has been preserved, but even so it is impressive. A number of long storage galleries branch off from a long central corridor, which is entered by way of a ramp from the north and eventually leads past a number of barriers in the form of stone slabs to the king's burial chamber. This is a new design. Its purpose was to provide room for an extensive quantity of grave goods including furniture, tableware, and

counted but named individually by reference to particular events, especially rituals and festivals.

Among these rituals the so-called Followers of Horus, a ceremony held every other year, is particularly important. It was soon linked with a "count," and sometimes the subject of such a count is more precisely defined, being described as the "count of gold and fields" or the "count of cattle and small creatures." It is therefore assumed that this was a countrywide census for tax purposes. These counting periods were renumbered within each king's reign, beginning with the number one. During the period of the Old Kingdom this led to the usual later method of dating by the years of the royal reigns. The impressions on vessel seals and the clay seals on bags, boxes, and doors are another important source for our knowledge of the organization of the early state economy. They name the institutions concerned, the royal central estate with its sub-sections, storehouses and workshops, and the administrative officials responsible. From such data we can reconstruct the picture of a palace economy built up around the royal court, organizing agriculture, crafts, and trade. There does not seem to have been an administrative system covering the entire country at this time.

We can only form a very tentative idea of the officials of this period, but the available evidence indicates that the holders of the highest positions were indeed to be found within the palace administration.

Foreign Policy

It becomes particularly clear in the field of foreign relations that the First Dynasty had ushered in a new period. Extensive and frequent provisions, in fact a complete household that was buried with the deceased. The old concept of the grave as the home of the dead has never been taken so literally. The same concept, although not on such a grand scale, is echoed in the tombs of the highest social class, but the idea is clearly fading in the Third Dynasty. We do not know what the superstructure erected over this tomb looked like, but everything suggests that it would have been a huge mastaba, possibly ornamented with niches. And we have a name stela of the king's successor, similar to those erected at the royal tombs of Abydos. The tomb to which this particular stela refers has not been discovered, but another gallery tomb, next to Hetepsekhemui's, was built for the third ruler, Nynetjer.

During the reign of this early Second Dynasty ruler, the royal necropolis in Abydos was abandoned, significantly indicating that the kings were part of the upper stratum of the aristocracy of the capital, and the connection with the origins of kingship in distant Upper Egypt, now becoming more and more of a provincial backwater, was losing its importance. Subsequently, however, two kings, Peribsen and Khasekhemui, once again favored the old Upper Egyptian sites for their monuments. In his titulatory on the palace facade in the "Horus name," King Peribsen also replaced the Horus falcon by the animal appropriate to the god Seth, whose cult was based in Ombos (also known as Naqada), the central settlement of prehistoric Upper Egypt. Other kings are known only from their names in inscriptions on stone vessels from Lower Egyptian sites, or simply from the later King Lists. Here we face the difficult question of how to allot the different names making up ancient Egyptian royal titularies to the individual rulers. The evidence as a whole has led to the conclusion that the kingdom split into Upper and Lower Egyptian parts again during the second half of the Second Dynasty period. This may be so, but it has to be admitted that the political circumstances of the situation remain entirely unknown.

Both kings, Peribsen and Khasekhemui, built their tomb complexes at Abydos. By situating their tombs in the old royal ceme-tery of the First Dynasty, and laying out huge walled ritual precincts ("valley precincts" or "forts," as they were called because of their appearance, still massive today although the term itself is inaccurate), they emphasized a direct link with the old tradition of Abydos.

The ground plan of the tomb complexes, however, makes it clear that they were structurally influenced by the gallery tombs of Saqqara. They too surround the king's burial chamber with storage areas branching off from a corridor, although in the loose desert soil here the entire complex had to be built of brick inside a single sunken pit, while at Saqqara the corridors and galleries could be cut directly out of the local schist stone. A crucial factor in this formal relationship is the fact that the "Upper Egyptian" kings of the Second Dynasty were from the upper classes of Memphis, and by no means represent the revival of an unbroken local Thinite tradition. Khasekhemui is also represented by important monuments in Hierakonpolis. He had monumental buildings erected in the temple of Horus there, and blocks from a gateway bearing relief work that is stylistically very much attuned to the canonical art of the Old Kingdom have been preserved. A number of valuable votive offerings also demonstrates the importance ascribed to the shrine by this ruler, who originally also called himself Khasekhem. Khasekhemui had another ritual precinct constructed outside the town of Hierakonpolis, in the style of the valley precincts of Abydos, and they too had stone blocks decorated with relief work. Besides this king's monuments, there are other indications that the main features of the art of the Old Kingdom were taking shape during the Second Dynasty. Two blocks with relief work from the Temple of Hathor at Gebelein (between Hierakonpolis and Thebes) are notable monuments of this period, and it was a long time before anything equivalent appears in Upper Egypt. In the aristocratic cemeteries of the Memphite area, relief work slabs showing the deceased seated at the funerary repast also make their first appearance. These slabs were set in the masonry "false doors" in the cult areas of the tombs, with inscriptions identifying the names and titles of the owner of the tomb and the ritual situation it was

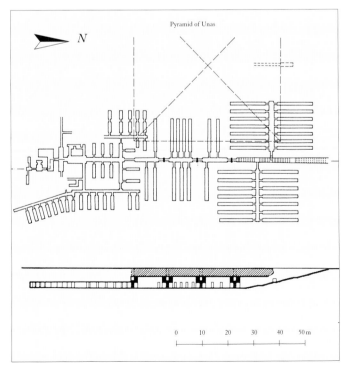

54 Tomb of King Hetepsekhemui
Saqqara; early Second Dynasty, ca. 2825 BC; ground plan and section (below).
The royal tombs of the early Second Dynasty used the technical possibilities of the soft rock of Saqqara to devise a new architectonic structure for the extensive storage areas already surrounding the tombs of the First Dynasty. Corridors with chambers branching off in a comblike pattern made a great deal of storage capacity available. Unfortunately these remarkable complexes have not been properly studied, and the plan as drawn is probably highly idealized.

55 Stela from the tomb of King Nebre
Saqqara; early Second Dynasty, ca. 2810 BC; red granite; H. 99 cm, W. 41 cm; New York, The Metropolitan Museum of Art, 60.144.
This item shows that the royal tombs of the Second Dynasty in Saqqara had name stelae, like the royal tombs of the First Dynasty in Abydos. As there, the ornamentation shows only the ruler's Horus name. These stelae too may well have been erected in the cult area of the tomb to identify its occupant.

56 Ritual precinct of Khasekhemui
Hierakonpolis; end of Second Dynasty, ca. 2720 BC.
The rectangular precinct was surrounded by a tall wall with a niche pattern and a monumental door. Inside, the remains of a building have been found; it has not yet been fully excavated. Since there are no indications of a tomb complex of Khasekhemui in Hierakonpolis, this seems to be a ritual precinct without any direct funerary connotations.

57 Relief slab showing King Khasekhemui
Hierakonpolis, the king's ritual precinct; end of Second Dynasty, ca. 2720 BC; granodiorite; H. 130 cm, W. 135 cm; Cairo, Egyptian Museum, JE 33896.
This block, part of a monumental gateway in the temple of Horus at Hierakonpolis, was decorated with a slightly raised relief. The scene has been ground down with a view to future reuse, so the image is now blurred, but nevertheless it is possible to make out the main image of the king and the goddess Seshat driving in the measuring poles for a temple building.

58 Statue of Khasekhem
Hierakonpolis; end of Second Dynasty, ca. 2720 BC; limestone; H. 62 cm; Oxford, Ashmolean Museum, E. 517.
The statue shows the king seated on a throne with a low back, wearing a narrow, calf-length cloak and crowned with the White Crown of Upper Egypt. The front of the plinth shows a personification of Lower Egypt, bound and struck down by an arrow. The whole plinth is surrounded by depictions of distorted corpses, and the number of dead is given at the front as 47,209.

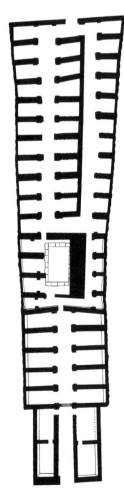

59 Ground plan of the tomb complex of Khasekhemui
Abydos, royal cemetery; end of Second Dynasty, ca. 2710 BC; entire L. ca. 70 m.
While the burial chamber at the center of the complex was made of limestone slabs, the other chambers were built of mud bricks. The structure of the ground plan seeks a compromise between a gallery tomb of the kind built in Saqqara and the technical limitations imposed by the desert soil of Abydos.

0   5   10 m

to serve. They were the germ from which the profuse pictorial ornamentation of the tomb complexes of great men in the Old Kingdom
were to develop.

The relationship between Upper and Lower Egypt in the second
half of the Second Dynasty is unclear. We do know that King Peribsen
was also honored by a funerary cult in Saqqara (although the date of the
establishment of this cult is not known for certain), and the existence of
a tomb in Saqqara for Khasekhemui has also been postulated. It was in
his reign at the latest that the relationship between the two parts of the
country was troubled by disputes and led to war. His votive offerings in
the temple at Hierakonpolis include large stone vases with inscriptions
describing a year as "Battle, defeat of Lower Egypt," and then the
symbol for the "Unification of Upper and Lower Egypt." Even clearer is
the evidence provided by the statues of Khasekhemui from the same
temple. Paradoxically, the phase of Upper Egypt's dominance came
irrevocably to an end with the victory of Upper Egypt over its Lower
Egyptian enemies, as recorded in the friezes on the statuary plinths.
The royal cemetery of Abydos was abandoned; however, the withdrawal
of the kings from their ancestral place of origin in This brought the
establishment of an administrative center for Upper Egypt whose
special position can be traced throughout the entire Old Kingdom
period. As with the founding of the First Dynasty, and as would be the
case many times in the future, the impetus for the creation of a unified
Egyptian state came from Upper Egypt, but structurally the north
always had the upper hand. And although the origin of the Egyptian
state lay in the policies of the Thinite dynasties, the development and
evolution of that state was to be shaped by Memphite influence.

1 Relief of Snefru
Wadi Maghara (Sinai); Fourth Dynasty, ca. 2620 BC; red sandstone; H. 112.5 cm, W. 133 cm; Cairo, Egyptian Museum, JE 38568.

King Snefru, as "Conqueror of Foreign Lands," smites a bearded Asiatic enemy with a mace. Under Snefru, worshipped as a god in the Sinai in later periods, the mining of copper and turquoise in the peninsula was intensified. The relief does not refer to any actual battle against nomadic peoples, but emphasizes the king's direct political and religious aura as protector of the Egyptians living and working in the area.

The Political History of the Third to Eighth Dynasties

Dieter Kessler

At the end of the Thinite Period (the First and Second Dynasties), which concluded the early history of Egypt, the country's political and economic center was finally fixed in the Memphis area. The distinguishing outward mark of the Old Kingdom (Third to Sixth Dynasties) consists of the gigantic pyramid tombs of its kings, appearing to defy time and decay. With some justice, the Old Kingdom may be called the age of the pyramids. However, behind the monumental stature of the pyramids themselves, suggesting the idea of huge power apparently concentrated solely on the person of the king, stands the will of an elite surrounding him. The prevailing economic system of the Old Kingdom was expressed in these buildings and the necropolises and pyramid towns attached to them. The striving for continued existence in the afterlife made provision for all members of the state community in this life and the next a necessity, and the king was at the center of this system of provision. He had power over the country, its inhabitants and its produce. He delegated that power to his officials, who in their turn were responsible for the people and property entrusted to their care. In the form of so-called "endowments to the dead," the powers thus delegated made provision in the immaterial world for the deceased official, and material provision for those to whom his funerary cult was entrusted. At the same time, all subjects had a part in the provision made by the royal funerary cult. Step by step, and parallel to the growing number of institutionalized cults in the country, such provision, at first limited to the capital, came to include the inhabitants of distant provinces. Extensive economic and religious developments lie behind the volume of building and the changes in the planning and location of the pyramid complexes of the Old Kingdom.

The Person of the Pharaoh in the Old Kingdom

The few available written sources for the early Old Kingdom do not enable us to draw any conclusions about the individual characteristics of the various kings. Later tradition portrayed some rulers, like Snefru, as good and others, like Cheops, as bad and cruel. These attributions need be taken no more seriously than similar evaluations in our own time. The queens were initially members of the royal house themselves; only in the later Old Kingdom were wives taken from the class of officials. Some of them assumed the responsibility for rule, since they ensured the succession.

The Development of Internal Policy in the Old Kingdom

The concentration of officials around the king was connected with the extension of the royal funerary complex. Provincial chieftains were replaced by civil servants sent out from the capital and controlled by it. Royal domains set up in the provinces – small economic units

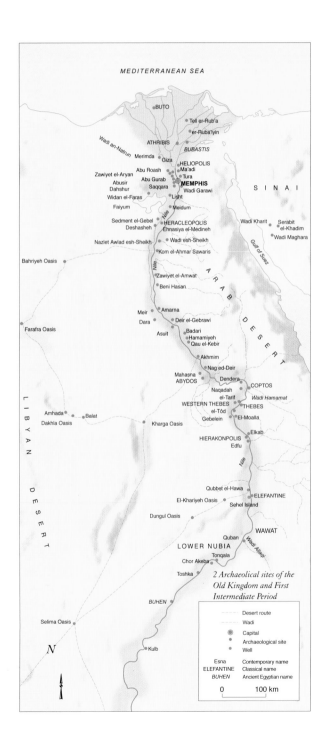

2 Archaeolical sites of the Old Kingdom and First Intermediate Period

3 Head of a statue of Mycerinus
Giza, the royal valley temple; Fourth Dynasty, ca.
2520 BC; calcite alabaster; H. 28.5 cm; Boston,
Museum of Fine Arts, 09.203.
Almost no political facts are known about the son
of Chephren and Queen Khamerernebti. His
pyramid was restored during the New Kingdom,
according to an inscription at the entrance. A
Saite period coffin inscribed with the king's
name, and dating some 2,000 years after his
death, was discovered inside the pyramid. His
original stone sarcophagus was lost at sea off the
English coast on its way to England by ship.

such as craft workshops, farming settlements, and fishing villages – delivered their products directly to the capital. The administrative regions were systematically organized. At the end of the Third Dynasty, under Pharaoh Huni, and the beginning of the Fourth Dynasty under Snefru, the construction throughout the country of small cult pyramids, not divided into chambers, was connected with these new royal domains: this is how the cult presence of the ruler was transferred to the provinces. The first provincial temples were dedicated under Mycerinus, and an increasing number of royal endowments was made available to the sacred complexes there.

During the Fourth Dynasty the army was commanded by royal princes. They led quarrying expeditions and supervised garrisons posted in the south (Elephantine) and the east (Heliopolis, Bubastis, the "Gate of Imhotep" where the trade route to Palestine began). Initially, the viziers who dispensed justice at this period were also drawn from their ranks. The kings of the Fifth Dynasty, descended from a family living north of Giza, concentrated on building temples to the sun, and the volume of complexes devoted to the cult of the dead at

Abusir was considerably reduced. These building complexes were now economically supported by the sun temples. Decentralization of the administration increased; even the viziers no longer had to be of princely rank. With Pharaoh Unas (ca. 2360 BC), a new family, perhaps from the Delta, came to power in unknown circumstances. The building of sun temples abruptly ceased, and the pyramid complex of Abusir was abandoned in favor of Saqqara. Now that the new god of the dead, Osiris, guaranteed religious transfiguration and provision for humanity, it was possible for an official to be interred outside the capital, in the provinces. Provincial administrative centres flourished. Abydos, the main center of the cult of Osiris, became the seat of the governor of Upper Egypt; the royal temple of Osiris-Khontamenti was fortified by royal decree.

Crucial reforms were carried out during the extremely long reign of Pepi II. The seat of the governor of Upper Egypt changed several times. Coptos, with its temple of Min, gained importance, and Thebes became the administrative center of the south. However, internal power struggles and murder at court (briefly placing one Nitocris,

sister of Pepi II, on the throne in 2218 BC) destroyed the infrastructure of the country and its supply network. The rulers who succeeded each other in Memphis in a series of brief reigns faced chaos in Upper Egypt: the region was splintering into several small, warring principal-ities. It was only with difficulty that the rulers in Memphis succeeded in restoring an administrative system that was generally acceptable to all parties. Nonetheless, the Memphite rulers were soon replaced by princes from Herakleopolis at the point of entrance to the Faiyum.

The Development of Foreign Policy in the Old Kingdom

Egypt had no external threats to fear during the Old Kingdom. However, it was well aware of the activities of the princes of the Nubian and south Palestinian regions, and kept a close watch on them. The annual festival rite in which the pharaoh repeated the ritual conquest of his enemies from all four quarters of the earth was a metaphorical way of asserting the superiority of the inhabitants of the Nile Valley. Potential enemies were magically destroyed by the ritual smashing of clay figurines. The purpose of foreign relations was to secure the trade routes and the neces-sary imports of raw materials. The increase in the building activities of the kings led to greater exploitation of sources of raw materials both at home and abroad, for instance the quarrying of calcite alabaster in Central Egypt, graywacke in the eastern desert at Wadi Hammamat, and basalt at Gebel Qatrani north of Lake Qarun in the Faiyum.

At the beginning of the Old Kingdom, probably under Djoser, copper mining was resumed in Wadi Maghara in the Sinai. The mining of its byproduct, turquoise, at Serabit el-Khadim must have begun not long after this time. Military control of the bedouin of the Sinai was a prerequisite of the industry.

Traditionally, timber for building was brought to Egypt from the harbors of the Levant, particularly Byblos. The construction of the necessary transport ships is repeatedly mentioned in the Egyptian annals. Numerous Egyptian items inscribed with royal names and

donated to the temple of the Near Eastern goddess Baalat at Byblos, linked here with the Egyptian goddess Hathor, indicate peaceful trade relations with that city. Egyptian objects have also been found at the trading center of Ebla (Tell Mardikh). Representations of stags and bears in royal mortuary temples of the Fifth Dynasty suggest gifts from foreign countries. A delivery of incense from Punt, somewhere in present-day Somalia or Eritrea, is mentioned for the first time in the reign of Sahura (ca. 2490 BC). Military actions were also frequently undertaken to secure trade interests.

Toward the end of the Fifth Dynasty, tomb decoration begins to show scenes depicting the conquest of Asiatic cities, seagoing vessels with Asiatic crews, and nomads of emaciated appearance. It is difficult to imagine that actual events such as battles in southern Palestine lay behind these subjects. Under Pepi I, however, at the beginning of the Sixth Dynasty, an attempt was made to extend Egyptian control to that area. Egyptian armies conducted several campaigns against bedouin "sand dwellers," and went as far as a mountain they called "Nose of the Gazelle," probably Mount Carmel in Palestine.

There was a campaign on a smaller scale against Libyan tribes in the reign of Snefru (ca. 2620 BC), in which 1,100 prisoners were taken. The trade routes in the south and in the western oasis were again threatened by armed Libyan raiders around 400 years later. As a result, an Egyptian "controller of oases" was specially stationed in Dakhla.

Also in Snefru's reign, at the beginning of the Fourth Dynasty, the records mention Egyptian campaigns in the south. Some 20,000 soldiers invaded Lower Nubia, stealing cattle and allegedly taking 17,000 prisoners in one campaign, and 7,000 more in another; the captives were put to work as laborers or auxiliary police. However, the large number of soldiers deployed casts light on the Egyptian plan to keep soldiers permanently stationed in the south and to build new fortresses, for instance at Buhen. This policy meant that the trade routes, the stone quarries and gold supplies from Wadi Allaqi in the eastern desert, and the quarries of hard stone in the west, could all be supervised.

Under Pharaoh Izezi (ca. 2405–2367 BC) there is evidence for the first time of an expedition going even farther south. Bartered trade products such as skins, ivory, and incense – and a dancing dwarf for the royal residence – probably came from the land of Yam in the Dongola basin. Caravan leaders from Elephantine ventured on this dangerous journey through the desert with the aid of native bedouin, interpreters, and soldiers. The route that could be traveled by donkey was known as the Oasis Road. By way of Bahriya, Dakhla and the small oases of Kurkur, Selima, and Dungul, it led to the region south of the third cataract.

The princes of Lower Nubia, themselves threatened by bedouin raids, basically supported Egyptian policy, and even supplied contingents of men for the campaigns in Asia at the beginning of the Sixth Dynasty. The threat to the trade routes increased only toward the end of the Sixth Dynasty. Under Pepi II, there was further fighting against intruders in Lower Nubia, and three expeditions to Yam were undertaken. A series of reports gives a clear idea of these eventful journeys. One expedition leader had to bring home to Elephantine the body of his father, who had died in southern Egypt, and the bedouin killed another expedition leader who was building ships by the Red Sea. As a result, trade with the interior of Africa soon ceased entirely.

6 Group portrait of Sahura with the local god of Coptos
Fifth Dynasty, ca. 2490 BC; anorthosite gneiss; H. 63.5 cm; New York, The Metropolitan Museum of Art, Rogers Fund, 1918, 18.2.4.

Sahura's pyramid is in Abusir, and his sun temple has not yet been rediscovered. The god accompanying him here carries the local emblem of Coptos, consisting of two falcons. Sculptural groups of this kind, showing the king with local divinities, are also known from the Fourth Dynasty.

7 Seated statue of Queen Ankhnesmerire II with her son Pepi II
Probably from Saqqara; Sixth Dynasty, ca. 2270 BC; calcite alabaster; H. 39.2 cm; New York, The Brooklyn Museum, Charles Edwin Wilbour Fund, 39.119.

Queen Ankhnesmerire II, from a local princely family of Abydos, ruled for her son while he was under age. The type of the mother and child figure therefore has some basis in reality, although Pharaoh Pepi II is shown in this illustration as an adult.

Royal Tombs from the Age of the Pyramids

Rainer Stadelmann

Until recently the transition from the Thinite era to the Old Kingdom seemed to have been marked by distinct political changes, and to have been a cultural turning point. However, new research into the tombs in the cemeteries of Abydos and Saqqara shows us that there was neither a dynastic change nor a cultural breakthrough. It appears from seal impressions that Djoser, first king of the Third Dynasty, brought provisions for and sealed up the tomb in Abydos of Khasekhemui, the last king of the Second Dynasty. Several kings from the beginning of the Second Dynasty had already sited their tombs – spacious galleried complexes with massive superstructures – in the central area of Saqqara, the royal cemetery of the Third Dynasty. Khasekhemui – Djoser's father or father-in-law – seems to have had both a large tomb at Abydos and an enormous gallery tomb in the form of a "Buto-type" mastaba in Saqqara. The troubling tendency for single rulers to have two or more tombs is encountered frequently in Egyptian history, and it cannot be satisfactorily explained by interpretations of some of these structures as cenotaphs, or memorials.

For the ancient Egyptians the preservation of the entire body was undoubtedly an essential and fundamental condition for life after death. Besides this there were, early on, other ritual totems for preserving the deceased king's physical presence and spirituality. These are, in order of importance: the portrait statue, the royal stela, and the royal tomb. These various images and different homes for the deceased king – mummy, statue, stela, pyramid, and tomb – were first brought together in monumental architectural form in about 2680 BC in the tomb precinct of Djoser, constructed in view of the royal palace.

To this extent the reign of Djoser marks an important watershed, the start of a magical period, in which Egypt emerges from its dark early history, and the brilliance of the Old Kingdom begins: the Age of the Pyramids. This is how the Egyptians themselves saw it, and in Djoser's reign they recognized a real beginning, a new era, although the ancient Egyptian view of life was in fact cyclical rather than historical. It was seen as a succession of recurring events, as in nature, structured by annual festivals and the royal jubilees.

In one of the few pseudo-historical documents from ancient Egypt, known as the "Turin Royal Papyrus," from the beginning of the Nine-teenth Dynasty – a list of kings with their dates – the name of Djoser is given special emphasis by the addition of a brief summary. That Djoser should be valued and honored in this way thousands of years later stems not, interestingly enough, from the political union or pacification of the country, or from foreign conquests, but from the fact that he was regarded as the initiator of monumental stone architecture, a role that historically he shares with his son and chief architect Imhotep.

Rough blocks of stone were occasionally employed in and on tombs of the Archaic Period, but Djoser and Imhotep discovered worked stone as a building material and with it created the first monumental architecture, buildings whose forms and symbols gave shape to the state of Egypt. In the stone buildings and courts, which were now "everlasting" thanks to the material, the idea was that the deified king should continue to celebrate, as was his lifetime role as ruler, the rituals and cult practices that ensured the preservation of the world order established by the gods. With death and deification this became his eternal task. Each king therefore had to construct his own tomb precinct and his own pyramid as palace for the next world, and as representation of the eternal Egypt of the afterlife.

This remarkable representation in stone of a state philosophy did not come about suddenly or arise out of nothing. By the reign of Djoser, Egypt had existed as a single country for several hundred years. With unification the old nomadic ways of the leading Upper Egyptian tribes of the First Dynasty were intermingled with the more settled, architectural culture of the peoples of the Delta region.

The different cultural traditions and contrasting geographical realities found their expression in funerary architecture. In the relatively narrow river valley of Upper Egypt the tombs lie mainly on the edge of the desert on either side of the Nile, protected from the annual floods. The earliest are shallow grave pits with a sand tumulus that rises just above the level of the desert. By contrast, the tombs of the earliest ruling class of the more urban state of Lower Egypt could only be built on the higher ground of inhabited sand banks, and deep shafts were ruled out due to the level of groundwater. The tomb was protected by its superstructure. From this feature developed a form of house-tomb with exterior walls decorated with niches, the "Buto-type" mastaba.

---

8 Mortuary complex of Djoser
Saqqara; Third Dynasty, ca. 2690 BC.
The tomb precinct measures 540 by 278 m, and is the oldest monumental structure in the world entirely built of worked stone. The monumental royal tomb in the form of a stepped pyramid, surrounded by stone chapels, cult buildings, and processional courts is an eternal cult setting for the king as mediator between the mortal and divine worlds. Built in lasting material, it is an ever-lasting image of Egypt and of Egyptian society. The Step Pyramid in the center is both tomb and royal palace for the afterlife; at the same time its stepped form presents an image of Egyptian society with king at the apex, his royal household, court officials, civil service, craftsmen, and peasants below.

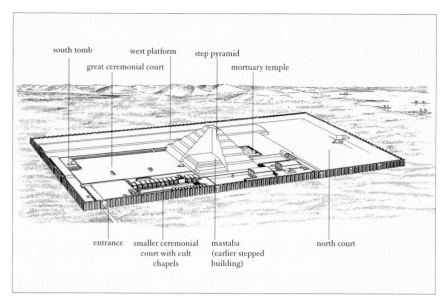

south tomb · west platform · step pyramid

great ceremonial court · mortuary temple

entrance · smaller ceremonial court with cult chapels · mastaba (earlier stepped building) · north court

9 Perspectival reconstruction of the Djoser complex
The development of the first example of monumental stone architecture can be seen best in the Step Pyramid. Originally there was a three-tiered step mastaba within a smaller tomb precinct that was altered in a second period of construction, first to make a four-step pyramid, and then finally altered to a towering six-step building. The increased height of the pyramid necessitated the enlargement of the precinct to the north and west.

10 The south face of the Step Pyramid
Saqqara, Djoser mortuary complex; Third Dynasty, ca. 2680 BC.
Beneath the broken facing of the pyramid the stepped mastaba of the original building is visible. It is noticeable that in the second building phase improvements were made in construction techniques. In constructing the stepped mastaba relatively small, convenient blocks of stone – somewhat larger than bricks – were still in use, laid in horizontal courses. But in the construction of the Step Pyramid large blocks were used. Further-more, in the first decade of building work in stone, improvements in construction techniques and economy of labor were made, namely the adoption of a building method using a series of layers, with the outer layers inclined approximately 18–20° toward the center, which automatically produced a gradient of 70–72° in the outer layer. In this way a considerable saving of labor could be made in the preparation of stone for facing. It also produced a reduction of weight of the building itself and a means of maintaining the correct angle of slope.

11 Statue of a provincial god
Probably from Saqqara, mortuary complex of Djoser; Third Dynasty, ca. 2680 BC; anorthosite gneiss; H. 21.4 cm, W. 9.7 cm; New York, The Brooklyn Museum, Charles Edwin Wilbour Fund, 58.192.
The figure of a deity stands in front of a tall rear panel, naked except for the loincloth hanging from a belt, holding a stone knife in his right hand and wearing a helmet-like wig. The iconographical details suggest the function of the figure as a provincial deity, while the execution suggests a date in the Third Dynasty. Along with other statues of a similar type and size, two of which are known, the examples here possibly stood in the small niches of the chapel in the *sed* festival court in the mortuary complex of Djoser. One might speculate that in their complete form in this spot they would have represented the provision of tribute from the whole country for the deceased ruler.

It can be shown that this type of tomb first appeared in a princely burial in Naqada and in the large niche mastabas at Saqqara from the beginning of the First Dynasty, which appear there suddenly in the reign of Hor Aha. These are refined tomb buildings of the Lower Egyptian house-tomb type, with massive, virtually solid superstructures, up to 50 m or 100 Egyptian cubits long, 15–20 m or 30–40 cubits wide, and over 5 m or 10 cubits high. Their whitewashed facades, punctuated by niches, were a magnificent display of royal presence above the northern cliffs of Saqqara. If they were not royal tombs or cenotaphs, then they were surely the tomb buildings of queens and the highest princes, impressive power architecture of the ruling dynasty.

The Mortuary Complex of Djoser

Before Djoser's mortuary complex there were differences in use of space between the Upper Egyptian royal tombs of Abydos and those in the Lower Egyptian royal cemetery. Djoser took forms that had developed in the separate regions through geographical and cultural differences, and combined them harmoniously in one complex and in a single tomb building. Superficially, it was dominated by the form and arrangement of palace tombs of the "Buto-type" mastaba. Thus far, scholars have sought to explain the origins of the Djoser precinct by a very abstract concept, namely as a construction that combines the two types that had existed alongside one another in Abydos for generations: the valley complex and the so-called tumuli of Abydos. However, since it became known that the Abydos royal tombs were not in fact burial mounds of any substantial height, but were covered by no more than a rather unattractive sand bank barely rising above the desert, this theory has become distinctly questionable. Far more likely is that in the construction of the Djoser complex, nearby tomb buildings in the royal cemetery of Saqqara, the "Buto-type" mastabas of the First and Second

Dynasties, were used as a model. Although we know little about the character of Djoser from contemporary sources – the only reliable information we possess are his buildings, his statue, and the reliefs depicting him – it seems nevertheless possible that he was responsible for the innovative concept of royal palace for the afterlife. He would have been supported by his kindred spirit, the architect Imhotep.

Recent experimental research into the layout of the building has shown that the tomb precinct was not originally conceived on such a gigantic and all-encompassing scale, but that it grew over a period of more than twenty years in several building phases, with alterations to the layout. At first the complex was to have been about half its size, extending 300 m from north to south, and 113 m east to west, but with the actual architectural elements already laid out and partially completed. The elements built in the first stage of construction included the 10.5 m-high stone enclosure wall with niched panels, the royal tomb with a mortuary temple to the north, the south tomb above the southern enclosure wall with a chapel, the facade of which has a distinctive frieze of uraeus cobras, the great ceremonial court between these two tomb buildings and the small ceremonial court in the eastern part. An important distinction between this and earlier royal tombs is the relatively precise orientation of the whole site to the four cardinals (the four compass points); the variation from the north–south axis, as it was then, was no more than 3°. The boundaries were marked by tall stelae bearing the names of Djoser and his queens, with the protective figure of the mortuary god Anubis. The superstructure of the king's tomb was planned from the very beginning as a three-tiered step mastaba that, like the south tomb, was oriented east–west; this had the effect of enclosing the great ceremonial courts to the south and north between the high buildings. Only in a second construction phase, when the three-tiered mastaba with the king's tomb and the south tomb were already nearly complete, was the superstructure of the mastaba converted into a stepped pyramid. In one of the earliest phases this was to consist of four tiers. This plan, as one can see on the east side where the structure lies open, did not develop beyond the first two tiers of the mastaba, at which point it was decided to extend the structure in breadth and height into a six-tiered pyramid 62.5 m in height.

The alteration of the step mastaba into a stepped pyramid gave the king's tomb its exceptional prominence within the entire tomb complex. In contrast, the shape of the south tomb remained as an elongated east–west-oriented mastaba, only just rising above the south perimeter wall. The presence of two tombs in one precinct with largely identical underground structures is one of the unexplained peculiarities of the Djoser complex. The fact that this double pattern carries on in the southern pyramids of later pyramid precincts does not simplify interpretation. Both burial chambers are built from large granite blocks at the bottom of a 28 m-deep shaft. Because of its internal dimensions, only the granite chamber under the north tomb can have served as a burial place. Various objects were discovered there in the last century including the gilded skullcap of Djoser. The tomb chamber of the south tomb, on the other hand, was too small; it was empty and without trace of a burial. Most likely that chamber contained a transportable, gilded wooden statue that was regarded as equivalent in importance to the body of the deceased king. Nevertheless, the south tomb, which was found empty, was sealed in a similar manner to the

tomb underneath the pyramid where the king's body was buried. The entrance to the granite chamber was through a round opening, which was sealed from above by a granite plug weighing several tons, and which must have been suspended in the antechamber up until the burial. The burial chambers are connected by a system of underground galleries that served to store the enormous quantities of provisions for the afterlife. On the east side of the shafts of both tombs a second system of galleries branches off to form a rectangular gallery around a section of solid rock. The walls of the galleries were decorated with blue-green glazed tiles.

A series of eleven shafts on the east side of the step mastaba led 30 m deep into galleries underneath the king's tomb. The royal family would have been interred in these, although only the five northernmost galleries were found to have been lined with stone or wood; several alabaster sarcophaguses were found for the burial of children, but no queen. The six southern galleries, on the other hand, were filled with incredible numbers (approximately 40,000) of stone vessels of varying shapes and containing a variety of different materials, among which were a number of vases bearing the names of kings of the First and Second Dynasties.

The raising up and widening of the original step mastaba into a six-tiered pyramid meant increasing the size of the ground plan and

14 Enclosure wall with entrance gate
Saqqara, mortuary complex of Djoser; Third Dynasty, ca. 2680 BC.
The niched perimeter wall had fifteen gates, of which fourteen were dummies. Only the tower in the southeast corner led into the main mortuary complex. This carefully reconstructed section of wall clearly shows its derivation from the brick building method of earlier days.

15 Entrance hallway
Saqqara, mortuary complex of Djoser; Third Dynasty, ca. 2680 BC.
Behind the entrance in the southeast corner of the complex stretched an entrance hallway 54 m in length, its roof supported by projecting spur walls. These are joined to half columns that closely resemble bundles of reeds in form and decorative effect.

16–18 The "Blue Chambers"
Saqqara, mortuary complex of Djoser; Third Dynasty, ca. 2680 BC.
Chambers and passageways were cut almost 30 m underneath the pyramid, as beneath the south tomb; architecturally and in their organization they represent sections of the palace for the king's use in the afterlife. Particularly remarkable is the covering of broad sections of the walls in turquoise porcelain tiles that were intended to represent the palace's wickerwork hangings and which have given their name to this apartment. The illustrations show a section of wall divided by false doorways, over each of which are set two windows. A reconstruction of one panel from the north tomb (the pyramid) gives an impression of these apartments in their original splendor (Cairo, Egyptian Museum; JE 68921; H. 181 cm, W. 203 cm), its main panel topped by an archway with so-called Djed pillars, symbols of permanence.

19 King Djoser running the cult race
Saqqara, Tomb precinct of Djoser, south tomb; Third Dynasty, ca. 2680 BC; limestone; H. of image ca. 110 cm.
Underneath the south tomb lies a network of galleries the organization of which represents the king's palace for the afterlife. There are false doorways with images executed in fine relief depicting Djoser engaged in cult ceremonies. Wearing the crown of Upper Egypt, he is here running the cult race in the "southern court of the west."

building over the mortuary temple to the north of the pyramid, and over the passageway into the tomb. To build a new mortuary temple in appropriate proportions, the complex had to be extended to the north and a court was needed for the delivery of offerings and provisions. A monumental altar, on which the offerings were brought each day to be consecrated, dominates the new north court. The entrance to the mortuary temple and the offerings place was guarded by a small chapel, leaning against the north side of the pyramid, known as the *serdab*. In this building was found the only surviving life-size statue of Djoser, which is an impressive image of the inaccessibility and divine dignity of the king in his afterlife.

When the complex was enlarged it took in on the west side an elongated structure that was hitherto regarded as a magazine, though this is very probably the Lower Egyptian tomb of Khasekhemui, last king of the Second Dynasty. The inclusion of this structure demonstrates the idiosyncrasies of Djoser and Imhotep in their design. The Djoser complex is not merely a model of the royal palace, as was previously assumed, but a representation in stone of Egypt in the afterlife. The south and north tombs are symbols for the royal cemetery of Abydos as well as of the Lower Egyptian palace. They are the religious centers of the royal cult. The south court that they enclose and the chapels of the small ceremonial court in the eastern section represent the land of Egypt and its shrines, the world of the living, which is the setting for the eternal cult ceremonies of the king. The north court symbolizes the wealthy marshes of the Delta, standing metaphorically for the offering place of the northern heaven; the western area with the elongated niche tomb symbolizes the "holy realm," the world of the dead. This stone image of Egypt in the afterlife is surrounded by a tall enclosure wall, which protects it from the chaos of the unordered world. This wall has as many as 15 gateways, yet only one functions as an entrance. Through its precise orientation to the north, following the course of the Nile, the complex is linked to the axis of the world, whose pole is the pyramid with the royal tomb, the palace of eternity.

This impressive invention of an everlasting Egypt in the afterlife developed gradually over a long period of construction. For the time being it must remain an open question whether the mere nineteen years given as the reign of Djoser in the "Turin Royal Papyrus" would have been sufficient to achieve this, or whether we need to double his years, which would be quite consistent with Old Kingdom ways of counting.

Djoser's Successors

None of Djoser's successors from the Third Dynasty completed his own tomb. Yet they made advances in construction techniques and brought clarity to the division of the underground magazines. The number of the courts was reduced, and they attempted to construct higher step pyramids. The mortuary complex of Djoser's son or grandson, Sekhemket, was first discovered in the 1950s at Saqqara, to the southwest of the Djoser complex. The tomb chamber contained a coffin that was apparently closed though empty, and which had probably been robbed in antiquity. Another, very much eroded step pyramid from the Third Dynasty stands 10 km further north, in Zawiyet el-Aryan. Huni, the last king of the dynasty, built a series of small, solid, step pyramids from Elephantine in the south to Athribis in the Delta; not pyramids with tombs, but royal monuments, as if they were towers for his palaces. His actual burial place has not yet been found. It is sometimes claimed that Huni began the step pyramid of Meidum, and that Snefru, first king of the Fourth Dynasty, completed it for him, although this thesis is no longer tenable. Huni's presence is not documented there. His tomb must have been in the region of Saqqara, where high officials of his time were buried. Besides this we can tell from graffiti on buildings and from inscriptions that during the Old and Middle Kingdoms no king finished a pyramid for his predecessor or took it over for himself.

The Reign of Snefru

The Pyramid Age begins around 2640 BC, with the long reign of Snefru, first king of the Fourth Dynasty; this was the most magnificent and magical period of Egyptian culture. In addition to architecture, the arts of relief sculpture and painting reach their absolute high points. Moreover, in the natural sciences and medicine, the foundations of knowledge and practice were laid that would remain valid for centuries, right into the Greek era. The belief in the sun god Re, creator of all things, dominated Egyptian religion, ethics, state, and society, which became open and receptive to those with the skills to work on great projects. These individuals formed the new class of "scribes" who were trained in the practical and theoretical management of the state. This group admitted princes alongside those who had risen by their merits. As guarantor of this system, the sun god Re gives power to the king, whose divinity consisted not in himself, but in his role as ruler. He is the "benign God," the god of the necropolis that it is his task to construct. Snefru's Horus name means "Lord of the world order," a title that later applies only to the sun god Re. Snefru's son Cheops identified himself with the sun god to such an extent in his pyramid complex and tomb that his sons and successors referred to themselves by the new royal title, "Son of Re."

Contemporary sources for Snefru's ancestry and character are rare. His mother Meresankh was probably a secondary queen of Huni, last king of the Third Dynasty, but the male ancestors of kings of the Old Kingdom are never mentioned directly because the king is by nature of divine parentage.

Besides his large pyramid structures, the principal achievements of the reign of Snefru were the campaigns in Nubia and Libya that brought substantial booty in both cattle and men. These were settled in thirty-five new royal estates in the Faiyum and in the Delta. Additional achievements that can be linked to this period include the construction of a new royal palace, possibly near Dahshur, with tall gateways of cedar wood, intensive ship building, the manufacture of life-sized royal statues in copper and gold, and an extremely large wooden harp.

Astonishingly, the building of the pyramids is not mentioned in contemporary documents, although it must have been the main event that took place during a king's reign. The building of a pyramid, along with the temple ceremonies, the performance of daily rituals that guaranteed the rising and setting of the sun, the passage of the seasons and the arrival of the Nile floods, is such a fundamental part of the king's natural lifetime task that it hardly needed mentioning. Besides, Snefru was without doubt the most impressive builder of the ancient world, constructing three large and two smaller pyramids in his long reign, using more than 3.6 million cubic metres of stone: one million more than his son Cheops used in his Great Pyramid at Giza. Nonetheless he is known in Egyptian tradition as a good, indeed excellent king, who addressed his subordinates, according to folk tales, as "friend" or even "brother."

The shape of the pyramid complex changed, under the influence of sun worship, from being a north–south-oriented rectangle into a square east–west complex, directed towards the rising sun. The east-west siting emphasizes a new element in the layout of the pyramid complex: the long causeway. It leads from the east, the land of the living, up to the pyramid tomb, ending at the mortuary temple that from this time onwards lies to the east of the pyramid. The entrance gate to the causeway develops into a valley temple, cult center of the pyramid town, in which the goddess Hathor and the king were worshipped as local deities.

The Pyramids of Snefru

Snefru built his first two pyramids, still in the form of step pyramids, at Meidum. A small, solid step pyramid formed a towering landmark above his palace at Seila, on the eastern edge of the Faiyum. His first full pyramid complex, 10 km to the east, includes a huge step pyramid, which was enlarged in a second building phase to the tremendous height of 85 m, and still dominates the view of the Nile Valley. Toward the end of his long reign Snefru "modernized" this pyramid, changing its form into that of a true pyramid.

Just as the form of the step pyramid had its roots in the preceding Third Dynasty, there were other innovations influenced by the orienta-

tion of the pyramid complex toward the sun's course, mentioned above, and in the system of tomb chambers. Among the cult buildings of the new pyramid complex the only reminders of the Djoser complex are the mortuary temple and the south tomb, which was constructed like the king's tomb as a small step pyramid directly to the south of the main pyramid. Certainly there is no true mortuary temple in Meidum, since the king was not to be buried there, but to the east of the pyramid lies a stela shrine with two stelae, which replace and physically represent the king. The tomb chamber system in the pyramid also differs from those of the Third Dynasty. The tomb chamber is no longer sunk deep into the subterranean shaft, but lies raised above the rock in the body of the pyramid. The entrance, or exit, on the other hand lies on the north side from now on, and remains in this position throughout the Old Kingdom. Through the tomb corridor leading up from the rock deep underground, the king would ascend to the everlasting stars in the northern sky, in order to meet the sun god in his barque there. The beginnings of a three-chamber system can be seen in the tombs of the First Dynasty: a tomb chamber proper, as well as two subsidiary chambers, which initially served to store the most important offerings for the deceased king. In the tomb of Djoser, the ante- and side-chambers were already conceived as having a religious function. Thus the ascent to the stars begins from the antechamber, and it is for this reason that the portcullis stones are decorated with stars. The eastern galleries of the "blue chambers" are the model palace for the afterlife. In the Fourth Dynasty the horizontal arrangement of the chambers is replaced by a vertical system, of which the Pyramid of Cheops provides the ultimate example.

At Meidum a trend was set by laying out a royal cemetery in regular rows to the northeast of the pyramids with the double mastabas

22 (opposite) Step Pyramid of Snefru
Meidum; Fourth Dynasty, ca. 2625 BC.
The Step Pyramid was constructed in two phases and was eventually rebuilt into a true pyramid toward the end of Snefru's reign. In

Roman times the pyramid's facing was removed to be made into stucco. Hence it is possible to see the steps again as well as the phases of the original Step Pyramid's construction.

23 View over south Saqqara towards Dahshur
In the foreground is the Mastaba el-Faraun, tomb of the last king of the Fourth Dynasty; to the right the pyramid of Pepi II from the

end of the Sixth Dynasty (ca. 2170 BC), and in the background the Bent Pyramid and Red Pyramid of Snefru, built between 2639 and 2581 BC.

of Snefru's sons and their wives. A huge single mastaba stands right by the northeast corner of the pyramid complex and thus in an important position. This was apparently built in a hurry and contains the burial of a nameless prince, probably the crown prince who died young in the early years of Snefru's reign. We can only speculate as to the reasons why in the fifteenth year of his reign Snefru should have abandoned his palace and the nearly complete pyramid at Meidum, and begun again nearly 50 km north, building a palace and a pyramid near Dahshur. Possibly it proved difficult to control the colonization of the Nile Delta and the trade routes from far away Middle Egypt. The new site near Dahshur, on the other hand, was very convenient. A natural basin for the harbor ensured the development of the region. To the east a trade route led to Sinai, and a wadi led to the western oases, and to the Faiyum. Conveniently sited limestone quarries for building material lay on both sides of the Nile.

A new opportunity was found for the now-idle workers and specialists in a bold undertaking that was to build a towering pyramid without steps, and with a gradient almost as steep as that of the stepped pyramid, to the extraordinary height of about 150 m.

It needs emphasizing here that the development from a step pyramid to the pure geometrical form of the pyramid proper is absolutely not inevitable. None of the other ancient cultures that built step pyramids made this advance. The progression from assembling step-shaped masses to form an artificial hill to the abstract geometrical form of the pyramid is a remarkable intellectual achievement that was the result of an extraordinary and unique gamble in the time of Snefru. Bold improvements were also made in the tomb chambers in the new pyramid, which because of its present form is known as the "Bent

24 The Bent Pyramid of Snefru
South Dahshur; Fourth Dynasty, ca. 2615 BC. This pyramid was originally intended to be nearly 150 m tall, with an even steeper gradient. As the ground underneath gave way an attempt was made to save the building by means of a thick facing layer, and by reducing the angle of slope. The system of chambers inside sank at the same time, and became dangerously fractured, forcing the building to be abandoned.

Pyramid." These were to have corbelled vaults, conceived at Meidum and perfected here, up to a height of 15 m. The ensuing alterations necessitated by subsidence and damage during construction resulted in a chamber system in this pyramid that is extraordinarily complicated and difficult to follow.

According to earlier religious descriptions of the king's afterlife, this took place deep in the underworld. For this reason the lowest of the three tomb chambers had to lie deep into the rock, as in the tomb of Djoser. The upward slope of the tomb corridor is also determined by the requirement for an undeviating passage up to the circumpolar stars. It therefore needed to begin deep in the rock below ground in order to lead to the desired exit, a short distance up the north face of the pyramid. The middle chamber is connected with the king's ascent to heaven, which is in turn represented by the tomb chamber above, although the ascent also actually lies in the direction followed by the tomb corridor.

In order to facilitate the excavation of a shaft of about 7 by 7 m and 22.5 m deep, a layer of marl and slate was put down first as at Saqqara. However, this was not adequate to support the weight of the stones. As the pyramid grew upward sizeable cracks appeared in the three chambers and in the corridor, and initially it was felt sufficient to repair these by filling. It became clear very quickly, however, that both the lower chambers and the entrance corridor were seriously damaged and could not be saved by any further alterations. Eventually all attempts at repair – even giving up the lower chamber and reducing the pyramid's angle of slope – proved useless. After fifteen years of building work the boldest of all pyramid projects had to be abandoned. Snefru began work on building a third pyramid.

The step pyramid at Meidum was modernized at the same time, and altered into a true pyramid. For the third of Snefru's great pyramids, the "Red Pyramid" at north Dahshur, the ground underneath was probably first tested, and the area increased to 220 m along the sides, and it was decided to employ a flatter angle of slope (45°). The method of building in layers, which in the construction of a true pyramid brought no economy of labor, was rejected and replaced by horizontal courses of stone. After the pyramids of Cheops and Chephren, the "Red Pyramid" is still the third largest, reaching 105 m in height. Everything about this building contributes to a harmonious, reserved and majestic effect. The system of chambers is also harmonious and easy to follow because they are laid out one behind the other. They are set only just below ground, and reached by an exit in the north wall nearly 30 m above ground, something that must have greatly inconvenienced the introduction of the funeral ceremony and the final blocking off of the corridor.

The foundations of a hastily completed mortuary temple in front of the east side of the pyramid, and the sad remains of a mummified corpse that were found in the tomb chamber, suggest that Snefru was eventually buried in this pyramid. The princes and princesses of the last years of Snefru's reign are buried in great stone mastabas in the eastern area in front of the two pyramids at Dahshur. These are massive rectangles of stone with smooth exterior walls. Only the east side seems originally to have had two niches, the more southerly of which bore the names of the deceased and perhaps a false door panel. In a small court to the front were possibly displayed two stelae with names and titles. Even the principal queen of this period, probably queen Hetepheres, had only a modest undecorated mastaba. She was, however, not buried in Dahshur but later in Giza, in her son Cheops' cemetery.

Under Snefru a period of construction lasting nearly fifty years brought remarkable advances in building techniques: in masonry, tunneling, the transport of stone and in structural engineering. The bitter experience of catastrophic collapse due to unstable ground led to extreme caution in the choice of sites. The organization and logistics of a building site profited from the experience of twice relocating the pyramid-building towns. The need for building materials, special types of stone, wood and copper for tools and equipment stimulated expeditions and trade with countries to the north. This brought greater awareness of the surrounding area. The civil service also grew in experience through its varied tasks and became an efficient instrument of central government.

The Pyramid of Cheops – Wonder of the Ancient World

Snefru's son and successor thus benefited from the best examples he could have in order to plan an even more ambitious pyramid for his own tomb. In order to avoid another ruined building he settled on a solid rock foundation, which he found in a commanding position on the ridge above what is now Giza. The new royal palace was erected to the east.

25 Isometric projection of the system of tomb chambers in the Bent Pyramid of Snefru
Subsidence in the stonework of the pyramid forced the reconstruction of the system of chambers. The two lower chambers (B, C) which, after the burial, could ideally serve only the spiritual nature of the deceased king, could be blocked up with stone. This meant that the passage to the tomb chamber (A) was also obstructed. It was therefore decided to add a second tomb corridor leading from the west (E, first corridor: D). Because of the higher level of the tomb chamber and the religious requirement for the tomb corridor to ascend, this finished nearly 33 m up on the pyramid's west side. Because of the subsidence no attempt was made to strain the corbel vault of the tomb chamber by connecting it directly to the second chamber, although this was subsequently done by means of a not entirely successful connecting corridor.

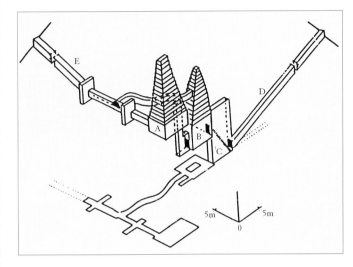

26 Bent Pyramid of Snefru
South Dahshur; Fourth Dynasty, ca. 2615 BC. View up into the corbel vault of the lower chamber inside the pyramid. The floor of the chamber spans an impressive 6.30 m by 4.96 m; the upper end of the vaulting is reduced to 1.60 m by 0.30 m, whereby the corbels jut out a distance of 15 cm each.

27 Northwest corner of the Bent Pyramid of Snefru
South Dahshur; Fourth Dynasty, ca. 2615 BC. On the exterior, attempts were made to prevent the fall of the mass of stone by means of a thick shell, and by a reduction in the angle of slope. But even the blocks of this facing were shaken free by the powerful ground movements.

28 The Red Pyramid of Snefru
North Dahshur; Fourth Dynasty, ca. 2605 BC.
After the catastrophe of the Bent Pyramid,
Snefru constructed a third pyramid about
2 km farther north (so-called after the red
iron-rich limestone of the core stonework), in
which he was finally buried. The harmonious
proportions of the exterior form and the
perfection of the system of tomb chambers
make it one of the most magnificent tombs of
the Old Kingdom.

*29 The pyramidion from the Red Pyramid of
Snefru*
North Dahshur; Fourth Dynasty, ca. 2605 BC;
limestone; H. 100 cm, W. 157 cm
The capstone of the pyramid was found
broken into pieces in the rubble by the east
side and reassembled. It is the oldest surviving pyramidion from a pyramid tomb of the
Old Kingdom, and may have been covered
with sheet metal.
Several fragmentary limestone blocks have
recently been discovered at the Pyramid of
Cheops at Giza, which must have belonged to
the pyramidion of the Great Pyramid.

30 The Red Pyramid of Snefru, tomb chamber
North Dahshur; Fourth Dynasty, ca. 2605 BC.
The burial chamber lies nearly 9 m above the
antechambers. It is an impressive hall 8.35 m
long and 14.64 m high, with a perfect corbel
vault, the impact of which surpasses even the
impressive Grand Gallery of the Pyramid of
Cheops. Later tomb robbers searching for
buried treasure burned the wooden grave
furniture and tore out the flooring.

The perfection of the proportions and construction of the super-structure exactly matches the planning of the system of corridors and chambers inside. To the present day, scholars have tried in a broadly positive spirit to attribute the pyramid's three chambers to three successive changes in the design. But it does not do justice to the architects who designed and executed this unique building so perfectly to suggest that, in the essential element of the pyramid's construction, that is the system of tomb chambers, they had proceeded without concept or design. Against this view is a conclusive argument in that the exterior construction and the layout of the chamber system work in perfect accord, and that neither inside nor out is there any suggestion of a change of plan. Recent research has shown that since the Thinite era royal tombs have had not just a single burial chamber but a series of three rooms or spaces, whose function has so far been only partially understood. Recently this realization has also provided evidence against pyramid mysticism, an epidemic of which is breaking out again, which suggests that hidden secrets, or even further treasure chambers, the "chambers of knowledge," were built into the chamber system of the pyramid of Cheops.

The upper granite burial chamber stands more or less isolated in the interior of the pyramid. Five relief chambers with granite beams weighing up to forty tons served to relieve the pressure. The uppermost has a gabled roof of magnificent limestone blocks that rest on the stones of the core construction. In the relief chambers are to be found various pieces of graffiti by construction workers that name Cheops, the only authentic evidence of the builder found in this pyramid. From

31 The Pyramids of Giza
Giza; Fourth Dynasty, ca. 2585–2511 BC. View from the south of the Mycerinus Pyramid with the king's small cult pyramid and the two step pyramids of his queens. In the background are the complexes of Chephren and Cheops.

the middle of the south and north walls of the burial chamber – and in the same way from the middle chamber – mock corridors lead toward the southern and northern skies. They provide a direct route up to heaven for the deceased king's soul. Previously these had been seen as ventilation shafts or telescopes for observing the skies. But it is certain that these corridors were originally sealed off and could only have served for the flight to heaven of the deceased king's soul.

It is characteristic of the conservative beliefs of the ancient Egyptians that alongside the predominant theology centered on worship of the sun, older ideas about an underworld afterlife in the depths of the earth were tolerated. This "chthonic" (underworldly) aspect is manifested in the rock chamber cut 30 m deep into the solid ground underneath. The corridor on the east side of the rock chamber, which would have led to a southern tomb underneath the pyramid, was never completed, which is why Cheops later built a small southern pyramid on the southeast corner of his pyramid enclosure, only discovered and excavated a few years ago. The middle chamber has a statue niche on the east side for a *ka* statue of the king and, like the granite chamber, has mock corridors leading to heaven. This chamber cannot ever have served as an actual burial chamber since it was not provided with a stone sarcophagus or a magical sealing by portcullises (stone plugs

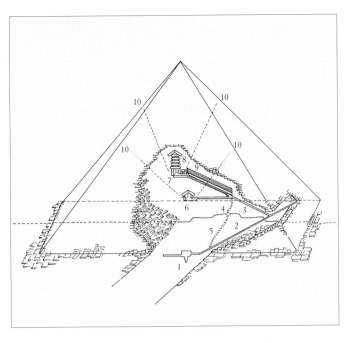

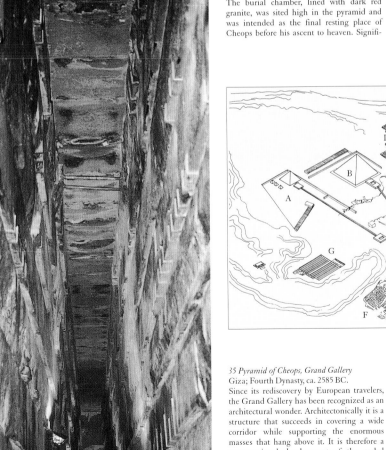

*33 Giza, isometric projection
of the pyramid of Cheops*
  1 Rock chamber
  2 Corridor leading
    downward
  3 Corridor leading
    upward
  4 Crypt
  5 Tomb robbers' passa-
    geway, or service shaft
  6 So-called Queens'
    Chamber
  7 King's Chamber
  8 Relief chambers
  9 Grand Gallery
  10 Ventilation shafts

*32 (opposite) The plateau of
the Pyramids at Giza*
This aerial photograph
shows the pyramid of
Chephren in the foreground
with its associated mortuary
temple and causeway. Diag-
onally behind is the pyramid
of Cheops, to the south side
of which can be seen the
museum for the great
funerary barque of the king.
To the west of the pyramid
of Cheops stretches the large
area with the officials' cemetery G 4000.

34 Pyramid of Cheops, King's Tomb Chamber
Giza; Fourth Dynasty, ca. 2585 BC.
The burial chamber, lined with dark red
granite, was sited high in the pyramid and
was intended as the final resting place of
Cheops before his ascent to heaven. Significantly, Cheops called his pyramid enclosure
"Cheops' horizon." By the west wall of the
chamber originally stood the simple sarcophagus (L. 227 cm, H. 105 cm) that today stands
aslant in the room. Its lid is missing, as is the
interment with the ruler's mortal remains.

35 Pyramid of Cheops, Grand Gallery
Giza; Fourth Dynasty, ca. 2585 BC.
Since its rediscovery by European travelers,
the Grand Gallery has been recognized as an
architectural wonder. Architectonically it is a
structure that succeeds in covering a wide
corridor while supporting the enormous
masses that hang above it. It is therefore a
constructional development of the corbel
vault in the Pyramid of Snefru.

*36 Giza, site plan of the pyramids and
mortuary temples*
In the foreground are tentatively placed the
pyramid town (F), and the royal palace (E)
mentioned in inscriptions.
A Pyramid of Mycerinus
B Pyramid of Chephren
C Pyramid of Cheops
D West cemetery
G Workers' village

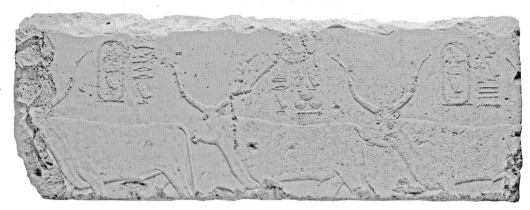

37 Procession of bulls
Lisht; Fourth Dynasty, ca. 2585 BC; limestone; H. 43 cm, L 129 cm; New York, The
Metropolitan Museum of Art, Rogers Fund
and E. F. Harkness Gift 1922, 22.1.3.
During the excavation of the Pyramid of
Amenemhat I and the surrounding necropolis at Lisht, numerous reused blocks were
found that originally came from royal buildings of the Old Kingdom in Giza and
Saqqara. Among them was this relief with its
representation of three long-horned bulls.
The surviving fragment belonged possibly to
a large scene in the valley temple of Cheops,
to which period it is dated by the cartouche, or
name ring, of that ruler.

*38 East side of the Pyramid of Cheops, with
queens' pyramids*
Giza; Fourth Dynasty, ca. 2585 BC.
Under the reign of Cheops, the king's mother
and the queens were given smaller pyramid
tombs of their own for the first time.

Immediately to the east of the king's pyramid
lay his mortuary temple, now almost completely destroyed, while behind the three neighboring structures for the queens stretched the
cemetery for more distant family members.

damaged by conditions underground. Undoubtedly both ships
provided transport for the king while he was alive and were to be at his
disposal in the afterlife. These are not the only ships found in this way.
As early as the First and Second Dynasties, kings were provided with
ships for the afterlife. To the east also lie three small pyramids, one to
the king's mother Hetepheres, main consort of Snefru, who outlived
him and died in her son's palace at Giza and was buried there; and the
others to the two main queens, Meretites and Henutsen, mothers of
Cheops' sons and successors, Djedefre and Chephren. The illegitimate
sons and daughters of the king were given huge, solid double mastabas
to the east of the queens' pyramids. High court officials, the architects
and even prince Hemiunu, the influential building manager of the
pyramids, were given tombs in the west cemetery.

The king himself was involved in the form of the tomb chapels
and their decoration, which is limited to scenes of the most important
offerings. These form a unique representation in monumental form of
state and society, in the strict hierarchies of the royal court and in the
imaginary world of the king's afterlife, in order that they might forever
serve him. They are also recipients of royal largesse and offerings from
the central royal mortuary temple.

We know as little about the person of Cheops as we do of other
kings of the Old Kingdom. The critique of his reign and achievements
handed down by Herodotus is a purely Greek reaction to architecture
that towers above everything on a human scale, and which for a Greek
could only signal mortal hubris. That he was Snefru's son, we know
only from the chance find of tomb equipment of his mother Hetepheres in a shaft burial at Giza. When she died, the queen was initially
buried in this shaft tomb, while her pyramid, the northernmost of the
queens' pyramids, was being completed to the east of the pyramid of
Cheops. Cheops is one of the younger generation of Snefru's sons and
was probably born when Dahshur was in the middle of its building
program, which would mean that he came to the throne when he was
about 25–30 years old. By this time, his older brothers the princes
Nefermaat and Rahotep, who were the architects of the pyramids at
Meidum and Dahshur, were already dead.

Cult and Pyramid Construction after Cheops

Never before or afterward in Egyptian history are the claims of divine
kingship so powerfully expressed. That this could be completed in the
twenty-three to twenty-six, or more likely thirty, years of his reign, is the
result of the remarkable training of the managers, architects, and
workers engaged in undertakings that had continued for half a century.
This enabled the participants to accomplish astonishing achievements:
the hollowing-out of rock beds to distances of 100 m; the preparation

released from above in the entrance corridors). Through the inclusion
of a closed cult area in the body of the pyramid, the precinct outside
was reduced to the mortuary temple, of which today only the basalt
paving remains. From the pattern of markings in the paving it can be
seen that the temple once consisted of a broad court surrounded by
columns and a chapel for mortuary offerings. Also added late, and only
after the south tomb in the rock beneath the pyramid had been abandoned, was a small cult pyramid in the southeast corner of the
complex. Fragments of statues of limestone and other stones are
evidence of its rich decoration. The necropolis was planned just as
precisely and carefully as the pyramid complex itself. Five shafts in the
rock to the east and south of the pyramid once contained funerary
barques – not solar barques – for Cheops. Both of the shafts to the
south were originally found sealed. The eastern shaft contained a royal
ship complete with rudder and rigging, broken into over 1,200 pieces.
Now reassembled, it measures 43.40 m long. The other barque burial
has not yet been opened, although recently video images were taken
through a bore hole that show that the ship it contains has been badly

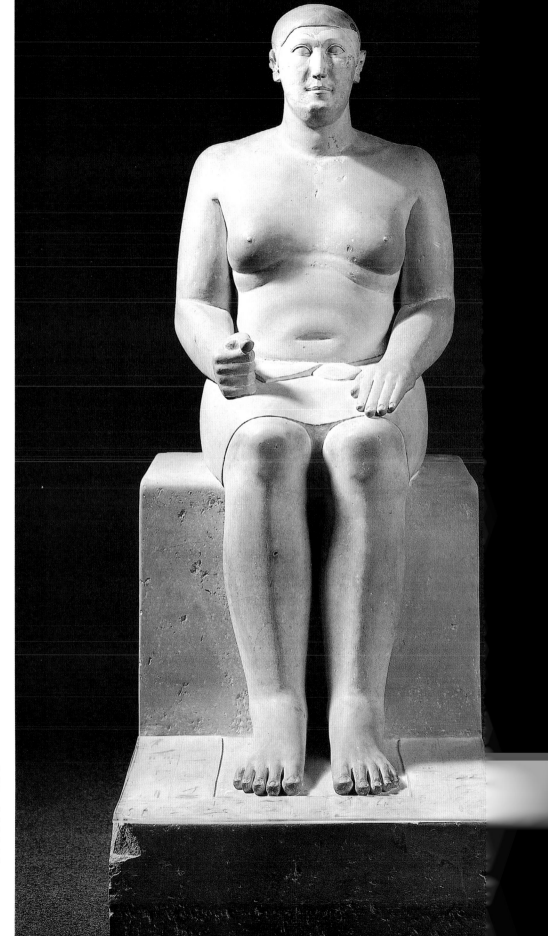

39 Seated statue of Hemiunu
Giza, west cemetery, mastaba G 4000; Fourth Dynasty, ca. 2580 BC; painted limestone; H. 155.5 cm; Hildesheim, Pelizaeus-Museum, 1962.
The vizier Hemiunu, Snefru's grandson, was entrusted by Cheops with the building of his pyramid. His impressive, life-sized tomb statue gives us the image of the type of individual from the time of Snefru and Cheops who built pyramids that could scrape the heavens.

and storage of incredibly heavy stones to provide a constant supply for the teams of workers; the design of ramps and transport routes that cost a minimum in time and materials and which still did not hinder the continuing process of surveying as the pyramids rose upwards. The details of how this was done are still largely unknown, although recent research into pyramid building using models by the German Archeological Institute in Cairo (DAI) has resulted in small initial ramps that could later be adapted. Although mention is still made of hundreds of thousands of workers, slaves, and bonded laborers, it is clear that the narrow building sites did not leave sufficient room for such large numbers of people. Our calculations suggest a number of workers not exceeding 20,000–25,000: quarrymen and stonemasons, sappers and carriers, bricklayers and plasterers, suppliers and servers of food, and then many engineers and architects. With the estimated total population of Egypt at around two million people, their numbers would have lain just below one percent of people who spent the whole year round building the pyramids. The main population of the country was hardly affected by the pyramid-building program. Even the costs and material assets for the building and its teams of workers remain within reason with this percentage.

A new class of men and their families, professional members of the court, administrators, and craftsmen, occupied the towns that surrounded the palace and pyramids. They were employed as priests and officers of the mortuary temple. It is these people who shaped the state, and enabled it to achieve ever greater accomplishments.

40 The Pyramid of Chephren
Giza; Fourth Dynasty, ca. 2550 BC.
Chephren's pyramid stands on a rise to the southwest of that of his father Cheops. For this reason and because of its steeper angle of slope, it appears taller, although in reality it is 3 m shorter than Cheops' pyramid. The steeper angle made it difficult for stone plunderers in the middle ages to remove the facing around the apex of the pyramid.

For a better understanding of the pyramids we must distance ourselves once and for all from the positivist viewpoint of the nineteenth century, and remember that the construction of the pyramids, the layout of the tomb chambers and the form and size of the mortuary temple were determined by religious ceremonies and the needs of the cult and by nothing else. The burial chamber system inside the pyramid and the form of the mortuary temple outside are interrelated. A complicated arrangement of the burial chambers corresponds to simple architecture in the mortuary temple and vice versa. The size of a pyramid is in no way a measure of the power and position of its builder. So for example, Djedefre, the son and successor of Cheops, began building his pyramid on a much smaller scale, but in such a commanding position at Abu Roash (north of Giza) that it dominates the landscape because of its location in just the same way that Cheops' pyramid does at Giza. Although unfinished, the mortuary temple of Djedefre was nevertheless adorned with many statues of the king of the highest quality.

This can be demonstrated more clearly by example of the complexes of Chephren and Mycerinus. Chephren was one of Cheops'

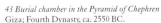

41 Valley temple of Chephren
Giza, the king's mortuary complex; Fourth Dynasty, ca. 2550 BC.
The valley temple creates the impression that it was carved from solid rock or projecting from the front of the pyramid structure. The rooms are encircled by gigantic walls and the effect of their plain granite architecture is impressively monumental. Originally the temple's core stones were faced inside and out with huge polished granite blocks.

42 Pillared hall in the valley temple of Chephren
Giza; the king's mortuary complex; Fourth Dynasty, ca. 2550 BC.
The sole decoration of this austere granite architecture was provided by smooth polished statues against the walls depicting the king as a visible symbol of divine power.

43 Burial chamber in the Pyramid of Chephren
Giza; Fourth Dynasty, ca. 2550 BC.
The chamber was rediscovered in 1818 by the Italian adventurer Belzoni, who wrote his name on the wall. The chamber system in Chephren's pyramid is simple compared to that of the Pyramid of Cheops. The broad and tall room still gives an impression of austere dignity. The black granite sarcoph- agus of the king was embedded in the ground before the west wall of the chamber. The accompanying lid which was originally anchored to the sarcophagus' sides by metal pegs was broken in two when the tomb was plundered. A rectangular trough on the south wall marks the location where the canopic box would have been placed.

44 Seated statue of Chephren
Giza, valley temple of Chephren; Fourth Dynasty, ca. 2550 BC; anorthosite gneiss; H. 168 cm, W. 57 cm; Cairo, Egyptian Museum, CG 14
Chephren's statues, especially this splendid seated figure with the protective Horus falcon, are cloaked in the dignity of divine kingship; their stone expression is cool, dismissive and directed past the viewer into the distance. Despite the idealization of the royal figure they remain masterpieces of indi- vidual portraiture, unmistakable images of Chephren. The "Falcon Chephren" originally stood, along with twenty-two other royal figures, in front of the walls of the pillared hall in the king's valley temple, and provided the centerpiece of the statue cult.

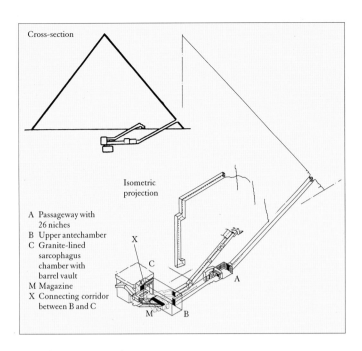

Cross-section

Isometric
projection

A Passageway with
    26 niches
B Upper antechamber
C Granite-lined
    sarcophagus
    chamber with
    barrel vault
M Magazine
X Connecting corridor
    between B and C

X

C

A

M   B

*45 Pyramid of Mycerinus: cross-section and
isometric projection*
The chamber system of the Mycerinus
pyramid is more or less the opposite of that of
Cheops. There the corridors lead upwards,
whereas in Mycerinus's case they descend
into the solid rock. The introduction to the
burial chamber of granite facing in the nar-
rowest of spaces is a remarkable and pio-
neering engineering achievement.

*46 Entrance and granite facing of the Pyramid
of Mycerinus*
Giza; Fourth Dynasty, ca. 2520 BC.
In the Fourth Dynasty granite became
increasingly important as a building material
because it was considered to be a precious
material. It also gained importance as a
symbol of permanence and eternity. Possibly
the entire Pyramid of Mycerinus was intended
to be faced in granite like his mortuary
temple. In this way form and symbolic material took precedence over monumentality.
The finding that of the facing's granite
blocks (max. 16 layers of stone) only those
immediately near the entrance had been
smoothed is striking and still inexplicable

*47 Pair statue of Mycerinus with Queen
Khamerernebty*
Giza, king's valley temple; Fourth Dynasty,
ca. 2520 BC; graywacke; H. 142 cm; Boston,
Museum of Fine Arts, 11.1738
This sculpture group was found together with
other completely preserved group statues in
the Mycerinus valley temple. The portraits of
the ruler, one example of which is shown in
the illustration above, are distinctly mannered.
His statues display an innovative system of
proportions; the king as athlete with powerful
thorax and a relatively small head, but with
fully modeled, almost gentle features.

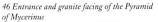

49 Pyramids and mortuary temple of Sahure
Abusir, Fifth Dynasty, ca. 2490 BC.
In the Fifth Dynasty (2504–2347 BC) the mortuary temple became the most important part of the complex. Originally the temple buildings of Sahure were enlivened by a variety of stone types, basalt paving, red granite paving stones and an elaborate decoration scheme with thousands of square meters of painted and inlaid reliefs. The pyramid behind was scarcely 50 m high and fitted harmoniously with the architecture as a whole, without dominating it.

48 The Pyramids of Abusir
Fifth Dynasty, ca. 2490–2420 BC.
The early and middle rulers of the Fifth Dynasty sited their pyramids at Abusir, between Giza and Saqqara. The constructions of Sahure, Neferirkare, and Niuserre are well preserved, and were studied and excavated along with their cult buildings by the German Oriental Society at the beginning of the twentieth century.

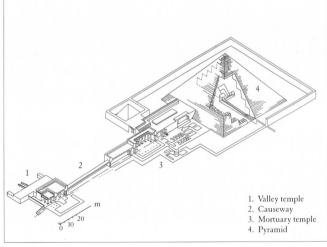

1. Valley temple
2. Causeway
3. Mortuary temple
4. Pyramid

50 Pyramid and cult buildings of Sahure: isometric plan
In the Fifth Dynasty the pyramid and valley temples became more important as sites of the offering rituals and worship of the deceased king. The size of the entire complex is certainly not comparable with the grandiose achievements of the Fourth Dynasty.

younger sons, and he came to the throne unexpectedly early after the death of his brother Djedefre. His pyramid was intended to equal the height of that of his father, which he achieved in fact through the choice of a slightly higher site and a steeper angle of slope. The system of chambers is so unusually simple that in the 1960s serious (but unsuccessful) attempts were made using the most modern scientific equipment to locate additional rooms. On the other hand, his pyramid temple and valley temple were very lavishly constructed.

In contrast, the burial chamber system in the considerably smaller pyramid of his son Mycerinus is characterized by an extraordinary succession of rooms that can only be compared with those in the Pyramid of Cheops. The chambers in the Mycerinus pyramid lead down into the solid rock, unlike those in the Cheops pyramid. But the mortuary temple of Mycerinus resembles that of Cheops in being dominated by a wide open court closed to the west by a chapel for offerings to the dead. Between Chephren and Mycerinus fits the four-year reign of Baka (Bikheris), one of Djedefre's sons, who planned and started work on a large pyramid in Zawiyet el-Aryan.

Complexes of the Fifth and Sixth Dynasties

The transition from the Fourth to the Fifth Dynasties passed peacefully, as is indicated by the biographies of high officials, which provide valuable historical sources. The few inscriptions do not reveal whether Khentkaus, mother of the first three kings of the Fifth Dynasty, Userkaf, Sahure, and Neferirkare, was the wife or daughter of Shepseskaf, last king of the Fourth Dynasty. Shepseskaf did not build a pyramid, but rather a huge stone mastaba at south Saqqara. It would be unwise to conclude from this that there were political or religious conflicts, for Shepseskaf had decreed the enactment of the mortuary cult, with offerings at the pyramids of his predecessors. The form of Shepseskaf's name cannot be distinguished from that of Userkaf, the first king of the Fifth Dynasty, who again chose the pyramid form for his tomb.

The shift of importance from pyramid to mortuary temple, which had established itself with Mycerinus, became the norm in the Fifth and Sixth Dynasties. The pyramids, which the kings of these dynasties constructed at Abusir and later at Saqqara, were considerably smaller, while the mortuary temples grew in size. The temples absorbed the entire east side of the pyramid. In this period there is hardly any further alteration in the architecture into an open temple for worship and an intimate temple for offerings, where the deceased king would receive the daily gifts in the company of the gods. The interior walls were richly painted with scenes on every surface. These showed the king's entry in the world of the gods, his rebirth through the heavenly goddesses, his triumph over the chaotic world beyond Egypt's borders and the daily gifts of offerings.

Administrative documents from the mortuary temples at Abusir tell us in detail about the bureaucracy that organized the supply and distribution of the considerable quantities of the offerings, from which the staff and priests ultimately lived, as in fact did the entire population of the pyramid town. The focal point of the pyramid town was the valley temple, whence the causeway ascended to the pyramid temple. In the valley temple the deceased king was also worshipped as a local divinity.

The offerings came first from the shrines of the sun god, temples that from the beginning of the Fifth Dynasty were built next to each of the royal mortuary complexes in the area of Abusir. These are "mortuary temples" for the daily setting of the sun god in the west. Architecturally they indeed resemble a royal mortuary temple, with a broad offering court, the main feature of which, however, was an obelisk, raised on a podium, in place of a pyramid. The offering was placed here first for the sun god, and then was taken to the royal mortuary temples in a kind of cult procession. We can conclude from the reliefs in the solar temples that the offerings made there to the sun god ensured the continuing cycle of rebirth of the world order.

The custom of building a new shrine to the sun god each time was abandoned at the end of the Fifth Dynasty, but this hardly represents a departure from the worship of the sun god Re that dominated Egyptian theology. The kings' names provide evidence here: they are all supplemented with "Re" and "Son of Re." But in the Sixth Dynasty there seems to have been a growing interest in the cult of Osiris and the concept of the afterlife in the underworld. This is not reflected in the architecture, but all the more in the pyramid texts that first appear at the end of the Fifth Dynasty, and in the prayers and wishes of private people. However, pyramid and temple architecture freezes into the pattern and scale found in the Fifth Dynasty.

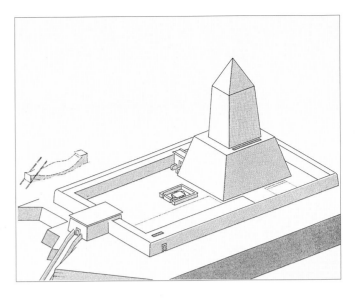

52 Solar temple of Niuserre: reconstruction
The religious focus of the complex is the massive obelisk, which reached a height of 56 m including the base. According to accounts in inscriptions, six rulers of the Fifth Dynasty built solar temples, although to date only two – the temples of Userkaf and Niuserre – have been located by archaeologists.

53 Solar temple of Niuserre
Abu Gurab; Fifth Dynasty, ca. 2420 BC.
The kings of the Fifth Dynasty each built their own shrines to the sun god Re on the edge of the western desert, in the middle of which, in place of a pyramid, stood an obelisk on a podium, with a large altar to the east. Each day offerings were consecrated there and afterward taken to the temples.

55 *King Neferefre*
Abusir; mortuary temple of Neferefre; Fifth Dynasty, ca. 2450 BC; pink limestone; H. 17.2 cm; Cairo, Egyptian Museum, JE 98171.
Because his reign was so short, Neferefre's pyramid never rose above the first courses of stones, and his mortuary temple was completed in brick. Among the royal statues found there was this small seated figure, which shows the king with youthful face and holding a ceremonial mace.

56 *King Userkaf*
Abusir (Abu Gurab); Fifth Dynasty, ca. 2500 BC; schist, H. 45 cm, W. 25 cm; Cairo, Egyptian Museum, JE 90220.
Userkaf did not build his pyramid at Giza but at Saqqara, as Shepseskaf, last king of the Fourth Dynasty, had done previously. Further north, in Abu Gurab, Userkaf consecrated the first solar temple, in which this head was found. The king wears the Red Crown of Lower Egypt.

54 *Causeway to the Pyramid of Unas*
Saqqara, pyramid precinct of Unas; Fifth Dynasty, ca. 2350 BC.
The causeway leads 800 m up from the valley temple to a monumental gateway of red granite into the mortuary temple in front of the east side of the pyramid, visible in the background.

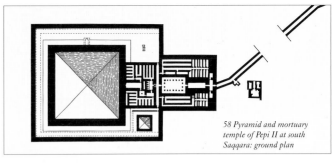

58 *Pyramid and mortuary temple of Pepi II at south Saqqara: ground plan*

57 *Sarcophagus chamber of King Unas*
Saqqara, Pyramid of Unas; Fifth Dynasty, ca. 2350 BC.
The tomb chambers of Unas were the first to be decorated with pyramid texts: a collection of spells intended to guarantee the continued existence of the deceased king. The lidless basalt sarcophagus of Unas still stands beneath the star-studded gabled roof of the sarcophagus chamber.

59 *Pyramid complex of Pepi II*
South Saqqara; Sixth Dynasty, ca. 2230 BC.
This is the last great pyramid complex of the Old Kingdom. Inside the king's pyramid are an antechamber, a burial chamber, and a corridor with pyramid texts. The precinct was enclosed by three smaller pyramids that were dedicated to the queens of the exceedingly long-lived king Pepi. Texts were found in the pyramids.

Yet it would be wrong to speak of a decline. The pyramids and temples of Kings Teti, Pepi I and Pepi II are technically perfect constructions, maintaining in their scale and proportions the standards of the Fifth Dynasty.

The causes of the end of the Old Kingdom are certainly not to be found in the exhaustion of the state and its resources through excessive pyramid building. The decline of the Old Kingdom began with the disintegration of the central administration during the exceptionally long reign of Pepi II. After his mortuary complex was completed the country lay idle for decades. During these years the provincial governors discovered that they could maintain their administration and rule without royal command and they became more or less independent. Thus the central administration was cut off from the resources of the provinces.

The construction of the pyramids was a moment that united belief in the person of the king and in the role of kingship, as well as an opportunity for individuals to progress through their own ability and be assured of a safe life both in society and in the afterlife. One can best compare the building of the pyramids with the construction of the great cathedrals in European cities of the Middle Ages, which were the work of religious urban communities on a scale similar to the pyramids, the product of a state united by religion. The cathedrals are the gathering places for a community of believers for common prayer and a common cult, the hope and preparation for salvation in the afterlife. The pyramid complexes are comparable to the extent that they ensured an afterlife for the people through the person of the king and his mortuary cult.

One could go so far as to compare the cult of the deified king in his pyramid complex, and here especially in the valley temple, with the cult of the saints to whom a cathedral is consecrated. Just as the saints share through their devotion in God's heavenly life after death, and the congregations strive to achieve the same through prayer, good deeds, and offerings, so the king's ascent into heaven and his union with the sun god ensures that his devout subjects will be able to share in the eternal afterlife. The intermediary role that the king had in the daily cult in this life, between the gods and the world order, is the same role he fulfills in the afterlife. The differences between the king's heavenly afterlife and that of his subjects in the "beautiful west" may seem great to us; yet in reality they are just a projection into the future existence of the divisions that exist in this world.

The Great Sphinx – A Puzzle is Solved

At 73.5 m long and over 20 m high the Great Sphinx is the most immense sculpture ever made by man. It shows a being that is part-lion and part-man, a creature metamorphosed into a divine being by the combined strength of a powerful wild animal and the intelligence of a human ruler. Earlier two-dimensional images of this creature as a griffin show it in action destroying the enemy. In the sculpture this

60 The Great Sphinx
Giza; Fourth Dynasty, ca. 2590 BC; limestone; L. 73.5 m, H. 20 m.
The Sphinx of Giza is the most colossal
image of a ruler from Egyptian history, and in
an extraordinarily impressive way it embodies
pharaonic divine kingship in the early Fourth
Dynasty. Restored several times in antiquity,
and first freed from the debris and sand
obscuring it in 1925–1932, the world-famous
statue is now threatened by surface water and
air pollution.

61 Head of the Great Sphinx
Giza; Fourth Dynasty, ca. 2590 BC; limestone; H. ca. 5.2 m, W. ca. 4.2 m.
The location of the Sphinx beside the valley
temple of Chephren has traditionally led to its
interpretation as a portrait of that ruler. But
careful research into the facial features and
iconographical details shows that the Sphinx
must have been carved during the reign of
Cheops. Egyptians of the New Kingdom
understood the monumental figure as standing for the sun god Harmachis.

power is tamed, controlled by human intelligence, and it has transformed into a divine, magisterial calm. Even if one agrees today that the
Sphinx is a work of the Fourth Dynasty, the attribution to either
Cheops, Djedefre or Chephren remains a matter of dispute. So far there
is no inscriptional evidence that clearly names any of these three kings
as the statue's creator. The mention made of Chephren on the sphinx
stela of Thutmosis IV (Eighteenth Dynasty) was, first of all, made a
good thousand years later and, secondly, stands today out of context: in
light of a similar text on the sphinx stela of Amenophis II it should
probably be explained as "resting place/horizon of Cheops and of
Chephren," in other words the necropolis of Giza. A small, unique
stela from the time of Ramesses of an "excellent scribe Monthu-her"
bears the earliest image of the two pyramids, of Cheops and Chephren,
with the Sphinx correctly shown in front of the Pyramid of Cheops.
The area in which the Sphinx stands was undoubtedly ground quarried
for stone to build the Cheops pyramid. Yet even this point is not
unequivocal evidence that Cheops constructed the Sphinx.

Some reevaluations and an analysis of stylistic criteria can take us
further. After Snefru in Dahshur, it was Cheops in Giza whose designs
and achievements are ultimately the finest. His pyramids, his temple,
and even his statues, as surviving fragments show, are at once innovative and supreme achievements. He is the great originator, the sun god;
his sons follow him. He is therefore the most obvious candidate to be
the inventor of the form of the Sphinx. The layout of the entire plateau
argues for this interpretation. The causeway of Chephren takes account
in its slanting course of something earlier, something important that
already stood there; from the situation as it stands this can only have
been the Sphinx. Stylistic considerations also point indisputedly toward
Cheops. The overall form of the Sphinx's face is broad, almost square.
On the other hand the features of Chephren were long, noticeably

narrower, the chin almost pointed. The Sphinx has the earlier, fully
pleated type of *nemes* headcloth as does the head fragment of a statue of
Cheops in The Metropolitan Museum, and still no band in the form of a
raised hem over the brow. This is the norm from Djedefre onward.
Under Chephren only the lappets of the *nemes* headcloth are pleated
and never the hood. The side wings of the Sphinx's *nemes* headcloth are
deeply hollowed, but with Chephren hardly at all. With Chephren the
headcloth corners curl up, but they do not do so with the Sphinx.

The Sphinx has a uraeus cobra placed on the lower edge of the
headcloth and in contrast to those of Chephren and Mycerinus it shows
high relief with naturalistic detailing of the serpent's neck and the scales
of its hood. The eyebrows of the Sphinx bulge powerfully forward, and
they are pitched high and slope down toward the temples. The eyes are
deep-set, but strongly modeled. They are large and wide open, to which
perhaps the monumentality of the head owes something. These wide-
open eyes are absolutely typical of sculpted heads from the time of
Cheops. The ears are fundamentally different from those of the statue of
Chephren. The ears of the Sphinx are very broad and folded forward,
those of Chephren elongated and situated closer to the temples.

A decisive criterion is the absence of a beard. Since the Sphinx has
no indications of hair on its chin, there certainly would not have been
one in the Old Kingdom. The god's beard is an innovation of the New
Kingdom, and it also included a platform, which was adorned with a
royal figure of the Eighteenth Dynasty. The small ivory statuette of
Cheops does not have a beard, nor do the heads attributed to him
(Brooklyn 46.167 and Berlin 14396), or the relief images. Whereas the
kings of the Fourth Dynasty that follow – Djedefre, Chephren, and
Mycerinus – all wear the ceremonial beard in relief and in modeled
form. Therefore all evidence suggests that the Great Sphinx, like the
great pyramids, is an original creation of Cheops.

62 (left) Statuette of Cheops
Abydos; Fourth Dynasty, ca. 2590 BC; ivory; H. 7.5 cm, W. 2.5 cm; Cairo, Egyptian Museum, JE 36143.
This miniature sculpture of Cheops is the only figure of the builder of the great Pyramids of Giza that is confirmed by inscription. The king wears the crown of Lower Egypt and a pleated kilt. In his right hand he holds the flail, symbolic of his power. The Horus name of Cheops is inscribed on the front of the simple throne, to the right.

64 Head of a king with Upper Egyptian crown
Provenance unknown; Fourth Dynasty, ca. 2590 BC; red granite; H. 54.3 cm, W. 29 cm; New York, The Brooklyn Museum, Charles Edwin Wilbour Fund, 46.167.
The remains of a strap from clothing on the neck indicates that the complete figure showed the king in his jubilee cloak (*sed* festival). The attribution to Cheops of this monumental head wearing the white crown of Upper Egypt rests on the stylistic analysis of the face, which is marked by its broad form, and especially a fullness across the cheeks.

63 (left) King Cheops
Probably from Giza; Fourth Dynasty, ca. 2590 BC; limestone, H. 13.5 cm; Berlin, SMPK, Ägyptisches Museum, 14396.
Although recorded in the collections of the Berlin Museum by 1899, this head has only recently been identified as representing Cheops. Quite exceptionally for a king of the Old Kingdom, the ruler wears a tight-fitting wig of tiny curls, above which is a diadem with star uraeus.

65 King Chephren
Giza, king's mortuary temple; Fourth Dynasty, ca. 2550 BC; anorthosite gneiss; H. 17.2 cm, W. 7.3 cm; Leipzig, Ägyptisches Museum der Universität, 1945.
Chephren provided many more statues for the cult buildings by his pyramid than his father Cheops. As is shown in the present example (left), Chephren developed a particular liking for the material gneiss. This fragment of the face with commanding ceremonial beard preserves the powerful features of the ruler.

67 Triad of Mycerinus
Giza, royal valley temple; Fourth Dynasty, ca. 2520 BC; graywacke; H. 96 cm, W. 61 cm; Cairo, Egyptian Museum, JE 46499.
In the valley temple of Mycerinus an expedition from Harvard University, led by the famous excavator George A. Reisner, found several group statues of the king together with the goddess Hathor and a local deity. This example depicts Mycerinus with the goddess of the seventh Upper Egyptian nome (province), who bears the emblem of her province on her head.

66 Head from a sphinx of Djedefre
Abu Roash, king's mortuary temple; Fourth Dynasty, ca. 2757 BC; sandstone; H. 26.5 cm; Paris, Musée du Louvre, E. 12626.
This head of a king with headdress from the unfinished pyramid precinct of Djedefre ranks as one of the most beautiful royal portraits of the Old Kingdom. Particularly impressive is the subtle indication of the anatomy of the face, which gives the countenance its great expressiveness. From the nature of the break, it is clear that the head once belonged to a sphinx portrait.

Daily Life in Eternity – The Mastabas and Rock-Cut Tombs of Officials

Hartwig Altenmüller

The Development of Funerary Architecture

The cemeteries of the Old Kingdom (2700–2200 BC) in Giza, Abusir, Saqqara, and Dahshur are but parts of a single, great royal cemetery at Memphis where high officials of the Old Kingdom were interred next to their kings. They are home-to-tomb structures characteristic of the Old Kingdom. In the provinces tombs of a similar size only appear toward the end of the Old Kingdom, from around 2200 BC. While royal tombs developed into the pyramid, the tomb architecture of officialdom retained the form of the mastaba. But here, too, stone building techniques began to take on new dimensions at the beginning of the Fourth Dynasty (2640 BC); the first nonroyal tombs in stone replaced funerary complexes constructed from mudbrick. In spite of the new construction techniques, however, the basic conception of the tomb changed little from the old mudbrick methods. The tomb continued to have two main areas, one above ground and the other below. The subterranean area was at first the more important one. It contained the burial chamber with an intricately fashioned sarcophagus of stone for the body of the deceased. In some tombs the exterior of these sarcophagi were formed like a palace (niche) facade. It seems likely that the person buried in it was to be identified as the inhabitant of a palace and this type of adornment indicated his personal rank.

At first, the sarcophagus below ground was surrounded by stored provisions. These were not intended for direct consumption by the dead but were to serve as reserves for eternity. Daily needs were met by the mortuary cult whose priests carried out their rites in the upper part of the tomb. Offerings were placed at a sacrificial site and taken up by the soul of the deceased. This cult site was marked by a "false door," which from the time of Cheops was protected by a tomb chapel that fronted the main structure. The walls of this tomb chapel were adorned with illustrations and texts whose primary representation was the deceased. He or she was shown either engaging in certain activities or as the focus of the actions of others. The individual nature of the

scenes is evident from inscriptions containing the names and titles of the tomb owner.

Tomb decoration depicted themes suited to the deceased's status. At the center of these were images of daily life. Because life in the hereafter was thought of in much the same way as mortal life, these images are uniquely able to depict the type of afterlife that the deceased imagined awaited him.

Further development of the range of images led to an increase in those depictions that applied themes from this life to the hereafter. The greater range of pictorial themes meant a greater need for rooms and wall space. This development temporarily came to an end with the tomb of the vizier Mereruka in Saqqara at the onset of the Sixth Dynasty around 2330 BC. The superstructure of his tomb consisted of a funerary palace of thirty-two decorated rooms, twenty-one of which were intended for Mereruka, six for his wife and five for his son Meriteti.

From the second half of the Old Kingdom, decorated tombs had long since ceased to be the privilege of the upper class of the court. Monumental tomb structures arose in the provinces on the model of the capital's necropolis. Because geography did not always allow for the building of a mastaba, tomb chapels were often designed as rock-cut tombs.

---

68 Western cemetery of Giza, mastabas of cemetery G 4000
Fourth Dynasty, ca. 2610 BC.
An innovation in tomb architecture occurred around 2610 BC under King Cheops. The royal cemetery in Giza was planned and laid out in rows with streets intersecting at right angles. The monuments were of a simple construction. Their superstructure consisted of a massive tumulus of stone with a rectangular foundation and sloping side walls. The burial was reached from the upper surface of the tumulus by means of a vertical shaft. From the outside these stone structures look like a "bank" or "bench," which in Arabic is "mastaba."

69 View of the exterior of a mastaba
The superstructures of the tombs have sloping walls that were smoothed when finished. The size and quality of the lime-stone blocks used as well as the general structural execution mirrored the social standing of the tomb's owner or the respective times. The sites for cult rituals were erected on the eastern side of the central structure. The main cult focus was protected by a projecting addition of mudbrick or stone. Later, this offering place was transferred to the interior of the upper structure. The tomb chapel in the interior of the complex consisted, in the early Old Kingdom, of a single L-shaped room.

70 Tomb of the royal manicurists, Niankhkhnum and Khnumhotep
Saqqara; mid-Fifth Dynasty, ca. 2450 BC.
Rock tombs were built in places where the local topography did not allow for a mastaba, or one of only limited form. The arrangement of its cult chambers oriented itself to the architecture of the walled-up mastaba. The range of images portrayed is also the same. The rock tomb of Niankhkhnum and Khnumhotep from the mid-Fifth Dynasty at Saqqara shows a unique solution: two cult chambers are connected with each other, one in the mastaba and one in the cliff. The mastaba was set in front of the cult chamber in the cliff after the latter's construction. Between the mastaba and the cliff chamber there is a portico in which the entrance to the burial chamber lies.

71 Plan of the tomb of the vizier Mereruka
Saqqara; Early Sixth Dynasty, ca. 2330 BC.
Two groups of rooms branch off from the tomb entrance, one to the east and the other to the west. In the eastern wing the cult rooms of the vizier Mereruka are situated, in the western wing those of his wife, the princess Watetkhethor. A third cult site extends from the northeastern corner of the hall of pillars in Mereruka's section. It was intended for Meriteti, the son of the deceased. Almost all the rooms in the family tomb are decorated. The exceptions are the storerooms in the northwest of the complex.

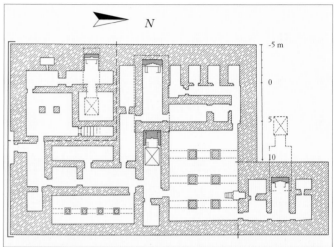

72 Entrance to the tomb of Merib
Giza (G 2100 Annex); early Fifth Dynasty, ca. 2500 BC; painted limestone; wall H. 285 cm; Berlin SPMK, Ägyptisches Museum, 1107.
The tomb chapel of the mastaba of Merib is situated on the east side of the central mastaba superstructure. To the left and right of the chapel entrance the deceased is pictured entering the tomb. His images face each other and he is accompanied by his sons. As a measure of their relative importance, the sons are depicted on a much smaller scale but nevertheless both as adults. In the architrave over the entrance to the cult chapel there is an offering formula to Anubis and a list of festivals. The offering formula consists of a spell that is repeated in this – or similar – form in almost every tomb: "An offering given by the king, and a offering given by Anubis, foremost of the divine booth. May he (the deceased) be buried (in) the western desert (as) a lord of veneration by the Great God after he has reached a ripe old age, (namely) the expedition leader and royal son, Merib." The list of festivals in the second line contains a request for invocation offerings on all the important annual necropolis festivals.

Funerary Repast Scene and False Door

The earliest examples of the adornment of a tomb chapel come from the end of the Third and the beginning of the Fourth Dynasties. Initially, interrelated scenes are still lacking, a few pictorial themes being indicated in key scenes. The oldest and most important example of this kind is the funerary repast scene that appears on the outside of the tomb, at first on a sacrificial plaque or slab and later in association with the false door of the tomb.

The early type of funerary repast scene depicts the deceased to the left of a table covered with bread. He or she reaches out with the right hand to the bread loaves spread out on the table and lays the left hand on his or her breast. The scene contains all the important information needed for its function. Inscriptions of names and titles make the necessary statements about the status of the deceased during his or her life. The funerary repast scene refers to the function of the tomb as the eternal dwelling place of the deceased. Its images and texts tell us about the quality of the offerings made since it lists by name the sacrifices placed on the table and distinguishes between these according to type and number. This depiction was standardized at an early date and established, in a legally binding way, just which offerings were to be brought to the deceased.

73 Slab stela of Iunu
Giza (G 4150); Fourth Dynasty, ca. 2590 BC; painted limestone; H. 39 cm; Hildesheim, Pelizaeus-Museum, 2145.
The slab stela of "the royal son" Iunu was found beneath a covering stone on the eastern exterior face side of a mastaba in Giza. The official was an overseer of the workforce during the construction of the Pyramid of Cheops. The stela of fine-grained limestone shows Iunu in a long robe of panther skin and seated to the right of an offering table. His name and titles are contained in the horizontal line across the top of the rectangular stone. The titles describe him as a member of the Vizier's Office. He was "Head of the Labor Divisions of Upper Egypt" and the "Greatest of the Tens of Upper Egypt." In the horizontal line over the table the offerings are listed: incense, ointment, figs, and wine. In the left-hand column three different types of linen are recorded. At the lower left are five storage granaries, each container listing a different type of grain.

The funerary repast scene forms the departure point for the entire wall decoration of the tomb chapel. Out of concern that the items listed in the funerary repast scene, which were required daily, might arrive too late or, at some time in the future, cease altogether, their continued provision was guaranteed by means of magical images. These include pictures of defiles of offering bearers as well as other images showing the production of gifts intended as offerings.

Depictions of offerings and their presentation by mortuary priests were originally found on the false door itself and were therefore directly related to the funerary repast scene. From there, however, they spread on to the surrounding walls of the tomb chapel until, finally, they fill

74 *False door of the royal daughter, Wenshet*
Giza (G 4840); Fourth/Fifth Dynasty, ca. 2500 BC; limestone; H. 223.5 cm; Hildesheim, Pelizaeus-Museum, 2971.
The standard false door imitated the door of a house with frame, lintel, and rounded drum for securing a curtain. Its placement in the tomb served to reinforce the idea of the tomb as a dwelling place. A good example of a standard false door is that in the tomb of the royal daughter, Wenshet. She is described in inscriptions as "the bodily daughter of the king, Priestess of Hathor, Lady of the Sycamore and Priestess of Neith, north of the wall." The usual offering formula is lacking. The decorative program indicates Wenshet's material provision and contains images of relatives and bearers bringing various offerings.

75 *Palatial false door*
Saqqara, rock-cut tomb of the court singers Nefer and Kahay; mid-Fifth Dynasty, ca. 2450 BC.
Another type of false door was represented by the palatial false door. It imitates the projections and recesses of a palace facade conveying the impression that the tomb behind was a palace. This type of false door can be seen from the Fourth Dynasty on. It is found only rarely, mostly combined with a standard false door. The palatial false door from this tomb stands between the false door of Nefer's tomb and that of his father, Kahay. It was used as the primary false door in connection with the later burial of the "leader of singers, (named) Khenu" (end of the Fifth Dynasty) and therefore has a name inscribed in the door recess.

up the entire cult chamber. The range of images of the early chapels therefore consists mainly of defiles of offering bearers and images of the sacrifice of cattle. In hindsight, the depictions in the early chapels can be seen to be representations of the items contained in the lists of the funerary repast scene. The essential role of these images lay in ensuring the continued production of offerings intended for sacrifice.

The production of sacrificial offerings transformed into images and their presentation refers to actions carried out in this life on behalf of the deceased in the next life. Series of images portraying the existence and social role of the deceased in the next life appear with increasing frequency in the Fifth Dynasty and are placed on an equal footing beside images that ensure the provision of offerings to him. The new images then set the tone for the type of images in the cult chamber. Pictorial cycles of agriculture and livestock prove particularly useful for the extension of the pictorial program because their output in the shape of bread and beer or in the form of animals for slaughter can be sacrificed to the tomb owner. Images of craftsmanship fulfill a similar function. These show the production of objects that, in the end, will be used for the construction of tombs.

Temporal and Spatial Structure of Tomb Images

The images in the tombs of the Old Kingdom set out to portray the existence of the deceased in the hereafter and their content is ordered accordingly. Because the afterlife was conceived in more or less the same way for all non-royal persons, the range of images found in the tombs of viziers, high state officials, court singers, royal hairdressers, and tradesmen does not differ greatly. The most important difference lay in their execution, which took into account the size of the tomb and the availability of the wall surfaces; this depended ultimately on the financial means of the deceased.

76 *False door*
Saqqara, offering chamber in the mastaba of the vizier Mehu; early Sixth Dynasty, ca. 2330 BC.
A third form of false door was that with cavetto cornice and torus moulding and post often used from the Fifth Dynasty onward. It mimicked the entrance to a cult building. The false door of Mehu is made of limestone, its red-brown paint imitates sandstone. The hieroglyphs are inset and painted in yellow. On the architrave and inner doorposts they contain sacrificial prayers to the gods of the dead, Anubis and Osiris – a good burial after an honorable old age is requested. In the vertical lines of the outer doorpost are inscribed the titles of the deceased. The inscription indicates that Mehu held the post of vizier and was the inspector of all important state offices in the land.

77 Goats grazing and net-fishing
Saqqara, east wall of the rock-cut tomb of the court singers Nefer and Kahay; mid-Fifth Dynasty, ca. 2450 BC.
In the northern section of the east wall in the tomb of Nefer and Kahay; there are depictions of rural labor. In the upper register, goats are shown grazing on trees. The foreman hands a written report over to the deceased. In the two registers below, there are scenes of net-fishing. The overseer of fishermen presents the largest fish of the catch to the deceased. The division of the registers in this section of the wall forms the base line for the depictions. In the middle of the upper register a second base line divides it briefly into two scenes. The resulting internal register shows young goats grazing.
The opposite method of forming registers can be observed in the way the fishing scene is depicted. Two registers are combined to make one large register and form an over-sized depiction of the action. In the topmost section the riverbank with the fishermen is shown; in the lower, water with fish caught in the net.

78 Driving cattle through a ford, construction of papyrus boats, cattle-rearing, and fowling with a clapnet
Saqqara, east wall of the rock-cut tomb of the court singers Nefer and Kahay; mid-Fifth Dynasty, ca. 2450 BC.
The images in the central section of the east wall are oriented toward the image of the deceased at the right end of the wall (not shown). The pictorial section unites a series of scenes whose common theme is rural life. The upper scene shows the papyrus harvest and construction of a boat; in the middle are scenes of cattle-rearing and a herd of cattle being driven through a ford. The lower register shows, on the left, the baking of bread and, on the right, various scenes in the lives of the fowlers. In the very lowest register there are depictions of dancing in front of a hut. Every group of scenes is drawn into a single unit; they appeal through their economy and precision. The shortening of the sequences is a result of the lack of available wall space.

79 *Two young steers being thrown to the ground*
Saqqara, tomb of the vizier Mereruka; early Sixth Dynasty, ca. 2330 BC.
This image shows two phases in the capture and subduing of animals destined for slaughter. To the left the steer is acrobatically thrown to the ground. To the right, the animal has been overpowered; its hind legs have given out, and its front legs are bent as it slowly collapses.

80 *Display of cattle*
Saqqara, tomb of the vizier Ptahhotep; end of the Fifth Dynasty, ca. 2350 BC.
The animals destined for sacrifice are from the estates of the deceased Ptahhotep. The cattle, ready for slaughter, are led out for counting by the estate foremen and their assistants. This takes place in the presence of Ptahhotep whose presence is indicated by the annotation to the scene: "Watching the inspection of cattle from the stalls of the estates and *ka*-houses of the endowments to the dead." At the head of the cattle drive is a magnificent ox with lyre-shaped horns and an amulet around its neck. The ox is led by a crippled cowherd. Physical disabilities of this kind were only shown in the rural population. Following the ox is a short-horned cattlebeast, driven on by blows from a stick. Both animals represent a large number of cattle of their respective breeds. The good condition of the animals shows that excellent care had been taken of them.

The wall surfaces of an Old Kingdom chapel intended for a planned series of images were composed down to the last detail. The wall was organized into sections and these sections linked with one another. The most important element for ordering the entire structure of the wall was the horizontal register. A wall area had several registers, generally of the same height. The horizontal registers were framed at the side by a long rectangular field, the height of the entire wall. This contains the enormous image of the deceased that bracketed the registers oriented toward it. The registers show individual scenes that can be arranged into groups or series. Depending on the availability of space to be decorated the depiction could be either detailed or brief. The scenes could be portrayed in abridged form or long narrative sequences.

While the image of the deceased does not occupy any definable time frame, the time sequence of registers is so arranged that the earlier event is at the top while the later one is in a lower register. Good examples of temporal ordering are to be found in images of agricultural labor. The scenes are linked in the same order as the seasons; plowing, sowing, stamping in of the seed, harvesting, threshing, filling of the storehouses, and calculating the yield of the harvest are all depicted one after the other. The sequence concludes with images showing the further processing of grain into bread and beer. A similar temporal order can be seen in images of cattle-rearing where one continuous chain of events is portrayed in a single register: a bull mounts a cow, a calf is born, the cow is milked and calves are raised. A somewhat shorter series can be seen for the production of wine where individual events extend from harvesting to the wine-pressing through to the filling of wine barrels.

Most image sequences express the spatial as well as the temporal dimension. In images of farming, depictions of labor in the fields are

82 South wall of the rock-cut tomb of the court singers Nefer and Kahay
Saqqara; mid-Fifth Dynasty ca. 2450 BC.
Behind the south wall of the cult chamber of Nefer and Kahay's tomb lies the statue room (*serdab*). It is situated behind the paneling and can only be recognized from the outside by the three horizontal slits that connect the *serdab* with the chapel. The slits can be seen above the deceased who is depicted looking to his right. They mark the spot where censing for the statues in the *serdab* took place. The main image, executed in relief, shows the deceased, Nefer, receiving offerings. He wears a pleated kilt and supports himself on a staff. His three brothers follow on behind. The tomb offerings are spread out before him and bearers bring additional offerings of fowl and small domestic animals. A small orchestra plays while the offerings are consumed. The deceased's richly adorned wife sits at his feet and partakes of the offerings.

81 Animal sacrifices
Saqqara, rock-cut tomb of the court singers Nefer and Kahay; mid-Fifth Dynasty, ca. 2450 BC.
On the south wall of the tomb of Nefer and Kahay there is a depiction of an animal being slaughtered. On the left its throat is slit and the blood collected in a bowl by a butcher who enters the scene from outside the frame. In the middle of the picture, the front shank is being separated from the body. At the far right, the shank and heart are being carried off to the sacrificial site by two assistants. The shank is carried on their shoulders, while the heart is held in their hands.
The images of sacrificing show different and somewhat unusual postures for the figures. The slaughtermen are in constant movement and some of them are pictured in quite contorted positions. In spite of the static medium in which they are portrayed, they have a lifelike effect.

followed by those of work in barns or storehouses. Similar relationships can be found where fishing and fowling with a throwing net are depicted; rural scenes are combined with those occurring in other contexts.

Occasionally the temporal and spatial dimensions overlap. In depictions of hunting in the desert, the prey is sometimes desert animals and sometimes that of the steppes. These animals are shown copulating and then giving birth. Similar displacements of time and space occur in boat journeys. In images of a river boat journey, the deceased appears as the passenger of a sailing ship in the same frame and at the same time as he is shown as the passenger of a galley.

Animal Sacrifices and the Provision of Offerings

An essential part of the sacrificial cult were meat offerings, most of which came from cattle. Hunting, however, was also an important source of meat, especially that of gazelles and antelope. Geese, ducks, and pigeons were also numbered amongst sacrificial animals. Fish had no place in sacrifices, although fishing was one of the activities frequently depicted in the tombs of the Old Kingdom.

The meat was offered up in either boiled or roasted form. It was placed at the tomb's offering place for ritual use by the deceased and was later removed and consumed by the priests of the mortuary cult. The offering of sacrificial meat was an event of great significance; through the meat the vital forces of the slaughtered animal were transferred to the deceased. The shank and heart of the sacrificial beast were thought to have a particularly revivifying effect. Both these parts were presented to the deceased in connection with the Opening of the Mouth ritual and played an important part in the resurrection rites carried out for the dead.

Because of the great life-giving qualities of the heart and shank for the recipient, images of animal sacrifice are always present in tombs of the Old Kingdom. The removal of the heart and cutting off of the shank represented integral parts of this ritual. Both these types of sacrificial scenes were executed with particular care and show clearly the vigorous movements of the butchers. They were also the first scenes in which conversations during work were recorded. The beliefs associated with the slaughter ritual had their origin in the "nomadic hunter-gatherer tradition" of prehistoric Egypt. The tradition persisted from prehistory into historical times. The slaughtered animal represented the object of the hunt. Before the sacrifice it was captured with a lasso, thrown to the ground, tied and killed according to ritual custom. Slaughtering was carried out with a flint knife that had long since disappeared from everyday use. The sacrifice was seen in this context as penance for a sinful act committed by the animal in the past. Its slaughter was seen as a positive act and sacramentally interpreted as the destruction of an enemy of the gods. In historical times, the sacrificial animals represented a valuable material possession. Thus the slaughter scenes in the Old Kingdom have a social aspect as well as a religious meaning. The sacrifice of animals served not only to resurrect the deceased and destroy divine enemies but also emphasized his or her wealth and power. Scenes of animal sacrifice can also be seen as a way of designating the deceased as the owner of an estate or large property.

This materialistic idea of recording wealth and power is also expressed in scenes of animal husbandry in tombs of the Old Kingdom. The herds are led forth in long processions and the animals counted individually. The result of the count always turns out to be highly favorable – any other result would have been inappropriate for a tomb representation.

Craftsmen and Market Scenes

In the tomb depictions of the Old Kingdom, the life of a typical representative of ancient Egyptian society was portrayed. The life of the elite was taken as the model for the afterlife of the deceased. A particularly good indicator of an individual's high social status is provided by the scenes of agricultural labor and cattle-rearing, images of fishing and fowling in the countryside as well as scenes of tradesmen working. In each of these the deceased is shown in a supervisory role.

The elevated position of the deceased and his proximity to the king is particularly apparent in the scenes of craftsmanship. The right to direct the activities of tradesmen was a royal privilege as the raw materials and goods being processed came from the possessions of the royal administration. The minerals for the metalworkers, for example, come from expeditions undertaken abroad or from the border areas of Egypt. Copper came from the Sinai or was supplied from Palestine (in the Old Kingdom perhaps even from Cyprus). Gold was mined in the eastern desert or in Nubia. This was also the case for wood, which was used frequently. It was harvested almost entirely abroad in Syria. Egypt itself is extremely poor in wood and has only the low-quality acacia or sycamore available in abundance. For this reason, Lebanese cedar – a valued import even in Egyptian prehistory – was particularly sought after.

The different varieties of African wood were also considered luxury products, especially ebony for making statues and furniture. Stone for the construction of tombs and their interiors was, in early times, donated by the king. It was mined in often-distant quarries and reached the royal residence on ships of the state administration from the area around the cataracts or Nubia.

Most artisans' products were destined for tomb furnishings. These were mostly objects that, in the early days of Egyptian culture,

83 Tradesmen and market scenes
Saqqara, south wall of the offering chapel in the tomb of the pyramid foreman Ti; end of the Fifth Dynasty, ca. 2400 BC.
The workers pictured in the tomb of Ti represent almost every type of trade. On the south wall of the main cult chamber a single scene shows sculptors, metalworkers, jewelers, carpenters, and leather workers going about their trades. A view into a carpenter's workshop shows aspects of his work: from left to right large planks are sawn, dowel is hammered into boxes, a smaller board is sawed into shape and a bed polished. The inscriptions state the titles of the tradesmen and their activities and contain their conversations. For example, a carpenter working with a saw calls to his colleague: "Give me another (saw-blade). (This saw-blade) is hot!"
In the lower register there is a scene of trading in the marketplace. Market business takes the form of bartering and has only local significance. Articles of everyday use are exchanged. At the left, a carver of seals offers his services. In the middle, unguents are traded for sandals and at the right fans are for sale. To the right also, sticks are traded for grain. The conversations of salesmen and buyers are recorded. A stick-dealer, for example, says: "Look! A fine stick, well dried, my friend. I want three hekats of wheat for it." The answer is: "Oh, it has a wonderful grip!"

84 Scenes of tradesmen

Saqqara, east wall of the cliff chamber in the tomb of the royal manicurists Niankhkhnum and Khnumhotep; mid-Fifth Dynasty, ca. 2450 BC.

A detailed series of tradesmen scenes is contained in the tomb of the two royal manicurists, Niankhkhnum and Khnumhotep, at Saqqara. Running from the top to the bottom, the registers show several workshops. At the top, sculptors fashion statues; in the middle, metalworkers produce objects for tomb furnishings; and at the bottom, jewelers knot broad collar necklaces.

The inscriptions refer to various details – to the activities being carried out, the titles of the craftsmen and the type of products being made, for example, "painting statues" by "the painter" or "buttoning broad collars by the jeweler."

The only conversations recorded in these scenes are between the metalworkers. One of these refers to the state of the molten metal in the crucible. The fire under the crucible is fed by four men blowing through long tubes; flames leap high at the sides. The foremen to the right of the workers announces the forthcoming casting with the following words: "The air is hot over the molten metal (which is called the brother of the sun). The molten state has been reached. Seize it (and begin to cast)!" Metal rods are produced which are then beaten by other metalworkers into sheets. The finished products are cult objects.

were placed as provisions in tomb storerooms but whose physical presence was later dispensed with. Pictures became the replacement for these missing tomb offerings.

The range of depicted products is limited. Metalworkers produced cult objects and jewelry while stonemasons manufactured stone vessels, statues or sarcophagi.

Woodworkers made religious objects and items for everyday use. Their work also encompassed traditional ship construction and the production of doors, columns, and shrines. The surplus of produced goods was sold on the market and made available to other tomb owners. The demand for goods traded on the market, however, was only able to satisfy fundamental needs. This market economy was a barter economy; goods were exchanged for goods. The standard measure of value was a unit of copper against which various commodities were assessed. Bartered goods derived mainly from domestic sources, the most common being food. The sorts of items offered included beer and bread, vegetables and fish, and smaller quantities of fish hooks, unguents, sandals, oils or cylinder seals. High-quality products from the royal monopoly were lacking – papyrus, for example.

The Journey to the "Beautiful West"

Although the tomb paintings depict daily life, they refer nevertheless to the hereafter, which was conceived of according to the standards of this life. It is possible, therefore, to comprehend ancient notions concerning the afterlife from the scenes and images in the tombs of the Old Kingdom.

Closer inspection reveals that non-royal notions of the afterlife display a similar variety to those of the royal house. In contrast to beliefs regarding the royal afterlife, the hereafter of the non-royal dead was not located in heaven with the gods but was under the earth in a world of ancestors and predecessors. The entire non-royal tomb culture is based on this assumption. This subterranean tomb was thought of as the dwelling place of the dead in the afterlife.

A series of seemingly contradictory beliefs was connected to this idea of the tomb as the hereafter of the non-royal Egyptian. If seen in the light of mythical thought, however, they do in fact appear consistent. Just as the deceased king ascended to heaven in different ways – on the wings of a bird, with the help of a locust, on the smoke from incense or with the aid of a heavenly ladder – so too the deceased reached his or her subterranean hereafter in different ways.

One old belief stated that, after death, the deceased was guided into the necropolis. In the course of the burial rites he or she was led somberly into the city of the dead and proceeded to live in a specially designated tomb chamber.

Another belief was based on the topographical location of the tomb. The hereafter was assumed to be located in such a way that the deceased reached the necropolis by crossing the Nile in a boat. This can be seen from the tomb inscriptions in which the deceased wished "to traverse the paths of the revered in great peace and to ascend to the mountain heights of the necropolis." The passage to the necropolis was often depicted in tombs as a journey in a river boat and is described in the associated inscriptions as a journey to the "Beautiful West." Depending on the prevailing winds a distinction was made between a river journey under sail and a journey in a rowed barge.

A third possibility was that of reaching the hereafter in the west by traveling overland. This wish, too, is expressed in tomb inscriptions. The deceased hopes to "attain the mountain heights of the necropolis" by land. The sedan chair was available for such land journeys to the "Beautiful West." The deceased is carried to the necropolis and the

85 Sedan chair procession
Saqqara, tomb of the estate overseer Ipi; early Sixth Dynasty, ca. 2330 BC; limestone; H. 112 cm; Cairo, Egyptian Museum, CG 1536.
The estate overseer Ipi is carried in a lavishly ornamented sedan chair. He sits under a sunroof and holds a short staff in one hand and a fly-whisk in the other. The poles of the sedan chair rest on the shoulders of the bearers, of whom only those on the right side can be seen. Those on the left are indicated by shading around the outlines of those on the right. Other accompanying individuals include servants with sunshades as well as the personal retinue of the deceased at the head of the procession. The bearers sing the so-called "Sedan Chair Song," in which they lament the burden of their work but also sing of the joy of having the honor of bearing the deceased. The text of the song is recorded in between the bearers. It contains the memorable refrain: "Better that the sedan chair (with the deceased) be occupied, than that it be empty."

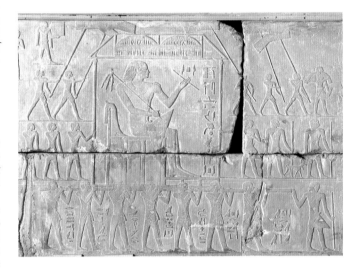

86 Journey to the "Beautiful West"
Saqqara, tomb of the vizier Mehu; early Sixth Dynasty, ca. 2330 BC.
The ship is shown with its sails raised. Some of the crew are at the oars while others pull the sails up. The deceased stands in front of the cabin amidships and supports himself on his staff. He observes the handling of the sails, which indicates a change in direction of the ship. This maneuver can be explained by the fact that the ship is about to arrive in the "Beautiful West." The deceased can be seen a second time in the cabin at the stern, this time lying lifeless on a bed. The inscription over the ship contains a song referring to favorable winds and the imminent arrival of the deceased in the region of the hereafter belonging to Hathor: "The gold (that is, the goddess Hathor) created the beauty of the beautiful (mummy). The beautiful (mummy) comes now to Hathor, Lady of the Sycamore. In peace, in peace to the western Mountain Land!"

87 Mock river-battle
Saqqara, tomb of the vizier Ptahhotep; end of the Fifth Dynasty, ca. 2350 BC.
The papyrus boats depicted in the tomb of the vizier Ptahhotep are traveling in a convoy on canals that branch off from the Nile. The water of the canals is teeming with fish and lotus blossoms; the goal of the convoy is the necropolis. For unexplained reasons, the transport of offerings is connected with mock battles, although the loaded boats are traveling in the same direction and the offerings are destined for the same deceased person. Perhaps the battles express the competitive spirit among the boat crews. Each boat would like to be the first to reach the place of offering and therefore attempts to divert the other boat from its course. The boats' cargoes consist of baskets of figs, fowl in a cage and, in the lead boat, a calf. The papyrus boat that brings up the rear of the convoy introduces an element of tranquillity to the hectic scene. Its passenger is the tomb's designer. The inscription contains an artistic signature seldom seen in ancient Egypt. It is "his beloved (of Ptahhotep) honorable artisan Niankhptah." During the journey, a meal of bread, fruit, and beer is handed to the artist. In the register above is a fowling scene with clapnets.

"Beautiful West" in a sedan chair on the shoulders of his servants. In order to lighten the load during the sedan chair procession, the "Sedan Chair Song" is sung. The bearers use the lyrics of the song to spur each other on; its text accompanies numerous scenes from the Old Kingdom. In some cases the deceased uses the more comfortable donkey sedan chair instead of the squatting or seated sedan carried by men.

The Deceased's Journey into the Papyrus Thicket

The hereafter was essentially modeled on the life in this world. The parameters for the hereafter were therefore fulfillment of one's duty and the inspection of work undertaken on the land and on the estates. The images of everyday life are placed firmly in this context. They consist of pictures of agricultural work, cattle-rearing, fishing and fowling, the production of food, and the craftsmen's activities. Besides these images of typical everyday life there are scenes showing the deceased journeying into the papyrus thicket. These images also refer to the regions of the hereafter and to the "Beautiful West;" in particular, they compare the hereafter with a mythical location. This location is the mythical landscape of Khemmis in the Nile Delta, where Isis gave birth to her son Horus in the papyrus thicket, and where she hid him from the depredations of Seth, the enemy of the gods. Here, Horus grew up under the protection of Isis.

In the mythical dawn of time, the papyrus thicket was Horus's place of birth and childhood. In the reality of the mortal world – the here and now – the wall paintings of the papyrus thicket became a place of rebirth and revitalization. The mythical function of the papyrus thicket is therefore transferred to the tomb; the tomb structure itself is seen as lying within the papyrus thicket. This idea is well expressed in those instances where images of the papyrus thicket occur on the tomb facade and entrance. Such conspicuous placement attests to the fact that the interior of the tomb is a papyrus thicket and that the tomb itself is a place of rebirth. The images of the funerary chapel therefore not only portray the daily life of the non-royal deceased in the hereafter, but also indicate the function of the tomb as a place of rebirth. A good example for the beliefs associated with this mythical place is provided by images showing the deceased hunting birds with a throwstick or fishing with a multi-pronged spear in the papyrus thicket. These expeditions generally show him in the company of his wife. He is therefore given the opportunity of being reborn from his own wife. The children of the deceased often depicted on the papyrus boat should be seen as younger versions of himself. In them, his rebirth has already been completed.

The papyrus thicket as a place of rebirth, at the same time, conceals a number of different dangers. Hostile forces, particularly the hippopotamus, threaten the incipient rebirth of the deceased. As potential enemies of the gods they are mercilessly driven from the presence of the deceased. He is assisted in this by helpers who have their home in the swamp. More than any other image in the tombs of the Old Kingdom, the scenes of the papyrus thicket highlight the connection of the tomb images with the hereafter and point directly to the rebirth of the deceased. The semantic associations of the papyrus thicket indicate its inseparability from the birth, growth, and triumph of Osiris's son, Horus, and confer on the deceased or tomb owner the comforting certainty that, through his rebirth in the papyrus thicket, he will overcome death.

88 Construction of papyrus boats
Saqqara, tomb of the vizier Ptahhotep; end of the Fifth Dynasty, ca. 2350 BC.
The building of papyrus boats usually takes place close to the papyrus thicket and in many cases is directly associated with a thicket representation. The boatbuilders work as a family and include their children in their tasks.

The children make themselves useful with simpler chores. In the tomb of the vizier Ptahhotep a child holds the ropes necessary for lashing the boats. During the work, a dialogue develops between father and son. The father, busy on the boat, calls to his son: "Oh my son Ikai, bring me the ropes!" The son answers promptly: "Oh my father, take this rope!"

89 Hunting birds with a throwing stick and spearing fish in the papyrus thicket
Saqqara, tomb of the royal manicurists Niankhkhnum and Khnumhotep; mid-Fifth Dynasty, ca. 2450 BC.
The collection of images shows both Niankhkhnum and Khnumhotep hunting in the papyrus swamp. On the left, Niankhkhnum prepares for the bird hunt while on the right his brother Khnumhotep is spearing fish.

Flocks of birds fly up at their approach on a papyrus boat. Some birds remain in their nests, which are depicted in a location that would not occur naturally – on the blossoms of papyrus plants. The breeding birds are also threatened by otters and wild cats. These predators approach the birds' papyrus bloom nests along unsteady stems. The deceased are accompanied on the hunt by their wives and eldest sons.

90 Hippopotamus hunt
Saqqara, tomb of the vizier Mereruka; early
Sixth Dynasty, ca. 2330 BC.
The hippopotamus hunt in the tomb of the
vizier Mereruka in Saqqara is counted
amongst the most important hunting scenes
in the Old Kingdom. Two boats, both crewed
by hippopotamus hunters, have cornered
three hippopotamuses. These have retreated
to the cover of an enormous aquatic plant at
the edge of the papyrus thicket. Huge locusts,
dragonflies and frogs can be seen on this
outsized plant. In comparison, the hippopotamuses are tiny. They face the hunters
approaching from left and right who launch
their harpoons at the animals. The detailed
depiction is of very high quality. This
contrasts with the incorrect proportions of the
objects, animals, plants, and people.

Living Images – The Private Statue

Helmut Satzinger

Egyptian museums and collections hold a great number of sculptures of standing, seated or squatting figures that differ from royal or divine images. In the Old Kingdom these so-called private statues were usually placed in tombs. Later on, statues were more often placed in temples – in the Late Period almost exclusively so. Those few statues made in prehistoric times – mostly of ivory or faience – come from sacred sites as well as tombs. However, it is not clear whether these were private, royal or divine statues. The same is true for the even rarer stone or wood sculptures of the Thinite Period. From this one can deduce that there may well have been temple statues in the Old Kingdom but evidence still remains to be found. The tradition of private tomb statues only really began in the Third Dynasty. They were first found in the tombs of princes and dignitaries in the necropolises of the ancient capital of Memphis, especially at Saqqara and Giza.

The statues were not openly displayed within the tombs. This is a particularly illuminating fact when it comes to assessing Egyptian art. It seems clear that being seen was not the primary function of the statue. Rather, its purpose lay in its mere existence in order to serve as a replacement body, a kind of "alter ego," for the deceased.

During rituals for the mortuary cult, food and drink were placed in front of the false door in the tomb chapel and incense was burned. When the deceased, or really his spirit, magically or ritually entered the statue, it became possible for him to consume these offerings through the statue. The statue could only perform this function if it was directly identified with the deceased. This was made possible by inscribing the statue with his or her name and providing it with individualized features or characteristics. In addition, there was a reviving ritual, the so-called Opening of the Mouth Ritual, performed on the statue by a priest. All Egyptian art, not only the fine arts, was suspended between reality and the demands of sacred standards. It was clear, even to the Egyptians of the Old Kingdom, that the sacred standards set for the world, that is, the way the world should be, were not always compatible with the harsh facts of reality. Art had to conform to the sacred norms; it had to present an ideal picture. That reality intruded, however, could not be avoided. Each individual work of art was thus a compromise between these two competing tendencies.

Where Did the Statue Stand?

Some funerary statues were placed in the tomb chapels where they could only be seen by those who serviced the mortuary cult; they were not therefore readily accessible. Typical for the Old Kingdom, however, was that the tomb statue was concealed from everyone. In King Djoser's pyramid a chamber for the tomb statue was built whose only connection to the offering place in the chapel was a slit (see p 86, no. 82). This type of tomb soon spread to private mastabas. To describe this room, archaeologists use the Arabic-Persian term *serdab*, meaning a cave or subterranean chamber. In other tombs, though, the statues were generally placed by the walls or in the niches of the cult chamber. The magnificent tomb of Hemiunu from the reign of King Cheops has two *serdabs*. In the tomb of his contemporary Kawab (as in the tomb of Prince Minkhaef), however, numerous statues were placed visibly in the outer chapel. Tombs with a *serdab* became more common only from the time of King Mycerinus on. In the late Fifth Dynasty the statue chambers became larger and more frequent. In Giza, Rawer, son of Itisen, had more than one hundred statues in twenty-five rooms for himself and his family. Toward the end of the Fifth Dynasty, statues of the deceased – and later those of servants – were placed within the tomb chamber.

This custom, which signaled a change in attitude toward both tomb and statue, finally led to the end of the *serdab* tradition. Moreover, the *serdab* is found only in conjunction with the mastaba. It was not used in the rock-cut tomb, which was characteristic for the necropolises of Upper Egypt – and thus for the further development of Egyptian tomb architecture after the Old Kingdom.

Who is Portrayed?

The basic answer is: those who were buried in the mastabas. During the reign of Cheops, these were primarily princes and dignitaries. At the end of the Old Kingdom they also included craftsmen and lower ranking officials who squeezed their modest tombs in between the

91 Seated statue of Princess Redji
Third Dynasty, ca. 2650 BC; diorite; H. 83 cm; Turin, Museo Egizio, cat. 3065. "The king's own daughter Redji" (the name in the inscription on the pedestal is read variously; for example, erroneously as Redief) is seated on a low-backed chair; the bow-shaped relief on the sides indicate that it is a wicker chair. Her attitude is upright; one hand rests on the thigh, the other below her breast. It is characteristic of Third Dynasty sculpture that her face appears lifelike and individualized, whereas her body seems stiff – although less so than in the work of the Early Dynastic period.

92 Seated figure of Khent with her small son

92 Seated figure of Khent with her small son
Giza; probably high Fourth Dynasty, ca. 2550 BC; limestone; H. 53 cm; Vienna, Kunsthistorisches Museum, ÄS 7507.

Khent was the wife of the high official Nisutnefer. She was probably buried in her own tomb shaft in the mastaba of her husband. Normally, wives did not have their own statue but were depicted together with their husbands. Khent, however, had her own statue placed in her own *serdab*. She sits erect on a broad, high-backed chair, her hands placed flat on her thighs. As with group

portraits of couples, a small boy, also worked from the same stone block, is depicted standing to the side of the chair. The pleat on one side of his head (the so-called sidelock of youth), the finger placed to his mouth and his nakedness characterize him as a small child according to the standards of Egyptian iconography. Stylistically, the sculpture belongs to a larger group of works of art from the Old Kingdom that replaced the realism of the Cheops and Chephren era with the idealization typical of the following period.

93 (below center) Group of standing figures of Memisabu and his wife
Probably Giza; late Fourth Dynasty, ca. 2520 BC; limestone; H. 62 cm; New York, The Metropolitan Museum of Art, 48.111.

In statues of couples, the woman usually places her arm around the shoulder of the man. Only rarely does the man place his arm around the shoulder of the woman. The possessive quality of this gesture is emphasized through the great difference in height. The woman encircles the waist of the man. Although traditionally described in all

previous literature as being a work of the Sixth Dynasty, it has recently been possible to attribute this group of figures to the late Fourth Dynasty. Its dependency in formal structure on royal figure groups of this period is unmistakable. Furthermore, the distinct tendency to an individual dissolution of the statuary structure of a group of figures is just as clear, marked here by the strong frontal orientation of the work, the parallel position of the official's feet, a very unusual gesture of embrace, and the slight leftward inclination in respect of the female figure.

larger mastabas. Mastabas were erected only for a single generation, normally a couple and their children if these died while still young. Thus we commonly find in a *serdab* either single statues of the deceased and his wife or both together. Children are never represented independently but rather in the company of their parents and usually on a very small scale. The children so represented had not necessarily died at a young age; at the time the statues were made they may already have been adults. The presence of children might only have indicated the desire for life after death. Sometimes, the woman at the side of the deceased is not his wife but his mother. Other combinations of two (two men, two women) and three (two men and one woman, etc.) individuals were also possible. Single statues of husband and wife could be placed in separate *serdabs*. Just as the deceased might have any number of single statues so, too, there are groups of statues in which he might be represented two or three times (so-called "pseudo groups").

The Relative Sizes of the Sexes

It is interesting to note the difference in proportions in the representations of men and women. Quite often they are of equal height or their difference in height merely reflects statistical reality. However, the woman is sometimes presented very much smaller than the man. Among these examples there are statues of couples in which the man sits while the woman stands. In these cases the significant difference in proportions can be explained by considerations of composition.

Examples of pairs in which the woman sits and the man stands are rare. In such cases the proportions of the seated and standing persons are about equal. The slightly larger size of the male figure is presumably due to the fact that these are high-ranking officials, that is, important personages. A woman could only possess such a high social status if she came from an equally high-ranking family.

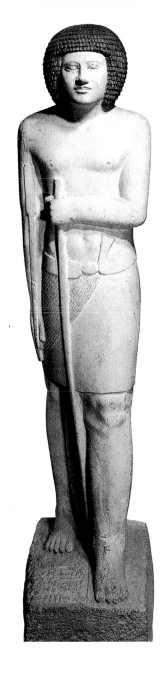
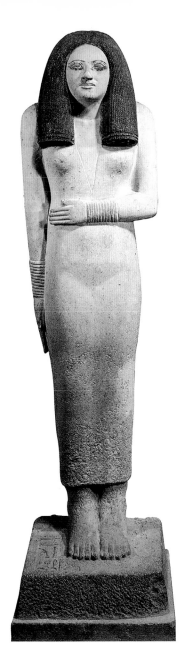

94 (opposite, right) Family group of Pepi
Giza; high Fifth Dynasty, ca. 2430 BC; limestone; H. 45 cm; Hildesheim, Pelizaeus-Museum, 17.
In this group of man, woman (Pepi) and child, the most striking feature is that the woman is larger than the man. Since the child is also larger than normal, the woman appears to have the dominant position. She holds the man by the shoulder and the upper arm, as is common for wives and mothers in group statues. Although the sculpture has an inscription on its base, the family relationship of this group is not clear. This is not least because the man and child both bear the same name: Rashepses. The man is called "her son" whereas the child is, according to the inscription, a "royal *wab* priest." The

simplest explanation is that the inscriptions have been accidentally swapped; the adult is indeed the woman's husband, a *wab* priest, and the child her son. In that case, the height and position of the woman is remarkable. It is also possible that they are two sons bearing the same name (as sometimes happened) or that they are son and grandson; it would then be surprising that the latter had a title and was therefore already an adult. Another possible explanation is to assume that it is a "pseudo group" – Pepi's son Rashepses would then be shown at two different ages. Whatever the correct explanation, this is a rare case of a family group dominated by a woman. Aside from formal aspects, the suggested dating is made on the basis of stylistic criteria .

95–97 Standing figures of Sepa (twice) and Nesa
Probably from Saqqara; Third Dynasty, ca. 2670 BC; limestone; H. 159, 165, and 152 cm; Paris, Musée du Louvre, A 36, A 37, A 38.
The three most outstanding large sculptures of the early Old Kingdom come from a single series. Two statues of the deceased and one of his wife were found in the same *serdab*. In the further development of Egyptian sculpture monolithic groups tended to replace single figures. If, as in this case, a person is represented twice we speak of "pseudo groups." The two statues are identical down to the smallest sculptural nuances. In contrast to later stone sculptures the man is shown holding a scepter and a staff. The sculptural

representation of insignia are problematic not only from a technical point of view; it is also difficult to place within the unconventional style of Egyptian sculpture. Whereas the sekhem scepter, according to depictions in reliefs, was to be held horizontally, the sculptor here has to present it vertically in order not to detach it from the body. The staff, too, had to be connected to the body for technical reasons. The style of the faces is individualistic, perhaps portrait-like. As is usual, the bodies are cursorily depicted. The arms pressed against the body appear stiff. This is characteristic for Third Dynasty sculpture when the transition from archaic art to the art of the classic Old Kingdom was already well advanced.

98 Standing figure of Babaef
Giza; probably early Fifth Dynasty, ca. 2480 BC; calcite alabaster; H. 49,7 cm; Vienna, Kunsthistorisches Museum, ÄS 7785.
Babaef is represented in a manner typical of the high Old Kingdom: standing erect, of athletic stature with wide shoulders, slim waist and powerful muscles. His gaze is directed ahead and slightly upward – toward the sun, according to a new interpretation, in order to indicate a desire for enlightenment. This figure of Babaef was found discarded together with other fragments in his Mastaba. Of all his different official functions it was that of "Manager of all the King's Works" that would have allowed the official access to the precious alabaster material used for his funerary figures.

99 Scribe
Saqqara; early Fifth Dynasty, ca. 2500 BC; painted limestone; H. 51 cm; Cairo, Egyptian Museum, CG 36.
The squatting figure is one of the best-known sculptures from the Old Kingdom. The idealization of Fifth Dynasty sculpture is paired here with clearly individualized features. We are unable to say whether the marked wrinkles on the side of the nose were a distinctive trait of the person portrayed. Nevertheless, this detail lends an individual touch to the attractive and engaging face. The natural effect is heightened by the inlaid eyes, although the corrosion of the copper border used to recreate the eye outline somewhat spoils this impression. The head is slightly turned, the eyes look slightly right. These features, also known from other, similar sculptures, seemingly show the scribe dutifully listening to dictation. With his left hand the man holds the open papyrus; his right hand presumably held a reed for writing.

Where couples are represented, the woman usually shows her affection through her posture and gestures; she lays her arm around his shoulders and perhaps grasps the man's arm nearest to her with her other hand. Other couples display a posture emphasizing equality by holding hands.

Types of Statues

In the course of the history of Egyptian sculpture a number of different postures developed that were often repeated and thus became part of the canon. Three basic forms were already present in the Old Kingdom. These are listed below.

The standing figure: Men show a distinct striding posture in which the weight largely rests on the back leg; it is therefore a static posture and only suggestive of striding. Women stand with legs together or display only a slight striding posture. The arms hang loose at the sides of the body and the hands are either open or clenched around a "stone core." In rare instances, there are some examples where one arm is bent and the fist placed at the opposite breast. Only wooden statues show the long staff, familiar from two-dimensional depictions, held in one hand.

The seated statue: The figures are seated on cuboid blocks. The bent arms rest on the thighs and often one hand is clenched around a "stone core."

The squatting statue: the figures, mostly men, sit cross-legged on a mat or on the ground. If the squatting figure has an open papyrus role on his lap he is considered a "reader;" if he also has a reed in his hand for writing, he is thought of as a "scribe." "Asymmetrical squatters," where one knee is drawn up, are rarely found. Rarer still are "kneeling figures" or those squatting on their heels.

100 Group statue of a standing man and his wife
Giza; Fifth Dynasty, ca. 2450 BC; painted limestone; H. 56 cm; Vienna, Kunsthistorisches Museum, ÄS 7444.
The sculpture shows the couple in a standard pose. Both man and woman are presented in the costume befitting their high social position; the man in a short loincloth, the woman in a long dress with shoulder straps and a wig. The woman, depicted in natural proportions in relation to the man, has one arm around his back and with the other touches his arm. The empty space between them is colored black, an iconographic sign that it is the background. The short inscription on the base limits itself to telling us the names of the people portrayed but does not provide any further information on their relationship.

101 Statue pair
Probably from Saqqara; early Fifth Dynasty, ca. 2500 BC; acacia wood; H. 69 cm; Paris, Musée du Louvre, N. 2293.
Wood is a material conducive to realistic representations. Both figures were worked separately. However, they are not only joined by a common pedestal (the original of which has been lost) but also by the woman's left arm, which embraces the man's back. Because she is very much smaller than the man her arm rests beneath his shoulder blades.
This unusual group portrait has found its way, along with the Salt collection, into the Louvre while its dating was for a long time a matter of controversy. The graphical nature of the facial style is especially indicative of the early Sixth Dynasty, belonging to the so-called 'second style' of Saqqara.

102 Statue of a brewer sealing a jar
Saqqara; Fifth Dynasty, ca. 2400 BC; painted limestone; H. 13 cm; Cairo, Egyptian Museum, CG 112.
During brewing it was necessary to smear the inner walls of the jar with clay to preserve the beer. The sculpture shows a servant at this task. The oval hollows at the front of the base were for three miniature model jars that complemented the sculpture.

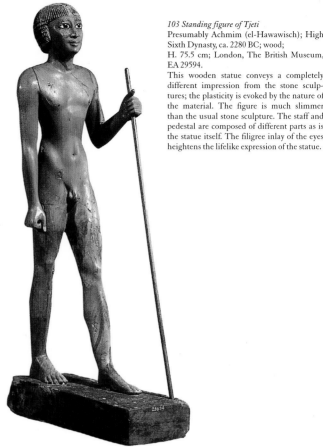

103 Standing figure of Tjeti
Presumably Achmim (el-Hawawisch); High Sixth Dynasty, ca. 2280 BC; wood;
H. 75.5 cm; London, The British Museum, EA 29594.
This wooden statue conveys a completely different impression from the stone sculptures; the plasticity is evoked by the nature of the material. The figure is much slimmer than the usual stone sculpture. The staff and pedestal are composed of different parts as is the statue itself. The filigree inlay of the eyes heightens the lifelike expression of the statue.

One should bear in mind that this terminology is of occidental origin and not Egyptian. Squatting was, in reality, the conventional seating position where-as sitting on a chair was something unusual. The hieroglyph of a seated figure 𓀀 means in Egyptian *shepses*, "noble," whereas the hieroglyph of the "asymmetrical squatter" 𓀃 was simply the sign for "man."

In the dynastic era seated statues were commonly made in stone whereas standing statues before the Third Dynasty were made only in wood. From this time on, the seated statue was the most common type of artifact, followed by standing figures and then squatting figures of all kinds. A special feature of the Old Kingdom are heads and busts that obviously have a different function from that of tomb statues. The same is true for the statues of servants shown preparing food or performing other kinds of duties; these developed only in the Old Kingdom. They are not individually marked (for example, inscribed with a name) but merely represent the task being performed. Standing statues are supported at the back by a pillar whereas groups of standing figures have a common back slab. Seated statues can also have a back slab that has the appearance of a high backrest. Besides freestanding statues there are also those carved from the rock face within the tomb.

The arms and legs of stone statues were connected to the body with pins. Statues made of limestone sometimes had freely worked arms. For technical reasons, this was not possible with figures made of hard stone. Wooden statues had no such technical restrictions with respect to the limbs; generally, these were carved separately and then attached to the body.

Reserve Heads

The rather sober-sounding term reserve heads (also called "replacement heads") is used for sculptures of life-sized heads found primarily in tombs of the Fourth Dynasty. More than thirty such heads are known, most of them from Giza. They were specifically made as individual heads and were not merely fragments of statues. Their intended placement is known from isolated examples; it was not the *serdab* but the bottom of the deep shaft leading into the burial chamber. More precisely, they were placed in niches in the wall that sealed the burial chamber off from the shaft. Most of the heads date from the time of Cheops and Chephren.

There have been many attempts to interpret the meaning of these objects and the motives for making and positioning them: firstly, the fear of literally losing one's head in the hereafter, be it through demons or natural decay; for this reason they have been called reserve or replacement heads. Secondly, they might have been substitutes for the tomb statue; and thirdly, they may have been intended to preserve the look of the dead even when the mummy decayed – mummification methods were not well developed at that time. This preservation was essential not only for life in the hereafter but also to enable the freely moving component of the self (the "soul") to identify the body.

A more recent theory – that these heads were part of a magical practice to prevent the dead from coming back and harming their descendants – has not found much support. There are even theories that claim that these heads might have been used as models of the tomb owner for statues or as decorations in his living quarters.

However, the placement of the heads indicates that they did not function as cult statues – that is, they did not enable the dead to receive offerings. Therefore their function must have been solely to preserve the individuality and appearance of the dead.

Stylization, Realism, Portrait

Human likenesses were portrayed in such a way as to suit them for eternity. This was achieved by stylizing certain aspects and features and this fundamental stylization dictated the way sculpture was represented. This idealization was at first concerned with the physical side of human existence. By and large the deceased were portrayed in a healthy and sound state. The sculpture obeyed a fixed ideal of proportions that determined the relation of the different body parts to each other. Apart from a few exceptions the dead appear of an indefinable age, neither young nor old, and show maturity as well as vitality. The bodies are strong and athletic, the posture is erect and their firm gazes are fixed straight ahead. The mood is equally neutral: neither happy nor sad, nor bound to a particular moment. They are neither engaged in a particular occupation nor do they belong to a certain milieu. The representation is altogether static.

This idealization also had a social aspect in that it expressed membership of the correct class and of a particular place in society. The choice of clothing befitting rank – including hairstyle and jewelry – illustrated this social status. (Jewelry originally had a magically protective function. In many cultures "beautiful" means "good" and "useful.") But it could also be expressed through posture or other attributes. For example, sitting on a chair indicated nobility. Similarly, a man represented as a scribe was characterized as a member of the elite. Furthermore, the figures may have been idealized for purely artistic reasons. Sculpture is not realistic, it does not reproduce exactly the human form in shape and proportion. Rather, it searches for stylistic tools and conventions in order to generate a distinctive and characteristic picture. The aim was to create the desired effect in the viewer – be it through a spontaneous visual impression or through knowledge of iconographic conventions – and to be accepted by society at large. These effects were achieved primarily through simplification (for example, in the details of the hairstyle) or through sculptural overstatement (for example, the embossed representation of brows and outlines of eyelids). The sculptural representation of an individual was more generously proportioned than in real life and also more strictly geometric.

However, it is important to note that there were varying degrees of stylization. In certain periods, for instance in the early Fourth Dynasty, tendencies developed that overcame those conventions. The face became fashioned more realistically, portraying a more mature age or even non-ideal body types, for example, corpulence or shortness. The necessity of idealization held realism in check. On the other hand, the religious purpose to which the pieces were put demanded that both the representation and the represented had individual characteristics. At first this was achieved through non-artistic means, that is, through the inscription. If the name and title of a person were specified then the work could be said to belong to a particular person. In addition, there were artistic means of graphic individualization or portraiture. Individualization without applying the techniques of portraiture is, in a sense, comparable with an amateurish caricature. Characteristic details are shown without the representation achieving the essence of a portrait. The intellect forces one to see that a person with such physical attributes can ultimately only be nameless. In a portrait, however, the viewer spontaneously identifies the person represented. The portrait is

104 Reserve head
Giza (Mastaba G 4350); Fourth Dynasty, ca. 2590 BC; limestone; H. 27,7 cm; Vienna, Kunsthistorisches Museum, ÄS 7787.
The function of the reserve heads must have been other than to serve as a surrogate body with which to receive ritual offerings in the mortuary cult. Stylistically, they are highly interesting because there are very few private sculptures from the first half of the Fourth Dynasty – a time when the development toward a naturalistic style reached its climax.

It is fascinating to observe the tensions between idealization and realism in individual works. Those showing the furthest development toward individualization, like this one, are astonishing and it can be assumed that they had something of the character of a portrait. An idealistic trait is, on the other hand, that it shows the figure in a completely neutral state, having neither emotions nor age, as was necessary for claiming a place in eternity.

supported by a realistic style, but portraits are nevertheless also possible in a non-realistic style. In modern art, there are expressionist, cubist and other types of portraiture that are all worthy of the name. Likewise, many of the Egyptian sculptures considered here have, despite their idealistic style, the character of portraits, even if we cannot clearly prove this.

Stylistic Developments

Compared to the Thinite era the faces of Third Dynasty sculpture seem strikingly alive – the bodies by contrast appear to be still pupating and not yet properly emerged from the material. Statues from the Fourth Dynasty sometimes display a considerable realism, like the grandiose bust of Ankhaef. Others show very individual features that seem realistic, for example the statue of Hemiunu (see p. 65, no. 39). Most reserve or replacement heads date from this period.

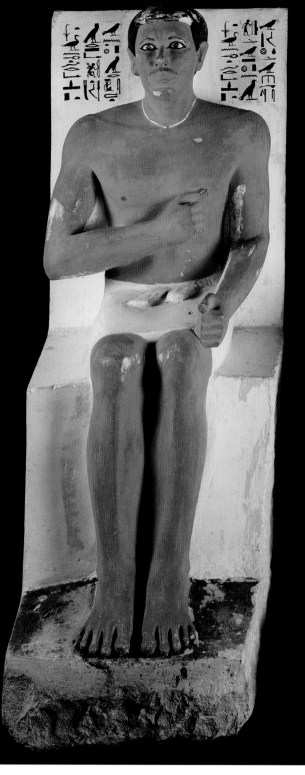
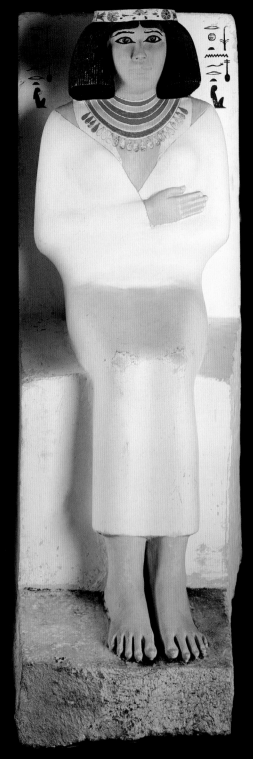

105 *Seated figures of Rahotep and of Nofret*
Meidum; Fourth Dynasty, ca. 2610 BC; painted limestone; H. 121 cm and 122 cm; Cairo, Egyptian Museum, CG 3 and 4.
These separate seated statues of a man and a woman form an ensemble. The seat with its high back and rectangular pedestal resembles the hieroglyph 𐃊 for throne. The statues show almost all their original paint and are a good instance of the conventions regarding the skin color of the sexes: brown for the man and yellow for the woman. The lifelike expression of the skillfully crafted faces is heightened by the inlaid eyes of white quartz and transparent rock crystal. The inscriptions for both statues are prominently placed in identical versions on the backs of the chairs next to the heads. Stylistically this pair of statues, with its facial features and relaxed postures, demonstrates a great step forward toward realism. They are therefore a connecting link between the works of the Third Dynasty and the realistic portraits of the reigns of Cheops and Chephren.

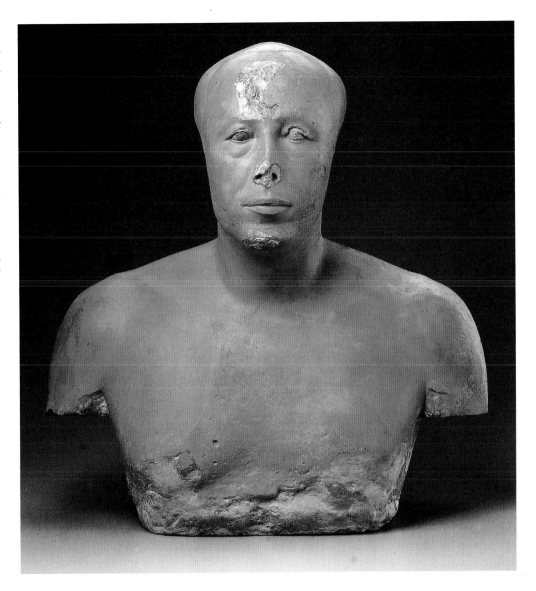

106 Bust of Ankhaef
Giza; Fourth Dynasty, ca. 2500 BC; limestone
with stucco; H. 50.6 cm; Boston, Museum of
Fine Arts, 27.442.
The bust of Ankhaef is unique for the art of
the Old Kingdom in its realism. Indeed, there
is scarcely anything even from later periods
that can compete with it in this sense. The
plasticity of the body is greatly differentiated,
particularly around the face. A high degree of
individuality is evident and, without doubt,
the bust bears a striking likeness to the person
portrayed – something we obviously cannot
prove. However, this bust is not a tomb statue
in the usual sense. This is not only just
because it is a bust, that is, a partial representation of a man, but also because of the
material it is made from and the production
technique. The stone has been coated with
stucco of different thicknesses and then
painted pink. The bust was discovered near a
small platform in one of the exterior mudbrick chambers in front of Ankhaef's
mastaba, and may once have formed part of a
composite statue.

In the late Fourth and Fifth Dynasty a distinctive type of sculpture
developed with round fleshy faces that seem almost interchangeable;
the bodies are depicted as athletic and full of strength. Since many
sculptures have been preserved from this period, this type is considered
representative of the Old Kingdom.

In the following period changes occurred that have arisen time and
again out of Classicism – that is, the distortion of Classicism. At first, the
idealized aspect becomes diminished, the representation becomes more
realistic and there is greater freedom in the way the posture is expressed.
Slowly, there appears a kind of expressionism that becomes typical for
the fine arts of the First Intermediate Period. The eyes grow large and
wide, the mouth becomes fleshier and the faces are no longer round and

full. The bodies are sometimes less well proportioned and one is
tempted to consider them unskilled work. However, such a judgment
would not do justice to the art of the later Old Kingdom. What they
show us is a new informality and freedom compared with the strictly
canonical artwork of the preceding Classical period.

The private statue of the Old Kingdom can only be understood in
its funerary context. A broad evaluation of these works and the context
in which they were presented enables us not only to gain an insight
into Egyptian society but also into the imagined world of the hereafter.
The beauty we perceive in these sculptures derives, on the one hand,
from the sense of beauty and style of their creators and, on the other,
because they were compelled to satisfy the demands of eternity.

The Political History from the Ninth to the Seventeenth Dynasties

Dieter Kessler

The Old Kingdom came to an end when a member of the house of Khety of Herakleopolis took over the Memphite throne under circumstances that are as yet unknown. The usual designation for the period to follow, the "First Intermediate Period," refers to a short phase of conflicts between the south and the north for dominance of the country. The new dynasty of the Herakleopolitans (Ninth/Tenth Dynasties) was only recognized from Lower Egypt to the area south of Asiut. Thebes was hostile from the outset. There the ruler of the city had overcome his opponents in the south. With the help of Nubian mercenaries and during the course of extended fighting, the Thebans succeeded in overpowering the Middle Egyptian blockade at Asiut. Under the leadership of Mentuhotep II (2046–1995 BC), the Thebans finally seized the Memphite throne as well, founding the Eleventh Dynasty. Mentuhotep was justified in calling himself "the unifier of the two lands." From a historical point of view, the reunification of the realm marks the beginning of the so-called Middle Kingdom.

The Position of the King in the Middle Kingdom

Since the Old Kingdom, belief in the absolute power of the king in a theological sense had been lost. The history of the following period is characterized by the antagonism between the king and powerful families who assert their influence in the provinces. With the help of literature and of theology, an attempt is made to strengthen the position of the king. The literary form of the "royal novel" serves as both justification and propaganda. The origin of the royal birth legend, declaring the king to be the son of god, dates from the Twelfth Dynasty.

Just as in earlier periods, the true person of the pharaoh during the Middle Kingdom also remains largely a mystery. The hymn to the king portrays the ruler as the ideal of an omnipotent father figure, whose education included training in warfare and hunting. But any intimate details about impulsive acts, of intrigues, and even murder, which surely also occurred at court during the Middle Kingdom, have generally not survived. A spectacular exception is the assassination of Amenemhat I.

Foreign Policy during the Middle Kingdom

The pharaoh's interests at this period regarding the Syro-Palestinian area concentrated primarily on the maintenance of trade routes. The Herakleopolitans had already strengthened the royal military presence at Qantir at the eastern arm of the Delta. Here began an important

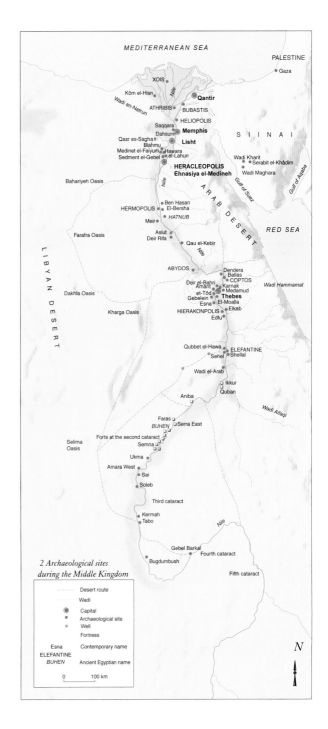

2 Archaeological sites during the Middle Kingdom

1 Standing figure of Mentuhotep II
Western Thebes, Deir el-Bahari; Eleventh Dynasty, ca. 2000 BC; sandstone; H. 183 cm; New York, The Metropolitan Museum of Art, 26.3.29.
The unifier of the kingdom Mentuhotep II

faced the dual tasks of securing political control and reorganizing religious affairs. The Theban gods Montu and Amun became national deities and were included in the great Theban line of ancestors.

3 Head from a sphinx of Sesostris I
Karnak; Twelfth Dynasty, ca. 1950 BC; granite; H. 38 cm; Cairo, Egyptian Museum, JE 38228 (CG 42007).
Upon his accession, Sesostris I first had to quell internal unrest. The king consolidated his rule and then began an extensive building program, particularly in Karnak where the so-called "White Chapel" has been preserved.

trade and military route toward Gaza. The so-called Walls of the Ruler, a blockade at the eastern border, was intended to prevent the immigration of bedouin tribes with whom sporadic conflicts took place at the beginning of the Middle Kingdom. Numerous Egyptian representatives spent time at the courts of the smaller city-states of the Near East. With their help, Egypt gained precise knowledge about the politics of their particular rulers. Artifacts of Egyptian products in Syria (Byblos, Qatna, Ebla) and Palestine (Hazor) as well as artifacts of Mesopotamian and Cretan products in Egypt (et-Tôd) have been identified from this period and attest to extensive long-distance trade contacts.

Already in the Eleventh Dynasty trade was also resumed with Punt (today in Somalia or Eritrea). In Sinai the turquoise mines were reopened. The Eastern Desert too became an area of economic activity. During the Eleventh Dynasty, amethyst (Wadi el-Hudi) and graywacke (Wadi Hammamat) were mined there and, during the Twelfth Dynasty (Gebel Zeit), galena as well. In the west, Wadi Natrun, whose inhabitants transported their own products and transit trade goods into the Nile Valley, was controlled from a fortress since the reign of Amenemhat I.

The Egyptians pursued control of Nubia step by step through military interventions. In the past, the princes there had placed their archers at the disposal of the Theban ruler. After the unification of the realm under Mentuhotep II, the lower Nubian area once again came under Egyptian influence as a supplier of raw materials. During the Twelfth Dynasty the Egyptians used large fortresses in the area of the third cataract to counter the threat of the kingdom of Kerma, which had prospered through trade with central Africa, and begun to expand from the Dongola Basin to both the south and the north.

Internal Developments in the Middle Kingdom

The victorious dynasty developed Thebes as its capital. Just at the moment of the new unification of the realm under Mentuhotep II, however, the provincial rulers, the so-called nomarchs, gained strength, to judge from the authoritarian tone of their tomb inscriptions. This is a possible indication that Mentuhotep II had to show them his gratitude in exchange for being accepted as king in Memphis. When the

4 Seated statue of Sesostris III
Hierakonpolis; Twelfth Dynasty, ca. 1860 BC; granodiorite; H. 54.5 cm, D. 35 cm, W. 19 cm; New York, The Brooklyn Museum, 52.1.
This statue belongs to the cult of Sesostris's rejuvenation and shows him at his preferred age, accompanying the renewal ritual at the *sed* festival. It is the cult image of a dynamic pharaoh striving for a centralized state. The officials who realized the significance of the image type adopted a similar appearance.

vizier Amenemhat overthrew the last ruler of the Theban dynasty, Mentuhotep IV, and seized the throne as the founder of a new dynasty, it also seems that not all governors simply went along with the new developments. Amenemhat I was only able to assert himself through internal struggles. He departed from the politics of his predecessors and deliberately chose to follow the traditions of the north. Near el-Lisht, south of Cairo, he built his new residential city, Itj-tawy, "Conqueror of the Two Lands," and a classical pyramid complex. As we can read in the "Teachings of Amenemhat," which was commissioned by his son Sesostris I and handed down for generations, Amenemhat I was murdered in his sleep as the result of a harem conspiracy. This unprecedented event led to chaos within both the royal family and the administration. The first task for the new pharaoh was therefore to consolidate territorial control. Structures were reorganized; the territorial borders were drawn anew. Thus the independent governors gradually became governors of the king.

Sesostris III continued the process of centralization and brought the sons of leading families to the royal court. Administrative power was concentrated at the royal residence, represented in particular by two viziers. The provinces' progressive loss of importance is reflected in the archeological discovery that these families no longer chose to build their tombs there. The most significant achievement of Amenemhat II was the colonizing of the Faiyum oasis, where he eventually built his pyramid. New land for the kingdom was gained through the organizing of a water supply to that area.

The short reigns of the last kings of the Twelfth Dynasty and those of the Thirteenth Dynasty in the approximately eighty years that followed suggest that there were violent conflicts over control of Egypt. Nevertheless, the administration remained for the most part intact, as is shown by preserved books of accounts. Neferhotep I, one of the last pharaohs of the Thirteenth Dynasty, was still powerful enough to maintain contacts with the ruler of Byblos. Shortly thereafter, however, Egypt seems to have dissolved into smaller territories for good.

The Hyksos

Foreigners who had settled in Egypt were employed in great numbers in the military, in trade, and in craftmanship already toward the end of the Twelfth Dynasty. At that time there was a second wave of immigration of settlers from southern Palestine and Syria as a result of violent upheavals there. From an archeological point of view, their presence in the area is proved by the singularity of their burial customs (donkeys' graves) as well as through artifacts dating from this period, among them pottery from Cyprus. The latter indicates the presence of groups of foreign merchants pursuing long-distance Mediterranean trade. A local ruler, Nehesi, Egyptian for "the Nubian," was finally able to gain independence and control a small area in the Delta along the trade route to southern Palestine with Avaris as its center. Today, such minor rulers are considered to belong to a period once thought to be fictitious, the Fourteenth Dynasty.

It seems as if a ruler from this group finally gained control of the Memphite throne. In a formal, historical sense this marks the end of the Middle Kingdom and the beginning of the so-called Second Intermediate Period. Later tradition grouped the foreign pharaohs under their Egyptian title "Rulers of the Foreign Lands" (Egyptian: Heka-khasut; Greek: Hyksos).

The following six so-called great Hyksos rulers of the Fifteenth Dynasty, with their capital in Avaris, were recognized as Egyptian pharaohs. They pursued a balance of interests with the regions farther to the south, including Thebes where the last descendants of the

5 Ka statue of King Hor in a shrine
Dahshur; Thirteenth Dynasty, ca. 1750 BC; wood, bronze, quartz; Cairo, Egyptian Museum, JE 30948 (CG 259).
This once-painted cult statue of an otherwise little-known Memphite king comes from a statue shrine in his tomb next to the brick pyramid of Amenemhat III in Dahshur.

6 Praying figure of Amenemhat III
Karnak; Twelfth Dynasty, ca. 1820 BC; black granodiorite; H. 110 cm; Cairo, Egyptian Museum, JE 36928 (CG 42014).
The king, who continued the centralizing policies of his predecessor, also adopted his predecessor's age type. Several granite statues of the ruler are known from Karnak.

Memphite rulers had retreated. The Hyksos' Semitic-Egyptian double names were intended to correspond to both groups of peoples. Their dominance was supported by a chain of settlements of alien populations in the eastern Delta and as far as southern Palestine, who profited from the trade. Thus vessels and scarabs bearing the names of Hyksos rulers have been found throughout the Mediterranean region.

Middle and Upper Egypt were divided into various spheres of power. In Thebes, minor rulers who seceded and assumed the ruling title are known as the Seventeenth Dynasty. In Middle Egypt and in the town of Gebelein, south of Thebes, the local rulers remained loyal to the Hyksos kings. Thebes began to arm itself in secret.

Seqenenre (ca. 1570 BC) initiated conflict with the Hyksos vassals but was killed in battle. His son Kamose eventually penetrated with his fleet as far as Avaris but was forced to turn back at the fortified walls of the citadel. It was only his brother and successor Ahmose, founder of the Eighteenth Dynasty, who about 1550 BC was able to expel the Hyksos rulers and reunite Egypt under the leadership of Thebes. This event is equated with the beginning of the New Kingdom.

The Tombs of the Pharaohs – Between Tradition and Innovation

Rainer Stadelmann

The long reign of Pepi II toward the end of the Sixth Dynasty turned out to be a "catastrophe" for Egypt. After the completion of his impressive pyramid complex dating from, at the latest, the first anniversary in the thirtieth year of his reign, nothing noteworthy happened for over thirty or even sixty years. Sculptors and painters were still partially engaged in working on private tombs, so in the artistic sphere the tradition of the royal cemeteries continued without interruption. The well-trained workcrews, stonecutters, masons, transporters, and engineers proceeded for decades without a state commission, thus the training of the next generation was also neglected and the organization forgotten. Projects for large pyramid complexes could therefore no longer be undertaken by the kings of the Herakleopolitan era in the area around Memphis. The few, only nominally known tomb complexes were surely small and possibly never completed.

First steps toward the construction of a monumental king's tomb of a completely different form were evident at Thebes in Upper Egypt, where the renewed unification of the realm originated. The minor kings or rulers of the Eleventh Dynasty in that area were buried in cliff-side tombs with large outer courts. The unifier of the kingdom, Mentuhotep II, gave this tomb type its monumental effect by choosing the wide valley of Deir el-Bahari opposite modern Luxor as a sort of courtyard for his tomb. This took the form of a terraced temple, which was expanded several times during his long reign, and included not a burial pyramid, but more likely a stylized primeval mound about 11 m high surrounded by an elevated portico with three rows of columns. Adjoining this to the west began the funerary temple proper, a large court with a portico, and a hypostyle hall with several naves including a sanctuary for the deified king and the god Amun.

The tomb itself is sunk fully 150 m into the mountainside and consists of a granite chamber with an alabaster shrine. During an early building phase, six shrines for princesses or priestesses of Hathor were constructed whose walls and coffins show scenes from the princesses' lives and of their function as priestesses with reliefs in the bold style of Upper Egypt. From the outer court a deep shaft leads under the bulk of the central structure where an empty coffin and the famous, black-painted, seated statue of Mentuhotep stood in a roughly hewn chamber. A long, wide ramp used for processions led from the flood-

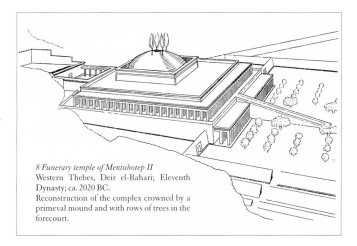

8 *Funerary temple of Mentuhotep II*
Western Thebes, Deir el-Bahari; Eleventh Dynasty; ca. 2020 BC.
Reconstruction of the complex crowned by a primeval mound and with rows of trees in the forecourt.

plain to the outer court with its rows of seated statues of the king under sycamores and tamarisks. At the southern and northern rims of the valley, the high officials of the late Eleventh Dynasty were permitted to build their sepulchres, splendid corridor tombs with courts sloping upward.

The kings of the Twelfth Dynasty left Thebes in order to establish the residence Itj-tawi, "Conqueror of the Two Lands," in the north near modern el-Lisht. There they resumed the traditions of pyramidal tombs, although with substantial construction changes. During the late Old Kingdom, a more or less standard measurement for pyramids of approximately 65–75 m (= 125–150 ancient Egyptian cubits) base length to a height of approximately 50 m (= 100 cubits) had become customary. Experience had taught that with these measurements a solid exterior facing would be able to hold even a loosely layered inner wall structure for a long time, which doubtless facilitated construction and shortened building time.

This knowledge is presumed to have still existed when Amenemhat I built his pyramid at el-Lisht since his tomb exhibits both these

7 *Tomb complex of Mentuhotep II*
Western Thebes, Deir el-Bahari; Eleventh Dynasty, ca. 2020 BC.
The tomb of the unifier of the kingdom, Mentuhotep of Thebes, is no longer a pyramid complex but a terraced temple with wide, tree-planted outer courts, porticoes, and a massive central structure ringed with ambulatories and crowned, not with a pyramid, but with a primeval mound. This important complex was rebuilt and extended several times before receiving its final form. The wide pit in the courtyard paving to be seen in the center of the picture marks the entrance to the passage that leads to the king's burial chamber. But even this hidden position could not defend the royal burial from being plundered by the grave robbers of antiquity.

9 *Statue of Mentuhotep II*
Western Thebes, Deir el-Bahari, funerary temple of Mentuhotep II; Eleventh Dynasty, ca. 2020 BC; painted sandstone; H. 138 cm, W. 47 cm; Cairo, Egyptian Museum, JE 36195.

The seated statue of Mentuhotep II was found – ritually buried – in an "Osiris tomb" under the burial structure. The face and body were subsequently painted black, that is the color of the god of the dead. Mentuhotep wears the white *sed* festival cloak, a very large ceremonial beard, and the Red Crown of Lower Egypt.

10 (below) *King Mentuhotep II*
Western Thebes, Deir el-Bahari, funerary temple of Mentuhotep II; Eleventh Dynasty, ca. 2020 BC; painted limestone; H. 38 cm, L. 98 cm; New York, The Metropolitan Museum of Art, Gift of the Egypt Exploration Fund, 1907, 07.230.2.

Among the numerous relief fragments discovered in the badly damaged funerary temple during excavation work in 1903–1907 by the Egypt Exploration Fund, the New York example is an important piece due to its size and its exceptionally well-preserved painting. The block originally belonged to a representation on the southern exterior wall of the sanctuary. It shows the king in adoration before Amun-Min (not pictured) while he himself is being followed by the goddess Hathor (right). Mentuhotep II wears the White Crown of Upper Egypt, a broad collar, and a garment with straps knotted over his shoulder. The king's divine nature is emphasized by a long ceremonial beard slightly rolled up at the end.

11 Temple relief of Amenemhat I
el-Lisht, funerary temple of Amenemhat I;
Twelfth Dynasty, ca.1960 BC; painted limestone; L. 190 cm, H. 35 cm; New York, The
Metropolitan Museum of Art, Rogers Fund,
08.200.5.
The first two rulers of the Twelfth Dynasty,
Amenemhat I and Sesostris I, once again built
their pyramids and accompanying cult
complexes in the area around Memphis, near

the village of el-Lisht. In the very badly
damaged funerary temple of Amenemhat I
the American excavators from the Metropolitan Museum (1906–1922) could find only a
few blocks of the original wall decoration.
The upper half of a lintel shown here has
attracted little attention thus far – surprisingly enough – although the piece with its
well-preserved painted decoration must be
considered one of the best examples of relief

sculpture under Amenemhat I. In
the center of the image, the ruler stands wearing a curled wig with the uraeus serpent, ceremonial beard, and broad collar. As symbols of
his power he holds a flail and a so-called
mekes symbol in his hands. He is flanked by
the falcon-headed god Horus (left), and the
necropolis and embalming god Anubis
(right); both gods hand him an ankh. The
scene is completed by the two goddesses of

the crowns and lands of Upper and Lower
Egypt, Nekhbet (left) and Uto (right) who
enter from both sides and, because of their
identical appearance, can be differentiated
only by the identifying inscription.

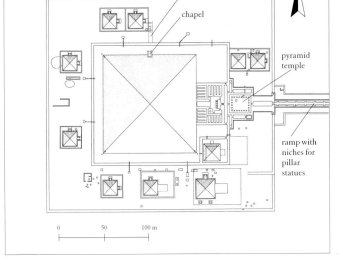

12 Pyramid of Sesostris I
el-Lisht; Twelfth Dynasty, ca. 1930 BC.
The kings of the Twelfth Dynasty resided
once again near the old capital of Memphis
and continued to construct pyramids like
those of their Old Kingdom predecessors.

Sesostris I focused for the most part on the
example of Sixth Dynasty pyramid complexes.
However, with a star-shaped skeletal structure
of limestone, his master builders discovered
new construction techniques.

13 Plan of the pyramid complex of Sesostris I
el-Lisht; Twelfth Dynasty, ca. 1930 BC.
Around the royal pyramid with its funerary
temple stand the small cult pyramids
and nine pyramids of queens. The king's

structure bore the name "Sesostris overviews
the two countries" and was fully surrounded
by an inner limestone wall displaying niche
decorations.

14 Seated figure of Sesostris I (detail)
el-Lisht, pyramid complex; Twelfth Dynasty,
ca. 1930 BC; limestone; H. 200 cm, W. 58.4 cm;
Cairo, Egyptian Museum, JE 31139.
Ten of these unfinished statues were found
in a pit in the area around the temple – apparently buried according to ritual. They are
portraits of a perpetually youthful ruler that
must have been destined for display in the
offering court. Perhaps this figure type no
longer corresponded to Sesostris I's taste,
which would explain why they were buried.

measurements and the building method. During construction, however, Amenemhat's master builders broke all rules of ethics and ignored the king's own instructions by stealing their materials from the funerary temples of the pyramids at Giza and possibly also at Saqqara and reusing them as core masonry.

This was surely not an act in pious commemoration of a great past, as it is sometimes explained, but deliberate theft by a state organization that apparently was no longer able to undertake the construction of large new pyramids.

This was to change during the reign of Amenemhat's powerful son and successor, Sesostris I. His pyramid, also at el-Lisht, was already somewhat larger and built with a new technique. A star-shaped skeleton supports the basic masonry, which as before consists of unworked stones. A strong facing made of solidly joined, fine limestone blocks once gave these structures the necessary solidity. It was only the removal of stones during the medieval Arabic period that caused the modern-day erosion of these pyramids.

The burial corridor was built of granite blocks. Today it ends below the water table, as does the burial corridor in the pyramid of Amenemhat I. Perhaps the burial chamber lay at the bottom of a deep shaft. The pyramid temple is a simplified copy of corresponding late Old Kingdom structures. The ramp differs from its precursors in the addition of a row of six engaged statues at its end and on each side. These may have replaced seated statues of Sesostris that were probably already carefully buried during the time of construction.

The inner pyramid complex was enclosed by a tall limestone wall, which was decorated both inside and outside with one hundred 5-meter high representations of the Horus name of Sesostris I in high relief. The relief fragments from the mortuary cult complex show the image of a self-assured, authoritative ruler – an image that is impressively confirmed by his statues and inscriptions. The queens and princesses were buried in nine smaller pyramids in the outer court of the larger pyramid.

The changes in the corridor and chamber system inside the pyramid on the one hand and in the outer pyramid complex on the

15 Pyramid of Sesostris III
Dahshur; Twelfth Dynasty, ca. 1860 BC.
This pyramid of Sesostris III – the earliest example of a pyramid constructed completely of mudbrick but faced with limestone – stands in an extensive pyramid complex that was first to revive the north–south orientation similar to that of Djoser. A hidden entrance leads to the barrel-vaulted burial chamber containing a splendid granite sarcophagus and decorated with niches. Around the pyramid lay the graves of twelve princesses buried with rich arrays of jewelry.

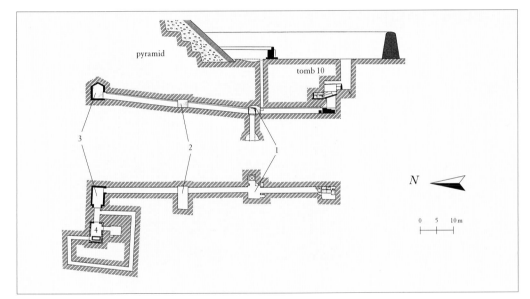

16 Passageway and burial chamber system of the pyramid of Sesostris II: plan
El-Lahun; Twelfth Dynasty, ca. 1875 BC.
The royal tomb lies not under the middle of the pyramid but southeast of it in the heart of the cliff. The shafts and corridors leading to the burial chamber make up a real labyrinth of false burial chambers, shafts, and forking corridors. The beginning of the burial corridor, hidden 16 m below the floor slab of the queen's tomb Number 10, led over a horizontal passageway to a barrel-vaulted hall (1) in front of which a vertical shaft, the entrance shaft proper, opened. From the hall a second shaft sinks deep down into the cliff; its end lies under the water table and can no longer be reached. From the northeast corner of the hall, the horizontal corridor climbs gently (6°46') to a passage chamber (2), from there again to the antechamber (3) from which one could reach the coffin chamber directly to the west or, turning south, by walking around the coffin chamber through a passageway with four turns and finally approaching from the north.

other shed light on the transformation of the world view and the concept of the royal afterlife. The experience of the plundering of royal tombs during turbulent periods inspired the master builders of the Middle Kingdom to devise ever more complicated safety measures. Portcullis stones were clearly no longer sufficient by themselves. During the course of the Twelfth Dynasty the entrances, which were traditionally set in the middle of the pyramid's north face, were placed in less obvious positions or in deep shafts. The entrance to Sesostris II's tomb at Illahun leads from the shaft of a tomb for queens outward and under the pyramid. Some corridors terminate in dead ends. The real burial corridors lead further at a higher level, turning corners to end finally in the royal burial chamber that is, for the most part, faced in granite. The coffin chambers are protected by massive sealing slabs and arches. The sarcophagi are in all cases made of costly red granite with niche decorations. The antechambers are developed into halls that would have served the maneuvering of the granite blocks but in which we can recognize the tribunal chamber of Osiris. The symbolism of the "Osiris tomb" was also clearly suggested by the planting of thick clusters of trees around the pyramid complex. The belief in an afterlife in Osiris's underworld, where the king and Osiris become one, now replaced to a large extent the heavenly afterlife with the sun god.

Through the worship of Osiris during the Twelfth and Thirteenth Dynasties, this god's cult site of Abydos became a holy city. The "Osiris tomb" was discovered in the First Dynasty royal cemetery in Umm el-Gaab, doubtless originally the tomb of a king of that time.

As a result, kings and private individuals of every class wanted to have actual tombs, symbolic tombs (cenotaphs), or stelae on the processional street at Abydos leading past the spot in order to identify themselves with Osiris. Sesostris III built a gigantic cliff corridor tomb at Abydos that contained three successive false tombs and an "Osiris tomb," the latter remaining incomplete. In its technique and religious concepts, this cliff tomb is a model for later royal tombs of the New Kingdom. Several of Sesostris III's successors in the Thirteenth Dynasty followed his example of constructing a symbolic tomb at Abydos. Perhaps the kings are even buried in these funerary structures.

19 Pyramid of Amenemhat III
Hawara; Twelfth Dynasty, ca. 1820 BC.
This limestone-faced brick pyramid stood in such an extensive complex of chapels and courts that the Greeks compared it with the labyrinth of Knossos. Hardly anything remains of the splendid decoration of columns, sculptures, and reliefs.

17/18 Double figure of Amenemhat III as god of the Nile
Tanis, Twelfth Dynasty, ca. 1820 BC; granodiorite; H. 160 cm, W. 100 cm; Cairo, Egyptian Museum, JE 18221 (CG 392).
Like other sculptures in the round of Middle Kingdom kings, the so-called fish-offering statue was removed to Tanis in the eastern Delta during the Twenty-first Dynasty where it was discovered during excavations in 1861. Judging from the characteristic facial features, the subject can unequivocally be indentifed as Amenemhat III, the last great ruler of the Twelfth Dynasty. The inscriptions between the figures, which mention Psusennes I, indicate that the monument was usurped. We can suppose with some certainty that the original location at the time of Amenemhat III was the funerary temple at the king's pyramid at Hawara, even if we cannot fully exclude the possibility of a provenance from the Sobek shrine in Shedit, the old capital of the Faiyum. The hairstyle of the two figures is particularly striking with thick braids and shield-shaped beards. Possibly Amenemhat III had adopted an archetype of the Nile god Hapi from the Predynastic period, whom the ruler embodies here; the numerous offerings support this interpretation – fish, poultry, and hanging lotus blossoms, which he may have added as guarantor of the fertility of the land. The perfect symmetry of the double statues, which supercedes all conventions, reflects the dualism of Upper and Lower Egypt.

20 Pyramidion of Amenemhat III
Dahshur; Twelfth Dynasty, ca. 1840 BC;
granite; H. 131 cm, base: 187 x 187.5 cm;
Cairo, Egyptian Museum, JE 35133 (35745).
The pyramidion of black granite was
decorated with the king's pair of eyes with
which he observes the journey of the sun in
the sun barques, which are also pictured on
the pyramidion.

21 "Black" brick pyramid of Amenemhat III
Dahshur; Twelfth Dynasty, ca. 1840 BC.
This pyramid has a core of brick and a limestone facing. The system of corridors and
chambers is labyrinthine, designed with
numerous antechambers and side rooms. The
pyramid showed serious signs of settling,
however, even prior to its completion. It was
therefore used only for the burial of queens
and princesses in secondary corridors and
chambers. Tombs for princesses were
constructed in the north of the pyramid. In
one of these shafts, the intact tomb of the
minor King Hor of the Thirteenth Dynasty
was found.

22 Pectoral of the princess Mereret
Dahshur, tomb of Mereret; Twelfth Dynasty, ca. 1840 BC; gold, carnelian, lapis lazuli, and faience; H. 7.9 cm, W. 10.5 cm; Cairo, Egyptian Museum, JE 30875.

While examining the pyramid complex of Sesostris III in 1894, the French excavator J. de Morgan came upon the tomb of the princess Mereret. As the daughter of Sesostris III and the sister of Amenemhat III, she possessed a lavish burial treasure that included this pectoral. It was produced in openwork technique of gold sheet with the picture contours soldered on as a base. The resulting cells were then filled with inlays cut to size. Under the symbol of the Nekhbet vulture, the motif is developed reflecting chapel architecture, symmetrical to an axis. On each side, Amenemhat III strides forward and with the scimitar-mace performs the "smiting of the foes," seizing each foe by the hair. The cartouches bear the throne name of the ruler while in the middle the title reads, "the perfect god, lord of the Two Lands and of all foreign lands who slays the Asiatics." On the reverse side, the image is repeated in chiseled technique.

23 Pectoral of Sit-Hathor-yunet
el-Lahun, tomb of Sit-Hathor-yunet, Twelfth Dynasty, ca. 1870 BC; gold, lapis lazuli, turquoise, carnelian, and garnet; H. 8.2 cm; New York, The Metropolitan Museum of Art, Henry Walter and Rogers Fund, 1916, 16.1.3.

In February 1914, workers digging for the English excavator W. M. Flinders Petrie at the pyramid of Sesostris II at el-Lahun chanced upon a shaft tomb that had already been plundered in ancient times. Careful examination of the chamber led to the discovery of the princess's jewels that, hidden in a small wall niche, had escaped the tomb robbers. These pieces of jewelry and toilet articles of Sit-Hathor-yunet, a daughter of Sesostris II, which closely resembled those from the hoard of Dahshur, were entrusted to Petrie by the antiquities authorities with the exception of four objects. Since British museums were unable to purchase the treasure, the jewels finally came to The Metropolitan Museum, among them the pectoral pictured here. In the center of the design is a raised cartouche with the throne name of Sesostris II over the kneeling figure of the god Heh holding a palm frond, the symbol for years of rule, in each hand. In addition, the figure of a tadpole, the numeral for 100,000, hangs from his left elbow. The central motif is flanked by two falcons of the royal god Horus, each of which carries a sun disk entwined by a uraeus cobra over its head. The message expressed by the pectoral is the ruler's claim to a mythically eternal life and reign. The classical elegance of this piece of jewelry, for which over 370 small inlays were fashioned, is emphasized by a long chain of gold and gemstone beads.

Sesostris III had nevertheless already ordered the construction of a grandiose pyramid complex at Dahshur which, in an expansion in the south, shows elements of the New Kingdom "Houses of Millions of Years." Outside the enclosure walls, entire ships were again buried in deep shafts, as had been customary during the Old Kingdom. His son Amenemhat III developed these changes further in his large pyramid complex at Hawara in the Faiyum. With its decorated chapels and rich array of statues, among them sculptural works of unusual form and expressive power such as the so-called fish-offering statues, this temple complex later impressed the Greek historian Herodotus so much that he believed it to be the original model for the Labyrinth.

The later pyramids at Dahshur and Hawara were built as solid constructions of unbaked mudbricks, as were the smaller, secondary pyramids for queens and princesses. The women were also buried in shaft tombs surrounding the pyramids, however. Astonishingly, the shaft tombs of the princesses of the Twelfth Dynasty, including the precious jewelry buried with the deceased, have remained for the most part untouched by thieves. The fact that they are intact suggests that the plunder of the Middle Kingdom pyramids took place only once knowledge of the precious objects in the secondary tombs had been forgotten.

Thus the passageways leading to the royal tombs were apparently uncovered only when, in relatively modern times, the limestone facing of the royal pyramids was removed and used for other purposes.

The subterranean complexes of the pyramid tombs of the late Middle Kingdom kings, however, become ever more confusing and complicated. Their construction resembles a Senet board game, a type of dice game with obstacles that the deceased played in his tomb in order to reach the netherworld. Presumably the pyramidal superstructures built over these elaborate subterranean complexes, which took years to erect, were hardly ever completed despite the fact that the crowning basalt pyramids with their inscriptions were already delivered, as in the tomb of Khendjer ("Eber") at south Saqqara. All of these complexes were surrounded by undulating enclosure walls, possibly representing the primeval waters, whereas the pyramid symbolizes the primeval mound rising from them.

The last impressive subterranean complex at south Saqqara seems particularly enigmatic. It consists of a sprawling system of corridors that turn many corners, and are planned on different levels, but then after several passage blockings, finally lead to a burial chamber chiseled out of a single block of quartzite weighing more than 150 tons. Upon the block rests a sealing stone of almost equal weight that, so it seems, was never lowered.

Despite all the effort to construct it, apparently this grave remained unused. Still it must have been the tomb, or perhaps the cenotaph, of one of the important kings of the Thirteenth Dynasty who was eventually buried in Abydos. As a result of waning centralized power, his successors in the final years of the Middle Kingdom, residents of Itj-tawy/el-Lisht as well as of Thebes, could erect only small brick pyramids that are known only through meager remains and written records.

A House for Eternity – The Tombs of Governors and Officials

Abdel Ghaffar Shedid

Architecture

The largely autonomous nomarchs, or governors of the Middle Kingdom, begin to build necropolises in their own provinces. We can recognize echoes of royal complexes and continuations of Old Kingdom traditions, but entirely independent developments are evident at individual necropolises.

During the First Intermediate Period, the necropolis of Mo'alla was created south of Thebes on the east bank of the Nile opposite that of Gebelein on the west bank. The traditional tomb form of the mastaba was still used at the necropolis of the royal residence near Memphis, though now in a considerably more modest form than during the late Old Kingdom. As a rule the superstructure is no longer accessible, and only the subterranean coffin chamber is decorated.

The most impressive necropolises of the Middle Kingdom are found in Upper Egypt and especially in Middle Egypt. For the most part, they are constructed at sites with striking natural features, in the cliffsides along the Nile, and have an imposing effect. The power and self-assurance of the ancient builders of the Middle Kingdom are felt by every modern visitor.

During the Eleventh and Twelfth Dynasties, necropolises were built on the steep slopes of the eastern mountain range at Beni Hasan and, to the south, at el-Bersha and Qau el-Kebir, as well as at Mir, Asiut and Deir Rifa on the western side of the Nile and, at the southern border of the territory, at Qubbet el-Hawa opposite Aswan.

Despite differing local developments, the aforementioned cemeteries share the same basic features: influenced by Old Kingdom traditions in building cliff tombs, and using rooms of the simplest design that continued until the Eleventh Dynasty. In the course of development, the concept of the tomb as a house for eternity was emphasized by elements borrowed from secular architecture. First, columns were included, then the tomb facade evolved into a columned portico. Finally, during the Twelfth Dynasty, a central axis from the entrance to the statue chamber at the rear wall of the offering room results from an alignment of successive chambers, thus assimilating the element of a procession or journey from concepts of the hereafter in tomb architecture.

The rulers' tombs at Asiut and Qau el-Kebir, unfortunately very poorly preserved, are among the largest non-royal complexes of the Middle Kingdom. Like the royal burial complexes, individual tombs were built in valleys and included a ramp, pylons, an atrium, a terrace with a hypostyle hall and a sunken room with pillars, and the cliff tomb proper with a transverse hall and statue chambers.

At Thebes, a special tomb type was developed in the necropolis on the west bank of the Nile, known as the Saff tombs. In the flat plain at the foot of the mountain, an outer court of generous dimensions is circumscribed by an enclosure wall. The tomb facade with pillars forming a type of gallery is hewn from the cliff. Along the tomb's central axis, a corridor descends to a cult chamber, and from there a shaft leads to the burial chamber. A second Theban tomb type clearly reflects the change in the concept of mortuary architecture. The tomb is now conceived as a representation of the tomb of Osiris and the underworld given form by a system of corridors leading deep within the mountain to the cult and burial chambers. This new type was important above all for the development of royal tombs during the New Kingdom.

The construction of large cliff tombs stopped abruptly when the governors under Sesostris III lost their power and independence.

Technique

The cliff tombs were carved out of the solid rock. In order to preserve the facade of the tomb, the cliff face was hewn in a vertical, even surface from the top to the bottom; the entrance or a narrow hypostyle hall was carved into the facade. While digging, builders worked a wide breadth of rock from the entrance towards the rear of the tomb, allowing for the carving of eventual architectural elements such as buttresses, architraves, and so forth. The leftover blocks of stone were transported to the outside in large pieces or were smashed. Stone hammers, copper chisels, and wooden mallets served as tools for this work.

The second step involved chiseling the walls to produce an even surface. Surfaces destined to be decorated with reliefs were filed smooth with stones. Any troublesome, uneven spots in the wall surface were leveled and smoothed with a mortar of limestone and sand that was laid on in varying thicknesses as needed. The final step in the preparatory work was the application of a distemper. This served as a painting ground that could support color yet prevented the raw stone from absorbing too much of the paint's binding agent. The distemper was kept in a neutral tone that blended with the original color of the stone and made corrections in the mortar invisible.

Colors used included blue and turquoise tones, which were already being synthetically manufactured, natural ochre with many variations of yellow, red, and brown, huntite or chalk white, and black made from soot. Presumably a water-soluble tempera based on resins and other organic matter served as a binding agent.

---

24 Coffin of the nomarch Djehuty-nakht (section of outer coffin, east wall)
el-Bersha, the grave of Djehuty-nakht (10A); Eleventh Dynasty, ca. 2020 BC; cedarwood, painted; length: 262 cm; Boston Museum of

Fine Arts, 20.1822-6.
Djehuty-nakht's large chest coffins are without doubt among the most magnificent coffins of all time. Especially the richly detailed paintings on the inside of the outer coffin

are considered to be an absolute masterwork of ancient Egyptian painting. All details of the composition – here the central figure of the grave's owner – are depicted with such an unsurpassed finesse of coloration

and style that on discovery of the grave (spring 1915) the coffin was at first considered to date from the heyday of the Twelfth Dynasty.

25 *Outer court and facade of the tomb of Sarenput I*
Qubbet el-Hawa (tomb 36); Twelfth Dynasty, ca. 1950 BC.
Following the model of royal tomb complexes, this tomb included a structure in the valley, from which stairs led up to a nearly square outer court. The facade is hewn from the rocky outcrop of red sandstone; in front was a narrow hall whose roof was supported by six pillars only partially preserved. At both ends of this hypostyle hall was a statue of the deceased in a niche. The six pillars bear inscriptions and representations of the tomb owner in sunken relief. The tomb facade itself shows several scenes: left of the entrance, the large figure of the deceased followed by a sandal-bearer and two dogs; adjacent to them on the left, Sarenput spears fish from a small boat; in the scene above he inspects cattle.

26 *View into the tomb of Sarenput II*
Qubbet el-Hawa (tomb 31); Twelfth Dynasty, ca. 1880 BC.
In this complex, the tomb architecture of Qubbet el-Hawa is at its finest. As in the royal burial complexes, the succession of rooms is strictly axial with an entrance hall, corridor, and cult chamber inside. The austerity of the first, undecorated room is striking with its six mighty, striated sandstone pillars. Nine steps lead up to the rear burial area. The long corridor with its barrel vault is punctuated on each side by three niches bearing half-figure statues of Sarenput in the form of the Osiris mummy. The passageway ends in the square cult chamber. From the entrance to the cult niche the ceiling height decreases from one room section to the next while the level of the floor rises; this has the effect of emphasizing the cult niche as the tomb's innermost sanctuary.

27 *View of the northeast corner of the tomb of Khety*
Beni Hasan (BH 17); Twelfth Dynasty, ca. 1950 BC.
This tomb is an example of the middle phase in the necropolis architecture of Beni Hasan. The rear half of the room is subdivided by two rows of three columns in the form of bunches of lotuses that run parallel to the entrance facade. They are joined to an architrave that continues as narrow pilasters on the side walls and down to the floor. These supports were not statically necessary; they recall the wooden columns of a dwelling in immortal stone and thereby clarify the notion of the tomb as a house for eternity. The original painting in ochre, red, and blue is still preserved on the graceful columns that imitate four lotus stems with closed buds.

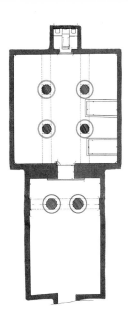

28 Floorplan of the tomb of Amenemhat
Beni Hasan (BH2); Twelfth Dynasty, ca. 1930 BC.
The succession of rooms consists of an outer court, a columned portico, the burial chamber, and statue niche.

29 Tomb of Amenemhat
Beni Hasan (BH 2); Twelfth Dynasty, ca. 1930 BC.
The stately design of the room is impressive. Four 16-sided columns stand in the nearly square hall. Two massive longitudinal architraves connect them in pairs and divide the room into three barrel-vaulted naves. The ceiling vault, which is decorated with a pattern, runs parallel to the east–west axis. The focus of the room's axis is the statue niche in the east wall containing the sculpture in the round of the deceased, his wife, and his mother.

30 Portico facade of the tombs BH 3, 4, and 5 (from left to right)
Beni Hasan; Twelfth Dynasty, ca. 1930 BC.
The tomb facades were cut vertically into the sloping cliffs, resulting in frontal courts bounded at the sides by the remaining rock. The facades of these latest graves in Beni Hasan are designed as porticoes with two 8- or 16-sided columns and a large architrave. These elements are borrowed from secular architecture and imitate a wooden veranda. The rectangular bosses over the architrave recall the protruding ends of ceiling beams; they are particularly clear on the facade of BH 3 (left). The form of the columns is defined as protodoric, and it anticipates the flutes and sharp edges of later doric columns.

31 Kitchen scene
Western Thebes (TT 60), Tomb of Antefoqer;
Twelfth Dynasty, ca. 1950 BC; painting on
stucco over stone.
Very little Theban tomb painting of the Middle
Kingdom has survived. Antefoqer, vizier under
Amenemhat I, built the tomb for his mother

Sened. It shows a wide variety of themes, including the scene here of women baking. They
pour the dough out of large, tall containers
into small clay pots with tapered bottoms. The
figures are well proportioned, but with their
angular movements and muted coloration
they have a stiff and simple air about them.

33 Donkey carrying sacks
Gebelein, mastaba of Iti; First Intermediate
Period, ca. 2120 BC; painting on stucco;
H. 84 cm; Turin, Museo Egizio, 14354h.
The animal is precisely rendered with sparing
contour lines and a clear distribution of color.
With the help of folding perspective, the

viewer is quite unambiguously made to
understand that the donkey carries two
wicker baskets on its back that are fastened
with ropes. The basket hanging on the far side
of the animal, which is normally invisible, is
folded upward in the painted image.

32 Papyrus thicket
Mo'alla, tomb of Ankhtify; First Intermediate
Period, ca. 2140 BC; painting on stucco.
The painter of this tomb found a wholly
original solution for the traditional scene of
the papyrus thicket. In severe abstraction he

first created a regular pattern of vertical
papyrus stems with umbels between them. In
order to soften this rigorous order, he placed
birds between them at irregular intervals. In
the register below, he used the finest of brushstrokes to add in turn the abstract pattern of

the fish, which are more characteristically
represented. A delicate pastel, soft coloration
makes an interesting contrast to the rigid
order. The subjects in the image are placed
next to each other without any overlap; the
artist has, however, taken care to vary the

spaces between them. He plays with the
porportions of his subjects and varies them
according to their significance for the content
of the image, not according to their true size.

Painting and Relief

In the private tombs of the Middle Kingdom, pure painting was often preferred over relief carving for the decoration of walls. This can be explained as not merely a consideration of cost, efforts to save time, or technical problems with poor-quality stone. Painting as the sole decorative element for Egyptian private tombs is nothing new; the earliest example, a tomb at Hierakonpolis, dates to predynastic times. Other examples follow from the Third Dynasty (the tomb of Hesy at Saqqara), from the Fourth Dynasty (the mastaba of Nefermaat and his wife Atet, the provenance of the famous geese of Meidum), and from the Sixth Dynasty (the tomb of Kaiemankh in Giza).

Both techniques were also used during the Middle Kingdom. While in the necropolises at el-Bersha, Mir, and Qau el-Kebir the wall pictures were executed as painted reliefs, the gigantic wall surfaces of Beni Hasan, for example, are decorated with paintings. Relief carving was used there only for the false doors. The owners of these large and elaborate complexes of the Twelfth Dynasty decided quite consciously in favor of painted decoration, surely since they appreciated the particular appeal of the possibilities in painting at that time. This expresses a new way of thinking on the part of the projects' commissioners.

Painting in the Middle Kingdom developed from the energy and enthusiasm that characterized the artistic renewal of the First Intermediate Period, during which innovations are clearly recognizable. It is a powerful style that consistently liberated itself from the canons of the Old Kingdom, from all superfluous elements and overly refined detail in favor of clear, well-defined order and easily comprehensible, unambiguous images. Most striking among the formal means of the First Intermediate Period is the clear picture composition, achieved, for example, through the avoidance of overlapping individual motifs.

A number of characteristic perspectives of an object are often combined, which is important for the clarity of representation. The

34 Birds in an acacia tree
Beni Hasan (BH 3), tomb of Khnumhotep II; Twelfth Dynasty, ca. 1880 BC, painting on stucco over limestone.
One of the most famous images from the tombs of Beni Hasan is this detail from the bird hunt scene. The background is formed by the tree with its sturdy trunk, finely forking branches, delicate green leaves, and yellowish blossom clusters. On top of that is a second layer with a variety of birds. The image is abstracted from nature, but the characteristics of color and pattern are so keenly typified that the individual birds can be identified without difficulty. Despite the complexity of the motif, the artist masterfully understood how to create a harmonious whole.

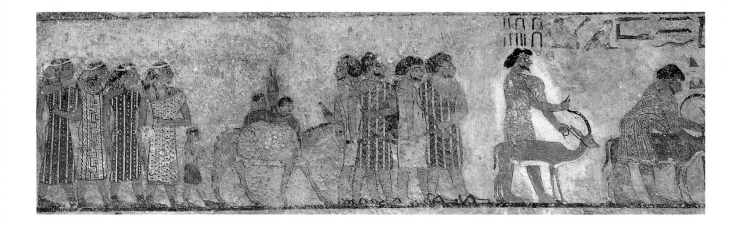

harmonious proportions of figures and an aesthetic, ideal body type no longer seem to be so important. The size of a represented object in a scene is determined by the significance of its function in life on earth.

The register line running from side to side and dividing the relief surface into horizontal bands is done away with entirely or is replaced by short baselines for individual figures or scenes. The established range of colors varies freely, resulting in completely new combinations. The new, creative use of color is particularly striking. Quite unique solutions are found, such as very strong color contrasts, a rather severely limited color palette, or the most delicate gradations of color, all betraying a sensitivity for special effects and a joy in the use of color.

Precisely this aspect is further developed by the painters of the Middle Kingdom. During the Twelfth Dynasty, a rich color palette of many different shades, free brushwork, the use of opaque color, smooth color transitions, and glazing techniques all mark a highly refined painting culture. The advantages of painting by itself, instead of the rather limiting possibilities of relief sculpture, are due to its ability to unfold freely over the picture surface.

Above all in scenes from nature, impressive moods are achieved through the differentiating of color nuances and the use of complex compositions. Airy landscapes that express, for example, the atmosphere of the desert or pastureland, are effective without a register line. Painted patterns are cleverly composed in order to fit the surfaces dictated by the architecture; cycles of themes are placed with a good deal of consideration.

At the climax of the development, complex compositions and variations on individual scenes are striking that work, for example, with multiple planes in space, the placing of one motif behind the other, overlapping, and even with attempts to paint in linear perspective, optical foreshortening, and effects of light and shade. In painting and reliefs a certain naturalism is attained through the most precise observation of textures, movements, and positions in space, of incidental details. This is the expression of a new interest in the endless variety of nature. The artists of this era develop a sensitivity for visually interesting details and relationships, they attempt innovations with evident pleasure in experimentation and also have, not least, the skill to transpose them technically.

Since the Twelfth Dynasty there is evidence of the use of auxiliary lines much like a proportional grid in the flat surface pictures. They were used on occasion for the sketching of rather large-format figures. The grid represents a further development of the system of coordinates used during the Old Kingdom to establish the proportions of figures with a vertical body axis and seven horizontal lines at the level of particular body parts. The proportional grid developed during the Middle Kingdom, which was based on a unit of measurement corresponding to the width of a fist, and which divided the height of a standing figure into 18 squares, was retained virtually unchanged in Egyptian art for over 1,000 years.

As has already been observed in architecture in earlier chapters, unique local styles developed in the Upper and Middle Egyptian regions. This is true for painting as well as for raised relief sculpture in private tombs. These appear lightly modeled, but do not achieve the freedom that painting does in wall composition. During the late Middle Kingdom, reliefs eventually show a tendency toward detailed, realistic representation. Those who commissioned the works made a conscious decision in favor of painting alone, however, since they preferred its possibilities for delicate interior drawing, gradations of color, and fine shading.

The themes are all familiar ones from the Old Kingdom; the function of subjects represented is still to provide the deceased with everything needed for the hereafter. Thus continuation into the First Intermediate Period and Middle Kingdom of scenes of agriculture, cattle-breeding, trades, hunting, and tables laden with food showed that these are still the most important subjects. The only truly new motif is the pilgrimage to Abydos, the illustration of the deceased's voyage along the Nile to the cult site of Osiris.

For the traditional themes, the artists of the Middle Kingdom devised a sheer endless variety of new compositions, approaches, and ways to embellish or develop motifs. The scenes come to life, their figures move with energy.

Although the objects represented were intended for the hereafter, the cliff tombs of the governors afford an exceedingly vivid picture of contemporary daily life, and even of particular events in the lives of the individuals who commissioned them. These men address the viewers of the images, wishing to communicate their eminence through the impressive and representative impact of their tombs.

36 The tomb owner at a table laden with food
Qubbet el-Hawa, tomb of Sarenput II;
Twelfth Dynasty, ca. 1880 BC.
The focus of the imposing tomb complex is this small cult chamber. The painted ceiling of the naos or shrine is divided in the middle by a band of hieroglyphs on a white ground and with red-brown zig-zag stripes painted on a yellow ground imitating a stretched mat. The side walls and the middle ground are framed by a colored border and from underneath by a base with several stripes; the background is an intense light blue. Sarenput II sits on a lion-legged chair and extends his hand toward the food table before him. His son brings him lotus flowers. The inscriptions include the name of the ruling king Amenemhat II twice in cartouches; on the left is a rarely occurring hieroglyph: the elephant, the sign for Elephantine.

37 Figure of a woman on a proportional grid
Qubbet el-Hawa, tomb of Sarenput II;
Twelfth Dynasty, ca. 1880 BC.
Under the partially flaking paint a grid is visible. It is painted black on the background of the wall and is, in part, quite imprecise in its measurements. Moreover, while tracing the figure, the artist did not keep exactly to the divisions of the space: the hairline and nose are placed at the "correct" axis of the grid, but other standard points of reference such as the shoulder and the armpits are placed with no regard for the rules. These imperfections, as well as the fact that only relatively few figures were painted this way, indicate that the proportional grid – at least in the private tombs – provided only a general orientation for the artist. It can by no means be understood as the exclusive tool needed to determine the proportions.

38 Group of offering bearers
Beni Hasan (BH 3), tomb of Khnumhotep II;
Twelfth Dynasty, ca. 1880 BC; painting on stucco over limestone.
A telling example for the layering of picture motifs in several levels is this group bringing offerings. The fowl are truly woven in between the high incense stands. A beautiful line is sought; the motif is characterized by smooth contours. At the same time this shows a refined painting culture with the finest gradations of color and a delicate composition in which the emphasis is on yellowish and red-ochre tones contrasting with different shades of turquoise. The interior patterns of the four animals display ever varying sequences.

39 The feeding of sable antelopes
Beni Hasan (BH 3), tomb of Khnumhotep II;
Twelfth Dynasty, ca. 1880 BC; painting on stucco over limestone.
The artist's inventive creativity manifests itself here in the composition of the group. Three planes in space are used in which first the lying, then the standing antelopes, and finally the herdsman keeping up the rear are arranged. The movements of this second herdsman are complicated. He seems to turn his back to the viewer and press his shoulders downward – creating an impression of perspective foreshortening of the shoulders. The way in which the group is unified as a whole is also masterful. The rounded back of the herdsman on the right is echoed in the horns of the standing antelope, and taken up again by the rear arm of the second herdsman.

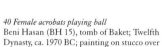

40 Female acrobats playing ball
Beni Hasan (BH 15), tomb of Baket; Twelfth Dynasty, ca. 1970 BC; painting on stucco over limestone.
A popular theme in the tombs of Beni Hasan is that of movement games and dances. Here four girls play an acrobatic ball game, shown in a strikingly concise drawing style. Each player sits on her partner's back and throws balls to the player opposite. The girls wear knee-length white dresses with straps, turquoise-colored faience jewelry on arms and ankles, and broad collars. Three long, thin braids ending in tassels are attached to their close-cropped wigs.

41 Herdsman
Meir (B2), tomb of Ukhhotep; Twelfth Dynasty, ca. 1900 BC; painted limestone.
A scrawny herdsman reduced almost to a skeleton, with matted hair and a ragged loincloth of fur leads three robust, well-tended cattle on a rope. This relief bespeaks a joy in striking contrasts and in the type-casting of people. The image almost qualifies as sunk relief; the background around the picture's subjects has hardly been worked; the contours are incised with lines of irregular width.

42 Wrestlers and a battle around a fortress
Beni Hasan (BH 2), tomb of Amenemhat; Twelfth Dynasty, ca. 1930 BC; painting on stucco over limestone.
The tombs of governors at Beni Hasan are famous for their depictions of wrestlers. A total of fifty-nine pairs of wrestlers in this tomb show the most widely varying sequences of movement, spectacular leaps and falls, and ever new grips and pulls. In order to better differentiate them, the opponents are represented in two different tones of brown. The two lower registers belong to a scene of a battle around a fortress. The marching soldiers are armed with spears, battle-axes, clubs, bows, and arrows. With the Egyptian soldiers march several Libyans who stand out with their colorful kilts and their fine chin beards. The lower register shows the journey to Abydos. This is the oldest inscribed depiction of this theme in Egyptian art.

43 The daughters of Djehutyhotep
El-Bersha (tomb 2), tomb of Djehutyhotep; Twelfth Dynasty, ca. 1900 BC; painted limestone; H. 80 cm; Cairo, Egyptian Museum, JE 30199.
The images in the tombs of el-Bersha are executed in paper-thin relief. The women with their slim bodies and severe, somewhat coarse, facial features seem relatively formal. Their headbands embroidered with blue and pink lotus flowers sit perfectly straight on their heads; the ends of the ribbons hang down stiffly. The artist has painted the thin red contour lines and, most of all, the internal detail in admirably accurate brushwork. The fashionable wigs are rendered with particular detail, their fine strands tied several times with red bands and their ends curled tightly around disks of carnelian, as are the large pectorals that hang from several rows of turquoise-colored faience chains.

Stelae

In the First Intermediate Period, painted funerary complexes such as those at Gebelein or Mo'alla are rather the exception. For the most part, the decoration of a cliffside tomb or a simple mudbrick mastaba was reduced to a stone tablet embedded in the wall. Similarly, at the Middle Kingdom necropolis of the residence at Memphis, the walls of the superstructures over the private tombs are virtually devoid of decoration; a simple stela is often the only surface on which texts and images appear.

This stela is the indispensable mimimum decoration of a tomb. In principle it contains three elements needed to ensure the afterlife of the deceased. First and foremost, the inscriptions must be mentioned along with their most important component, the offering text. This is a request for the provision of all necessary items for the afterlife. Also included in the inscriptions are prayers, the name of the deceased, his or her title, dates, and genealogical information. The second element of the stela is the representation of the tomb owner who thereby lives on in eternity; the third is the offerings table piled high with food, guaranteeing that the deceased will always be provided for.

In their artistic and technical execution, Middle Kingdom stelae vary considerably. Occasionally produced by simple mass production, the stelae were also affordable for members of the lower classes. Indeed, with their texts they are an important source for our understanding of the religious beliefs of these people. Most stelae of the Middle Kingdom have a vertical format, the upper edge is rounded, the figures are executed in low relief, and the text in sunk relief.

Funerary Sculpture

As in the Old Kingdom, the sculptural representation of the tomb owner during the Middle Kingdom was an essential part of the private tomb. Whereas this figure was once sealed in a chamber, the *serdab*, and thus hidden from visitors to the tomb, it now stood in a prominent position, for example in a statue niche, the focal point of the sepulchre. It is now obviously intended to be seen by the visitor and also meant to be a monument. In addition, the tomb statue retains its traditional function, to serve as a substitute image for the represented individual who, through it, could exist for all eternity and receive the mortuary cult. Unfortunately, almost no funerary statues have been preserved whole and in their original location, and it is therefore an exception when we can associate a statue with a particular tomb. The majority of tomb statues are of rather small size. Their often undifferentiated, schematic execution and rough styling lead us to surmise that they were mass-produced for members of the lower classes.

The classical poses of the Old Kingdom are still the most commonly used: the seated figure, signaling that the tomb owner is of an elevated social class, and the standing figure, suggesting his

44 Tomb stela of Amenemhat
Western Thebes; Asasif, tomb of Amenemhat (R 4); Eleventh/Twelfth Dynasty, ca. 1980 BC; painted limestone; H. 30 cm, W. 50 cm; Cairo, Egyptian Museum, JE 45626.
The members of a family are shown on this stela from the Asasif (tomb R 4). The father and mother sit on a lion-legged bench with a low backrest. The mother has a basket out of which peeks the handle of a mirror. Between the parents sits their son; they hold each other's hands and shoulders. The daughter-in-law at the right edge of the picture stands before the offering table on which pieces of meat, a string of onions, and lettuce are piled; under it are two loaves of bread. The horizontal line of hieroglyphs above this scene is carved in typical sunk relief; it contains funerary formulas and the names of the parents. The stela is a composition of intense and pure colors. The deep red-brown and yellow ochre skin colors, the white of the clothing, and the clear green of the hieroglyphs and jewelry all contrast equally well with the light blue background. The composition is tight and balanced; the rendering of the human figure now seems confident again compared to the style of the First Intermediate Period.

45 Stela of Antef
Western Thebes, Dra Abu el-Naga; Ninth Dynasty, ca. 2125 BC; limestone; H. 106 cm, W. 73 cm; Cairo, Egyptian Museum, CG 20009.
The stela comes from the tomb of Antef, governor of Thebes and inspector of priests in the necropolis of Dra Abu el-Naga. It is a so-called false door stela that borrows the false door framing elements of the cavetto cornice and torus moulding. The deceased can in an abstract sense emerge from the hereafter through the leaves of the double door in the lower center of the stela to receive any needed provisions. To the right and left of the door, offerings of animals are presented by small servant figures, and a bull is slaughtered. The middle field of the stela is filled by the depiction of the tomb owner under a baldachin; he is accompanied by figures bearing sandals and whisks, and a servant hands him beer. The food provisions are piled in front of the baldachin. The three upper lines of hieroglyphs bear the offering formulas. The composition is characteristic for the period: the pictured objects are placed next to each other and are simple, clear, and neatly arranged.

46/47 *Cuboid statue of Hetep (above)*
Saqqara, tomb of Hetep; Twelfth Dynasty, ca. 1975 BC; painted limestone; H. 85 cm; Cairo, Egyptian Museum, JE 48857.
Cuboid statue of Hetep (below)
Saqqara, tomb of Hetep; Twelfth Dynasty, ca. 1975 BC; painted gray granite; H. 74 cm; Cairo, Egyptian Museum, JE 48858.
Both cuboid statues from the tomb of Hetep are among the earliest examples of this new statue type. Their composition and carefully considered, detailed decoration demonstrate particularly well the concept of resurrection underlying this figure type. The figures were found in two adjacent chambers of the tomb, their faces turned toward the rising sun. The

granite statue stood in the southern chamber toward Upper Egypt; the limestone statue stood in the northern chamber toward Lower Egypt. The cuboid statues represent the moment in which the deceased frees himself from a compact form; head, arms, and legs are already in the light. This compact unit can be compared to the "primeval mound" out of which, according to Egyptian belief, the world emerged. The deceased wishes to take part in the perpetually repeating diurnal and nocturnal journey of the sun god. The inscriptions define the granite figure as corresponding to the daytime journey; the limestone statue represents the nighttime journey.

48 *Group statue of Ukhhotep*
Mir, tomb of Ukhhotep; Twelfth Dynasty, ca. 1860 BC; gray granodiorite; H. 37 cm, W. 30 cm, D. 14 cm; Cairo, Egyptian Museum, JE 30965 (CG 459).
This family portrait comes from the tomb of Ukhhotep, one of the last governors of Middle Egypt. He is shown with his two wives and daughter. The four figures stand in strict frontality in seemingly stiff poses against a stela with a rounded top. At each edge of the stela are a papyrus and lotus plant, the

heraldic emblems of northern and southern Egypt. Ukhhotep is framed by two incised udjat eyes, which serve to connect him to the Egyptian cosmos. The figures' hairstyles and clothing reflect contemporary fashion, and their names and titles are inscribed on their garments. The somewhat coarse rendering of the faces makes for little differentiation between man and woman. The proportioning of the bodies is also typical: slim, with a high, thin waist and exaggeratedly long limbs.

49 *Standing figure of Nakhti*
Asiut, tomb 7; early Twelfth Dynasty, ca. 1950 BC; painted acacia wood, with inlaid eyes; H. 179 cm; Paris, Musée du Louvre, E11937.
During the First Intermediate Period and the beginning of the Middle Kingdom, wood was still used frequently for funerary statues. Stylistically, this standing figure of the vizier Nakhti, with its highly elongated proportions, is typical for this period. The calf-length kilt is rendered in smooth planes meeting at sharp edges; the body and head are only flatly and sparingly modeled. A particular gesture distinguishes this figure from many other similar statues: Nakhti places his right hand in a fold of his kilt.

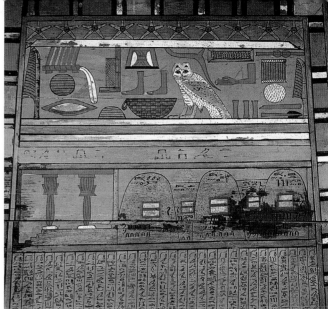

50 Coffin of Senbi (detail)
Mir (B1); Twelfth Dynasty, ca. 1920 BC; painted wood, H. 63 cm, L. 212 cm; Cairo, Egyptian Museum, JE 42948.
This rectangular coffin is an especially fine example of the notion of the coffin as a home for eternity. The architectonic details, the base and posts of the wooden construction, the doors with their two leaves, the finely patterned mats, and bands with which the facade is hung are all delicately painted. The artist has achieved a pleasing contrast of colors by emphasizing variations of green and red-brown with more intense fields of color dispersed between them.

51 Coffin of Sepi (detail)
El-Bersha, tomb of Sepi (III); Twelfth Dynasty, ca. 1920 BC; painted wood; W. 65 cm; Cairo, Egyptian Museum, JE 32868.
While the exteriors of the coffin bear only simple bands of hieroglyphs, the interior walls are richly painted with pictorial motifs in notably fine brushwork. At the foot end illustrated here, coffin texts appear on the bottom half; above, under the hieroglyphic sign for the heavens decorated with stars, the text reads: "Provided for by Isis, who is at your feet, General Sepi, the justified." Large storage silos with a columned front hall are pictured in the register below.

continued ability to move. Figures of scribes are only rarely produced. A new type that emerges in various private tombs is the mummiform niche figure. A second new figure type originally developed exclusively for Middle Kingdom private sculpture continued for over one and a half millennia into the Late Period: the so-called cuboid or block statue. The represented person squats on the floor with bent knees and wrapped in a cloak. The whole body seems to be enclosed in a cube; only the head, and sometimes also the feet, arms, and hands are included outside the geometric form.

Primarily hard stones such as diorite or granite, which are difficult to work, are preferred to wood as the material of choice. The technical perfection of the sculptures is striking. Even in the hardest stone, fine details and delicate modeling is achieved and the surface is polished to a velvety shimmer.

Several iconographic details can be identified as typical for the Middle Kingdom. Examples include the long kilt worn by men that reaches from the chest or hips as far as the ankles, or the wide cloak that wraps around the entire figure, terminating at the chest. The men wear either heavy shoulder-length wigs or wigs with pointed ends reaching down to the chest, or their heads are clean-shaven. On the wigs for the women, the two locks of hair with ends rolled up in tight curls are particularly outstanding. The facial expression has become more individualized; the sculptors emphasize characteristic, realistic features.

Sculptured heads at the beginning of the Middle Kingdom still exude above all power and energy; but during the course of their development the expressions become softer. The face is clearly readable through the wide eyes, often large and high-set ears, and the mouth; the elements are juxtaposed like the hieroglyphs of an inscription. With their emphasis on large, simple planes, their dignified and individualized facial features, and the merging of the abstract, cubic form with realistic, plastic detail, the private sculptures produced during the Twelfth Dynasty are among the finest creations of Egyptian sculpture.

Coffins

The coffins of the Middle Kingdom show rich decoration. In private coffins, locally differentiated types developed. For the most part their form and painted decoration reflect the notion that they serve as a home for eternity. The most common coffin type is made of single planks of wood in a rectangular form, with an exterior painted with architectural and decorative elements borrowed from the construction of houses. During the course of the Middle Kingdom, anthropoid (human form) coffins appear for the first time as inner coffins are painted to represent a mummy swathed in linen. This coffin form became the most important during the New Kingdom.

The coffin is oriented facing east; consequently at or near the head end a pair of eyes is often painted, enabling the deceased to "see" outside. He or she could thus observe the sun rising in the east, watch the journey of Re throughout the day or his or her own participation in it, and observe the mortuary rites taking place in the tomb. Here we most often see the depiction of a false door that was to allow the soul of the deceased to leave and enter. Among other motifs, the so-called frieze of tools should be mentioned, a listing of useful objects in pictorial form of which the deceased can make use in the hereafter.

On the inside walls are offering formulas and lists. Also included are the so-called coffin texts, a collection of spells intended to accompany and protect the deceased on his journey to the hereafter.

Shabtis, Servant Figures, Models

"O you *Shabti*, if I am obliged to perform any task that is performed in the underworld – that is if a man there is ordered to the performance of his task – then oblige yourself (to) that which is done there, to cultivate the fields and irrigate the banks, to ferry over the 'sand' (fertilizer) of

52 Statuette of a woman bearing offerings
Western Thebes (TT 280), tomb of Meketre; Eleventh Dynasty, ca. 1990 BC; painted wood; H. 123 cm, W. 17 cm; Cairo, Egyptian Museum, JE 46725.
This relatively large, particularly beautifully worked figure of a servant also comes from the tomb of Meketre. She must be understood as the personification of a donation who offers her gifts. On her head she carries a woven basket containing four clay pots sealed with conical lumps of clay. In her right hand she holds a duck. This symbolic representation is already familiar to us from the long rows of offering bearers in Old Kingdom wall reliefs and paintings. The slim figure of the woman wears elaborate clothing and jewelry. Over her close-fitting dress is a net of red and turquoise-colored tube beads; the lower hem and the straps are decorated with several different patterns. Multi-colored bracelets and anklets complete her elegant outfit.

53 Funerary figure (Shabti) of Djaf.
Twelfth Dynasty, ca, 1800 BC; surpentinite; H. 11.6 cm; Basel, Antikenmuseum Basel und Sammlung Ludwig, inv. BSAe 1021.
The figure of Djaf is styled in a pure mummy form and fitted with a straight wig. The inscription on the body contains an offering formula invoking Osiris, the god of the dead. The official title of the grave's owner is given as manger of the main accounting office. During the Twelfth Dynasty such funerary figures represented a substitute body for the dead person. It was first during the change from the Twelfth to the Thirteenth Dynasty that their function as deputies for work in the afterlife was defined and the figures inscribed with chapter six of the Book of The Dead. They were then known as Shabtis, and in the following period became an indispensable part of funerary equipment.

the east and the west. 'I will do it, I am here', you should say." This text appears at the end of the Twelfth Dynasty on the so-called *shabtis*, small, mummiform figurines laid in tombs and fashioned mostly of stone, wood, or faience. The name *shabti* ("answerer") explains their function. They are "answer figures," who must respond to their master's order to work and, on his behalf, take upon themselves the unpleasant tasks of irrigating and fertilizing in the life beyond, labors regarded as drudgery compared to the work of ploughing, sowing, and harvesting. Since the beginning of the Middle Kingdom they form part of the burial equipment, at first only for private individuals. As precursors of the figures, one might consider the small, substitute mummies, the naked wax or clay figures wrapped in bandages and buried in tiny coffins in order to replace the mummy of the deceased in case of damage or destruction. Some of the *shabtis* can be identified as belonging to particular tomb owners due to the names and genealogical information inscribed upon them. As of the Twelfth Dynasty they also bear offering formulas.

A further group of statuettes that were also produced exclusively as burial equipment are the so-called servant statues that are shown carrying out particular tasks. Contrary to the function of the *shabtis* as representatives of the tomb owner, the function of servant statues is also fulfilled by tomb reliefs and paintings: as statues, reliefs or paintings, they ensure the continuing existence of the tomb owner in the hereafter, provide him with food, uphold the social status prescribed by his public offices, and entertain him.

While Old Kingdom servant statues as individual sculptures are made of limestone with relative care, during the Middle Kingdom they are for the most part fashioned in wood and painted. Since the First Intermediate Period, several individuals could be mounted on a board and combined to create model groups. These figural groups are comple-

mented by the appropriate surroundings, buildings, craftsmen's tools, and so forth. Thus entire slaughterhouses, bakeries, carpenters' and weavers' workshops are assembled, as well as diverse models of ships for travel, trade, or for the journey to Abydos, for example, but also ships with troops of soldiers commensurate with the tomb owner's office.

Such scenes are already familiar from the decorative programs on the walls of the great Old Kingdom mastabas where they are separated into single motifs and juxtaposed in registers. But now the groups of models include the surroundings of the action and, in their three-dimensionality, gain a sense of space. Furthermore, within that space they can show the interplay of several separate yet simultaneous activities involving many figures, making the scene seem more lifelike and realistic, like a modern-day snapshot.

The groups are placed in the tombs in order to complement the wall paintings or to serve as substitutes for them. With their rich variety of motifs, they provide for the afterlife of the tomb owner in every way. Typical scenes include farming and cattle-breeding, the storage of goods, the preparation of foods and the production of widely varying objects for everyday use.

The single figures in these models differ greatly in style and technical execution; some are finished very neatly and with great care. Most of them show the mark of a practiced and sure hand, but also appear to have been made quite quickly, in which case fine detail and the working of the surface are unimportant.

During the Middle Kingdom it became usual to place the models in the shaft or the subterranean burial chamber where they were safer from tomb robbers. The sites where they are found are concentrated in Middle and Upper Egypt. Only at the beginning of the Twelfth Dynasty does the production of these servant figures come to an end.

54 Assessing the cattle (model)
Western Thebes (TT 280), tomb of Meketre; Eleventh Dynasty, ca. 1990 BC; painted wood, H. 55.5 cm, L. 173 cm, W. 72 cm; Cairo, Egyptian Museum, JE 46724.
Cattle are driven before several farmers and herdsmen in order to be counted for taxation purposes. Scribes and officials sit in a small pavilion on a raised platform whose roof is supported by four delicate columns in the shape of bundles of papyrus. The tomb owner himself sits in a chair, observing the procedure. In front of him, a delinquent cattle-herd is being punished by flogging.

The figures in the model groups represent no particular individuals; they remain anonymous and their sole purpose is to fulfill an important function for the continued existence of the tomb owner. The decisive difference from sculptures representing the tomb owner or his or her family is that with the servant figures the artist freely varies the canon of figural representation and makes numerous exceptions to the usual rules. A great variety of poses are often shown almost exaggerated, with sweeping gestures; rigorous composition and frontality were abandoned. Portraiture too can play no part here. The facial expressions are unforced, the proportioning is, on the whole, careless. But it is precisely in this way that they gain in expressive quality and do not seem staged but rather grant us – although intended for the hereafter – a glimpse of earthly life in Egypt during the closing years of the third millennium BC.

Between Heaven and Earth –
Temples to the Gods in the Middle Kingdom

Regine Schulz

In ancient Egypt, temples were meeting places for humans and gods, the living and the dead. They symbolized and guaranteed the existence and permanence of creation. This guarantee was secured on the one hand through the daily practice of the cult and observance of the festivals, and on the other through the magical power evoked by the concept of the shrine with its architectural layout and program of texts and images. The different levels of this system stem from a common notion, but were only effective as a whole. In its content, the cult rituals performed in the temples is to be understood as communication between a human and a deity whereby the initiative is taken by the human, and the god functions as the beneficiary of the cult ritual.

Temples were considered part of heavenly and earthly reality. Inside them on a heavenly plane, the gods were provided for and given satisfaction by the king; in the exterior region on the earthly level, humans were heard by the gods. Mediators between these levels were the king and his attending priesthood. The king possessed a double function, however, as he performed not only the cult of the gods but was himself also the beneficiary of a cult. The concept and practice of the cult in Old and Middle Kingdom temples to the gods can only be reconstructed to a very limited extent, however, due to the buildings' poor state of preservation. Texts that could give clues about them exist only as fragments or do not tell us much of value.

From the Cultic Hut to the Temple of the Gods

Cults of kings and gods characterized life in Egypt from prehistoric times. The first cult image or fetish huts consisted of a wooden framework and woven mats. Their exterior form varied and was independent of the object of the cult, its function, or its location. In early dynastic times, mudbrick structures began to replace these more transitory constructions, and by the beginning of the Old Kingdom at the latest, stone was also used for door frames, supports, and shrines. The spatial articulation of these complexes began to be ever more differentiated, and evidence suggests that, next to the chamber holding the cult image, there were also visitation rooms and offering table rooms.

The image and text program, that is the decoration of these buildings, can no longer be reconstructed. It is certain, however, that besides the cult images in the sanctuary, there were also figures in the temple or the exterior area, which facilitated the meeting of the humans and the gods.

The Gods and the Omnipotence of the King

This picture changes at about the time of the pyramid age. Whereas for earthly and heavenly sites in this world, that is for residential buildings, palaces, and temples to the gods, mudbrick continued to be used as building material, for the deceased king huge stone complexes for the funerary cult were created. Temples constructed exclusively of stone, such as the Sphinx Temple at Giza or the obelisk-like solar shrines built with masonry, must be seen as exceptions for they stood in direct relationship to the royal pyramid complexes. Accordingly, their function lay not only in the joining of heaven and earth, but also in the joining of this life with the next. For the pharaoh was believed to be the divine Horus and son of the sun god, and was thus the guarantor for all aspects of creation. Creation was not thought to be a completed act, and needed continual confirmation as well as individual and constant renewal through every newly enthroned king.

The Gods and the King – A Powerful Partnership

The steady waning of royal domestic political power during the Sixth Dynasty led to the collapse of the Old Kingdom, to the internal division of the land, and to a deep-seated religious crisis. The trust in pharaoh's omnipotence was destroyed, and the presence of the gods on earth was endangered. Now humans were responsible for life on earth while the hereafter was the responsibility of the mythical god-king Osiris, who was independent of the actual circumstances of this world.

It took over 150 years before Mentuhotep II (Eleventh Dynasty) managed to reunite the country and inspire new trust in the religious

55 *Sphinx of Amenemhat II*
Tanis; Twelfth Dynasty, ca. 1900 BC; red granite; H. 204 cm, L. 480 cm; Paris, Musée du Louvre, A 23.
The original location of this powerfully rendered sphinx is unknown and only a few traces of Amenemhat II's inscription are preserved, since the monument was usurped several times. The name of the Hyksos ruler Apophis as well as those of the kings Meren-ptah and Sheshonq I can be made out. Thus we can assume that the sphinx first stood in the Hyksos capital Avaris, was taken from there to the city of Pi-Ramesse and finally to Tanis during the Twenty-second Dynasty. In its almost brutal directness, brought out by the sculptor's metallically clear carving, the Louvre sphinx can be regarded among the greatest masterpieces of Egyptian royal sculpture of all time.

56 Mentuhotep II at the festival of renewal
Armant, temple of the king; Eleventh
Dynasty, ca. 1990 BC; limestone; H. 80 cm,
W. 135 cm; New York, The Brooklyn
Museum, Charles Edwin Wilbour Fund,
37.16 E.
The block from Armant shows two scenes: to
the left, Mentuhotep II during the *sed* – the
race for the renewal of his royal power and, to
the right, the king before the goddess Yunit, a
companion of the god Montu in Armant. The
finely modeled flat relief, compared to the
very powerful, undetailed style of Thebes,
suggests the increasing influence of Memphite
schools of artists in the Theban area.

57 Mentuhotep II
Dendara, scene from the king's chapel;
Eleventh Dynasty, ca. 2010 BC; limestone;
H. of the king's figure 90.5 cm; Cairo, Egyptian Museum, JE 46068.
Mentuhotep II regarded Hathor as his special
patron goddess. As her primary cult site in
Dendara he had a small royal cult chapel
constructed. The scene showing the enthroned
ruler comes from this building. In one hand
he holds the flail, while the other is extended
toward the offerings heaped before him. The
Horus falcon hovering over him gives the
king life.

58 (opposite) Obelisk of Sesostris I
Heliopolis; Twelfth Dynasty, ca. 1925 BC; red
granite; H. 20.41 m.
On the occasion of his renewal festival, Sesostris had two massive obelisks erected before
the Atum temple at Heliopolis. Obelisks
symbolized the close link between the king
and the sun god and thus ensured the perpetual regeneration of creation. Their development began with examples executed in
masonry in the shrines to the sun of the Fifth
Dynasty from Abu Gurab. They received
their final form only later at Heliopolis with a
tall shaft and pyramidion point.

59 "Osiride pillar" of Sesostris I
Karnak, Amun temple; Twelfth Dynasty, ca.
1950 BC; painted limestone; H. 158 cm;
Luxor, The Luxor Museum of Ancient Egyptian Art, J.174.
So-called Osiride pillars were erected in front
of the facade of the Amun temple at Karnak
during the reign of Sesostris I, probably to
flank the main entrance. The statue pictured
here is well preserved; only the separately
worked crown and the legs have been lost.
The body of the figure is shaped like a
mummy, the arms are crossed, and each hand
emerges from the white-painted wrappings
holding an ankh. A large beard with a turned
up end reaches down to the hands. All
of these elements are typological and iconographical references to Osiris, the god of the
underworld. The existence of Osiride statues
of kings in front of facades or pillars at other
temples of the Middle Kingdom has also been
documented, for example at Armant or
Abydos. They must be clearly distinguished
from standing royal statues wearing the *sed*
cloak that suggest the individual renewal of
the king's power. In a clever fashion, through
the "Osiride pillars," the perpetuation of the
actual king's cult in this life is extended by the
mythical perpetuation of Osiris, king of the
underworld, thus ensuring the creative power
of the god worshipped in the temple.

principle of the cult as a guarantee of creation. The fundamental belief
was that the gods chose the ruler and imbued him with the necessary
legitimacy so that he in turn could see to the preservation of world
order, ward off chaos, and provide for both humans and gods. The cult
of the king thus became a permanent element in the cult of the gods,
and chapels for royal statues were integrated into divine temples. In the
pictorial program of these chapels, motifs such as the designation,
provision, and coronation of the king by the gods as well as the
conquest of enemies by the ruler (as in Gebelein or Dendara) were of
primary importance.

A type of mixed architecture in brick and stone was characteristic
of many sacred buildings of this period. Some complexes were
conceived as analogies for the rooms of secular dwellings, which
underlined the connection to life on this earth. On the other hand, the
relationship of these temples to the hereafter was reflected by other
elements. Mummiform pillar statues of the king exemplify this concept
expressing the connection between the material ruler and Osiris.
Among the oldest examples of this type are those erected for Mentuhotep II in the temple of Montu at Armant, near Thebes.

Temples for Eternity

Countless building projects were undertaken during the forty-five-year
reign of Sesostris I. This king built temples of stone at almost all the
country's important cult sites; these replaced the older brick constructions. Monuments were consecrated not only to gods, but also to
deified ancestors such as Snefru and to patron deities such as Heqaib
in Elephantine. The variety of the decorated shrines corresponded to
the many forms of divine presence for the enhancement of royal power.

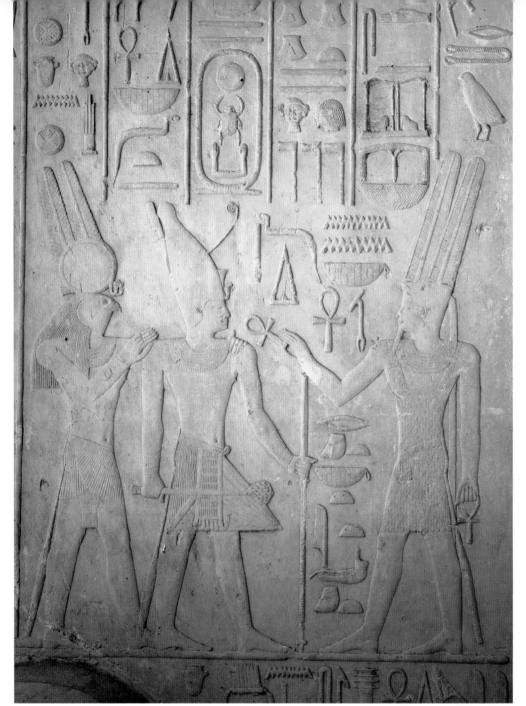

60 *Amun receives Sesostris I*
Karnak, "White Chapel," pillar relief; Twelfth Dynasty, ca. 1925 BC; limestone; H. of the entire picture field ca. 260 cm.
The sixteen pillars of the "White Chapel" are decorated on all sides with inscriptions and a total of sixty picture fields. The pictorial program shows the king's cult rituals before Amun, who is shown in his various aspects, as well as the god's granting of life, permanence, and protection. Here the falcon-headed god Montu leads the king to Amun, who extends an ankh toward him. The inscription above the scene tells that the event takes place in conjunction with the king's festival of renewal. Such representations complement the actual event with an eternal cult – since it is depicted in stone – and therefore signify cultic perpetuation.

61 (*opposite*) *The "White Chapel" of Sesostris I*
Karnak, Open-air Museum; Twelfth Dynasty, ca. 1925 BC; limestone; surface area: 6.54 x 6.45 m.
The way station of Sesostris I known as the "White Chapel" is considered a treasure of ancient Egyptian architecture and relief sculpture. Two ramps lead up to a pillared structure raised on a platform. A balustrade and architrave topped by a cavetto cornice and torus moulding and roof enclose the room. The original site of the chapel is disputed, though it might have stood in the axis of the Amun temple.

Along with the rise of the god Amun in the Middle Kingdom came the importance of his cult site of Karnak. Sesostris I had the older buildings completely replaced.

The front of the complex consisted of an open garden surrounded by columns and a group of Osiride pillars in front of the facade; the rear consisted of a succession of three central cult and auxiliary rooms. A cult image shrine of Amun made of granodiorite, which was found south of the seventh pylon, must also have belonged to the main temple.

Another building of Sesostris I in Karnak ranks among the most beautiful of the Middle Kingdom. The so-called "White Chapel," a way station erected on the occasion of the king's first festival of renewal

(*sed*), was torn down during the New Kingdom and its materials rebuilt into the foundation of the pylon of Amenophis III. The structure, which today has been almost completely reconstructed from the original blocks, has sixteen pillars and two access ramps opposite one another. A pedestal stands in the middle that might have held a double figure of the King with Amun-Re-Kamutef; today only the foot slab remains. In conjunction with his renewal festival, Sesostris I also created new complexes in Heliopolis and erected two tall obelisks in front of the Atum temple.

The kings of the late Twelfth Dynasty spread their cult and building programs far beyond the borders of Egypt. They commissioned

temples in Amara and Semna in Nubia, and also in Serabit el-Khadim in Sinai. In Egypt proper, numerous statues and stelae were consecrated, and temples extended or rebuilt. Amenemhat III paid special attention to the Faiyum and constructed numerous complexes there.

One of these is the cult site of Biyahmu with two 18-m-high colossal statues (now destroyed) of the deified king. In Medinet Madi he consecrated a small temple to the crocodile god Sobek and the goddess Renenutet, and in old Shedit, modern Medinet el-Faiyum, he remodeled the Sobek temple. A series of statues showing the king in extremely unusual vestments or as a sphinx with an enormous lion's mane surely also came from there.

Certainly, the few Middle Kingdom temples that still exist show heterogeneous basic structures, but included in almost every case are a sanctuary tract with cult image chambers, an offering table hall, and a visitation hall along with a court area. Each of these temples must be understood as an independent, powerfully evocative complex. Landscape and architecture, surface images and inscriptions, statues and obelisks form a conceptual whole in which gods and kings play their parts.

62 Lintel: Sesostris III brings offerings before Montu

Medamud, temple of Montu; Twelfth Dynasty, ca. 1860 BC; limestone; H. 107 cm, L. 225 cm; Paris, Musée du Louvre, E 13983.
Montu, god of war and of the province of Thebes since ancient times, was highly regarded among the rulers of the Middle Kingdom. His most important cult site was in Medamud. Sesostris III completely rebuilt and considerably expanded the temple there. The lintel, now in the Louvre, comes from this complex. It derives from a passage that led to a room for the storage and preparation of offerings. An inscription on both sides of the passage, which also reports that Sesostris III erected the gate "for his father Montu … of fine, white limestone", refers to this function. The picture field of the lintel is divided into two parts whose compositions mirror each other. Each of the halves shows Sesostris II presenting offerings to Montu. The figures of the king with their offerings face outward from inside the room and are protected by the winged sun disk, symbol of the heavenly deity of Edfu. To the right, the king hands the god Montu a conical *shat* cake and, to the left, a conical loaf of white bread. In both cases Sesostris III wears a royal headdress and a kilt with bull's tail; the falcon-headed Montu wears a god's kilt and a tall feathered crown with a sun disk and double uraeus cobras. The god holds a *was* scepter and an ankh, symbols of life and prosperity.

63 Sphinx of Sesostris III

Twelfth Dynasty, ca. 1860 BC; anorthosite; H. 42.5 cm, L. 75.5 cm; New York, The Metropolitan Museum of Art, 17.9.2.
This powerfully expressive sphinx is characterized by an apparent contrast between the deeply lined, gaunt features of an aging Sesostris III and the muscular massiveness of the lion's body. Yet both elements equally communicate a great sense of self-assurance, and the head raised high emphasizes the alert tension of the body, creating a harmonious whole.

Living Images – The Statue Programs of the Temples

A divine sculptural image in the round worshipped by the cult was an essential part of every temple in ancient Egypt. These cult images have almost all been lost since they were completely or partially made of precious metals and were therefore stolen and melted down. Two-dimensional images on temple walls show that for the most part the statues must have been standing or enthroned figures. They were believed to be living images and thus elements of the divine being, which is why only the king or a priest acting on the king's behalf were permitted to approach them. Outside the sanctuary too were figures of gods fashioned primarily of stone and approachable by initiated individuals such as priests and leading administrators. Only the barque with the processional statue was on display for the entire population during large festivals.

The Multifunctional Nature of Royal Sculpture

Statues of kings were indispensable components of every temple to the gods; they were also believed to be alive. Since their exact provenance can be reconstructed in only a very few cases, we must surmise their function on the basis of their appearance. The statue type plays an important role here, suggesting various functional levels. Royal statues can take on an active as well as a passive role. As supreme lords of the cult, they move before the gods, for example, in the form of offerings or praying figures who kneel or stride forward. As embodiments of divine and royal power, they demonstrate the guarantee of creation through the king, such as in the form of sphinxes. They are worshipped and provided for by humans as the cult focus, shown as either standing or enthroned figures. They enjoy the protection and acknowledgment of the gods as chosen individuals. We find them in statue groups, for example, in which king and god touch each other. Iconographic elements identify the depicted individual as well and emphasize his function, such as the unusual attire of the so-called priest figure of Amenemhat III or the ankh symbols held by the pillar statues of Sesostris I. As a third and definitive element, the body and facial features play a central role in determining the expressive effect of the figure. Analogous to the king's titulary, each and every ruler established his own formal criteria that still allowed for functional and stylistic variations. If we observe the development in royal portraits of the Eleventh and Twelfth Dynasties, significant differences become apparent: concentrated mass and powerful weight for Mentuhotep II, formulaic symmetry for Sesostris I, taut intensity for Amenemhat II, great concentration and force of will for Sesostris III, and energetic severity for Amenemhat III.

In principle the appearance thus leads from great formalism and a "hieroglyphic" composition of details over a balanced aesthetic to psychologizing naturalism.

64 Temple of Qasr el-Sagha
Qasr el-Sagha; Twelfth Dynasty, ca. 1880 BC; limestone; W. 21 m, D. 7.80 m.
One of the few Middle Kingdom temple complexes still well-preserved today was created during the late Twelfth Dynasty on the west bank of the Qarun Lake in the Faiyum oasis. It consists of seven adjacent cult image chambers and a common offering table room. Forecourts or halls are absent, as are an enclosure wall and the entire image and text decoration. Consequently the temple must have remained incomplete and was probably never used for cult rituals.

65 (below) Bust of Amenemhat III
Probably Faiyum, Sobek temple; Twelfth Dynasty, ca. 1810 BC; copper alloy with remains of inlays of gold, silver, electrum, and rock-crystal; H. 46.9 cm; private collection, Switzerland.

Royal metal statues are attested since the Old Kingdom (such as the over-life-sized statue of Pepi I from Heliopolis), and were part of the temple statue programs. Very few of them have been preserved, however, since most were stolen and melted down. This piece is without a doubt a masterpiece of the metal-worker's art. It remains unclear whether the figure was once standing or enthroned, since the lower body was produced separately and has yet to be found. The large headdress was attached separately; the headband, which ensured a harmonious transition to the forehead, is missing. The face betrays great expressive power. The form of the face, the energetic thrust of the jaw, the dominant chin and naturalistic eyebrows are elements known from other portraits of Amenemhat III. The extremely large mouth, the wide set of the small eyes, prominent, long nose, and the very reserved modeling of muscles and wrinkles depart from the typical image of the king, however. One might ask, therefore, if a separate portrait was developed for royal metal statues, or if the bust must be dated somewhat later and was perhaps created for Amenemhat IV.

66 (above) "Priest figure" of Amenemhat III
Medinet el-Faiyum, Sobek temple; Twelfth Dynasty, ca. 1830 BC; granodiorite; H. 100 cm; Cairo, Egyptian Museum, JE 20001.

The bust of the "priest figure" of Amenemhat III belonged to an over-life-sized statue of the king. It was found at Shedit, the primary cult site of the crocodile god Sobek in the Faiyum. The costume of the figure is unique. The ruler wears a heavy, braided wig, the animal skin, and a heavy chain around his neck. The ceremonial beard, which was held by extremely wide chin straps, and the cobra over his forehead have been broken off. To the right and left of the wig, the king holds two narrow divine staves with falcon heads. Thus the prototype was created for the royal staff bearer, a statue type that only reappeared late during the New Kingdom. The identification of the figure is unquestionably Amenemhat III, due to the characteristic facial features. The statue's function is disputed, but the unusual attire and the animal skin, however, refer to a particular cult ritual so that the designation "priest figure" is certainly acceptable.

67 Squatting figure of Sesostris-senebefni
Probably Memphis; Twelfth Dynasty, reign of Amenemhat III, ca. 1830 BC; sandstone, H. 68.3 cm; New York, The Brooklyn Museum, Charles Edwin Wilbour Fund, 39.602.
Squatting figures with the legs drawn in to the body and arms crossed over them occur for the first time during the Middle Kingdom. They stood in tombs in connection with a cult path, or in temples. The body position is meant to demonstrate unambiguously the privilege of participation in the cult for a king or god and the provisions required for it. Sesostris-senebefni includes his wife in this privilege. The god appealed to in the offering formula is Ptah-Sokar, lord of the necropolis of Memphis.

68 Statue of Sobekemsaf
Probably Armant; Thirteenth Dynasty, ca. 1700 BC; granodiorite; H. 150 cm; Vienna, Kunsthistorisches Museum, ÀS 5051/5801; base slab with feet; Dublin, National Museum of Ireland, 1889.503.
The standing-striding figure of the Theban governor Sobekemsaf probably once stood in the Montu temple in Armant since the offering formula addresses "Montu of Thebes, resident of Armant." The considerable corpulence of the man's body, the unusual size of the statue for a private sculpture of the Middle Kingdom, and the kilt of honor, which juts out strongly and is pulled high over the chest, manifest the importance of this high official whose sister was an important royal wife of the Thirteenth Dynasty.

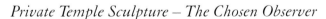

Private Temple Sculpture – The Chosen Observer

While both divine and royal sculpture was directly involved in the magical safeguarding of the cults, the statues of other persons bore a completely different significance. During the Old Kingdom, statues of private individuals who were neither kings nor gods were most likely placed along the paths of cults and processions. Since the Middle Kingdom at the latest, such figures could also be seen in the temples themselves. They represent individuals who did not actively partake in the cult, but who enjoyed the privilege of being present and "observing" the rituals. They were thus involved in the temple's redistributive system. The inscriptions on the figures also suggest their association as participants in cult ritual, since they contain for the most part formulas invoking participation in the provision of offerings for the divinity. Many of these statues show a squatting position with the legs folded under the body, or the knees held up and pressed close to the body.

Such a squatting pose suggests a passive position of repose and is suitable for neither the gods nor the king. In order to guarantee the permanence of this participation in the cult and the resulting provision in an enduring manner, both in this life and the next, a new iconographic element is added: a cloak wrapped tightly around the body. Combined with the crossed arms and partially covered hands, it suggests the aspect of Osiris. During the late Middle Kingdom, standing figures were also added. Their arms hang close to the body and their hands are either at their sides or extended in the front along the kilt.

The individuals represented are high-ranking priests or officials who also in reality were directly involved in the cult. With this development the Egyptian temple during the Middle Kingdom opened itself to non-royal persons in two phases. As "observers," they were granted access to the temple and later, as worshippers, were even allowed to participate in the rituals of the cult.

The Political History of the Eighteenth to Twentieth Dynasties

Dieter Kessler

The New Kingdom presents itself to the modern observer as the period in which Egypt achieved its greatest territorial expansion and produced its most famous royal personalities. Its starting point, however, is the revolt of the Thebans in Upper Egypt against the Hyksos whose stronghold was based in Lower Egypt. By about 1570 BC the Hyksos ruler controlled only the northern part of the country from his capital of Avaris in the Delta. The first attack by the Thebans under Kamose, who had previously already conquered the Hyksos followers in Middle Egypt, had been repelled. The Hyksos king now tried in vain to establish contact with the ruler of the Nubian kingdom of Kerma in order to engage Thebes on two fronts. His messenger was captured on the oasis road.

The second attack under the future Theban ruler Ahmose was more successful. Memphis was captured, and the Theban fleet appeared before Avaris. Finally, the city surrendered. Ahmose took over the citadel of the city, which he then extended and decorated with Minoan frescoes among other motifs. The main force of the Hyksos had withdrawn to the southern Palestinian town of Sharuhen. After a three-year siege, this bastion also fell and the region came once more under Egyptian influence.

For historians, the expulsion of the Hyksos and the reunification of the Kingdom under Ahmose marks the beginning of the so-called New Kingdom. The political history of the first half of the New Kingdom is marked by gradual territorial expansion into Asia Minor and Nubia. The borders of Egypt were redefined. At the end of the campaigns of conquest, the southern border was situated deep in what is now Sudan near Abu Hamid, north of the fifth cataract, while the northern border presumably extended as far as the Euphrates to a country called Naharin.

Egypt rose to become a "world power." However, the territory beyond the Nile valley was hardly controlled to its full extent. Although the larger and smaller city states of Palestine were controlled by Egyptian "advisers," they were left under the rule of the local princes. This can at best be described as imperialism geared to the exploitation of raw materials and the control of trade routes. There is a vast discrepancy between the contemporary claim in the ancient sources that Egypt ruled the world "as far as its outer edges" and the actual extent of Egyptian power. Egypt never succeeded in permanently pacifying central and northern Syria. The pharaohs were in competition there with the princes of other large states, first with the Mitanni, rulers of the federation of Hurrian city states beyond the Euphrates, and then with the Hittites. Nonetheless, Egypt achieved a position of power in the Mediterranean region and remarkable cultural dynamism as a result of its foreign policy successes and internal political stability.

1 Kneeling figure of Hatshepsut
Western Thebes, Deir el-Bahari, Eighteenth Dynasty; ca. 1460 BC; red granite; H. 75 cm; Berlin, SMPK, Ägyptisches Museum, 22883. By building her funerary temple in Deir el-Bahari, Hatshepsut rivalled the temple of Mentuhotep II from the Middle Kingdom, which had hitherto been the destination for festival processions. As is customary in a funerary temple, Hatshepsut is portrayed in sacrificial pose. She is holding a ritual water vessel.

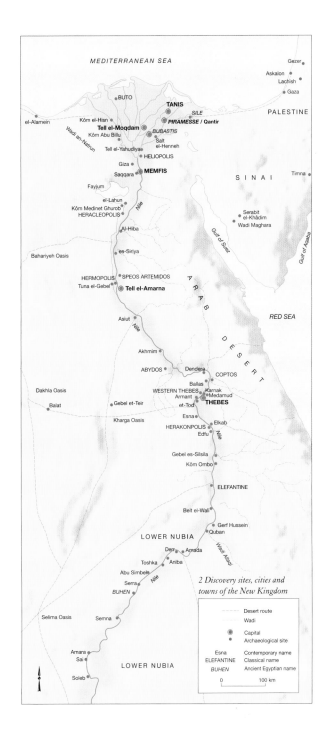

2 Discovery sites, cities and towns of the New Kingdom

3 Upper part of a statue of Thutmosis III
Eighteenth Dynasty, ca. 1450 BC; grano-
diorite; H. 45.5 cm; Vienna, Kunsthistorisches
Museum, ÄS 70.
Of all this pharaoh's many achievements, it is
not his military conquests that posterity has

deemed worth mentioning, but rather the
writings ascribed to him and his erudition.
Under Thutmosis III, the Guidebook to the
Netherworld, the so-called Amduat, which
presents the Egyptian view of the underworld, first appears in the royal tomb.

Internal Developments in the Early New Kingdom

Under Ahmose and his successor Amenophis I ("Amenhotep," to use
the Egyptian form of the name), long-overdue reforms following the
reunification of the Kingdom were introduced, such as the standard-
ization of the administration, laws, the calendar, and worship. The
deification of Amenophis I and his spouse in later years ultimately goes
back to the binding nature of the rules that he introduced at this time.
The region of his funerary temple at Thebes later became an important
oracle site where decisions were sought in official matters.

The new rulers fostered the importance of the royal family within
the divine cult. Thus a princess from the royal family generally
assumed the ritual and – because of the oracle of Amun – also politically influential office of "God's Wife of Amun" at Thebes. From the
time of Amenophis I on, owing to the concentration of political power
and financial means there, the cult and processional sites of the local
Theban god Amun were enlarged as never before, and Amun was
elevated to chief god. The ensuing temple building activity of each
ruler encompassed not only Thebes, but the whole country. Never
before had a single deity achieved such a position of religious and political supremacy over the other gods of the Egyptian pantheon.

Hatshepsut and Thutmosis III

The royal family resided in palaces near Karnak and farther to the
northwest at Deir el-Ballas. However, the military training of the
princes and especially the heir to the throne was conducted in the
Memphis region. The harem established at the entrance to the Faiyum
near Abu Gurab appears to have been the scene of power struggles for
the royal succession. Thus, the succession of the young Thutmosis III,
son of a concubine of Thutmosis II, who had been designated the royal
heir, could not be accomplished. Supported by an oracle of Amun at
Thebes, a court faction elevated to the throne as regent his half-sister
Hatshepsut, the daughter of Thutmosis I, who was already God's Wife
of Amun in Thebes. We owe her spacious funerary temple at Deir el-
Bahari in Western Thebes to Hatshepsut's efforts to legitimize her
coup in religious and political terms. With its unique series of paintings, which fits extraordinarily well into the landscape, the building
contains the first attestation of the divine birth of pharaoh.

Hatshepsut was not the first female to rule alone as a Horus
pharaoh. Nonetheless, the co-regency of Hatshepsut and the young
Thutmosis III has constantly led to fanciful speculation about the
nature of their relationship. Upon her death and that of the incumbent
high priest of Amun, the influence of the priesthood seems to have
come to an end. Both appear to have become the victims of internal
power struggles. All we know is that, following the death of Hatshepsut, Thutmosis III, who commanded the army in Memphis, terminated the festival cult in her funerary temple and also overturned her
statues. Her sanctuary inside the temple at Karnak was also
dismantled.

Under Hatshepsut, only five minor campaigns had been necessary in Nubia; this does not justify creating the image of a peaceable
female pharaoh who is confronted by a warlike Thutmosis III. Thutmosis III's name was handed down and presumably honored accordingly, particularly on scarabs, over the course of a millennium, probably
also in connection with his construction of his new stone festival building centrally located in the temple in Karnak. His personality, which
one can certainly describe as energetic, is hardly mentioned in the
sources apart from references to his passion for hunting. The king gave
a personal demonstration of his bravery on a spectacular hunt of 120
elephants on a plain by the Orontes river. All the same, an officer did
have to rescue the king, who was being threatened by an elephant, and
save him from an awkward situation.

The Push into Syria and Palestine

After conquering southern Palestine in a bold expedition to the
Euphrates, Thutmosis I had asserted Egyptian claims to Syria vis à vis
the king of Mitanni. During the regency of Queen Hatshepsut the
conflicts concerning trade routes and spheres of influence must have
intensified. The real adversary in this regard was the prince of Kadesh
in Syria, who amassed an anti-Egyptian coalition. After the death of
Hatshepsut, the Egyptian armies under Thutmosis III advanced to
Gaza. The enemy army was surrounded at the city of Megiddo, which
surrendered after a seven-month siege. Numerous city states now recognized Egyptian sovereignty. The ruler of Assur, who was anti-
Mitanni, established contacts with the pharaoh.

The objective of the subsequent campaigns, which lasted twenty
years, was to gain control of central Syria. At the mouth of the Orontes,
two Egyptian fleet bases were built, from which rapid advances could
be made against Kadesh. Thutmosis III established a lasting system
of control and administration for Syria and Palestine, for which a

governor of the eastern foreign countries held supreme responsibility at court. At points of major strategic importance on the Bekaa plain in Syria, at the mouth of the Orontes, in Gaza and perhaps also in Damascus, Egyptian regional administrations and garrisons were established. The princes of the Palestinian city states continued to be controlled by Egyptian advisers, and their sons were brought up at the royal court in Egypt together with the crown prince.

The Push Southwards

The fall of the last bastions of the Hyksos led immediately to an Egyptian attack on the enemy in the south. In the region of Elephantine and Lower Nubia, individual Egyptian city governors had come to an arrangement with the ruler of Kerma. Even Ahmose had used military might against them. Then, under Thutmosis I, came the well-prepared attack on the center of military power, Kerma. The city was overrun and the kingdom of Kerma destroyed (ca. 1500 BC). With the aid of his fleet, the pharaoh continued his advance southwards as far as the border of the conquered kingdom. Between the fourth and fifth cataracts, a border stela marked the southernmost point reached by the Egyptian armies. The internal African trade routes that converged here thus came under Egyptian control.

The entire region was placed under the control of an Egyptian viceroy who bore the title of "King's Son of Kush," and whose jurisdiction stretched far northwards into the eastern desert region near Elkab. The Nubian princes continued to serve as go-betweens, guaranteeing regular deliveries of tribute and the use of local labor. However, their sons, just like those of the Near Eastern princes, were brought to the Egyptian court and raised there together with the crown prince, in order to ensure their future loyalty. Although minor revolts constantly broke out in the ensuing period, all of Nubia was now under the pharaoh's influence. The income from the south was administered in the temple district of Amun at Thebes.

The state cult of the king and his ancestral gods Amun, Horus, and Ptah was instituted in the major trade and garrison centers with numerous new temple complexes, particularly in the region of Kerma (Sai, Soleb, Napata) in the south. Powerful fortresses at the edge of the Wadi Allaqi ensured the profits from Nubian gold that became increasingly important to Egypt's economy and prestige.

The enormous tribute exacted from the northern city states and Nubia flowed into the royal treasury at Thebes and altered Egypt's economic power. Even in the time of the Hyksos, groups of foreign merchants and artisans with foreign goods had flooded into Egypt. Perhaps triggered by the volcano eruption on the Mediterranean island of Santorini, the naval supremacy of the Minoans on Crete also collapsed. The subsequent conquest by Mycenae allowed for vastly increased exchanges of goods in the region, and Egypt participated as vigorously as did other states. Egyptian gold was very popular with foreign princes and Egyptian products reached the far corners of the Aegean region. From the pharaoh's court, specialists, particularly physicians and interpreters, were sent to foreign princes.

Conversely, semi-finished products and raw materials as well as workers came to Egypt. Tradesmen from Syria, Asia Minor, Crete, and

4 Statue group of Amenophis III with the crocodile-headed god Sobek
Dahamsha; Eighteenth Dynasty, ca. 1360 BC; calcite-alabaster; H. 256.5 cm; Luxor, The Luxor Museum of Ancient Egyptian Art, J. 155.
In connection with the *sed* festivals of Amenophis III, from the thirtieth year of his reign on, increasing numbers of statues in the form of animals appear. This statue group originates from a local temple of Suchos (Sobek) south of Thebes at which sacred crocodiles were also kept. Ramesses II later inscribed his name on the statue.

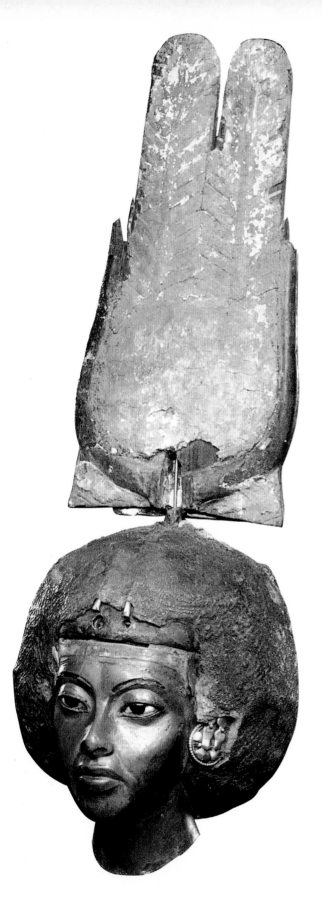

6 (right) Statue group of Akhenaten and Nefertiti
Tell el-Amarna; Eighteenth Dynasty, ca. 1340 BC; limestone; H. 22.5 cm; Paris, Musée du Louvre, E. 15593.
Like their full-formed figures, the intimacy of the royal couple holding hands is deliberate. The statue was part of the royal cult in a (residential) chapel of Amarna. Both figures achieve union and rebirth with their physical person rather than in their mythical and divine role.

other neighboring regions built ships in Egypt for the royal shipyards at Memphis; smelted metals and glass production experienced significant growth; prisoners of war worked for the armorers in Thebes. Nubians were commonly employed as elite troops and as police.

Iron for the pharaoh was produced near Kumidi in the Lebanon. Mining for turquoise at Serabit el-Khadim in the Sinai was resumed. Tastes and fashions changed. Even the jewelry of the royal family of Ahmose clearly shows elements borrowed from the Mediterranean. The influence of foreign advisers on the king grew steadily, and numerous words of Semitic origin entered the Egyptian language.

Amenophis II and Thutmosis IV

Under the successors of Thutmosis III, Egypt's military might extended further. His son Amenophis II continued the campaigns in Syria. His grandson Thutmosis IV, who also received his training with the army, seems to have put his policies into practice largely with the army's assistance. At that time, the ruler of Mitanni in the north was facing increasing pressure from the new superpower, the Hittites, and sought to reach an agreement with Egypt. Thutmosis IV was therefore able to appoint a king acceptable to him in the country of Nukhasse, south of Aleppo. He also accepted an offer made by the king of Mitanni and took the latter's daughter into his harem with a large retinue. Military and political power during this period was exercised in the royal palace at Memphis.

New Concepts at Royal Court

Under the succeeding reign of Amenophis III (1388–1351/50 BC), Egyptian dominance in Syria initially appeared undisturbed, and in Nubia only minor military operations were necessary to retain control. In addition to his military upbringing, the new ruler prided himself on having performed a series of supreme physical feats in his youth, which at that time was regarded as part of the ideal accomplishments of a ruler. On commemorative scarabs he announced his marriage to Tiye, the daughter of an influential court official from the Akhmim region. At the age of eighteen, diplomacy bestowed upon him another concubine, Gilukhepa, daughter of the ruler of Mitanni, who brought considerable property in Syria and Palestine into the marriage. Toward the end of his reign, another princess from Mitanni was accepted into the harem. The rulers of Babylon, Assur, and Arzawa in Anatolia also attempted to arrange political marriages as a reaction to the increasing military might of the Hittites and their growing influence in the regions of northern Syria.

5 Head of Queen Tiye wearing crown with raised headdress
Abu Gurab; Eighteenth Dynasty, ca. 1350 BC; yew wood, gold foil, inlays; H. 9.5 cm (not including the crown); Berlin, SMPK, Ägyptisches Museum, 21834.
The royal harem at the entrance to the Faiyum, where numerous princesses resided with their retinues, was controlled by the Great Wife of the King. The famous head and the newly assigned crown of the wife of Amenophis III probably originates from a dynastic cult at the harem. As Queen Mother, Tiye played an important role in the royal cult of Akhenaten at Tell el-Amarna, even after the death of her husband.

7 *Fragment of a seated statue of Ramesses II*
Thinis (San el-Hagar); Nineteenth Dynasty, ca. 1270 BC; granodiorite; H. 80 cm; Cairo, Egyptian Museum, CG 616.
After the Ramesside era, the statues of Ramesses II were transferred to the new royal residence of Thinis. The sophisticated refinement and love of splendor displayed by society's elite during the Ramesside Period seems to be reflected in the soft lines of this beautiful statue.

The king soon appears to have lost any interest in military operations. He became obese and was plagued by illness. For his *sed* festival, the most important royal festival to celebrate the thirtieth anniversary of his reign, he had prepared a radical move. He transferred his royal residence from Memphis southward to the western side of Thebes, where he built an extensive palace complex complete with its own harbor installation near Malqata. A new religious fervor, in which the king was greeted daily as the image of the sun, gained acceptance at the court. North of the palace, a huge mortuary temple was built by the architect Amenhotep, son of Hapu, who was later deified. In the temple courtyard, new statues of the tutelary deities of the royal *sed*

festival, including some in the shape of animals, were erected. Great royal *sed* festival buildings were erected throughout the land as well as in Nubia (such as the temple of Soleb).

The new palace ideology manifested itself in the emergence of the god Aten, the usual term for the sun disk. According to this ideology, the king united with it in a secret procedure, becoming visible again as its reflection in the morning. The court reduced the importance of the Theban-influenced Amun in relation to the national sun god, thereby causing a confrontation with resident Upper Egyptian families. Initially, however, the conflict was concealed by the arrival of high-ranking officials from Memphis who strengthened the king's influence locally.

The decorations on the tombs of these individuals at Western Thebes, for instance the vizier Ramose or Kheruef, the administrator of the Queen's property, who had magnificent rock-cut tombs built for themselves in Western Thebes, reflect the wealth and breadth of thought of this period. Daughters of Amenophis III and Tiye were given the title of "Great Wife of the God" in order to strengthen the dynastic cult and political responsibilities at the temple of Amun.

The Religious Revolution of Akhenaten

Even as crown prince, Amenophis IV, the son of Amenophis III and Tiye, married to Nefertiti, the daughter of a palace official from Akhmim, would have been involved in discussions on the dynastic cult of the king and his sun god. He must have planned the replacement of Amun by the palace god Aten very early on. The king abolished the cult of Amun from Karnak, but not the organization of the temple, and to the east he built a temple complex of Aten to replace it. Nefertiti and her eldest daughter Meritaten performed there the sacred function of the earlier "God's Wives." The property of Amun was rededicated in rigorous fashion by erasing the name of Amun throughout the land.

In the fifth year of the king's reign, the entire court, including the king's mother Tiye, moved to a new capital in Middle Egypt, the newly founded city of Akhetaten, "horizon of Aten" (modern Tell el-Amarna). The royal palace there, along with the palace temple of Aten and a funerary temple, became the new ritual center. The king's tomb was built in the eastern desert far from the surrounding tombs of court officials. The king, who personally acted as the ritual mediator in his capital, changed his name to Akhenaten to coincide with the move. There was a conscious attempt to break free from the religious norms associated with the old cult. The expressively ugly statues of the ruler show a new type of king, based on a changed canon of artistic proportions.

Even in the production of stone blocks, new structural dimensions were introduced. Linguistic forms from the colloquial language of the time, which we call "Late Egyptian," gained acceptance in official documents. The dynastic cult with images of the king and queen replaced the traditional tutelary gods in the shrines.

From the twelfth year of the king's reign, however, a reversal of the radical nature of the reforms is to be noted. Around this time, Akhenaten had to devote more time to dealing with foreign policy matters, as the Hittites were continuing their efforts to gain influence in Syria via Kadesh and other city princedoms. The preserved cuneiform script correspondence from the palace archive in Tell el-Amarna tells of intensive Egyptian efforts to assess the situation in neighboring regions correctly.

The ruler of Byblos repeatedly warned Egypt about the ruler of Kadesh. In order to protect the Egyptian administration, groups of Nubians were even resettled in Palestine. Ultimately, however, Egyptian policy banked on diplomatic marriage. Akhenaten thus married a daughter of the Babylonian Kassite ruler.

A second queen who appears on monuments of the period, one Kiya, may be identical with a daughter of the ruler of Mitanni. Following the death of Nefertiti and Kiya, Meritaten, the daughter of Akhenaten and Nefertiti, appears to have assumed the office of Great Wife of the King in the cult.

Akhenaten died without a designated successor. Soon after his death, his reforms were abandoned, Amun was rehabilitated and reintroduced to his temples. The capital of Akhetaten was abandoned in favor of Memphis, and the royal tomb of his successor was built once

8 Victory stela of Merenptah (the so-called Israel Stela)
Western Thebes, mortuary temple of Merenptah; Nineteenth Dynasty, 1208 BC; granodiorite; H. 318 cm; Cairo, Egyptian Museum, JE 31408 (CG 34025).
The stela text, which is written in a poetic style, announces first and foremost the victories over the Libyans in the fifth year of the king's reign. There is an added comment on the fact that calm also reigned in Palestine. The tribal name of Israel is mentioned for the first time: "Israel lies waste, its seed does no longer exist."

again at Thebes. Following the death of Ankhkheperure, who ruled only briefly and who may be identical with Smenkhkare, his widow appears to have written the famous letter to the Hittite king in which she requested him to send her a prince as a husband. The Hittite king made sure that the offer was a serious one before sending a prince, whose murder at the Egyptian border must then have given the Hittites a reason to march into northern Syria.

Under the influence of General Ay from Akhmim, another daughter of Akhenaten and Nefertiti, Ankhesenamun, was married to the young Tutankhamun, from whose short reign only the famous burial treasure has been preserved. After the early death of the young king, which is still an unexplained mystery, the elderly Ay himself acceded to the throne but also died soon afterwards.

The Rule of the Generals: The Ramesside Period

The army under the commander-in-chief Horemheb at Memphis does not appear to have automatically accepted Ay's accession to the throne. Eventually, Horemheb usurped the throne himself and moreover let himself be confirmed in Thebes by an oracle of Amun. As his successor, he chose his military deputy by the name of Ramesses, whose reign marks the second half of the New Kingdom. This era is generally called the "Ramesside Period" (Nineteenth/Twentieth Dynasties).

Horemheb, Ramesses I, and especially Seti I carried out internal political reforms. Under the latter, the erased names of Amun were restored at many of the old shrines and Akhenaten was declared a heretic king. For economic and strategic reasons, the Ramessides founded a new capital in the eastern Delta, near the old Hyksos capital. The city of Ramesses ("Pi-Ramesse") was situated at the beginning of the road to Palestine, which was becoming increasingly important militarily and was well-protected with wells and forts. The city was a sprawling complex with various temples to the state gods, palaces, and military installations, including extensive stables and weapons factories in which Hittite shields were even made for auxiliary troops. The raw material copper was delivered from the newly opened mines at Timna (Israel).

From the city of Ramesses the Egyptian armies were able to advance rapidly against Palestine and Syria, which were threatening to break away from Egypt. Trade in the area was disrupted by nomadic warrior troops, which Egyptian sources call Hapiru and whose name is perhaps found again in those of the Hebrews. Finally, the country of Amurru with its center of Kadesh openly allied itself with the Hittites. Military intervention became inevitable.

Seti I's successor, Ramesses II, eventually carried out a large-scale attack on the trouble-spot Kadesh, probably with the intention of preventing the Hittite troops from joining forces with those of the king of Amurru. The widely dispersed Egyptian army fell into a trap; it was thanks only to the ill-discipline of the enemy who were pillaging their camp that the king managed to withdraw south. The country of Amurru was thus lost. The ultimately indecisive battle of Kadesh, proclaimed as a victory on Egyptian temple walls, signified a turning point in relations with the Near East. Both sides realized that a complete military victory could not be achieved. Moreover, the king of the Hittites faced internal political difficulties in his own country, with epidemics and famines contributing to his problems. The Egyptians and Hittites thus concluded a detailed peace treaty that established the status quo and ended hostilities. Both versions, in cuneiform script in the Hittite capital of Hattusa and in hieroglyphs in Egypt, have been preserved. Later, Ramesses II even married a Hittite princess.

This king, who died at the age of over ninety, launched into tremendous building activity that was based on the intensive mining of Nubian gold. Almost all the settled centers in the country received new sacred buildings in the name of the pharaoh. His son Khaemwese was responsible for the restoration of old cults. The branches of the royal family consisted of almost ninety sons and daughters, with several daughters holding the office of "Great Wife of the King." Along with temple construction, the provisioning of numerous military units of foreign tribes bound to the royal temple institutions also occurred, in particular the large numbers of colossal standing statues of their ruler. New land had to be opened up with the aid of foreign military colonists whose leaders were rewarded with temple sinecures. The apparent

9 Seated statue of Seti II with ram's head emblem
Thebes; Nineteenth Dynasty, ca. 1195 BC; sandstone; H. 143 cm; London, The British Museum, EA 616.
Under Seti II, who lived at Pi-Ramesse, new fortresses were built in Palestine. Turquoise mining in the Sinai continued during his reign. Seti's monuments are also found in Upper Egypt and Nubia from Abu Simbel to Karnak. There is some dispute as to whether a revolt broke out against him there and in Nubia at the beginning of his reign.

climax of pharaonic self-portrayal, which manifested itself in the royal buildings, is an indication of the growing economic supply crisis into which Egypt was sliding.

The political situation was also changing in the west. Libyan tribes were growing restless, perhaps as a result of the appearance of foreign ships carrying groups of the so-called "Sea Peoples" from the Aegean region. Under Ramesses II a chain of fortresses was built for the purpose of protecting the coast to the west of Alexandria. Subsequently, under his son Merenptah, the Libyans, who had joined forces with bands of Sea People warriors, mounted their first attack on the Delta, which was repelled by the Egyptians.

After Merenptah's reign, a civil war between the north and south shook Upper Egypt. Under Ramesses III, the situation became even more dangerous. The Hittite kingdom had collapsed as a result of the attacks by the Sea Peoples, who cut off the trade routes and devastated the coasts of Asia Minor and Cyprus. The towns in the countries of Alalakh, Ugarit, and Carchemish, were destroyed. By land and by sea, various ethnic groups moved along the Phoenician coast in the direction of Egypt; the sources mention Sherden (Sardinians?), Lycians, Turshas, Akhiyawa (Acheians?), the Peleset (Philistines), and others. From the west, the Libyans attacked. In a combined land and sea battle, the enemy was repulsed.

Ramesses III's victory and booty were tremendous. The booty was used to extend the temple of Medinet Habu, which was surrounded by mighty walls and served as a fortress. Ramesses III considered himself the descendant of the victorious Ramesses II and he expressed this both in words and in buildings, for example by copying the latter's funerary temple. Nevertheless, he was unable to prevent trade and payments of tribute gradually coming to a standstill. The Philistines established themselves in Gaza and Ashdod before the gates of Egypt.

The provisioning of new mercenary forces and the lack of income from Palestine, along with perhaps the reduced gold revenue from Nubia, accelerated the economic decline. In Thebes the workers at the royal tombs went on strike. Ramesses III had become old and finally fell victim of a harem conspiracy.

Control of Upper Egypt increasingly slipped from the grasp of the succeeding Ramesside kings. The deplorable state of internal affairs, corruption, and violence led to renewed unrest. The Libyan mercenaries who had been brought into the country eventually plundered Theban temples. The Viceroy of Nubia, Panehsi, waged a private war against Amenhotep, the High Priest of Amun of Thebes. Although Ramesses XI, who had his residence in the Delta, still celebrated the festival of the "Renewal of Birth," an attempt to take a new political direction and restore stability, in the end he could only stand and watch as pharaonic power at Thebes was lost. Herihor, the general and High Priest of Amun at Thebes, established a dictatorship that was defined by an oracle of the Theban god and underpinned by a theocracy.

10 Ramesses III as staff-bearer
Karnak; Twentieth Dynasty, ca. 1170 BC; granodiorite; H. 140 cm; Cairo, Egyptian Museum, JE 38682 (CG 42150).
After groups of the Sea Peoples (Philistines, Shikelesh (Sikulans), Sherden and Danaeans) had settled in Canaan, Ramesses III endeavoured to consolidate his position by accepting soldiers from the Sea Peoples into the Egyptian army and building new garrisons in southern Palestine. The tremendous building activity in Thebes also belongs to this phase. This statue with a ram's staff as a cult symbol belongs to one of the processional rituals at the temple of Amun in Karnak.

The Temples – Royal Gods and Divine Kings

Regine Schulz and Hourig Sourouzian

Thebes – The City of Amun

Waset in ancient Egypt, named Thebes by the Greeks after the settlement of Djeme, rose to become Egypt's religious center during the New Kingdom. It was here that the tombs of the kings, the cult establishments of the state god Amun-Re and for a time even the royal residence were situated. On the east bank of the Nile lay Karnak with the temple complex of Amun-Re, the cult palace of the king, and (during the Eighteenth Dynasty) portions of the state administration with the vizier's office. In the reign of Akhenaten, the great Aten temple was established here, but it was abandoned immediately after the death of this king. South of Karnak were the residential districts, stretching as far to the south as the temple at Luxor. On the west bank lay the royal residence, the Valley of the Kings, the Valley of the Queens, the mortuary temples of the rulers together with smaller shrines to tutelary gods and gods of the dead, the temple of Amun-Re-Kamutef at Medinet Habu, the settlement for the necropolis workers and artists of Deir el-Medineh, and finally the countless tombs of officials. Amenophis III moved the royal residence from the north to the far south of the western city district. There he built the huge port installation of Birket Habu and established the magnificent palace complex of Malqata on its west bank.

Even when the state administrative seat moved back to Memphis and later to the city of Ramesses ("Pi-Ramesse") in the eastern Delta, Thebes remained the religious center. The city continued to be the place of Amun, a god of all-embracing divine power. Besides that, the other state gods (Ptah, Re-Harakhty and, during the Ramesside Period, Seth) now also played an increasingly important role. However, the kings stayed in Thebes only on periodic visits to the city, although they continued to be buried there until the end of the Twentieth Dynasty.

The great festival processions played an absolutely crucial role in the cult activities at Thebes, linking places of mythical significance with one another. In the Thutmosid Period, there were four such places of importance: Karnak and Luxor on the west bank of the Nile, and Deir el-Bahari and Medinet Habu on the east bank. Whereas the Opet Festival, which was held on the east bank, involved the maintenance of heavenly and earthly power, the Festival of the Valley, linking the east and west banks, focused on the regeneration of creation and the continuance of this life and the hereafter. The cult establishments at Deir el-Bahari subsequently diminished in importance and their place was taken by the later funerary temples of the kings and their built-in shrines to the gods. At the end of the New Kingdom the mortuary temple of Ramesses III at Medinet Habu together with the place of creation and renewal of Amun-Re-Kamutef finally became the religious and administrative center of all of Western Thebes.

The Temple City of Karnak – State Shrine and Site of Creation

In the course of the New Kingdom, Karnak developed into a huge temple city, consisting of numerous cult establishments, processional routes with shrines at various stages along the route, palaces, administrative buildings and storehouses. Its name was Ipet-sut, the temple "which counts the cult establishments." Here major new state religious concepts blended into a new theological system with Amun at its head. Without replacing the other gods, Amun took on their essence, thereby becoming the original god and god of creation, the god of the sun and the heavens, the omnipresent, always active King of the Gods and Father of the Kings who were to guarantee the world order.

Karnak was likewise the administrative center of the estate of Amun, to which the royal mortuary temples on the west bank of the Nile and Luxor temple also belonged. Countless priests and officials were needed to maintain the cult activities. Although the king in his capacity as chief cult overseer was actually responsible for each ritual activity himself, he could not always be present everywhere, so in reality it was the priests who conducted the sacrifices and said the prayers. At the top of the hierarchy was the high priest together with three other "servants of the god." They were in charge of four groups (phyles) of *wab* priests, who were responsible for the temple cult and alternated every four months. The majority were officials and must thus be thought of as laypersons. The ritual and "recitation" priests, on the other hand, were specially trained and performed their duties on a full-time basis.

11 Osiride pillars of Thutmosis I
Karnak, temple of Amun-Re; Eighteenth Dynasty, ca. 1500 BC; sandstone; total original H. ca. 5 m.
Between the fourth and fifth pylons, Thutmosis I furnished his court with thirty-six Osiride pillars that stood along the walls in deepened niches. The arms of the mummiform figures are crossed over the breast and emerge clearly from their wrappings. They hold signs of life in their hands. Their heads are for the most part badly damaged; they originally wore tall state crowns, uraeus serpents, and the divine beard that curled at the end.

The actual administration of the temples was structured in the same way as that of the state. The enormous economic power of the shrine, which was reflected in extensive estates, livestock, staff and officials of all kinds and, last but not least, the temple treasure, enabled the high priests at Karnak to gain more and more influence over internal politics. Ramesses III alone allowed 240,000 hectares of land and 86,486 staff to be made over to Amun.

The temple complex at Karnak consisted of three large districts: in the center stood the establishments of Amun-Re, in the south those of Mut and in the north those of Montu. Whether the northern district was dedicated to the god Montu as early as the New Kingdom or not until the Late Period is not certain, as it may originally have been an area for the royal cult as well. From the early Eighteenth Dynasty on, the facilities were constantly expanded and rebuilt until eventually the Amun district alone covered an area of 123 hectares. Beyond the actual Amun temple and the accompanying buildings on the eastern and southern axis the following establishments were built in the early and mid-Eighteenth Dynasty: in the north, the temple-like treasury of Thutmosis I, the Ptah temple of Thutmosis III and a temple of Amenophis III whose attribution to Montu is disputed; in the east, a sun cult establishment of Hatshepsut and Thutmosis III with a single 33 m-high obelisk (now in Rome) and in the south, a temple dedicated to the royal cult of Amenophis II.

Under Akhenaten, whose religious ideas were focused solely on the god Aten, all building activity in these districts was halted, the cult was discontinued and the names and images of many gods, especially Amun, were destroyed. Instead, the king erected extensive cult establishments in east Karnak for his sun god Aten. After the death and condemnation of this ruler the old cults were resumed and the shrines restored where necessary.

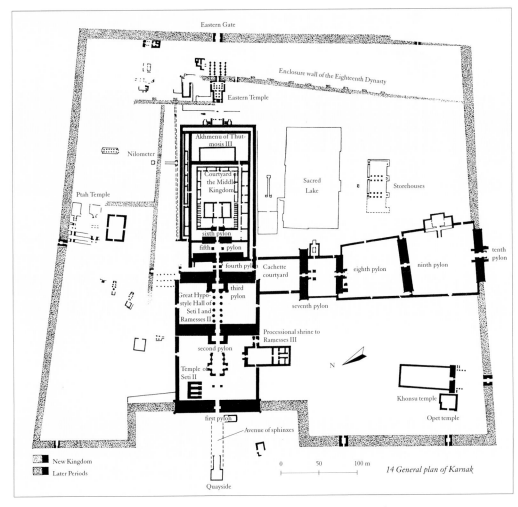

13 *The temple city of Karnak*
Watercolor: Cécile, illustration for *Description de l'Egypte*, 1798–1801.
This picture was painted during Napoleon Bonaparte's great Egyptian campaign. The engineer Cécile was a member of the scientific team accompanying the French whose task was to make a written and pictorial record of all the noteworthy cultural and natural monuments. The result was the monumental twelve-volume edition of the *Description de l'Egypte*.

12 (opposite) *General plan of Thebes:*

1 Tombs of the kings (Biban el-Moluk)
2 Funerary temple of Hatshepsut
3 Temple of Thutmosis III
4 Temple of Mentuhotep II
5 Deir el-Medineh
6 Hathor temple
7 Qurnet Murrai
8 Palace of Amenophis III
9 Birket Habu
10 Colossi of Memnon
11 Shrine to the primeval god
12 Luxor temple
13 District of Montu
14 District of Amun
15 Amun temple
16 District of Aten
17 District of Mut

Names of the mortuary temples:
a Temple of Ramesses III
b Temple of Ay and Haremhab
c Temple of Amenophis III
d Temple of Merenptah
e Temple of Thutmosis IV
f Temple of Ramesses II (Ramesseum)
g Temple of Thutmosis III
h Temple of Ramesses IV
i Temple of Seti I
j Temple of Amenophis I

14 *General plan of Karnak*

15 *"Alabaster Chapel" of Amenophis I*
Karnak, temple of Amun-Re, barque sanctuary; Eighteenth Dynasty, ca. 1505 BC; calcite alabaster; H. 4.51 m, L. 6.76 m, W. 3.59 m; Karnak, Open-air Museum.
The barque sanctuary dedicated to Amun-Re was commissioned by Amenophis I toward the end of his reign and was only later completed by Thutmosis I. The architect Ineni used valuable calcite alabaster from Hatnub as well as copper and gold for its construction, in order to cover the wooden doors that unfortunately have not survived. The blocks were found reused in the third pylon of Amenophis III.

16 *Amenophis I in a cult procession*
Karnak, temple of Amun-Re, section of the exterior wall of the "Alabaster Chapel;" Eighteenth Dynasty, ca. 1505 BC; calcite alabaster; H. of detail ca. 80 cm.
In Egypt, the royal portrait was an integral part of the royal identity, which was redefined for each ruler. The face of Amenophis I is marked by a very large, hooked nose, while the eyes, ears, mouth, and chin appear rather small. These striking characteristics diverge somewhat from the harmonious ideals current at the time and consequently they were not transferred to the divine portrait, for which more measured features were chosen.

The Establishments of the Eighteenth Dynasty
Regine Schulz

The kings of the New Kingdom saw it as one of their primary tasks to extend and decorate constantly the state temple at Karnak. It is difficult to reconstruct the early phases of construction, as almost all the establishments were later demolished and only a few fragments remain. The founders of the Eighteenth Dynasty, Kamose and Ahmose, erected monuments in Karnak, and Amenophis I began a program of expansion. He restored the original Middle Kingdom temple, built a ring of chapels around the temple's court and erected an entrance gate 10.40 m high (equivalent to 20 Egyptian cubits). On the central axis running from west to east, his famous barque sanctuary built of calcite alabaster probably stood in front of the courtyard. Two other chapels built by this king, of which only a few blocks remain, were inspired by the famous "White Chapel" of Sesostris I (see Middle Kingdom, Schulz, no. 61). Together with the latter they may have stood in the area of the temple or on the secondary north–south axis. Thutmosis I gave the buildings a new, more expansive framework and surrounded the area with a stone enclosure wall. An establishment for the royal cult erected farther to the east can probably be attributed to him. The first two pylons (numbers four and five according to our modern numbering), with a hypostyle hall in-between and two 21.80-m-high obelisks in front of the entrance, formed the western end of his extension to the Amun temple. Thutmosis II added another pylon and in the festival court that was thus created in front of his father's obelisks he erected his own smaller pair. Later, under Thutmosis IV, this festival court was further decorated with beautiful wall reliefs. The pylon and obelisks, together with many other buildings from preceding periods, subsequently fell victim to Amenophis III's alterations. Their blocks were used as fill for the huge pylon built by that king (number three) which, with its 40-m-high flagstaffs now formed the external end of the temple's western face. Not until the transition from the Eighteenth to the Nineteenth Dynasty was the front of the temple moved farther westward through the construction of Horemhab's pylon (number two) and the Great Hypostyle Hall that he had possibly planned but which was only built by Seti I and Ramesses II.

Hatshepsut's Construction Program – Cult and Legitimization

Hatshepsut also began her program of construction with a series of alterations. Between the Middle Kingdom temple and the eastern pylon (number five), a complex comprising chambers with cult paintings and sacrificial rooms was built, some of the architecture and decoration of which have been preserved. The center of this series of rooms may have been the barque sanctuary of Amenophis I, which was later dismantled,

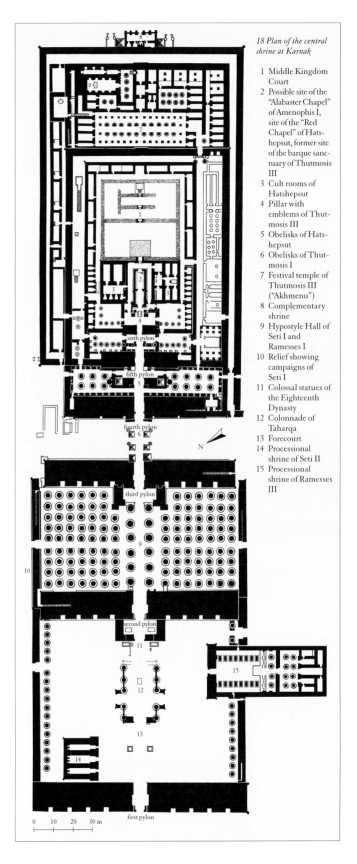

18 Plan of the central shrine at Karnak

1 Middle Kingdom Court
2 Possible site of the "Alabaster Chapel" of Amenophis I, site of the "Red Chapel" of Hatshepsut, former site of the barque sanctuary of Thutmosis III
3 Cult rooms of Hatshepsut
4 Pillar with emblems of Thutmosis III
5 Obelisks of Hatshepsut
6 Obelisks of Thutmosis I
7 Festival temple of Thutmosis III ("Akhmenu")
8 Complementary shrine
9 Hypostyle Hall of Seti I and Ramesses I
10 Relief showing campaigns of Seti I
11 Colossal statues of the Eighteenth Dynasty
12 Colonnade of Taharqa
13 Forecourt
14 Processional shrine of Seti II
15 Processional shrine of Ramesses III

17 (opposite) Obelisks of Thutmosis I and Hatshepsut
Karnak, temple of Amun-Re; Eighteenth Dynasty, ca. 1505 and 1464 BC; red granite; H. 21.80 m (Thutmosis I) and 30.43 m (Hatshepsut).
After Thutmosis I had added major extensions to the temple of Amun-Re, he erected two large obelisks for his "father Amun-Re" in front of the entrance at the "double gate of the place of worship." Only the southern obelisk still stands today. His inscription refers to the fact that the tips of these monuments were clad in gold; Hatshepsut had also gilded her obelisks, which stood in the hypostyle hall of her father. The text on the northern pillar states that "their upper halves consisted of electrum from the best of all the mining areas." The treasurer Djehuty, who supervised the work on the obelisks, goes even further, stating in his tomb that they were covered with "electrum along their (entire) length," which may be regarded as an understandable exaggeration.

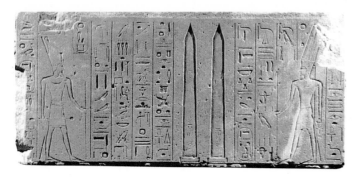

19 Obelisk dedication by Hatshepsut
Karnak, temple of Amun-Re, "Red Chapel;" Eighteenth Dynasty, ca. 1460 BC; sandstone; H. 60 cm, L. 131 cm; Luxor, The Luxor Museum of Ancient Egyptian Art, J 138.
In front of the central shrine of Amun-Re, Hatshepsut constructed a barque sanctuary closely connected with her two obelisks in the hypostyle hall of Thutmosis I. Both long sides of the chapel tell of the dedication of the obelisks on the one hand, and of the sanctuary on the other. Both scenes are inserted into a parallel series of motifs that consist of three sections: consecration of gold, donation of the monuments, some of which are clad in gold, and the coronation of the ruler. Therefore, Hatshepsut's coronation, and thus the legitimization of her rule, is seen as the result of her cult guarantee to Amun-Re.

and her own barque sanctuary built of sandstone, which is named the "Red Chapel" after the color of the building material. This chapel was demolished after her death, however, the small blocks being used as fill for the pylon built by Amenophis III.

Another alteration undertaken by Hatshepsut concerned the hypostyle hall of Thutmosis I. The queen removed a number of the columns and erected two obelisks over 30 m high to the right and left of the cult path. She added two columns in the north wing that may have been intended to mark the spot where Amun-Re designated her pharaoh. In addition, she surrounded the Amun complex and the eastern cult establishment built by her father with a large enclosure wall. On the eastern side, on the central temple axis, a colossal shrine of calcite alabaster with cult scenes, a so-called complementary shrine, was erected, and to its left and right, two large obelisks, of which only fragments have survived.

The two large obelisks inside the shrine are in better condition. The northern obelisk is still completely intact and large fragments of the southern one have been found. What is unusual is that in addition to the inscribed columns, ritual and coronation scenes are also depicted. The tips and perhaps parts of the shafts as well were originally clad in precious metal off which the sunlight would have gleamed. The great significance of the obelisks is shown, among other things, by the fact that both in Hatshepsut's mortuary temple and on the "Red Chapel" blocks their transportation and dedication are described and illustrated.

Generally speaking, one can assume that the hypostyle hall, the obelisks and the "Red Chapel" form a programmatic whole. By emphasizing her royal and divine origins, Hatshepsut endeavored to legitimize her claim to the throne. As the daughter of Thutmosis I and the wife of Thutmosis II, she continued the cult of Amun-Re and thus ensured the preservation of the Dynasty.

Like Thutmosis I, she erected obelisks and extended the temple, decorating it with gold, in return for which the God's Father Amun-Re was to guarantee her selection as king, her coronation, and the continual renewal of her reign.

However, the depictions on the "Red Chapel" show not only the ruler Hatshepsut, but also her stepson and co-regent Thutmosis III. They present offerings to Amun-Re together; nonetheless, the coronation scenes refer solely to her. Thus, all the queen's building initiatives were carried out in the name of both regents, even if Thutmosis III played only a supporting role, such as can be seen on the obelisks.

Thutmosis III at Karnak – Amun-Re and the Power of the King

Thutmosis III's great festival temple, the Akhmenu, has to be seen as his most important building project after the death of Hatshepsut. This complex replaced an older building probably dating from the time of Thutmosis I, and was dedicated to the creative power of Amun-Re and the royal power needed to maintain the world order. The living ruler was regarded here as directly related to the divine being.

The building faced north and was situated at right angles to the main axis behind the Middle Kingdom temple. The entrance was at the south end and could only be accessed via the central shrine of Amun-Re. It led to a unique hall that was modeled on a large tent for the royal renewal rites. The entire complex is therefore connected with the king's *sed*, and the great building inscription even tells of his personal involvement in the planning. In the nave of the hypostyle hall stood two rows of ten columns shaped like huge tent poles.

20 (opposite, bottom) Squatting figure of Senenmut with Princess Neferure
Probably from Karnak, temple of Amun-Re; Eighteenth Dynasty, ca. 1475 BC; grano-diorite; H. 100 cm; Berlin, SMPK, Ägyptisches Museum, 2296.
Senenmut, overseer of the treasure of Amun and mentor of the king's daughter Neferure, was one of the most important figures during the reign of Hatshepsut. There is no other official of the Eighteenth Dynasty of whom so many monuments and innovative artistic creations are known. The "teacher statues" form a special group in this regard. Together with another (Cairo, CG 42114), this statue probably formed a pair and stood in Karnak. In both cases Senenmut squats on the ground with his legs drawn up. He holds Neferure in his arms. His robe completely encloses the bodies of both figures, and the entire block figure is inscribed. Senenmut's name was later erased, for he had fallen out of favor.

21 Standing statue of Thutmosis III
Karnak, temple of Amun-Re; Eighteenth Dynasty, ca. 1450 BC; graywacke; H. 90.5 cm; Luxor, The Luxor Museum of Ancient Egyptian Art, J 2.
This statue, in classical standing pose with the left foot forward, belongs to a series of figures that were probably created for the festival temple of Thutmosis III. They are remarkable in terms of their extremely high quality and are characterized by the symmetry of their proportions, outstanding surface treatment, and the classical physiognomy of the ruler.

The lower side aisles, on the other hand, had simple pillars. A small chamber in the southwest section contains the so-called King List of Karnak, providing a chronological inventory of the ancestors of Thutmosis III. To the east of the festival hall were additional rooms. On the east–west axis was the chamber with cult scenes for the king who was connected with Amun-Re; to the south of this was an area for Sokar, god of the dead, and to the north, a sun cult establishment. This combination partly reminds one of the funerary temple complexes of Western Thebes where similar arrangements can be found.

The Egyptians' general intent here was to establish magically and ritually divine creative and regenerative power in connection with the guarantee of royal creation. This interpretation is supported by, among other things, the varied depictions of flora and fauna that fill the bottom wall register in the room described as a "botanical garden" between the royal and sun cult areas.

In the central shrine, Thutmosis III, late in his reign, demolished the barque shrine of Hatshepsut and replaced it with one of his own. Prior to this, he had established the Hall of Annals containing reports of his military campaigns and erected two unique emblematic pillars. In addition, he built the fourth pylon, the easternmost gateway in the entire complex. The obelisks erected by his predecessor were covered up, so that they were no longer visible in the temple interior; in their place, in front of the fourth pylon, a pair of obelisks was erected, of which, only a few fragments have withstood the ravages of time.

22 (opposite) Western facade of the Festival Temple (Akhmenu) of Thutmosis III
Karnak, temple of Amun-Re; Eighteenth Dynasty, ca. 1450 BC; sandstone; area of the temple 78.76 x 38.84 m.
In the first years of his autocratic rule, Thutmosis III had a festival temple, which was given the name of Akhmenu, built to the east of the inner sanctum of the temple of Amun. The name refers to this establishment's function as the place of "transfiguration," where divine and royal power combine to preserve creation.

23 "Archery stela" of Amenophis II
Karnak, temple of Amun-Re; Eighteenth Dynasty, ca. 1410 BC; red granite; H. 170 cm, W. 234 cm; Luxor, The Luxor Museum of Ancient Egyptian Art, J 129.
This representation, intended to demonstrate the strength and skill of the ruler, shows the king in a chariot. With his bow drawn he shoots at a post covered with copper and at a copper target, while his team of horses charges at full gallop. The relief block, together with another, which today can be found in Cairo (JE 36360) and which depicts the "smiting of the foes," may have belonged to a large gate dedicated to themes of victory.

24 Emblematic columns of Thutmosis III
Karnak, temple of Amun-Re; Eighteenth Dynasty, ca. 1450 BC; red granite; H. 6.77 m.
During the final years of his reign, Thutmosis III redesigned the central section of the temple of Amun. In front of his barque sanctuary he erected two unique monuments, the so-called emblematic columns. On their northern and southern sides they display in bold, raised relief the papyrus and lotus, the heraldic plants of Upper and Lower Egypt. The eastern and western sides, on the other hand, show the king in sunk relief being embraced by Amun-Re, Mut, Hathor, and Amaunet.

25 "Botanical garden"
Karnak, temple of Amun-Re, festival temple of Thutmosis III; Eighteenth Dynasty, ca. 1450 BC; sandstone; H. of the register ca. 110 cm.
The hall in which the so-called botanical garden is located was used for the manifestation of creation in this world. This is reflected among other things in the decoration scheme preserved only in the bottom section of the wall. New knowledge gained from the observation of nature during the course of the Syro-Palestinian campaigns of Thutmosis III must also have had some influence on the extremely varied representations of flora and fauna.

26 (opposite) Thutmosis III's triumph over the enemies of Egypt
Karnak, temple of Amun-Re, seventh pylon; Eighteenth Dynasty, ca. 1450 BC; sandstone; total W. of the pylon 63.17 m.
The scene on the pylon's western tower shows the motif of the king smiting his enemies, which can almost be seen as a kind of coat of arms. Thutmosis III takes a huge swing with his mace to kill a large group of enemies seized by the hair. Beneath his feet the names of the conquered cities and peoples are listed in three rows.

27 Southern facade of the eighth pylon with colossal figures of the king
Karnak, temple of Amun-Re; Eighteenth Dynasty, ca. 1455 BC; sandstone; W. 47.43 m. Hatshepsut erected the eighth pylon on the southern axis of the temple of Amun. In front of it stood six colossal seated figures that today are very badly damaged. The statues probably represent Hatshepsut, her co-regent Thutmosis III, and some of her predecessors as well.

The North-South Axis of the Amun Temple

From the Middle Kingdom onward, a secondary axis led from the central temple to the district of the goddess Mut, wife of Amun, situated to the south. It was probably Hatshepsut who replaced the older cult establishment of Mut with a new building that was later extended. In addition, throughout the area, Amenophis III set up hundreds of statues representing the lion-headed goddess Sakhmet.

In the New Kingdom, the cult route inside the Amun precinct that led southward consisted of several courtyard complexes with large gateway structures (seventh to tenth pylons). There must have been chapels in the first courtyard on the secondary axis as early as the Middle Kingdom, which Amenophis I had restored and probably also extended. Hatshepsut created an outer border with her eighth pylon, in front of which huge seated images of the ruler and figures of Amenophis I and of Thutmosis II respectively were erected. To the north, Thutmosis III added the seventh pylon, thereby dividing the courtyard.

At the entrance, he erected a pair of obelisks (the western one of which today stands in Istanbul), as well as two colossal statues. Thus, this king alone erected five large obelisks in Karnak. Amenophis III doubled the length of the cult axis and marked the edge of the district to the south with a 35-m-high pylon (number ten). An avenue of sphinxes led from here to the precinct of Mut and from there another avenue led to Luxor Temple. It was Horemheb, finally, who was the last to construct a pylon (number nine) erected on this secondary axis. It was added between the eighth and the tenth pylons, the latter already completed by Horemheb. The two courtyards created in this way were surrounded with a new enclosure wall. In addition, the royal cult temple of Amenophis II was dismantled and re-erected on the eastern side of the entrance courtyard.

Thus, by the end of the Eighteenth Dynasty, the secondary axis of the Amun precinct had attained its maximum area. In the huge courts created stood countless statues of priests and officials who, by virtue of their location, could participate in the cult activities permanently.

28 *The excavation of 1913 by the tenth pylon at Karnak*
Pairs of statues of Amenhotep, son of Hapu (ca. 1360 BC), and Paramessu (ca. 1300 BC) at the foot of the western colossal figure of King Horemheb at the southern facade of the tenth pylon.

The four figures presented in the classical pose of the scribe must have played a special role in the temple. Amenhotep, son of Hapu, was the leader of the festival at Karnak, while Paramessu (the later King Ramesses I) was the vizier and thus the highest official in the land. Their statues were almost certainly used as mediators between humans and gods. The location of their discovery probably does not correspond to their original location; the fact that the statues are in pairs suggests that they were positioned on both sides of a cult route.

29 *Scribal statue of Amenhotep, son of Hapu*
Karnak, temple of Amun-Re, tenth pylon; Eighteenth Dynasty, ca. 1360 BC; granodiorite; H. 128 cm; Cairo, Egyptian Museum, JE 44861.

Under Amenophis III, Amenhotep, son of Hapu, was personal adviser to the king and the éminence grise at court. His most important titles were "Director of all the royal works" and "Leader of the Festival" at Karnak, that is to say the king's representative at the great celebrations in the temple. After his death he was deified and worshipped as the god of medicine. Special powers were attributed to his statue, as is indicated by the smooth polish in the middle of the rolled papyrus on his lap: this is the result of the rubbing of countless human hands.

30 *Profile of a column statue of Akhenaten*
Karnak, Aten temple; Eighteenth Dynasty, ca. 1348 BC; sandstone; H. 141 cm; Luxor, The Luxor Museum of Ancient Egyptian Art, J 53. The statue shows the characteristic facial features of Akhenaten's early style that was obligatory for his representations at Karnak: small slanting eyes, an extremely long, narrow nose, a full, prominent mouth, cracked (nasolabial) lines running down from the sides of his nose to the corners of his mouth and a greatly extended round chin.

The Aten Temple at Karnak – Attempt at an Alternative Design

Amenophis IV, who later changed his name to Akhenaten, turned away from Amun and the gods associated with him soon after his accession to the throne. Instead, he began the construction of several shrines to his god Aten to the east of the Amun precinct at Karnak. In terms of their architecture these structures differed considerably from the temples of the other deities.

Aten manifested himself in the sun, which sends its life-giving rays to earth. Therefore, he was not depicted in human, animal or hybrid form as were other divinities, but as a sun disk whose rays end in human hands. There were no closed sanctuaries containing a statue of the god, but instead open courtyards with altars were used as places of worship. One of the shrines was the place where the Benben Stone, a stone monument in the form of a stela, was erected and, since very ancient times, had been regarded as the cult symbol of the creative power of the sun god.

The principal temple of Aten at Karnak was called Gem-pa-Aten, which can be translated literally as "finding of Aten," a name that refers to the king's active role and the first morning encounter with the sun god.

Of the sandstone complex, only a few remains of foundations can be found today, for it was demolished by the rulers of the late Eighteenth and early Nineteenth Dynasties following the condemnation of the heretic king. However, tens of thousands of small blocks with relief scenes as well as fragments of statues have survived, since they were reused in the construction of later shrines, and particularly of the second, ninth and tenth pylons at Karnak. Because the blocks were used as fill, much of their decoration appears in its original condition.

The original building had an eastward orientation and an area of approximately 130 by 200 m. It consisted, among other things, of a long open courtyard surrounded by colonnades. In front of the columns stood five statues, each one meter high, showing the king in a magnificent pleated loincloth and wearing various wigs and crowns. His hands were folded over his chest and held the royal insignia, the crook and flail. The shape of the figures is unusual, with overly long limbs, an extremely corpulent, feminine-looking stomach and upper thighs, and a very slender waist. The facial features, too, are overly long and gaunt, with narrow, slanting eyes, a long, narrow nose, a mouth with extremely full, prominent lips, and a strong, extended chin. Although these features are exaggerated, they come across as sensitive and expressive.

The decoration on the temple walls can be reconstructed in its basic form with the aid of the reused blocks. Unlike his predecessors, under Akhenaten all the representations were carved in sunk relief. The scenes show, among other things, the king with his wife Nefertiti and his daughters presenting offerings to Aten. The hands of the rays of sunshine hold out symbols of life and prosperity to them.

Other scenes depict, among other things, sacrificial offerings being prepared, the Festival of Renewal (*sed* festival) of the king, the palace complex or a parade of soldiers. The range of paintings shows a completely new design with hitherto unknown themes and details, the great number and variety of motifs resulting in a small-format method of representation.

The figures of the royal family in particular show a clear break with the balanced style of the period of Amenophis III, which appears almost overly aesthetic. As with sculpture in the round, the shapes of the bodies are characterized by the opposites of slenderness and corpulence, with the mannerist length of the neck, arms, and fingers being revealed even more clearly in this instance.

Akhenaten's attempt to place beside the newly formulated state dogma an equally altered image of mankind may be described as inspired and revolutionary. The image of the ruler, in particular, combines cerebral rapture and fruitful creative energy, and in this way demonstrates his divine quality.

The Buildings of the Ramesside Period
Hourig Sorouzian

The Nineteenth Dynasty is distinguished by intensive construction activity. The cult structures throughout Egypt had to be restored or re-established, as most of the temples to the gods had been closed or even destroyed during the Amarna Period. Under the Ramessides Thebes was, and remained, the cult center of the god Amun-Re.

The Great Hypostyle Hall

The construction activity during the brief reign of Ramesses I, the founder of the Nineteenth Dynasty, focused above all on his tomb in the Valley of the Kings and on the vestibule of the second pylon at the then main entrance to the temple of Amun at Karnak. His son and successor Seti I continued this work by beginning the construction of the immense Hypostyle Hall in the courtyard, which was once open, between the second and third pylons. The Hall was 104 m long and 52 m wide, and with a height of 24 m it was the largest hypostyle hall ever built. More than just an extension of the existing structure, it is a true temple in its own right that, from this time on, became the starting point for the processions of the two great Theban festivals. It bore the name "The Temple of Seti-Merenptah shines in the House of Amun."

The row of columns along the temple axis comprises two rows of six colossal columns each, the capitals of which imitate the shape of opened papyrus umbels. These rows in the nave, with a height of 22.40 m, are higher than in the rest of the Hall. The two side aisles comprise seven rows of columns each, in the shape of bundled papyrus columns with a closed capital. Each row has nine columns, and each innermost row flanking the central colonnade contains square columns at both ends instead

of the bundled papyrus shape. In all there are 134 columns that form an immense papyrus maze, immortalized in stone. The columns are not monolithic, but are constructed of massive drums. They stand on high, round bases, while the top edge is made up of square abaci upon which the colossal architraves supporting the roof beams rest. The difference in height between the nave and side aisles allowed for the incorporation of clerestory windows. These are windows made up of lattice work, through which the light falls onto the main aisle. The resulting basilica form of the Hypostyle Hall was implemented previously in the festival hall of Thutmosis III, but never before on this uniquely grand scale.

In the center of the Hall a diagonal axis runs between the two gates in the southern and northern side walls. This created a north–south axis in addition to the dominant east–west axis, as a processional route between the Karnak and Luxor Temples. When Seti I died after a reign of just under eleven years, the Hypostyle Hall, which was unfinished, and its series of paintings were completed by Ramesses II. The northern half, the decoration of which was begun under Seti I, is carved in raised relief, while the paintings on the southern half of the wall were completed under Ramesses II in sunk relief. The lower sections of the column shafts are decorated with papyrus leaves and at the top with offering scenes and cartouche friezes bearing the names of the royal builders, which for the most part were later usurped to bear the names of the last Ramesside rulers. The interior walls of the Hall are decorated with a variety of motifs and designs. Several series of paintings show the king being introduced by gods to the Theban triad of Amun, Mut and Khonsu, the recipients of his obeisance and offerings. Depictions of the liturgical purification of the king by gods alternate with those of his coronation and enthronement in the temple, the presentation of the scepter and the entry of the king's name in the leaves of the sacred *ished* tree in heavenly Heliopolis. The great impor-

36 (below) The entrance to the temple of Amun-Re
Karnak; buildings from the late Eighteenth to Thirtieth Dynasties, ca. 1300–340 BC.
In the Ramesside Period, a road flanked by ram-headed sphinxes led from the quayside to what is now known as the second pylon (W. 99.88 m). At that time, this gateway, erected as early as the Eighteenth Dynasty under Horemheb, formed the facade of the temple. Later, inside the forecourt area, other buildings were added and eventually, probably in the Thirtieth Dynasty, the entire complex was completed with another pylon facing west.

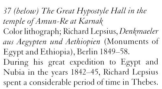

37 (below) The Great Hypostyle Hall in the temple of Amun-Re at Karnak
Color lithograph; Richard Lepsius, *Denkmaeler aus Aegypten und Aethiopien* (Monuments of Egypt and Ethiopia), Berlin 1849–58.
During his great expedition to Egypt and Nubia in the years 1842–45, Richard Lepsius spent a considerable period of time in Thebes. He produced a series of maps of Karnak, and devoted particular attention to the columns of the Great Hypostyle Hall. The color engraving shows, in the foreground, the high nave with papyrus columns and latticed windows in the sides of the high walls, and behind it, the lower southern side aisles with bundled papyrus columns.

tance of the processions of images of the gods in the sacred barques is shown by the main registers both of Seti I and of Ramesses II. The interior walls are decorated exclusively with cult activities and festival processions, giving an insight into the rituals that were performed in the temple hall itself.

By contrast, on the exterior walls, the conquest of chaos through the king's victories over foreign enemies is portrayed. On the northern exterior wall are shown the military campaigns of Seti I against the bedouins in the eastern deserts and in Palestine, as well as against the Libyans and Hittites. On the southern exterior wall can be found relief scenes from the famous battle of Ramesses II against the Hittites at Kadesh and extracts from campaigns mounted by this ruler against Asians and Libyans. The Great Hypostyle Hall is therefore a stone representation of Egypt and its environment, of the ideal world of the gods and the cult practiced within the country, and of the threatening,

chaotic world beyond its borders, which the king time and again must repel. The papyrus columns themselves symbolize the "Black Land," that is to say Egypt under the flooded Nile from which it arises each year with moist black soil like the primeval mound of the myths of creation.

Of all the statues that stood in front of and inside the Hypostyle Hall and which repeated in three-dimensional form the relief representations on the walls of the Hall, none remains today. It is only in front of the vestibule of the pylon (number two) that two colossal statues from the Thutmosid Period have survived through the millennia, one of them only in fragments. Ramesses II had them reinscribed, and Seti II and Ramesses IV had their pedestals and bases renewed. The custom of re-inscribing and reusing statues of earlier kings should not be looked upon as appropriation; on the contrary, the king retrieves them from oblivion so that offerings might be presented to them again.

38 (opposite) Seti I offering floral bouquets
Karnak, temple of Amun-Re, northern section
of the Hypostyle Hall; Nineteenth Dynasty,
ca. 1280 BC; sandstone; H. of the scene approx.
200 cm.
Floral bundles were a common sacrificial
offering to the gods, along with wine and
bread. They represent the desire for pleasure
and continuous life-giving strength. In
connection with Amun, bouquets also had a
special significance. The "bouquet of Amun
at Karnak" is offered not only to the god by
the king, but also, with the same designation,
to the deceased as a regeneration wish.

*39 Triad of Ramesses II between Mut and
Amun*
Probably Karnak; Nineteenth Dynasty, ca.
1270 BC; red granite; H. 174 cm; Turin,
Museo Egizio, Cat. No. 767.
The triad shows the king enthroned between
the pair of gods from Karnak, Amun and Mut.
Ramesses II here assumes the role of the son of
god and, in addition to wearing his royal headdress, is crowned with divine ram's horns, the
sun disk, and ostrich feathers. Although there
is a clear physical distance between the figures,
the mutual embrace points to the ruler's close
connection with these divinities.

40/41 Seti I's military campaigns
Karnak, temple of Amun-Re, northern external
wall of the Hypostyle Hall; Nineteenth
Dynasty, ca. 1285 BC.
The battle reliefs of Seti I refer to campaigns
against the Hittites and against Syro-Palestinian tribes, including the Shasu bedouins.
The scenes on this wall show the victories of
the ruler leading his army in a chariot or on
foot. The individual vignettes show the siege
of a fortress, the crushing of foes, and the
presentation of enemies during the triumphant return. The members of his royal household are already there to greet him on Egypt's
eastern border. The latter is formed by a canal
with frolicking crocodiles and by defensive
towers used for purposes of fortification.

42 Processional shrine of Seti II
Karnak, temple of Amun-Re, first court; Nineteenth Dynasty, ca. 1195 BC; sandstone; H. 7.40 m, W. 22.33 m, D. 13.86 m.
In the temple forecourt which was originally open (today, through the later addition of the first pylon, it is the first internal courtyard), Seti II erected a shrine with three chapels at which the barques carrying the cult statues of Amun-Re, the goddess Mut, and the moon god Khonsu stopped to receive offerings during the processions.

43 Royal colossal statues
Karnak, temple of Amun-Re; second pylon; Eighteenth/Nineteenth Dynasty, ca. 1300–1200 BC; red granite; H. ca. 11 m.
In front of the entrance area of the second pylon from the time of Horemheb, several colossal figures dominate the area. The southern statue on the left side, wearing a Double Crown, and originally one half of a pair, was sculpted during the reign of Thutmosis III and usurped by Ramesses II during the Nineteenth Dynasty. The northern colossus, which was replaced in 1954, suffered a similar fate. Pinadjem I had the inscription restored during the Twenty-first Dynasty, while the statue itself is from the time of the Ramessides.

44 (left) Colossal standard-bearing statue of Seti II

Karnak, temple of Amun-Re, first court; Nineteenth Dynasty, ca. 1195 BC; sandstone; H. 4.65 m, Paris, Musée du Louvre, A 24.

Seti II built several processional statues as standard-bearers in front of his processional shrine in the forecourt at Karnak. One of these colossal statues can be found today in the Louvre. It shows the king wearing a Double Crown over a spherical wig and a festive pleated loincloth. A massive divine staff leans against his left shoulder and in his right hand he holds a partially opened papyrus roll.

45 East temple of Ramesses II

Karnak; Nineteenth Dynasty, ca. 1270 BC. Ramesses II built an additional temple to Re-Harakhty and Amun, who "hears the prayers," to the east of the central temple district. Two large figures of Osiris flank the entrance in front of the central axis. Later, in the Twenty-fifth Dynasty, Taharqa added a kiosk with papyrus columns.

The Edifices in the First Court

From the quay in front of the temple an avenue of ram sphinxes of Amun-Re, bearing the name of Ramesses II, led to the vestibule of the Great Hypostyle Hall. To the north of this processional avenue, Seti II later built a shrine with three divisions, a way station for the barques of the Theban triad. In front of it stood colossal statues of the king in the form of standard bearers. Today they stand in the Museo Egizio in Turin and in the Louvre in Paris. Other statues of this type, some of them life-sized, stood in the entrance to the Hypostyle Hall. Today they are preserved both in the hall's interior and in the Cairo Museum. It was the only building activity undertaken by Seti II, in addition to his tomb, which he commissioned in Western Thebes. This again shows

the great significance attached to the processions of the divine barques on the occasion of the two great annual festivals during the Nineteenth Dynasty. At least once at the beginning of his reign, every king had to lead the festival processions personally; from then on statues could take the place of the royal persona. This is why each king visited Thebes in the first year of his reign and immortalized himself for posterity with a monument bearing his name. At the start of the Twentieth Dynasty Ramesses III likewise ordered his own processional shrine to be erected to the south of the processional route's main axis. It is a proper temple with its own pylon flanked by standing statues of the king. A courtyard surrounded by Osiride columns and a vestibule form the entrance to the shrine, which was used as a way station and offering place for the three divine barques during the processions.

The Eastern Temple of Ramesses II

Parallel to the extensions to the main temple in the west, Seti I and Ramesses II also erected edifices in the east section of the temple of Amun. Fragments of large sphinxes bear witness to an eastern processional route. The older eastern temple dating from the Thutmosid Period was restored. In the wide empty space in front of it, Ramesses II built a temple to Re-Harakhty, which was dedicated to the cult of the rising sun. At its entrance stood two large statues of Ramesses II in the form of Osiris.

Perhaps the most beautiful and certainly the most famous statue of Ramesses II in dark granite derives from the interior of this temple. The young king is represented seated on the throne wearing the Blue Crown, a long pleated robe, and sandals, and he holds the *heka* scepter in his hand. A gentle smile characteristic of all of Ramesses II's original statues transfigures his face. Today the statue is in Turin.

The importance of the many processions and their routes in the large temple complex is shown by the fact that to complete the round trip between the main and eastern temples the procession had to make its way around the enclosure wall of the Thutmosid temple. For that reason Ramesses II completely decorated the exterior wall of this older temple with offering scenes. Thus the temple and its cult activities, which were of course closed to most people, became "transparent" and accessible to those involved in the processions.

The Cachette Courtyard in front of the Seventh Pylon

On the north–south axis of the great temple, already in existence since the Eighteenth Dynasty, the Ramesside kings left numerous dedications inscribed on both sides of the processional route. After the Great Hypostyle Hall had been completed, Ramesses II again redesigned the courtyard in front of it to the southeast, in front of the seventh pylon. Here, the point at which the two main axes of the temple met formed a kind of intersection for the large processions. For this reason we find find large inscriptions, relief representations, and stelae of almost all the rulers of the Ramesside Period in this area.

Of unique importance is the inscription of Ramesses II on the exterior of the western court wall, which contains the peace treaty between Egypt and the Hittite king, the first known treaty in history. Toward the middle of the court, on the eastern side, is the triumphal inscription of his son and successor Merenptah, in which the latter celebrates his victory over the alliance of Libyans and Sea Peoples. Numerous texts tell of temple foundations, gifts and the erection of royal statues, representations of the gods, and private sculptures.

Over the centuries kings and the highest dignitaries filled the courtyards and routes from the pylons to the inner sanctuaries along the processional routes with statues and stelae of all sizes and every type of material. Thus it is not really surprising that eventually, in the Late Period, thousands of these statues and statuettes that previously lined the processional routes had to be buried in this courtyard for reasons of space.

46 Statue of Ramesses II seated on the throne
Karnak, east temple; Nineteenth Dynasty, ca. 1270 BC; granodiorite; H. 194 cm; Turin, Museo Egizio, Cat. No. 1380.
This seated statue of the young Ramesses II originally stood in the eastern temple at Karnak. It shows the king with the Blue Crown, wearing a magnificent, finely pleated robe and holding the royal crook in his right hand. To the right and left, beside the king's legs, are the figures of his son Amunherkhopeshef (right) and his wife Nefertari (left). The statue is often described as a work of Seti I. The iconography and facial features are, however, clearly those of the young Ramesses.

47 Ramesses II before the deified queen Ahmose-Nefertari
Karnak, temple of Amun-Re, southern enclosure wall; Nineteenth Dynasty, ca. 1270 BC; sandstone; H. of the register ca. 220 cm.
The scene shows Ramesses II in front of "Ahmose-Nefertari, god's wife, god's mother, great wife of the king, ruler of the Two Lands." She was the wife of Ahmose, founder of the dynasty, and the mother of Amenophis I. Together with the latter, she was worshipped as a deity. Ramesses II meets her here in the presence of the gods and receives from her the guarantee of "life and health."

48 Kneeling figure of Ramessesnakht
Karnak, "cachette;" Twentieth Dynasty, ca. 1150 BC; statue: graywacke, pedestal: calcite-alabaster; H. 40.5 cm; Cairo, Egyptian Museum, JE 37186 (CG 42163).
The High Priest of Amun Ramessesnakht belonged to the elite class of Theban society and held his office during the reigns of Ramesses IV to Ramesses IX. The figure shows him in a kneeling pose with the statue group of the divine triad (Amun, Mut, and Khonsu) in front of him on a pedestal.

49 View of the external enclosure wall of the temple
Karnak, temple of Amun-Re; Eighteenth/Nineteenth Dynasty, ca. 1450–1210 BC.
The large enclosure wall surrounding the precinct of Amun-Re and also encompassing the festival temple of Thutmosis III was erected as early as the Thutmosid Period. Ramesses II decorated parts of the outer walls with scenes of the rituals that were actually performed inside the temple.

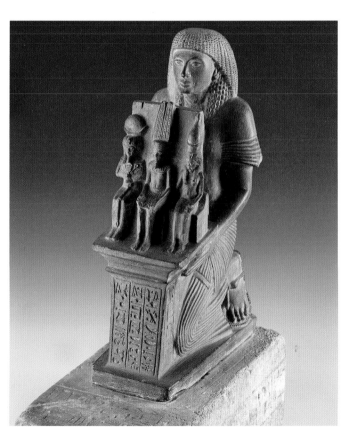

50 The "court of the cachette" at Karnak
Karnak, temple of Amun-Re, innermost court on the north–south axis with the seventh pylon; Eighteenth Dynasty, ca. 1460 BC.
The cache of statues called the "court of the cachette," which was discovered at the beginning of the twentieth century, played an important role since the Middle Kingdom. The east and west enclosure walls of this court were decorated with ritual scenes under the Ramesside rulers. On the western exterior wall Ramesses II also placed scenes of the battle against the Syrians as well as the text of the Egyptian version of the peace treaty with the Hittites dating from the twenty-first year of his reign.

During the years 1903–1906 they were recovered there by the French archaeologist Georges Legrain. It was a difficult undertaking, severely hampered by the high groundwater level.

The portraits of the gods in the innermost chambers, the barque sanctuaries, the vestibules and the hypostyle halls functioned as the recipients of the rich and varied offerings presented by the king. They embody in three-dimensional sculpture what was also expressed in two-dimensional relief on the temple walls. Accordingly, this also explains the plethora of royal statues showing the ruler standing, kneeling, stretched out on the ground or as a reclining sphinx. With their hands extended, these figures present either sacrificial offerings in the form of vessels or sacrificial plaques or, last but not least, cases with documents.

Outside the inner sanctuaries and the inaccessible halls, where the processions made their way through the courtyards and to the pylons in the presence of the priests and high officials, stood statues of royal standard bearers. They represented the person of the king in stone and thus in permanent form; they ensured that he participated in the ceremonies that only he could lead.

Likewise, other colossal statues and huge sphinxes stood outside the actual temple, in the broad forecourts. They bore the king's features, even though they represented the manifestation of the gods. As a result, the common people, who themselves were of course not admitted to the temple interior proper, could perceive and experience them. By their otherworldly size, these sphinxes and colossi suggested the existence of the divine forces and made them effective for the world of mankind. They were the recipients of all manner of sacrificial offerings, and countless individuals turned to them with their requests and prayers. In addition, high-ranking officials who enjoyed the privilege of participating in the processions were given permission to erect their own statues in the vicinity. These also offered themselves as mediators between the people and the gods.

51 Sphinx of Ramesses II with a "vase for Amun"
Karnak, "cachette;" Nineteenth Dynasty, ca. 1260 BC; hard sandstone; L. 30 cm, H. 18 cm; Cairo, Egyptian Museum, JE 38060 (CG 42146).
This sphinx of Ramesses II presents the king as divine cult ruler. Above the lion-shaped body rises the human head with the *nemes* headdress and royal beard. Unlike other sphinxes, this one shows human hands that hold a sacrificial vessel for the god Amun.

52 Standing statue of Amenophis II
Karnak, "cachette;" Eighteenth Dynasty, ca. 1420 BC; graywacke; H. 68 cm; Cairo, Egyptian Museum, JE 36860 (CG 42077).
This figure of Amenophis II was discovered in the Karnak "cachette" in 1904. The king wears a bag wig with uraeus serpent and the royal kilt. The facial features appear balanced in their proportions, idealized and youthful. The figure stands out from other portraits of Amenophis II by virtue of its much more energetic expression.

Luxor Temple – Renewing the Power of God

The temple complex at Luxor was considered the site of the primeval mound and southern residence of the god Amun-Re. It was used for purposes of renewal in several senses of the word. During the Opet festival Amun-Re moved from Karnak to Luxor in order to effect his own regeneration and strengthen the king's divinity by uniting with the divine life-giving forces. During the festival of the decade the god was brought from Karnak via Luxor to Medinet Habu on the west bank, to ensure the continuance of creation.

The Structures of the Eighteenth Dynasty
Regine Schulz

Exactly when the oldest building was erected on this site is a matter of dispute; however, it is certain that the Thutmoside rulers built a large temple structure. Within the broad courtyard of Ramesses II still stands a processional shrine with three barque chambers for the divine family of Karnak: Amun, Mut, and Khonsu. The red granite papyrus columns in front of the facade and the architrave date from the time of Hatshepsut. Ramesses II subsequently reused and re-inscribed these architectural components with his own name. It is as yet uncertain whether such a shrine already stood here under Hatshepsut or whether the individual elements were taken from another structure.

Amenophis III replaced the main Thutmosid temple with an enormous new building. The entrance leads through a large colonnade with two rows of seven papyrus columns 21.20 m high into an open courtyard. The latter is surrounded by double rows of bundled papyrus columns and leads into a hypostyle hall to the south that is slightly elevated. The colossal standing figures of Amenophis III, which were later moved by Ramesses II into his courtyard, must have stood here. The total number of columns (twelve by eight) in the courtyard and the hall refers to the Hermopolitan concepts of creation connected with Amun that are based on a number of eight primeval gods. The following hall also has eight columns. In the southeast, a chapel branches off it in which the royal *ka* statue, where the divine life-giving force of the ruler resides, was erected during the Opet festival. Along the temple axis come the offering table chamber, the barque sanctuary, and another hall, oriented at right angles to the axis with twelve columns, which was defined as the mythical place

53 Luxor Temple with a pylon and colossal statues of Ramesses II
Color lithograph; David Roberts, *Egypt and Nubia*, London 1846–1849.

In 1838, just a few years after the western obelisk had been removed, the English artist David Roberts drew the entrance pylon, still deeply buried, of the sacred precinct at Luxor.

54 General plan of Luxor Temple

1   Barque sanctuary of Amenophis III
2   Court of Amenophis III
3   Colonnade with scenes of the Opet festival (Tutankhamun and Horemheb)
4   Court of Ramesses II
5   Processional shrine (built partly by Hatshepsut)
6   Entrance pylon of Ramesses II
7   Obelisks of Ramesses II

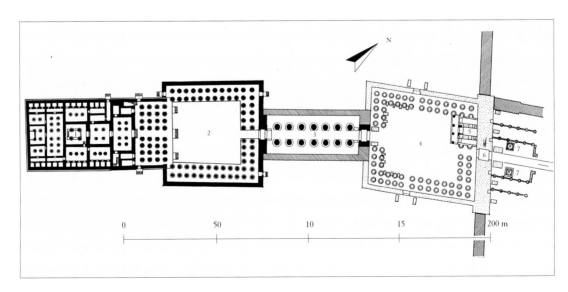

55 Festival Court of Amenophis III
Luxor Temple; Eighteenth Dynasty, ca. 1370 BC; sandstone; area of the court approx. 54 x 56 m.
The festival court of Amenophis III was one of the most impressive architectural achievements of the New Kingdom. Here the rituals of the great festivals were performed and here the king presented himself endowed with divine powers. The enormous size of the court, which was surrounded by a veritable forest of columns, far exceeded anything that had existed previously. Unlike in the immense entrance colonnade, here columns were erected, the fluted shafts of which represent bundles of papyrus. Unfortunately, most of the walls of the court have been lost, and the variety of scenes can no longer be ascertained.

57 Colonnade hall of Amenophis III
Luxor Temple; Eighteenth Dynasty, ca. 1355 BC; sandstone; H. 21.20 m.
The great entrance colonnade at Luxor Temple was built toward the end of Amenophis III's reign. The massive columns imitate papyrus plants with open umbels. It is uncertain whether the architectural work was already fully completed under Amenophis III or whether Tutankhamun finished the project. Originally, upon completion, this entrance hall was enclosed at the sides and the top and large clerestory windows shed light into it. Today, however, the ceiling and upper sections of the walls are missing.

56 Barque shrine in the first court of Luxor Temple with columns and architraves erected by Hatshepsut
Temple of Luxor, Eighteenth Dynasty, ca. 1465 BC; red granite.
The barque shrine in three sections standing in the court of Ramesses II has columns and architraves dating to the reigns of Queen Hatshepsut and Thutmosis III. Ramesses II integrated them into his own sanctuary. When the inscriptions were being rewritten, it was forgotten in two places to change the feminine form of the word "beloved" to the masculine form, so they can clearly be attributed to Hatshepsut.

58 Processional figure of Amenophis III
Luxor Temple, "cachette;" Eighteenth Dynasty, ca. 1370 BC; sandstone, H. 2.10 m; Luxor, The Luxor Museum of Ancient Egyptian Art, J 838.

The figure of Amenophis III on a processional sledge may be considered unique. Although the standing pose of the king with his left foot forward can be described as classical, the connection to a sledge has had no parallel to date in terms of sculpture in the round. The combination of a pedestal and a high back pillar points to the fact that it was not the king who was represented on a sledge here, but rather his statue. It wears the Double Crown of Upper and Lower Egypt with the uraeus serpent above the forehead, a royal beard, and a magnificent kilt with a decorative uraeus garland in the center. The slightly roughened areas on the chest and arms were probably gilded and point to a decorative collar, a pectoral, and armbands. Under Akhenaten, the name of the god Amun in the inscriptions was erased and subsequently never restored, raising the question as to whether the statue was still in use after the Amarna Period.

59 Coronation of Amenophis III
Luxor Temple, southern wall of the hall of appearances; Eighteenth Dynasty, ca. 1370 BC. Directly behind the Great Hypostyle Hall was the hall of appearances. Here the deification of the living king and his *ka* force took place, which had to be repeated each year. In the decoration of the room the coronation ritual plays a central role. This scene shows Amenophis III in front of his father Amun who lays his hand on the ruler's crown, made up of many different royal and divine elements including the ram's horn of Amun. In his right hand the king holds the royal crook and in his left, a sign of life that refers to his divine qualities.

of the path of the sun and behind which the three cult image chambers of the Theban triad are located. To the east of the barque sanctuary are two rooms in which the so-called birth legend is depicted, which tells of the divine origin and the selection of the king by his father Amun-Re.

The range of statues in the temple cannot be fully reconstructed, though a sensational discovery made in the courtyard of Amenophis III in 1989 indicates the great variety of figures that once existed there. In a deep pit, a total of twenty-six three-dimensional images of kings and deities dating from the New Kingdom and the Late Period were unearthed. The most spectacular individual item is the standing figure of Amenophis III on a sledge, but the group portrait of Horemheb before the god of creation Atum (see p. 434, no. 24), by virtue of its perfectly preserved state, also shows the importance of this find. Judging by the pottery recovered from the pit, the burial of the figures can be linked to the redesign of the rear temple rooms for the cult of the Roman emperor in ca. 300 AD.

60 Tutankhamun making offerings
Luxor Temple, part of the northern wall of the colonnade hall; Eighteenth Dynasty, ca. 1325 BC; sandstone, height of the face ca. 35 cm.
After Tutankhaten had changed his name to Tutankhamun and left Amarna, there was a clear return to the values and norms prevalent before the Amarna Period. In art the idealizing tendencies of the reign of Amenophis III were revived, but the experience of Amarna could not be denied, as indicated among other things by the treatment of the human figure. This representation of the king shows him wearing the Blue Crown (in Egyptian: *Khepresh*) as he burns incense and offers a libation to the god (not included in the illustration). As is so often the case with memorials to Tutankhamun, Horemhab, the last king of the Eighteenth Dynasty, also had this cartouche containing the boy king's name overwritten with his own.

The Opet Festival

After the iconoclasm of the Amarna Period, the kings of the late Eighteenth and early Nineteenth Dynasties restored the temple and commissioned the scheme to decorate the great colonnade hall. The representations of the "Beautiful Festival of Opet" on the interiors of the walls were begun by Tutankhamen and completed by Seti I. During the Thutmosid Period, the celebrations lasted for eleven days. The barque and statue of Amun-Re was carried overland from Karnak to Luxor and for the return journey transportation on the Nile was chosen. After the Amarna Period, the procedure changed. The festival was extended by several days until towards the end of Ramesses III's reign it lasted as long as twenty-seven days.

Furthermore, both journeys were now undertaken on the Nile, and Amun-Re was accompanied by Mut and Khonsu. The Luxor reliefs represent the individual stages in the procedure. First, the king presents offerings to Amun-Re and Mut in Karnak and confirms for the god the renewal of his cult establishments (north wall). Next, he donates incense and water purifications in front of the portable festival barques of Amun, Mut, and Khonsu, which still rest on their pedestals

in Karnak (west wall). From there, they are taken to the quayside together with the king's barque, loaded onto large river barques and towed by sailing boats and hauling teams to Luxor. The pharaoh's river barque was accompanied on the riverbank by soldiers and chariots, and the barque of Amun-Re that followed it was escorted by rejoicing priests, musicians, and singers. Upon their arrival in Luxor, the barques of the divine family were carried to their shrines, past sacrificial altars, musicians, and dancers. The king made his way to the temple to offer sacrifices there to Amun-Re and Mut, together with the priests (south wall). The return journey to Karnak (east wall) was completed in similar fashion. There, the king again entered the temple to be strengthened by the regenerated Amun-Re and to hand him a floral bouquet. During this encounter the god is accompanied by his creative companion Amaunet.

The Expansion under Ramesses II
Hourig Sourouzian

The Nineteenth Dynasty judiciously continued the work of renewal. Seti I contributed to the functioning of the temple by performing restorations and adding ritual scenes to specific areas. When the young Ramesses II himself arrived in Luxor to lead the Opet festival in the first year of his reign, he decided, in addition to other building projects, to construct a wide courtyard and a tall pylon in front of the great row of columns of Amenophis III. Construction began immediately and only two years later the pylon was finished. In front of the pylon Ramesses II erected six colossal statues and a pair of obelisks. Today, only one obelisk and three colossi remain standing, the others lie in

61 Transportation of the barques during the Opet festival
Luxor Temple, western wall of the colonnade hall (detail); Eighteenth Dynasty, ca. 1325 BC; sandstone, H. of the register ca. 120 cm.
The scene shows the transportation of the divine barques of Khonsu and Mut from the temple at Karnak to the quayside, whence they are to make their way to Luxor. The team of bearers is accompanied by fan-bearers, priests offering incense and water, and four so-called lector priests who pray and supervise the procession. Their dress differs from that of the others by means of a leopard slung over their shoulder.

pieces on the ground. The second obelisk was sent to France as a gift of Mohamed Ali in 1836 and today it towers above the Place de la Concorde in Paris.

After the fifth year of Ramesses' reign, the dramatic events of the Battle of Kadesh were depicted on the façade of the pylon; a few years later, the colossal statues stood in place complete. The decoration of the interior walls of the courtyard with the procession at the Opet festival, led by the royal princes, was now also finished. The cycle of scenes is oriented toward the temple pylon, whose facade is depicted twice in relief. The courtyard is surrounded by a portico consisting of two rows of bundled papyrus columns.

At a later stage Ramesses II also set up colossal standing statues between the columns, some of which are reused statues of Amenophis III while others are originals from the time of his own reign, imitating those of his predecessor from the Eighteenth Dynasty. The longitudinal axis of the courtyard branches off to the east in relation to that of the rest of the temple, as it is oriented exactly to the temple at Karnak. The lateral axis established the link between Luxor Temple and the west bank, where since the early Middle Kingdom the kings erected their mortuary temples.

65 *(opposite) Colossal seated statue of Ramesses II*
Luxor Temple, first court at the entrance to the colonnade (western colossus); Nineteenth Dynasty, ca. 1260 BC; black granite, H. ca. 7 m.
The figure of the king sits enthroned and bears the proper name of *Ra-en-hekau,* "sun of the ruler of foreign lands," which may refer to the beneficial aspects for foreign lands of Ramesses II's rule. His wife, Queen Nefertari, is represented in sculpture in the round in front of the throne, beside the king's right leg.

64 *Facade of the entrance pylon*
Luxor Temple; Nineteenth Dynasty, ca. 1260 BC; sandstone, W. 65 m.
Originally, six colossal statues and two obelisks erected by Ramesses II stood in front of the pylon. Of these, two seated figures flanking the entrance and a standing statue have survived in their original location. The western obelisk was given to the French king Louis Philippe as a gift by the Egyptian viceroy Mohamed Ali in 1829. Since 1836 it has stood in the Place de la Concorde in Paris.

62 *Entrance pylon with avenue of sphinxes*
Luxor Temple; Nineteenth Dynasty (and later), ca. 1260 BC.
A 2.5-km avenue with two rows of 365 human-headed sphinxes led from the precinct of Amun at Karnak to Luxor Temple. These sphinxes (their inscriptions date them to the Thirtieth Dynasty) thus differ from those with ram's heads (symbolic of the god Amun) that stood before the first pylon in Karnak.

63 *Representation of the entrance pylon*
Luxor Temple, first court, relief on the western half of the southern wall; Nineteenth Dynasty, ca. 1260 BC.
The carving shows the temple pylon with two obelisks, tall flagstaffs, and statues of Ramesses II. In keeping with ancient Egyptian perspectival principles, the statues are shown in profile rather than head-on. A second representation of the pylon is found in the same court on the rear side of the pylon.

66 Court of Ramesses II
Luxor Temple; Nineteenth Dynasty, ca. 1260
BC; sandstone, L. 57 m, W. 51 m.
With this impressive courtyard complex and

the concluding pylon Ramesses II extended
Luxor Temple to a total length of 254 m. The
courtyard was surrounded on three sides by a
magnificent colonnade, between the columns

of which colossal standing statues were
erected. To complete this arrangment, besides
erecting statues of his own, Ramesses II also
reused older statues of Amenophis III, whose

names had been erased during the Amarna
Period and had thereby lost their significance.

67 *View of the second court of the mortuary temple of Ramesses III at Medinet Habu* Colored lithograph; David Rogers, *Egypt and Nubia*, London 1846–1849.
This view of the courtyard as it was in the nineteenth century clearly shows the columns of a church built into it in the fifth/sixth centuries. This reuse of temple sites was not at all unusual, since building material was readily available, and it provided an effective means of counteracting the demonic spirits of the ancient gods who still inhabited the site.

68 *The colossi of Memnon during inundation* Colored lithograph; David Roberts, *Egypt and Nubia*, London 1846–1849.
Until the modern High Dam at Aswan was built, the Nile flooded the entire fertile plain each year. The floodwaters often reached to the very edge of the desert, swamping the area of the mortuary temple of Amenophis III, with its two gigantic colossi.

The Temples of Western Thebes – The Cult of the Dead and Veneration of the Gods

The Eighteenth Dynasty Temple Complexes
Regine Schulz

At the beginning of the New Kingdom, Thebes increased enormously in importance, for it was Theban nomarchs who had driven out the Hyksos and succeeded in reuniting Egypt. Amun-Re, the Thebans' chief divinity, rose to be god of the empire, and his close link with the royal house was reflected in the temple complexes. The funerary temples of the kings were completely replanned and now were situated separate from their tombs at the edge of the Theban necropolis, abutting the desert. They were intended not only for the mortuary cult but also for the veneration of Amun-Re and of the living king who was united with him. Conversely, the temples dedicated to the gods were now also shrines for the royal cult.

An important element in cult ritual was the "Beautiful Festival of the Valley." Amun-Re, in the form of his processional statue, would set out from Karnak and cross the Nile in order to visit the sacred sites on the West Bank and so ensure the continued existence and provisioning of the deceased. Originally the processional route probably ended at a shrine to Hathor, the patron-goddess of Western Thebes, in the valley of Deir el-Bahari. Later the route changed, the funerary temples of the deceased kings served as way stations, and the building dedicated to the living ruler became the festival procession's final destination; this was the place where the combination of god and pharaoh was made manifest. In the post-Amarna era at the latest, the procession of the Festival of the Valley was enlarged: now the barques of Mut, Khonsu, and Amaunet as well as statues of deceased kings and other persons of high rank joined the procession.

At the beginning of the Eighteenth Dynasty the temples dedicated to the royal cult in Western Thebes were still exclusively oriented toward the valley of Deir el-Bahari. Amenophis I built a temple for himself and for his wife Ahmose-Nefertari along the processional route at the edge of the desert, and an additional shrine to Amun-Re in the valley. Hatshepsut even transferred her funerary temple to the valley basin. By contrast, the later rulers of the Eighteenth Dynasty chose the edge of the desert for their mortuary cult buildings and placed them side by side between the processional route to Deir el-Bahari and the shrine to the primeval god Amun-Re-Kamutef at Medinet Habu. Thutmosis III did, however, have an additional temple complex for Amun-Re and Hathor built at this location.

Most of the funerary temples of the Eighteenth Dynasty are in a very poor state of preservation; the sequence of the rooms and their decoration can be reconstructed only to a very limited extent. However, since the basic structure of the temple of Hatshepsut at Deir el-Bahari, which has survived, is also found in the better preserved buildings of the Ramesside Period, it seems probable that this form also resembles that of the now-destroyed complexes of the Eighteenth Dynasty. Each of these temples has courtyards where the festival rituals took place, and here the royal guarantee of maintaining the cult and the divine guarantee of power were pictorially fixed and thereby magically safeguarded. At the center of the main cult area are one or more rooms used for sacrifices, the barque sanctuary, and the room with the cult images associated with the worship of Amun-Re and the king. On the south side is the area actually dedicated to the mortuary cult, with a false door and rooms with offering tables, a chapel for ancestor worship, and a cult palace. On the north side is an open courtyard for worship of the sun, with an altar in the middle. The temple also has additional rooms for patron-gods or gods of the dead such as Hathor and Anubis, Osiris or Sokar; but the position of these chapels varies considerably and they may actually be outside the main building.

In addition to the temple complexes devoted to the royal cult, the small temple of Medinet Habu also played an important role. This place was held to be the site of the Primeval Mound, where creation first manifested itself. Here Amun-Re was venerated as Kamutef, that is to say in an aspect that reflected the god's ability continuously to renew himself. The oldest building dates to the Eleventh Dynasty, and probably sprang from a desire to establish the local Theban god Amun as an autonomous creator-god. Hatshepsut and Thutmosis III completely

altered the original layout. The new building, measuring 13 by 29 m, consisted of the barque sanctuary of Amun-Re surrounded by an aisle of pillars and behind it six rooms with religious functions behind it. Every ten days the decade-festival was held, when Amun-Re came from Karnak via Luxor to Medinet Habu in order, by mythical rites, to ensure the continuation of the world.

The Temple of Hatshepsut at Deir el-Bahari – The Staircase of Amun-Re

Djeseret, "Holy Place," was the name given by the ancient Egyptians to the valley of Deir el-Bahari. Here was the threshold between this life and the next, here they worshipped Hathor, the patron-goddess of Western Thebes, and here the unifier of the kingdom, Menhotep II, who was later venerated as a divinity himself, had created his splendid temple. This was a place of great significance to the early Thutmosid rulers too, and Hatshepsut chose it as the site for her funerary temple. It was called Djeser-Djeseru, "the Holy of Holies," and the valley temple, causeway, and way station were the final destination of the Festival of the Valley procession. It is astonishing that despite several changes this tremendous building project was completed in only fifteen years (years 7–22 of Hatshepsut's reign). Some of the most

69 The valley of Deir el-Bahari in Western Thebes
Side by side directly beneath the limestone cliffs are the funerary temples of Hatshepsut (on the right) and Mentuhotep II of the Eleventh Dynasty. Between them, on a slightly raised platform, are the remains of the temple of Thutmosis III. Some of the mountain paths were already in use in the New Kingdom, and the modern road also follows the route of the ancient causeway to Hatshepsut's temple.

senior priests and officials were charged with the design and with supervising the building works. Among these Senenmut, a favorite of the Queen and an éminence grise at court, played a prominent role: he was even allowed to depict his own image in many "secret" places in the temple. Before Hatshepsut's death, however, he fell from grace, his name was effaced and most of the images of him were destroyed.

The temple building, oriented toward the west, is on three ascending terraces or levels; the levels, each arranged as a courtyard, are separated by narrow halls placed in front of the steps. Centrally placed ramps lead to the two higher terraces. The large front courtyard, with pools and rows of trees, had on its far side two halls, open to the facade, with half-columnar pillars and columns. The representations in these halls portray the ruler's guarantee, both mythic and real, of a cult. They show the transportation and the dedication of great obelisks of Karnak, the consecration of a temple and the donation of statues, and men driving calves and hunting in a papyrus thicket. On the lower terrace is a second courtyard with pillared halls. The northern hall tells of the

70 King and Queen of Punt

Western Thebes, Deir el-Bahari, mortuary temple of Hatshepsut, Punt chamber; Eighteenth Dynasty, ca 1470 BC; painted limestone; H. 36 cm; Cairo, Egyptian Museum, JE 14276.

The main purpose of the journey to Punt was the exchange of goods. To the Egyptians the most important raw materials were incense, myrrh, and gold, but ivory, ebony, and animal skins were also highly prized. The fragments of relief show the king of Punt with his wife and their entourage welcoming the leader of the Egyptian expedition. The artist carefully portrayed the queen, who evidently suffered from obesity.

71 Portrait of Thutmosis I

Western Thebes, Deir el-Bahari, mortuary temple of Hatshepsut, upper terrace; Eighteenth Dynasty, ca. 1470 BC; painted limestone; H. 41 cm; Hildesheim, Pelizaeus-Museum, 4538.

This block once formed part of a relief showing the ruler presenting offerings to the god Amun-Re. It was in one of the rear niches in the west wall of the large courtyard where sacrifices were made. Thutmosis I, the father of Hatshepsut, wears a composite crown consisting of many divine and royal elements and has the long beard, slightly curling up at the end, of a god, which identifies him as the deceased Osiris-king.

72 Transportation of myrrh trees

Western Thebes, Deir el-Bahari, mortuary temple of Hatshepsut, Punt chamber; Eighteenth Dynasty, ca. 1470 BC; painted limestone; H. of this detail ca. 40 cm.

Along with myrrh resin, entire trees complete with their roots were imported from Punt. They were dug up, packed into baskets, and loaded onto the ships. The accompanying inscriptions for the scenes state that thirty-one such trees arrived in Thebes.

73 Pillar of the Hathor chapel
Western Thebes, Deir el-Bahari, mortuary temple of Hatshepsut; Eighteenth Dynasty, ca. 1465 BC; painted limestone.
To the south of the Punt chamber is the small shrine to the goddess Hathor, the patroness of Western Thebes. The pronaos and entrance hall consist of columns and pillars with emblems of Hathor or capitals depicting her. They may be regarded as a transposition into stone of the sistrum that was used as a musical instrument to summon divine beings and appease them, and which was especially associated with the cult of Hathor.

divine descent of Hatshepsut and of her being chosen king by her father Amun-Re. Although the idea of the divine birth of pharaoh is attested from the Old Kingdom onward, this is the earliest pictorial representation of it. It may have been prompted by a desire for additional legitimacy, in order to justify Hatshepsut's claim to the throne and her co-regency with Thutmosis III. The theme of the southern hall is the great expedition to Punt ordered by the queen. The scenes depicted include the seagoing ships used for the journey, the round pile-dwellings of the natives, the king of Punt with his obese wife and retainers, the region's flora and fauna, and the goods that the Egyptians took home to present to the god Amun-Re.

To the right and left of the middle terrace are separate groups of rooms. On the northern side is the chapel of the jackal-headed god of the dead, Anubis. It consists of an anteroom with twelve sixteen-sided pillars and a corridor with a sharp turn that leads to the inner sanctuary. The scenes of ritual sacrifice ensure both the supply of provisions for Anubis and the return to life of Hatshepsut in the next world.

To the south a chapel to Hathor was added in a later phase of construction. It had its own causeway leading up to it and a front courtyard with twenty-four columns, each with two images of the face of Hathor, and eight pillars flanking the entrance. The scenes on the walls indicate that this is not only a shrine to the goddess but also a place designed to legitimize the deified Hatshepsut. Another ramp leads to the upper terrace, on which the great courtyard for sacrifices is situated. The facade of the entrance hall is fronted by a row of Osiride pillars, with a row of columns behind it. The passage in the center leads through to the open courtyard for sacrifices, which was originally surrounded by a double row of sixteen-sided pillars; only in front of the west wall was a third row added. The west wall has niches for statues, while the east wall preserves remnants of a series of scenes. Continuing the line of the temple's axis, the barque sanctuary, with its arched ceiling, and the room for cult images dedicated to Amun-Re and Hatshepsut, reachable by a short flight of steps, were built into the cliff. On the south side of the terrace were the false palace and the vaulted mortuary cult rooms for Hatshepsut and her ancestors, while on the north side were an open courtyard dedicated to the sun-god Re-Horakhty and side chapels for the royal family and Anubis.

About twenty years after Hatshepsut's death, Thutmosis III began to excise her memory as pharaoh. Her statues were destroyed, her images and the cartouches bearing her name were effaced. At first Thutmosis III planned to continue to use his predecessor's temple for the worship of Amun and Hathor, and therefore had her statues

75 Figure of Hatshepsut enthroned
Western Thebes, Deir el-Bahari, mortuary temple of Hatshepsut; Eighteenth Dynasty, ca. 1470 BC; crystalline limestone; H. 195 cm; New York, The Metropolitan Museum of Art, 29.3.2.
Probably the most beautiful statue of the queen in the ceremonial costume of a reigning pharaoh, this piece unites her official status in an ideal manner with the subtly captured physical form of a woman. It may be assumed that this seated figure was originally situated in the room for mortuary cult offerings on the upper terrace.

76 Plan of the upper terrace of the mortuary temple of Hapshepsut
Western Thebes, Deir el-Bahari; Eighteenth Dynasty, ca. 1470 BC.

1 Osiride pillar
2 Festival courtyard
3 Barque sanctuary
4 Room for cult images
5 Area for mortuary cult of Thutmosis I
6 Area for mortuary cult of Hatshepsut
7 Sanctuary dedicated to the Sun
8 Cult palace

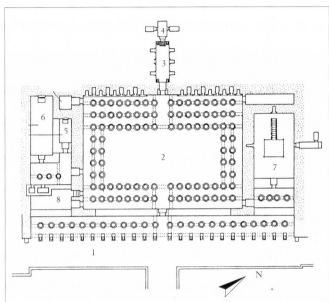

hacked from their positions and her name replaced by that of Thutmosis II or his own. In the end, he decided against this adaptation and in his final years erected a new building that stands, on a higher level, between the temples of Mentuhotep II and Hatshepsut.

The architecture of Hatshepsut's terraced temple and the images it contains reflect the various levels of operation. Aspects such as the real and the mythic guarantee of a cult, the protection, selection and justification of the ruler by the gods, the desire for regeneration in the afterlife, and the constant ensuring of the continuation of creation were all part of a system that emphasized the direct family link between the dynasty of the Thutmosids, but especially Hatshepsut, and Amun-Re.

From the very beginning of the excavation and restoration work carried out in the temple at the end of the nineteenth century, isolated fragments of statues of Hatshepsut continually came to light. But it was not until the 1920s, in the course of the excavations conducted by the Metropolitan Museum of Art, that archaeologists were able to recover a sizeable number of representations of the queen, which allowed for the reconstruction of an entire series of statues.

An avenue of about 120 sandstone sphinxes lined the causeway and continued right into the building's front courtyard; here, at the northern and southern corners of the facade of the hall, were two colossal Osiride pillars, 7.25 m tall. There were sphinxes made of limestone and red granite on the lower terrace. Twenty-six Osiride pillars stood in front of the entrance hall of the upper terrace, and there were others in the niches in the rear wall of both the barque sanctuary and

Thanks to the work of the Schweizer Institut für Bauforschung (Swiss Institute for Building Research), it has been possible to reconstruct the ground plan of the great court (90 by 90 m) – the only part of the mortuary temple for which this has been possible. On all four sides the courtyard had triple rows of papyrus bundle columns that were 14.20 m tall. Only on the east side was there a fourth row. Between the columns a total of thirty-six statues of the king were erected, eighteen for each half of the courtyard.

In the design of the courtyard two different levels of meaning are fused together. On the first level the papyrus bundle columns signify regeneration and protection, and the royal statues represent all-embracing kingship and the guarantee of the cult of Amun-Re.

It is the number of statues that leads to the second level of meaning. The number thirty-six (4 x 9) combines the idea of the totality of space (4 = the totality of the four cardinal points) with the absolute multiplicity of all life forms (9 = 3 x 3: the number 3 in Egyptian signified the plural of things and beings, and 9 the plural of the plural and thus the totality of all forms and variations). Consequently this number stands for the king's cultic guarantee of creation.

the courtyard used for sacrifices. Inside the courtyard there were four colossal kneeling figures holding wine vessels, and smaller figures between the pillars, also in the attitude of offering bearers. There may have been, among other figures, seated statues of Hatshepsut in the mortuary cult rooms and side chapels. The different types of Hatshepsut statues are part of a total design representing the various rituals and activities in the temple. They are not mere decoration but an indispensable means for conveying functional information. Distinct functions were indicated by the posture and iconography of the figures. Some served as the recipients of offerings in the sacrificial cult of the king, while others were actors, turned to stone, in the ritual communication with the gods. On principle the queen presented herself, in accordance with dogma, as a male pharaoh: only two seated statues show her in female dress and with female physical characteristics.

The Funerary Temple of Amenophis III – A Fortress for Eternity

The largest mortuary temple of the entire New Kingdom was built by Amenophis III, and it is unclear whether it was ever completely

77 The colossi of Memnon
Western Thebes, mortuary temple of Amenophis III; Eighteenth Dynasty, ca. 1360 BC; sandstone; original H. 21 m.
The famous seated statues of Amenophis III, modern symbol of the Theban necropolis, survive to greet the visitor, although the entrance pylon they once fronted has not

survived. That they have been admired for centuries is shown by the many graffiti dating from antiquity on the legs of the colossi. Originally erected as divine manifestations of Amenophis III, the two statues are in danger of toppling over due to the instability of the subsoil on Kom el-Heitan, as the site is now known.

finished. It was situated not at the edge of the desert, like the other temples, but further to the east in what is now fertile land. The wall surrounding the complex was 8.5 m thick and enclosed an area of 700 by 550 m. Inside, in addition to the main temple, there were gardens and pools, and a separate shrine to the Memphite god of the dead, Sokar.

At the entrance to the temple grounds two seated statues of the king, 20 m tall and made of sandstone, still remain. The proper name, "Ruler of Rulers," on the southern colossus points to the unlimited divine power possessed by the king. An earthquake in the year 27 BC created a large crack in the northern colossus, and from then on the rise in temperature each morning caused it to emit a squeaking sound that was interpreted as a lament. This was explained by the legend of Memnon, the mythical king of Ethiopia, who was said to have been

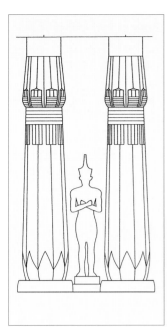

79 Colossal head of Amenophis III
Western Thebes, mortuary temple of Amenophis III; Eighteenth Dynasty, ca. 1360 BC; sandstone; H. 131 cm, W. 102 cm; London, The British Museum, EA 7.

This head belonged to a colossal statue of the king, about 9 m tall, which was placed with others between the columns of the great sun court. The materials used for these statues and the type of crown they wear together reflect an all-pervading dualistic principle based on the bipartite nature of the country. Sandstone, obtained from the quarries of Gebel el-Ahmar near Heliopolis, and the Red Crown point to Lower Egypt, while the red granite from the Aswan quarries used in other statues and the White Crown symbolize Upper Egypt. On this principle the figures were divided between the northern and the southern half of the courtyard. Despite the monumental scale, the facial features appear harmonious and show the characteristic traits prescribed for the image of Amenophis III as ruler. These include the almond-shaped eyes with a broad band for the upper eyelid, the broad-ridged, small nose, and the full mouth edged with a sharp ridge. By the extreme abstraction of this language of forms, the divine manifestation of Amenophis III is impressively represented.

killed by Achilles in the Trojan war but to have been resuscitated through the efforts of his mother Eos and placed among the immortals. This association may have been due on the one hand to a certain similarity of pronunciation between "Memnon" and the vocalized form of the throne name of Amenophis III, which was probably Nimmuria, and on the other hand to the early morning timing of the statue's "cry of lament," since Eos was seen as the goddess of the dawn. After the statue was restored in AD 199 under the Emperor Septimus Severus the phenomenon disappeared, but the idea that the northern colossus was an embodiment of Memnon lived on. Nowadays that name is applied to both colossi.

The temple of Amenophis III is now almost completely ruined. Its front part consisted of three courtyards with brick pylons forming their entrances; behind these was a courtyard measuring 86 by 85 m surrounded by three (on the west side four) rows of papyrus bundle columns that were once a dizzying 14.2 m tall. Of the main building, we only know with certainty of the hypostyle hall toward the entrance; it is no longer possible to reconstruct the rooms that lay behind it.

Both the variety and the quality of the statues in the complex as a whole must have been most impressive. Pairs of colossal seated statues of the king adorned the front of the first three pylons, and Osiride pillars and sphinxes in the courtyards. There were also many statue groups, of widely differing sizes, and an extensive collection of single statues of gods. Especially worth noting are the many statues of the lion-headed goddess Sakhmet and the unusual finds, such as sphinxes with the bodies of crocodiles or jackals, a life-size sculpture of a hippopotamus, and colossal figures of jackals.

In addition, on the north and south facades of the large courtyard, 8-m-tall standing figures of the king made of sandstone (north) and red granite (south) were placed between the columns. In this courtyard were also two huge stelae (north stela 9.7 m, south stela 8.6 m), on which the king addresses Amun-Re and Ptah-Sokar-Osiris. One of the texts tells of the manner in which the temple was built. It reads: "He built for him (Amun) a temple on the western side of Thebes, a fortress of eternity … of sandstone, the whole of it faced with gold; its … floor is of silver, all its gates of electrum … (It is) richly furnished with statues of the Lord (King) made of granite, sandstone and all kinds of jewels, which have been worked superbly and for eternity."

This most magnificent of the funerary temples in Western Thebes was abandoned toward the end of the period of the Ramessides. Parts of the huge facility must already have been demolished during the Nineteenth Dynasty because blocks corresponding to it were found in the foundations of the nearby funerary temple of Merenptah. However, as indicated by the titles of priests, it was used for religious services (albeit in a reduced form) well into the Twentieth Dynasty.

The Buildings of the Nineteenth and Twentieth Dynasties

Hourig Sourouzian

The Temple of Seti I at Qurna

As soon as he came to the throne Seti I began construction of his temple at the very north of the necropolis. He evidently wished to place his temple so that it would serve as Amun-Re's first resting place when he came in procession from Karnak. This was the first of a series of temple buildings that was continued by his successors, building farther to the south each time. These temples on the west bank of the river all bore the designation "House of Millions of Years," an expression of the hope that they would last for ever. They were not exclusively dedicated to the mortuary cult of the king but on the contrary were primarily way stations for the divine barques that came across the river from Karnak during the procession of the Festival of the Valley.

The temple of Seti I at Qurna, a splendid sandstone building, is a veritable fortress of the gods that served as a model for all later funerary temples. It is surrounded by a high, whitewashed enclosure wall of unbaked mudbricks with square, protruding towers – a revival of an ancient tradition from the time of Djoser. The processional route coming from the east ended right in front of the first pylon. This was built of unbaked bricks, covered with white plaster and colorfully painted, while the gateway and the passage through were of limestone and sandstone respectively.

In front of the temple building were two courtyards, one behind the other. On the south side of the first courtyard, the "festival court of the subjects," stood a ritual palace. There the reigning king showed himself at the Window of Appearances during the "Beautiful Festival of the Valley;" after his death he was represented by his cult statue that, in a royal barque, was able to take part in the various ceremonies and sacrificial acts. An innovation was a portico of closed papyrus bundle columns on the facade of the temple. Here Seti I was breaking with the tradition of preceding dynasties, which had preferred terraces with a frontal pillared portico.

On the facade is a depiction of the barque procession of the Theban Triad during the Festival of the Valley, accompanied by the barques of the deified Queen Ahmose-Nefertari and the king. This shows that the rituals conducted in the temples on the west bank were dominated by the festival processions. Three tall, wide gateways in the facade allowed access to the three main parts of the temple that were situated side by side.

The northern part, dedicated to the sun cult, consisted of a large courtyard, open to the sky, with the altar for offerings in the center. The southern part contained the rooms for the royal mortuary cult; its front section, which is better preserved than the rest, contained a chapel for Seti's father, Ramesses I. A false door provided a link between this group of rooms and the royal tomb.

The central part of the temple is entirely dedicated to the Festival of the Valley and to Amun. The processional route, on which the axis of the temple lies, led to a columned hall, with openings to six side rooms. In one of these the royal barque was kept, and the opposite one shows the deceased king being united with Amun, who thus becomes the god Seti-Amun, the god of the temple. This is the most important cultic event in the temple, and the raison d'être of the entire complex. A vestibule leads to the barque sanctuary of Amun-Re and the rooms on either side of it, dedicated to Mut and Khonsu. When the barques of those gods arrived, they remained in these rooms temporarily in order to receive offerings. At the very back was a large chamber with four pillars and a false door, which on the one hand showed the god Amun the way to the west, and on the other hand gave the deceased king access from his tomb eastwards into the temple, where he could receive the daily offerings and take part in the rituals of the cult.

In the northern part of the temple were the vaulted storerooms, which could be reached through the rooms used for the distribution of offerings. These storerooms within the temple's enclosure wall are also an innovation of the Nineteenth Dynasty: previously, the offerings were delivered directly from the temple storerooms of Amun at Karnak. From now on the funerary temples had their own administra-

tion and agricultural land from which they could draw their own supplies, even though they remained subject to the temple of Amun. Their organization was comparable to that of the large monasteries of medieval Europe.

Of the temple's numerous statues and sphinxes, which flanked the passageways and were still in place when nineteenth-century travelers viewed the site, there remain only the pedestals of the two large sphinxes resting against the rear side of the first pylon, and the double crown of a colossal statue. At the death of Seti I the temple was still unfinished; it was his son and successor, Ramesses II, who completed it and also provided much of the wall decoration.

The Ramesseum – The Mortuary Temple of Ramesses II

In the very first year of his reign, and while still completing his father's temple, Ramesses II began to build his own temple to the south. J.F. Champollion, the decipherer of hieroglyphic writing, admired this temple ruin more than any other, and gave it its now famous name of "Ramesseum." It was here that for the first time on the west bank pylons were built of stone. On the inner face of the pylon leading into the first courtyard are lively scenes in relief of the battle of Kadesh, the most important event of the early years of Ramesses II's reign. In the same courtyard there once stood the colossal statue – at 19 m the tallest of all the colossal statues on the west bank at Thebes – which is now broken and lies on the ground at the entrance to the second pylon. On the north side of this courtyard standing figures of the king, majestically attired, towered in front of the portico's pillars. On the south side was as usual a ritual palace, of which now only the column bases survive. The scenes of victory, the palace, and colossal statues all indicate that the first court was dedicated to the glory of the reigning king. Here too the peace treaty with the Hittites was only inserted later. The

second courtyard was flanked on the east and west sides with a portico with Osiride pillars, but on the north and south sides with a double row of papyrus bundle columns. The temple's facade with its raised portico is decorated with sacrificial scenes. Below these the king's sons march in a festival procession into the interior of the temple. Three ramps that are still preserved today lead to the three gateways in this facade, clearly delineating the tripartite plan of the temple.

At the sides of the middle ramp were two seated figures of the king; the exceptionally beautiful head of the statue on the northern side now lies in the courtyard, but of the statue on the southern side only the throne and the lower part of the body have remained in the Ramesseum. The torso and head, made of light gray, fine-grained granite that turns reddish toward the head, was removed in 1816 by G. Belzoni on the instructions of British Consul-General Henry Salt and sold to The British Museum, where as "Young Memnon" it was greatly admired. The main entrance in the facade opens into a hypostyle hall that is larger and far more developed in style than that of Seti I. The basilica-like central nave consists of two rows of papyrus columns, six in each row, with open capitals of papyrus umbels. The side naves each have three rows of six papyrus bundle columns with closed capitals. The extaordinary effect of this hall, perhaps the most beautiful hypostyle hall in Egypt, derives from the clear spatial structuring, the harmonious proportions of the columns and the good state of preservation of the bright colors. A series of three smaller rooms, in each of which the ceiling is supported by eight columns, led to the holy of holies, which has unfortunately been completely destroyed. The first room is called the "astronomical room" because of the personified stellar constellations depicted on the ceiling; its walls show the barque procession.

The procession is led by the crown prince, who is followed by a number of other sons of the king. On the right-hand side of the rear wall is a magnificent portrayal of Ramesses' coronation in the heavenly Heliopolis. Ramesses II sits, holding the insignia of the kingdom, in the shade of the holy *Ished* tree, while Atum and Seshat inscribe his name on the leaves of the tree. The extensive vaulted storerooms sur-

84/85 Fallen colossus of Ramesses II
Western Thebes, mortuary temple of Ramesses II ("Ramesseum"); Nineteenth Dynasty, ca. 1260 BC; red granite; original H. 19 m.

Massive fragments of the colossal statue "Ramesses – sun of the foreign rulers" lie today in front of the temple's second pylon. Almost 19 m tall and weighing around 1,000 tons, the statue, made of the finest Aswan red granite, was the largest seated statue in Western Thebes and was already much admired in ancient times for its size, consummate technology, and fine execution. This view is taken looking out from the interior of the temple past the colossus, into the first courtyard and toward the inner side of the entrance pylon (width 69 m) with its representations of the king's battle against the Hittites at Kadesh.

86 Second court and hypostyle of the famous "Ramesseum"
Western Thebes, mortuary temple of Ramesses II; Nineteenth Dynasty, ca. 1260 BC; sandstone; ground plan of the temple building 58 by 183 m.

On the east and west sides of the second court, opposite each other, were two rows of eight Osiride pillars 11 m tall. Two massive seated figures (the bust of "Young Memnon" was part of one of them) were positioned before the entrance to the hypostyle. This consists of two rows of six columns with open papyrus umbel capitals, and six rows of six smaller papyrus bundle columns. The harmonious proportions of the columns and the good state of preservation, including some of the original painting, make this hypostyle one of the most impressive in all Egypt.

87 (opposite) Upper part of a colossal statue of Ramesses II
Western Thebes, mortuary temple of Ramesses II ("Ramesseum"), second court; Nineteenth Dynasty, ca. 1260 BC; granite; H. of surviving section 267 cm; London, The British Museum, EA 19.
This incomparably beautiful bust of Ramesses II, known as "Young Memnon," is made of light gray, fine-grained Aswan granite with a reddish tinge toward the head. When this statue was set up in The British Museum in London in 1817, it caused a worldwide sensation.

88 Columns with open and closed papyrus capitals
Western Thebes, mortuary temple of Ramesses II, hypostyle; Nineteenth Dynasty; ca. 1260 BC.
The capitals are decorated with a delicate, originally multi-colored design of leaves. Above the points of the leaves of the open capitals runs a decorative band with cartouches bearing the throne and birth names of Ramesses II.

89 Transportation of the bust of "Young Memnon"
Hand-colored lithograph; Giovanni Belzoni, *Six New Plates*, London 1822.
In 1816, at the instigation of the British Consul-General, Henry Salt, Giovanni Belzoni dragged the upper part of the statue from the "Ramesseum" to the Nile, then by ship to Alexandria and from there to London. This difficult feat of transportation laid the basis of Belzoni's fame.

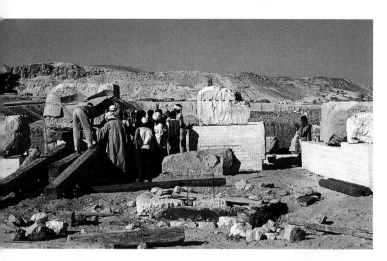

rounding the temple are mostly well-preserved and indicate the importance of the goods that were stored in them.

The Temple of Merenptah

Of the works of Ramesses II's successors in the Nineteenth Dynasty, only the ruins of the temple of Merenptah south of the "Ramesseum" are still visible. Apart from some minor divergences it is a copy of the temples of his predecessors. His complex was built largely by re-using materials from the neighboring buildings of Amenophis III. About a century ago, the British archeologist W.M. Flinders Petrie found the triumphal stela of Merenptah in the first courtyard of this temple. The text tells of Merenptah's victories over the alliance of Sea Peoples and Libyans who had invaded Egypt in the fifth year of his reign.

Recent excavations have revealed what remained after the temple was plundered in the nineteenth century for limestone for lime kilns and sandstone for the extraction of saltpeter. Large limestone blocks from the first columned hall give an impression of former splendor; there are representations of the barque procession, scenes of sacrifices, as well as thousands of sandstone fragments, many still bearing traces of paint, from the walls of the rooms and of the holy of holies. Fragments of numerous statues, among them the lower part of a bust discovered by Petrie, bear witness to the destruction. In the temple's second courtyard large pieces of three colossal statue groups were discovered, showing the king accompanied by gods. These were originally sculptures of Amenophis III, but were newly inscribed with the name of Merenptah and re-used. Other colossal statues from the reign of Amenophis III, among them jackals and sphinxes, as well as large blocks of limestone with colored reliefs and magnificent scenes of the feast of the king's jubilee, were used in the foundations of Merenptah's temple and therefore survived in good condition.

Medinet Habu – Ramesses III's Castle of the Gods

The last of the Theban mortuary temples was completed by Ramesses III at the southernmost point of the necropolis, very close to a small temple built by kings of the Eighteenth Dynasty above the sacred site of the Theban Primeval Mound. The very well-preserved temple complex of Medinet Habu completes our understanding of the "Houses of Millions of Years." The actual temple, like that of Seti I, is surrounded by a wall with protruding towers; it is a veritable fortress of the gods. Somewhat later in the reign of Ramesses III a much larger wall of considerable height was built to enclose the complex, which had since been enlarged with storerooms and administrative buildings. Access to the complex as a whole was by two gateway towers, like those of a fortress, on the east and west sides. From the better-preserved east gateway one can see that despite its forbidding appearance it is the core building of a multi-storied royal palace, with a limestone gateway in the middle and broad, multi-storied side wings built of brick. The core building contained high, airy sitting rooms with large windows; the eastern window was perhaps a royal Window of Appearances.

The exterior decoration immortalizes Ramesses III's victories over the Libyans and Sea Peoples, while the rooms inside show scenes of genuine family life. The king is seen playing a board game with his daughters; perhaps this is the Senet game, which is directly related to themes of the afterlife. Ramesses III stayed in these "gate palaces" when he visited Thebes and took part in the festivals. It is possible that he was even killed in one of these two palaces in a harem conspiracy.

90 Modern excavations in the first hypostyle
Western Thebes, mortuary temple of Merenptah; Nineteenth Dynasty, ca. 1210 BC.
The crew is engaged in the excavation and relocation of the great blocks in the first hypostyle hall. Merenptah's mortuary temple was largely built of re-used limestone blocks from the neighboring temple of Amenophis III. Merenptah even used statues and sphinxes of that Eighteenth Dynasty king for the foundations of his temple.

91 Bust of King Merenptah
Western Thebes, mortuary temple of Merenptah; Nineteenth Dynasty, ca. 1210 BC; gray granodiorite; H. 91 cm; Cairo, Egyptian Museum, JE 31414 (CG 607).
This bust was part of a monumental seated statue of the king from his mortuary temple at Thebes. It is the idealized portrait of a youthful ruler and certainly does not reproduce the actual features of Merenptah, who was at least fifty years old when he ascended the throne.

92 The "High Gate" of Medinet Habu
Western Thebes, mortuary temple of Ramesses III, eastern entrance; Twentieth Dynasty, ca. 1155 BC; brick, faced with sandstone blocks; H. 19 m.
In Ramesses III's last years his mortuary temple was extended to form an occasional royal residence at Thebes. An 18-m-high enclosure wall now surrounded an area of 205 by 315 m. Along with administrative buildings, stables, barracks, and parade grounds, an imposing residential palace was built on both east and west. Each had a central section consisting of a three-story stone gateway containing high-ceilinged, airy rooms, with side wings of brick adjoining it.

Behind the gateway there is, to the right of the temple axis, an older small temple dating from the Eighteenth Dynasty, which was constantly used and extended down to Roman times. On the left-hand side of the processional route the chapels for the God's Wives of Amun were built during the Twenty-sixth Dynasty, so that they could participate in the festivals associated with the processions and in the cult of the Primeval Mound. Here above all it becomes clear that the chief function of all the buildings on the west bank was connected with the great procession of the "Beautiful Festival of the Valley." The temples of Medinet Habu marked the end of the festival route.

The first pylon of the main temple is the best preserved in Western Thebes. Its external walls bear the traditional scene of the king "smiting his enemies," in the presence of Amun on the south wall and Re-Horakhty on the north wall. The wall reliefs in the first courtyard, which are also well-preserved, immortalize the king's campaigns and victories against the Libyans and Sea Peoples who had invaded Egypt for the second time and whom Ramesses III had to repel, like Merenptah before him, in hard-fought battles on land and sea at the Egyptian border. On the northern side of the courtyard is a row of pillars with statues of the king in splendid attire. Facing him, a portico of papyrus columns with open capitals forms the facade of the temple palace; this is the best preserved palace in the Theban area, and its remains have moreover been restored in an exemplary manner. The Window of Appearances is in the middle of the facade, with the two entrances on either side. They lead first into a hall of columns, whose vaulted ceiling was once supported by palm columns. Behind this is a throne-room with the essential side-rooms, a bathroom, and a bedroom for the king, as well as three small apartments for princes or the royal retinue. It is clear that this palace was a model of a royal residence, each of whose main elements was represented here by a room. This palace was not, however, used as an actual residence, for it lacks certain essential quarters, such as a kitchen and stables. Moreover, it would probably have been too small for the Ramessides, who were accustomed to the greatest luxury. It existed solely for the ceremonial appearance of the living king during the processions. Only after his death did he, in the form of a statue, inhabit the temple palace. A false door on the rear wall of the throne-room enabled the spirit manifestation of the king to enter the palace from his tomb in order to take part in the sacrificial offerings.

93 Forecourt and first pylon at Medinet Habu
Western Thebes, Medinet Habu, mortuary temple of Ramesses III; Twentieth Dynasty, ca. 1160 BC; sandstone; H. of pylon 24.45 m, W. 67.80 m.
The great pylon of Medinet Habu is the best preserved in all Thebes. It originally had four tall flagpoles, which were named after the goddesses Nekhbet and Uto, Isis and Nephthys. The outer facades of the pylon's two towers show the triumphant king smiting

his enemies in the sight of the great gods of the empire (Amun-Re and Re-Harakhty), who present him with the sword of victory. Above the actual gateway was a sanctuary to the sun. The large forecourt incorporated, on its northern side, the older and deeply venerated Eighteenth Dynasty temple to Amun as primeval god. Later, in the Twenty-fifth and Twenty-sixth Dynasties, the God's Wives of Amun built their mortuary chapels on its southern side.

94 Ramesses III hunting wild animals
Western Thebes, Medinet Habu, mortuary temple of Ramesses III, rear wall of the southern pylon tower; Twentieth Dynasty, ca. 1160 BC.
This representation – unusual in a mortuary temple – is on the rear side of the pylon, next

to the passage to the temple palace. In battle and hunting scenes such as this the artist was permitted to depart from the strictly conventional positioning of figures in well-ordered registers. The ensuing "disarray" is what makes this type of image so lively and dynamic.

95 View looking into the second inner court
Western Thebes, Medinet Habu, mortuary temple of Ramesses III; Twentieth Dynasty, ca. 1160 BC.
Behind the great pylon were two large courtyards. The first was dedicated to warding off chaos, and showed extensive battle scenes, among them the battle against the Sea Peoples. On the southern side was a Window

of Appearances leading to the cult palace outside the temple building. The second court was dedicated to the great festivals that took place. In front of its eastern and western sides stood Osiride pillars, and in front of the northern and southern sides papyrus columns. Almost every one of the figures in front of the pillars was destroyed in Christian times, in order to build a church.

However, judging by the inscriptions added later to the doors of the columned hall, it seems that the impoverished priest-kings of the Twenty-first Dynasty did use this building as an official palace.

From the first courtyard a ramp with a staircase led through the portal of the second pylon into the second temple courtyard, the festival courtyard; the images here, with colors often in an excellent state of preservation, are entirely devoted to the processions. The colored reliefs showing parts of the "Beautiful Festival of the Valley," the Min festival with the statues of the deceased kings, and the Sokar festival with the ceremonial barque processions indicate how beautiful the decoration of the temple walls must once have been. A raised portico with broad, squat, painted Osiride pillars and unusually deeply cut inscriptions gives access to the hall of columns. This room in basilica form is flanked by chapels assigned to the royal ancestors, guest divinities and the royal barque. Although the ceiling and the upper sections of the walls and columns have been demolished, this hall feels oppressive and gloomy, probably chiefly because the massive columns are placed so close together. Their bases almost touch and reach right to the processional way. Here we are far removed from the airy design of Seti I's hall of columns or the grandeur of the hypostyle hall in the "Ramesseum," although Ramesses III took the latter as his model. A mystic heaviness and gloom pervades the interior of the temple. Cramped suites of rooms lead to the sanctuary on the axis of the temple and to the storerooms at the sides. The small courtyard of the sun to the north and the cult rooms for the deceased king to the south are squeezed in at the sides under the high outer walls.

Between the inner enclosure wall of the temple and the temenos wall with its two groups of gateway buildings, a later building phase added houses for the priests, administrative buildings, barracks, stables, ponds, and gardens. Wells, which also served to measure the level of the Nile ("Nilometers"), provided water for the complex. In the troubled period after the end of the Ramesside Period, this residential precinct, with the storerooms, barracks, and temple palace, finally became the seat of the priest-kings (at first ruling only over Thebes) of the theocratic state. The high temenos walls gave protection against attacks by nomadic bands of robbers. Thus the ideal fortress of the gods had finally become a fortified royal city in real life.

The Great Temples around the Country

The Temples of the Eighteenth Dynasty
Regine Schulz

Immediately after the consolidation of the country, intensive construction work began in order to reinforce the cultic presence of the reigning king throughout the land. Thus Ahmose, the founder of the Eighteenth Dynasty, restored the temple of Ptah at Memphis, and established places of worship at Abydos, Karnak, Armant, and Buhen (Nubia), amongst other sites.

Under his son Amenophis I and the following Thutmosid rulers, sacred buildings in almost all the important places in the country were restored, extended, or built anew. Amenophis II can be shown to have had ordered construction projects in over thirty different places.

The most costly program, however, must be that commissioned by Amenophis III as an expression of Egypt's enormous economic power at the height of the Eighteenth Dynasty. The cult objects placed in his temples show variety and innovation. Hundreds of statues of gods and kings, some re-inscribed and appropriated by later rulers, have survived entirely or in part; there are over forty colossal statues alone.

During the Amarna Period the cult of Aten and of the deified king Akhenaten had replaced worship of most of the other gods. From the fifth year of Amenophis III's reign, the center of building activity was Akhetaten, the modern Amarna. The temples of other gods, especially those of the god of the empire, Amun, were closed and fell into disrepair. Tutankhamun described the situation on his famous restoration stela: "His Majesty, however, ascended the throne when the temples of the gods and goddesses … were almost forgotten, their shrines were beginning to decay and to become mounds of rubble overgrown with weeds, their sanctuaries were as if they had never been …" The rulers of the post-Amarna Period were thus engaged in a vast restoration program, and the old temples were not merely renovated but also extended and newly fitted out. Nonetheless, it was only under the Ramesside kings of the early Nineteenth Dynasty that actual building once again took place on a large scale, and no other ruler ordered the construction of as many new temples as Ramesses II. Whereas some of the Ramesside temples are very well preserved, many buildings of the Eighteenth Dynasty have left behind only a few blocks, sections of foundations or isolated monuments, as the buildings were often built over and extended, and surplus stone was used elsewhere. The acts of destruction continued right down to modern times. Thus on Elephantine as late as the mid-nineteenth century a completely intact way station built by Amenophis III was demolished so that the blocks could be used as raw material for the local lime kilns.

96 The Satet temple
Elephantine; building phase of the Eighteenth Dynasty, ca. 1460 BC; sandstone.
This temple with an aisle of sandstone pillars was commissioned as a completely new building by Hatshepsut. It was demolished in ancient times and its stones were re-used. It has therefore been possible to recover a large number of the original blocks from the foundations of the Ptolemaic temple complex that succeeded Hatshepsut's building, and so to reconstruct the lost temple from the early New Kingdom. This building can thus be counted among the few examples of Eighteenth Dynasty sacred architecture outside Thebes.

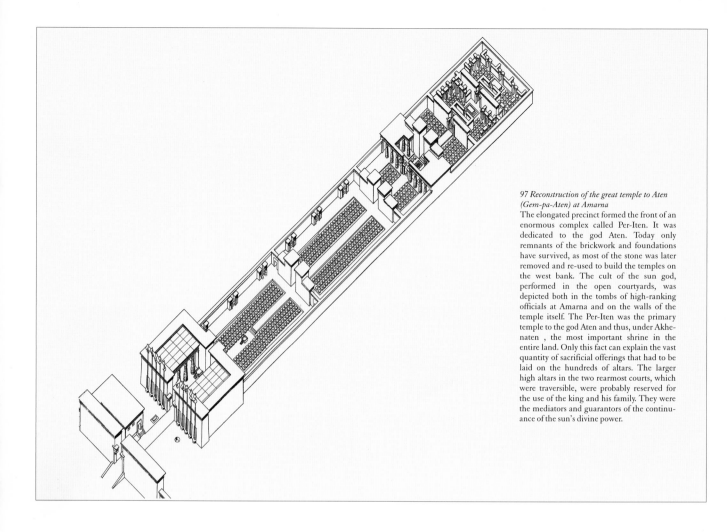

The Temples of Amarna – Sun Worship and Royal Cult

In the fifth year of his reign, Akhenaten decided to leave Karnak. He located his new capital, which he named Akhetaten ("Horizon of the Sun") and which is now called Tell el-Amarna, in a place in central Egypt hitherto untouched by cults. On one of the many rock stelae that marked the city boundaries he gave an account of the choice of this location: "I will build Akhetaten for my father Aten in this place ... which he himself created in such a way that it ... is enclosed by mountains and pleasant to him." On the east bank of the Nile, in the middle of the town, was the large temple complex dedicated to the god, the Per-Aten ("House of Aten"). Like so many Egyptian buildings sacred to the sun, the temples here are roofless. Here were the bipartite main temple, the site of the Benben Stone of primeval myth, and innumerable sacrificial altars. The two parts of the main temple were 350 m apart, shared the same axis and were oriented toward the east. The rear complex consisted of two courtyards and was regarded as a holy of holies. The square front courtyard had on the outside two walls projecting outward and on the inside columned halls at the sides and a central high altar. Between the columns were groups of statues of Akhenaten and Nefertiti. A ramp led up to a gateway and on to the terrace behind it with the second

courtyard that was surrounded by roofless chapels. On a dais in the center was the shrine, open at the top, to the sun god. Statues of the royal couple stood in this courtyard as well.

Like the temple of Aten at Karnak, the front section here was called Gem-pa-Aten. The building, measuring 210 by 32 m, was divided into two parts consisting of a series of uncovered courtyards with gateways. A large pylon formed the entrance to the front part, and behind it was a front courtyard. At the far side of this was the great hall of columns with an uncovered central passage; tall flagpoles stood in front of the hall. Behind the hall were two enormous courtyards each with 224 sacrificial altars. The rear part was less spaciously arranged. Here too the entrance area consisted of a front courtyard and a columned hall, followed by a smaller court with sacrificial altars. The last two courtyard units were again each surrounded by unroofed chapels, and each had a high altar.

To the south of the Per-Aten a small cult building was erected; this was called Pa-hut-Aten ("temple of Aten"). It was surrounded by an enclosure wall with bastion-like protrusions, and consisted of three courtyards with entrance pylons and a bipartite holy of holies similar to that of the larger temple. Although this building was designed in the style of a temple to Aten, the orientation of its axis toward the rock-cut tomb of Akhenaten, and the fortress-like form of the enclosure wall, also found in some Theban funerary temples, suggest that it served an

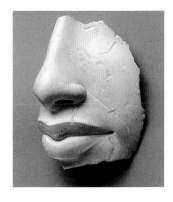

99 *Fragmentary face from a statue of Akhenaten*
Amarna, great temple of the Aten; Eighteenth Dynasty, ca. 1345 BC; hard limestone; H. 8.1 cm, W. 5.1 cm; New York, The Metropolitan Museum of Art, Edward S. Harkness Gift, 26.7.1395.
Although merely a fragment, this piece can be identified with certainty, based on the shape of the lips and the treatment of the line from the nose to the edge of the mouth, as part of a slightly under-life-sized statue of Akhenaten dating from his early years at Amarna. The type of limestone used, with its marble-like quality, was especially popular with sculptors at that period because it lent itself to a high degree of surface polish.

98 *Sanctuary in the great temple to Aten*
Hermopolis, originally Amarna; Eighteenth Dynasty, ca. 1340 BC; limestone; H. 22.7 cm, W. 26.9 cm; Boston, Museum of Fine Arts, 63.961.
Part of a larger whole, this block has preserved a representation of the sanctuary area of the temple. At the center is the main altar, heaped with an overabundance of offerings and flanked by two standing figures of Akhenaten. It also shows additional altars, incense burners on stands and the doorways leading to small side chapels.

100 *Grain field*
Hermopolis, originally Amarna; Eighteenth Dynasty, ca. 1340 BC; limestone; H. 23 cm, W. 52 cm; New York, The Metropolitan Museum of Art, Norbert Schimmel Gift, 1985, 1985.328.24.
Long-bearded heads of wheat, gently swaying in the breeze, give this representation its naturalistic character. Although the larger context of this scene is not known, it immediately calls to mind a passage from Akhenaten's great hymn to the Aten: "Your rays suckle the fields; when you rise they live and grow for you."

101 *The royal family under the "Aten with rays"*
Amarna, Great Palace; Eighteenth Dynasty, ca. 1345 BC; calcite-alabaster; H. 102 cm, W. 51 cm; Cairo, Egyptian Museum, RT 30.10.26.12.
At the heart of the newly defined state dogma of Amarna was the reciprocal relationship between the king and his sole god, Aten, who manifested himself in the image of the sun-disk. Here Akhenaten and Nefertiti each bring two vessels for libations for Aten; they are followed by their eldest daughter, Princess Meritaten. The exaggerated representation of the facial features and physiognomy should not be seen as "realistic" but has religious meaning: the king and queen possess the quality of fertility gods. They are active components of creation and can ensure its continued existence by means of the Aten cult. This block formed part of the balustrade of a ramp in the great royal palace.

102 (opposite) Portrait of Akhenaten
Amarna, northern part of the city, sculpture workshop of Thutmose (house P 47); Eighteenth Dynasty, ca. 1340 BC; grayish-white plaster; H. 26 cm; Berlin, SMPK, Ägyptisches Museum, 21351.
This life-sized head of Akhenaten consists of two joined halves, the shape of which was taken from a finished portrait of the ruler and then moulded in plaster. The original figure showed the king wearing the Blue Crown. The facial features illustrate the more balanced late style of his royal portraits.

103 Torso from a statue of Queen Nefertiti
Probably from Amarna; Eighteenth Dynasty, ca. 1345 BC; dark red sandstone; H. 29.5 cm; Paris, Musée du Louvre, E 25409.
Scarcely veiled by a pleated garment knotted beneath the right breast, the queen's torso gives unsurpassed expression to femininity and the idea of fertility. The sensuous modeling of the body seen in this illustration renders this figure one of the masterpieces of Egyptian sculpture.

104 Bust of Nefertiti
Amarna, northern part of the city, sculpture workshop of Thutmose (house P 47); Eighteenth Dynasty, ca. 1340 BC; painted limestone; H. 50 cm; Berlin, SMPK, Ägyptisches Museum, 21300.
Perhaps comparable only to the gold mask of Tutankhamun, the world-famous bust of Nefertiti epitomizes the beauty and perfection of ancient Egyptian art. The queen wears her characteristic headdress, the so-called Nefertiti cap crown, with a diadem band and uraeus cobra over the brow. She also wears a broad collar with a floral design. One is impressed by the harmonious proportions of this work as well as the polychromed painting. This bust was discovered in 1911, during excavations in the workshop of Thutmose conducted by the German Oriental Society, where it served as the prescribed model to be followed in the production of the queen's statues.

additional purpose as a royal mortuary temple. At the southernmost edge of the city there were two additional sacred buildings with unroofed chapels, gardens, and pools, which were possibly thought to mark the sites of the sun god's birth and creation.

At the death of Akhenaten all building was halted, and the town was soon afterward abandoned and never resettled. In the early Nineteenth Dynasty Ramesses II demolished the temples. He used the remaining blocks of stone as filling material for his temples at Hermopolis, the old cult center on the west bank of the Nile opposite Amarna. The foundation trenches and brickwork were all that remained in the "City of the Sun." Despite the almost total loss of the temple buildings, however, it has been possible to a large extent to reconstruct their architecture with the help of reliefs depicting them that have survived in the tombs of officials at Amarna.

The Images and Sculptures of Amarna

The intensive excavations carried out at Amarna by German and British archaeologists uncovered a number of outstanding works of art.

The walls of the temples and palaces had been almost completely destroyed and the statues broken, yet parts of the painted floors, and fragments of paintings, fallen reliefs and tiles, as well as pieces of statues, still remained. Objects removed to other sites and blocks re-used in later buildings complete the picture.

But works of art were also found in the residential areas of Akhetaten. These include domestic altars with depictions of the royal family beneath the rays of the sun, as well as sculptor's models and unfinished figures from the workshops. All these finds afford a good overview of the artistic development that took place in Akhetaten. They show that the highly dogmatic stylistic norms of the early phases in Karnak and Amarna were replaced by moderate and idealizing tendencies.

Toward the end of Akhenaten's reign another new stylistic trend emerged, in which the aim was to be as faithful as possible to nature. Some of the most striking examples of the latter two phases come from the workshop of the sculptor Thutmosis. They include the world-famous bust of Nefertiti and numerous portraits of her daughters, as well as the impressive plaster masks and heads in a style so naturalistic that it may be seen as a first step toward a new portrayal of the human figure.

The Temples of the Ramesside Period
Hourig Sourouzian

Although the kings of the late Eighteenth Dynasty had reinstated the cult of Amun-Re in Thebes, the buildings sacred to the other gods in the country had also been destroyed or abandoned and had to be restored. It was the aim of the Ramessides' huge building program to restore all cult sites, with the result that there are buildings and artifacts of this period in almost all the religious centers in the Nile Valley.

Memphis – The Sacred District of Ptah

At Memphis the Nile riverbed had moved farther eastward in the course of the New Kingdom and so created space for the Nineteenth Dynasty to erect new buildings in front of the gates of the temple of Ptah. First a processional road was made, ending at the southern gate where today the famous colossal statue of Ramesses II in crystalline limestone lies – without doubt the most perfect sculpture of the reign of Ramesses II in the Memphite area. Temples, chapels, and statues bordered the newly created avenue. A beautiful little temple built by Seti I was dedicated to Ptah and to the goddesses of Memphis. Only at this way station have the statues groups been preserved, showing in three-dimensional form what is depicted in low relief on the side walls.

Several temples, one of them dedicated to the goddess Hathor, were built in the reign of Ramesses II. He was also responsible for the great pylon on the west side of the enclosure wall of the Ptah temple, of which only the blocks at the very base can be seen today. Colossal statues stood in front of it, flanking the entrance to a great columned hall. By the northern gateway of the large enclosure wall was a group of two statues representing Ramesses II with Ptah-Tatanen, now in Copenhagen's Glyptothek, and a colossal sphinx, now in the University of Pennsylvania Museum in Philadelphia. By the eastern gateway stood the colossal statue of red granite that was set up in 1954 as a symbol of the new Egypt in the square (renamed "Midan Ramesses" – Ramesses Square) in front of Cairo's railway station, where it now suffers from the effects of modern environmental pollution.

Some hundreds of meters to the east of the Ptah district are the ruins of a temple built by Ramesses II and a building erected by Merenptah that was approached through a monumental gate. Associated with it was another building sacred to Ptah and a splendid temple palace, the walls and columns of which were adorned with multi-colored faience tiles. The last kings of the Ramesside Period contented themselves with preserving their names on the already existing buildings. They probably did this not only out of a desire to appropriate the buildings but also because they recognized that the organization of almost all cult buildings worked extremely well and that it was only necessary to endorse and guarantee the existing endowments. Moreover, it was probably felt that, given the increasingly unsettled times, any new building programs had little prospect of being realized.

105 Colossal standing statue of Ramesses II (detail)
Memphis, temple of Ptah; Nineteenth Dynasty, ca. 1275 BC; crystalline limestone; H. of surviving part 10.95 m; Mitrahina, Archeological Park.
This standing figure, now lying horizontally, once towered before the southern portal of the temple of Ptah. Of the colossal statues of the ruler, this is one of the highest quality; the proportions are harmonious, and the technical execution and surface polish are superb. The mild yet august facial expression is characteristic of the early style of the reign of Ramesses II.

106 Remains of Ramesses II's hypostyle and western pylon
Memphis, temple of Ptah; Nineteenth Dynasty, ca. 1270 BC.
Of the exquisite Ptah temple, which Herodotus was still able to admire on his Egyptian travels in the fifth century BC, only remnants of the foundations, isolated blocks of stone and drum-shaped column sections remain. Nevertheless it can be shown that the pylon was 74 m wide, and that the hypostyle contained four rows of four papyrus columns that were probably 13 m tall.

Heliopolis – Site of the Primeval Mound of Re

Heliopolis, once a center of very intensive building activity, has now been robbed of almost all its monuments. An extremely high proportion of them were transported to other sites in Egypt, and from Greco-Roman times onward even taken abroad. We know from texts that have been recovered of the existence of temples dedicated to the sun god Re, to Atum, and to Hathor, of a great avenue of sphinxes, and of obelisks, but we can now form only an uncertain impression of them. A model of Seti I's temple, found in Tell el-Yahudiya near Heliopolis and reconstructed at the Brooklyn Museum, shows the entrance to the temple district.

On the site itself only a few remains from the New Kingdom have been preserved, and these were only recently uncovered. They are the remnants of a broad avenue, once bordered by temples with statues of the king fronting their facades. At the end of the avenue was a monumental gateway with papyrus bundle columns inscribed with the name of Ramesses III; it evidently led into a great temple. Some distance away lay a column of red granite – this has now been restored to its upright position – that bears an inscription from the fifth year of the reign of Merenptah and glorifies his victory over the Sea Peoples. This monument, which probably once bore a statue or an emblem, is the prototype of the memorial columns familiar to us from Greco-Roman times.

107 Statue group of Ramesses II with the god Ptah-Tatanen
Memphis, temple of Ptah, northern entrance; Nineteenth Dynasty, ca. 1260 BC; red granite; H. 335 cm; Copenhagen, Ny Carlsberg Glyptothek, ÆIN 1483.
Among the many sculptures erected by Ramesses within and in front of the Ptah temple are group statues showing the king together with divinities. As shown by this dyad of Ramesses II with the god Ptah-Tatanen, they are manifestations of the king together with the lord of the temple. Through this conjunction the deified aspect of the king was represented most effectively and became the object of veneration by the subjects.

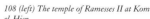

108 (left) The temple of Ramesses II at Kom el-Hisn

Heliopolis; Nineteenth Dynasty, ca. 1270 BC. Kom el-Hisn is part of the extensive temple complex at Heliopolis. Here, at the side of the processional route, once stood a way station of Ramesses II. By the Late Period and especially under the Ptolemies, the temples of Heliopolis had already been robbed of their monuments and statues, which were then set up in the new royal residences such as that at Alexandria.

110 The victory column of Merenptah

Heliopolis; Nineteenth Dynasty, ca. 1206 BC; red granite; H. of column 5.42 m, Diam. 82 cm; Heliopolis, magazine.
Beside the processional avenue to the obelisk temples of the Middle Kingdom, Merenptah erected a column on which he glorified his victory in his fifth year over an alliance of Libyan tribes and the Sea Peoples of the north. Set into the abacus is a square key by which a figure might have been held in place. This victory column is thus a direct model for those of classical antiquity, such as the columns set up by the Roman emperors Trajan and Marcus Aurelius.

109 Monumental stela of Ramesses II, from the eighth year of his reign

Mansheit es-Sadr, near Heliopolis; Nineteenth Dynasty, 1271 BC; limestone; H. 210 cm, W. 106 cm; Cairo, Egyptian Museum, JE 39503 (CG 34504).
The upper part of the stela shows Ramesses II, accompanied by the goddess Hathor, before the falcon-headed Re-Harakhty. The god hands him the insignia of kingship. The long inscription beneath the pictorial lunette reports that the young king stayed at Heliopolis and consid-

ered how he might give pleasure to his father, the sun god Re-Harakhty, by means of monuments for his temple: "He traveled through the desert (...) near Heliopolis (and came) to the Red Mountain (quarry area). There His Majesty found a mighty block of quartzite the equal of which has not been found since the time of Re, (and) it was taller than an obelisk of granite." The king gave this block to his sculptors, who within a year fashioned it into the colossal statue "Ramesses, Miaamana, the god."

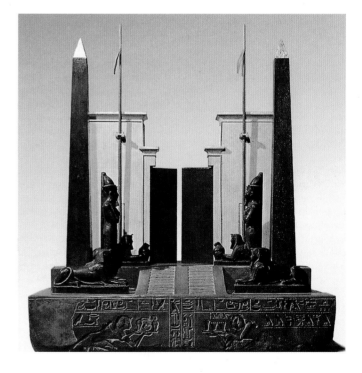

111 Ancient model of a temple portal at Heliopolis

Tell el-Yahudiya; Nineteenth Dynasty, reign of Seti I, ca. 1285 BC; sandstone; L. 112 cm, W. 87.5 cm, H. 28 cm; with reconstructed superstructures; New York, The Brooklyn Museum, Charles Edwin Wilbour Fund 1949, 49.183 and 66.228 (reconstruction).

Slots in the top surface of the model's base allow a pylon gateway in front of which were two obelisks, two standing royal statues in ceremonial costume and two pairs of sphinxes. In the images running around the sides of the base Seti I can be seen in a "kneeling run," making offerings to the gods Re-Harakhty and Atum.

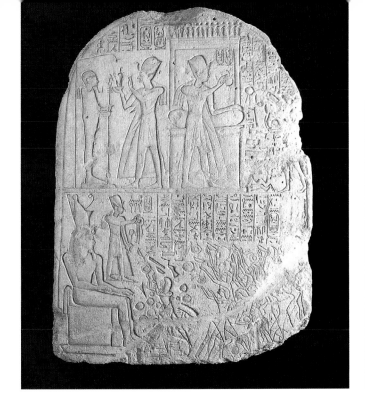

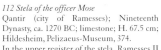

112 Stela of the officer Mose
Qantir (city of Ramesses); Nineteenth Dynasty, ca. 1270 BC; limestone; H. 67.5 cm; Hildesheim, Pelizaeus-Museum, 374.
In the upper register of the stela, Ramesses II makes an offering to the god Ptah, "he who answers prayers," and from his palace window dispenses the gold of honor to the

officer Mose. In the lower register Ramesses II stands next to his own colossal seated statue, which bears the name "Ramesses, sun of the rulers," and presents gifts to Mose and his soldiers. We know from similar stelae that in the city of Ramesses (Pi-Ramesse) there were numerous seated and standing colossal statues, some of them over 20 m tall.

113 Tanis, view of Ramesside buildings and statues
After abandoning the splendid city of Ramesses, the rulers of the new Libyan dynasties (from about 1045 BC) transported statues, columns, and architectural features from Pi-Ramesse to Tanis, their new seat in the Delta, and reused these in their temples

there. As a result, when excavations began in the nineteenth century, Tanis was declared the richest "open-air museum" of the Nile Delta. Even today, after most of the sculptures have been removed to the museums of Cairo and of Europe, Tanis must still be regarded as the Delta's most impressive ancient site.

Pi-Ramesse – The Temples of the City of Ramesses

Papyri and stelae tell of the great new royal residence in the eastern Delta. Founded by Seti I, it was enlarged, embellished, and praised by Ramesses II, who gave it his name, "Pi-Ramesse the victorious" – the city of Ramesses. The extensive palace formed the center of the city; the temples of the great gods of the empire, Amun, Re, and Ptah, and that of the family god, Seth, were placed around the palace at each of the four cardinal points, and oriented toward it. In the square in front of the palace Ramesses II erected four colossal statues; the remaining fragments suggest that these were the largest free-standing statues in Egypt, over 21 m tall. We know them only from representations on stelae, where they were portrayed as objects of veneration and of the cult – the visible manifestation of the gods in the person of the king. Through them the individual could convey his petitions to the gods. When they were erected, land and property were assigned to them to provide for their cult, and this was recorded for all time on memorial scarabs. With a view to celebrating the many jubilees of his reign, Ramesses laid out great festival courts in front of the temples and the palace and planted them with a forest of obelisks.

This city is named in the Bible as the place where the Children of Israel suffered oppression, and early archaeologists in Egypt, who believed in the historical truth of the Bible, were particularly eager to find it. However, most of the stone buildings of Pi-Ramesse were demolished in the Twenty-first Dynasty and later, and their compo-

nents were removed to be used as building material for the temples of the new capital, Tanis. Thus numerous decorated blocks bearing the names of Ramesses II and the gods of Pi-Ramesse have been found at Tanis: entire doorframes of granite, parts of architraves, numerous broken obelisks, columns, and many fragments of colossal statues, some of them on such a huge scale that the eye of one of the standing granite colossi is 42 cm across and a foot is over 3 m long. Other colossi were made of sandstone, and numerous smaller statues were of granite. There are statues of gods and kings, and groups of two or three statues of the king together with gods, as well as great sphinxes and colossal statues of Middle Kingdom kings that were reinscribed by Ramesses II or his son Merenptah. Statues of priests and high-ranking officials were also been brought there.

Altogether about fifty sculptures from Pi-Ramesse have ended up at other sites or in museums around the world; they represent an exemplary collection of the sculptor's art that could form one of the most beautiful and impressive of open-air museums. No wonder that for a long time people were convinced that the great ruins of Tanis actually were the famous Pi-Ramesse. More recent excavations have, however, provided incontrovertible proof that ancient Pi-Ramesse was, in fact, close to present-day Qantir. The town extended over several square kilometers as far as Tell ed-Dab'a where the earlier Hyksos capital Avaris has also been uncovered. Scattered in the fields at Avaris are the sparse remains of that once-splendid royal city and its magnificent monuments.

Abydos – Home of the Cult of Osiris

Abydos – once a religious center of great importance, a place of pilgrimage from early times, and the home of the cult of Osiris, god of the dead, whose tomb was thought to be here – had been abandoned during the Amarna Period. To make amends for this sacrilege, Seti I designed and built a temple on the processional route there, on the "terrace of the great god" from the temple of Osiris to his tomb at Umm el-Gaab. This, probably the most beautiful and exquisitely built temple erected to any god in the land of the Nile, was a "House of Millions of Years" dedicated to all the major gods and all the earlier kings of Egypt.

The Temple of Seti I

In front of his own temple Seti placed a memorial chapel for his father Ramesses I. The images there, in fine high relief of the best quality, show us the family of Seti I, his father Ramesses I, and his brothers, all making sacrifices to the divinities of Abydos. The great temple of Seti I, built of the finest limestone, is dedicated not only to the divine triad of Abydos – Osiris, Isis, and Horus – but also to the great gods of the empire, Amun of Thebes and his circle, Re of Heliopolis, and Ptah of Memphis, and to the king himself. The ground plan and the architectonic design are clear and perfectly realized, the ensemble of representations and statues follows a strictly orthodox pattern, and the technical execution and artistic quality are of the highest order. This temple thus provides the best example of the art of the Nineteenth Dynasty at its peak. Moreover, the detailed scenes of the daily rituals associated with cult statues are uniquely well preserved, allowing us to gain a deeper understanding of the religious ideas underlying them.

Steps of a ceremonial nature lead to the raised platform on the quay, where a canal once led to the Nile. In front of the temple building were two courtyards, one behind the other, of which a memorial text records that "their pylons reached up to the sky." The exterior wall of the front hall of columns is in the form of a portico with Osiride pillars. It has seven gates, which led into the seven sanctuaries of the gods, so that each sanctuary had its own gateway and axis. The central sanctuary was dedicated to Amun-Re and the Theban triad, whose barques are represented in bright colors on the walls. To the right of it were the sanctuaries of Osiris, Isis, and Horus, and to the left those of Ptah, Re-Horakhty, and the deified Seti I. With the exception of the Osiris sanctuary, each chapel had on its rear wall a false door giving magical access to a cenotaph (false tomb) that was located underground behind the temple. At his death the king would become Osiris and his mortuary cult would be established there. The sanctuary of Osiris was the only one that genuinely opened into an additional group of rooms that lay behind. This consisted of two columned halls, each with three chapels, which were dedicated to the three divinities of Abydos – Osiris, Isis, and Horus.

From the second columned hall of the main temple a corridor, whose west wall was decorated with a list of names of earlier kings from the First Dynasty to Seti I, branched off and led to two further sets of rooms, chapels of the gods of Memphis and sanctuaries in which statues, barques, and paraphernalia for the processions were kept. Outside the temple, as at the Theban mortuary temples to the east, there were extensive brick-built storerooms. At the death of Seti I this extraordinary temple was still incomplete. The young Ramesses II personally led his father's funeral procession to Thebes and made a stop at Abydos, where he made a solemn vow to complete his father's temple and to set up the statues that were still lying in the courtyards – a vow that he fulfilled.

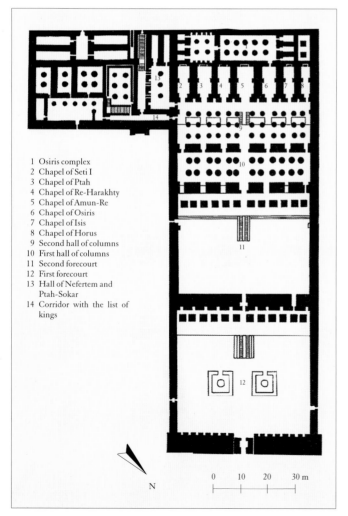

114/115 Temple of Seti I at Abydos
Nineteenth Dynasty, ca. 1285 BC; limestone; ground plan of the temple building.
Seti I's temple is famous because of its excellent state of preservation. It was his own mortuary temple and "House of Millions of Years," close to the most sacred necropolis in Egypt, home of the cult of Osiris, and at the same time a memorial temple to the great divinities of the empire, Re, Amun, Ptah-Sokar, Osiris, and Isis. The finely executed, colored reliefs are among the most accomplished works of art produced during the New Kingdom.

1 Osiris complex
2 Chapel of Seti I
3 Chapel of Ptah
4 Chapel of Re-Harakhty
5 Chapel of Amun-Re
6 Chapel of Osiris
7 Chapel of Isis
8 Chapel of Horus
9 Second hall of columns
10 First hall of columns
11 Second forecourt
12 First forecourt
13 Hall of Nefertem and Ptah-Sokar
14 Corridor with the list of kings

0   10   20   30 m

N

116 View into the second columned hall
Abydos, temple of Seti I; Nineteenth Dynasty, ca. 1285 BC.

The second columned hall in the temple of Seti I at Abydos is divided into two parts. The front occupies two-thirds of the floor area and has, like the first columned hall, twenty-four papyrus bundle columns. In the rear, gently sloping ramps lead up to the entrances to the seven chapels of the gods that form the sanctuary area. In front of these entrances are twelve plain columns without capitals.

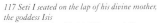
117 Seti I seated on the lap of his divine mother, the goddess Isis

Abydos, temple of Seti I; Nineteenth Dynasty, ca. 1285 BC; plastered and painted limestone. This relief shows the king wearing a finely pleated ceremonial loincloth, with a broad collar, golden royal cap, and a uraeus above his forehead. In his right hand he holds the crook as a symbol of kingship. His feet rest on a footstool with the sign for the "Unification of the Two Lands." Isis looks into the boy's face and with one hand raises his chin. In a motherly gesture she places her other hand protectively on the back of his head.

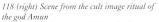
118 (right) Scene from the cult image ritual of the god Amun

Abydos, temple of Seti I, chapel of Amun; Nineteenth Dynasty, ca. 1285 BC; painted limestone.

In each of the temple's six chapels of the gods (the sanctuary dedicated to Seti I has a different scheme of decoration), the daily ritual associated with the cult images is depicted. This consists of a prescribed series of actions to be performed by the king in the presence of the image of the god, or by the priests acting on his behalf. The sequence of rituals, of which we are fortunate to have here a complete pictorial record, contains the following elements: entering the sanctuary, opening the shrine containing the cult image, the appearance of the god, falling down before the god, praising and offering gifts to the god, taking the cult image from the shrine, cleaning the image, clothing it, handing over insignia, ointments, and cosmetics, concluding by cleaning the floor, replacing the image in the shrine, wiping away footmarks, extinguishing the torches and closing the shrine.

The scene reproduced here shows the shrine with the cult image of Amun being opened by Seti I: specifically, it shows the seal from the previous day being broken.

119 (opposite) Kneeling figure of Seti I
Abydos, temple of Seti I; Nineteenth Dynasty, ca. 1285 BC; gray granodiorite; H. 114.3 cm; New York, The Metropolitan Museum of Art, 22.2.21.
This figure shows Seti I kneeling to present the gods of Abydos with a tray of offerings. The foot of the plate is formed by the hieroglyph *ḳa*, "sacrifice," on a lotus bud. Despite the extensive damage, this statue conveys an impression of the beauty and elegance of sculpture in the reign of Seti I.

The Temple of Ramesses II

On the same processional route to the temple of Osiris at Abydos, Ramesses II also built a temple of his own. This too was a way station and a funerary temple, but the ground plan was different from that of his father's temple. Notwithstanding that, it was no less richly decorated, and it too included chapels for the divinities of Thebes and Abydos, for the nine gods of Heliopolis, and for the underworld god, Wepwawet. The barque of his father Seti I also had a way station sanctuary inside the temple. The wall decoration, some of which has retained its beautiful coloring, has a wide range of subject matter. There are representations of ceremonial processions in the courtyards, the parade of the gods of the Nile bringing products from their nomes, and portrayals of the gods in their chapels. The main theme is the festival procession, in which the reliquary for the head of Osiris is carried in procession from the temple of Osiris to his presumed tomb in the cemetery, dating to the Predynastic Period, at Umm el-Gaab.

Egyptian Temples in Nubia

After the expulsion of the Hyksos from Egypt the pharaohs of the New Kingdom made determined efforts to regain their influence in Nubia. Doubtless one of the main reasons for Egypt's great interest in Nubia was that country's rich natural deposits of gold. Many military campaigns are documented, and Thutmosis III finally succeeded in advancing almost as far as the fourth cataract. An Egyptian administration was established with its seat at Aniba, the fortresses of the Middle Kingdom were repaired, towns were founded, and new temples built. Despite this, there were repeated rebellions. It was not until the reign of Amenophis III that the region seems to have been substantially pacified and completely subject to Egyptian influence.

The Temple of Amenophis III at Soleb – The Shrine of the "Lord of Nubia"
Regine Schulz

Amenophis III erected several cult buildings in Nubia, of which the most impressive was situated about 500 km south of Thebes on the west bank of the Nile at Soleb. He called it "He who appears in Maat" (principle of the order of the cosmos), a designation that was also a part of his own Horus name within the royal titulary.

The temple was dedicated to Amun-Re and to Amenophis III as the divine "Lord of Nubia." In his divine form he acquired cosmic status and wore a sickle moon and full moon above the royal headcloth as identifying signs. His costume also included the beard and the loincloth of a god, and the ram's horns of Amun. In the temple the king had a dual function. As a god he was, like the other gods, the object of a cult, and as a king it was he who performed the ritual acts. So it is not surprising that in one picture Amenophis III is offering a sacrifice to his own deified image.

120 View into the second court of the temple of Ramesses II at Abydos
Nineteenth Dynasty, ca. 1270 BC.
To the northwest of the temple of Seti I at Abydos, his son Ramesses II built his own temple to the triad of Abydos – Osiris, Isis, and Horus. The complex is also dedicated to the royal cult and to the House of Millions of Years of Ramesses II.

121 Ramesses II's processional barque
Abydos, temple of Ramesses II, barque sanctuary; Nineteenth Dynasty, ca. 1270 BC.
Several smaller chambers directly adjoin the courtyards; one of these is a room for the royal processional barque, which is, accordingly, depicted on the side walls. In the center of the barque is the figure of the enthroned king, shown to be a deified ruler by the ram's horn behind his ear. The barque of the pharaoh played an important part in the festivals at Abydos, and was carried at the head of the procession of the emblem of Osiris.

122 Figure of a lion carved for Amenophis III
Gebel Barkal; originally Soleb, temple of
Amenophis III; Eighteenth Dynasty, ca. 1360
BC; red granite; H. 117 cm, length 205 cm;
London, The British Museum, EA 2.
Both majestic calm and stern vigilance are
embodied in this figure of a lion that, with a
counterpart, probably originally flanked the
entrance to the monumental kiosk in front of
the temple's second pylon. The two lions
represent a deified manifestation of Amenophis III and link him mythically to the

cyclical aspects of the moon and sun. The
pose with the forepaws crossed is a variation
previously unknown in animal sculpture.
Like the figure of a ram from the Gebel
Barkal, both lions – after Tutankhamun and
Ay had usurped some of the inscriptions –
were taken by the Meroitic king Amanislo
(third century BC) to Gebel Barkal, where
they were discovered by Lord Prudhoe on a
journey of exploration to the Sudan, shipped
to England, and finally, in 1835, donated to
The British Museum.

*123 Temple of Amenophis III at Soleb, viewed
from the southwest*
Soleb; Eighteenth Dynasty, ca. 1360 BC.
This temple complex, built in connection
with his first festival of renewal (*sed*), marks
the southernmost point reached by an enormous building program set in motion by
Amenophis III throughout the country. This
temple served not only as an impressive
demonstration of Amenophis's claim to
sovereignty in the "foreign" territory of Nubia,
but also as a stage for the presentation of a
cult, with the manifestation of the deified
king at its center.

124 The god Amun as a ram
Gebel Barkal; originally Soleb, temple of
Amenophis III; Eighteenth Dynasty,
ca. 1360 BC.
As one manifestation of Amun, the god of the
empire, several colossal figures of rams
flanked the processional route leading up
from the landing quay to the entrance pylon
of the temple of Soleb. Between the ram's
front legs stands the mummiform figure of
the ruler, protected by the divinity. Horns,
ears, and the sun disk were once separately
worked in precious metals (the statue now
bears modern replacements). Reduced as it is
to the characteristic formal elements, this
representation may be seen as a masterpiece
of ancient Egyptian animal sculpture. The
inscription running around the base
celebrates the beauty of the temple. This
ram was discovered in 1845, not at Soleb
but farther south in the temple of Amun at
Gebel Barkal, where it had been brought
during the Twenty-fifth Dynasty under
King Piye.

After four extensions, the temple of Soleb was the largest Egyptian cult complex in Nubia. It began as a tripartite central building with rooms for barques and cult images. Later a hall with twenty-four columns with palm-leaf capitals, a courtyard with pillars around it, and the first pylon were added. Next, another courtyard with the second pylon was built. The papyrus bundle columns for this courtyard, the kiosk in the center at the front with four palm columns, two obelisks, and six colossal statues of the king were all added last. Finally, an avenue of criosphinxes led to the third pylon, which was built into the great surrounding wall. Of the temple's original decoration program little has survived.

The second courtyard contained a series of scenes showing the festival of royal renewal, at which not only Amenophis III but also his wife Tiye and his wise counsellor Amenhotep, the son of Hapu, appear. At the bottom of the column shafts in the hypostyle hall are lists of the names of subjugated tribes. Among these names is the designation "Shasu bedouins of Yahweh;" this may possibly be one of the earliest recorded references to the later god of the Israelites.

The Buildings of the Ramesside Period
Hourig Sourouzian

In the New Kingdom it became increasingly customary for kings in the desert regions on both sides of the Nile Valley and especially in Nubia to build rock-cut temples. Some of the Nineteenth Dynasty examples, for instance Seti I's temple in the Wadi Mia, were placed close to wells on the routes to the gold mines; others, like Merenptah's Hathor chapel at El-Babein, were built actually within the mining areas, where the extraction of the sought-after raw materials had already created

large caverns. In Nubia the temples were intended to help spread the Egyptian cult of the gods, and Ramesses II founded no fewer than six new temples for this purpose. Each of these was a masterpiece, and each has preserved at least some of its former beauty and individual features. Beit el-Wali is famous for its finely cut reliefs, and the temple of ed-Derr for the many colors of its wall decorations. The Gerf Hussein complex, now submerged beneath the waters of Lake Nasser, was outstanding for the numerous sculpted triads on the walls of the courtyard and in the columned hall, while the notable feature of Wadi es-Sebua was its overwhelmingly impressive avenue of sphinxes.

The Rock-cut Temples of Abu Simbel

There is no doubt that Abu Simbel represents the absolute artistic peak of this type of architecture. One can see in this monument the ideal embodiment of the architectural type and religious content of the Nubian temples. As we admire this magnificent building we may gain some inkling of the greatness and the creative imagination of Ramesses II, the young king who created it, who was little more than fifteen years old when he gave the order for its construction.

The complex comprises two sacred buildings that complement one another. The large temple houses the cult of the three great gods of the empire, Amun, Re-Horakhty, and Ptah, together with that of the deified king. In the smaller temple Ramesses II links himself with the goddess Hathor, who is embodied in the Great Wife of the King, Nefertari. The seated colossi in front of the great temple and the standing colossal figures fronting the facade of the small one are there to demonstrate, in this distant province, the overwhelming power and

125 *Sphinx of Ramesses II in the temple of Wadi-es-Sebua*
Wadi-es-Sebua; Nineteenth Dynasty, ca. 1260 BC; sandstone; H. 4.80 m.
The avenue of sphinxes in this temple is considered to be the best-preserved dromos of the Nineteenth Dynasty. The large number of surviving figures has led to its being called the "Valley of the Lions." The sphinxes in the first courtyard have human heads, those in the second have falcon heads and a smaller statue of the king in front of the breast. The inscriptions on the sphinxes indicate that Ramesses II erected them as a monument to his father Amun-Re.

126 *Avenue of sphinxes at Wadi-es-Sebua*
Nineteenth Dynasty, reign of Ramesses II, ca. 1260 BC.
Originally on the bank of the Nile before being relocated, this temple was linked to the river by a quay. On each side of the temple entrance stood a statue of the king and a sphinx. An avenue of sphinxes led through two courtyards to a pylon in front of which stood two monumental statues of the king holding a staff. The actual temple building was behind this, inside the rock. Like the temple of Derr, the rock temple of Wadi es-Sebua was relocated in 1964 and is now situated 4 km farther to the west.

greatness of the pantheon of the Egyptian gods, represented by the images of the divine king and his family.

Inside the temple complexes, the depictions of sacrifices and festive barque processions also show Egypt as a land that is inhabited and blessed by the gods and where the divine order of the cosmos is upheld by the king. One aspect of this representation shows the king, as guarantor of that order on earth, warding off the dangers that threaten Egypt. Accordingly, we find here once again a depiction of the great battle and "victory" of Ramesses II over the Hittites at Kadesh.

The broad, high-ceilinged hall hewn out of the rock, with its eight pillar statues of the king, grows narrower toward the west as it leads into the second hall of pillars, and the ceiling becomes lower and lower until the holy of holies presents something like a rock-hewn cave. The gods of the temple – Amun-Re, Re-Horakhty and Ptah, that is to say the Ramesside gods of the empire – are seated against its west wall, together with the deified king. The orientation of the temple is such that twice a year, on February 20 and October 20, the rays of the rising sun illuminate all four statues, a fact that has recently been hailed with much publicity as the wonder of Abu Simbel. There is insufficient evidence to prove that the dates are those of Ramesses II's birthday and the anniversary of his coronation.

127 The Great Temple of Ramesses II at Abu Simbel
Abu Simbel; Nineteenth Dynasty, ca. 1260 BC; sandstone; depth within the rock 60 m.
Abu Simbel represents the absolute pinnacle of the architecture of the Nubian rock temples. Begun in the early years of the reign of Ramesses II, the Great Temple was completed before the twentieth year of his rule. The facade, which takes the form of a pylon, is dominated by four colossal seated figures, 22 m tall; the southern ones entitled "Ramesses, Sun of the Rulers" and "Ruler of the Two Lands," the northern ones named "Ramesses, loved by Amun" and "Loved by Atum." Above the entrance Ramesses II is depicted sacrificing to the lord of the temple, Re, whose attributes together with his statue form Ramesses II's throne name, Usermaatre. The temple itself is carved out of the Nubian sandstone, 60 m deep, and contains two pillared halls, store-rooms, and a sanctuary situated deep in the rock. In 1964–1968 the temple, together with the small temple of Abu Simbel, was dismantled and moved to a hill behind the original temple site in order to save it from the rising waters of Lake Nasser following the construction of Aswan High Dam.

Between 1964 and 1968 a unique international collaborative project saved both temples of Abu Simbel from the rising waters of Lake Nasser; they were sawn into blocks and then reassembled on higher ground nearby. Technically this relocation was as great a feat as the construction of the temples under Ramesses II. But the unique manner in which the temple blended with its surroundings, the special quality of its romantic setting in the Nubian river landscape with its farms and palm-trees, could not be saved.

128 (below) The sanctuary of the Great Temple
Abu Simbel; Nineteenth Dynasty, ca. 1260 BC.
Behind the Hall of Appearances and the room with the tables for offerings is the temple sanctuary. There, in a statue group, Ramesses II is united with the three great gods of the empire, Ptah, Amun-Re, and Re-Harakhty, beside whom he appears as a divinity of equal status. The temple was so oriented that it was only on the days of the equinoxes (February 20 and October 20) that the rays of the rising sun illuminated the entire group.

129 The Small Temple at Abu Simbel
Abu Simbel; Nineteenth Dynasty, ca. 1260 BC; sandstone; depth in the rock 21 m.
The smaller temple, to the north of its larger counterpart, is dedicated to Queen Nefertari in her roles as the goddess Hathor, the king's beloved, and the mother of the royal children. On the facade (28 by 12 m), on either side of the entrance, statues of the king, 9.50 m tall, alternate with statues of the queen. Beside the figures of Nefertari stand smaller ones of the princesses, while the princes flank the statues of the king.

130 The pillared hall in the Great Temple
Abu Simbel; Nineteenth Dynasty, ca. 1260 BC; sandstone; H. of pillars 8 m.
Behind the facade of the Great Temple is a pillared hall (17.70 by 16.50 m) with two rows of four roof supports in front of which were colossal standing figures of the king reaching to the ceiling. They wear the ceremonial kilt, royal beard, and crowns of the Two Lands, and hold in their hands the crook and flail. Like the seated statues in front of the facade, these statues too were given titles indicating that they represented the deified ruler.

The Valley of the Kings

Matthias Seidel

Wadi Biban el-Moluk, the Valley of the Kings: surely no other topographical term is so immediately associated with the concept of the power and glory of the pharaohs, nor is there one that so excites modern imagination. It was in this valley of the Theban western mountains, approximately three miles from the Nile, that all the rulers of the New Kingdom were buried after and including Thutmosis I.

Only Akhenaten and his family provide the exception. Several factors may have determined the choice of location. With the founding of the Eighteenth Dynasty, Thebes was elevated to the role of Egypt's new royal capital, and burial was sought out near the city. The isolated desert wadi was perceived by the necropolis administration to be easily guarded and supervised, and to fulfill the security requirements of a royal place of rest. Events were to prove this to be an erroneous judgment.

The site of the necropolis in the west was generally justified by religious concepts that defined the cyclical trajectory of the sun (the west: sunset or the underworld) as an important prerequisite for the king's existence in the next world. The goddess Hathor had moreover been particularly venerated in Western Thebes since the Middle Kingdom. The "Lady of the West," the deity in the form of a cow, was closely linked with the ruler's existence in the afterlife. Reminiscent of the tradition of royal mortuary complexes, the highest elevation of the western mountains (450 m), which dominated the valley in the form of a pyramid, was known as the "Horn of Qurna."

Pragmatic reasons lay behind the fundamental decision to lay the dead king to rest in a rock-cut tomb instead of a pyramid. The associated funeral cult was established in a specially constructed temple on the edge of the fertile land. Neither the massive stone structures of the Old Kingdom pyramids, nor the ingenious systems of corridors within those of the Middle Kingdom, had been able to fulfill their main purpose, namely to guarantee the protection of the royal mummy and the burial equipment.

The valley area can be divided into two arms, the eastern arm forming the Valley of the Kings with the majority of the royal tombs, and known as the "great district" or simply "the valley" in the ancient Egyptian texts. By contrast, the western arm contains only the tombs of Amenophis III and Ay. The concentration in the eastern valley can be explained by the fact that in the early part of the Eighteenth Dynasty

the towering rock formations allowed the excavation of particularly well-concealed sites. An indication of the constant need for secrecy is provided by the official Ineni in his biographical tomb inscription, where in reference to the royal tomb he writes: "… I saw how the rock tomb of his majesty was dug in isolation, no one seeing, no one hearing." Nevertheless, as time progressed, free space became short, and the Ramesside rulers of the Nineteenth and Twentieth Dynasties occasionally had to locate their tombs in the flatter areas toward the middle of the valley.

Early Tourists, Adventurers, and Scholars

In the age of classical antiquity Egypt was regarded as a land of wonders and mysteries. Of central interest to the first influxes of visitors were not only the pyramids, but also the area of tombs and temples at Thebes. Even Roman emperors were overwhelmed by the remains of the civilization of the pharaohs. In the Valley of the Kings there are over 2,000 examples of graffiti in the ten tomb sites that were accessible in Roman times, all inscribed by visitors, and bearing witness to the interest shown by these tourists of antiquity. On the walls they left both their own names and those of their home town, praised the beauty of the pictures and expressed their regret at their inability to understand this art.

Numerous wall inscriptions also show that in the following period (fourth–sixth centuries) some of the royal tombs, such as those of Ramesses IV and VI, served as homesteads for Christian hermits.

With the Islamization of Egypt in the seventh century AD, the valley fell into a long period of neglect. It lasted until 1738, when the English clergyman Richard Pococke twice entered the Valley of the Kings and published the first overall plan as well as some individual ground plans in his book *Observations on Egypt*. The decisive impetus for the increasing interest in ancient Egypt was provided by the scientific results of the Napoleonic expedition of 1798. Among the numerous scholars and artists was Vivant Denon, who reached Thebes in 1799 with the troops of General Desaix. Because of the prevailing state of war Denon was only able to work in the Valley of the Kings for three hours and moreover under the most difficult conditions, a circumstance about which he complained bitterly in his memoirs. In the late summer of the same year the two French engineers, Jollois and de Villiers, followed in his footsteps, and were successful in locating the tomb of Amenophis III.

131 The Valley of the Kings
An isolated desert valley of the Theban western mountains was chosen by the rulers of the New Kingdom as the site for their final resting places. Once the daily streams of tourists have left, the valley still exudes even today an atmosphere of the peace and grandeur of death.

132 The inner valley
Many of the most important royal tombs are located in the central area of the valley. With the exception of the tomb of Tutankhamum, the tombs of the Ramesside Period (Nineteenth/Twentieth Dynasties) were openly visible and equipped with sealed doors.

KV 7: tomb of Ramesses II
KV 8: tomb of Merenptah
KV 9: tomb of Ramesses VI
KV 16: tomb of Ramesses I
KV 17: tomb of Seti I
KV 35: tomb of Amenophis II
KV 57: tomb of Horemheb
KV 62: tomb of Tutankhamun

133 Burial chamber in the tomb of Amenophis II
Western Thebes, Valley of the Kings (KV 35); Eighteenth Dynasty, ca. 1410 BC.
The walls of the burial chamber are equipped with a complete version of the Amduat (Book of the Underworld), while the six columns were decorated with representations of the king in front of the most important underworld and protective deities, Osiris, Anubis, and Hathor. The ceiling is designed throughout as a starry sky.

134 Seti I before the sacrificial table
Western Thebes, Valley of the Kings, tomb of Seti I (KV 17); Nineteenth Dynasty, ca. 1285 BC; color lithograph from: G. B. Belzoni, *Narrative of the Operations and Recent Discoveries in Egypt and Nubia*, London, 1820. In 1817 the Italian adventurer Giovanni B. Belzoni discovered the tomb of Seti I. The colors of the wall paintings had been preserved in their original splendor, and he copied them by means of drawings and wax moldings. The resulting copies were exhibited with overwhelming success to an astonished public by Belzoni in 1821/22. Although Egyptian hieroglyphs had not yet been deciphered, the drawings were greatly appreciated and easily comprehensible.

The most controversial figure ever to set foot in the Valley was the Italian Giovanni B. Belzoni. In the service of the British Consul-General, Henry Salt, Belzoni employed his workers in an intensive search for buried and hidden tombs. A brief period of a few days in October 1817 produced the greatest successes in Belzoni's career in archaeological excavation. The entrances to the tombs of Ramesses I and Seti I were cleared and soon afterwards Belzoni was standing in one of the greatest royal sepulchers of any age. The rock-cut tomb of Seti I became known in the literature as "Belzoni's tomb."

Before 1850 there were two additional large undertakings that contributed to progress in the investigations of the Valley. In 1829, with the aid of a team of artists and architects, Jean François Champollion, the decipherer of hieroglyphs, and Ippolito Rosellini copied numerous inscriptions and representations in the sixteen already known tombs. The work of the Prussian expedition under Richard Lepsius was even more productive. Commissioned by his king, Friedrich Wilhelm IV,

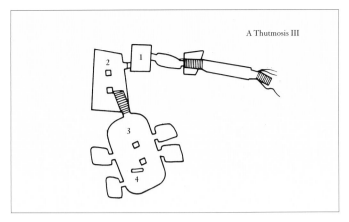

A Thutmosis III

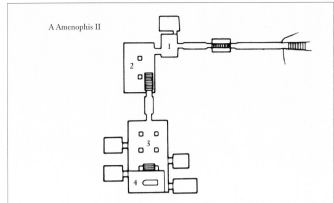

A Amenophis II

135 *Basic types in the development of New Kingdom royal tombs*
A with right angle axial turn (Eighteenth Dynasty: Thutmosis III, Amenophis II)
B with displaced axis (late Eighteenth Dynasty: Horemheb)

C with straight axis (Nineteenth and Twentieth Dynasties: Merenptah, Ramesses IV)
1 shaft space
2 first pillar room
3 burial chamber
4 sarcophagus

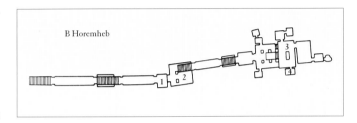

B Horemheb

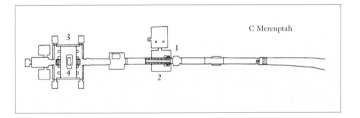

C Merenptah

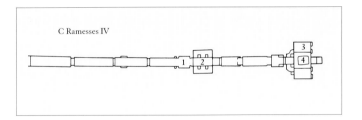

C Ramesses IV

Lepsius worked in Egypt in the years 1842–45 and spent a good six months studying the tombs of the pharaohs. He compiled all his results in a monumental twelve-volume work, the famous *Denkmaeler aus Aegypten und Aethiopien* (Monuments of Egypt and Ethiopia).

There were no new sensational finds in the Valley until 1898, when Victor Loret discovered the important tombs of Thutmosis III and Amenophis II. A few years later the New York businessman, Theodore M. Davis, appeared on the stage. He held the excavation concession for twelve years beginning in 1902. Bent on success and rather obstinate in nature, Davis went through several excavation leaders, among them the young Howard Carter. Davis could not complain about lack of success. The tombs of Thutmosis II, Thutmosis IV, Queen Hatshepsut, Siptah, Horemheb, and the tomb treasures of Yuya and Tuya, the parents-in-law of Amenophis III, more than compensated him for his financial investment. Of the strong conviction that the opportunities in the Valley were now "exhausted," Davis transferred his excavation rights to Lord Carnarvon. It would later become evident that he had stopped his excavations a mere two meters from the entrance to the tomb of Tutankhamun. The discovery of this tomb, the greatest triumph in the Valley of the Kings, thus fell to the Englishmen, Carter and Carnarvon.

Modern Egyptology of course continues its research on the royal tombs. Recently this has become more and more involved with conservation measures to preserve these unique products of the world's cultural heritage for future generations. Moreover, the Valley still holds surprises, as is underlined by the "rediscovery" a few years ago of the monumental tomb complex for the sons of Ramesses II.

The Architecture

In principle the architectural development of the royal tombs can be considered as a case of "expansion and extension." Great changes occurred between the small tombs, albeit just as deeply cut into the rock, of the Thutmosid rulers (Eighteenth Dynasty) and the monumental corridor tombs of their successors (from Horemheb onwards). The scale of the corridors provides a good illustration. While corridor height during the Eighteenth Dynasty was a good two meters (Amenophis II, Thutmosis IV), it had increased up to a height of four meters in the tombs of the last Ramesside kings (Twentieth Dynasty). Even within short periods of time, there was no absolute or inflexible tomb plan, and each king varied the layout of the various chambers, at least in detail.

The characteristic right angle turn in the axis of the tombs of the early Eighteenth Dynasty was intended to symbolize the winding path through the underworld. By contrast, the division in two, with the displaced axis, which occurred for the first time under Horemheb and remained the model for the Nineteenth Dynasty, harks back to mythological dualism. The upper axis was attributed to the sun god Re-Harakhty (meaning East) while the lower one corresponded to the god of the dead, Osiris (meaning West).

136 Tomb plan of Ramesses IV
Thebes; Twentieth Dynasty, ca. 1150 BC; painted papyrus; H. 24.5 cm, L. 86 cm.; Turin, Museo Egizio, 1885.
Although some inconsistencies can be seen in comparison with the actual architecture of the tomb, the Turin papyrus contains the complete version of an ancient Egyptian tomb plan. This is possibly a first draft from the office of the vizier responsible for the project. In the center, described in the accompanying text as "gold house," lies the chamber with the sarcophagus, which is surrounded by several shrines. The following rooms were used to house the *shabtis*, or were designated as treasuries. The wavy outline containing the dotted pattern around the tomb depicts the mountain landscape in which the rock-cut tomb was located.

In the Twentieth Dynasty the tomb plan was simplified and characterized by a straight axis in order to give priority to the solar aspect. A particularly significant area within the spatial plan was the shaft, which closed off the first section of the tomb. In terms of its depth and design, with or without chamber, it could be rendered in very different ways. The shaft may initially have been planned to keep the periodic and later deluge-like rainfalls from reaching the burial chamber, but subsequently it was understood as the symbolic tomb of the chthonic god of the underworld, Sokar. It certainly never had the function of defending or misleading tomb robbers, since the back wall (passageway) had to be rapidly blocked and decorated immediately after the funeral of the ruler. The resulting difference in the quality of the wall decorations thus provided a purely optical indication of the continuation of the tomb architecture. After the reign of Ramesses III (Twentieth Dynasty), the space was still planned, but the shaft was dispensed with.

Work on the Royal Tomb

Immediately after the ascent to the throne the work would generally begin on the tomb of the new ruler. Sometimes a significant period of time would elapse, as is evidenced by the note on an ostracon (limestone flake) for the tomb of Ramesses IV: "Year 2, second month of the

137 Burial chamber in the tomb of Horemheb.
Western Thebes, Valley of the Kings (KV 57); Eighteenth Dynasty, ca. 1033 BC.
The incomplete images in the pillar room of the burial chamber clearly reveal the working method that was employed: the red-lined preliminary drawings with corrections in black, which the sculptors of the relief and inscriptions followed, progressing from bottom to top. The final stage was the painting. The theme of the scene depicted is taken from the fourth hour of the "Book of Gates."

138 In the company of the Gods
Western Thebes, Valley of the Kings, tomb of Thutmosis IV (KV 43); Eighteenth Dynasty, ca. 1390 BC.
The decoration for the anteroom to the burial chamber included images of the deities presenting the sign of life to the king. The tomb of Thutmosis IV marks the first time this theme occurs. Hathor, protective goddess of the necropolis, the jackal-headed Anubis, and finally Osiris, mummiformed god of the dead, all stand opposite the ruler against the "golden" background of the wall.

inundation, day 17; the vizier Neferrenpet came to Thebes, accompanied by the officials, Hori and Amunkha … they went into the Valley of the Kings, in order to find a place for the construction of the tomb of Ramesses IV." In the Eighteenth Dynasty every king appointed an official whom he trusted personally to be the building manager for the tomb. In the Ramesside Period, by contrast, this office was held by the vizier, to whom the supervision and guidance of the work process was entrusted and who was responsible for it.

The administration of course possessed precise documentation (on papyrus) on the already existing tombs in the valley, and this was consulted in order to avoid infringing on other sepulchers, an event that did indeed happen in the case of the tomb of Ramesses III. Throughout the entire New Kingdom the work itself was executed by the craftsmen and artists from Deir el-Medineh. These individuals lived with their families in the settlement built to the south of the necropolis; they were allowed to build their own tombs in its immediate vicinity. In ten-day shifts the workers came in teams of 40–60 men over the mountain tracks to the Valley of the Kings. Under the leadership of the foreman the pharaoh's team was split into two groups, the "left" and the "right" side. The work commenced with pure quarrying, a rapid process in the soft Theban limestone. There would only be difficulties when they struck large outcrops of flint or crumbly deposits of stone. The resulting rubble was removed from the tomb with baskets. Subsequently the walls were smoothed by means of chisels, and if necessary repaired with plaster filling. After completion of the basic work, preliminary drawings were applied in several stages as preparation for the final decoration. The painting of the walls formed the final stage of the operation.

Although most kings of the New Kingdom had a sufficiently long reign at their disposal to complete their tombs, the majority of the tombs nevertheless show incomplete sections. In the case of Horemheb's tomb one almost has the impression that the workers stopped work from one minute to the next. After the ruler's death the priority lay on completion of the tomb decoration, which could be done during the seventy days of the embalming ritual. The work in the tomb was thus restricted to the most essential elements.

139 The twelfth hour of the Amduat
Western Thebes, Valley of the Kings, tomb of Thutmosis III (KV 34), coffin chamber; Eighteenth Dynasty, ca. 1450 BC.
In the final, twelfth night hour, the figure of the sun god (in the small barque) narrows down to form an enormous snake 120 cubits (ca. 62 meters) long, and then turns into a scarab in the morning sky, starting the course of another day. The upper end of the wall is traditionally completed by the cycle of a sky hieroglyph decorated with stars, a colored band, and a kheker frieze (stylized bundle of reeds).

The Decoration Program

Although during the Eighteenth Dynasty the decoration included only the walls of the burial chamber and columns, the anteroom, and the shaft area, the situation changed significantly in the Ramesside Period with the decoration of the entire tomb with pictures and texts. The method of execution changed from pure painting to raised and then to sunk relief (Nineteenth/Twentieth Dynasties). The complex significance of the magnificent pictures in the New Kingdom royal tombs have become comprehensible only after the most intensive research. At

140 The king sacrifices to the goddess Isis
Western Thebes, Valley of the Kings, tomb of Horemheb (KV 57); Eighteenth Dynasty, ca. 1300 BC.
Dressed in a royal headdress and short loincloth, Horemheb stands before the goddess Isis and hands her two containers with wine. Thanks to their almost complete state of preservation and high quality, these murals in the tomb of Horemheb are among the most exquisite products of two-dimensional art of the New Kingdom.

world") undertook the attempt at a complete description of the underworld in words and pictures.

In the central register of the individual depictions of the hours, the barque of the sun god moves through the twelve night hours with his accompanying retinue on a kind of antithetical Nile, where continued travel from one hour to the next is only possible by the utterance of a password by the goddess Isis, the "magical one." While the action itself is always shown with respect to the sun god, the outer areas show the inhabitants of the underworld who are brought to life by the god as he passes through. Even physical dangers have to be overcome. Thus Apophis, the enemy of the gods, lies in wait on a sandbank in the shape of a gigantic snake who tries to scoop the water of the underworld river away from the barque and prevent it from advancing. The termination of the sun's cycle would be tantamount to the end of the world. Consequently Apophis is conquered by Re, and his body is portrayed cut into pieces by knives.

It is only in the tomb of Horemheb, the last king of the Eighteenth Dynasty, that an additional book of the underworld, the so-called Book of Gates, was incorporated into the scheme of decoration. Like the Amduat it also portrays the night journey of the solar barque. The separation of the individual hours is not achieved by the use of a longer block of text, as in the Amduat, but by the depiction of the fortified gates that give the book its name.

Particularly noteworthy among the books of the underworld from the later years of the Ramesside age is the Book of Caverns. Here the division into twelve is abandoned and replaced by the frequent reproduction of the sun's disk. The sequence of pictures is typically interrupted by scenes such as the image of Nut, and the accompanying texts contain many litanies.

Parallel to the idea of the sun god's journey through the underworld is the concept of the solar cycle running its course within the body of Nut, the goddess of the sky. While this heavenly sphere is manifested in the royal rock-cut tombs of the Eighteenth Dynasty by a flat ceiling decorated with stars, the Nineteenth Dynasty (after the reign of Seti I) employed a vaulted ceiling with an "astronomical map" in the burial chamber.

In the ensuing Twentieth Dynasty this decoration is replaced by the books of the heavens, which use the long outstretched figure of Nut as their central pictorial motif. The relationship between the king and

At the beginning of the twentieth century the great Egyptologist Adolf Erman still considered the images to be "muddled fantasies" and the "flights of fancy of individual people."

It is particularly the Amduat, the oldest and, until the Amarna Period, the only book of the underworld used, that provides a deep insight into the concept of the nightly journey of the sun god through the realms of the underworld. It was of primary importance that the occupant of the tomb participated in this journey and, like the deity, regenerated himself in an eternal cycle.

Under the title "The Writings of the Hidden Chamber," the appropriate version was initially painted on the walls of the burial chamber and was thus displayed in the immediate proximity of the deceased king. The cursive form of hieroglyphs and figures on an ochre-colored background thereby translates the papyrus draft onto the larger scale of the wall surfaces. Around 1500 BC and in line with the earlier beliefs, the Amduat (which means: "that which is in the under-

142 (opposite) The king between the "souls of Pe and Nekhen"
Western Thebes, Valley of the Kings, Tomb of Ramesses I, founder of the Nineteenth Dynasty, ca. 1290 BC.
The short reign of Ramesses I, who founded the Nineteenth Dynasty, prevented the construction of a tomb of normal size; it ultimately consisted of only the burial chamber. This picture shows the ruler kneeling in a gesture of jubilation between the animal-headed figures of the "souls of Pe and Nekhen," powerful spirits that represent the ancient mythical tradition of royalty in the duality of Upper and Lower Egypt. The painting style reveals a close relationship with the murals in the tomb of Horemheb.

143 (overleaf) The course of the sun
Western Thebes, Valley of the Kings, tomb of Queen Tausret (KV 14); Nineteenth Dynasty, ca. 1190 BC.
Above the large winged form of the sun god with his ram's head are additional manifestations of Re as a child, a beetle, and the sun, moved by two pairs of arms reaching down and flanked by the deceased with their *ba* souls. The two powerful triangles symbolize darkness and the waters through which the sun travels on its nightly journey. The representation forms the final picture of the "Book of Caverns" and is to be found on the right-hand short side of the burial chamber.

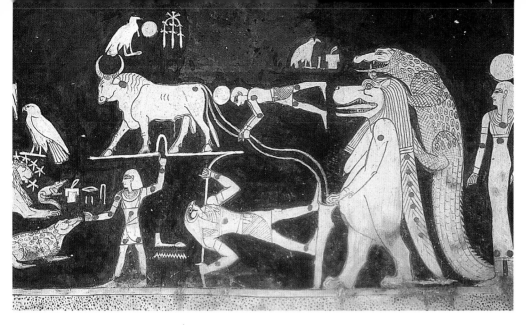

141 Ceiling images of the burial chamber of Seti I (detail)
Western Thebes, Valley of the Kings, tomb of Seti I (KV 17); Nineteenth Dynasty, ca. 1280 BC.
Above the mummy of the deceased king in his coffin appears the magnificent vaulted ceiling of the monumental burial chamber with its famous "astronomical ceiling." The extensive picture includes lists of stars, decan stars and constellations, such as Orion, Sirius, and the Big Dipper (Taurus). In this manner the ruler could ascend directly into the sky as a *ba* soul in the form of a bird.

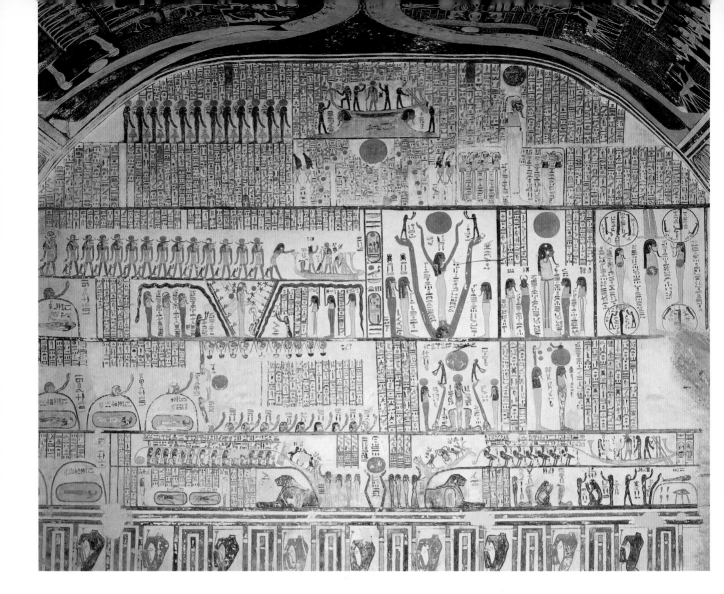

144 Raising of the sun's disk
Western Thebes, Valley of the Kings, Tomb of
Ramesses VI (KV 9); Nineteenth Dynasty, ca.
1135 BC.
The underworld books of the Ramesside
Period, such as the "Book of the Earth" in the
burial chamber of Ramesses VI, emphasize
the role of the earth gods (for example
Tatenen, Geb) in the night journey of the sun.
In this scene the oversized arms of Nun, the
personification of the ancient waters, lift up
the sun's disk.

the most important underworld deities is documented in the scenes on
the pillars of the burial chamber or its anterooms. The range of pictures
is continually extended throughout the New Kingdom.

The Royal Sarcophagi

In terms of dimensions the stone sarcophagi of the New Kingdom
pharaohs follow the general development of the tombs themselves.
While those of the early Eighteenth Dynasty still show relatively
modest proportions, it is during the reign of Amenophis III that the
beginnings of a monumentalization are seen that culminates in the
massive sarcophagi of the Ramesside Period (Nineteenth/Twentieth
Dynasties) weighing up to several tons.

The external form often initially resembles a cartouche (oval
enclosing the king's name), as does the design of the burial chambers
until the reign of Thutmosis III. The Amarna Period brings a
change in design that was in essence retained by the succeeding kings
Tutankhamun, Ay and Horemheb. The figures of the protective
goddesses Isis, Nephthys, Selket, and Neith now appear on the four
outer corners of the sarcophagus, while the base and edges are treated
separately.

From the reign of Seti I, the sarcophagi of the Ramesside Period
reproduced the semi-sculptured figure of the Osiris king on the lid,
almost always accompanied by the goddesses Isis and Nephthys. Moreover, it became customary to use several stone sarcophagi, each fitting
into the next.

The range of pictures and accompanying texts in the Eighteenth
Dynasty was subject to a clearly structured basic scheme that placed
the late pharaoh in the protection of four canopic gods, the
embalming god Anubis, and the four goddesses from the Osiride
circle. Canonized in the same way, Nut, the sky goddess, appears
in the interior of the sarcophagi. By contrast, the Ramesside
sarcophagi are dominated by the widespread use of the books of the
underworld.

145 Sarcophagus of Thutmosis I
Western Thebes, Valley of the Kings, tomb of Hatshepsut (KV 20); Eighteenth Dynasty, ca. 1470 BC; sandstone; L. 225 cm, W. 82 cm; Boston, Museum of Fine Arts, Gift of Theodore M. Davis, 04.278.
The royal sarcophagi of the early Eighteenth Dynasty were all worked from sandstone, since there was a perceived connection between the cult of the sun and this material, which was quarried near Heliopolis, city of the sun. The decoration program was also redesigned at this period. The two long sides show the four sons of Horus in pairs (protective gods of the canopic jars) and the god Anubis. On the short sides appear the images of the protective goddesses Isis (foot end) and Nephthys (head end). The upper side of the lid is decorated with a royal cartouche. This sarcophagus was initially designed for Hatshepsut after her ascension to the throne. On the occasion of the transfer of her father's mummy it was inscribed afresh for the latter and removed to the queen's tomb.

146 Sarcophagus of Horemheb
Western Thebes, Valley of the Kings, tomb of Horemheb (KV 57); Eighteenth Dynasty, ca. 1300 BC; painted red granite; L. 272 cm, W. 115 cm.
It had presumably become customary since the time of Amenophis III to reproduce the protective goddesses Isis, Nephthys, Selket, and Neith with outstretched wings in relief on the corners of the royal sarcophagi. The vaulted lid had split already in ancient times and was carefully repaired with the aid of wedges, so-called "swallowtails."

147 Sarcophagus of Thutmosis IV
Western Thebes, Valley of the Kings, tomb of Thutmosis IV (KV 43); Eighteenth Dynasty, ca. 1390 BC; painted sandstone; L. 300 cm, W. 160 cm.
In the center of the undecorated tomb chamber the king's monumental sarcophagus still stands, its scale large enough to hold several inner sarcophagi. The number of texts has been increased, and the images of protective deities follow the basic Thutmosid pattern. The painting has been remarkably well preserved in its restricted range of colors that combine harmoniously with the basic tone of the sandstone.

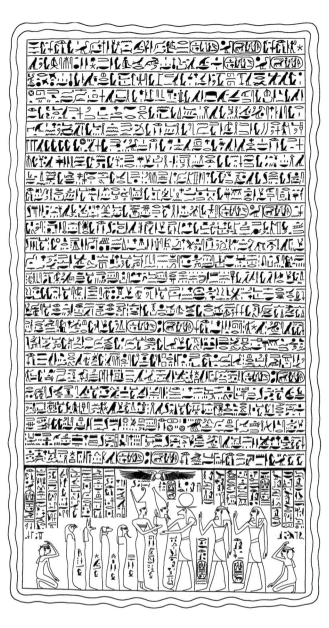

148 Face from the sarcophagus of Ramesses VI
Western Thebes, Valley of the Kings, tomb of
Ramesses VI (KV 9); Twentieth Dynasty,
ca. 1135 BC; green conglomerate; H. 83.8 cm;
London, The British Museum, EA 140.

The most beautiful fragment to have been
recovered from the badly damaged stone
sarcophagus of Ramesses VI was the mask of
the ruler from his anthropoid inner
sarcophagus.

*149 Inscription from the lid of the outer
sarcophagus of Merenptah*
Western Thebes, Valley of the Kings, tomb of
Merenptah (KV 8); Nineteenth Dynasty, ca.
1205 BC; red granite; L. 410 cm, W. 220 cm.
Merenptah's sarcophagus arrangement consisted of a total of four individual parts,
nesting one within the other. While the three
outer sarcophagi were worked from red
granite, calcite alabaster was used for the
inner anthropoid sarcophagus. The heavy lid
of the outer sarcophagus, weighing several

tons, is completely covered by an otherwise
unknown text and accompanying images.
The long inscription contains a hymn of the
goddess Neith to the dead king. The picture
shows him in the form of Osiris, embraced by
the sun god Re (right) and Neith, greeted by
the gods of creation Shu and Geb (following
on the right). They are joined by the four
canopic gods (left) while Isis and Nephthys
complete the scene on both outer ends as
wailing mourners.

150 Lid of the second coffin of Merenptah
Western Thebes, Valley of the Kings, tomb of
Merenptah (KV 8); Nineteenth Dynasty, ca.
1205 BC; red granite; L. 345 cm, W. 150 cm.
Built to resemble a king's cartouche in its
basic form, the lid bears the almost three-

dimensional figure of the deceased Osiris-
king. The hands folded over the breast hold
the royal insignia of the crook and flail. The
exhaustive texts and pictures provide extracts
from the underworld books of the Amduat
and the "Book of Gates."

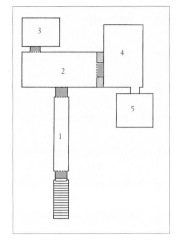

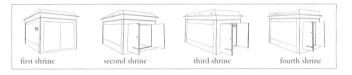

151 The seal of Theban necropolis
After the burial of the king, both the main entrance and the passageways to the side and burial chambers were blocked with layers of stone. These were then smoothed over with plaster stucco onto which the official seal of the necropolis administration was stamped, probably with the aid of a wooden seal. The example illustrated here shows the nine traditional enemies of Egypt bound below the figure of the recumbent Anubis and the king's name ring (cartouche).

152 Plan of the tomb of Tutankhamun
Western Thebes, Valley of the Kings (KV 62); Eighteenth Dynasty, ca. 1325 BC. The king's early and unexpected death was almost certainly the reason that only an abbreviated sort of emergency tomb with four small rooms could be prepared for him.
1 entrance corridor
2 antechamber
3 side chamber
4 burial chamber
5 treasure chamber

Even the choice of working materials reveals differing priorities. Initially (until Thutmosis IV), sandstone was used, but by the Nineteenth and Twentieth Dynasties it was only granite or other types of hard stones. Calcite alabaster appears to be the standard material for the inner sarcophagus of the deceased ruler, at least for the early Nineteenth Dynasty. Only the tomb of Tutankhamun gives us an idea of the original splendor of the gilded sarcophagi with their inlay work. It cannot, however, be assumed that all the kings of the New Kingdom were provided with a final sarcophagus made of pure gold.

Tutankhamun the Golden Pharaoh

On November 4, 1922 the workmen of the English archaeologist Howard Carter hit upon the first steps of the entrance to the tomb of Tutankhamun. At the time Carter surely could not have known that he had succeeded in unearthing the most sensational find in archaeological history.

Yet the discovery was no accident, but the result of a well-planned search. In 1914 Lord Carnarvon, who was financing the undertaking, had taken over the concession in the Valley of the Kings, but it was not until 1917 that actual excavations began. After years of failures and in the face of considerable costs Carnarvon had wanted to end his commitment to the Valley in 1921. However, Carter's offer to finance the new campaign from his own pocket should they fail again so impressed him that he consented to a last attempt. Carter did indeed possess enough indications as to the existence of the tomb of Tutankhamun, a ruler in the Eighteenth Dynasty whom history had obscured until then. That this of all tombs was the only royal one to escape the ancient tomb robbers with a virtually intact decoration was due to a very fortunate circumstance. The tomb of Ramesses VI (Twentieth

153 View into the antechamber of Tutankhamun's tomb during excavation
Western Thebes, Valley of the Kings (KV 62); Eighteenth Dynasty, ca. 1325 BC.
When Carter entered the antechamber he was confronted with an overwhelming sight, albeit a confusing one. Against the rear wall standing

next to each other were three ritual beds shaped in the form of animals. Over and below them were furnishings, boxes, and chests. Piled up opposite were the individual dismantled parts of the royal chariots. They were in such disarray that even the slightest contact with them threatened their total collapse.

| first shrine | second shrine | third shrine | fourth shrine |

154 The shrines of Tutankhamun (diagram)
Four gilded wooden shrines fitted one into another and almost completely filled the burial chamber. Before the actual burial the individual parts therefore had to be set up in the burial chamber in the right order.

Although they were marked, Carter discovered that the original workers had made many mistakes in putting the shrines together. Thus all the shrine doors, for example, pointed in the wrong compass direction.

Dynasty) lay directly above that of Tutankhamun, and when the former was dug out, the entrance to the latter was buried under tons of rubble and thus saved from any further attempts at disturbance. Even Carter had once stopped his digging at this spot in order not to prevent tourists from visiting the Ramesside tomb.

Tutankhamun's early and unexpected death after barely ten years of rule meant that no proper tomb had been prepared for him. The burial therefore took place in a small, fairly shallow-lying sepulcher. A small flight of steps leads directly into the corridor, which ends in the antechamber and which was originally filled with stones. When Carter and Carnarvon stood in front of the still walled-up corridor they could

156/157 *Outer shrine of Tutankhamun (details)*
Western Thebes, Valley of the Kings, tomb of Tutankhamun (KV 62); Eighteenth Dynasty, ca. 1325 BC; gilded wood, stucco; H. 275 cm, L. 508 cm, W. 328 cm; Cairo, Egyptian Museum, JE 62218.
The exterior of the first shrine is decorated in an alternating sequence arranged in pairs: the tyet signs (knot amulet of Isis) and djed pillars (cult symbol of Osiris). The background is inlaid with blue faience. Only the two door panels contain a small image area, representing the crouching figure of Osiris.

scarcely contain themselves with anticipation. Carter first carefully removed a few stones and then used a candle to illuminate the opening he had created. Lord Carnarvon's impatient question as to whether Carter could see anything was answered with the now-legendary words, "Yes, wonderful things." In the course of the continuing excavations and with the valuable support of the scientific staff of the Metropolitan Museum of New York, Carter was able to bring to the surface nearly 5,000 individual objects of breathtaking and unparalleled beauty. Among these were the shrines and sarcophagi, the golden mask of the youthful king, his throne chair, figures of deities and kings, and exquisite jewelry, all of it now famous throughout the world. All had been piled up together in the woefully cramped tomb. There was only one disappointment amid all this success. Carter found no written documents, no papyri. Furthermore he was able to establish that tomb robbers had penetrated the tomb on two occasions, primarily searching for the valuable anointing oils and jewelry. The thieves were probably caught, or at all events disturbed, as they had had to flee, and the tomb was subsequently resealed. In the heat of events, however, the priesthood did not take

much trouble to restore the original order. In particular, the small pieces of jewelry had simply been thrown back at random into the boxes.

The planned scientific analysis of the find was denied to Carter, for he died in 1939, an isolated and lonely figure, although not from the "curse of the Pharaohs." Research on the tomb treasure continued nevertheless. There are still many questions awaiting satisfactory answers. The gleam of the gold should, however, not hide the fact that the significance of the find was primarily that of its unique state of completeness. Projections of the quantities of gold in the tombs of other rulers of the New Kingdom who ruled for far longer than Tutankhamun have no value whatsoever. The question as to the cause of death of the approximately eighteen-year-old Tutankhamun also remains a matter of speculation. Repeated investigations of his mummy have not been able to establish any illness or other convincing proof of a violent end.

The Shrines

In the burial chamber a total of four shrines, each without a base, enclosed the actual sarcophagus, which in turn contained the inner coffins of the king. Their symbolic function is determined by the shape of the roofs, which are derived from various types of shrines. While the slanted double vaulting of the first shrine resembles a *sed* festival pavilion, the other shrines are modeled on Egyptian chapel types, the

155 *(opposite) Door panels of the second shrine*
Western Thebes, Valley of the Kings, tomb of Tutankhamun (KV 62); Eighteenth Dynasty, ca. 1325 BC; gilded wood stucco; overall measurements: H. 225 cm, L. 375 cm, W. 235 cm; Cairo, Egyptian Museum, JE 62368.

Executed in hollow relief, the scene on the left door portrays the ruler before Osiris, god of the dead. Tutankhamun wears the headdress with the double crown, a pleated kilt down to his calves with a sash, and an attached uraeus cobra. Behind him stands the goddess Isis, wife of Osiris.

158 The first sarcophagus
Western Thebes, Valley of the Kings, tomb of Tutankhamun (KV 62); Eighteenth Dynasty, ca. 1325 BC; gilded and inlaid wood; L. 224 cm.
The outer coffin with the remains of the royal mummy is still in the sarcophagus and is a chief attraction for visitors to the Valley of the Kings. The dead god-king holds his crook and flail in his hands. When the tomb was discovered, a small wreath of flowers from the funeral ceremony was still to be found around the symbols of power on his forehead, the Nekhbet vulture and uraeus cobra.

159 The middle coffin
Western Thebes, Valley of the Kings, tomb of Tutankhamun (KV 62); Eighteenth Dynasty, ca. 1325 BC; gilded and inlaid wood; L. 204 cm; Cairo, Egyptian Museum, JE 60670.
The king wears the classic royal headdress and the pleated divine beard. The feather pattern on the body of the coffin particularly required elaborate and painstaking work. In a kind of cloisonné technique the individual pieces were cut from colored glass and set into gold mountings. The cost in time alone for the production of this coffin is impossible to estimate.

160 The mummy with the golden mask of Tutankhamun
Western Thebes, Valley of the Kings, tomb of Tutankhamun (KV 62); Eighteenth Dynasty, ca. 1325 BC.
Because of the extravagant use of anointing oils that over time chemically charred the corpse, the mummy of Tutankhamun was in a very poor state compared to other mummies that had been torn from their coffins by tomb robbers soon after burial. Carter was able to rescue nearly 150 amulets, pieces of jewelry and other items of the king between the bandages of the mummy.

161 The sarcophagus
Western Thebes, Valley of the Kings, tomb of Tutankhamun (KV 62); Eighteenth Dynasty, ca. 1325 BC; painted sandstone; L. 275 cm, W. 147 cm.
The wonderful stone sarcophagus with the four winged protective goddesses on its corners is sealed off above by a hollow-molded sill. The lid is made of red granite but was painted over yellow and thus matched the color of the lower part. There appears to have been an accident during the transportation of the lid, since it is broken in two pieces. It was nevertheless used, despite its defective state of repair.

162/163 *The gold sarcophagus*
Western Thebes, Valley of the Kings,
tomb of Tutankhamun
(KV 62); Eighteenth Dynasty, ca.
1325 BC; gold with inlays; L. 188 cm;
Cairo, Egyptian Museum,
JE 60671.
A miracle of the goldsmith's art, the
innermost coffin is made of solid
gold with a total weight of 110.4 kg.
The design is generally similar to
that of the middle coffin and the
inscriptions are engraved with the
utmost delicacy of draftsmanship.
The coffin's entire beauty only
became apparent when Carter
removed a layer of the dried
anointing oils, generous quantities
of which had been poured over the
coffin by the priests at the funeral.

following two on an Upper Egyptian type, and the fourth and final one
on a Lower Egyptian type. Made of cedar wood planks covered with a
layer of gilded stucco serving as base for the decoration, all the shrines
have double doors at their eastern end, which are sealed by means of
three ebony bolts running in large copper housings. It was only the
sight of the unbroken seal on the door of the second shrine that finally
convinced Carter he would be the first human being for over 3,000
years to see the undamaged body of Tutankhamun.

In addition to images and inscriptions on the shrines taken from
the Amduat and spells from the Book of the Dead, there are also
demons from the underworld, protective deities, and the ruler in the
presence of the most important netherworld gods. The complete
scheme of decoration offers a meaningful extension to the paintings on
the burial chamber wall, which due to lack of space were only able to
represent their scenes in an abridged and fragmentary form.

The dismantling of the shrines, an essential but painstaking task,
took over eighty-four days, and was a brilliant feat of skill and patience.
Before transportation to Cairo, the crumbly stucco layer first had to be
secured by means of paraffin wax. Unfortunately, Carter did have to
bear one loss, although through no fault of his own. In the space
between the first and second shrines there was a wooden framework
that supported a huge, linen cloth or pall (5.5 m x 4.4 m), covered with
gilded bronze rosettes sewn onto the cloth. The archaeologists were
particularly concerned about this fragile piece. During the period when
Carter was in dispute with the Egyptian authorities, work was often
halted, and the cloth suffered irreparable damage from unchecked
exposure to the open air. After his return Carter commented to the official representative on the pitiful state of the cloth, "Well, it is your cloth,
not mine, but it is the only one in the world."

The Coffin Assemblage

Before the discovery of the tomb of Tutankhamun, the opulence of the
sarcophagi associated with such a royal burial was quite inconceivable.
The coffins found in the concealed chambers of the royal mummies at
Deir el-Bahari in 1881 had been robbed of all their precious metals and

164/165 The golden mask
Western Thebes, Valley of the Kings, tomb of Tutankhamun (KV 62); Eighteenth Dynasty, ca. 1325 BC; gold with inlays; H. 54 cm; Cairo, Egyptian Museum, JE 60672.
The famous mummy mask of the youthful pharaoh was beaten from thick gold plate and the details were created in inlaid colored glass paste and various decorative stones (lapis lazuli, obsidian, quartz, feldspar). "Gold is the flesh of the gods" – surely no other Egyptian work of art illustrates this better than the mask of Tutankhamun. While the front breast plate exhibits a banded collar with falcon head clasps, the rear bears a text, relating individual parts of the face to specific Egyptian deities.

were thus only a pale shadow of what the world was to see later. A total of three anthropoid coffins for Tutankhamun fitted precisely one into another and enclosed the mummy of the dead pharaoh with his gold mask. He joined the gods as the Osiris king, and the crook and flail insignia together with representations of the goddesses Nekhbet (the vulture of Upper Egypt) and Wadjet (the serpent of Lower Egypt), attached to his brow all embodied his rank as ruler in both this world and the next. The inner coffin demonstrates particularly impressively the huge investment expended in material and labor in the preparation of the pharaohs' tombs of this period.

After Carter had lifted the lid of the sarcophagus in 1924, he made an interesting observation. On the base of the sarcophagus were gilded wooden chips strewn about. They must have been chipped away from the upper foot end of the outermost coffin, since this spot had to be painted with black bitumen resin. It was only during interment that the ancient artisans realized that the assemblage of coffins did not fit precisely into the sarcophagus, and resorted to the above, albeit very crude, solution to the problem. A pure design mistake? It seems hardly likely when one considers the otherwise great precision of their work.

It becomes clearer when one realizes that many of the very famous Tutankhamun objects were not produced specifically for his tomb, but were incorporated into the tomb treasure of the young king after the abandonment of the interment of Akhenaten and Smenkhkare, his immediate predecessors. Even in the inner lower part of the golden coffin with its inscriptions (citations from the Book of the Dead), a square piece had been cut out in the area of the head before the lid could be closed over the mummy with the golden mask.

The Canopic Shrine

In addition to the sarcophagus with its shrines, the canopic chest was an essential part of the basic furnishings of every New Kingdom royal tomb, since the intact state of the entrails was absolutely vital to the completeness of the body of the mummy. At the beginning of the Eighteenth Dynasty it was still a simple box made of sandstone in which the four individual jars were placed. The canopic chest was then set up directly in the burial chamber next to the sarcophagus. Since the

166 The goddess Selket
Western Thebes, Valley of the Kings, tomb of Tutankhamun (KV 62); Eighteenth Dynasty, ca. 1325 BC; gilded wood; H. 90 cm; Cairo, Egyptian Museum, JE 60686.
The finely modeled figures of the protective goddesses were executed identically in terms of external appearance (long pleated costume and bag wig), and can only be distinguished from each other by the emblems over their heads. In the case of the goddess Selket it is the strongly stylized form of a scorpion.

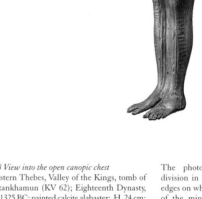

167 The canopic shrine
Western Thebes, Valley of the Kings, tomb of Tutankhamun (KV 62); Eighteenth Dynasty, ca. 1325 BC; gold with gilded stucco; H. 198 cm; Cairo, Egyptian Museum, JE 60686.
Indispensable, and as finely worked as the shrine and coffin assemblage for the king's mummy, the canopic shrine was designed for the separate burial of the vital organs. Above a sledge-like structure is an external baldachin with two uraeus friezes, one part-way up the structure and another around its crown. At the sides the shrine is surrounded by the four protective goddesses Isis, Nephthys, Selket, and Neith with their arms outstretched. The style of these figures is still indebted to the artistic heritage of Amarna. The canopic shrine formed the centerpiece of the so-called treasury.

168 View into the open canopic chest
Western Thebes, Valley of the Kings, tomb of Tutankhamun (KV 62); Eighteenth Dynasty, ca. 1325 BC; painted calcite alabaster; H. 24 cm; Cairo, Egyptian Museum, JE 60687.
The photograph shows the rectangular division in the interior of the chest and the edges on which the lid rested. Only the heads of the miniature coffins placed inside are visible from this angle.

169 Lid of the canopic chest
Western Thebes, Valley of the Kings, tomb of Tutankhamun (KV 62); Eighteenth Dynasty, ca. 1325 BC; painted calcite alabaster; H. 24 cm; Cairo, Egyptian Museum, JE 60687.
The interior of the canopic chest has four cylindrical cavities that were closed individually with lids in the form of a portrait of the king's head from the shoulders upwards. The king's features are emphasized by economically but skillfully painting them onto the translucent, high-quality material.

170/171 The canopic chest
Western Thebes, Valley of the Kings, tomb of Tutankhamun (KV 62); Eighteenth Dynasty, ca. 1325 BC painted calcite-alabaster; H. 85.5 cm; Cairo, Egyptian Museum, JE 60687.
Within the shrine the actual canopic chest stood on another gilded wooden sledge and was covered with a large pall or cloth. Attached once again to its corners are the quartet of the protective goddesses. The accompanying inscription refers both to these goddesses and to the four canopic gods Amset, Hapi, Duamutef, and Qebehsenuf, who were responsible for protecting the royal organs.

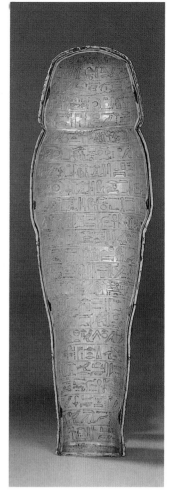

172–174 The coffin for the organs
Western Thebes, Valley of the Kings, tomb of Tutankhamun (KV 62); Eighteenth Dynasty, ca. 1325 BC; gold with inlay; H. 39.5 cm, W. 11.5 cm; Cairo, Egyptian Museum, JE 60691.
The deceased king's vital organs were packed in four miniature coffins decorated in gold repoussé and placed in the canopic chest. Their outer design resembles Tutankhamun's large middle coffin, the inlays consisting of glass paste, obsidian, and carnelian. On the interior surfaces are citations from the Book of the Dead.

175 The ba bird
Western Thebes, Valley of the Kings, tomb of Tutankhamun (KV 62); Eighteenth Dynasty, ca. 1325 BC; gold with inlay; H. 12.5 cm, W.33 cm; Cairo, Egyptian Museum, JE 61903.
This important amulet in the form of a royal *ba* bird lay directly on the linen bandages of the mummy. With outstretched wings and the shen rings in the claws of each foot, this amulet combines a falcon's body with the head of the ruler. According to ancient Egyptian concepts, the *ba* was an aspect of human existence. This *ba* soul could leave the tomb in the form of a bird, take up contact with the world of the living and return to the mummy.

176 Scarab pendant
Western Thebes, Valley of the Kings, tomb of Tutankhamun (KV 62); Eighteenth Dynasty, ca. 1325 BC; gold with inlays; H. 9 cm, W. 10.5 cm; Cairo, Egyptian Museum, JE 61886.
This elegant piece of jewelry was surely worn by Tutankhamun during his lifetime. It shows the winged scarab as representing the morning sun god Khepri. Its significance goes far deeper, however, for the combined symbols of the sun disk, the beetle, and the three lines above a basket form the throne name of the king – Nebkheperure – and thus visibly integrate his person into the cyclical course of the sun.

177/178 Tutankhamun's ivory chest
Western Thebes, Valley of the Kings, tomb of Tutankhamun (KV 62); Eighteenth Dynasty, ca. 1325 BC; wood, ivory, and bronze; H. 48.5 cm, L. 72 cm, W. 53 cm; Cairo, Egyptian Museum, JE 61477.
The precious chest consists of wood veneer with ivory and has a domed lid. On the sides are hunting scenes in the midst of vegetation, but it is the picture on the lid that deserves special attention, since its style so closely resembles the art of Amarna that the entire chest must have been made in Tutankhamun's early years, when the king still resided at Akhenaten and was called Tutankhaten.
In a casual pose the child pharaoh leans on a long staff and receives two large bouquets of papyrus, lotus flowers, and poppy capsules from Queen Ankhesenamun. Fascinated by its artistic perfection, Carter labeled this piece of carving in colored ivory as an "unsigned picture of a great master."

These paintings, executed in minute detail, undoubtedly belong to the supreme achievements of ancient Egyptian art. The rectangular chest has four low post-like feet and a domed lid. Originally it was used to keep the royal sandals, but during his investigation of the contents Carter also found clothes, jewelry, and a partially gilded headrest. The "disorder" came about because the priests did not take the trouble to restore the original order when they cleared up after the brief raid by the tomb robbers. Although the pictures in their symmetrical arrangement of the two war and hunting scenes do integrate the ruler into the action itself, this is not a depiction of real events. Rather it reveals the king as triumphing over chaos, which is symbolized on the one hand by the dead animals of the desert and on the other by the traditional enemies of Egypt, the Syrians in the north and the Nubians in the south.

Surrounded by a pattern of rosettes and other ornamental moldings, the fictitious picture on the south side of the chest shows Tutankhamun's battle against the Nubians, who, on the evidence of the chaos of dead bodies and fleeing soldiers, are clearly already defeated. By contrast there is clarity and order in the Egyptian army with the pharaoh at the head in his chariot, portrayed in exaggerated dimensions and dominating the entire field of view.

reign of Amenophis II the material of choice was increasingly calcite alabaster, which subsequently became obligatory. The Twentieth Dynasty on the other hand appears to have preferred sets of monumental canopic jars without any chests.

The canopic assemblage from the treasure of Tutankhamun consists of an outer baldachin, the gilded shrine on a sledge surrounded by the figures of the four protective goddesses and the canopic chest itself with golden miniature coffins under the portrait heads inside. Whether such complex versions were also produced for succeeding rulers must remain an open question, given the current state of archaeological finds.

The images and inscriptions of all the individual elements are dedicated to the protection of the entrails. An example is the short recitation of the goddess Isis: "Words, spoken by Isis: 'My arms conceal what is in me. I protect Amset (canopic god), who is in me, the Amset of the Osiris king Tutankhamun, the justified one.'" There is much to be said for the theory that this unique assemblage for the royal canopic jars was not originally made for Tutankhamun's burial, but for one of his immediate predecessors, Smenkhkare. Traces of the latter's erased cartouches, or name rings, can be found on all four small golden coffins, and even the facial features of the lid closures do not reflect those of the youthful king.

The Cache of Royal Mummies

Around 1875 increasing quantities of objects such as shabtis or papyri from the Book of the Dead began to turn up in local and then European art circles. The Egyptian authorities became vigilant and conducted intensive inquiries into the origins of these very interesting objects. The trail eventually led to the Abd el-Rassul family in Thebes, whose activities as royal tomb robbers were well known. Despite brutal interrogation methods, no confessions could be wrung from the primary suspects, and they had to be released from detention.

It was not until 1881 that Mohammed Ahmed Abd el-Rassul broke the silence and revealed the long-kept secret. He led Emil Brugsch, representative of the director general of the antiquities administration, to the concealed entrance of a tomb, immediately to the south of the valley of Deir el-Bahari. A vertical shaft led 12 m down to a 70-m-long passageway that in turn ended in a final chamber. In the light of the burning torches Brugsch was overwhelmed by what he saw. Distributed around the tomb lay dozens of coffins with the mummies of the New Kingdom's greatest rulers, among them such illustrious names as Thutmosis III and Ramesses II, as well as those of the high priests of the Twenty-first Dynasty and their relatives. Since the knowledge of such a huge "treasure" would spread like wildfire

180/181 The throne of Tutankhamun
Western Thebes, Valley of the Kings, tomb of Tutankhamun (KV 62); Eighteenth Dynasty, ca. 1325 BC; wood, gold and silver sheet, opaque glass, and semi-precious stones; H. 102 cm, W. 54 cm, D. 60 cm; Cairo, Egyptian Museum, JE 62028.

Surely the most beautiful and best-known piece of furniture from the tomb treasure of the young god-king is his throne chair, which was worked in the traditional form of a wildcat throne, with lions' heads as the decoration on the front corners. Between the legs, the braces, which have now largely broken away, represented the emblem of the "Unification of the Two Lands." The armrests are designed in the form of winged serpents, each of which bears a double crown. Apart from its purely material and artistic value, the throne also has an historic signifi-

cance as the cartouches of the ruler and his wife on the back still show their early name forms Tutankhaten and Ankhesenpaaten. This is an indication that this splendid piece of furniture originates from the first year of the king's rule when he was still living in Amarna. The scene on the back, situated beneath the shining sun disk, symbol of the god Aten, plays a role in its dating. A king – usually recognized as Tutankhamun because of the inscription – is sitting here in a casual manner on a comfortable chair, dressed in a long pleated kilt and broad collar and a composite crown of many parts. The queen stands before him, and with her right hand straightens her husband's collar, while in her left hand she holds an ointment container. She herself wears an ankle-length gown with sashes, a broad collar, and a tall plumed crown over the wig with its uraeus frieze.

Behind the couple is another collar on a table decorated with festoons of flowers.

The breathtaking virtuosity of the artist in the execution of this scene reveals itself in the use of various materials such as silver and gold sheet, colored opaque glass, faience, and semi-precious stones. For the design of the royal kilt alone, nearly 500 minute splinters of material were used, all of which had to be cut with precision to the millimeter.

Apart from its significance as a unique piece of furniture, the throne – like so many other objects from the tomb treasure – provides an opportunity to check its original ownership in addition to establishing an accurate date for its production. Upon closer inspection of the image it becomes obvious that the inscriptions were added, and alterations to the crowns of both persons depicted carried out, at a later date. Furthermore, the facial

expressions of the royal couple may not in reality be identifiable with Tutankhamun and Ankhesenamen, but rather with those of a ruling couple on the throne in Amarna shortly before the death of Echnaton. The throne was eventually used for Tutankhamun, who had died unexpectedly early.

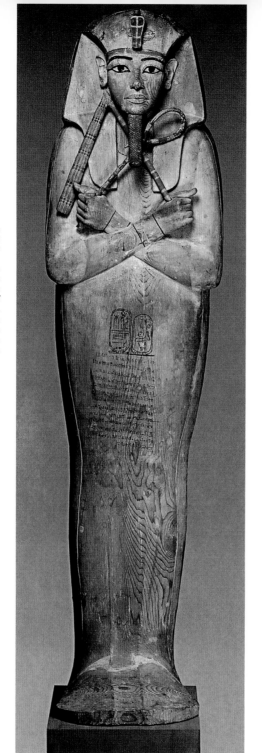

182 Papyrus Leopold II (single sheet)
Probably from Thebes; Twentieth Dynasty, ca. 1110 BC; papyrus, with hieratic text; H. 45.5 cm; Brussels, Musées Royaux d'Art et d'Histoire, E 6857.
The text, a court record from the sixteenth year of the reign of Ramesses IX, contains the confession of a tomb robber who with his accomplices had broken into a royal tomb of the Seventeenth Dynasty in Western Thebes. The incident is described in detail: "...we collected the gold which we found on the venerable mummy of this god (that is the king), together with his amulets and jewels which were around his neck...."

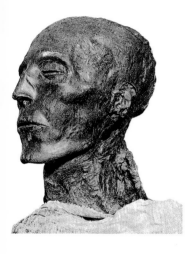

183 Head of the mummy of Seti I
Western Thebes; cache of the royal mummies of Deir el-Bahri; Nineteenth Dynasty, ca. 1279 BC; Cairo, Egyptian Museum, CG 61077.
The mummy of Seti I is one of the best-preserved royal mummies of the New Kingdom. It is an impressive testament to the high art of embalming at this period.

184 Lid of the coffin of Ramesses II
Western Thebes, cache of the royal mummies of Deir el-Bahri; Nineteenth Dynasty, ca. 1215 BC; painted wood; L. 206 cm, W. 54.5 cm; Cairo, Egyptian Museum, JE 26214 (CG 61020).
The mummy of Ramesses "the Great" was not found in its original coffin. The coffin's facial features above all show that in the process of re-interring mummies during the Twenty-first Dynasty a spare coffin from the late Eighteenth Dynasty was used. All the gold inlay was removed, and the insignia and the uraeus on the forehead renewed. Under the cartouches of Ramesses II are several lines of hieratic inscription explaining the rehousing of the mummy, which allowed it to survive the millennia concealed at Deir el-Bahari.

185 Mummy of Ramesses III
Western Thebes, cache of the royal mummies of Deir el-Bahri; Twentieth Dynasty, ca. 1150 BC; painted wood; L. 168 cm; Cairo, Egyptian Museum, CG 61083.
A four-line inscription in hieratic script on the linen bandages of the mummy of Ramesses III reports on its restoration (effectively a rewrapping) in the thirteenth year of rule of Smendes at the beginning of the Twenty-first Dynasty (ca. 1055 BC), that is about 100 years after the king's actual burial in the Valley of the Kings. The commission was granted by the high priest Pinodjem to two necropolis officials, the process being described as "Osirification." Above the inscription is the winged image of Amun with a ram's head and an ostrich feather fan in the talons of each foot.

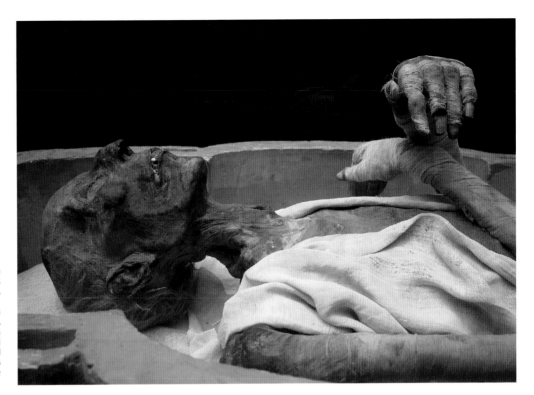

among the local inhabitants, Brugsch preempted all possible reactions, and had the whole find recovered, loaded, and transported to Cairo within forty-eight hours and under the strictest guard. Over forty coffins with their mummies and thousands of burial artifacts including papyri, shabtis in their boxes, wooden statues, and vessels reached the Egyptian Museum, which at that time was located in Boulaq. To explain the overall significance of the cache at Deir el-Bahari, Maspero shortly thereafter put forward a theory that was accepted for quite some time, namely, that the priesthood of the Twenty-first Dynasty had rescued the mortal remains of the rulers from final destruction after their tombs had been plundered by bands of robbers. More recent research has, however, proved that the history of the royal mummies in Western Thebes has to be regarded as considerably more complex.

Over the course of the New Kingdom there were repeated break-ins to individual royal tombs. The perpetrators must have been employees and workers of the necropolis. They were interested above all in the valuable materials such as embalming oil, glass, high-grade woods, and precious metals (gold, silver, bronze), which could be easily reused without attracting attention.

When the necropolis administration discovered a robbery, the affected tomb was closed and resealed after the necessary repairs had been carried out. Such a procedure is documented by a restoration inscription in the tomb of Thutmosis IV, which is dated the eighth year of Horemheb's reign. It was only toward the end of the Ramesside Period, when the country was shaken by internal political unrest and a catastrophic economic situation under the kings Ramesses IX–XI, that the plundering increased and included the entire necropolis.

A particular group of texts has revealed fascinating information about these circumstances to us, the so-called tomb robbery papyri. As official trial records, they give the names of tomb robbers, document their testimony with precise accounts of the incidents, or note the course of judicial investigations. In the unfortunately incompletely preserved Papyrus Mayer B (Liverpool), stolen objects made of bronze, copper, and cloth are listed in detail, and it is reported that the five thieves were able to share almost 50 kg of metal among themselves.

Nevertheless, the whole truth is not revealed by the information on the papyri; these make the tomb robbers listed there appear almost as amateurs. During the turbulent reign of Ramesses XI the king's actual area of influence was reduced to Lower Egypt, while at Thebes it was now the high priests of Amun who exercised real power. The latter for their part were entangled in a continuous feud with the viceroy of Nubia, Panehsi. In order to finance this petty war in the south, which lasted until the death of Ramesses XI, the high priest Piankhi resorted to the unthinkable. He allowed the Theban necropolis with the tombs of the kings, queens, and officials to be plundered freely. His agents roamed the necropolis searching for intact graves in order to gain precious artifacts.

Even in the early Twenty-first Dynasty the official hunt for gold continued. The mummies of the pharaohs robbed of their treasures were collected together in various tombs including, for example, that of Seti I. One of these temporary "storage depots" remained intact until its discovery in 1898 in the tomb of Amenophis II and concealed, among others, the bodies of Thutmosis IV, Amenophis III, Merenptah, and Ramesses VI. They had largely been rewrapped, often using the numerous linen bindings from former temple property, and roughly laid out in the available coffins. Even throughout the Twenty-first Dynasty the royal mummies continued to be accommodated at these collection points.

Finally, during the rule of Sheshonq I (ca. 930 BC), most of the mummies were transferred, via a further temporary site, to the family tomb of the high priest Pinodjem II at Deir el-Bahari, where the god-kings were disturbed once more in their final resting place by a modern tomb robber.

The Valley of the Queens

Friederike Kampp-Seyfried

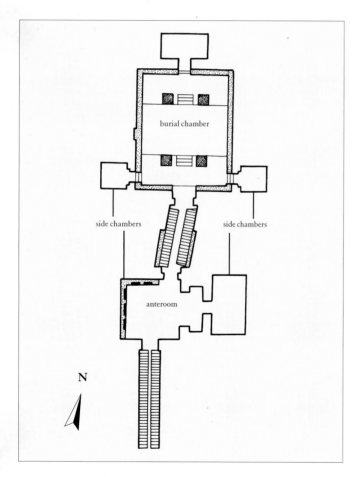

187 *Floor plan of the tomb of Queen Nefertari* Western Thebes (QV 66); Nineteenth Dynasty, reign of Ramesses II, ca. 1250 BC. While the tombs of princesses or anonymous queens consisted only of a main chamber and one or two side chambers, those of the important and named queens were much more complex in design. As the example of the tomb of Nefertari illustrates, its design includes two fairly large rooms placed one behind the other, and from which up to five additional side chambers branched off. The second principal room, the burial chamber, may also be extended with four pillars and an axial niche and/or chamber.

In addition to the famous "Valley of the Kings" and the immediately adjacent "Western Valley," there are still more necropolis areas on the west bank at Thebes, in which both kings and their relatives were buried. These include the cemeteries of the early Eleventh Dynasty in the area now known as El-Tarif, as well as the valley of Deir el-Bahari with two adjoining side valleys to the south that were used in the later Eleventh and early Twelfth Dynasties. In the Seventeenth Dynasty the royal cemeteries shifted toward the north, to the necropolis that today is called Dra Abu el-Naga. At the beginning of the Eighteenth Dynasty, when the pharaohs had chosen the Valley of the Kings for their sepulchers, the royal family members were buried in several desert valleys that lay farther south. These southern wadis also include the "Valley of the Queens."

In contrast to the Valley of the Kings with its steep, craggy cliffs and relative isolation, the Valley of the Queens is a broad, sweeping wadi that climbs gently up toward the Libyan mountains, easily accessible from the Nile floodplain and therefore in no way resembling a hidden, secretive burial place. The tombs, moreover, are not concealed, but are dotted around both sides of the dry wadi, which only rarely carries any water.

While both the name "Valley of the Queens" and "Valley of the Kings" slightly misleadingly suggest a rather restricted "clientele," the ancient Egyptian name Ta-set-neferu for the modern Arabic Biban el-Harim is a more neutral term. According to the most recent, very plausible suggestion for its translation, the ancient Egyptian name, until recently understood to mean "place of perfection," was originally "place of the (royal) children." This translation comes closest to the actual use of this region from the Seventeenth and early Eighteenth Dynasties on, namely, as a place of burial for princes, princesses, and some private individuals, who among other things may have been involved with the upbringing of the royal children. The earliest burials of two queens can be proved to date to the reign of Amenophis III. It was only at the beginning of the Nineteenth Dynasty that this valley really became the favorite burial place for the wives. At the same time it retained its original function as the burial place for the royal children, as is shown by the well-known princes' tombs from the reign of Ramesses III.

Of more than ninety-eight tombs in existence today, over half are not attributable to their original owners, as the sites contain too little decoration, are undecorated, remained unfinished, or no longer contain any identifiable objects. Nevertheless, the particular architectural design does often suggest a possible attribution, since the types of floor

188–190 Tomb of Nefertari (various views)
Western Thebes (QV 66); Nineteenth
Dynasty, reign of Ramesses II, ca. 1250 BC.
The masterfully worked reliefs and paintings
in the tomb of Nefertari are among the most
beautiful examples of Egyptian mural decoration from the New Kingdom. As well as finely
executed details on clothing, crowns, and
hieroglyphs, the artists succeeded in bringing
out nuances of facial modeling and folded
linen by means of color shading.
The examples selected here are located in the
area around the first side chamber and initially show the view of the corridor (below),
which is flanked by the gods Khepri (left) and
Re-Harakhty with the goddess Hathor
(right). Nefertari is led on both sides by
deities into this passageway, as is illustrated by
the example of the striding goddess Isis.
Among the images within the chamber is the
vignette for Spell 94 of the Book of the Dead,
in which Nefertari receives a writing palette
and a water bowl from the ibis-headed god
Thoth (far right).

plan vary in their features according to the gender and rank of the occupant and the era in which he or she lived. Apart from the simple shaft tombs that can generally be attributed to non-royalty, the larger tombs can be categorized into three groups: the simple, plain princesses' tombs, the corridor-type princes' tombs and finally the elaborately designed tombs of the queens.

The most important of the decorated queens' tombs is certainly that of Nefertari, one of the seven "great royal wives" of Ramesses II. Four other wives were also honored with a tomb in the valley.

Since the tomb's entire decoration program concentrates on the queen's future in the next world, it is not surprising that Nefertari is hardly portrayed as the seated recipient of cult or sacrifice. This is to be seen in the sites of veneration of contemporary private tombs that are above ground. Nefertari instead faces the gods as the individual performing the cult, or alternatively as the one introduced by the gods.

In the upper section are portrayed the arrival of the queen in the kingdom of Osiris, her transfiguration and the court of the underworld. In the next descending corridor Nefertari experiences the gradual transition into the kingdom of the god of the dead, before finally completing her metamorphosis in the burial chamber by becoming Osiris and achieving immortality.

The tomb of Nefertari illustrates the ambiguous position these tombs in the Valley of the Queens occupy between the royal and private conceptions of the netherworld. Even if the use of royal architecture and decoration is evident, for example, the corridor architecture, the four-pillar arrangement in the burial chamber or even representations of the Book of the Gate, these people were nevertheless denied the great royal books of the underworld. In their place are vignettes of the Book of the Dead, otherwise known only from contemporary private burial sites.

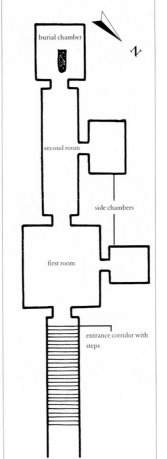

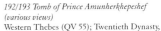

192/193 Tomb of Prince Amunherkhepeshef (various views)
Western Thebes (QV 55); Twentieth Dynasty, reign of Ramesses III, ca. 1160 BC.
Although princes' and queens' tombs were architecturally different, they nevertheless shared many aspects of the decoration program. So it is that one usually sees the worship or encounter with various gods. In the case of the queen she faces the gods as an independent individual, while the prince always requires the mediating function of his father, in this case Ramesses III, who leads his son into the corresponding scenes.

194 Ground plan of the tomb of Prince Amunherkhepeshef
Western Thebes (QV 55); Twentieth Dynasty, reign of Ramesses III, ca. 1160 BC.
Princes' tombs, in contrast to the tombs of queens, usually consist of two long corridor rooms, which lead into a rectangular, often somewhat wider burial chamber. Side chambers may lead off all of these rooms.

191 (opposite) Tomb of Nefertari, the mummy of the sun god
Western Thebes (QV 66); Nineteenth Dynasty, ca. 1250 BC.
The cyclical course of the sun contains the concept of mutual interchange of the sun god and the god of the dead, Osiris, who in the underworld was considered to be the corpse of Re. The central divine concept is as follows: while on the one hand the mummiform body belongs to Osiris, the ram's head with the sun disk reveals itself to be Re, whose name is mentioned in the title. The message of the picture is furthermore explained in a short statement: "It is Osiris rests in Re; Re it is who rests in Osiris." The two wives of Osiris, Isis (right) and Nephthys (left) revere and embrace the mummy of the sun god. Each is wearing a white hairbag wig with their hieroglyphical name sign above it.

Overcoming Death – The Private Tombs of Thebes

Friederike Kampp-Seyfried

There are three famous necropolises whose private tombs are so incredibly well preserved that they are usually cited as the models of their respective ages, that is, the three great epochs of ancient Egyptian history. Each of the three necropolises was used over a long period of time and contained tombs of private individuals who held senior positions, although they did not belong to the royal family.

The Old Kingdom is represented by Saqqara and the mastabas of the administration and elite classes of the time, while Beni Hasan, and the rock-cut tombs of the local rulers, represents the Middle Kingdom. The New Kingdom is symbolized by the necropolis of Western Thebes. Each of these cemeteries is, of course, only one site among many. The following remarks are therefore only applicable to the specifically Theban features of the private tombs of the New Kingdom, and cannot necessarily be applied to other private Egyptian necropolises.

The necropolis of Western Thebes extends over the massif on the west bank opposite modern Luxor. Most of the rock-cut tombs here date to the Eighteenth and Nineteenth Dynasties, although the site had been used long before that. Western Thebes is used generically here as the term for the conglomeration of settlements that in turn give the necropolis its name, among them Deir el-Medineh and Qurna.

Tomb Architecture

The typical Theban rock-cut tomb is a complex burial structure, the central parts of which, namely the inner cult and burial chambers, were cut out of the adjacent hills and cliffs. The simplest version of such a tomb complex consisted of a single chamber cut horizontally into the rock, from which a vertical shaft led down into the burial chamber below.

While such "single chamber tombs" were often built by privileged members of a very small upper class, the highest-ranking officials had virtual "rock-cut palaces" constructed for them, with chambers that could be the size of halls and containing several rows of columns or pillars. An easy way of imagining the archetypal Theban official's tomb

195 View toward the hill of Sheikh Abd el-Qurna
Entrances to numerous rock tombs can be identified behind the modern town of Qurna. Particularly prominent are some of the portico facades of the Saff tombs, deriving from the Arab word for "row." The funerary hill of Sheikh Abd el-Qurna was the most prestigeous burial location for the elite of Thebian court officials at the height of the Eighteenth Dynasty. The almost triangular mountain peak that can be made out on the left is known as "el-Qurn, the horn," which dominates the necropolis of Western Thebes and the Valley of the Kings as a kind of natural pyramid.

196 Stelophorus statue of a court official
Presumably West Thebes; Eighteenth Dynasty, reign of Amenophis III; ca. 1380 BC; limestone, painted; H. 26 cm; London, The British Museum, EA 24430.
Especially during the Eighteenth Dynasty, statuettes of this kind, so-called stelophori, were placed in small niches in the facade above the grave entrance. The tomb's occupant (the name has been removed from the text) is depicted kneeling in an attitude of worship with raised hands, holding in front of him a stela inscribed with a hymn to the sun. Looking to the east he greets the rising sun: "Worshiping Re as he rises and until he sets throughout life."

is to divide it vertically into three sections and then to project this pattern onto tombs from the Eighteenth and Nineteenth Dynasties.

This leads to a better understanding of the marked changes in the design of tomb structure. The Amarna Period, the reign of Akhenaten during the later part of the Eighteenth Dynasty, represents a decisive turning-point in this development.

The above-mentioned vertical division of the tomb and each of the individual components corresponded to particular significant ritual functions crucial to understanding the overall plan. If this framework is now applied to a typical tomb of the Eighteenth or Nineteenth Dynasties, a number of interesting differences emerge. The upper, solar level has a strong relationship to the cult of the sun god. During the Eighteenth Dynasty, its role as an independent structure seems to

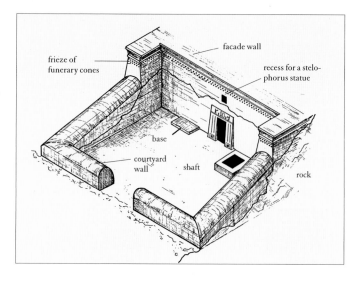

Site	Function	Architectural Form
1 Upper Level	Aspect of solar cult, sun worship	Superstructure in the shape of a chapel or pyramid or a facade recess with a stelophorus statue
2 Middle Level	Site for worship and ceremonial cults, social monument to the tomb occupant	Courtyard and horizontal inner tomb chambers such as transverse and longitudinal hall and chapel
3 Lower Level	Aspect of Osirian cult, realization of landscapes of the next world, and resting place of the body	Subterranean burial complex with shafts and corridors, ante-chambers and side rooms, and a burial chamber containing the sarcophagus

be of low priority. It can, however, be made an integral part of the overall courtyard and facade architecture, for instance, by means of a so-called stelophorus, or stela-bearing, statue placed within a facade recess.

During the Ramesside age, on the other hand, the upper level is realized, whenever possible, in the form of an independent brick pyramid erected above the rock-cut chambers. This, in turn, can be furnished either with a recess for a stelophorus statue, or an interior chapel chamber.

Initially the middle level subdivides into two sections: the courtyard situated in front of the tomb interior, and the interior chambers of the tomb. The courtyard of an Eighteenth Dynasty tomb is usually laid out in terraces and is dominated by a lavishly constructed facade that can be seen from a distance. The lower side walls enclosing the courtyard and the termination at the front were as a rule constructed with rounded wall balustrades. Enclosed in this way, the tomb's outer courtyard played an important role during burial and memorial festivities, particularly since during the Eighteenth Dynasty the access to one of the burial complexes was usually situated in the outer courtyard.

The appearance of the courtyards underwent a fundamental change at the beginning of the Ramesside Period. While in the Eighteenth Dynasty the facade, with its imposing appearance and its integrated stelophorus statue recess, partly took over the function of the superstructure, it almost completely disappeared in that form during the Nineteenth Dynasty. There was now a high wall of uniform height surrounding the outer courtyard on all sides. These walls served simultaneously as support for the roof construction and as an inner portico surrounding the courtyard. On the exterior, the entrance to the courtyard was marked by a brick pylon reminiscent of temple architecture.

The entire architectural, visual, and textual design of the Ramesside outer courtyards therefore delineates that part of the tomb as a

197 Reconstruction of the facade and outer courtyard of an Eighteenth Dynasty tomb
Ca. 1550–1290 BC.
This reconstruction is one of several possible variants designed to underline the dominant aspect of the construction of the facade wall of Eighteenth Dynasty tombs. Such walls terminated at the top in the form of a torus molding and cavetto cornice, typical features of ancient Egyptian buildings. As a further decorative element, several rows of so-called funerary cone tiles, marked with the name and title(s) of the tomb owner, could be inserted below the molding. The funerary cones stood out against the whitewashed facade like a band of red dots. Sometimes there was a niche for a stelophorus statue above the tomb entrance. Another characteristic feature for this period was the absence of any stelae in the outer courtyard, and the placement of a shaft within the courtyard.

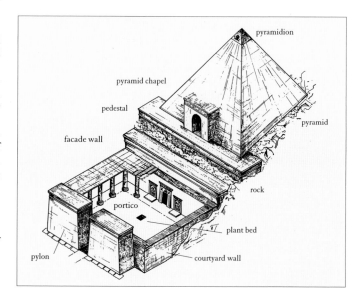

198 Attempted reconstruction of the layout of the superstructure and courtyard of a tomb of the Ramesside Period
Ca. 1290–1070 BC.
By contrast with the tombs of the Eighteenth Dynasty, the appearance of a Ramesside tomb is dominated by the pylon towers of the outer courtyard and a brick pyramid above the tomb. Inside the courtyard and protected by the colonnaded portico, the tombs of particularly elaborate design were complemented by decoration on the courtyard walls and above all on the tomb facade. Decorative elements included the "facade stelae", which whenever possible were carved out of the rock to the left and right of the tomb's entrance. The central feature of the courtyard was often a kind of "miniature garden" with a group of trees. The planting of a sycamore ensured that this embodiment of the "tree goddess," who provided water and nourishment, was close to the tomb.

kind of temple courtyard, particularly since during that period the outer courtyard shaft complexes virtually disappear.

While the structure of the Eighteenth Dynasty outer courtyards can be clearly separated from those of the Ramesside Period, this is not the case with the spatial arrangement in the interior chambers of the tomb. Here no such obvious differences are initially discernible.

The ground plan most frequently employed throughout the entire New Kingdom is based on the so-called inverted T-shape. This means that, proceeding from the entrance that determines the axis of the tomb, one first enters a room placed perpendicularly to the axis (the transept hall). Adjoining this is the so-called longitudinal hall in the same axis as the tomb. Apart from the simplest tombs, the "single chamber tombs" mentioned above, the T-shaped basic plan can be extended and modified in many different ways, for instance by means of pillar and column arrangements.

There are, nevertheless, architectural features present in the interior chambers that clearly indicate whether a tomb complex dates to the Eighteenth Dynasty or to the Ramesside Period. They include details such as stelae, false doors, or statues of deities. While during the Eighteenth Dynasty, stela and false doors were often placed opposite one another on the narrow side of the transept hall, in the Ramesside Period the stelae are usually found on the tomb facade, and the false door is often omitted altogether. The Ramesside artisans also occasionally placed divine statue groups inside the tomb chapels, something that would have been unthinkable during the Eighteenth Dynasty.

The two components of tomb architecture introduced so far served the worship of the gods as well as the cults surrounding the festivities, the worship, and the provision of the tomb occupant. The actual tomb has not yet been mentioned. As a rule, the New Kingdom Theban tombs provided two ways of gaining access to the "subterranean" level of the complex, namely the vertical shaft and the so-called sloping passage. The latter could be negotiated on foot and sloped to a greater or lesser degree, sometimes leading down to the lower level via a number of bends. The design of these tunnel systems was probably influenced by the Egyptians' visualization of the underworld. During the early Eighteenth Dynasty the vertical shaft system was preferred, while the Ramesside Period gave precedence to the sloping passage. Nevertheless, it should also be mentioned that more often than not provision was made for both burial systems to be incorporated when a large rock-cut tomb was planned. One system would have been used for the actual burial of the deceased while the other probably fulfilled some specific ritual function. If a tomb complex featured both a shaft and a sloping passage, the latter usually led to the burial chamber containing the sarcophagus of the tomb's occupant. Often these chambers were no more than simple undecorated rooms with four small recesses in the walls where the so-called magic bricks could be positioned. Only rarely were these rooms given any decoration, one example being the tomb of Sennefer.

Tomb Paintings

The principles of architectural design of the tombs themselves are often clearly discernible, even if the tombs are in a poor state of preservation. Sadly, the same cannot be said for the decorative design, since it is largely only fragments that remain. Nevertheless, it is possible to identify typical patterns and distinguishing features in the decorative content of both the Eighteenth Dynasty and the Ramesside Period.

Following our three-part model, we will first deal with the decoration of the upper level, with its superstructures, pyramids, and facade recesses, which was primarily dedicated to the cult of the sun god.

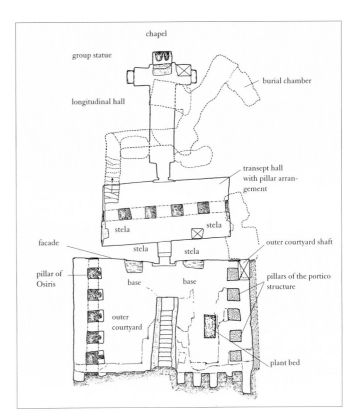

199 Tomb of the senior domain administrator to Amun Amenemope (ground plan)
Western Thebes (TT41); Eighteenth/ Nineteenth Dynasty, reign of Horemheb/Seti I, ca. 1300 BC.
This ground plan is a very clear example of the characteristic features of a Theban tomb of the early Ramesside Period. The outer courtyard is constructed on a lower level and surrounded by a portico construction. Outer courtyard stelae are placed in front of the facade to the left and right of the entrance, and there is a bed for plants inside the courtyard. The interior consists of a transept hall with four pillars, a longitudinal hall and a chapel with statue recess. Access to the underground burial complex can be gained via stairs located in the left-hand corner of the transept hall.

Exposed to the weather and the sunlight, the decorative elements were executed in relief, as exemplified by the stelophorus stela texts or the pyramidia. The inner chambers of the Ramesside pyramidal chapels, on the other hand, were decorated with paintings, whose themes served primarily to establish references to Osiris, the god of the underworld, and in this way acknowledging the second function of the pyramid as symbolic of a funeral site.

The decorative program of the "middle level" involved the courtyard and the interior chambers. Here, too, it can be observed that the decoration of the exterior surfaces was carved in relief. It must also be borne in mind that the outer courtyard of an Eighteenth Dynasty tomb was generally not decorated except for the framework area of the tomb entrance. Only in the Ramesside Period did decorations increasingly begin to appear in the form of texts and images in the courtyard and on the facade, in particular on the "facade stelae" mentioned previously.

On entering the tomb's interior chambers on the middle level, one is finally faced with a wide spectrum of different scenes and subjects, which have transformed the Theban tombs today into monuments of unparalleled artistic interest. Be that as it may, it is not the skills of the artisans, the captivating colors or the stylistic details that are our prime concern at this moment. Instead, our interest will focus on the choice of subjects, and their content, function, and meaning.

200 Pyramidion of Ptahemwia
Nineteenth Dynasty, Ramesside Period, ca. 1200 BC; limestone; H. 42 cm, W. 28 cm; Leiden, Rijksmuseum van Oudheden, AM7W.
The upper termination of private brick pyramids had a "pyramidion" whose lateral surfaces could be decorated. The texts and depictions refer to the course of the sun. In the present example, this is achieved by the juxtaposition of the sun god Re-Harakhty and the god of the underworld Osiris, since according to ancient Egyptian beliefs, the sun on its nocturnal course through the underworld united with Osiris at midnight. But it is likely that pyramidia were not only used as capstones for pyramids. They probably also served as miniature copies of "large" pyramids and as such were placed, for instance, in the outer courtyards of tombs. There is also evidence that pyramidia served as donations to temples.

201 "Pyramid stela" of Amenhotep
Probably from Saqqara; Nineteenth Dynasty, reign of Seti I, ca. 1290 BC; limestone; H. 120 cm, W. 67 cm, D. 14 cm; Vienna, Kunsthistorisches Museum, ÄS 178.
This type of tomb stela terminating in a triangular, pyramid-shaped top did not appear until the Ramesside Period and is common in the context of Memphite tombs. Here, too, the pyramidal top was likely to have assumed the function of a pyramid; such stelae thus bore all the most important aspects of an entire tomb complex in condensed form. These were first, the aspect of the cult of the sun god in the "pyramidion;" second, the worship of the god of the underworld, Osiris, and the simultaneous reception of the deceased into the hereafter (in the upper level of the stela); and third, the provision of the deceased in the hereafter by his relatives (in the lower level of the stela).

If one were to design the prototype of a T-shaped tomb of the Eighteenth Dynasty for this purpose, one would have to bear in mind from the very outset that four essential areas of the complex are invested with a particular representative content.

The first is the entrance area. Here we find a representation of the tomb owner striding into or out of the tomb, accompanied by his wife or the members of his family. When he is "leaving" the tomb, he is portrayed next to a hymn in praise of the rising sun. If there were a companion piece on the other side showing the tomb occupant entering the tomb, this would be directed toward the setting sun or toward Osiris, god of the underworld. These decorative subjects are so closely related to the tomb entrance area that they are later found in the repertoire of Ramesside tombs.

The second and third areas are the narrow ends of the transept hall, the so-called secondary places of worship. As mentioned above, the stela and the false door are part of the decoration of the transept hall and are as a rule placed opposite one another along the narrow end of that chamber. With its autobiographical texts, the stela takes over the function of self-representation and description of the tomb owner for posterity. The false door, on the other hand, serves as a point of contact between this world and the next, where "contact" can be established with the deceased and offerings presented. This door disappears completely in the Ramesside Period when the stelae were given a different decorative content and placed outside on the facade. Here, a passage into the next world actually existed in the form of the sloping passage. Instead of stela and false door, the subsidiary places of worship were usually furnished with statues of the tomb owner and his wife, or the narrow end was integrated into the overall decorative program.

The fourth area is the primary place of worship represented by a statue recess: at the end of the longitudinal hall, the ideal Theban tomb has a recess or a chapel for the statue of the tomb owner and his wife who, as embodiments of the deceased, were intended to receive offerings. This function was still maintained in tombs of the Ramesside Period, but the status of the statue chapel was often upgraded to a kind of temple sanctuary with additional statues of deities. The decorative themes of these four areas of the tomb were already clearly established, and were also frequently the only areas where decoration was actually

completed, since they represented the most important focal points for
worship and contemplation. In addition to these four areas, other decorative motifs were distributed over the remaining walls according to
rather less fixed rules. For example, in the Eighteenth Dynasty, the
immediately visible images on the walls opposite the entrance included
depictions of the tomb owner facing and paying homage to his lord, the
king. Other instances showed the tomb owner receiving offerings and
victuals during a banquet.

The decorative repertoire of the transept hall in the Eighteenth
Dynasty included images from so-called daily life, with depictions of
agricultural activity, scenes from the tomb owner's professional
employment, or even of hunting for desert animals, fish, and birds.
While the scenes relating to the tomb owner's professional life again
emphasized his social standing and the agricultural genre scenes
helped guarantee the provision of the deceased in the hereafter, it is
likely that the hunting scenes can be interpreted on other more
complex levels touching on the ritual area of religious concepts, in
particular that of re-birth and reproduction.

In the longitudinal hall we now find a greater emphasis on the
passage into the realm beyond. Often there are detailed depictions of the
funeral procession and the pilgrimage to Abydos, as well as the so-called
"opening of the mouth" ritual. With its many individual vignettes and
the rather static representation of the process, the opening of the mouth
ritual shares nothing in common with the much livelier compositions in
the transept hall depicting subjects from this world, rather than the next.
Another factor useful in the dating of tomb paintings is the division of
the walls into pictorial sections, so-called registers (horizontal levels) and
"picture strips." Eighteenth-Dynasty registers were arranged to be "read"
from bottom to top and often included numerous subsidiary scenes

204 *Banquet scene in the tomb of Userhat*
Western Thebes (TT 56); Eighteenth Dynasty, reign of Amenophis II–Thutmosis IV, ca. 1397 BC.
In tomb decoration, a significant amount of space is dedicated to festive banquet scenes, since participation in the feast guaranteed the integration of the deceased into the circle of his relatives and acquaintances. No distinction is made in the pictures between family members who are still alive and those who are already dead; after all, the meeting shown in such scenes abolishes the boundaries between this world and the next. The scenes are represented in an idealized fashion in line with the ritual aspect of depicting offerings presented before the tomb owner. In the other registers the stylistic measures further include the subdivision of scenes into smaller sequences. By virtue of their arrangement in groups, these achieve a certain degree of variety and liveliness.

depicted in great detail that contribute greatly to the charm and attraction of the images. In the Ramesside Period, however, the decorative wall layout was completely different.

Here the register style was abandoned in favor of the so-called "picture-strip style" that clearly divides the walls into two strips of different thematic content. The "line of separation" is realized by means of a horizontally arranged strip of inscriptions or ornamentation. Thematically, the uppermost register is reserved for the level of the world of the Gods, whereas the lower register served to establish the connection to the cult for the tomb owner. The thematic shifts that can be traced here are only too obvious. While the main objectives during the Eighteenth Dynasty were the self-representation of the tomb owner, his social integration, and the cult for his persona, during the Ramesside Period there was a shift toward veneration of the gods on the part of the tomb owner. The entire tomb complex increasingly acquired the character of a "mortuary temple."

A different use of stylistic devices seems to run parallel to the thematic changes described. In religious scenes dependent on ritual, the stiff hieroglyphic character of Egyptian painting and relief work still remains. Nevertheless, during the Eighteenth Dynasty, subjects dealing with the world of the living were depicted with the full range of painting variation in order to imbue them with a livelier, more real, and representative impact.

It remains to mention the decoration of the underground level. Here, too, painting was employed as a medium, both in the Eighteenth Dynasty and in the Ramesside Period. Since in both periods this area focused on the context of the hereafter, they hardly differed in terms of subject. If one disregards for the moment the tomb designs in the workers' settlement at Deir el-Medineh, one finds that only very few burial chambers were decorated with a textual and a pictorial program.

Tomb relief

While we have illustrated the thematic content of tomb decoration with numerous examples of painting, the other medium, relief decoration, should not be ignored. Apart from the fact that the mural decoration of a large number of tombs was completely or at least partly executed in relief, this particular type of decoration was indispensable to the overall conception of a tomb with superstructure and exterior structures. A number of factors determined which of the two techniques was chosen.

From the early Eighteenth Dynasty onward, the technique of the sunk relief was used for the decoration of exterior structures. Apart from the optical effect of catching the light, it was more weather-

205 *Statue recess in the tomb of Nefersekheru*
Western Thebes, (TT 296); Nineteenth Dynasty, reign of Ramesses II; ca. 1250 BC.
The primary ritual focal point of a tomb is normally constituted by the statues of the tomb owner and his relatives sitting in a kiosk or shrine. The statues may either be smaller sculptures made separately of wood or stone, or almost life-sized figures carved out of the adjoining rock, as in the example illustrated here. During the Ramesside Period, statue groups like that of Nefersekheru may, however, also be found in the secondary cult area of the transverse hall, especially if the main ritual site is occupied by the figure of a deity (here, the figure of Osiris placed in the recess opposite the entrance).

206 Hunting in a papyrus thicket, in the tomb of Nakht
Western Thebes (TT 52); Eighteenth Dynasty, reign of Thutmosis IV, ca. 1390 BC. Without doubt, the hunting scenes in the papyrus marshes are among the most beautiful and eye-catching representations found in Theban tombs. Standing on a papyrus skiff, the tomb owner is seen with his wife and children catching either fish or birds respectively. The formal garments underline the character of this luxurious pastime. It is fairly safe to assume that here, too, the subject is imbued with a ritual character that is further emphasized by the arrangement of the scenes, which face one another and whose design is repeated. Nevertheless, the detail employed in the figures, their rela- tionship to each other, and the naturalistic rendering of the flocks of birds all bring a lively animation to the pictures.

207/208 *Tomb owner, called Kiki, and his wife
– scene in the tomb of Samut*
Western Thebes (TT 409); Nineteenth
Dynasty, reign of Ramesses II, ca. 1250 BC.
*Tomb owner and his wife, from the burial
chamber of Sennefer*
Western Thebes (TT 96b); Eighteenth
Dynasty, reign of Amenophis II; ca. 1410 BC.
The difference in the use of stylistic and
compositional means between the Eighteenth Dynasty and the Ramesside Period is
illustrated in the above comparison of two
pictures, similar in many aspects, as each
shows a married couple. There are several
differences in the details of the garments and
accessories. The wigs of the Ramesside
couple lie in a flatter position on top of their
heads, which, because of their sloping
foreheads, appear altogether smaller than the
heads of Sennefer and Meret. By contrast, the
wig of Raya, Kiki's wife, reaches almost down
to her hips and is decorated not only by a very
wide ornamental band around the forehead,
but is also held together by another band at
the neck. Meret's plain dress, with its one
strap, leaves part of the breast exposed, and is
painted a flat white. In the Ramesside Period,
the wife's garments are replaced by a soft
robe with sleeves, with the arrangement of
the folds indicated by a few brush strokes.
Even Kiki wears not only a close-fitting
undergarment with short sleeves and a
simple loincloth, but also a gossamer-thin
gown with wide sleeves which allows the
contours of his body to show through. The
figures of Sennefer and Meret with their stur-
dier limbs (compare their wrists and ankles
with those of Kiki and Raya), the coloring
and the flat manner of painting appear altogether more robust and static, more like
"symbols" or hieroglyphs than the slimmer
representations of Kiki and Raya.

209/210 *Funeral procession and journey to
Abydos in the tomb of Userhat*
Western Thebes (TT 56); Eighteenth Dynasty,
reign of Amenophis II–Thutmosis IV,
ca. 1397 BC.
*Divine worship and funeral procession in the
tomb of Neferrenpet*
Western Thebes (TT 178); Eighteenth
Dynasty, reign of Ramesses II, ca. 1250 BC.
Registers and picture strip style:
The two examples illustrate the change in the
stylistic and compositional treatment of the
two-dimensional representation. In both
pictures, the depiction of the funeral procession constitutes an essential motif. In the
tomb of Userhat, this scene is distributed over
four registers, and there appears to be no
greater separation from the register of the
journey to Abydos (lowest register). By
contrast, the sequence of the scenes of the
funeral procession in the Ramesside tomb of
Neferrenpet is depicted only in the lower half
of the wall space. The sequence of scenes
shown above, representing the worship of
gods, is separated by a wide ornamental band
with inscriptions. In this way, a striking
distinction is achieved between the scenes
of worship in the upper view in which the
tomb owner plays an active part, and the
sequences in the lower "pictorial strip" in
which the tomb owner is the passive recipient
of ritual acts.

211/212 Banquet scene in the tomb of Nakht
Western Thebes (TT 52); Eighteenth
Dynasty, reign of Thutmosis IV; ca. 1390 BC.
Banquet scene in the tomb of Rekhmire
Western Thebes (TT 100); Eighteenth
Dynasty, reign of Thutmosis III–
Amenophis II, ca. 1479–1397 BC.

The subjects of these images were primarily
intended to be read "hieroglyphically." It was
only in the depiction of mourners in funeral
processions and in subsidiary scenes of more
comprehensive themes that a certain creative
freedom was applied. The numerous banqueting scenes in particular provided an
opportunity to explore such possibilities by
means of composing smaller groups of
people. The examples reproduced here illustrate a rejection of the fixed and timeless
sequence of picture after picture, toward a
more individual, spontaneous, and ultimately
more realistic manner of representation. This
was achieved by means of a staggered arrangement of the seated ladies and singers, by
a turn of the head accompanied by a gesture
of the hand or a slight turn of the body, or even
by an acceptance that the traditional patterns
of representation could be dis-regarded.

resistant. If the quality of the stone was not sufficient for such a treatment, separately worked building components were used.

For the decoration of the interior chambers, in many cases the
only suitable medium was painting, since the quality of the stone was
not adequate. The process of carving relief was more intensive than
painting because of the greater number of work stages, ranging from
the preliminary drawing and development through to the final
painting. The "cost factor" of this prestigious technique of decoration
should therefore not be underestimated, and this probably accounts for
the fact that there are only very few tombs decorated solely by relief work.

Apart from these criteria, we have been able to establish that the
choice of decorative medium generally followed the fashions of the age
in question, and that these preferences might well vary according to the
intended effect of the pictures. Thus, the stiffer, pictographic low relief
was employed frequently in the interior tomb chambers at the beginning of the Eighteenth Dynasty, whereas during the heyday of painting
during the reigns of Amenophis II and Thutmosis IV it was hardly used
at all. It then enjoyed a revival, reappearing later in a refined version
under Amenophis III.

Subsequently, in the post-Amarna era at Thebes, a pluralism of
styles are again encountered. Painting tended to be used for scenes
from the life of the tomb owner, while raised, sunk, and stucco relief
were favored for the more religious subjects. The increasing trend
toward more religious themes during the Ramesside Period resulted in
a leveling out of these differences in the use of relief and painting,
producing a style that was independent of the technique used. Once
again a certain stiffness appears, and the use of signs and symbols,
which gave painting an increasingly mannered look.

213 Tomb of Sennefer
Western Thebes (TT 96 b); Eighteenth Dynasty, period of Amenhotep II, around 1410 BC.
The tomb of Sennefer constitutes one of the rare examples of a decorated underground structure. Sennefer was the mayor of Thebes under Amenhotep II, and his burial chamber was decorated throughout with texts and pictures (vignettes) from the Book of the Dead. The view from the interior of the four-pillar chamber shows the low access that was blocked up after the funeral. The guardians of this closed-off area are two Anubis jackals enthroned on shrine-like structures. Sennefer and his wife Merit are turning toward the entrance in order to "come out of the earth and see the disk of the sun every day", as is written in the accompanying texts.

214 Relief depicting a supper and banqueting scene in the tomb of Benja
Western Thebes (TT 343); Eighteenth Dynasty, period of Tuthmosis III, around 1450 BC.
At the beginning of the Eighteenth Dynasty it is very difficult to define the differences between "relief" tombs and "painted" tombs. They relate very closely to one another in terms of the stiff and hieroglyphic structure of the sequence of pictures, the color scheme, and the style in which they have been decorated. In our illustration a gentle highlight is required to reveal the slightly elevated relief work that is restricted to the contouring of large outlines and the indication of a few details.

Tomb Sculpture

Apart from the use of statues within tombs, the focus of our discussion here, the temple courtyards were also important sites for the emplacement of private statues. It was hoped that the statue's presence would ensure participation in the daily offerings and thus "provision" in the vicinity of the deity.

The repertoire of temple statues included groups of seated figures like that of Sennefer, which initially appears to be a tomb statue, statues of seated scribes and individuals at prayer, statues holding a naos (shrine), and the so-called block (or cuboid) statues.

Apart from ceremonial sites for smaller effigies of deities, there is evidence that there were statues or busts of ancestors in private houses. While expressing veneration for deceased forebears, these statues also constituted a transition to tomb sculpture, particularly since this type of statue also appears in tombs.

The examples of sculpture from tombs of the New Kingdom can be classified into several groups, according to the context in which they were used. If we take as a starting point our arrangement of the private tomb on three different architectural levels, the following types of statue can be assigned to the appropriate categories.

The superstructure (pyramid or superstructure chapel) with solar aspect contains a stelophorus statue with a hymn dedicated to the sun god or, in a few cases, a so-called block or cuboid statue.

The middle level (courtyard and site of ceremonial worship) with ritual functions served the cult for the deceased (and for deities). It included the statues of people at prayer in the outer courtyard and in the interior chambers of Ramesside tombs, as well as ancestor busts and statues depicting the tomb owner as the recipient of offerings and rites from members of his family (in other words, the very essence of a tomb statue). Statues of gods were also found in the chapels of Ramesside tombs. Funerary objects were deposited in the lower level, which had an

215 Banquet scene in the tomb of Ramose
Western Thebes (TT 55); Eighteenth Dynasty, reign of Amenophis III, ca. 1370 BC. Among the technically most perfect raised reliefs from Egypt are the examples in the tomb of Ramose. The art of relief work reached its peak in the reign of Amenophis III, and contrasts strongly with the almost total absence of reliefs in the early Eighteenth Dynasty. An extremely fine method of processing the surface was employed to render all nuances in great detail, not only for wigs, collars, jewelry, and gowns, but also for parts of the face, such as the contours of cheeks and eyelids. The impressive effect of these depictions is further emphasized by the absence of a final decoration in paint, which here is applied only to outline the eyes.

Osirian aspect (burial complex, shafts and sloping passages, burial and subsidiary chambers). These included standing statues of the tomb owner or his wife, small figures of servants and so-called accompanying female sleepers (figurines of females, usually lying on beds, which in the context of the goddess Hathor can also be interpreted as fertility symbols). There would also be numerous *shabtis* at the tomb owner's disposal to act as laborers on his behalf in the next world.

Returning to the wall decoration of officials' tombs, we may recall that the tomb owner appeared there together with his wife in a variety of scenes, seated on a chair or bench. The couple were usually shown receiving food and offerings during a feast or ceremony of sacrifice to the dead. The visitor bearing offerings would see the tomb statue as a three-dimensional embodiment of the deceased. These tomb statues were in most cases placed in the ritual center of the site of worship, the chapel. Whenever possible they were carved out of the surrounding rock so that they could provide the best possible guarantee of the permanent presence of the dead person. However, neither the statues nor the two-dimensional representations on the wall were intended to render the individual concerned in a realistic, portrait-like manner. With the exception of only a few individual features, they complied with a contemporary, abstract ideal influenced partly by royal sculpture, which tended to portray people in the prime of their lives wearing the clothes of the time with the appropriate status symbols.

Investigations of the Theban area suggest that the group of the smaller, more delicate standing statues and wooden statuettes originally were placed in the hidden underground burial complex. According to their inscriptions, these figures, too, were supposed to receive offerings in their role as representatives of the deceased. Owing to the location of their placement, however, they did not form part of the daily offering ritual of the cult focus. It was only the medium of their inscriptions that could guarantee them permanent and adequate sustenance.

The Tombs of Deir el-Medineh

It would be remiss to examine the Theban necropolis without including the tombs of Deir el-Medineh, especially since that group deserves particular attention for a number of reasons. The systematically laid out settlement of Deir el-Medineh is situated in a rather isolated spot behind the hill of Sheikh Abd el-Qurna. Since the Eighteenth Dynasty it was the home of the craftsmen and painters whose task it was to construct and decorate the royal tombs. As an independent social group that had achieved a certain degree of prosperity, the craftsmen laid out their own tombs directly next to their settlement. The earliest structures from the Eighteenth Dynasty tended to be simple, undecorated shaft tombs containing one or two burial chambers. Nevertheless, it was in these simple tombs that some of the few examples of complete burial equipment were discovered, which included among other things the statuette of Ibentina. Most of the decorated tombs of Deir el-Medineh date, however, to the Ramesside

216/217 Wall relief from a Ramesside tomb
Saqqara; Nineteenth Dynasty, ca. 1292–1186/85 BC; limestone; H. 51 cm, L. 105 cm; Cairo, Egyptian Museum, JE 4872.
Food offerings before the family in the tomb of Neferhotep
Western Thebes (TT 50); reign of Horemheb/ Seti I, ca. 1319–1279 BC.
A comparison of these two compositions highlights the differences between the Memphite and the Theban stylistic devices of relief production. Both works were probably made at about the same time, and the genre chosen – a funeral relief and a banquet – cannot necessarily be compared. Nevertheless, the viewer is captivated by the liveliness of the Memphite female dancers who are shown by using just a few relatively coarsely drawn lines. In Memphis the artistic forms of expression of the Amarna Period were developed further, culminating in the apparent use of perspective, the reproduction of figures by means of overlapping, or depicting them in groups or staggered arrangements. The Theban artisans, on the other hand, returned to a stiff, canonized manner of representation in ritual compositions.

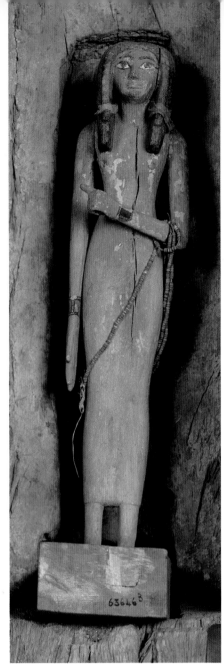

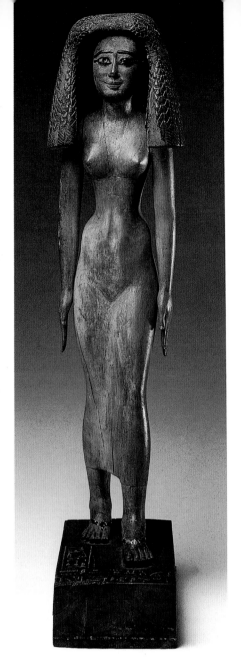

218 Seated statue of Tjanuni

Western Thebes (possibly TT 76); Eighteenth Dynasty, reign of Thutmosis IV, ca. 1390 BC; limestone; H. 56 cm, W. 15.8 cm, D. 35.7 cm; Vienna, Kunsthistorisches Museum, ÄS S63.

The type of the cloaked statue appearing in the Middle Kingdom illustrates how an abstract and idealized manner of representation could be achieved with very simple means. These statues no longer belonged to the inaccessible *serdabs* of the Old Kingdom, but were erected in temples and tombs, thus taking on publicly representative functions. The cloak imparts a serene unity to the figure and at the same time covers up nearly all the body contours, even those that remain appearing to be reduced to a minimum. The painted limestone statue of Tjanuni followed this tradition. It may therefore be regarded as a typical example of this abstracted type of sculpture that renounced any superfluous embellishments and was conceived in clear-cut outlines. The figure depicted in that idealized fashion was thereby given a timeless quality.

219 Statuette of Ibentina

Western Thebes, Tomb of Satnem (TT 1379); Eighteenth Dynasty, reign of Hatshepsut–Thutmosis III, ca. 1450 BC.; wood, H. 31.8 cm; Cairo, Egyptian Museum, JE 63646 A/B.

The simple, unadorned figure of Ibentina is particularly suitable for illustrating the context in which such statuettes were originally placed. In many cases there were placed in small shrines or boxes. The decoration, a small string of faience beads, was moreover probably not an isolated example; the same applies to the additional wrapping of many of the figures in a piece of cloth.

220 Statuette of Iimernebes

Thebes; Twelfth Dynasty, ca. 1900 BC; wood; H. 48 cm, W. 9.5 cm, D. 21 cm; Leiden, Rijksmuseum van Oudheden, AH 113.

Even in the Middle Kingdom there were small-sized, finely worked standing statuettes made of wood that, like the small servant figures, belonged to burial chamber equipment in their role as effigies of the deceased. The choice of material meant that such statuettes could be fashioned much more delicately than comparable figures made of stone. Thus it was possible, for example, to eliminate the back pillar, the arms did not need to adopt a stiff supporting position on the body, and the stance of the legs meant that no connecting fillet was necessary. In many cases the arms and wigs were worked separately and joined to the figure at a later stage. This method permitted a particularly fine execution of the individual parts, as is illustrated in an especially attractive manner by the example above.

221/222 Group of statues of Sennefer and Senai
Karnak; Eighteenth Dynasty, reign of Amenophis II, ca. 1410 BC; granodiorite; H. 134 cm, W. 76 cm, D. 65 cm; Cairo, Egyptian Museum, JE 36574 (CG 42126).

Group of statues of Neye and his mother Mutnofret
Probably from Thebes; Nineteenth Dynasty, ca. 1200 BC; limestone, H. 54 cm, W. 25 cm; Munich, Staatliche Sammlung Ägyptischer Kunst, Gl.WAF 25.

The group of statues including Sennefer does not come from his tomb but from the Amun temple of Karnak. Nevertheless, it is conceivable that a similar sculpture would have been placed inside his tomb as a statue of ritual worship. As was the case with the wall paintings, differences in artistic design can be perceived when they are contrasted with the group of statues from the Ramesside Period. The abstracted cube form of the stool supporting the statue in the group from the Eighteenth Dynasty becomes a chair in the Ramesside group, this being achieved by working the side parts in relief and by lowering the seat in a slightly concave shape. Here, as in the two-dimensional pictures, the Ramesside figures are slimmer, and the plain loincloth and the simple dress with straps found in the Eighteenth Dynasty are replaced by richly pleated garments. Furthermore, the statue of Mutnofret is no longer painted in the idealized, stereotyped yellow that symbolized female skin in the Ramesside Period, but is instead finished in a more naturalistic reddish-brown hue.

Period. Thanks to their unique state of preservation they are among the most impressive tomb complexes of the New Kingdom.

If one looks at the paintings in these chambers with their vibrant colors, then the thematic content of the scenes from the various chapters of the Book of the Dead may at first sight appear strange, militating against any comparison with the tombs of the officials in the remaining parts of the necropolis. However, when one recalls the architectural structure and layout of a tomb as explained in the chapter dealing with the private Theban tombs, the background of the three levels also helps clarify the principle behind the tombs of Deir el-Medineh.

In the Ramesside Period, the upper, solar cult level was usually realized by the construction of a brick pyramid. Apart from a recess for a stelophorus statue or for a small stela with a hymn to the sun god, most pyramids were constructed to provide enough space for a small barrel-vaulted chapel. This chapel could take over the function of the site of worship on the second level.

Larger tomb complexes in Deir el-Medineh were, however, also constructed with the chambers of the middle level that are already familiar. The corresponding pictorial repertoire we know from the Ramesside tombs of the other parts of the necropolis is also to be found here. The bad state of repair of the pyramid chapels that unite the two levels, and the small number of the sites of worship situated in the traditional location in the rock therefore lead to the misleading impression that we are now faced with a completely different tomb conception. Moreover, the lower,

226 Illustration of Spell 110 from the Book of the Dead in the burial chamber of Sennedjem Western Thebes (TT 1); Nineteenth Dynasty, reign of Seti I/Ramesses II, ca. 1279 BC.
One of the best-known vignettes from the Book of the Dead is the depiction of the so-

called "Iaru," the field of offerings or of reeds. This is a paradisiacal location in the world beyond, surrounded by water, where the tomb occupant – here accompanied by his wife – works the fields. The deceased cannot reach this place of secure provision until he

has experienced transfiguration and has passed the Judgment of the Dead. Only then can the wishes be fulfilled that are quoted in the spell's heading as follows: "O to be powerful there, to be transfigured there, to plough the land there and to harvest, to have

sexual intercourse there, and to do everything that is done on earth."

"Osirian" level shows an extraordinary arrangement that underscores this perception. The architectural differences that exist here between the tombs of the officials and the tombs of Deir el-Medineh can certainly not be explained merely in terms of the limited space available, but must also be set against the social status of the groups concerned. The thematic content of the representations is, however, adapted to the Osirian level and is by all means comparable to the few decorated burial chambers of the officials' necropolis. Recalling the decoration in the burial chamber of Sennefer, it becomes clear that vignettes from the Book of the Dead were already integrated into that Eighteenth Dynasty chamber.

What is admirable about the decoration of the tomb complexes of Deir el-Medineh, apart from their excellent state of preservation and their brilliant colors, is the artistic skill that is so evidently displayed. While pre-

liminary outlines are so often obviously discernible extending even to the smallest details and the inscriptions, here they are found only in the large lines outlining the figures and for the general articulation of the wall space.

The subsequent steps in the painting process were executed without the aid of any preliminary drawings and are testimony to the incredible skill of the painters. With vigorous brushstrokes and a sure sense of the structuring and coloring of the surfaces, they created pictures of astounding liveliness out of subjects that we would consider as rather stiff and formal. The unusual attraction of these paintings lies in the generous handling of the flowing lines largely without correction, the sketchy details often indicated merely by a few strokes of the brush, and the application of paint that in places resembles that of watercolor.

The Hidden Tombs of Memphis

Matthias Seidel

After the death of Akhenaten, his successor Tutankhamun left Akhetaten, the "city of the sun" (modern Tell el-Amarna), after residing there for some time. However, the seat of government did not return to Thebes, but moved to Memphis. The time-honored capital of Egypt, Memphis had certainly remained an important administrative center and garrison town during the Eighteenth Dynasty, but it now entered upon a short period during which it flourished once again. As Memphis rose once more to political prominence, the nearby necropolis at Saqqara came into increasing use. The cemeteries of the New Kingdom lay close to the pyramid of Teti (from the Sixth Dynasty), where excavations have uncovered several small funerary chapels, but nothing else apart from some isolated stone blocks. The much larger area containing mortuary structures of the late Eighteenth and the Nineteenth Dynasties, however, extends southward from the causeway leading to the pyramid of Unas (Fifth Dynasty), not far from the Step Pyramid of Djoser. Evidence of the existence of this necropolis area was provided by over 500 limestone fragments of relief held for decades by many museums throughout the world. Until some twenty years ago, however, the precise location of the tombs from which this interesting material derived was unknown. Only in 1975 did systematic investigation of the New Kingdom complexes begin, with an expedition organized by the Egypt Exploration Society of London in association with the Rijksmuseum van Oudheden of Leiden, and led by the British Egyptologist Geoffrey T. Martin. Unlike the private tombs of Thebes, conceived purely as rock-cut tombs, the tombs in the funerary complexes of Saqqara have superstructures above the ground, and only the shafts containing the burial chambers penetrated the bedrock below.

The Tomb of Horemheb

On January 14, 1975, only a few days after fieldwork began, the excavators found the tomb of Horemheb, supreme commander of the Egyptian army in the time of Tutankhamun. Like so many tombs at Memphis, his funerary complex had been lost since the nineteenth century and was even thought to be completely destroyed. Only a few reliefs, of a quality equal to the great masterpieces of New Kingdom relief sculpture, provided information about the distinguished official who was to conclude his career by ascending the throne as the last Eighteenth Dynasty ruler. The sources tell us nothing about the descent and origin of Horemheb, but his obvious connection with the cult of the Horus of Herakleopolis in Middle Egypt seems to indicate that this city in the eighteenth Upper Egypt nome was his birthplace. A rapid rise through the official and military hierarchy brought Horemheb to the top of the administrative system. He and Ay, who held the title of "father of the god," ruled the country as regents for the child pharaoh Tutankhamun. Beside Horemheb's position as generalissimo of the army, he held such titles as "Chief Spokesman of the Land" and "Deputy of the King at the Head of the Two Lands," indicat-

227 Tomb of Horemheb; view of the courtyard complex with reconstructed columns
Saqqara; Eighteenth Dynasty, ca. 1325 BC.
A massive entrance pylon leads to the first court of the tomb's superstructure. The court is surrounded by pillars, nearly all of which have been restored or in some cases completely reconstructed.

ing that he had almost unlimited power, and his influence must have had much to do with the choice of Memphis as the capital. That decision was followed only a short time later by his plan to build a funerary complex in the officials' cemetery in Saqqara. It was not virgin ground; many Fifth and Sixth Dynasty mastabas of the Old Kingdom had to be cleared away first, and some of their stone was reused. Even the nearby funerary precinct of Djoser served to provide stone for Horemheb's tomb. The masonry consists chiefly of unfired bricks of Nile mud faced with limestone blocks.

In the course of his unimpeded rise the general extended his tomb twice, so that in its final phase the superstructure (with a total length of around 49.5 m) was more like a private funerary temple. Such lavish architecture was reserved solely for the highest dignitaries in the land, clearly and permanently distinguishing their tombs from the usual funerary chapels of lower ranks of officials, which were built on a smaller scale.

The entrance is marked by a mighty pylon over 7 m high, leading to the first court, which is paved with stone and surrounded by pillars 3 m high in the form of bundles of papyrus reeds, forming a double row on the west side. Only a few scenes of the original wall decoration have been preserved in situ. Those that can still be made out include a vivid depiction of daily life in a military camp, unique in its wealth of detail. Some of the pictorial elements exist only in outline, and the relief work on them was never carved.

This fact may indicate that the tomb's final construction phase (the pylon and the first court) was carried out during the brief reign of Ay, Tutankhamun's immediate successor, and consequently work on the relief decoration of the walls was incomplete when Horemheb took to the throne, for as the incumbent ruler he commissioned the construction of a rock-cut tomb commensurate with his royal rank in the Valley of the Kings: the former general was never buried in his tomb in Memphis. Most of the statues of Horemheb found on the site by the excavators were also in an unfinished condition.

Beyond the first court follows a large rectangular statue room, flanked by two narrow storage magazines. The room had a vaulted brickwork ceiling, which has now collapsed. The walls here were also of brickwork that had been whitewashed and then painted, as the very faint traces of surviving color indicate. Under Ramsses II a cult was set up in this area to the deified Horemheb, who was regarded by the Ramesside rulers as the ancestor of their own dynasty. Having no son of his own, Horemheb had nominated Paramessu, a high-ranking military officer, to succeed him, and as Ramesses I this man was to found the Nineteenth Dynasty. The statue room opens into a second and rather smaller court, likewise with an arrangement of pillars in the form of papyrus bundles running around it. The walls of this court bear reliefs, and parts of them been preserved up to a height of 2.25 m.

228 Horemheb at the funerary repast
Saqqara, tomb of Horemheb; Eighteenth Dynasty, ca. 1325 BC.
The relief on the door jamb of the passage into the statue chamber shows the tomb owner sitting at a table. He wears a curled wig in several layers, a long linen robe, and sandals. His left hand reaches for the stylized loaves of bread, and he holds a scepter of office in his right hand. Only after Horemheb's accession to the throne was a small uraeus cobra added to his forehead, as a token of his royal status.

229 Scribe statue of Horemheb
Probably Memphis; Eighteenth Dynasty, ca. 1325 BC; granodiorite; H. 89.5 cm; W. 71 cm; New York, The Metropolitan Museum of Art, Gift of Mr. and Mrs. V. Everit Macy, 1923, 23.10.1.
Although we have no direct evidence, it is tempting to suppose that this famous scribe statue of Horemheb originally came from his tomb complex at Saqqara. The classic posture of the scribe, with crossed legs and an unrolled papyrus on his lap, distinguishes this high official as a member of the administrative hierarchy. He wears a wig with wavy tresses, a shirt-like garment with wing sleeves, and a pleated apron.

230 The chariots of Horemheb
Saqqara, tomb of Horemheb, east wall of second court; Eighteenth Dynasty, ca. 1325 BC. Behind the figure of the generalissimo Horemheb, several small registers show his teams of chariots and horses. This section shows two chariots with their drivers, one of them leaning casually over a horse's back. Besides the rare finds of chariots and bridles, it is the fine detail of depictions such as those in Horemheb's tomb that provide us with an idea of the chariot as a war machine. In consideration of the tomb's owner, it is no wonder that so many depictions are to be found here.

231 Scribes at work
Saqqara, tomb of Horemheb, east wall of second court; Eighteenth Dynasty, ca. 1325 BC. Four military scribes squat on the ground in pairs with their legs crossed, industriously recording tributes paid to the Egyptian court on their unrolled papyri. The portable containers for their writing instruments are shown in front of them. Two other officials stand behind, the direction of their eyes and their gestures indicating the adjoining scene, which shows the large figure of the tomb owner supervising the procession of several registers of prisoners.

232 Syrian and Hittite prisoners
Saqqara, tomb of Horemheb, south wall of second court; Eighteenth Dynasty, ca. 1325 BC; limestone with traces of paint; Leiden, Rijksmuseum van Oudheden, H.III.OOOO. Besides identifying the general provenance of the prisoners by means of their clothing,

beards, and hairstyles, the Egyptians took care to portray each figure with individual features. They succeeded particularly well with the Hittite pair (left), while the emotional representation of the pain-racked face of a Syrian with his head thrown back (right) could hardly be improved.

233 The Triumph of Horemheb
Saqqara, tomb of Horemheb, south wall of second court; Eighteenth Dynasty, ca. 1325 BC; limestone with traces of paint; entire length ca. 360 cm; Leiden, Rijksmuseum van Oudheden, H.III.OOOO, H.III.PPPP.
Arms raised in jubilation, the commander of the Egyptian army, Horemheb, stands before the enthroned king Tutankhamun and his wife (adjoining on the right). Horemheb receives the distinction of the "gold of honor"

from the ruler; it consists of heavy necklaces of gold disks, some of which already hang around his neck while others are placed on him. Behind the triumphant Horemheb, two long registers show a procession of his West Asiatic and Hittite prisoners, led past by Egyptian soldiers and officials. Women carrying children are held only by the arm, but the male prisoners all wear wooden handcuffs and have ropes around their necks.

The theme of the relief decoration depicts several scenes of the triumph of Horemheb, shown as a victorious general presenting long lines of prisoners – Asiatic, Libyan, and Nubian – to the young pharaoh Tutankhamun, who awards him the distinction known as the "gold of honor." The dense composition of these images, the genuinely dramatic concept of the events that they narrate, and their masterly execution make them the finest of all examples of relief work of this type. Along with the military images, scenes of funerary ritual are depicted on the walls. They include an extensive sequence showing offerings being presented, professional mourners, and the slaughter of sacrificial cattle.

A shaft leads down from the inner courtyard to the underground burial chamber 28 m below ground level. Although it was originally planned for Horemheb himself, initially his first wife was the only occupant of this extensive system of shafts and chambers, which is laid out on several levels. However, fragments of writing on the grave goods led scholars to the sensational conclusion that Horemheb's second wife, Queen Mutnedjmet, must also have been buried in her husband's tomb in Memphis, rather than being laid to rest in the Valley of the Queens. The burial chambers of both women had been plundered by tomb robbers in antiquity. At the western end of the tomb, the central room for the sacrificial cult follows directly on from the second court. This room was flanked on both sides by undecorated chapels. A brickwork pyramid with a stone pyramidion on top, now lost, was erected above the ceiling of the cult chamber, in the manner shown on many of the tomb reliefs of Memphis.

The Tomb of Maya

The license for the British and Dutch team to excavate was originally granted with the aim of rediscovering the tomb complex of Maya. When the Prussian expedition under Richard Lepsius was working, at Saqqara in 1843, it removed some blocks from the accessible part of the superstructure of this tomb and took them back to Berlin.

Lepsius indicated the approximate location of the tomb on a plan of the necropolis, and published the reliefs in his famous and monumental work *Denkmäler aus Ägypten und Äthiopen*.

Unfortunately almost all the Maya reliefs were among the losses sustained by the Ägyptisches Museum in Berlin during the Second World War.

In addition, the Rijksmuseum van Oudheden in Leiden took a particular interest in the person of this official, since three fine seated statues of Maya and his wife Merit have been in its possession since the 1820s, and they undoubtedly came from the tomb in Saqqara.

Work on the excavation of the tomb of Maya did not begin until 1987, although the excavators had already come upon its underground

234 Seated statue of Maya
Saqqara, tomb of Maya, Eighteenth Dynasty, ca. 1325 BC; limestone; H. 216 cm; Leiden, Rijksmuseum van Oudheden, AST 1./1.1.5.
Maya is seated, as befits a high official, on a chair with tall backrest; in his left hand he holds a linen amulet hanging down.

He wears a bipartite wig with lower lappets finely curled. With its rounded physical forms and sensitively depicted features, this over-life-sized seated statue of Maya is among the outstanding works of private sculpture from the end of the Eighteenth Dynasty.

235 Seated figure of Meret
Saqqara, tomb of Maya, Eighteenth Dynasty, ca. 1325 BC; limestone with traces of paint; H. 190 cm; Leiden, Rijksmuseum van Oudheden, AST 2.
Meret wears a finely pleated robe and sits on a

chair with a high backrest. Her face is surrounded by a heavy wig, depicted in great detail and falling almost to her waist. As "temple songstress of Amun" Meret holds a cult object, the *menat*, in her left hand, against her torso.

complex by chance a year earlier, when they were following an interconnection branching off from the shaft of another tomb. The architecture of Maya's tomb, only a few meters away from the tomb of Horemheb, is very similar in extent and structure to that of his superior officer and later king.

As "Head of the Treasury," Maya was one of the men at the very top of the administrative hierarchy, and he had held that important office in the time of Tutankhamun and Ay. In his other function as "chief overseer of construction projects in the place of eternity," Maya was responsible for the planning and furnishing of the tomb complexes of the last three kings of the Eighteenth Dynasty. It was probably for this reason that he was granted the privilege of donating two items to the funerary treasure of Tutankhamun: a fine *shabti* figurine and a model of a bed with an Osiris figure of the king lying on it. Later, Horemheb also entrusted the supervision of his ambitious building projects in the imperial temple of Amun-Re at Karnak to Maya.

The tomb complex of this high official, which is laid out east to west, is entered through a broad pylon that bore large relief depictions of Maya in the passageway. The first court beyond the pylon was paved with brick, and only its western side has a series of six papyrus bundle pillars. Next to it, the large statue chamber leads into the inner court, which has an arrangement of pillars running around it, like its counterpart in Horemheb's tomb.

Most of the wall reliefs are devoted to such religious subjects as the funerary procession or worship of the Hathor cow, but the themes also refer to the professional life of the tomb owner, who is shown registering prisoners and their cattle. A short procession of offering bearers is particularly well preserved. The main cult chamber and two side chapels lie at the western end of the courtyard, but even in times of classical antiquity they had already lost their limestone facing and relief decoration. The architecture of the tomb as a whole has suffered severely from the theft of stone, both in antiquity and at a later date (in the eighteenth century), and only a small percentage of the original decoration has survived.

However, the excavators found compensation in the form of a remarkable discovery. Several rooms of the underground complex, including the burial chambers of the official and his wife, were fully decorated and show the couple venerating the gods of the dead. A striking feature is the fact that the color palette of the paintings is primarily restricted to a golden yellow tone, obviously in reference to the transfigured condition of the dead husband and wife.

236 Maya praying to Osiris
Saqqara, tomb of Maya, pylon passageway; Eighteenth Dynasty, ca. 1325 BC; painted limestone; H. 65 cm.
The well-preserved paint on this block gives some idea of the original coloring of the reliefs. The scene shows the tomb owner and his wife Meret (only her hand is visible behind his shoulder), praying with raised hands to Osiris, god of the dead, whose enthroned figure appears to the left of the couple.

237 Figures bringing offerings
Saqqara, tomb of Maya, second court; Eighteenth Dynasty, ca. 1325 BC; limestone.
Wearing elegantly pleated garments and heavy wigs, the figures in this procession bear offerings of incense, flowers, and birds. Their faces are not individual portraits, but are rendered in the stylized manner that was the general rule in the time of Tutankhamun.

Tanis and Thebes – The Political History of the Twenty-first to Thirtieth Dynasties

Dieter Kessler

A special feature of the period following the New Kingdom and known as the Third Intermediate Period is the existence of two centers of power. The new royal residence of Tanis in the eastern Delta, to which the new Twenty-First Dynasty moved from the Ramesside capital, stood in opposition to Thebes in the south. The Theban high priest of Amun was also a military leader who safeguarded his power base by building a chain of fortresses running north from Middle Egypt. Political actions were sanctioned by allegedly divine decisions pronounced through oracles. However, efforts were made in the south toward formal recognition of the Delta pharaohs. The existing river transport system utilized by the temple of Amun and the distribution of temple possessions all over Egypt called for nationwide cooperation. Repeated efforts to restore unity were made through family connections between Tanis and Thebes. The office of the "god's wife of Amun" in Thebes was of considerable political significance because of its oracular function, and consequently it was often held by princesses from the north.

The kings of Tanis built their stone tombs inside the imposing walls of the temple precincts of Amun of Tanis. At Thebes, on the other hand, royal tombs were systematically opened and the mummies they contained moved to other graves. Since control of Nubia and with it Nubian gold had been lost at the end of the Ramesside Period, the gold from these reopened tombs was reused for new purposes. The Theban families lived largely from temple benefactions. There was often internal opposition to the family of the all-powerful High Priest of Amun; these efforts were quelled by exiling offenders to the oases of Kharga and Dakhla.

The kings at the residence city of Tanis, well situated for traffic on a distributary of the Nile, maintained trade contacts with Byblos and Assyria (whose strength was now increasing), and were soon involved once again in Palestinian affairs. A daughter of King Siamun (ca. 979–960 BC) was given as wife to King Solomon, with the city of Gezer as her dowry. In a political alliance with Solomon, Siamun conquered the Philistine cities of Ashdod and Sharuhen. Egyptian craft items, particularly scarabs, were widely distributed in Palestine at this period, and soon an independent native style with the adaptation of Egyptian motifs developed in the Syro-Palestinian area.

The Rule of the Libyan Princes (ca. 946–736 BC)

To an increasing extent, the Tanite rulers were marrying into the Libyan warrior nobility that had long been resident in Egypt. One Shoshenq of the Libyan Meshwesh tribe, the Biblical Shishak, was the founder of the Twenty-second "Dynasty from Bubastis," but reigned in

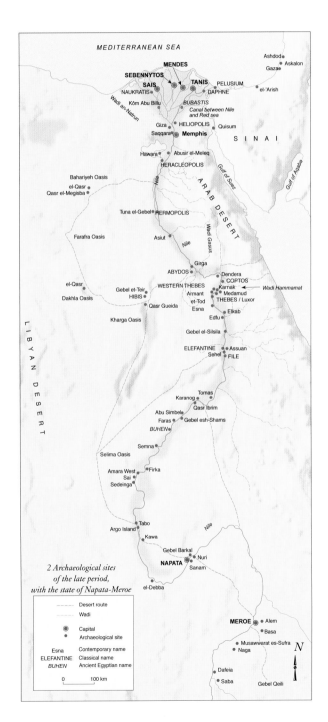

2 Archaeological sites of the late period, with the state of Napata-Meroe

1 Statue of Osorkon I
Heliopolis; Twenty-second Dynasty, ca. 920 BC; bronze, gold; H. 14 cm; New York, The Brooklyn Museum, Charles Edwin Wilbour Fund, 57.92.

There was relatively little stone sculpture in the time of the kings of Libyan descent, but the technique of bronze-working became very sophisticated. The king bears designs showing gods on his breast.

3 Colossal head of Shabako
Karnak; Twenty-first Dynasty, ca. 715 BC; red granite; H. 97 cm; Cairo, Egyptian Museum, JE 36677 (CG 42010).
The double uraeus and the facial features around the mouth betray the origin of this head from the south. The Kushite ruler installed governors appointed by himself in the Delta, but deliberately avoided confrontation with the Assyrians on the eastern border.

Tanis. He also succeeded in asserting his authority in Upper Egypt, and installed one of his sons as high priest. A Libyan relative became prince of Herakleopolis. Sheshonq I, like the kings of the previous dynasty, intervened actively in the politics of the Palestinian states. Campaigns against the cities of Judah and Israel were conducted from Gaza and went as far as Megiddo. To avert the destruction of Jerusalem, Rehoboam of Judah delivered up all the treasures of the temple to the pharaoh in the year 925 BC.

The Libyan royal house, increasingly confined to Tanis and Bubastis in the subsequent period, finally had to accept a new division of Egypt into two spheres of power, both legitimizing their authority by royal title. The new monarchy, regarded as the Twenty-third Dynasty (756–714 BC), was based in the north in the city of Leontopolis in the eastern Delta, where there was probably a royal residence, and in the south at Thebes. However, the new kings had close family ties with the Tanite house.

The Libyan prince of Herakleopolis occupied an increasingly influential central position, and eventually he too gave himself the title of king. Herakleopolis, which controlled its own means of shipping

and transport, could administer its lands independently. Namlot, the Libyan prince of Hermopolis, emulated the prince of Herakleopolis by similarly declaring himself king.

In the western Delta, the "princes of the Libu [Libyans]" gained independent control of an area reaching from Sais to the gates of Memphis. Ultimately, they even held the post of High Priest in Memphis. They profited from the traffic route of the western arm of the Nile, along which an increasingly large quantity of international trade passed to Memphis. The Nile inundation began to reach very high levels in the eighth and ninth centuries BC, resulting in an increasingly wet climate – and as a result great changes occurred in the settlement of large areas of the Delta and Upper Egypt.

The Rule of the Kushites
(Twenty-fifth Dynasty, ca. 750–655 BC)

Once direct Egyptian military rule had been removed from Nubia, new regions and cultures arose, and consolidated their positions in

4 Head of a statue of Amasis
Twenty-sixth Dynasty, ca. 560 BC; sandstone; H. 28 cm; Baltimore, Walters Art Gallery, 22.415.
Although many scandalous stories were told about him, this king was very popular with the Greek mercenaries because of his Greek wife, his demonstrative adoption of a soldier's way of life and his preference for drink. His conciliatory attitude to political opponents enabled him to integrate various different groups of the population into the economic life of the country.

constant internal warfare against nomadic groups. The centers of this part of Kush were the old settlement sites of Napata, Dongola, and Sais, which lay on major trade routes. The Kushite chieftains continued to use the Egyptian temple buildings on their lands to legitimize their position, and they eventually succeeded in gaining control of Lower Nubia. It was only a matter of time before the Kushite ruler was accepted by the ruling families of Thebes as the new pharaoh by decree of Amun, thus initiating the Twenty-fifth Dynasty.

The Amun of Karnak and the Amun of Napata were theologically related, and the Kushite coronation ritual, involving journeys to such sacred places as Napata, Kawa, and Pnubs, imitated Egyptian ceremonies. However, certain matriarchal aspects recognized by the Kushite monarchy were of native origin. The Kushite rulers introduced what is known as the "Kushite Renaissance" in Egypt, a period during which ancient religious writings were resurrected and cult reforms instituted.

Their northern neighbors reacted to this new threat when Tefnakht of Sais declared himself king and founded the Twenty-fourth Dynasty of Sais (ca. 740–714 BC). After long campaigning, the Kushite ruler Piye conquered him and the petty kings of Middle Egypt. The Delta princes formally recognized the Kushite king as sole ruler, but the power of the Saite princes continued unabated.

The Assyrian Threat

In 722 BC the troops of the Assyrian empire occupied Israel after the fall of Samaria, and now posed a threat to the princes of the Delta. After long hesitation, the Kushites eventually decided to lend active support to the Delta states in their struggle. In 701 BC the Assyrian king Senacherib defeated the Egyptian army sent against him, but for reasons that are not known refrained from taking Jerusalem.

After several unsuccessful attempts, Assyrian attacks on Egypt finally succeeded in 671 BC. Memphis was taken, and the Egyptian cities in the eastern Delta came under Assyrian influence. The princes of Middle Egypt collaborated with the Assyrians, but the Delta princes were constantly conspiring against the occupying power. The result was a series of executions, and only Necho, prince of Sais, was confirmed in his office. In 664 BC the Assyrian army reacted to Kushite revolts by marching on Thebes and looting the city. Mass deportations to Assur followed, and a large number of exiled Egyptians were gathered in that city. However, the southern part of Upper Egypt continued in its allegiance to the Kushite king.

The Reign of the Kings of Sais: Beginning of the Late Period (664–525 BC)

The king of Sais formed a powerful army of Carian and Ionian mercenaries. When the Assyrians faced serious difficulties at home with their enemies Elam and Babylon, Psammetichus I, regarded as the founder of the Twenty-sixth Dynasty, embarked on the first steps toward independence. He first turned against the princes of the Delta, and then moved on to Thebes with the support of Herakleopolis. The god's wife of Amun, a Kushite princess, was forced to adopt the daughter of the Saite king as her successor to the post. Egypt was united again in the year 656 BC.

The Saites provided military security for the Egyptian borders by building new fortresses, partly occupied by foreign mercenaries and exiled Jews. They built Daphnai (Tell el-Defenneh) in the east, and garrisons were stationed at Elephantine in the south and the fort of Marea in the west. Under the reign of Amasis at the latest, another fortress was added at Migdol, south of Pelusium in the Sinai. A strong fleet was formed under Necho II, who also initiated the project to build a canal through the Wadi Tumilat, linking the Nile to the Red Sea. In addition, he is said to have circumnavigated Africa, but the accuracy of this report is disputed.

In the south, Psammetichus II marched on Nubia in 591 BC with Carian and Greek mercenaries to counter the influence of Napata. Thereafter, all traces of the Kushite rulers of Egypt were systematically removed.

The Assyrian empire came under increasing pressure from the emerging major power of the Medes, and it now received support from Egyptian troops. Under Necho II they even invaded Palestine, where they defeated King Josiah of Judah at Megiddo, and went as far as Carchemish and Harran. The Phoenician cities were forced to pay tribute. After several successful battles, however, the Egyptian army was utterly annihilated at Carchemish and Hamat in 605 BC. The Babylonians pressed swiftly on to Palestine, which was lost to Egypt once again.

Egypt's contacts with the Mediterranean area increased. Treaties were concluded with Croesus of Lydia and Polycrates of Samos, and valuable votive offerings were made at Delphi and Cyrene. Part of Cyprus became Egyptian. King Apries sent troops to help the Libyan prince of Cyrene in his struggle against the Greeks who had settled there. The army was defeated; the soldiers mutinied, and when

General Amasis was sent to settle the matter they promptly made him king. Amasis won the ensuing civil war battle outside the gates of Memphis, in which Apries fell but was buried in Sais with due ceremonial by his opponent. Amasis, who married a Greek woman from Cyrene, was regarded as friendly to the Greeks and had the reputation of being a heavy drinker. His task was to integrate the foreign troops in Egypt. The Greeks (including some Cypriots) were allowed to found a trading colony in Naukratis in the western Delta. A garrison of Greek and Carian mercenaries now protected Memphis.

Amasis was the real founder of the "Saite Renaissance." Once again, old documents were collected, relief sculpture styles from earlier tombs were copied, and the cults of dead kings revived. New arrangements were established for royal tutelary gods, provincial deities, and religious districts. Lower Egyptian demotic, a much abbreviated development out of hieratic script, became the official script. New rules governed the royal cult, and, as a result, Amasis was regarded, even centuries later, as an ideal lawgiver.

Amasis's building projects were extensive. He made magnificent extensions to the temple of the Neith of Sais and the family necropolis. New temples in the oases of Bahariya and Siwa served the local garrisons, and Amasis also founded the temple of Isis at Philae.

The Rule of the Persians (First Persian Period, Twenty-seventh Dynasty, 525–401 BC)

In 525 BC the Median Persians moved against Egypt with the aid of a Phoenician and Cypriot fleet. The Egyptian army was betrayed by Greek mercenaries and crushed at Pelusium, and after another attempt at resistance the Egyptian pharaoh was executed. Udjahorresnet, the Egyptian naval commander and a priest of the goddess Neith in Sais, defected to the Persians and became one of their advisers. Egypt was now a satrapy of the Persian empire.

The great king Cambyses occupied Memphis and executed many Egyptians; others were deported to Persia, and these initial measures established Cambyses' reputation for cruelty. Soon, however, Cambyses and later Darius I, true to the conciliatory policies of their predecessor Cyrus, were seeking recognition from the Egyptians. Darius had a new legal code drafted, and the winged Persian sun god Ahuramazda was equated with the Egyptian solar deity.

The temple of Horus of Edfu received many gifts of land, and the great king paid special attention to military control of the oases, where several temples were constructed. The building of the canal through the Wadi Tumilat was completed, but turned out to be a failure.

During the First Persian Period, Memphis increasingly became a center of international transport, and Aramaic joined demotic as the second written language.

Greek travelers, including Herodotus, visited Egypt and left descriptions of the sights of the country and its "strange" religious rites. Herodotus also tells us that the Egyptians considered Greeks unclean. A dispute arose in Elephantine between the Jewish Aramaic community and the priests of the ram god Khnum, and ended in violence; one of the points at issue was the custom of the slaughter of the Passover lamb.

6 Architectural plate depicting Nectanebo I
Alexandria; Thirtieth Dynasty, ca. 370 BC; graywacke; H. 123 cm; London, The British Museum, EA 22.
The architectural element categorized as a plate is decorated on both sides with reliefs and is often described as a column barrier. Usually however, such barriers are worked from a single block, while this example possessed further connecting plates as can easily be deduced from the decoration and inscriptions. Although found in Alexandria, the object originated from a building in Heliopolis. The better preserved side shows a palace facade as a basic decoration, above which the kneeling figure of Nectanebo I makes an offering of a tall loaf of bread. The king who was descended from a distinguished general's family wears a tight fitting crown cap with the Uraeus.

The Last Native Dynasties (401–332 BC)

Several rebellions by native Egyptians against Persian rule took place, instigated and supported by the Persians' Greek enemies, but each one failed. One such revolt was led by the Libyan Prince Inaros, who asked Athens for armed naval aid against the Persians. The Athenian venture in Egypt ended with the complete annihilation of the Greek mercenaries and the execution of Inaros. More successful was the Libyan Amyrtaios, whose rule is counted as the Twenty-eighth Dynasty (404–399 BC). He first asserted himself against the Persians from the western Delta, and in 402 BC was recognized all over Egypt.

Eventually, Amyrtaios was deposed by the founder of the Twenty-ninth Dynasty, Nepherites I (399–393 BC), from Mendes in the Delta, who sent assistance in the form of grain supplies to Sparta in its struggle against the Persians. King Nepherites was probably also buried in Mendes. His successor Hakoris (392–380 BC) concluded alliances with Athens and Euagoras of Cyprus against the Persians. Egyptian coins were minted for the first time to pay his army of mercenaries, which was commanded by the Athenian Chabrias. He repelled a Persian attack in 385 BC.

The dynasty came to an end amidst internal confusion. General Nectanebo, whose family hailed from Sebennytos in the Delta, deposed Nepherites II (380 BC) and founded a new dynasty, the Thirtieth. Nectanebo I managed to repel the Persian army that invaded the Delta in 375 BC, assisted by the great satrap revolt in Asia Minor against the king of Persia. Nectanebo II (360–343 BC) employed a mercenary army led by the Spartan Agesilaos in his defensive battles against the Persians. Finally, however, the Persians occupied the Delta in 343/42 BC and founded what is known as the Second Persian Period of rule, which ended only with the campaign of Alexander the Great.

Assimilating the Past – The Art of the Late Period

Elisabeth Siebert

The Temples

Although the Egyptians constructed numerous buildings even after the end of the Twentieth Dynasty, very little of it has been preserved compared to the wealth that survives from the New Kingdom. Upon his accession to the throne, moreover, it was incumbent on every pharaoh to take stock of the country's temples, ascertain their architectural condition and the state of their cults and perform any necessary maintenance. There is evidence that this royal duty was duly observed in the form of extensions or new buildings for all the country's major temples. The Kushite rulers of the Twenty-fifth Dynasty built their residences, tombs, and large temple complexes to both Amun and their native gods in their Nubian homeland, but they did not neglect the great temples of Egypt. At Karnak, for instance, colonnades were built before and behind the temple building, and various smaller sanctuaries were erected within the temple precincts. It can be assumed that many new buildings were constructed in the new royal capitals of the Twenty-first to Thirtieth Dynasties in the Nile Delta: at Tanis, Bubastis, Sais, Mendes, and Sebennytos. However, from classical antiquity until modern times they were used as stone quarries, so that very little is left to be seen even of the impressive layout of the city of Tanis, which itself was built with materials brought from the Ramesside capital. Little more than the ground plan remains today of the great temple of Amun, Mut, and Khonsu, built on the model of the temple at Karnak.

In Bubastis, the temple of the goddess Bastet has now disappeared entirely, and only the gateway of the festive hall of Osorkon II (Twenty-second Dynasty) can be reconstructed from the scattered ruins. Its relief ornamentation shows one of the most complete depictions we have of the *sed* festival, the jubilee celebration of the royal reign. The ruins of Sais served as a source of building material for the nearby city of Rosetta. In Mendes only a granite naos, 7 m in height and originally one of a set of four, still towers above the ruins of the temple built by Amasis (Twenty-sixth Dynasty) and now entirely destroyed. A similar although smaller shrine built by Nectanebo II (Thirtieth Dynasty) stands in the sanctuary of the temple of Horus at Edfu. The only temple of the Late Period to have been preserved complete is the temple at Hibis, built in the Kharga Oasis during the Twenty-seventh

Dynasty by Darius I. An innovation in the building program of the Late Period is the introduction of the *mammisi*, a simple structure located in front of the main temple, and from the Ptolemaic Period on surrounded by an ambulatory with intercolumnar screen panels. It symbolizes the birth-house in which the divine child was born and raised. The earliest *mammisi*, in Dendara, dates from the time of Nectanebo I.

---

7 Osorkon II and his wife Karomama making offerings
Bubastis, gate of the king's festival hall; Twenty-second Dynasty, ca. 855 BC; red granite; London, The British Museum, EA 1077.
Osorkon II celebrated his first royal jubilee two decades after his accession to the thone, and on that occasion he erected a ceremonial portal in front of the temple of the goddess Bastet. Many of the blocks with reliefs depicting the course

of the festival are today in various museums around the world. This block, now in London, shows the royal couple presenting offerings to a deity (the figure on the left is broken off). The parallel scene, on a relief block in the Ägyptisches Museum, Berlin, shows the couple making symbolic restitution of the "Eye of Horus" to the crown goddess of Upper Egypt, Nekhbet; the god Horus had lost his eye in his duel with Seth.

8 Naos built by Amasis for the god Shu
Mendes, main temple; Twenty-sixth Dynasty, ca. 550 BC; granodiorite; H. 7.85 m, W. 4 m.
Although the fish-goddess Hatmehit and the "ram of Mendes" were venerated in Mendes, capital of the "dolphin" nome of Lower Egypt, Pharaoh Amasis (570–526 BC) built a temple here that was also dedicated to the gods Geb, Re, Osiris, and Shu. Four towering shrines to these gods, each consisting of a

single block of stone, stood in the innermost sanctuary on a base of several layers of lime-stone blocks. Only the naos of Shu still stands erect on the site today; the others are in ruins. The shrines had an internal wooden partition that divided them into two compartments, the lower intended for a fairly large stone statue of the deity and the upper probably for cult utensils.

9 Cult chapel of King Taharqa
Kawa (northern Sudan), temple of Amun;
Twenty-fifth Dynasty, ca. 680 BC; sandstone;
H. 257 cm, W. 395 cm; Oxford, Ashmolean
Museum, 1936.661.
Upon succeeding to the throne every Kushite
ruler made a "journey of accession" to the
most important cult sites of his Nubian
homeland, including the temple of Amun in
Kawa. Pharaoh Tarharqa (690–664 BC)
subsequently erected a cult chapel between
the pillars of this shrine. The reliefs show him
offering to Amun, Mut, Khonsu, and the war
god Montu, who was also worshipped in
Thebes.

*10 Barque sanctuary of Philip Arrhidaeus
(southern outer wall, segment)*
Karnak, Temple of Amun-Re; Greek Period,
ca. 320 BC; red granite, painted; register H.:
ca. 130 cm.
After the surprise death of Alexander the
Great in Babylon in 323 BC, his mentally
deficient half-brother Philip Arrhidaeus
(ruled 323-317 BC) was proclaimed king by
the army. Although he never set foot in Egypt,
the central barque shrine of the Karnak
temple was replaced by a new construction
in his name. As was the traditional manner,
the hard stone reliefs were only partially
painted, while the style used was that of
work from the last indigenous Dynasty, the
Thirtieth. On the south wall of the shrine
several registers are reserved for the themes
of royal coronation and the stations of the
great barque procession of the god Amun-Re.

11 Temple of Hibis

Kharga Oasis; Twenty-seventh Dynasty, reign of Darius I, ca. 500 BC; sandstone; L. 44 m, W. 19 m, H. ca. 8.5 m.

When the Persian Achaemenid Dynasty conquered Egypt and set up the Twenty-seventh Dynasty there, the country formed the western frontier of their empire. Two shrines, the temple of Qasr Gueida and the temple of Hibis, were built under Darius I at this most westerly outpost of the Persian sphere of influence, in the Kharga Oasis in the Libyan desert; both were dedicated to the god Amun. They were intended to provide magical and ritual protection for the imperial frontier. Kharga, once an important center of traffic and trade and situated at the start of a caravan route to Lower Nubia, experienced new prosperity in the Persian Period through the construction of underground irrigation channels. The temple of Hibis was built ca. 500 BC, possibly on the site of an earlier shrine of the Twenty-sixth Dynasty, and according to an inscription was constructed "of fine white stone, with roofs of Libyan acacia wood and with bronze from Asia." The ground plan of the palace of Darius in the Persian city of Persepolis is remarkably similar to the plan of this temple. Moreover, the use at Persepolis of features such as the cavetto cornice, the winged sun disk and the style of floral ornamentation on the column capitals shows that Egyptian architecture had made a deep impression on the Persian ruler.

12 Intercolumnar panel showing the New Year's ritual

Probably from Sais; Twenty-sixth Dynasty, ca. 600 BC; green slate; H. 120 cm; Vienna, Kunsthistorisches Museum, ÄS 213.

This stone slab can best be identified as a free-standing panel once set between the columns of an open kiosk, since it has relief work on both sides. In the lower area, it also shows the "palace facade" pattern typical of the base of a structure, and is crowned with the frieze of uraeus motifs that always marks the upper, terminal portion of an architectural component. The side shown here depicts the kneeling ruler successively "cleansing" the baboon god known as the "great white one" with four containers of water, bringing bolts of fabric to clothe the four-headed snake god "he who lives through his magic power," and worshipping the six-legged snake goddess "she of the nose." The building was probably already founded under Psammetichus I, as an inscription on one of its barriers (now in The British Museum in London) indicates, but his successors Necho II and Psammetichus II continued using it and completed it respectively. The name rings of Psammetichus II are on the Vienna piece. Every year the images of the gods were carried up from the darkness of the sanctuary to such kiosks on the temple roof, to renew their powers in the sunlight.

13 Bowl of General Wendjebauendjed
Tanis, the general's tomb (no. III); Twenty-first Dynasty, ca. 1000 BC; silver, gold plate, and glass; H. 2.5 cm, Diam. 18 cm; Cairo, Egyptian Museum, JE 87742.
While no vessels made of precious metals were found among the burial equipment of Tutankhamun, apart from a silver vase in the shape of a pomegranate (they may well have vanished without trace having been taken by ancient tomb robbers), the royal necropolis of Tanis has provided many vessels of gold and silver. One of the finest pieces, a silver bowl with a glass rosette set in its center and an internal gold plate section decorated with relief work showing fish, ducks, naked women swimming, and water plants, does not in fact come from a royal burial. This bowl was part of the funerary treasure of a high dignitary, the general and high priest Wendjebauendjed, who was granted the high honor of a burial place in the tomb of his lord, the pharaoh Psusennes I. According to the inscription, the king gave it to his subject during the general's lifetime as a "token of royal favor."

Royal Tombs

Very few royal tombs of the period following the New Kingdom have been preserved or excavated. However, we can gain a good idea of their appearance from accounts in classical antiquity, for instance by Herodotus, and from comparison with the tombs of other members of the royal house.

At the beginning of the Third Intermediate Period, a completely new form of royal burial was introduced and remained in use until Ptolemaic times: the tomb was a chapel within the temple precinct. In both this choice of location and their situation and structure, the royal tombs no longer obeyed the familiar traditions of the pyramid tombs of the Old and Middle Kingdoms or the rock-cut tombs of the New Kingdom in the Valley of the Kings. The rulers were now interred in their various royal capitals in the Nile Delta. One reason that the necropolis in the Valley of the Kings was abandoned at the end of the New Kingdom may have been the increasing insecurity of Thebes; tomb robbery was now frequent, and even the royal tombs were not spared. Major factors favoring the temple as the new burial site were proximity to the sanctuary itself and the fact that the tomb would be secure within the most strongly walled part of the city.

Characteristics of Late Period royal tombs include their placement in the courtyard of a god's temple, the chapel-like form of their superstructures, and the spatial proximity of the cult area and the tomb itself, a feature that had been abandoned during the New Kingdom. By comparison with private tombs of the same period, the underground tombs and their superstructures are quite small. Their importance lay less in the architectural execution of their layout than in the sanctity of the location and a possible historical precedent.

The tombs of the kings of the Twenty-first and Twenty-second Dynasties are in the southwest corner of the temple precincts of Tanis. The underground tombs found intact by Pierre Montet in 1939 proved to be rich treasure chambers, but while nothing was left of the unfired mudbrick superstructures, their existence can be inferred from the massive ceiling structures. This hypothesis also derives support from

14 Mummy mask of Psusennes I
Tanis, tomb of Psusennes I; Twenty-first Dynasty, ca. 995 BC; gold with lapis lazuli and glass inlays; H. 48 cm, W. 38 cm, thickness of gold plating 0.6 mm; Cairo, Egyptian Museum, JE 85913.
In all, four golden mummy masks were found in the royal tombs of Tanis. They are the masks of kings Psusennes I, Amenemope, and Sheshonq II, and of General Wendjebauendjed. The first is the finest, and is surpassed only by the world-famous mask of Tutankhamun. Unlike the mask of Tutankhamun, the mask of Psusennes bears no inscription, but it too shows the royal headdress with the uraeus, the pleated divine beard, rolled at the end, symbolizing the deification of the ruler as Osiris, and the broad collar. However, the inlaid work of blue lapis lazuli and glass is restricted to the area around the eyes and the band tying the beard; nor does it delineate the stripes of the headdress. The mask was found still lying over the face of the ruler's mummy, which had been interred in several coffins and sarcophagi nesting one inside the other.

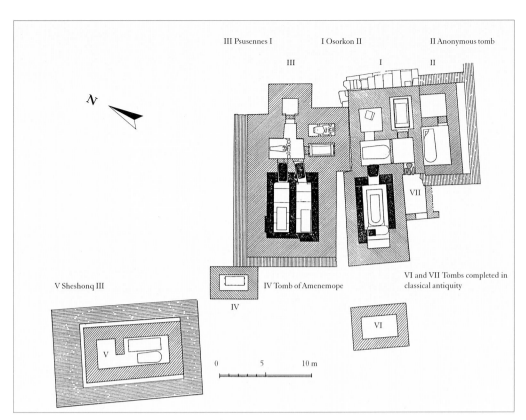

15 Ground plan of the royal tombs of Tanis
Twenty-first and Twenty-second Dynasties, ca. 1040–800 BC.

Detailed analysis of the building sequence of this series of royal tombs, numbering six in all and constructed by the kings of the Twenty-first and Twenty-second Dynasties in the southwest corner of the temple of Amun in Tanis, shows that some of their occupants have changed places. Tomb no. III, of Psusennes I, the second king of the Twenty-first Dynasty, in which Sheshonq II of the Twenty-second Dynasty was also later buried, partly overlaps the foundations of tomb no. I lying next to it, which can only have been commissioned by Smendes, founder of the Twenty-first Dynasty and Psusennes' predecessor on the throne. However, remains of the burials of Osorkon II, his successor Takelot II of the Twenty-second Dynasty and the contemporary Prince Hornakht were found in the same tomb. At least two canopic jars from the grave goods of the ousted Smendes are now in collections in Boston and New York.

It has been possible to identify the tombs to the west of this group as those of Amenemope (tomb IV) and Sheshonq III (tomb V). Sheshonq I obviously had to make way for a later ruler, whose stone canopic chest (now in Berlin) has been preserved.

16/17 (left and above) Tomb chapels of the "god's wives of Amun," and section of the facade
Medinet Habu, outer court of the temple of Ramesses III; Twenty-fifth/Twenty-sixth Dynasties, ca. 750–585 BC.

During the Late Period the "god's wives of Amun," the highest secular office of female representatives of the Theban divine state, erected their tombs in the court that lay between the monumental portal to the temple precincts of Ramesses III and the sanctuary of Medinet Habu itself. Where mudbrick super-structures were built over the stone burial chambers, as in the tomb of Shepenupet I, they have not survived. The two tomb chapels in the area are still preserved complete; they were both commissioned by Shepenupet II, daughter of the pharaoh Piye, the southern chapel for her predecessor Amenirdis, sister of Shabako, the northern chapel for herself. The latter was not completed, so that her successor Nitocris, daughter of Psammetichus I of the newly arisen Twenty-sixth Dynasty, could be buried here with her mother Mehetenusekhet.

the situation of the rooms, half a meter below ground level in antiquity, and the fact that they had to remain accessible for later burials. The burial chambers themselves, constructed of limestone blocks from older buildings, contained the remains of kings, high officials, and members of the royal family. Most of the the rooms are hardly larger than the sarcophagi they contain, and are ornamented with painted reliefs showing scenes from the netherworld books and devotional texts. Most of the sarcophagi did not originally belong to the occupants of the tombs, not necessarily because of the difficulty of obtaining new stone from distant Upper Egypt; there may also have been a wish to ensure religious validity by using what was old. The mummiform inner coffins were gilded or made of silver, and the coffin of Sheshonq II bears a falcon's head. Some of the mummies wore gold masks and rich jewelry.

Other funerary complexes of high-ranking members of the royal family are known to us from the temple precincts of Memphis. These tombs were underground burial chambers ornamented with images of the underworld, and in construction and situation may be compared with the complexes in Tanis, Sais, and Medinet Habu. The Kushite kings of the Twenty-fifth Dynasty constructed pyramid tombs in the necropolises of their capital, Napata, in northern Sudan.

The tomb chapels of those princesses of the Twenty-first to Twenty-sixth Dynasties who occupied one of the highest and at this time most influential of religious offices, the position of "god's wife of Amun," are in the precincts of Medinet Habu, the mortuary temple of Ramesses II in Western Thebes. The origins and function of these princesses indicated their close relationship to the kings, and their tombs resemble the royal tombs of the period. The excellent state of preservation of two of these chapels, built not of mudbricks but of stone, allows us a glimpse of a typical royal tomb of the Late Period. Access to the courtyards of these relatively small chapels (about 10 x 15 m), with pillars running around them, is through a pylon with a wooden portico in front of it. The cult building itself lies beyond the courtyard, and apart from a narrow ambulatory is almost entirely occupied by a room with a vaulted ceiling. The coffin was let down into the bottom of a shaft directly below this ceiling.

The ground plan of the Theban chapels corresponds quite closely to Herodotus's account of the royal tombs of Sais. He tells us that all the kings of the Twenty-sixth Dynasty from the Saite nome were buried in the courtyard of the temple of Neith at Sais, and describes the tomb of Amasis as a great stone hall with a portico of palm columns, ending in two doors behind which lay the coffin. The tombs of Sais have not yet been excavated; since items from the royal funerary equipment of Apries, Psammetichus I, and Psammetichus II exist in various museum collections, it seems likely that they were plundered a long time ago. The tombs of the Persian rulers of the Twenty-seventh Dynasty are not in Egypt but in Naqsh-i Rustam in Iran. The royal tombs of the Twenty-eighth to Thirtieth Dynasties very probably followed the chapel tomb model and were situated in the residence cities of Mendes and Sebennytos respectively. From the time of the Twenty-first Dynasty, it can be said that there was a new type of royal tomb, and one in marked contrast to the private tombs of the same period, although no real explanation has yet been found for the nature and origin of this significant development.

18 Tomb of Montemhet in the Asasif
West Thebes (TT 34); Twenty-fifth/Twenty-sixth Dynasties, ca. 650 BC.
One of the largest of the Late Period tombs in Thebes was that of the dignitary Montemhet, who contrived to remain in office as mayor of the Egyptian capital of Thebes even during the great political turmoil of the late Kushite era (Twenty-fifth Dynasty), the brief period of foreign rule by the Assyrians, and the follow-ing Saite Period (Twenty-sixth Dynasty). In addition, Montemhet held the high priestly office of a "fourth prophet of Amun." The first court of his tomb, between the entrances to the side chambers, is decorated with large panels of symmetrically arranged pairs of papyrus plants. The owner of the tomb himself is depicted in relief on both sides of the entrances.

19 Late Period tombs
West Thebes; Twenty-fifth/Twenty-sixth Dynasties, ca. 750–525 BC.
Many tombs were built during the Twenty-fifth and Twenty-sixth Dynasties, particularly in the Asasif, the area lying just in front of the valley of Deir el-Bahari, where the procession of the divine barque of Amun led to the terraced temple of Queen Hatshepsut during the Opet festival. The entrances of these tombs faced the processional route, which follows the modern paved road (seen at left in the picture). The mudbrick pylons in front of the entrances are particularly striking features, while the tomb complexes behind them – the tomb of Montemhet is in the foreground and that of Pabasa behind it – consist of one or several subterranean open courts with an extensive, branching system of corridors and shafts with subsidiary underground rooms opening off of them.

The Tombs of Private Individuals

Priests and officials of the Third Intermediate Period preferred collective or family burial places, and older tombs were often reused for this purpose, not just out of economic considerations but for reasons of security. The trials of tomb robbers in the not-so-distant past had made their mark, and so had the operations carried out to retrieve the stolen royal mummies of the New Kingdom, who were themselves reburied in collective tombs.

Expensive, elaborately decorated tombs were avoided; the most important mythological scenes were depicted on the coffins, which were generally made of cartonnage and wood. Shortage of space left room for only a small selection of such scenes, and an extensive papyrus Book of the Dead was added to the burial. The painting of coffins and papyri reached an artistic peak at this period.

Although tombs of the Late Period are to be found in every necropolis of the contemporary settlements, the most important places of burial were still Thebes and Memphis.

The tombs of the Twenty-sixth Dynasty at Memphis were built to a different plan from that of the monumental structures in the Theban necropolises of the same period. Total protection from tomb robbers was the prime consideration, and an ingenious security system was devised. The sarcophagus lay at the bottom of a vertical shaft, sometimes more than 30 m in depth, inside a walled burial chamber with skylights. The shaft was filled with sand, and the burial itself took place through a narrower vertical side shaft linked to the main shaft by a short brick vault. Finally, the skylights of the burial chamber were opened for sand to be poured in. Then the linking passage was destroyed and the subsidiary shaft was also filled in with sand. There was

20/21 Scenes from the tomb of Menena
West Thebes (TT 69); Eighteenth Dynasty, ca. 1395 BC; plastered and painted limestone.
22 Scene from the tomb of Montemhet
West Thebes (TT 34); Twenty-fifth to Twenty-sixth Dynasties, ca. 650 BC; limestone; H. 23.9 cm; New York, The Brooklyn Museum, Charles Edwin Wilbour Fund, 48.74.

New artistic developments after the political unrest of the Third Intermediate Period led to an increase in deliberate borrowing from older models. The high officials of Thebes were inspired by the rock-cut tombs of the New Kingdom. The motif of a mother sitting under

a tree and suckling her child, held in a broad cloth against her body, while she helps herself from a basket of fruit, occurs in both the tomb of Menena and the tomb of Montemhet, although the later version has taken over only the basic motif.

The other picture, only the upper part of which has been preserved, can also be reconstructed by comparison with a parallel scene in the tomb of Menena, showing a young girl removing a thorn from the foot of another girl sitting opposite her. It is certain that the tomb of Menena provided the model, if only because there are no other known scenes using either motif.

23 Torso from a statue of Osorkon I
Byblos; Twenty-second Dynasty, ca. 900 BC;
sandstone; H. 60 cm, W. 36 cm; Paris, Musée
du Louvre, AO 9502.
This fragment of a statue was found in
Byblos, where a local ruler added a dedicatory
text to the goddess of the city, the "Lady of
Byblos," in Phoenician alphabetic script.
There is controversy over the question of why,
and above all when, this Egyptian statue
showing the ruler with the uraeus serpent
and a form of wig especially popular in the
Amarna Period came to be in the Libyan
coastal city, and over the time that elapsed
between its creation and the addition of the
secondary inscription. A point at issue is
whether Osorkon I, in placing the cartouche
containing his name on the chest – a very
unusual arrangement for a royal statue – was
appropriating a work of art from the time of
Horemheb, or whether he was only borrowing from the style of the earlier period.

origins of this festival date from the beginning of the Middle Kingdom,
and it flourished again in the Late Period.

With the inclusion of various elements of other architectural
forms, such as private dwellings, rock-cut tombs of the New Kingdom,
and the royal mortuary temples, new tomb forms developed, but not in
compliance with any single concept. Features of the Theban tombs of
the Late Period include their freestanding mudbrick superstructures,
the presence of an open courtyard sunk into the bedrock (in reference
to the tomb of Osiris at Abydos), and subterranean rooms opening off
the courtyard. Many details in the structure of these buildings reinter-
pret older forms, some of them long disused, such as vaulted door
frames, niches or the so-called "palace facade" patterns in the superstructures, and funerary cones or mudbrick pyramids of private tombs
of the New Kingdom.

The program of tomb decoration likewise harks back to structural
elements of earlier periods. Individual depictions, pictorial sequences
and texts in imitation of those in nearby but much older tombs,
frequently appear in the extensive complexes of the Saite tombs in
Western Thebes. However, like the decoration of the tombs at
Memphis, they cannot really be called copies. These borrowings are
never slavish reproductions of their models, but are a selection and
rearrangement of old motifs, perhaps chosen for reasons of individual
preference, and complemented by details from other monuments.

Although the origin and age of the models themselves cannot
usually be determined, a style developed that was unmistakably
specific to the Late Period. This phenomenon, described not entirely
accurately as "archaism" or a "renaissance," is sporadically attested
earlier, but it became increasingly common from the time of the
Twenty-fifth Dynasty, perhaps reflecting a desire to revive aspects of
former political greatness and religious efficacy. Motifs were probably
taken from pattern books and/or direct study of the originals.

Between the Twenty-sixth Dynasty and the Ptolemaic Period, only
a few tombs can be dated with certainty. Various necropolises contain
rock-cut tombs, shaft tombs, and tombs within temple precincts.

Freestanding Sculpture

The few surviving royal sculptures of the Third Intermediate Period
continue the traditions of the New Kingdom on the same high artistic
level. Immediately after the Twentieth Dynasty it was still common for
private individuals to acquire New Kingdom statues, either retouching
them or usurping them by changing the inscription. New statues of
this period show a decline in the variety of types depicted and a
tendency toward simplification exemplified, for instance, by the cuboid
or block statue with its clear geometric surfaces. However, these
smooth surfaces were seldom left empty, but were frequently covered
with inscriptions or figurative representations.

The direct juxtaposition of private individuals with deities brings
the bronze statue, until now rather insignificant as an artistic genre, to
a period of great popularity. The bronzes include sculptures of the

now a reservoir of 2,000–3,000 cubic meters of loose sand above the
coffin, effectively preventing tomb robbery, since the sand would have
flowed unstoppably toward any intruder.

The decoration program of the burial chambers consists of Old
Kingdom pyramid texts; however, they were not copied word for word
from the nearby pyramid of Unas but compiled from other and sometimes more complete versions. Small mudbrick structures, now lost,
stood above the shaft, so that in their own way these complexes may
have resembled the Saite royal tombs.

The Theban tombs are fundamentally different from their
contemporary counterparts at Memphis in their monumental dimensions and their complexity, but they do display certain similarities with
earlier Memphite tombs of the New Kingdom. The great funerary
complexes of high officials of the Twenty-fifth and Twenty-sixth Dynasties are in Western Thebes, in the Asasif, a plain just in front of the
valley of Deir el-Bahari. They are generally close to the old processional
routes along which the cult image of Amun-Re was borne through the
necropolis on the occasion of the "beautiful festival of the valley." The

24 Head of a statue of Taharqa
Probably Karnak; Twenty-fifth Dynasty, ca. 670 BC; gray granodiorite; H. 36.5 cm, W. 24 cm; Cairo, Egyptian Museum, CG 560. This head, found in Luxor, has been identified as a portrait of the Kushite ruler Taharqa, the most important ruler of the Twenty-fifth Dynasty, from the remains of an inscription on the back pillar behind it. However, stylistic features such as the rounded face, broad nose, and massive neck allow us in any case to date this head accurately to the Twenty-fifth Dynasty. Further significant features include such iconographic details as the double uraeus serpent, now broken off, that was set on the roughened stone of the "Kushite cap," formerly gilded and with the traditional pharaonic Double Crown rising above it.

25 Colossal head of a Kushite ruler
Probably from Karnak, the temple of Amun-Re; Twenty-fifth Dynasty, ca. 700 BC; red granite; H. 35 cm; Cairo, Egyptian Museum, CG 1291. This head, broken from a monumental standing figure, is among the best examples of royal freestanding sculpture of the Twenty-fifth Dynasty. The S-shape of the clearly executed nasolabial folds and the structure of the eyebrows make identification with Pharaoh Shebitku (Shabataka) very probable. On his head, the king wears the characteristic "Kushite cap" with a broad band around the forehead and the double uraeus, in this case almost entirely destroyed.

greatest artistic refinement as well as simple votive offerings in the form of small figures of gods and animals.

After centuries during which their land of Kush had remained under the Egyptian sphere of influence, the Nubian rulers of the Twenty-fifth Dynasty felt themselves to be the legitimate successors of the pharaohs. They represented themselves in the Egyptian tradition but with their own Kushite style, typically showing a round head with African features above a sturdy frame. Iconographic innovations include the double uraeus on the forehead, the close-fitting cap, or the addition of a ram's head amulet around the neck. The style of private sculpture continued to imitate that of the royal statues. At the same time, there were still statues in the tradition of the New Kingdom, or even looking back formally or stylistically to earlier epochs. The first "portraits of old age," so popular during the Twenty-seventh Dynasty, also make their first appearance at this time.

Under the Saite pharaohs of the Twenty-sixth Dynasty, Egypt once more enjoyed a period of economic stability and cultural flowering. Unfortunately, however, only a few incomplete examples of dated royal sculptures or works can be definitely ascribed to this period. The kings usually wear the Blue Crown. Their facial expressions are greatly idealized, although the effect is not a muted one. A large amount of private sculpture has been preserved. The most preferred material was a hard, dark stone, notable for its polished or very glossy surface. The most frequent type found is the theophoric statue, in which a standing, kneeling or squatting donor holds the figure of a divinity in front of him, either freestanding or in a naos. A new fashion detail of costume appearing at this period is the bagwig.

Despite formal and iconographic references to earlier epochs, the statues can be accurately dated. They are not mere imitations but, quite apart from the high quality of artistry and craftsmanship, they make an unmistakable statement of their own, while including a number of assimilated elements. The slight smile worn by both royal and private statues is a stylistic feature that was a conspicuous characteristic of the period and even found its way into Greek art.

No royal sculpture from the Persian Period has been preserved apart from a headless statue of Darius found outside his palace at Susa.

26 Head of a statue of King Amasis
Sais; Twenty-sixth Dynasty, ca. 550 BC; graywacke; H. 24 cm; Berlin, SMPK, Ägyptisches Museum, 11864.
In the Saite Period and the following dynasties, the graywacke quarried in the Wadi Hammamat enjoyed a popular revival as a material for statues and architecture in both the royal and the private spheres. This head, assumed on stylistic grounds to represent King Amasis, shows the most typical stylistic feature of its time, which has found its way into the terminology of art history as the "Saite smile" and may even have influenced the features of archaic Greek *kuroi*. However, the *nemes* or royal headdress with a uraeus serpent (now broken off) worn by the Saite ruler here is the exception rather than the rule among royal figures of this period. The king is more frequently shown wearing the *khepresh* or Blue Crown, perhaps to distinguish his dynasty from the preceding Kushites, who never wore this form of crown.

27 Torso of a standing figure of Nectanebo I
Probably Delta; Thirtieth Dynasty, ca. 370 BC; gray granite; H. 68.5 cm; London, The British Museum, EA 1013.
Under the last dynasty of native rulers all forms of art as well as architecture saw a last, brief flowering. Royal and private sculpture is characterized by the formative influence of a stylistic return to the classical late period of the Twenty-sixth Dynasty. Most striking is the three-part upper body musculature modeling which also bestows a natural, athletic aura on this torso of a standing figure in London. The King is wearing the the traditional short apron with his name cartouche carved on the belt buckle. Originally, the high white crown or the more compact blue crown would have belonged to Nectanebo's regalia.

This statue, created by Egyptian artists, originally stood in the temple of Heliopolis. A unique feature of the work is that while it followed Egyptian formal requirements in structure and execution, it showed the king in purely Persian clothing and with Persian weapons. The private sculpture of the time shows a certain trend toward realism, perhaps deriving from the sculpture of the Middle Kingdom. Faces marked by old age appear with increasing frequency. Often the clothing and ornaments shown are Persian, as in the standing figures of Ptahhotep (now in The Brooklyn Museum) and Udjahorresnet (now in the Vatican).

Only a few sculptures of the following dynasties have so far been found. They represent a further development of the works of the Twenty-sixth Dynasty, and can sometimes be distinguished from them only with difficulty. The bodies are even more perfectly modeled, and the surfaces polished to a high sheen. A new type of statue occurring at the end of the Late Period is the genre known as the *statue guérisseuse*, which was equipped with magical symbols and covered with magic spells, and was supposed to protect its donor or a worshipper from misfortune. Magical statues of this kind enjoyed much popularity in the Ptolemaic period.

28 Standing statue of the "god's wife of Amun" Karomama

Probably Karnak; Twenty-second Dynasty, ca. 870 BC; bronze with gold and silver inlays; H. 59 cm; Paris, Musée du Louvre, N 500.

The art of bronze sculpture reached a new peak in Egypt during the Third Intermediate Period. Although iron was known at the time, the finest examples of the technique are the cast bronzes overlaid with gold, silver or electrum (an alloy of gold and silver), or niello (iron sulfide). Even *shabti* figurines such as those found in the royal tombs of Tanis were made of bronze. One of the finest works of this period is the standing figure of the "god's wife of Amun" Karomama, which is ornately decorated with colored and precious metal inlays. Since there were several noble ladies of the same name (the wives of Sheshonq I, Osorkon II, and Takelot II were all named Karomama), there was much scholarly dispute over the precise identity of this statuette. Although she was once considered to represent the wife of Takelot II, a daughter of the high priest Namlot and the mother of Osorkon III, she has now been definitively identified as the granddaughter of Osorkon I.

29 Standing figure of Montemhet

Karnak, temple of Amun-Re, the "cachette;" Twenty-fifth to Twenty-sixth Dynasties, ca. 650 BC; granodiorite; H. 139 cm; Cairo, Egyptian Museum, JE 36933 (CG 42236).

Montemhet's activities in a period of constant change are reflected in the varying style of his many portraits, a large number of which have fortunately survived. This standing figure, seen in the act of striding forward, was found in the "cachette court" at Karnak in 1904; with the muscular modeling of the body, the short, massive neck, and the full face with clearly marked nasolabial folds, a broad, flat nose, and the indication of tear sacs under the eyes, it still reflects the Kushite tradition, while Montemhet's later free-standing statues derive from the more academic, restrained style of the early Saite Period.

30 Naophoric standing figure of Udjahorresnet

Probably Sais; Twenty-seventh Dynasty; green basalt; H. 70 cm; The Vatican, Museo Gregoriano Egizio, 196.

Udjahorresnet began his career as the commander of the Egyptian fleet under the last two Saite rulers, Amasis and Psammetichus II, and reached the height of his power during foreign Persian rule under Cambyses and Darius, whom he served as an indispensable adviser. This information is provided by the extensive biographical inscription on the surface of the Persian robe he wears in his naophoric statue. He holds a small open shrine with a figure of Osiris, perhaps being carried in the annual procession to the temple roof. The statue shows the moment at which the priest stops and sets the naos with its pillared plinth on the big toe of his left foot.

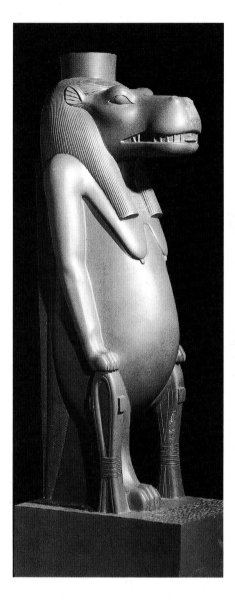

31 Statue of the goddess Thoeris
North Karnak, chapel of Osiris-Padedankh; Twenty-sixth Dynasty, ca. 615 BC; green slate; H. 96 cm; Cairo, Egyptian Museum, CG 39194.
As in the human freestanding sculpture of the Saite Period, the rounded modeling of the body shapes dominates this standing figure of the hippopotamus goddess Thoeris in polished slate. As guardian deity of pregnant women, she is shown as pregnant herself. Lion's claws and the crocodile tail running down her back symbolize her defensive qualities, also expressed in what amounts to a kind of inscription, since she is supporting herself on two specimens of the looped hieroglyph *Sa* ("protection"). The figure was found in a limestone shrine (Cairo, CG 70027) to the north of the temple of Amun in Karnak; the shrine was given to the "god's wife of Amun" Nitocris, daughter of Psammetichus I, by the chief domain administrator Pabasa, and provides evidence of the growing importance of animal cults in the Late Period. The original location of the find (1874) shows that the statue's shrine possesed an opening level only with the head of the goddess' statue. Visitors to the temple could establish direct eye contact with the deity to present their requests and make offerings. The decorated shrine was built into a brick chapel dedicated to Osiris.

32 Headless standing statue of DariusI
Susa, east of the palace; Twenty-seventh Dynasty, ca. 490 BC; hard grey limestone; H. as preserved 246 cm; Teheran, Iran Bastan Museum.
This over-life-sized standing figure of the Persian king Darius shows the ruler in Persian dress, but standing on a plinth bearing Egyptian motifs. It was found in Darius's capital of Susa in 1972, where it stood outside the palace gate; it was manufactured, however, in Egypt. The sculpture bears inscriptions in three languages (Egyptian, Elamite, and ancient Persian) on the folds of the robe. The front of the plinth shows the unification of Upper and Lower Egypt, symbolically performed by two Nile deities linking their emblemic plants. On the sides, also in pharaonic tradition, personifications of defeated peoples are depicted above oval city circles inscribed with the names of their Persian satrapies. However, these peoples of the empire are not shown in fetters, as usual, but with their hands raised, so that they are in fact "supporting" the statue of the ruler on his plinth. Unfortunately, the excavators' hopes of finding either the head or a better preserved figure of the king on the other side of the palace gate have not been fulfilled.

33 Standing statue of Iret-Hor-ru with Osiris
Karnak, temple of Amun-Re, "cachette"; Twenty-sixth Dynasty, ca. 600 BC; green slate; H. 56 cm; Baltimore , The Walters Art Museum, 22.215.
This small statue shows the official with a long apron and a braided wig which leaves the ears free. With both hands he holds in front of him the cult figure of Osiris, god of the underworld, who is depicted in his canonical appearance with Atef crown and insignia. This type of statute, with numerous variations, enjoyed great popularity from the New Kingdom onward, and was especially to be found in the field of temple sculture. Iret-Hor-ru, who bore numerous titles, held office in the Amun temple at Karnak, as had his father and grandfather before him. In the inscription he is given the titles of "Father of the God" and "Priest of Amun-Re, King of the Gods." This statue to him was donated by his son who bore the name of the ruling monarch, Necho. Also taking into account discernable stylistic criteria, the dating of the statue to this period of the Twenty-sixth Dynasty can be considered certain. It was discovered in 1905 during the renowned "cachette" excavations at Karnak, and at first transfered to the safe keeping of the Cairo museum before its official sale in 1911.

34 Portrait of an old man
Probably Memphis; Twenty-seventh Dynasty, ca. 450 BC; graywacke, H. 25.1 cm, W. 18.1 cm; Paris, Musée du Louvre, N 2454.
During the Twenty-seventh Dynasty, as we know from the few sculptural works that can be dated with certainty from inscriptions, the style of the Saite Period was continued and further developed into lifelike portraiture by the introduction of realistically executed features. This bust of an anonymous dignitary, with the "Saite smile" on a full-lipped mouth that wears an otherwise skeptical expression, probably dates to the period of Persian rule. However, the vividly modeled face, full and rather slack, with crow's feet at the corners of the eyes, a slight double chin and a double fold around the neck is reminiscent of portraits of the Middle Kingdom in its abandonment of a purely idealized approach.

35 Cult figure of a falcon god
Probably Twenty-seventh Dynasty, ca. 500 BC; silver and electrum; H. 27 cm; Munich, Staatliches Museum Ägyptischer Kunst, on loan from the Bayerische Landesbank.
The valuable material from which this divine figure is made suggests that it was not a votive offering from a wealthy donor, but the cult figure kept in the innermost sanctuary of a temple, formerly accessible only to the pharaoh and the high priest. The composition of the trace elements in the silver makes it likely that the figure was made during the period of Persian rule, when silver was imported into Egypt by the Persians and was in more general use than at earlier periods. Small iconographic deviations from the rule, such as the slightly curved upper part of the "Lower Egyptian" section of the double crown could be interpreted, however, as an indication that the figure may actually have been made by Persian metalworkers.

36 The Tyszkiewicz statue
Thirtieth Dynasty, ca. 350 BC; black granite; H. 68 cm; Paris, Musée du Louvre, E 10777.
This statue, called after its former owner, belongs to the *statue guérisseuse* type, a figure covered all over with magical texts and pictures. Most such figures are of high dignitaries who were elevated to the rank of patron saints after death. The statues, erected in temples, had water poured over them; as it ran down the sacred figure, the water was supposed to absorb magic powers, and was then often collected by worshippers in small bowls set into the plinth of the statue for that purpose and taken away for use as a medicinal fluid. Here the statue is holding an apotropaic stela with a depiction of Horus as a divine child averting evil.

The Political History of the Ptolemies and the Imperial Roman Period in Egypt

Dieter Kessler

The advance of the Macedonian king Alexander the Great from Greece into the heart of the Persian empire also brought an end to Persian rule in Egypt. The Macedonian troops marched into Memphis in 332 BC. Alexander founded the new capital of Alexandria on the site of an Egyptian port in a good position for traffic on the western arm of the Nile, and moved on by way of Marsa Matruh into the Siwa Oasis, where he had himself confirmed king by the oracle in the temple of Amun.

Alexander established an internal policy that would also be binding on his successors by holding his coronation ceremony in Memphis according to Egyptian ritual, recognizing indigenous oracles, and recruiting members of the last native Egyptian ruling house into the army. He was both pharaoh of Egypt and king of Greece to the Egyptians and Greeks who assembled at state festivals. The Greek eagle of Zeus and the divine standards of the theriomorphic Egyptian gods now stood side by side.

Alexander's religious policies were based on those of the Thirtieth Dynasty. He rebuilt the sanctuary of the temple of Luxor, and at a later date his successors rebuilt the sanctuary of Amun at Karnak. The ideology behind associating himself with the divine ancestors of the pharaohs also provides the background of the literary tale of the "Deceit of Nectanebo," which narrates the story of a liaison between Alexander's mother Olympias and Nectanebo II. After Alexander's death in Babylon, his general Ptolemy transferred his corpse to a tomb in Alexandria that has yet to be found, and where a dynastic cult was instituted in his honor.

The Rule of the Greeks (323–30 BC)

The position of the Greeks on the pharaonic throne became part of the international politics of Hellenistic Greece and its vassal states. At first, Egyptian foreign policy was determined by disputes over Alexander's inheritance. Ptolemy II's fleet tried to reassert the old Egyptian claims on Cyprus, and also conquered parts of the south coast of Asia Minor and bases on the coasts of Greece and Crete. Quarrels flared up over the Palestinian areas lying between the Syro-Mesopotamian kingdom of the Seleucid dynasty and Egypt.

In Egypt, Alexander's general Ptolemy at first ruled formally in the name of the generally recognized successors of Alexander himself, Philip (III) Arrhidaios and Alexander IV, Alexander the Great's son by the Bactrian princess Roxana, but in 305 BC Ptolemy crowned himself pharaoh. With the assistance of Egyptian and Greek advisers, he tried to unite these two diverse ethnic groups, usually divided by their religious practices, at the state ceremonies of the festivals of Osiris and the New Year, using a set of sacred rituals for the purpose. They included the elevation of Serapis (equated with the ancient Egyptian god Osiris-Apis) to chief god of the Greek rulers. The Serapeum of Alexandria, where Egyptian divinities and their sacred animals are also present, received its own Greek temple to Serapis, with a Greek statue of the god over 10 m high, next to the sanctuary of Osiris, Isis, and Harpocrates that was central to the festivals. The cult of Serapis, with which the cults of the ruling house and of Osiris and Isis were linked, spread swiftly from Alexandria throughout the Mediterranean area, partly with the Ptolemies' encouragement through the construction of new sacred buildings in their more far-flung holdings.

Alexandria had its own civic laws and thus occupied a special position within Egypt. The Hellenistic and Egyptian ways of life in the city merged to create a unique Alexandrian style. Ethnic groups from the entire Mediterranean region settled in Alexandria, not least because it was the point of intersection of many trade routes. The shipping route along the Red Sea, in particular, was extended. Luxury goods such as incense, spices, fabrics, and rare animals were brought to Alexandria. Ptolemy II (282–246 BC) staged a magnificent show for the people of the city, featuring a much-admired ceremonial procession with elephants, panthers, and other exotic beasts.

From the time of Ptolemy II's reign, the population of Alexandria became noticeably more Egyptian. Isis and Osiris now held out the hope of salvation to Greeks as well as to Egyptians, and Egyptian representations stood next to Greek statues.

The royal palace of Alexandria was the scene of court intrigues, often of a bloody nature, but the library of Alexandria and the large

1 Cleopatra VII
Probably Mauretanian; post 30 BC; marble; H. 28 cm; Berlin, SMPK, Antikenmuseum, 1976.10.
As the last regent of the Ptolemaic ruling house, Cleopatra VII was one of the most outstanding personalities on the political scene of her time. The queen's keen intellect and personal magnetism played a more important role than her supposed beauty in the classical sense; judging by contemporary portraits of her on the coinage, she was not in fact particularly beautiful. This posthumous Greek portrait of the queen may come from Mauretania, where her daughter Cleopatra Selene was married to Juba II of Mauretania. Her son was assassinated by Augustus for political reasons. Augustus allowed portraits of Cleopatra to be created after her death for private purposes.

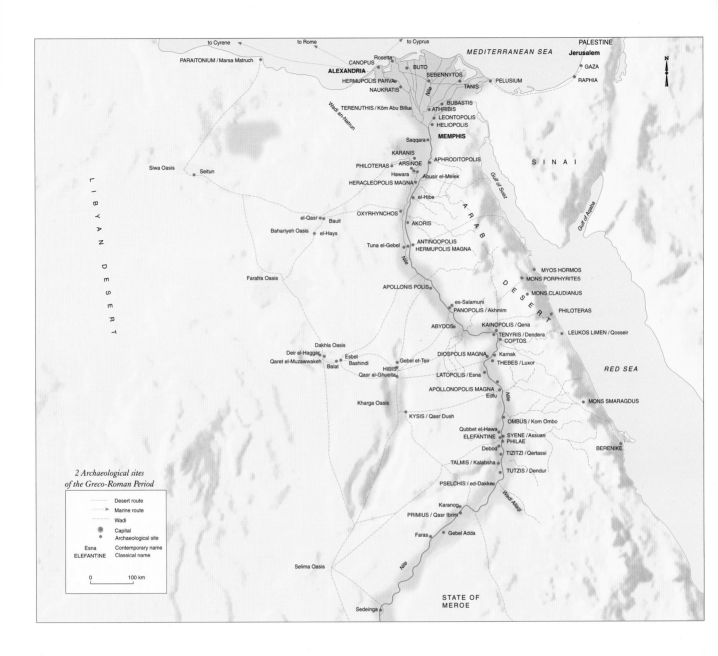

2 Archaeological sites
of the Greco-Roman Period

·········	Desert route
––►––	Marine route
– – –	Wadi
◉	Capital
•	Archaeological site
Esna	Contemporary name
ELEFANTINE	Classical name

0   100 km

number of scholars at court also made it a center for the collection of old traditions. Around 250 BC, Manetho of Sebennytos wrote a history of the pharaohs, drawing on the old king lists. Poets such as Kallimachos and scientists such as Eratosthenes, who calculated the circumference of the earth, were typical representatives of the famous Alexandrian school of scholarship.

The differences between the city of Alexandria and the rest of the country, the Khora, were enormous. The social position of native Egyptians there was not clearly delineated, and tension between different groups of the population was increasing. The Egyptians now became acquainted with the "blessings" of a money-based economy side by side with their traditional trade by barter. The official languages were Greek and, for the common people, Demotic. The relatively small number of Greeks in the interior of the country were landowners or administrative officials stationed in the provincial cities. Meanwhile,

the great mass of Egyptians continued to live by the ancient laws and rules of their traditional religion.

The Faiyum, where the Greek military colonists had settled, was a special legal case. Royal financial officials such as Zeno, known to us from the preservation of his papyrus archives, became large landowners in this area. Improvements in the water supply provided by a channel (the modern Bahr Yussuf) and by reservoirs meant that new fields could be cultivated as royal domains, and more than one harvest a year could be gathered. Another exceptional case was the Greek city of Ptolemais, founded by Ptolemy I in the Theban nome near Abydos, with a dynastic ruler cult on the model of the cult of Alexander. Yet a third special legal position was that of the Dodekashoinos or "twelve-mile strip" south of Aswan, which was a royal domain. The planned settlement policy of the Ptolemies and improved irrigation by means of canals and a new kind of scoop waterwheel (the *saqiya*, worked by draft animals) opened up new agricultural areas everywhere. Egypt's population rose to a total of between five and six million.

The Greeks encouraged the maintenance of temples and restored almost all of them throughout the land. In the interests of the state finances, the Ptolemies established a number of cult statues and small chapels, to whose upkeep Egyptian religious communities had to contribute; service to the cult center was divided into ten-day periods (decades), and the administration sold these as shares to Egyptian families. Every cemetery had its centers for the state cultic festivals of both groups of the population, with an Osireion and an animal cemetery for the sacred animals appropriate to the Egyptian tutelary gods who took their form.

The conduct of indigenous cults was left to the priests of the Egyptian temples, and their temple schools became guardians of the tradition. Greek influence was consistently kept away from cult practices and hieroglyphic literature. On the other hand, the Greek administration controlled and determined developments through royal decrees issued by temple synods. The administration of a cult's material possessions and oracular proceedings were subject to bilingual organization. Political oracles for the ruling house of the Ptolemies in Alexandria were imparted and written down in Demotic. The chief Greek administrative official of a region – first the nomarch and then the strategos – was also high priest of the indigenous Egyptian temple. There is clear Greek influence on the Demotic writings of the royal scribes, and particularly on fictional literature.

Under Ptolemy II (282–246 BC) and Ptolemy III (246–222 BC), a dynastic cult of the royal family was introduced, beginning with the veneration of the deceased queens Arsinoe II and Berenice II. Egypt suffered a severe economic crisis during the time of Ptolemy IV (221–204 BC), after victory in the battle of Raphia against the Syrian King Antiochus III (216 BC), when it was necessary to provide for many Egyptians who had been recruited into the Egyptian army at short notice. In Upper Egypt, internal conspiracies at the royal court, corruption, and misadministration led to years of decline of the central authority and the recognition of two rival kings (206–186 BC).

3 Head of a statue of Ptolemy I
Probably from the Faiyum; ca. 280 BC; white marble; H. 26 cm; Copenhagen, Ny Carlsberg Glyptothek, JN 2300.
This head is probably a posthumous portrait of the founder of the dynasty. Despite its Greek appearance, the surface features point to the Egyptian tradition. Ptolemy I's policy of integrating the Greeks in Egypt maintained the principles of Alexander the Great.

The Ptolemaic Kingdom and Meroe

In southern Egypt, the Kushite kingdom with its center in Napata was at first cut off from developments in the north after the campaign of Psammetichus II in the Twenty-sixth Dynasty. The royal house retained Egyptian forms of worship, with Osiris and Isis playing a prominent part in the cult of the dead. Only after the third century BC did temple walls depict such native gods such as Sebiumeker, who took human form, the elephant and snake gods and the lion-headed Apedemak.

The Kushites continued to maintain trade relations with the "great king" of Persia, but exploited the weakness of the rulers of the Second Persian Period to assert their own influence in Lower Nubia, which eventually became Kushite again. The Kushite kings increasingly resided in the more southerly city of Meroe, which marked the end of a major trade route. Eventually a king named Ergamanes (ca. 270–260 BC) had himself buried in Meroe, perhaps as part of a dispute with the priests of Napata. The necropolis of Meroe contained steep pyramids with Egyptian cult and burial chambers, and the indigenous language quickly found its way into the cult of the dead. Meroitic cursive script was developed for this purpose, and experiments were also made with a script derived from Egyptian hieroglyphs.

The Kushites were powerless against the heavily armed troops of Ptolemy II. In 275 BC the Egyptian army invaded Lower Nubia, with the specific purpose of gaining access to the gold of the Wadi Allaqi. Ptolemy II founded the city of Berenice Panchrysos ("the All-golden") to the east. The Kushites themselves took advantage of Egypt's weakness at the time of the rival kings in Thebes (from 204 BC) to extend their influence to Lower Nubia again. They reinforced their claim to the island of Philae by continuing construction on the Egyptian temple of Arensnuphis, and finally came to an agreement with Ptolemy IV. Access to the temple at Philae was kept open for visitors from the south. The Ptolemies and Kushites collaborated in constructing the temple of Thoth at Dakke in Lower Nubia and the temple of Amun at Debod. Old theological connections were revived, and the Horus falcon god of Edfu was linked to the "southern Horus," the Horus of Kush.

The Dodekaschoinos became a kind of free trade zone as far as Hierasykaminos, 120 km south of Aswan. However, the Ptolemies still controlled the area, and with it the gold mines in the Wadi Allaqi, which now resumed production.

The End of Greek Rule

The invasion of Egypt by King Antiochus IV of Syria in 168 BC led to the revolt of one Dionysios Petosarapis in Alexandria; social unrest

erupted in Memphis, the Faiyum, and Thebes. After the expulsion of the foreign troops a need for reforms was felt: both monetary reform and measures affecting the temples and religious communities. The subsequent great period of new building on the Egyptian temples under the last Ptolemies was connected with these economic changes. At a time when the presence and power interests of Rome were gradually increasing in Egypt, a period of oppressive social injustice, the greatest temples of the country were rebuilt or renovated: they included the temple of Opet in Karnak, the temple of Horus at Edfu (on which work was concluded in 70 BC), the temple of Hathor in Dendara, and the temple of Isis and Harpocrates on the island of Philae. These constructions were financed by the ordinary people of Egypt under the cult community system, and as a result they usually went on for decades. The economic importance of the temple centers united the priests of the protected temple sanctuaries with the people who lived locally. Once again, religious knowledge was collected in the temple schools. The distant pharaohs now played only a cultic or formal part in the life of the temples, and the inscriptions often simply mention "Pharaoh" in general instead of giving the ruler's name.

In the second and first centuries BC Egypt fell under the influence of Rome. The country's grain crops went to Rome, and Roman senators determined Egyptian politics. The long reign of the ineffective Ptolemy VIII (164 and 145–116 BC), marked by passivity, and the involvement of the royal house in violent internal power struggles had particularly devastating effects on the population. Once again the indigenous Egyptians rebelled. In 131/130 BC a man named Harsiese inscribed his name in a cartouche (royal ring) at Thebes and el-Hibe as the last native ruler. The religious provincialism of the people, who were attached to their own city gods and sacred animals, led to bloody conflicts between regions with different theocratic leanings, and hatred of the multinational groups of soldiers often connected with the necropolis temples and their autocratic actions did the rest. On one occasion, a Roman who killed a sacred cat by accident was actually lynched.

It remained only for Cleopatra VII (51–30 BC) to bring the country's independence to a dramatic close. She came to an agreement first with the Egyptian priesthood and then with the Roman rulers to support her against other potential claimants to the throne. She succeeded in establishing a liaison with Julius Caesar, whom she had invited to Alexandria, although during his visit to the palace of Alexandria a dangerous nationalist revolution broke out (47 BC). During the fighting the famous library of Alexandria was destroyed by fire, with devastating consequences for the transmission of a vast amount of knowledge.

Cleopatra bore Caesar a son named Caesarion, whom she used skillfully in Egypt's interests after Caesar's death. She had both herself and Caesarion depicted on the temple walls at Armant and Dendara to legitimate his status. Her later open parade of her love affair with Mark Antony, the Roman tribune and Caesar's political heir, concealed an attempt to reassert the Ptolemaic claim to her possessions in Cyprus and Cilicia, and she thereby linked herself to Mark Antony's fate. Octavian, Caesar's adopted son and later the emperor Augustus, cleverly encouraged hostile reaction to the couple's reputedly Egyptian and Hellenistic (and profoundly un-Roman) life of luxury and vice. The end of the story was a Roman one. After defeat at the sea battle of Actium (31 BC) and the death of Mark Antony, Cleopatra committed suicide with a venomous snake. Her son was killed by Augustus and her daughter Cleopatra Selene married off to Juba II of Mauretania, who proudly added the Egyptian symbols of Isis to his coinage. Egypt itself, however, became a Roman province in 30 BC under the rule of an imperial prefect.

4 Standing figure of Ptolemy II
Probably from Heliopolis; ca. 260 BC; red granite; H. 266 cm; Vatican, Museo Gregoriano Egizio, 32.
Ptolemy II, surnamed Philadelphos (brother-loving), asserted Ptolemaic claims to land in conflicts with Antiochus I of Syria. His campaigns against Kush and Arabia safeguarded the trade routes. The first exchange of envoys with Rome took place in 275 BC.

5 Standing figure of Arsinoe II
Probably from Heliopolis; ca. 260 BC; red granite; H. 270 cm; Vatican, Museo Gregoriano Egizio, 31.
This is a cult statue of Ptolemy II's deified sister and wife, equated in the inscription on this statue with the daughter of Geb by Isis. Arsinoe was a daughter of King Lysimachus of Thrace.

6 *Colossal head of Augustus*
Probably from Athribis; ca. 50 AD; marble; H. 79 cm; Alexandria, Greco-Roman Museum, 24043.
Augustus did not encourage work on Egyptian temples; he had developed a dislike for supposed Egyptian decadence in his conflict with Mark Antony and Cleopatra, and abhorred the animal gods of Egypt. However, he himself was accepted into the dynastic cult of the Egyptian temples established for both Greeks and Egyptians. This head is a posthumous portrait.

porphyry quarries of Mons Porphyrites and Mons Claudianus in the eastern desert, and granite and alabaster from Aswan and the eastern desert, were taken to Rome and later to Constantinople. The squares and circus arenas of the Roman empire were adorned with obelisks and Egyptian statues. The mysterious rites held in the sanctuaries of Isis in Italian cities were a medley of Egyptian and Egyptianized features. The emperor Hadrian, who had Egyptian advisers, seems to have had a personal preference for the Greco-Egyptian cults, even if it arose chiefly from antiquarian interest, like the Egyptian style of his villa at Tivoli near Rome. When the new city of Antinoopolis in Middle Egypt was founded in honor of Hadrian's lover Antinous, who drowned there during the emperor's Egyptian journey, a cult of Antinous was established within the Egyptian ritual.

Cosmopolitan Alexandria of the Roman Period experienced frequent unrest for political, social or religious reasons. In the city, traditional ancient Egyptian theology became connected with Greek, Jewish, and at a later date Christian ideas, and it survives to this day in concepts of the Trinity, the Ascension, and the image of the Madonna and Child. The cult of Serapis and Isis still rivalled Christianity in the third century AD.

At first the indigenous Egyptians of the rest of the country kept their associations with the Egyptian temples. New legal regulations governed the conduct of cults. Temples were constantly rebuilt or converted in the names of Roman rulers. The late temple inscriptions at Esna display a depth of religious thinking hardly ever attested before. The temple at Philae was kept open even in Christian times, until the period of Justinian (AD 527–565), because of its attractive nature and its connections with non-Egyptian peoples; it contains the latest Demotic inscriptions.

From the middle of the third century AD, Upper Egypt was laid waste repeatedly by invasions of the nomadic Blemmyes from the south, and the Dodekashoinos had to be abandoned to them. As a consequence, state support for the indigenous cults ceased, but the Upper Egyptian population in particular remained true to "heathen" practices and the worship of sacred animals, even in the fourth and fifth centuries AD, when large parts of Egypt had converted to Christianity. Mummification was still practiced in the seventh century AD, even by Christians. Emperor Theodosius passed a law prohibiting pagan cults, and the assassination of the philosopher Hypatia of Alexandria by fanatical monks in AD 425 marks the end of the pagan Alexandrian school of philosophy. The history of pharaonic Egypt ended in the late imperial Roman Period, but traditions of ancient Egyptian intellectual history lived on for a long time in Coptic Christianity, and their influence is felt to the present day.

Egypt as a Roman Province

Augustus stationed several legions in Egypt. When Prefect Gaius Petronius marched on Napata in 23 BC it was in reaction to earlier Meroitic incursions into the Aswan area. South of the Dodekashoinos, the Romans defended a zone of thirty *shoinoi* as their own sphere of influence. Meroe was opened up to trade with the north and experienced a new period of prosperity, leading once again to the construction of many temple buildings in the Egyptian style in the fertile area of the "Island of Meroe," the plain of Butana northeast of Khartoum. Only the arrival in Lower Nubia of new nomadic tribes, the Nubians and Blemmyes, gradually brought intermediate trade with Africa and with it the prosperity of Meroe to an end. Around AD 350 a campaign conducted by King Ezana of Aksum (Ethiopia) against the Blemmyes and Kushites led to the fall of Meroe.

Egypt meanwhile experienced the fate of a plundered imperial Roman province. Grain, papyrus, and valuable hard stone from the

A World Order in Stone – The Late Temples

Dieter Kurth

The modern traveler on a classic tour of Egypt will see, among other sights, the great and well-preserved temples of the Greco-Roman epoch. They date from the time of the Ptolemaic dynasty that succeeded Alexander the Great and ruled Egypt for some three centuries, and from the period directly following the Ptolemies, when the country lost its independence became part of the Roman Empire in 30 BC.

These foreign rulers deprived the Egyptians of their political independence but not their religion. Although the temples were under state control, they retained their landed property and their priesthood systems, and with the aid of royal and private donations the Egyptians were even able to build new sanctuaries or extend those that already existed. The temples organized portions of the economy to that end, structuring areas of public life with temple festivals, for instance, and providing the new masters of Egypt with religious legitimacy.

That legitimacy was expressed in the portrayal of the foreign kings on temple reliefs, performing acts of worship before Egyptian gods exactly as their indigenous predecessors of the past had done. Under some of the Ptolemies, processions bore golden statuettes of the living king along with them, and erected statues of him in temples for veneration, while the deceased kings of the dynasty appeared on temple reliefs with the gods, to be worshiped side by side with them.

Of over a hundred temples of that period, six of the large buildings, and smaller temples, have been comparatively well preserved: these are the temple of Mandulis at Kalabsha, the temple of Isis at Philae, the double temple of Haroeris and Sobek of Kom Ombo, the temple of Horus at Edfu, the temple of Khnum at Esna, and the temple of Hathor at Dendara. The temples at Edfu and Dendara have survived the two millennia since their construction almost intact, and are therefore ideal illustrations of the characteristics of a temple complex of the Greco-Roman Period.

Tradition and Innovation in Temple Architecture of the Greco-Roman Period

The custom of embedding the holy of holies deep within the temple is not an invention of the Greco-Roman Period, but the contemporary builders deliberately adopted it systematically and consistently. The visitor to the temple at Edfu steps into a world sheltered from everything outside, its order determined by a symmetry that creates an atmosphere of peace (see p. 298, no. 9, plan of the temple at Edfu).

Only after walking a considerable distance from light to twilight, with the floor gradually rising while the ceilings become lower and the doorways narrower, does the visitor reach the innermost part of the temple and the sanctuary (5) where the principal cult image of the deity stood within a shrine (B).

On the way to the innermost sanctuary, the visitor passes through the massive gateway of the pylon (A) and comes to the great open courtyard (1). This is bordered by a symmetrical row of pillars accompanying the visitor to the entrance of the temple's outer hall (the pronaos). Here he reaches the largest enclosed room of the temple (2), with its ceiling resting on eighteen columns. From there he proceeds to the inner pillared hall, the "Hall of the Appearance" (3), into which the image of the god moved from the twilight of the innermost temple during the procession. Next come the hall of offering (4) and the hall leading to the sanctuary. A passage (C) runs around the sanctuary, leading to eight chapels, two of which in turn lead to additional rooms (6–15). The sanctuary, surrounded by chapels on three sides, is an architectural feature found in similar form in many other temples of the Greco-Roman Period.

Another architectural feature of Late Period temples can be better illustrated by the temple of Hathor at Dendara (see p. 301, no. 16, plan of the main temple of Dendara): this is the *wabet*, the "pure chapel" and the open court in front of it (A). The many portable statuettes of the deities were brought out into the court, where elaborate offerings were made to them. In the *wabet*, the divine statuettes were anointed, clothed, and ornamented to prepare them for the festival of "unification with the solar disk."

The beginning of the new year was the most important although not the only occasion for celebrating the festival of unification with the solar disk. During this festival the divine statuettes were removed from the temple's lower crypts and taken into the *wabet*, where they were clothed, adorned with their insignia, and finally carried by many priests up the western stairway (B) to the temple roof. The procession led to the kiosk at the roof's southwest corner. Here the statuettes were exposed to the rays of the sun, thus absorbing vital power for the new year. Finally they were carried back into the temple down the eastern stairway (C). The *wabet*, therefore, was only a part of the great stage for the New Year festival, which also involved the crypts, the stairways, and the kiosk on the roof.

The roof of the temple of Dendara has two other chapels on it as well as a kiosk. Each of these chapels consists of a courtyard and two adjoining rooms. Like the comparable roof chapels of other contemporary temples, they were intended for the special cult of Osiris in the month of Choiak. Cult areas on the temple roof are attested since the New Kingdom; however, they were usually open to the sky and intended for the cult of the sun god.

As in earlier times, the main temple in buildings of the Greco-Roman Period was set within an extensive precinct (see no. 17, plan of the Dendara precinct) where kings of centuries past had commissioned numerous sanctuaries and other structures. For instance, during the late Roman Period Dendara contained within its great enclosure wall a chapel of the Eleventh Dynasty, a *mammisi* (birth-house) of the Thirtieth Dynasty, a Ptolemaic chapel, a temple of Isis dating from the time of Augustus, a large temple of Hathor built in the late Ptolemaic to the early Roman Period, a *mammisi* of the Roman Period, a sacred lake, a

7 Pronaos of the temple of Hathor
Dendara; imperial Roman Period, first century AD. The pillars, shaped like a musical instrument called the sistrum, show the head of Hathor facing in all four directions, filling the great space with harmony.

8 Edfu: view of the court from the roof of the pronaos
Reign of Ptolemy VIII to Ptolemy XII, ca. 164–55 BC.
The southern side of the court ends at a pylon some 35 m in height, and the east and west sides are surrounded by a 10-m-high wall. A covered set of pillars, a peristyle, stands in front of the pylon and the wall. The architectural ensemble creates the impression of an enclosed space, its harmony resting on the perfect symmetry of the structural elements.

9 Edfu: ground plan of the temple
Reign of Ptolemy VIII to Ptolemy XII, ca. 164–55 BC.
The ground plan shows the perfect axial symmetry of the design. The central corridor (A–C) conducted a visitor entering the temple straight to the sanctuary, passing from light to dark, from spacious to narrow, and right into the center of the surrounding architecture, focusing attention on the holy of holies within. The stone enclosure wall, 10 m high, ran from the pylon on the southern facade and surrounded the main temple on three sides. The temples of other cult sites had enclosure walls, but only in Edfu has this defensive work of the sanctuary been preserved almost intact.

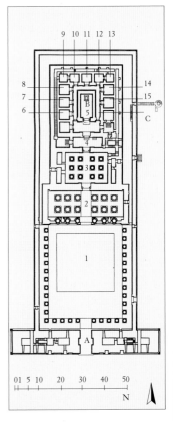

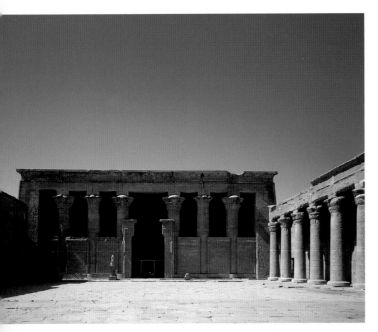

10 Edfu: view of the northern end of the courtyard and the facade of the pronaos
Reign of Ptolemy VIII to Ptolemy IX, ca. 164–81 BC.
The high intercolumnar panels are typical of temple architecture of this period, and so are the richly ornamented composite capitals of the pillars and the pierced lintel above the centrally situated main entrance. While the intercolumnar panels and the pierced lintel occur sporadically during the New Kingdom, composite capitals do not show their full, varied splendor until the temples of the Late Period. To the left of the central entrance of the pronaos is an image of the lord of the temple, Horus Behedeti, in his form as a falcon wearing the Double Crown.

sanatorium, and a number of wells. In addition there were several more sanctuaries outside the enclosure wall.

The construction of the *mammisi* as a separate structure is another peculiarity of Greco-Roman temple architecture. The ritual of the birth festival of the child of the local divine triad was celebrated annually in this birth-house.

The child god in Dendara was the youthful Ihy, son of the Hathor of Dendara and the Horus of Edfu. The story behind this ritual dates at least to the reign of Queen Hatshepsut, when it was performed on her behalf as female successor to the reigning pharaoh. According to the birth legend her mother was a mortal queen and her father the god Amun. Now, however, under foreign rulers, a traditionally minded priesthood transferred the action entirely to the divine sphere.

Variety of Form in Greco-Roman Temple Architecture

The layout of the main temples of Edfu and Dendara is quite similar. On closer examination of their ground plans, however, one can see clear differences, for instance in the number of pillars supporting the ceilings of the two pillared halls, and the side chapels of the inner pillared hall. A visitor to Dendara cannot fail to notice the unique facade of the temple of Hathor with its pillars in the form of the sistra sacred to the goddess.

The temple architecture of the Greco-Roman Period is often accused of being monotonous. Only a superficial glance, however, can give this impression, as is shown by a closer comparison of the temples of Edfu and Dendara. If we look at other temples of the same period the picture becomes even more diverse. For example, the layout of the temple of Isis at Philae is altogether unique (see p. 303, no. 22, plan of the temple of Philae). The sanctuary of the main temple, with its three chapels standing in front of the rear wall (1), corresponds to a New Kingdom type. There is no inner pillared hall, and the courtyard between the outer pillared hall and the pylon (2) is very small. Instead, there is a large courtyard (3) between this pylon and another, outer pylon. On the eastern side an arrangement of pillars borders the courtyard, and a *mammisi* stands on its western side. A door leads from the west tower of the outer pylon to the entrance of the *mammisi*.

Between the outer pylon and the Thirtieth Dynasty kiosk (6) is a spacious outer courtyard flanked by two long, covered ambulatories on its east and west sides. All these features derive from the nature and development of the local cult, upon which the architectural changes are directly based, but the shortage of space on the island as a building site may also have been a factor.

The main temple at Kom Ombo also shows quite a different design (see p. 304, no. 26). It has two sanctuaries, from which two central passages lead to the pylon through all the rooms of the temple. This double structure (now partially destroyed) reflects local theology, since two principal gods and their triads were worshipped at Kom Ombo. The right half (seen from inside) belongs to Haroeris, his wife Tasenetneferet and his son Panebtawy, and the left half to the divine family of Sobek, Hathor, and Khonsu.

However, no strict distinctions are made in the decoration of the temple. A number of ritual scenes connected with Sobek and Haroeris appear in the other god's half, and the effect of any rigid parallelism is thus avoided.

The temple has other unique features. In contrast to the temples of Edfu and Dendara, the *wabet* is on the right-hand side (next to the innermost sanctuary of Haroeris) and there are not two but three halls

between the sanctuaries and the inner pillared hall. Again in deviation from the Edfu and Dendara model, the main temple at Kom Ombo is surrounded by two stone walls and thus has two ambulatories. Finally, six chambers and a central stairway are set into the back of the inner peripheral wall.

The many smaller temples of the Greco-Roman Period also have their own specific architectural features. For instance, the wealth of different forms of the composite capitals in the pronaos of the temple of Esna is particularly striking. The basic shape of one or more open papyrus umbels bears vegetal decoration carved in raised relief. While some are highly stylized, other occasionally organic forms come closer to nature.

Only scant remains are preserved of a small temple to Osiris and Isis on the island of Bigga. They include a gate to the nearby quay where ships moored after bringing priests over from the island of

11 View of the courtyard and facade of the "pure chapel" or wabet
Dendara, temple of Hathor; reign of Augustus, ca. 30 BC–AD 14.
The "pure chapel" and the offering court in front are part of the architectural setting for the festival of unification with the solar disk. The name *wabet* may have been adopted from the anointing hall of the classical period; in both areas, bodies were prepared for resurrection. In one case – the royal and private sphere – it was the body of a deceased person; here in the temple it was the body of the god dying in the annual cycle of the seasons.

13 *View of the roof of the temple of Hathor*
13 View of the roof of the temple of Hathor
Dendara; reign of Augustus, ca. 30 BC–AD 14.
At the back, to the right, is the kiosk where the
main ceremony of the festival of unification
with the solar disk was celebrated.

Philae to make offerings at the tomb of Osiris, which was thought to
lie here. The gate was originally built and decorated in purely Egyptian style, but at a later date its passageway was reconstructed in the
Greco-Roman manner of classical antiquity. The reconstruction
affected only the central section of the older building and its Egyptian
decoration, so today the gate as a whole bears an unusual hybrid style.
The two columns at the entrance with their composite capitals are the
main feature of the temple ruins beyond the gate. Considering the
general destruction around them, it is remarkable that these columns
have survived the passage of time almost intact.

The layout of the temple of el-Qala (see p. 304, no. 27), some 40
km north of Luxor on the east bank of the Nile, is very unusual. This
small temple has two central passages intersecting at right angles, one
running east to west, the other south to north. The former leads, as
usual, straight from the entrance in the building's narrow facade to the
main sanctuary; the latter sets out from an entrance in the long
southern side, crosses the other central passage, and ends in an additional sanctuary on the far side of the temple. This additional sanctuary was used for the rites of the festival annually celebrating the
return of the "Distant Goddess." The goddess was the eye of the sun
god, and the sun goes south once a year. Most Egyptian temples
welcomed the Eye of Re returning from the south with a festival, but in
el-Qala the festival had special local features.

*12 Courtyard and facade of the western roof
chapel of Osiris*
Dendara, temple of Hathor; reign of Augustus, ca. 30 BC–AD 14.
The mysteries of Osiris were performed in the
roof chapels. The rituals included the traditional production of Osiris figures from earth
and grain, and then regularly watering them.
After a while the grain germinated and the
body of the god put forth shoots, symbolizing
the resurrection of Osiris and with him all
creation. The previous year's "grain
mummy," which had been kept for a year, was
brought down from the roof and probably
buried in the necropolis of the ancient gods in
Dendara. The walls of the roof chapels of
Osiris contained many texts and images
narrating these events.

14 View of the facade of the pronaos
Dendara, temple of Hathor; first century AD.
Six columns in the form of the sistra of
Hathor divide the facade of the building. The
capitals of these columns show the head of
the goddess Hathor, with a human face and
cow's ears, wearing a heavy wig and crowned
with the sistrum, her musical instrument;
Hathor was the tutelary goddess of dance and
music. Santuary Inscriptions and archaeo-

logical finds show a long cult tradition of
ritual building in Dendera, as is also the case
with other veneration sites of long standing.
A shrine to Hathor may be presumed to have
stood here since the end of the Old Kingdom
(Sixth Dynasty), and probably even earlier.
After several extensions in the following
periods, the present large construction
replaced a mostly unknown New Kingdom
temple during the Greco-Roman epoch.

15 Roman mammisi
Dendara; second century AD.
A covered ambulatory runs around the main
building, with columns and intercolumnar
panels on the outside, a typical architectural
feature of this "birth-house." The panels
shown here (from the south side) show the
emperor Trajan making offerings to Hathor,
who is suckling her son Ihy, and to Hathor
and her husband Horus of Edfu (first scene

on the left). On the tall abacus above the
composite capitals, the god Bes appears in the
pose of the god Heh. Bes thus serves the
mammisi in a multiple function: his own role
as a god assisting women in childbirth –
helping with the birth of the divine child –
and as Heh, god of the air who held up the sky
and personified eternity – giving the breath of
life to the divine child and bestowing safety
and everlasting existence on the building.

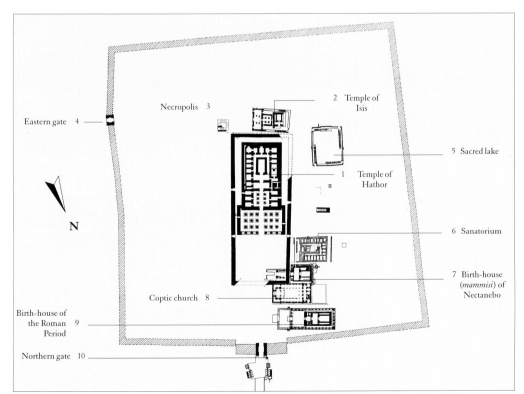

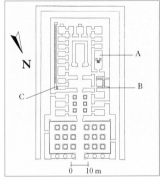

16 Dendara: ground plan of the temple of Hathor
There is a striking similarity between this plan
and that of the temple at Edfu, of the Ptolemaic Period, which must have served as its
model. In Dendara, however, the structural
elements of enclosure wall, courtyard, and
pylon, which were part of the original design
here too, were never completed.

17 The sacred precincts of Dendara
The precinct is surrounded by a high wall of
unfired mudbricks. Its northern gate lies on
the axis of the main temple. The processional
route led out through this gate and past a late
Roman complex of wells to the channel
connecting with the moorings on the banks
of the Nile near a kiosk.

18 (right) Interior of the pronaos
Edfu, temple of Horus; reign of Ptolemy VIII, ca. 164–116 BC.
The view is from the west down the central passage to the door in the east wall. From the south, the rays of the sun shone into the great hall over the panels of the facade, bathing part of the reliefs on the columns in bright light. The reliefs on the twelve inner columns are devoted to the great divinities of all of Egypt. The king presents them with their favorite offerings, and as representative of the whole country thereby welcomes them to the temple of Edfu.

19 Western peristyle
Edfu, temple of Horus; reign of Ptolemy VIII to Ptolemy XII, ca. 164–55 BC.
Sunlight falls into the covered ambulatory from the east, casting the shadows of the columns on the floor and wall.

20 Hathor sistrum columns
Philae, temple of Isis; Kiosk of Nectanebo I; Thirtieth Dynasty, ca. 370 BC; sandstone; H. of the columns ca. 3.60 m.
Already in antiquity, the small Kiosk of Nectanebo I was removed from its original (now uncertain) location and rebuilt directly on the docks. Above the capitals, which are decorated with plant motifs, the columns used here depict Hathor's four-sided face with cows' ears and surmounted by shrines.

This is typical of the specific type of sistrum column also found at Philae in the birth-house and the eastern colonnade of the great court inside the main temple; it impressively enhances the religious ritual within sanctuaries of Hathor or Isis. Columns of this order convey a very different impression from the purely composite columns in the Horus temple at Edfu, whose capitals adorned with plant motifs decorate only those parts of the chamber immediately below the ceiling.

21 The temple complex of Philae after its reconstruction on the island of Agilkia
Agilkia is aligned in much the same direction as the island on which the temple originally stood. In the center is the *mammisi* with its ambulatory; behind it, the inner courtyard between the two pylons to north and south; to the left, behind the smaller pylon, is the main temple of Isis; and to the right, in front of the larger pylon, is the long forecourt extending to the island's southern tip. In the background, the modern constructions in the water indicate the original location of Philae.

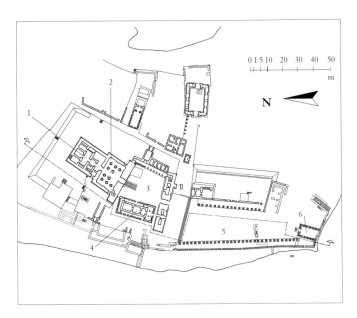

22 Ground plan of the temple complex of Philae
Here also the sacred precinct contains many other sanctuaries as well as the main temple. It is also clear that the original planning concept of the buildings took the geographical conditions found on the island into account, as can easily be seen by the bend in the axis of the Isis temple. 40,000 stone blocks had to be moved during the transfer.

23 The gateway on the quay in Bigga
Period of Augustus, ca. 30 BC–AD 14.
Coming from the island of Philae, processions moved through this gateway to the tomb of Osiris once every ten days, and also on festival days. Multiple building phases have brought elements of the architecture of classical antiquity (the round arch, and egg and dart molding) into proximity with Egyptian architecture and wall decoration.

24 Pronaos of the temple at Kom Ombo, view of the facade from the Nile
Reign of Ptolemy XII, ca. 80–51 BC.
The intact central part of the facade has two main entrances. Two central passages run parallel through the entire temple to the sanctuaries of Haroeris and Sobek respectively.

25 View from above of the temple at el-Qala
Imperial Roman Period (Augustus to Claudius), ca. 30 BC–AD 50.
The buildings of the modern impinge on the outer walls of the temple. The photograph clearly shows two sanctuaries with two central passages that intersect at right angles.

26 Plan of the temple precinct at Kom Ombo
The double central passage and the two stone enclosure walls distinguish this sanctuary of Sobek and Haroeris from other Egyptian temples of the same period. The position of the *mammisi*, the birth-house, now largely destroyed, corresponds to the same feature at Edfu.

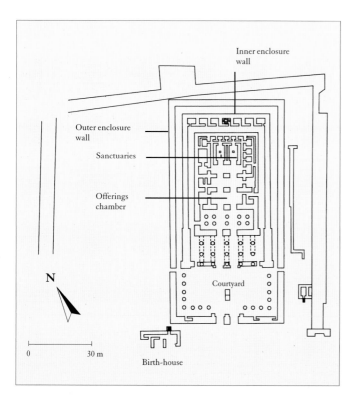

27 Ground plan of the temple of el-Qala
South of the main sanctuary is the *wabet*, the "pure chapel." The location of the additional sanctuary is a peculiarity of this temple, which otherwise echoes the architecture of its time, for instance in the ambulatory around the main sanctuary, with subsidiary chapels opening off it.

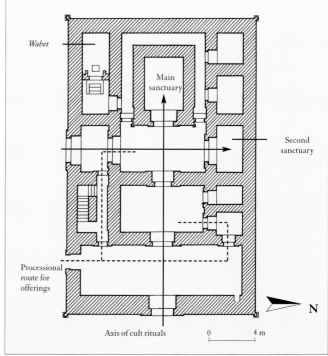

Themes of Temple Decoration

Temple decoration can be classified in several different ways, according to one's perspective. We may distinguish between three categories, depending on whether the decoration relates primarily to the temple, the king, or the god.

Elements of decoration relating primarily to the temple present it as a reflection of the world, appropriate to the cosmic dimensions of the deity. These include the structural depiction of columns as plants and the ceiling as the sky. Elements relating primarily to the king include scenes of the ruler entering the temple and being cleansed, crowned, and embraced or having his royal functions bestowed on him by divinities. By far the majority of all the pictorial images and texts, however, relate to the gods, so the first question to be asked is: which gods were still benefiting from new temples or the extension of their existing temples in the Greco-Roman Period?

In general they were the great and ancient deities of the land such as Amun, Khnum, Geb, Haroeris, Hathor, Horus, Isis, Min, Montu, Neith, Osiris, Re, Sobek, Thoth, and so on. However, new temples were also built for divinities who were originally less important, but whose cult was expanding at this late period. They include, in Roman

times, the temple of Tithoes (Tutu) at Ismant el-Kharab (Kellis) in the Dakhla Oasis, and the temple of Serapis and Isis in Qasr Dush in the Kharga Oasis. At this time the leading priests in the many cult centers of Egypt were developing a considerable variety of theological systems, on the foundations of the old tradition but animated by a desire to create something of their own. The theologians of the various cult centers were in contact and exchanged ideas, adopting them from one another or providing stimulus for new concepts. Consequently, there was a broad background of commonly shared ideas, and in the foreground a wealth of local peculiarities that were also reflected in temple decoration.

As in the past, a king in traditional Egyptian regalia is shown making offerings to a number of different divinites. Although he is not in actuality Egyptian but only a foreign ruler, he was still the only individual allowed to approach the divine powers as high priest of Egypt. The ancient royal dogma still applied in the world of these late temples, stating that only the king of Egypt could sacrifice to the Egyptian gods. Moreover, the gods must receive those offerings if the well-being of the country were to be assured.

These offering scenes may be divided into the royal and the divine, corresponding to the two protagonists involved, and the set

28 Composite capitals in the pronaos of the temple of Khnum
Esna; Imperial Roman Period, first to second centuries AD.
This selection shows two of the eighteen capitals inside the building. In contrast to the temple of Edfu at Esna, and with one exception, there is no symmetrical axial arrangement of the different types of capitals inside the building.

29 The ceiling of the pronaos in the temple at Dendara
Imperial Roman Period, first century AD.
The sky goddess Nut gives birth to the sun, whose rays fall on Dendara (left, shown upside down). The zigzag lines on Nut's robe reflect the sky as water. The barques of the star gods float on the water, with the decans in the top row: second from the left, for instance, Isis-Sothis is shown as a recumbent cow, and to her right Orion as a man turning to look behind him.

30 Room 24 in the temple of Horus
Edfu; reign of Ptolemy IV, ca. 221–204 BC.
Ptolemy IV receives an "annunciation." The
king kneels under the sacred *ima* tree and
"receives from the hand of his father" Horus
Behedeti the document confirming his legitimate succession to the throne. The goddess

Nekhbet (right) bestows on him the blessing
of an endless reign "as king on the throne of
Horus." Horus and Nekhbet hold palm
fronds as symbols of a never-ending succession of years; the hieroglyph signifying
"jubilee of the reign" is attached to the curved
ends of the fronds.

31 Room 24 in the temple of Horus
Edfu; reign of Ptolemy IV, ca. 221–204 BC.
Hathor embraces King Ptolemy IV. The
goddess wears the vulture diadem above her
long wig and on top of it her crown, which

consists of cow's horns and the solar disk. The
image adds pictorial emphasis to the text,
which states: "King Ptolemy IV, beloved of
Hathor the Great, Lady of Dendara."

dialogue transpires between king and god. The king's gifts are very
diverse in nature. Many scenes show actual objects such as food,
flowers, fabrics or amulets. Other gifts consist of a demonstration on
the part of the king, who kneels before the divinity and prays to it,
dances before it, shows himself to be a victorious ruler by smiting the
god's enemy before the god's own eyes, or performs symbolic acts of
various kinds.

A major theme of temple decoration is the protection of the sanctuary and its gods. In Edfu, among other things, there are four companies of tutelary deities each with its leader; the leaders are depicted as
hybrid creatures with the heads of a falcon, a lion, a serpent, and a bull.
The images of such beings are placed at the most vulnerable areas of
the temple: the main entrances and the enclosure wall.

Large parts of the ornamentation are devoted to temple festivals.
The festival calendar on the pillars of the temple at Esna consists solely
of texts. The gate of Hadrian at Philae bears both texts and images
connected with the processions to the tomb of Osiris (Abaton) on the
island of Bigga. Long sequences of scenes in the temple of Horus at
Edfu show the god's victory festival and the procession to the sacred
precinct of Behedet. The roof chapels of the temple of Hathor at

Dendara provide the most detailed depiction of the Choiak festival, a
ritual guaranteeing the annual resurrection of Osiris.

One of the major festivals celebrated at Edfu was the Victory of
Horus, beginning on the twenty-first day of the sixth month (Mekhir).
The images and texts recounting events in the story are on the inner
surface of the western section of the enclosure wall. The second register
of this wall contains the narrative text of the cult legend divided into
separate sections. The significance of the festival derives from the
legend, and its episodes are shown in the scenes depicted in the first
register, and followed by the legend of the cult and the festival of
victory, each in four scenes.

Cult Reliefs and the Narrative Text –
The Victory of Horus

The events narrated in the cult legend began with a rebellion against
the sun god Re, weakened by old age. It broke out suddenly at Aswan in
Lower Nubia. Horus of Edfu hastened to his father's aid and defeated

32 Offerings chamber
Edfu; reign of Ptolemy IV, ca. 221–204 BC.
Ptolemy IV (right) offers Horus bread and a
staff bearing an artistic flower arrangement.
Before him, the bull-headed god Mnevis asks
Horus (in the name of the king) to eat the
warm loaves on the offerings table: "Come O
god, hasten to all your foods that are hot!
[…]. Countless loaves of good flavor lie daily
on your offerings table, that you may taste
and eat of them […]." The king describes the
flower arrangement, addressing the god in
these words: "[…] flowers of the field grow by
virtue of your sweat [water] and your sunlight
[…]." The god answers the king: "[…] I am
pleased with the gifts you have brought, and I
will cause Egypt to bring you gifts […]. I give
you plenty of good things [food], that you
may give of them to the living."

33 Scene on the side of the western pylon tower
Philae, temple of Isis, first pylon, third regi-
ster from top; reign of Ptolemy XII,
ca. 80–51 BC.
Ptolemy XII kills the enemies of the Horus of
Buhen. "Be glad, O [Horus], protector of

your father, for your enemies lie dead beneath
you!" runs part of the royal speech. The god
answers: "I will strengthen your arm against
your enemies." The Christian cross to the
right of the god's head indicates the possible
perpetrators of the damage to the relief.

34 Enclosure wall of the temple of Horus
Edfu; reign of Ptolemy IX to Ptolemy X;
ca. 116–88 BC.
"He-of-the-mighty-bellow," runs the name of
the god, boding ill to anyone who tries to
climb the enclosure wall of the temple of

Horus, for Urhemhem, in the shape of a bull-
headed falcon, has stationed himself at its
highest point.

Scenes from the myth of Horus

Edfu, temple of Horus; inner ambulatory, western interior of the enclosure wall; reign of Ptolemy X–Alexander I, ca. 100 BC.

35 In this scene, the victory festival approaches its climax. To the left, the king feeds a goose, a ritual act symbolizing among other things victory over his enemies. At the center the priest, representing the deified Imhotep, reads from the book of ritual, and to the right the slaughterer goes about his business, although no blood is spilt, for the ritual slaughter of the enemy is performed on a figure made of dough. Then each of the gods is given part of the body of the hippopotamus, so that they may eat it and participate in the destruction of Seth. It is Isis, however, who instructs her son Horus on their correct distribution: "Give his front thigh [...] to your father Osiris [...]. Let his shoulder be taken to Hermopolis for Thoth [...]. Give his hips to Horus of ancient days [...]. But mine is his front part, and mine is his back part, for I am your mother [...]." The text closes with triumphant spells, each to be uttered four times, including: "Rejoicings daily for Horus, joy for his father every day! [...] Horus Behedeti, the great god, lord of heaven, triumphs over his enemies in overthrowing him [Seth]."

36 The scene shows the seventh and eight episodes of the harpoon ritual. Standing on land, the king raises his arms in veneration. Before him, and from each of two boats, Horus spears the hippopotamus he holds on a rope bound to a harpoon that has already been plunged into the creature's flesh. A tutelary god keeps watch behind Horus, armed with spear and dagger.

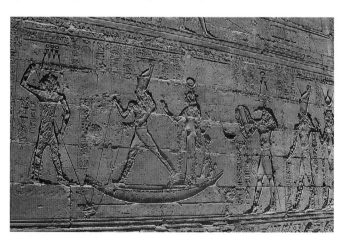

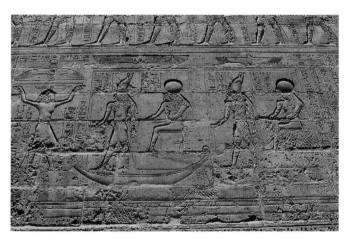

37 In contrast to the cult legend in which the gods featured alone, the king now takes an active part in the course of the festival. He stands at the left in the picture. Opposite him, in the barque, Horus says: "We will stab that coward [Seth] with our two harpoons." Behind Horus, Isis raises her protecting hand. She says: "I will strengthen your heart, my son Horus; seize the hippopotamus, your father's enemy!" Thoth reads from the festival scroll: "O fair day of Horus, lord of the land, son of Isis, the very well beloved, lord of the triumph, heir of Osiris [...]." Behind Thoth comes Horus of Edfu, carrying the harpoons, and then his mother Isis. The depiction of divinities twice in the same scene is a common phenomenon, but different aspects of the same god are usually represented.

38 The king raises up the sky beneath the sun god, who appears as a winged scarab. With the words "Your heaven belongs to you, [Horus] Behedeti, brightly feathered one!" he expresses the quintessence of the entire myth: the annual victory of the sun god over his enemies. The shrine to the right, on land, shows the temple of Edfu with its principal gods Horus Behedeti and Re-Harakhty; in the left-hand shrine, on board the ship ready to leave, we see the same gods, but with the difference that Re-Harakhty is now described as "king of Upper and Lower Egypt." This is where the course of the narrative starts: "In the three hundredth and sixty-third year of the reign of the king of Upper and Lower Egypt, Re-Harakhty, his Majesty was in Nubia [...]." Rebellion breaks out there, and there is good reason for it on this particular day (a year in the sun god's reign counts as a day), for the three hundredth and sixty-third day of the year was the birthday of Seth, the leader of all rebels.

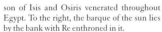

39 The victorious journey north has now reached Middle Egypt and the vicinity of Herakleopolis, a major cult center of Osiris. Osiris himself stands in the shrine on the left, with Isis before him: "she who is rich in magic […] who repels the enemy in [the cult center of] Naref." In the center, Horus of Edfu and Harsiese stab an enemy together. The two gods look the same, to show that the local Horus of Edfu was equated with Harsiese, the son of Isis and Osiris venerated throughout Egypt. To the right, the barque of the sun lies by the bank with Re enthroned in it.

40 In their flight, the enemies have reached the eastern Delta, the home of the Horus of Mesen, who fought his enemies in the shape of a lion. Consequently the Horus of Edfu changed "into a lion with the face of a man, bearing the *Hemhem* crown, with claws sharp as a knife," and tore his enemies to pieces, as shown on the plinth in the center of the scene. Left, one of the harpoonists sails away towing the barque of the sun god. The god himself stands in his shrine to the right, with Thoth in front of him and Horus of Edfu in the bows. Thoth is a constant companion on the journey, and at many points he explains what is going on, in his character of omniscient deity. In this scene his magic spells calm the water so that the fleet of Re will suffer no damage.

41 From the bank, the king kills the hippopotamus. The figures approaching behind him are "the children of the king, the team of Horus, the harpoonists of the lord of Mesen [Horus], the strong harpoon hunters of Horus Behedeti who strike to make an end of all his enemies […]." They say: "Come, let us go to the [sacred] lake of Horus, that we may see the falcon in his ship, that we may see the son of Isis in his ship of war […]." Isis kneels in the bows of the ship, taking an active part in the battle and encouraging her son: "Be steadfast, Horus! Do not flee from the hostile water creatures! Do not fear the enemies in the river. Do not listen when he [Seth] begs for mercy!" Isis herself is also on the ship of war carrying Horus: "Take your ship of war, O my son Horus, for I am the nurse carrying Horus over the water, hiding him in the dark wood of her planks."

The ship is described thus: "[…] for the perfect rudder moves in its place like Horus on the lap of his mother Isis. The tillers sit fast in their mountings, like the vizier in his residence. The mast stands firm on its foot, like Horus having taken possession of this land. This perfect sail is of radiant color like the goddess [of the sky], Nut the Great One, pregnant with the gods. […] Straps beat on its sides like warriors when they begin to fight with cudgels. The planks are close friends, not one of them moving before the others […]."

42 This scene is acted out in Edfu. Horus has struck his enemies blind and deaf, and they have destroyed each other. Re is invited to view the battlefield, together with the warrior goddess Astarte, "lady of horses, mistress of the war chariot." Both are on the right in the picture. In the boat, before the enthroned Re, stand the goddess Hathor of Dendara and her husband Horus of Edfu. On land we see one of the harpoonists, a companion of Horus in battle.

43 Pylon of the temple of Horus
Edfu; reign of Ptolemy VIII to Ptolemy XII, ca. 164–51 BC.
The goddess Hathor wears a composite crown; its elements are not a random combination, but reflect the content of the ritual scene to which it relates.

44 (opposite) Inner room of the western roof chapel of Osiris
Dendara, temple of Hathor; reign of Augustus, ca. 30 BC–AD 14.
This scene does not depict the resurrection of the god in the usual way with images of sprouting grain. The body of Osiris lies on his bier, mourned by Hathor-Isis (left). However, the god is not dead. He holds his erect member, and Isis hovers above it in the form of a female sparrowhawk. According to the myth, she will receive the seed of Osiris and give birth to Horus, in whom Osiris lives again.

his enemies, who fled north down the Nile, pursued by Horus and Re. At a number of places in the Nile Valley Horus vanquished the enemies of Re, chasing them on ahead of him until they reached the Mediterranean. The sun god and his son then returned to Nubia without encountering any more enemies on their way. Back in Nubia, however, rebellion broke out once more, and Horus again successfully battled his enemies until he arrived in Edfu as the victor.

There are complex layers of meaning behind this cult legend. The central idea is that of the Egyptian kingship of Horus, embracing spheres both earthly and divine. The continuance of the earthly kingship is endangered by enemies when one ruler succeeds another, and it must be fought for every time. The divine paradigm is the death of Osiris, murdered by his brother Seth; the son and legitimate successor of Osiris can enter upon his kingdom only after defeating Seth. However, in the text of this particular narrative these recurrent events are seen in parallel to the annual journey of the sun. At the winter solstice Re is in the south, an old, dying sun in the annual rhythm of the seasons and vulnerable to attack by enemies. His successor Horus of Edfu fights successfully and goes north, growing stronger and stronger as the sun of the New Year, until, at the summer solstice, when his powers begin to wane, he moves south again and the next cycle begins.

The climax of the ceremony celebrating the victory of Horus in Edfu was the performance of a ritual drama, probably staged on the sacred lake. One can imagine the citizens of Edfu forming the audience, and they may even have taken part in the play itself, for instance uttering the cry, "Strike, Horus! Strike!" always heard from a number of voices when the harpoon of Horus plunged into the body of an enemy. The events in the drama include flashbacks, lyrical descriptions of the protagonists and their equipment, division of the action into separate parts by the ritual involving ten harpoons, and as the finale that crowns the drama, the slaughter of Seth in the form of a hippopotamus. Each harpoon is described in the same phrasing; only the parts of the hippopotamus's body change: "The first harpoon drives into his nose […]. The second harpoon drives into his forehead […]. The tenth harpoon drives into his feet." Seth in the shape of a hippopotamus is entirely destroyed from head to foot.

Repetitions of this nature are quite common; they impart urgency to the words and appeal to the audience. In general, the dramatic effect of the play seems to have derived less from the action than from the language in which it was expressed.

In view of the wide variety of ritual scenes, one may wonder what actual cult actions corresponded to them. Some are probably quite a faithful reflection of contemporary reality, for instance the offering of incense or water, or a procession. Others derive from a ritual drama such as the victory festival of Edfu. In the actual celebration of the cult the story was sometimes imitated in miniature, for instance by stabbing wax figures of the enemy. Other events were merely indicated by gestures, and still others simply took the form of the presentation of small, freestanding sculptures of the god.

Finally, it betrays modern prejudice to claim that the relief sculpture of Late Period produced no original art (see the figure opposite). Certainly there were some unimaginative and poorly executed works, as there were in every period, but at the same time new and well-executed concepts emerged, and the quality of craftsmanship was high.

Tomb and Burial Customs After Alexander the Great

Joachim Willeitner

Egyptian and Greek Mortuary Customs

The Egyptians sustained close contacts to Greek culture since at least the Twenty-sixth Dynasty. During the reign of Psammetichus II, Milesian merchants and mercenaries settled in Naucratis in the western Delta, and in about 560 BC, Pharaoh Amasis declared the town the only Greek free-trade zone in Egypt. Religious conceptions as well as burial customs show, however, that in this age of the last independent Egyptian dynasties, native and foreign traditions still existed side by side without any overlap. Greek residents in Egypt did not mummify their dead, for example. It was Alexander the Great who first attempted to unite aspects of pharaonic and Greek culture following his conquest of the land of the Nile. To be sure, this was not motivated by Egyptophilia, but by his calculating desire for political power.

It is precisely in the cult of the dead during the subsequent Hellenistic Period, primarily in regard to the furnishing of subterranean burial complexes at the new capital of Alexandria, that the synthesis of pharaonic and Macedonian concepts of the afterlife is particularly clearly reflected. While triglyph friezes and other architectural articulations were borrowed from the Greeks, lintels were made in the traditional Egyptian form of a cavetto cornice and torus molding with the winged sun disk; furthermore, uraeus cobra friezes, sphinxes, and other native motifs can be found. Still, research has gradually revealed that this apparent fusion of mirroring architectural components and figural elements is often only decorative "scenery" that was not understood or perhaps misunderstood, and one may by no means conclude that this reflected the adoption of underlying religious conceptions.

The Tomb of Alexander

Alexander the Great's tactic of adopting foreign customs as his own was particularly clear at the time of his campaign to the oracle of Amun in the Siwa oasis. There he declared himself the son of the god Amun, thus legitimizing his claim to world rule. Alexander's particular affinity to that site near the modern Libyan border has repeatedly interested those hoping to locate the final resting place ("Sema") of the

Macedonian ruler there. The ancient sources (Strabo, Zeno, Lucian), however, place the burial site at Alexandria's government district Brucheion. The as-yet-undiscovered tomb of Alexander was most likely decorated with Greek as well as pharaonic motifs and with elements that can be seen in the nonroyal necropolises and catacombs of Alexandria. The same can be supposed for the tombs of the succeeding Ptolemaic kings in the direct vicinity of Alexander's tomb, which have also never been found. As an aside one might note that Alexander, according to the account handed down by Diodorus, planned to erect a mortuary pyramid for his father Philip to match the size of Cheops' Great Pyramid.

Hellenistic Funerary Architecture in Alexandria

The Ptolemaic dynasty continued Alexander's politics of fusion. But purely Greek customs, among them also those for the mortuary cult, often lived on unchanged among the new upper class, who at any rate looked down upon the Egyptians as "barbarians." The most striking

47 Wall painting from a hypogeum
Wardian (Alexandria); Roman Imperial Period, second/third century AD; painted limestone; Alexandria, Greco-Roman Museum, 27029.
This tomb, the only painted tomb from the small necropolis of Wardian that unfortunately cannot be attributed to a particular individual, shows the oldest representation of a *saqiya*, a water-wheel pulled by oxen. This scene, as well as the wall painting perpendicularly adjacent to it, which decorates a pillar crowned by a herm, is painted in purely Hellenistic-Roman style. In the same tomb, however, the motif of a bird as a representation of the soul comes from the traditional Egyptian repertoire. Its depiction in profile already recalls the style of ancient Egyptian precursors even though the bird is also reminiscent of Greek representations of sirens.

48/49 Sarcophagus chamber in the hypogeum of Kom esh-Shugâfa
Alexandria; Roman Imperial Period, first/second century AD; limestone.
Alexandria's oldest and largest catacomb sprawls over several levels under the Kom esh-Shugâfa, the "hill of rubble." More clearly than in any other tomb complex, the figural decorations in the central cult room here show the pharaonic-Mediterranean stylistic mixed, for example in the figure of the jackal-headed Egyptian embalming god Anubis wearing the uniform of a Roman legionnaire. Immense complexes like this one, comprising several hundred loculi and a large triclinium (banquet hall) for the funeral meal were no longer organized and managed by families but by "burial societies."

Some of the hypogea in western Alexandria contained wall paintings instead of reliefs, such as those found in March 1952 during
construction on the Tigrane-Pasha road and in a reconstructed burial
chamber (probably the first century AD), today in the area of Kom esh-
Shugâfa; a painted burial site of the second or third century AD was
found under the four subterranean burial sites of the necropolis in the
Wardian quarter, which was discovered in 1960.

The Tomb of Petosiris – Cultivating Tradition in the Nile Valley

The most vital expressions of largely unadulterated pharaonic art are
not in Alexandria, but in the old religious centers of the country farther
to the south. According to architectural evidence and relief decoration
in newly constructed temples such as Dendara or Edfu, the fact that
Egyptian traditions continued at this time is due less to the rulers in the
north than to local priests and members of cult communities.

Important information on the dates and familial relationships of
these individuals is supplied most often by the inscriptions and images
on their tomb stelae, discovered at a number of different sites, although
the circumstances surrounding their discovery are only very rarely
documented. This is why we often know nothing about the form of the
respective tombs. Depending on topographical factors, deep shaft
graves were also hewn into the rocks of the valley cliffs, or dug into the
floor of the desert. (These probably had superstructures that are no
longer preserved.) Older complexes were reused in many cases. Thus a
complex of Ptolemaic funerary stelae comes from the rock-cut tombs of
Qubbet el-Hawa near Aswan, a cemetery already constructed in the late
Old and early Middle Kingdoms.

This period marked the end of the custom of removing the
entrails of the deceased during mummification and storing them separ-

example is their custom of cremating the deceased – an unimaginable
procedure for the Egyptians who considered the mummified corpse as
indispensable for resurrection. The most important archaeological artifacts in this context are the "Hadra vases," urns for cremation ashes
named after the southeastern quarter of Alexandria where these containers were first discovered in a necropolis.

Most of the subterranean cult rooms (hypogea) of the Ptolemaic
Period found at Alexandria, such as Shatbi, Mustapha, Pasha, Ezbet
Mahlouf, Gabbari, and Anfushy, provide evidence, not of cremation,
but of burials. The corpses were shoved horizontally into deep rock-
cut niches or niches of masonry ("loculi"). The openings of these
loculi, which were densely placed next to and above each other, were
finally sealed with a stone slab that was sometimes decorated with
pharaonic motifs such as a false door. Even if the tomb complexes
possess decorative elements such as pedestal platforms crowned with
winged sphinxes, or torus mouldings and lintels decorated with the
winged sun and other traditional pictorial elements, the ground plans
of burial structures where the loculi were accessible through a connecting sunken court, are Greek in style, and resemble the plans of dwellings. Even the most outstanding of these complexes, the catacomb of
Kom esh-Shugâfa, where the figural decoration in the central cult
room is in a pharaonic-Mediterranean combined style, ultimately
follows this tradition although it was only built during the Roman
Imperial Period.

51/52 Representations in the pronaos of the tomb of Petosiris
Tuna el-Gebel; early Ptolemaic Period, ca. 300 BC; painted limestone.
Aside from the use of hieroglyphic script, the relief decoration in the front room of Petosiris's tomb reveals motifs from the traditional ancient Egyptian repertoire, showing agricultural scenes such as plowing and the grape harvest, or craftsmen at work. However, the figures wear Greek clothing, are rendered in some instances in Egyptian oblique or even frontal perspective, and are shown in a plastic style strongly influenced by Greek art. Furthermore, the products made by the craftsmen on the tomb reliefs, such as furniture and drinking vessels, look Achaemenid-Persian rather than Egyptian.

53 (right) Inner coffin of Petosiris
Tuna el-Gebel; early Ptolemaic Period, ca. 300 BC; pine, glass inlays; L. 195 cm; Cairo, Egyptian Museum, JE 46592.
During clearance of the tomb of Petosiris in 1920, the excavators came across the plundered burial chamber. The tomb robbers had left behind the tomb owner's two anthropoid wooden sarcophagi that lay one inside the other within the stone sarcophagus. Unlike the outer coffin of yellow-plastered sycamore, the inner coffin made of pine was extremely well preserved. According to the tomb inscription, another coffin of juniper for Petosiris' daughter Tjehiau once existed but is now lost. The filigree molding of the hieroglyphic inlays in colored glass, which extend over the cover in five vertical columns and quote Spell 42 from the Book of the Dead, make the inner wooden coffin an acknowledged masterpiece.

54 Wall paintings in the tomb of Petosiris
Qaret el-Muzawaqqa (Dakhla oasis); Roman Imperial Period, probably first/second century AD.
Not far from the temple of Deir el-Haggar, unearthed only several years ago, the burial mound Muzawaqqa rises in the northwest of the Dakhla oasis. Two of the countless rock-cut tombs, those of Petubastis and Petosiris, are decorated with paintings. In the front room of the Petosiris tomb, the tomb owner appears dressed in a pallium, tunic, and sandals and holds a text scroll in his hand. Before him a considerably smaller figure presents funerary offerings in liquid and solid form, followed by a Nile god bearing a tray of offerings. Here again, traditional Egyptian and Hellenistic motifs and stylistic elements are mixed.

55 Tomb of Siamun
Gebel el-Mawta (Siwa oasis); early Ptolemaic Period, early third century BC.
In the tomb of Siamun in the Siwa oasis, Egyptian gods appear in traditional costume, such as the vulture goddess as protectress of the tomb owner. Similarly, the ceiling shows the typical vultures and hawks with spread wings, the traditional star patterns, and hieroglyphic script. Only the clothing of the tomb owner and his family, and above all his full beard, cropped close to the chin, are un-Egyptian. As these are neither typically Greek nor characteristic for a Libyan, Siamun's ethnic origins remain a point of dispute.

56 Funerary stela
Kom Abu Billo (Terenuthis); Roman Imperial Period, second/third century AD; limestone; W. 44 cm; Recklinghausen, Ikonenmuseum, 564.
The "Terenuthis stelae," named after the site of their discovery, show the deceased either frontally in a pose of adoration, that is, with characteristically raised arms or (as here) reclining on a couch and leaning his weight on one arm while holding a drinking vessel in the other outstretched hand. Dogs and birds are often included on the remaining surfaces, seemingly with no particular significance; to the right, a hawk is perched on a stela with a rounded top upon which the name of the deceased was surely once inscribed. Although most of the people buried in the necropolis of Terenuthis practiced the Christian religion, these are reminiscences of Anubis, the ancient Egyptian god of the dead, and of the falcon deity, Horus.

57 *Mummy portrait of a woman*
Hawara (Faiyum), probably 24 AD; painting in tempera on canvas; H. 42 cm, W. 32.5 cm; Berlin, SMPK, Ägyptisches Museum, 11411.

58 *Male mummy portrait*
Er-Rubiyyat (Faiyum); probably third century AD; encaustic painting on wood; H. 36 cm, W. 22 cm; Hildesheim, Pelizaeus-Museum, 3068.

59 *Female mummy portrait*
Er-Rubiyyat (Faiyum), probably early third century AD; tempera on wood; H. 38 cm, W. 23 cm; Munich, Staatliches Museum Ägyptischer Kunst, ÄS 1.

For the mummy portraits in the Faiyum, the portrait of the deceased was painted as a rule almost life-sized on a primed wooden panel. For the most part the encaustic technique was used, that is the pigments were dissolved in wax and the colors, which as a result glowed richly, were then made plastic through warming and applied more with the spatula than with a paint brush, as was the case for the male face with dark hair and full beard (opposite page, left, above). Tempera painting, as seen in the portrait of a woman with short, wavy hair and pearl earrings (opposite page, right, above) was used less frequently. Only rarely was the portrait painted directly on the linen cloth covering the face, which was pulled tight and smooth and backed with a lining. For this type of mummy portrait, the picture of the lady Aline (left) dating from the Tiberian period (stretched and framed in modern times) is surely the finest example.

ately in the tomb in canopic jars. The bandaged mummies were decorated with a plastered and painted, sometimes also gilded type of cartonnage that could cover individual body parts (head, chest, feet) or the entire torso in one piece, much like a lid. The bodies were then laid in several coffins, one inside the other, whose mummiform covers from the Ptolemaic Period are distinguished by ample wigs made up of strands of imitation hair, a strongly concave abdominal area, and a plinth at the foot end. This ensemble was finally bedded in a large sarcophagus of stone, which, in the case of especially opulent burials, might be decorated with mythological scenes of the underworld.

The magnificent coffins found at Tuna el-Gebel, the Hermopolis of antiquity in Middle Egypt and belonging to the early Ptolemaic family tomb of the high priest of Thoth, Petosiris, his wife, and his son, have become particularly well-known. The stone superstructure over the burial shaft, built in the style of a Ptolemaic temple, is unique.

Whereas the reliefs on the facade are worked in the traditional style, the images in the column-less antechamber behind it show a very interesting stylistic mixture. Everyday scenes of farming and trades are represented in a fashion reminiscent of older tombs, but the people are depicted in a totally un-Egyptian, early Hellenistic style with overlaps and oblique perspectives.

On the other hand, the cult chapel at the rear, which is supported by four pillars and located directly over the burial shaft, is decorated in traditional pharaonic style with religious and mythological scenes associated with earthly life. Here the Greek influence came to a halt literally on the threshold to the netherworld.

The tomb of the high priest Petosiris had already achieved a certain status in antiquity. This is demonstrated by many other mud-brick tombs that were built around this burial site, primarily during the second century AD.

Treasures from the Oases

Surprisingly enough, apart from Alexandria, the best-preserved tombs with wall paintings from the Ptolemaic and Roman Periods can be found in the oases of Egypt's western desert. Since the name of a king is mentioned in none of these tombs, the complexes and their decoration cannot be dated precisely. The most beautiful tomb is doubtless that of Siamun in the Siwa oasis with its oblong burial chamber dug horizontally into the mountain ridge of Gebel el-Mawta. It most likely dates from the early Ptolemaic Period. In addition, the neighboring tomb, called the "crocodile's tomb" because of its striking decorations, and the tomb shared by an anonymous man and his wife Mesu-Isis, are dated to the Ptolemaic Period, whereby the latter complex was re-used during the Roman Empire and wall niches were added in order to accommodate additional bodies.

The rock-cut tombs of Qaret el-Muzawaqqa ("painted hill of rock") in the northwesternmost corner of the Dakhla oasis were first built in the Roman Period, in the first or second century AD. Wall paintings grace two of the tombs, the single-room tomb of Petubastis and the later tomb of a different Petosiris with two rock-cut chambers placed one behind the other. Here we see traditional Egyptian gods and motifs, but they seem misproportioned and show Hellenistic-Roman influence.

This influence becomes particularly clear in the tomb of Petosiris with its images rendered in perspective and the portrayal of the tomb owner in generously draped Roman dress. Similarly, ceiling paintings with entirely un-Egyptian representations of the zodiac and other

60 Coffin cupboard of Padichons
Abusir el-Melek; Roman Imperial Period, first century AD; painted wood; H. 250 cm; Berlin, SMPK, Ägyptisches Museum, 17039. The production of mummy portraits was apparently so expensive that on average only every fiftieth corpse was provided with one. The deceased who did have such portraits were not buried in a cemetery immediately but were kept in their own houses for a certain period, standing in their own mummy cupboards. These pieces of wooden furniture, of which several have come to light at Abusir el-Melek at the edge of the Faiyum, have double doors that could be opened when one wanted to allow the deceased, whose portrait could then look out from the cupboard, to participate in family life. The mummy of a 61-year-old man that was once contained in the coffin cupboard of Padichons has been lost.

61 Male mummy with portrait
Hawara; Roman Imperial Period; second/
third century AD; L. 175 cm; Berlin, SMPK,
Ägyptisches Museum, 11673.
By now many more than 700 detached
portrait panels have been discovered, but few
completely bandaged mummies with portraits
have been preserved. Apparently both men
and women of the period dressed according to
the current fashions of the Roman imperial
family, so that at least an approximate dating

of the pictures is possible through comparisons of hairstyles and jewelry in the
mummy portraits with representations of the
emperors and their wives. Despite the
unmistakably Egyptian facial features, this
portrait (encaustic painting on wood) on a
complete mummy wrapped with the
"coffered" bandaging technique shows stylistic similiarities with representations of the
Roman emperor Caracalla (AD 198–17).

personified constellations can be found in contemporary rock-cut
tombs in the Nile Valley, such as in the badly damaged necropolis of
Salamuni north of Akhmim.

At the other end of the Dakhla oasis, a tomb chapel in the village
of Esbet Bashendi, likewise dating from the first or second century AD,
is built of stone blocks on a square ground plan. It was built in
conjunction with other, now destroyed burial structures for a high official with the un-Egyptian name Qetiinus. The interior is divided into
six rooms. The rear center room is decorated with traditional motifs
from the Egyptian cult of the dead. They were executed not as wall
paintings, however, but as sculptural reliefs.

In the neighboring Kharga oasis, the largest Roman and contemporary early Christian necropolis in Egypt stretches across the flat crest
of the Bagawat mountain. What began here as a "pagan" cemetery was
taken over without interruption by Christians; moreover, the early
Christians also continued the custom of mummifying their dead. Texts
found in the south of Kharga prove that both Christian embalmers and
others who adhered to traditional pharaonic religious conceptions
coexisted peacefully and practiced their profession side by side.

It has also been proved that a comparably seamless transition
from pre- to early Christian burials took place at the western edge of
the Nile Delta in the necropolis of the ancient city of Terenuthis, today
Kom Abu Billo. There American archaeologists came upon not large
tomb chapels but only low-lying superstructures of mudbrick, resembling miniature copies of Old Kingdom mastabas. The funerary stelae,
which researchers call "Terenuthis stelae" because of their unmistakable decoration, were set into the walls of their narrower sides.

Roman Influence – Plaster Masks and Mummy Portraits

Through the influence of Roman portrait painting, the custom of
fitting mummies with more or less naturalistic representations of the
deceased surfaced in Egypt during the first few centuries AD.

In the Nile Valley, particularly in the Middle Egyptian area,
plaster or cartonnage masks were used for this purpose. Actual
mummy portraits painted on wood were apparently limited to the
Faiyum oasis. The mummy bandages, which for the most part were
wrapped in a complicated lozenge pattern resembling the coffered
ceiling of some Renaissance buildings, were applied so that the area
above the face, where the wooden board with the portrait of the
deceased was placed, was left open. Apparently the subjects of the
portraits, who are almost always shown at the "ideal" age, posed for the
pictures while they were still alive and first hung the paintings in their
houses.

In Christianized Egypt it was still the custom not to bury the dead
immediately, but to keep them in their houses for a certain time. When
Emperor Theodosius forbad the custom as pagan superstition in an
edict in the year AD 392, the residents of the Faiyum were forced to
remove all of their dead from the houses and bury them in large mass
graves at sites such as Hawara. Plunderers who attacked these graves as
early as the end of the nineteenth century cut the wooden portraits out
of the mummies so that all archaeological context for them was lost.

The dominance of Christianity finally led to the demise of pharaonic burial customs and its rich tomb equipment; in this regard at least
the ensuing era was one of cultural impoverishment.

63/64 Mummy labels of Pesentaluros
Akhmim; Roman Imperial Period, second/third century AD; wood; L. 8.7 cm, H. 5.3 cm; Brussels, Musées Royaux d'Art et d'Histoire, E 397.

If all mummies with portraits had been unearthed in the course of planned excavations during which the exact circumstances of their discovery were carefully noted, these funerary portraits could be dated more precisely, for the body was often tagged with wooden labels that recorded the name and official titles of the deceased. A large group of

such mummy labels comes from the Middle Egyptian town Panopolis, modern Akhmim. The inscription was painted on in most cases or, more rarely, was incised into the wood. While some labels bear texts in Demotic script on both sides, others show Demotic on one side and Greek on the other, such as this example which was once attached to the mummy of the Akhmim townsman Pesentaluros.

62 Mummy mask of a woman
Mir; Roman Imperial Period, early first century AD; linen covered with plaster and painted, cotton imitation of hair, necklace of glass and faience; H. ca. 55 cm; Berlin, SMPK, Ägyptisches Museum, 2/89.

This plastered and painted cartonnage mask of a woman belongs to an ensemble of four mummy masks of the early Roman Imperial Period from the Middle Egyptian town Mir. She wears separately made earrings, a necklace and, in her black-dyed cotton hair, a wreath of blossoms made of fine plaster leaves. Her earrings and bracelets as well as the gold-worked bands of her wrapped garment (chiton) reflect Roman fashion. By contrast, the pictorial frieze with representations of gods that frames her head is traditionally Egyptian in both its motifs and its style.

Sacred Kingship

Thomas Schneider

Kingship represented one of the keystones of ancient Egyptian culture. The Roman emperors in Egypt still bowed to its traditions; the last to do so was Decius (249–251 AD), who brought offerings to the god Khnum in the pronaos of the temple at Edfu three and a half millennia after the first evidence suggesting the existence of Egyptian kingship. Within that period, the interpretation of the institution changed, but in itself it remained fundamentally intact. Upon his accession to the throne the king became "a human in the role of a god" (E. Hornung), the successor on earth of the god Horus "upon the throne of (the god) Geb." The individual, temporal person of the ruler and the transcending, idealized being from the ideology were united within him. The tension between claims and reality did not contradict the Egyptian concept of kingship, but corresponded to pharaoh's dual nature, which comprised both human and divine aspects.

The Titulatury and Official Apparel of the King

Purely with regard to outward appearance, the fundamental continuity of Egyptian kingship is manifested in the titles held by the king, which name him as the current representative of kingly rule and determine his political program, in the only minimally varying royal insignia, and finally in representations of royal behavior prescribed by dogma. The royal titulary is composed of a (canonical) succession of five names that are binding for all time. The "Horus name" characterizes the king in the role of the god Horus, whose rule over the world was delegated to the monarch. The second title is the "nebty or Two Ladies name" (Egyptian: *nebty*: the two female rulers), referring to the Upper Egyptian vulture goddess Nekhbet and the Lower Egyptian cobra goddess Wadjet as protectresses of the king. The third part of the royal titulary is the "gold name" (once read as the "golden Horus name"), the significance of which is still unclear. The fourth and fifth titles are the most frequently encountered. In contrast to the other royal names, they are

encircled by name rings (cartouches). They are the prenomen introduced by the title "King of Upper and Lower Egypt," and the nomen, or name given to the king at his birth. The given name follows the expression "son of Re" since the king, from the Fourth Dynasty on, was believed to be the son of the sun god Re.

Another form of royal expression is the king's official apparel, which signified both his power and protection. His dress and insignia date in part from the Archaic Period; the bull's tail, for example, refers to the animal powers of the Early Dynastic Period and the bull nature of the king. Other animals in whose form the king can appear are the falcon and the lion. The king wears various kilts, often the so-called *shendyt* kilt, but depending on the time and the occasion also cloaks, shirts, certain types of shawls, or a panther skin. The king's head is usually adorned with a crown – for example the White Crown of Upper

1 Forearm cuff of Thutmosis IV
Tell el-Amarna, house Q 48.1; New Kingdom, Eighteenth Dynasty, ca. 1388 BC; ivory; L. 11.2 cm; Berlin, SMPK, Ägyptisches Museum, 21685.
This cuff, which once protected the arm of an archer against the snapping string of his bow, represents Thutmosis IV (1397–1388 BC)

striking down an Asian with his scimitar. The motif of the Egyptian king, who – in fact or in ritual – vanquishes his foes and thus preserves the order of the world, dates from the earliest periods. To the left, the war god Montu hands the king a sword "so that he might cut down the princes of every foreign land."

2 Inner coffin of Psusennes I
Tanis, tomb of the ruler; Third Intermediate Period, Twenty-first Dynasty, ca. 994/3 BC; silver; L. 185 cm; Cairo, Egyptian Museum, JE 85912.
The coffin depicts Psusennes I in the form of a mummy in full regalia. He wears the royal *nemes* headcloth, the uraeus cobra at his forehead, and, as insignia, the crook and the flail.

Although the coffin does not display the craftsmanship of the golden coffins of the New Kingdom, the extensive use of silver constitutes a real innovation in the field of royal funerary provision. The question of whether the amount of precious metal needed for this was won by state plundering of tombs remains a point of controversy.

3 Lintel inscription of Amenophis II
Giza, Harmakhis temple; New Kingdom, Eighteenth Dynasty, ca. 1400 BC; limestone; H. 53 cm, w. 126 cm; Cairo, Egyptian Museum, JE 55301.
This architrave from the temple of Amenophis II (1428–1397 BC) at the Great Sphinx of Giza shows the two most important elements of the royal titulary in the two lines of inscription beneath the winged sun, each repeated symmetrically to the right and left of the central ankh symbol. The upper line shows the prenomen "Re, great are his images" preceded by the title "King of Upper and Lower Egypt" and followed by the epithet "beloved of Harmakhis." The second line shows the nomen "Amun is satisfied," followed by the epithet "divine possessor of Maat" and preceded by the title "Son of Re."

Egypt, the Red Crown of Lower Egypt, the Double Crown of the unified land, or the Blue Crown (*khepresh,* the so-called war helmet). But pharaoh also wears a cap, the striped *nemes* headcloth, or an uncovered wig. The uraeus cobra rears up from his forehead, protecting the king from enemy forces. Insignia of the king's power are usually the crook and the flail.

The King and Maat

The majority of representations show the king not in his historical individuality, but in the role he assumes in order to preserve and expand the created world, to which he is bound by cult and religion. The basis for his actions is Maat, the fundamental concept of the Egyptian world view. Maat signifies the correct structure of life and the world – as well as social solidarity and the responsible governing of the land. According to a statement in the royal morning ritual, the sun god placed the king on earth to realize Maat and destroy Isfet, that is chaos and injustice. At the same time, the king is also bound to Maat; he stands not above the order, but rather is tied into it. Gods, kings, and human beings live from Maat; in an important cult ritual, the king presents a figure of Maat as an offering to the god. The individual king here is only the current, transitory performer of this eternal task in a long line of predecessors and successors, a fact of which he is fully aware.

Since the king is the guarantor of world order, the world is threatened with destruction at his death. With his accession, the successor to the throne thus creates the world anew and symbolically reunifies Upper and Lower Egypt. The mentioning of the new king's first military campaign or his mere depiction as field commander, without his ever actually having waged war, should be understood in this context.

Accounts of the dawning of an age of salvation with the beginning of a particular king's reign are offered by hymns to the accessions of Merenptah and Ramesses IV, for example: the new king is scarcely upon the throne and already refugees return home, the hungry are satisfied and the thirsty can drink, the naked are clothed, those quarreling are peaceful, injustice is conquered, and Maat has returned. On the other hand, political writings of the Middle Kingdom, through their drastic descriptions of periods without a ruler, make the kingship appear all the more vividly as an instrument of salvation.

According to the royal ideology, the heart of the king, his thoughts, and his will are divine; he is omniscient and perfect. The king's words mean the right decision in war, the fair judgment; they are the convincing speech and also the magical declaration that creates new things. The hymn to Amun in Papyrus Leiden I 344 says of the god Amun: "Your essence is that which is in the heart of the king of Upper Egypt: his rage is directed at your enemies. You are seated upon the mouth of the king of Lower Egypt: his words answer your instructions. The two lips of the lord are your shrine, your majesty is within him: He pronounces upon earth that which you have determined." And a noteworthy passage about the Hyksos ruler Apophis (ca. 1550 BC) states: "Whom (the god of wisdom) Thoth himself instructs and in whose mouth (the goddess of writing) Seshat has spat."

The Birth and Regeneration of the King

The divine ancestry of the king, who was already selected "in the egg," is the theme of royal birth legends. According to the three known cycles of scenes (for Hatshepsut in Deir el-Bahri, for Amenophis III in the Luxor temple, and for Ramesses II in the Ramesseum), the earthly queen conceives the future king from a god. During the Old Kingdom this was Horus or Re, during the New Kingdom Amun, and in the Ramesside Period Ptah as the ram from Mendes. The child is formed by the god of creation Khnum, is born, and named. He is cared for by divine wet nurses, and is finally acknowledged as pharaoh.

Further forms of legitimizing the king are his inheritance of the throne from his father – similar to the mythological transfer of kingship from Osiris to his son Horus – or his special election by a god. Concrete political stabilization was achieved since the Middle Kingdom when, prior to his death, the incumbent king named the successor to the throne as his co-regent.

In order to regenerate himself and ensure that the salvation of his reign would last, the aging king, for whom the texts prophesied an unending number of years of rule, usually celebrated the so-called *sed* festival (festival of renewal) for the first time after thirty years of rule and then every three years thereafter. On the evening before, a statue of the king was buried, symbolizing his death, while on the following day the king, in an analogy for the nightly regeneration of the sun, would once again "appear" rejuvenated on the throne, be crowned again, and prove his new vitality by running a race before the gods.

Amenophis III boasted to have been the first king to celebrate the *sed* festival again "in accordance with the old texts" since "no earlier generations of humans since the time of Re had performed the *sed* festival (correctly.)"

By the admission of aging, the king's human nature manifests itself – which, in numerous fairy tales, stories, and also depictions, stands in stark contrast to the ideal image conveyed by the ideology. Here we meet, among others, the lustily carousing King Amasis, the treacherous King Sasobek or, in a homosexual episode, King Neferkare.

The King as Patron of the Land and Controller of the World

After his coronation we meet the king as military commander, commissioner of buildings, performer of the cult, and patron of the land of Egypt. All of his actions in these capacities served the constant renewal of creation and the "expansion of that which exists" (E. Hornung).

According to tradition, the king is the nourisher and provider of the country, who thus protected the subjects in their life, sparing them from hunger, poverty, and violence. One text corpus known as the loyalist instructions describe the salvation secured through the king's rule: "He is the realization of that which is in hearts, his eyes look through all bodies. He is the sun god under whose leadership man lives, whoever is in his shadow will be rich in servants. He is the sun god, through whose rays man sees, who illuminates the Two Lands more than the sun (…). He allows more to become green than a high inundation of the Nile, and he thus fills Egypt with fruit trees."

The entire world was available to the king without restriction, through the magical power of his word. On the Quban stela we read about Ramesses II: "When you speak to the water: 'Come out of the mountain!,' then the primeval ocean hurries forth at your word." This availability is much more concrete, however, in the areas of economy, jurisdiction, and territorial administration.

4 Figure of King Pamay offering wine
Third Intermediate Period, Twenty-second Dynasty, ca. 780 BC; bronze; H. 25.5 cm; London, The British Museum, EA 32747.
The image of the kneeling king in an attitude of offering, here Pamay (ca. 785–774 BC) wearing the White Crown of Upper Egypt, is first seen in the reign of Pepi I (ca. 2335–2285 BC). This type of representation shows the ruler as the bearer of offerings and the performer of the daily cult before the gods; he is thus the guarantor of communication between the human and divine worlds.

UC.14786

The king is the lord of Egypt, which was entrusted to his care by the gods; he is thus fundamentally the sole owner of the land and all that it produces. He has royal privileges (expeditions and trade), economic monopoly, and can do as he pleases with the spoils of military campaigns as well as with the mineral resources of foreign dominions (Sinai, Nubia). As the supreme authority he holds all administrative positions requiring decisions and represents the highest legal agency concerned with the enforcement of laws in Egypt.

The king as controller of the world, who vanquishes the chaos symbolized by Egypt's enemies in the frequently depicted scene of "smiting the foes," is a permanent motif (topos) in the royal ideology. The king combats the rebellion of the foreign enemies (required by the ideology) and simultaneously strives to extend creation as it exists by pushing the borders of Egypt into Asia and Africa. The king is the ruler of the world who has power over "all land and all foreign lands," "whose southern border reaches as far as the wind and whose northern

border advances to the end of the ocean" (from an inscription from Buhen). The chaotic counter-world is also symbolized by the wild animal kingdom against which the king charges in the hunt for large beasts (lions, elephants) – his exclusive privilege.

The King as Performer of the Cult

The king had obligations not only to humans but to the gods as well. He was expected, according to a text from the morning ritual, to "satisfy the gods with divine offerings and bring funerary offerings for the transfigured dead." The fulfilling of the cult and the construction of cult buildings were duties reserved for the king alone; in practice, though, he delegated cult functions to priests. The king was the mediator between the gods, who were only indirectly present on earth in their temples and cult statues, and the people. Communication with

5 (opposite) Ptolemy VIII Euergetes II crowned by Nekhbet and Wadjet
Edfu, Horus temple; Ptolemaic Period; ca. 130 BC.
Ptolemy VIII Euergetes II (ruled 164 and 145–116 BC) is installed as ruler of the Two Lands by Nekhbet and Wadjet, the goddesses of Upper and Lower Egypt. He wears the so-called *shendyt*-kilt, the bull's tail, the double crown composed of the Red Crown of Lower Egypt and the White Crown of Upper Egypt, the ritual royal beard, and the uraeus cobra at his forehead. Above the king are two cartouches bearing his nomen and his prenomen.

6 Sesostris I performing the ritual race before the god Min
Coptos, Middle Kingdom, Twelfth Dynasty, ca. 1926 BC; London, University College, Petrie Museum, 14786.
The relief shows Sesostris I (1956–1911/10 BC) performing the ritual race before the god Min on the occasion of the *sed* festival – the royal festival of renewal – thus proving his regenerated strength and ability to rule. He wears the Red Crown of Lower Egypt, the royal kilt with the bull's tail, and holds two ritual objects. His prenomen is shown in the cartouche over his left hand.

the gods, necessary for the stability of the world, could only be maintained through the maintenance of the cult. To return for a moment to the aftermath of the reign of Akhenaten, the so-called restoration stela of Tutankhamun impressively conveys what turning away from the gods signified as a final consequence: "When His Majesty (Tutankhamun) appeared as king, the temples of the gods and goddesses from Elephantine to the marshes of the delta (…) were in the process of being forgotten; their shrines were beginning to disappear because they had turned to hills of rubble, overgrown with weeds, and their cult image chambers were as if they had never been, their halls a footpath. So the land experienced a sickness, and the gods turned their backs on that land. When they sent soldiers to Syria to extend the borders of Egypt, they had no success. If someone beseeched a god in order to ask something of him, he did not come at all. If someone beseeched a goddess in the same way, she also did not come at all. Their hearts had become weak in their forms and they destroyed what had been created." Neglecting the cult, whose maintenance was believed necessary to appease the gods and secure their beneficial power for the country, was thus tantamount to the destruction of the world.

Our knowledge of ancient Egypt is shaped by the monuments that the kings constructed throughout the land. Building "enduring" monuments (from the meaning of the Egyptian word for "monument") was one of the king's main tasks. In addition to the construction of his own burial site, the erection of temples for the country's many divinities was a priority.

The Kingship in History

Compared to the continuity of the fundamental characteristics of royal ideology and the ritualized conception of history, clear shifts in the concept of kingship can be recognized during the three millennia of Egyptian culture.

The origin of Egyptian kingship can be traced in its rudiments as far back as the second half of the fourth millennium BC. Proof for the existence of kingship and royal ideology since at least 3200 BC includes the first presumably royal tombs at Hierakonpolis (with paintings) and Abydos (where a ruler's scepter and early kings' names were discovered), splendid palettes and decorated clubs, and the original form of the Palermo Stone (a list of the kings down to the Fifth Dynasty).

Compared to the knowledge from earlier research, the broadening of our perspective based on these finds "creates a less heroic but more plausible image of the evolution" of Egyptian kingship (J. Baines). The assessment of the king's position since the Old Kingdom has also changed in the course of Egyptological research. It was once supposed that the king during the Old Kingdom was considered divine, and later developments were interpreted as a gradual decrease of that divinity and increase in the humanity of his office. Today it is clear that the king was believed to be human during the Old Kingdom as well. Ideally, he fulfilled his role so perfectly, however, that he was equal to the gods and his essence could be indentified with theirs, above all with that of the sun god. Since the reign of Amenophis III (1388–1351/50 BC), the king's identity approached that of the sun god Re, and he was worshipped already during his own lifetime. In a text from the reign of

7 Striding king with a figure of Maat
New Kingdom, Nineteenth Dynasty, thirteenth century BC; gilded silver; H. 19.5 cm; Paris, Musée du Louvre, E 27431.
This statuette from the Nineteenth Dynasty shows the king dressed in a kilt and wearing a cap with the rearing uraeus cobra. He offers a figure of the goddess Maat, the basic order of the cosmos, to a god standing before him (now missing). The statuette expresses the king's duty to guarantee the proper and just functioning of the world during his reign.

Ramesses II (the decree of Ptah-Tatenen), he is described, for example, as "the living (creator-god) Khnum," as "divine king, (…) who was born as the (youthful sun god) Khepri, whose body is Re, who was born of Re, whom Ptah-Tatenen conceived." Here he is "son," "image," and "form" of the god who put him on the throne, "wearer of the double crown, son of the White Crown, inheritor of the Red Crown, he who unified the Two Lands in peace."

The Middle Kingdom emphasized the indispensability of kingship for the well-being of the state and society. A potent statement can be read in the "Instruction addressed to King Merikare": "the kingship is a good office."

At this period and increasingly during the New Kingdom, the actions of the king are no longer taken for granted but are explained and often characterized as unique historical deeds. Thus we read about the conquests of Thutmosis I that such things "could not be found in the annals of the predecessors since the followers of Horus (the Early Dynastic Period kings)." Of particular interest here is the account of the battle at Kadesh by Ramesses II, whose intention it apparently was to prepare the historically unique peace treaty with the Hittite empire. Furthermore, an additional New Kingdom tendency becomes clear in this account: gods now increasingly influence the course of history, causing the importance of kingship to decline and, in the Twenty-first Dynasty, leading to the theocracy of Amun in Thebes. To an extent unknown until that time, the kings of the Late Period encouraged the modeling of Egyptian culture on the past. They and their subjects now lived consciously in "a world of remembrance comprising thousands of years which (…) appears overwhelmingly visible before their eyes and (…) is chronologically and historically illuminated in every nook and cranny" (J. Assmann). The borrowing of

the Egyptian term for king, *Per-aa,* "the great house," in the Hebrew tradition also occurs during this time, which explains how the term "Pharaoh" became common in modern usage.

The true demise of Egyptian kingship signified the triumph of Christianity, which replaced the belief in the king as savior of the world, the son of the sun god, with the belief in the savior and son of god, Jesus Christ.

It was once assumed that kingship of ancient Egypt, whose major features also strongly influenced the kingdom of Meroe in the Sudan, constituted the starting point for sacred kingship in Africa (G. Lanczkowski). Additionally, it was also one of the so-called "undercurrents" in the Hellenistic-Roman image of the ruler, and thus was also indirectly part of the medieval concept of the divine right of kings and the dual nature of the monarch (S. Morenz). Today, however, we tend to assume the universality of the idea of kingship that developed a number of cultural manifestations in many different places.

8 King Herihor and his wife Nedjmet in adoration before Osiris
Book of the Dead of Herihor; Twenty-first Dynasty, ca. 1070 BC; painted papyrus; London, The British Museum, EA 10541.
This illustration depicts King Herihor, the high priest of the Theban Amun and his wife Nedjmet worshipping the judge of the dead Sokar-Osiris in the final judgment scene of the afterlife. Continued, successful existence in the hereafter depended on the weighing of the personality (represented by the heart), whose character and integrity had to equal that of Maat, the ideal of honesty (Book of the Dead, Spell 125).

Beauty and Perfection – Pharaonic Art

Rita E. Freed

Throughout the world, over the course of millennia, Egyptian art has delighted the eye, earning the admiration of countless travelers and museum visitors. Serving as a foundation for Western art, it continues to inspire artists today. Nearly all can recognize it as being Egyptian. For although the civilization that created these monuments endured for some three millennia, the basic tenets of its art – a translation of its world view into two and three dimensions – changed remarkably little. Concepts such as the ideal form for the human figure, perspective, movement, and hierarchy were all codified within the first few dynasties and, with only occasional exceptions, remained unchanged.

Although their works are universally admired and their production was prolific, ancient Egyptian artists per se are unknown. With rare exceptions, sculpture was left unsigned, and seldom can an artist known from other sources, such as a tomb inscription, be matched to a specific work. Yet artists were surely respected, as their quality of life at Deir el-Medineh, the village inhabited exclusively by the workers who built and decorated the New Kingdom royal tombs, clearly demonstrates. Uniqueness and individuality – aspects central to artists today – were irrelevant and even undesirable in ancient Egypt. The job of an artist was to reproduce, exactly and according to strict guidelines, the model before him. A statue acquired individuality and specificity only by means of the inscription added to name the subject represented, rather than through any reproduction of that subject's unique characteristics.

The result, whether statue, relief, or entire monument, was magically brought to life by a priest through the "opening of the mouth" ceremony. A statue thereby animated would serve for eternity as the home for the soul, or *ka*, of its owner. This soul might leave and return at will in the form of a bird, known as the *ba*. As a statue of a god became that god, and served as an object of worship, so could reliefs similarly be brought to life, to perform for eternity the activities represented, such as the production of food and material goods or the presentation of offerings to the gods, which were essential for eternal life and well-being. The close connection between religion and art is further demonstrated by the training of artists in the "House of Life," an institution located in or around a temple. Priests may also have received training in the same institution.

In light of the reasons cited above, it is understandable that the concept of art for art's sake virtually did not exist in ancient Egypt. The same monuments showcased as artistic masterpieces in today's museums enjoyed a very practical and critical significance. Yet that did not stop the people for whom they were created from commissioning and creating beautiful works. In fact, many of the finest works in sculp-

ture, relief, and painting were not meant to be seen by outside eyes, but buried in tombs with their owners. Not until the Middle Kingdom were sculptures incorporated into temple decoration in a significant way, often placed in areas where the general populace might see them. Understandably, a rich repertoire of types of sculpture, both royal and private, developed for temple contexts to show the closeness of man to his gods.

Although Egyptian artists made use of a wide range of materials for sculpture, including stone, wood, terra-cotta, bronze, faience, ivory, and glass, stone was by far the most common, perhaps because of its permanent qualities. Limestone, sandstone, and granite were quarried in great quantities close to the Nile River, thus easily transportable to the desired location. Other stones such as quartzite, basalt, anhydrite, or diorite, were prized for their color, hardness, or ability to accept a high polish, and expeditions were dispatched to retrieve them even though their quarries might be in distant and inhospitable areas. Ever practical, stonecutters appear to have roughed out the approximate shape of a sculpture while the stone was still in the quarry, thereby avoiding the need to transport more stone than was necessary. This practice also indicates that quarrying expeditions were project-specific. Some of the finest quality and sensitively carved sculptures known from Egypt were made of wood, usually imported, although unfortunately only a small percentage have survived. From the Old Kingdom on, superb works were also made of copper and, later, of bronze.

The earliest sculptures in Egypt date from around the beginning of the fourth millennium BC and already display some of the characteristics of later Egyptian monuments, particularly the ability to express much with an economy of effort. The human form was reduced to its most essential elements, which were rendered simply but expressively. Clay rolled into cylinders served as the arms and legs on a female torso that was abstracted into clay triangles and cones. Yet this simply made (and now headless) figure, which was found at the Badari site, exhibits a latent sexuality. Similarly, an oval of clay from the settlement area of Merimda, with eyes of punched circles, a pinched nose, and a slit for a mouth (see p. 8, no. 1) displays a lifelike pathos, despite the fact that it measures only a few centimeters.

The appearance of sculpture on a colossal scale coincides with the increasing complexity of social organization in Egypt, that is around the time that the country underwent unification. Using many of the same stylistic devices as the earlier works, particularly the reduction of forms into simple geometric elements, examples such as the Min colossi from Coptos project an eerie, other-worldly aura. It is significant that these first colossal works are representations of gods.

Relief sculpture from the beginning of the third millennium BC already demonstrated such a successful ability to translate three-dimensional forms into two dimensions that it would be repeated for the remainder of dynastic Egypt. There is no better example than the famous Narmer palette, a document as important for the development of Egyptian history, religion, and writing as it is for art history. On the main side a large-scale figure of King Narmer faces right, wearing a

9 Triad of Mycerinus
Giza, valley temple of the king, Old Kingdom, Fourth Dynasty, ca. 2520 BC; greywacke; H. 83.5 cm, W. 39.3 cm; Boston, Museum of Fine Arts, 09.200.
The characteristic facial features of Mycerinus

are repeated in the face of the enthroned goddess Hathor (with cow's horns and a sun disk) as well as in the face of the provincial goddess. This group of three figures is one of eight triad sculptures found in the king's valley temple at Giza.

10 Stela of Heku
Saqqara; Middle Kingdom, Thirteenth Dynasty, ca. 1700 BC; limestone; H. 51.5 cm; New York, The Brooklyn Museum, 37.1347E.
The sculptor Nefertem chiseled his name in large letters on the lower edge of this stela, which he created for the official Heku and his family. It is one of the few cases in the over 3,000 year-old history of Egypt in which a particular relief can be ascribed to an artist known by name.

11 Incomplete figure of a criosphinx
Gebel el-Silsila, quarry (east); New Kingdom, Eighteenth Dynasty, ca. 1370 BC; sandstone; L. ca. 210 cm.
The quarry of Gebel el-Silsila was an important source of sandstone used to build temples and fashion sculpture. Here we see a roughly hewn sphinx which – perhaps because of a material flaw – was never transported out of the quarry.

royal kilt and the Upper Egyptian crown. The most characteristic view of each element of the king's body is represented in its most recognizable way, with profile and frontal views combined to convey effectively a message of strength, stability, and forward motion. Accordingly, the face is in profile but the eye is frontal. The broad frontal shoulders and chest emphasize the king's royal power, while the legs, shown in profile with one advanced ahead of the other, add both dynamism and stability. In short, the two-dimensional representation is a hieroglyph, an abbreviated way of conveying the greatest amount of information with a minimum of effort.

Size indicates importance. The king is always significantly larger than his attendants, as he is on the Narmer Palette, and he frequently dwarfs his wife and children as well. He may equal the gods in stature – a reflection of the divinity of the royal office – but he never surpasses them. In the private realm, tomb owners are also identifiable by their size, which may be four or five times that of the workers on their estates.

The Early Dynastic or Archaic Period was a time of trial and experimentation, and this is evident in both royal and private sculpture. A splendid example of the latter is Hetepdief from Memphis. The relatively balanced proportions of the body on the Narmer Palette have not been translated into three dimensions here: rather, the eye is immediately drawn to the head. With its wig of echeloned curls and precisely drawn features, the head is the most detailed aspect of the figure. It is also proportionally the largest, projecting forward. In comparison, the body is reduced to a cubic mass where limbs and torso virtually blend together with little articulation of individual aspects. Perhaps because there was a question as to whether or not the stone was able to withstand its own weight, the neck – a narrow, vulnerable area – has been eliminated entirely. Cleverly, however, the potentially awkward transition between head and body has been masked by the enveloping wig. In royal sculpture of approximately the same period, such as the statue of Djoser from his funerary precinct, the king's *nemes* headdress serves the same function.

By the Fourth Dynasty, the Pyramid Age, in sculpture in the round and in relief, the Egyptians had perfected both the conception and the rendering of their idealized body form, and this would serve as the standard until the advent of Christianity. From the Old Kingdom on and with rare exceptions, an ageless, classical beauty was the ideal, and this is nowhere better seen than in the statue of Mycerinus and his queen, Kamerernebty (see p. 330, no. 9). Regal and impassive, the king gazes straight ahead into an indefinite beyond. His eyes are naturalistically rendered and almond-shaped, his nose straight with a slightly bulbous tip, his straight lips betray no hint of emotion. Not only kings, but males in general sported broad shoulders, small waists, muscular legs, and unlined, impassive facial features. Women had narrower shoulders, slim hips, and small round breasts, and these features were given additional emphasis by clothing that conformed exactly, but modestly, to the body's contours. In general, although details such as facial iconography or clothing style changed with each dynasty, the model set by the reigning king was followed by his subjects.

Traditionally, standing males were depicted with the left foot forward, although their weight remained on the rear (right) leg. Women's feet were most often together in a more passive stance,

13 Standing statue of a high-ranking official
Probably Faiyum; Middle Kingdom, Twelfth Dynasty, ca. 1800 BC; copper, silver; H. 32 cm; Munich, Staatliches Museum Ägyptischer Kunst, ÄS 7105.
This statuette from the late Twelfth Dynasty, a masterpiece in copper, is one of the earliest Egyptian examples of a hollow cast figure. As with several stone statues of this period, a kilt wrapped high above the hips covers the official's corpulence.

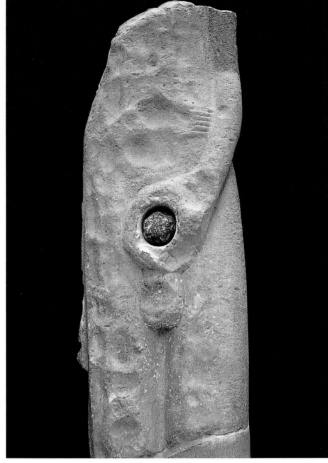

14 Two female idols
Predynastic Period, Naqada I, ca. 3800 BC; bone; H. 10.6 cm and 12 cm; London, The British Museum, EA 32142, 32139.
Because of its softness, bone was a popular raw material for naturalistic figures during the Predynastic Period. Incised lines and stamped holes emphasize the sexuality of the two female figures, who were probably expected to guarantee the fertility of their owners in this life and, through resurrection, in the next.

15 Colossal figure of the god Min
Coptos; Predynastic Period, Naqada III, ca. 3100 BC; limestone; H. 168 cm; Oxford, The Ashmolean Museum, 1894.105 d.
The larger than life-sized, columnar statue in this illustration – simply sculpted but power-ful in its effect – shows Min, the male god of fertility who was worshipped throughout all periods in Egypt. Recent research has proved that the incised signs on the side of the statue indicate place names.

although queens and goddesses might advance the left leg slightly, as does Mycerinus' queen. The differing roles of men and women were further emphasized by their skin color. Because men worked outdoors in the fields or on the river, their skin was of a ruddy color, while women, traditionally engaged in such indoor tasks as cooking or weaving, had skin of a yellow hue.

In order to reproduce the ideal body forms exactly, regardless of size, method, or medium, artisans used a grid for the standing figure that consisted of eighteen squares (in most periods). Underlying this grid was the concept of a canon of proportion, the idea that different parts of the body were related to each other by natural ratios. The basic unit was the standard cubit, which equaled the distance from the elbow to the tip of the thumb. A standing figure measured six cubits. The cubit could be further subdivided into four and a half palms (the distance across four fingers and the thumb), six handbreadths (the width of four fingers), or twenty-four digits (one finger width). Each grid square measured one palm, and body parts fell on or between specific grid squares. Unfinished statues as well as sculptor's "models"

– small-scale representations in either relief or sculpture in the round – show grid lines in red paint (generally) in the case of the former, or delicately incised in the case of the latter.

In different ways and at different times, the rules of human representation outlined above were often broken. By the Middle Kingdom, around the time of Sesostris II, the image of the king underwent a transformation both in art and in literature. The idealized, eternally youthful face acquired unmistakable signs of age: foreheads creased with wrinkles, heavy overhanging brows, bags underneath the eyes, and deeply furrowed faces became the norm. These stern countenances inspired both awe and fear, particularly when placed in or around temples in areas that were visible to passersby. The second half of the Middle Kingdom was also a time when private sculpture, particularly on a small scale, proliferated. This coincided with a time when the worship of Osiris, god of the dead, expanded to the general populace. Many of these sculptures were found at Abydos, the city where Osiris was buried and resurrected, and expressed the owner's desire to be similarly reborn.

16 Kneeling statue of Hetepdief

Memphis, Old Kingdom, Third Dynasty, ca. 2650 BC; red granite; H. 39 cm, W. 18 cm; Cairo, Egyptian Museum, CG 1.

Hetepdief kneels on the ground with both hands on his knees as a sign of worship. Both his pose and the statue's provenance (Memphis) implies that the figure was once placed in a temple. The names of the first three kings of the Second Dynasty are chiseled onto his right shoulder; possibly Hetepdief belonged to their cult.

17 Decorated palette of King Narmer

Hierakonpolis; Dynasty 0, ca. 3050 BC; graywacke; H. 64 cm; Cairo, Egyptian Museum, JE 32169

On the primary side of his famous palette, King Narmer raises his arm to smite his foe. This monument from the beginning of Egypt's dynastic history displays the traditional emblems of kingship, such as the White Crown of Upper Egypt, the ceremonial beard, and the bull's tail.

18 Portrait of Nefer

Giza, Western Cemetery (G 2110); Old Kingdom, Fourth Dynasty, ca. 2550 BC; limestone; H. 95.2 cm; Boston, Museum of Fine Arts, 07.1002.

On this doorjamb from a private tomb, the treasurer Nefer is pictured three times as large as the scribes opposite him who report about the accounts of his properties. Nefer's prominent aquiline nose can also be seen on the "reserve head" of the high-ranking official. The two images are rare examples in Egyptian art for the rendering of portrait-like characteristics.

The art of the New Kingdom is noteworthy for its deliberate attempts to divorce itself from the troubled countenances of the late Middle Kingdom, and to return to the aloof signature of the Old Kingdom. Even Hatshepsut, the woman who ruled as king in place of her stepson Thutmosis III, is depicted with the ageless impassive gaze, broad shoulders, slender waist, and left-foot-forward stance of her male predecessors. When Thutmosis III assumed the throne upon Hatshepsut's death, he expanded Egypt's empire to its greatest extent, opening it to range of new materials and ideas that would find expression in the art of the next few reigns. The New Kingdom witnessed a great flowering of tomb painting, particularly in Thebes, and many of these works featured foreign peoples bearing tribute or trade goods from their native regions. The details of each nationality's physiognomy and dress were captured and caricatured in much the same way as the Egyptians stereotyped their own depictions.

Although many of the basic themes of the tombs – including large-scale figures of the tomb owner seated at a table of food, receiving offerings, or overseeing the activities on his estate – reproduce those found in tombs of the Old and Middle Kingdoms, often the way they were done betrays an unmistakable New Kingdom stamp. The frenzied panic of the animals fleeing their pursuers in the tomb of Userhet, or the coyness of the servant girl who has her back to the viewer in the tomb of Rekhmire demonstrate the New Kingdom artist's skill in capturing detail, movement, and emotion. The extent of Aegean influence on the tomb paintings of this time is undergoing re-evaluation in light of the recent discovery in Tell el-Daba of palace paintings believed to have been executed by Minoan artists.

The rich subject matter of the New Kingdom paintings often challenged artists to resolve issues of perspective, and they did so in the characteristically Egyptian manner of depicting each element's most salient aspects. For example, a vignette from his tomb features Sebekhotep and his wife refreshing themselves beside a pool in the garden of his estate. In order to make the pool recognizable, it had to be drawn from an aerial perspective, that is, as a rectangle. The fish and lotuses in the pool, however, are shown in profile, as is the lush landscape of surrounding trees.

Although the official portrait of the king had changed dramatically in the Middle Kingdom, the sleek, slender body form remained unchanged from the Old Kingdom. But even that would undergo an alteration in the New Kingdom, during the latter years of the reign of Amenhotep III, when the king would develop an unmistakable paunch. The most dramatic transformation of the kingly image would take place during the reign of his son, Amenhotep IV. All semblance of reality is abandoned in representations of this monarch. His grossly elongated face is marked by narrow slit eyes slanted dramatically downward, high and pronounced cheekbones, a long, narrow nose flaring at the nostrils, and V-shaped lips echoing the pendant shape of the chin. For the first time, the king's long, concave neck is marked by furrows, and collarbones protrude from his emaciated upper torso. This stands in marked contrast to his grossly swollen hips and hanging belly. Not only the king, but his wife, six daughters, and members of his court are depicted in the same exaggerated fashion.

Some five years into his reign, Amenhotep IV (who changed his name to Akhenaten) moved his capital to Amarna and inaugurated a tremendous building program. It is on reliefs from both the sacred and secular buildings of Amarna, including private houses, that yet another rule of Egyptian royal representation was broken. For the first time, the king abandoned his exclusively formal image. Instead he is depicted in his role as an affectionate father kissing his children, who sit playfully in his lap or clamber over his body. His wife, Queen Nefertiti, is similarly depicted. Entirely different emotion is exhibited in the royal tomb at Amarna, as the royal parents grieve at the death of their second daughter.

22 The desert hunt of Userhat

Western Thebes, tomb of Userhat (TT 56); New Kingdom, Eighteenth Dynasty, reign of Amenophis II, ca. 1410 BC; Painting on plaster ground.

With immovable calm the royal scribe aims his bow – in clear contrast to the wild confusion of the fleeing animals. Low bushes and undulating lines suggest the desert.

23 Ramesses II at the battle of Kadesh

Western Thebes, funerary temple of the king (Ramesseum), first pylon, New Kingdom, Nineteenth Dynasty, ca. 1270 BC. Ramesses' war chariot charges at the army of the Hittites who, faced with the force of this attack, fall in a disorderly heap. The contrast between the heroic figure of the king and the confusion of the fallen soldiers is reminiscent of hunting scenes in private tombs, such as that of Userhat.

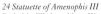

24 Statuette of Amenophis III

Probably Thebes; New Kingdom, Eighteenth Dynasty, ca. 1360 BC; Serpentine; H. 22.5 cm; New York, The Metropolitan Museum of Art, Bequest of Theodore Davis 1915, 30.8.74.

Recent research has proved that the representations of Amenophis III created toward the end of his reign, and above all for his anniversary celebrations, portray him as a clearly overweight man. A royal torso is rendered in this way for the first time in Egyptian history.

21 Praying figure of Hatshepsut

Western Thebes, Deir el-Bahari, funerary temple of the queen; New Kingdom, Eighteenth Dynasty, ca. 1465 BC; red granite; H. 242 cm; New York, The Metropolitan Museum of Art, 28.3.18.

As in most of her statues and despite her sex, Hatshepsut is portrayed here with the male insignia of kingship: the *nemes* headcloth, the uraeus, a false beard, and a short kilt. Also characteristic for this statue type is the advanced left foot. Numerous statues of various sizes and materials decorated Hatshepsut's funerary temple at Deir el-Bahari until they were removed by her stepson and successor Thutmosis III.

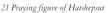

25 Altar panel
Amarna; New Kingdom, Eighteenth Dynasty, ca. 1340 BC; limestone; H. 32 cm; Berlin, SMPK, Ägyptisches Museum, 14145.
Under the life-giving rays of the Aten, Akhenaten's only god, the king and his wife Nefertiti play with their young daughters. This stela was found in the shrine of a home in Amarna, where it once served as the focus of prayers.

26 Relief image of an aging official
Probably Saqqara; New Kingdom, Eighteenth Dynasty, ca. 1310 BC; limestone, H. 14.4 cm, W. 31.3 cm; New York, The Brooklyn Museum, Charles Edwin Wilbour Fund, 47.120.1.
A lined forehead, sagging cheeks, and a wrinkled forearm mark this portrait of an old man. Such intense attention to realistic detail is typical for some works of the post-Amarna period.

28 Kneeling figure of King Shabako
Late Period, Twenty-fifth Dynasty, ca. 710 BC;
bronze; H. 16 cm; Athens, National Museum,
ANE 632.
King Shabako kneels praying before a (now
missing) divinity. Even if his name weren't
engraved on his belt, he could be identified on
the basis of the close-fitting cap, the double
uraeus, and the necklace with ram's head
pendants as one of the Kushite conquerors of
Egypt.

27 Maya and Merit
Saqqara, tomb of Maya; New Kingdom,
Eighteenth Dynasty, ca. 1320 BC; limestone;
H. 158 cm; Leiden, Rijksmuseum van
Oudheden AST 3.
The statue group shown here is among the
most exceptional examples of private sculp-
ture in the round of the late Eighteenth
Dynasty. It depicts the treasurer Maya and his
wife Merit, a temple singer of Amun. The
couple is elegantly dressed for eternity.
Although the artist did not adopt the extreme
style of the Amarna Period, the naturalistic
quality of their faces reflects the legacy of
Amarna. Maya held office under Tutankhamun as well as under Horemheb.

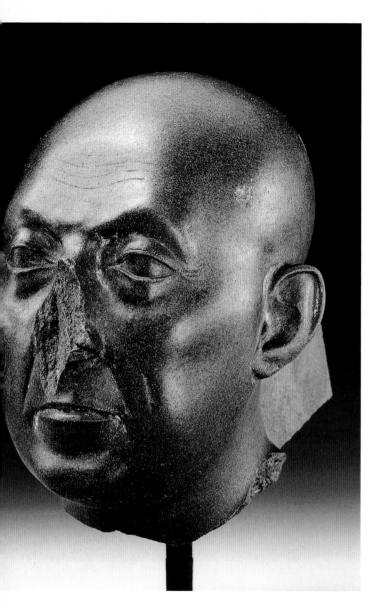

29 The Boston "Green Head"
Saqqara; late fourth century, ca. 330 BC; dark green slate; H. 10.8 cm; Boston, Museum of Fine Arts, 04.1749.

Albeit rarely, Egyptian artists did occasionally create portraits throughout Egyptian history. The thin wrinkles on the forehead, the "crow's feet," and a wart – lifelike detail chiseled into this fist-sized piece of hard stone – make the Boston "Green Head" one of the most important such portraits. The man's shaved head implies that this is the scalp of a priest.

These glimpses into the intimate moments in the life of the royal family are unprecedented, and would never be repeated in Egyptian art.

Although many of the eccentricities of the Amarna style softened even during the Amarna Period, the artistic legacy of Amarna persisted well after Akhenaten died and the city was abandoned. The three-dimensionality of the facial features, particularly the eyes, sensuous mouth, wrinkles on the neck, pronounced breasts, and protruding stomachs, and general attention to detail are all aspects of Amarna's heritage. But perhaps most important of all is the ability of the post-Amarna works to elicit emotion through gesture or detail. Even during the Ramesside Period, a creative license existed that might not have been possible without the Amarna interlude.

The art of the era of Ramesses the Great is noteworthy both for its scale and quantity. Colossal statuary, temples, and even entire towns appeared from the Delta south into Nubia to honor the king as both god and ruler and to celebrate his exploits. Ramesses claimed countless more as his own by substituting his name – and sometimes his image – on a predecessor's monument. Although by no means the first to practice the art of usurpation, he did it on an unprecedented scale. His bravery and military savvy during his battle to reclaim the strategically important city of Kadesh from the Hittites was celebrated in relief and accompanying text on temples throughout the land, even though in reality the debacle itself had ended in a stalemate. Episode by episode, the events leading up to the confrontation, the fight itself, and the aftermath were all recorded sequentially in Egypt's most detailed and extensive narrative works.

The art of Egypt's Late Period is noteworthy for its assimilation and adaptation of foreign concepts and iconography into millennia-old ideals. When the Nubians conquered Egypt in the Twenty-fifth Dynasty, their rulers were depicted in traditional pharaonic poses and dress. However, their facial shape and features as well as their regalia were distinctively Nubian, including a cap crown with double uraeii (the significance of which is yet to be satisfactorily explained), and a neck and shoulder piece featuring images of Amen represented as a ram's head.

In a political attempt to associate themselves with times of Egypt's greatness, subsequent dynasties made deliberate attempts to return to the timeless ideals of earlier eras, copying earlier styles. At the same time, artists experimented with the iconography of age and even portraiture, which represents another anomaly in Egyptian art. Since a statue was associated with a specific individual through the addition of the owner's name and not through the specificity of its representation, and since the Egyptian ideal encompassed not only an ideal body form but an ideal facial type as well, portraiture was unnecessary. This makes sculpture like the Boston "Green Head" particularly special. Although this Memphite priest exhibits the furrowed countenance of an older man, his face is not merely a stereotypical representation of age, as the Middle Kingdom examples are. The shape of his skull, his tight-lipped expression, and the striking asymmetry of his face, which includes a wart on his left cheek, leave no doubt that a specific individual is represented. Although he is the product of pharaonic Egypt's later years, nearly every era in Egyptian history produced a few examples of what may be called true portraiture.

When Egypt fell under the yoke of Greece and later Rome, foreign rulers made great efforts to gain the support of the local populace and powerful priesthood by showing themselves in what they understood to be traditional pharaonic garb, at times in combination with the muscular bodies and *contrapposto* poses of the Classical world. This ill-fitting blend was almost never seen in the private realm, where native Egyptian and Classical styles were understood, admired, and even juxtaposed, but seldom combined.

30 Standing figure of Ir-aa-Khonsu
Probably Karnak, temple of Amun-Re, "cachette," Late Period, Twenty-fifth/ Twenty-sixth Dynasty, ca. 670 BC; black granite; H. 43.5 cm; Boston, Museum of Fine Arts, 07.494.

This striding statue of Ir-aa-Khonsu dating from the first millenium BC copied the youthful body and clothing type as well as the pose that had been common nearly 2,000 years before. Only subtle details of proportion, modeling, and engraving, as well as the highly polished, hard stone, distinguish this statue from those created during the Old Kingdom.

Hieroglyphs – Writing and Literature

Stefan Wimmer

The Origin of the "Holy Pictures"

The town of Abydos in Upper Egypt is known to many visitors in Egypt as the main location of the Osiris cult. The oldest royal tombs in the country, which date from the Predynastic Period, are situated a few kilometers behind the famous temple of Seti I. According to artifacts recently unearthed during excavations in the necropolises by the German Archaeological Institute in Cairo, the date of the origin of writing in Egypt has been adjusted earlier by several centuries. Until now this time frame was assumed to have been around 3000 BC. As a result an old question has been raised again, namely as to the possible dependence of the development of writing in Egypt on the approximately simultaneous developments in Mesopotamia and Iran. The early picture symbols of the Near East, out of which a simple form of the so-called cuneiform characters soon developed, were apparently invented for economic reasons. Stories and myths as well as messages of the greatest variety could be passed down orally and transmitted without difficulty. Trade purposes, however, required a dependable record of simple facts such as expenses, revenue, or accounts.

The Egyptians themselves explained the unprecedented cultural achievement of writing in quite a different way: as a gift of the gods – or, to be exact, of the god Thoth. As the moon god, he was responsible for chronology as well as for what we would generally call science, and thus above all also for writing and scribes.

The Egyptians called their writing *medu-netjer*, "the god's words," while we give it a semantically very similar name, the Greek-influenced "hieroglyphics" (from *hieroglyphikòs grámmata*), "holy signs." Anyone who has ever admired the enigmatic combinations of plants and body parts, geometric figures and birds, which are often lovingly rendered in great detail, will be able to understand the idea of "visual poetry" and appreciate the Egyptians' certainty of divine inspiration behind their hieroglyphs.

The Use of the Hieroglyphic Script

It is remarkable that in Egypt, unlike in neighboring Mesopotamia, it is not possible to trace a long phase of development during which a system of writing gradually crystallized out of common images used throughout millennia for rock art and the decoration of vessels. Hieroglyphic writing emerged more or less suddenly as an essentially complete system that would then endure basically unchanged for over three and a half thousand years. The oldest textual artifacts consist only of the writing of individual terms. These are labels for the contents of vessels or names and titles of people or places, such as on tomb stelae or votive offerings to the gods. Indirect references suggest, however, that complete books existed as early as the First Dynasty (ca. 2950 BC).

At the other end of the history of hieroglyphics is a temple inscription on the island of Philae from the year AD 394. By that time, hieroglyphs had long been comprehensible only to a few remaining priests of ancient Egyptian religion. The Byzantine Empire, which at that time had supremacy over Egypt, forbade the "pagan" cults whose "divine words" then faded into oblivion for centuries. Christianity in Egypt brought with it the introduction of Greek letters for the Egyptian language, complemented by some genuinely Egyptian signs for sounds that were unknown in Greek. This Coptic language and writing system continues to be used today in the liturgy of the Egyptian Christian church.

Reading and Understanding Egyptian

Modern scientific research into ancient Egyptian culture began with Napoleon's campaign in Egypt. Soon thereafter, the discipline of Egyptology was born. The Frenchman Jean-François Champollion (1790–1832) eventually succeeded in deciphering the hieroglyphic and hieratic scripts. Other preparatory work preceded this success, such

31 The Rosetta Stone
Rosetta, Ptolemaic Dynasty, 196 BC; basalt; H. 118 cm, W. 77 cm, D. 30 cm; London, The British Museum, EA 24.
It was on the eighteenth day of the second winter month in the year 9 of the reign of King Ptolemy V – March 27, 196 BC – that the assembled priests in Memphis issued a decree regarding the coronation of the king – who had only just celebrated his fourteenth birthday. The Ptolemaic Dynasty, of Macedonian origin, remained part of the Hellenistic world even upon the throne of the pharaohs. Here Greek was the *lingua franca*. At that time, the Egyptians used Demotic script for their own language, while sacred texts – and this priestly decree was one such sacred text – were written in the time-honored hiero-glyphs. Thus the decree was publicized throughout the land sometimes in Greek, sometimes in Egyptian (in hiero-glyphs, Demotic, or in both types of script). On one particular stela, the text was carved in all three scripts, one after the other. This large, black basalt stone was discovered in the port city el-Rashid – called Rosetta by Europeans – during Napoleon's Egyptian campaign in 1798. Upon the surrender of the French, the stela, despite its weight of 762 kg, was taken to London and has since been on display in The British Museum. As the key to deciphering hieroglyphs, the stone became a sort of cornerstone of the new science of ancient Egypt – and is now one of its most famous monuments.

	Represented object	Phonetic transcription	Conventional pronunciation
	vulture	ꜣ	a
	reed leaf	j	i or y
	double reed leaf	jj	y guttural sound (unknown in English)
	forearm	ꜥ	a
	quail chick	w	u or w
	foot	b	b
	stool	p	p
	horned viper	f	f
	owl	m	m
	water line	n	n
	mouth	r	r
	court ground plan	h	h (as in English)
	twisted wick/flax	ḥ	strongly aspirated h
	placenta(?)	ḫ	ch as in Scottish loch
	animal belly with tail	ẖ	h as in whispered word huge
	door bolt	s	voiced s
	folded cloth	s	unvoiced s
	pond/pool	š	sh
	slope	q	k palatal k as in queen
	basket with handle	k	k
	jar stand	g	hard g
	loaf of bread	t	t
	tethering rope for animals	ṯ	ch as in chin
	hand	d	d
	cobra	ḏ	j as in judge

32 The characters for single-consonant sounds
This list shows the range of consonants in the Egyptian language. Vowels were not written. Of the approximately 800 characters in the hieroglyphic script, some were used to denote sounds (phonograms), others denoted meanings (ideograms); some could fulfill both functions. Thus the character is used in texts that refer to a man; stands for a house. On the other hand, (a hoe) stands for the sound *mr* and can be written for all terms that contain this syllable, completely independent of their meaning (for example: "to love," "cedar," "harbor," "to spoil," and others). In the same way, the character can also stand for the sound *pr*. For differentiation, so-called determinatives are added that categorize the term but are not actually pronounced: = "to come out," = "house." The vertical stroke indicates that the symbol should not be read phonetically but as its true word meaning. Of the phonograms, most indicate a combination of two consonants, a few correspond to three, and each of the characters listed here corresponds to one only. These twenty-five signs were never considered individually by the Egyptians themselves. The concept of a system of writing based on an alphabet – so natural for us – was unknown to them, which is why it would also be incorrect to speak of a "hieroglyphic alphabet" here. On the contrary: in the final centuries (Ptolemaic and Roman Periods), the Eygptians' complex system of writing was expanded many times over with new, sometimes similarly read symbols.

as that of the Swede Johan David Åkerblad (1763–1819) and the Englishman Thomas Young (1773–1829).

For Champollion, the key to understanding was the realization that the hieroglyphs, despite their outward appearance, were in fact not a pictorial language such as Chinese, for example, where every sign stands for an entire word. He arrived at this conclusion on the basis of the Rosetta Stone, which bears a priestly decree from the Ptolemaic Period in three different scripts and two different languages: in hieroglyphs, in Demotic script (the language is also Egyptian) and in Greek.

Champollion counted over 1,400 hieroglyphs, which corresponded to just under 500 words of the Greek version. He correctly supposed that the royal names Ptolemy and Cleopatra, which were found in the Greek text, were contained within the conspicuous king's rings or so-called cartouches in the hieroglyphic text – and then in principle had only to read them letter for letter. Other names of kings followed on other documents, and finally, step by step, other words unfolded before him, then grammatical forms, and finally a syntax: no longer just the writing, but truly the language itself. Certainly Champollion's knowledge of Coptic was of great help to him. Champollion published his admirable accomplishment in 1824 in a 400-page work entitled *Précis du système hiéroglyphique des anciens Égyptiens*. In 1836, several years after his untimely death, his *Grammaire égyptienne* was published, followed by his *Dictionnaire égyptien* in 1841.

The Work of Egyptologists

Since then, generations of Egyptologists have worked to resurrect the Egyptian language. Today research has progressed to the point where almost all texts, as far as their state of preservation allows, can basically be understood. Most of the exceptions are the specially devised, cryptographic texts that priests developed during the Ptolemaic and Roman Periods. Of course the Egyptians themselves left behind neither a dictionary, nor a grammar of their language. Thus discussions among philologists, as far as semantics are concerned, but above all regarding a precise understanding of grammatical forms and syntactic foundations, will certainly continue, even if one point or another can be clarified. With the help of modern linguistic methods, for example, new approaches have been attempted in recent years.

Particular dissatisfaction is often felt due to the fact that the actual pronunciation of Egyptian is unknown. Since only consonants were written, with no vowels in between, Egyptologists make use of an artificial "pronunciation aid": researchers simply agreed to pronounce the so-called half-consonants ꜣ (aleph, a glottal stop), ꜥ (ayin, a deep guttural sound), *j* or *jj* and *w* as a, i, and u and otherwise to add an e between other consonants. In the meantime many specialists have made progress with the reconstruction of the actual pronunciation. This is possible on the one hand through inferences made on the basis of the Coptic language, and on the other hand through contemporary

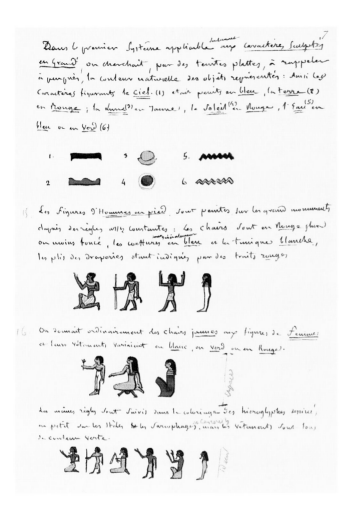

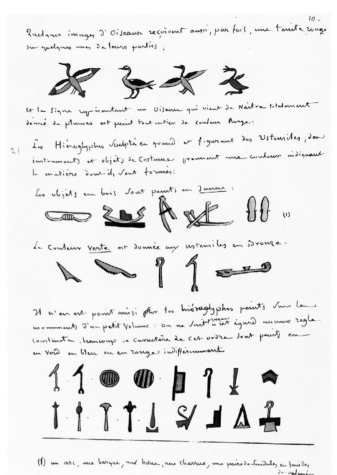

transcriptions of Egyptian words and, above all, names in cuneiform characters. Perhaps in the not-too-distant future we can expect further progress on this front. Today we know, for example, that the name of the Pharaoh Akhenaten really was pronounced "Akanyati." The conventional scientific phonetic transcription is $3ḫ$-n-Jtn and is pronounced "Akh-en-iten."

33 Examples of hieroglyphs from Champollion's Grammaire égyptienne of 1836 Champollion also hoped to express the "visual poetry" of hieroglyphs in the first scientific grammar of Egyptian. A selection of beautiful hieroglyphic signs embedded between the black letters of our modern script, which by comparison seems a mere monotonous chain of empty symbols, makes it clear that, in Egypt, writing and art were by no means considered separate fields. Subsequent grammars for Egyptologists do without such elaborate presentation. In the past, standardized hieroglyphic typesetting fonts were commonly used, or each author drew his or her own signs; nowadays, computer-generated hieroglyphs are more common.

Types of Script

Hieroglyphic script is above all a formal, monumental script, that is it was used particularly for inscriptions on monuments that were built to last. We find hieroglyphs carved in or painted on the walls of temples and tombs, on objects of burial equipment, on stelae of all types, on pieces of jewelry, and so forth. As for content, hieroglyphic texts are concerned with everything intended to be captured in writing for eternity, in particular religious texts, historical and political inscriptions, and biographies. Slightly abbreviated, so-called cursive hieroglyphs were written in ink for certain papyrus manuscripts. The famous Book of the Dead was written this way, for example.

On the other hand, secular texts intended for limited use chronologically were written in another type of writing called hieratic script. This developed through the rapid and flowing writing of hieroglyphic forms, although both scripts seem to have developed at about the same time. The two types of writing were used side by side. It is correct to speak about a cursive style of writing, and as an analogy one might compare our modern, handwritten cursive script with printed type.

Depending on the type of text and the personal handwriting of the scribe, the appearance of hieratic texts can vary much more widely than is the case for hieroglyphs. Anyone who has had to guess at rather than read a particularly illegibly written letter can imagine something of the challenge that some hieratic texts pose for Egyptologists.

During about the seventh century BC the script was simplified further and practically stenographically abbreviated. The result of this third Egyptian script was Demotic, which then took over the function of the hieratic script. Demotic became the script for everyday use, although hieratic remained in use for religious texts. This situation was

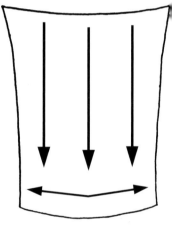

34/35 Unguent vessel bearing the name of King Pepi II
Old Kingdom, Sixth Dynasty, ca. 2240 BC; calcite-alabaster; H. 15.5 cm; Berlin, SMPK, Ägyptisches Museum, 14280.
Hieroglyphs can be written horizontally from right to left and vice versa or in columns from top to bottom. In each case, the signs are oriented so that they are turned in the direction of the reader – in the same way that people who are speaking together turn to face each other. Written characters were not merely functional linear shapes, but were considered to be "holy images" similar to living beings possessing a soul.

36 *Lintel bearing a curse against tomb robbers*
Giza, tomb of Meni; Old Kingdom, Sixth Dynasty, ca. 2250 BC; limestone; Munich, Staatliche Sammlung Ägyptischer Kunst, Gl. 24. a.
The reproduction of the text in hieroglyphs and the transcription have been adapted to the direction of the translation.

37 *Scripts*
Besides hieroglyphs, a variety of cursive scripts were always in use.

Hieroglyphs					
Hieroglyphic cursive					
Hieratic (literary script)					
Hieratic (non-literary script)					
Demotic					

described by Greek observers with the terms "Demotic," that is "the people's writing," and "hieratic," or "writing of priests."

The Process of Writing

The paper upon which this book was printed was ultimately derived from a Chinese invention. And yet already the word "paper" refers to the fact that the invention of an incomparably more advantageous material for writing than stone and clay tablets was another cultural achievement of great consequence from the land of the pharaohs.

From the stems of the papyrus plant (Cyperus papyrus L.), strips were cut that were then pressed together in two layers, one horizontal and one vertical. Several pages made this way were glued together to form rolls. The longest known roll of papyrus measures more than 40 m. Rolls of twenty pages and a length of 1.5 to 2 m were more common, however. The height of the roll varies; it is often between 16 and 20 cm, and the maximum is approximately half a meter. Fresh papyrus was white and turned a yellow-brown color only after much time had passed.

Before an Egyptian scribe applied his pen, he first sprayed a few drops from a small water pot as an offering to Thoth, the god of writing. He kept this small container with him in order to stir up the dry, solid ink, which might be compared to the paints in a modern painting set. Black ink was made of soot. Red, made from ochre or hematite, could be used, for example, for the date or for the beginnings of new chapters and – just like today – for corrections. The ink was applied with a thin rush, and a scribe usually held one at the ready behind his ear like a status symbol. The end of the stem was chewed to form a type of brush at the moment it was needed. Some scholars maintain, however, that the other, smooth end was used for writing while the chewed end can hardly be explained better than our "chewed pencils" can today.

The scribe sat cross-legged on the ground with his kilt pulled tight by his knees, thus forming the writing surface. The papyrus scroll was rolled open a little to the right. The direction of the writing therefore came about quite naturally: vertical lines one after the other from right to left. The disadvantage was that, for right-handed scribes, the still-moist ink could be smudged by the hand as it worked across the page. During the Twelfth Dynasty, horizontal lines began to be used, which in hieratic and Demotic script read from right to left without exception. Contrary to our orientation, this was the original alignment of all types

38/39 Scribe's palette
Saqqara; New Kingdom or later; wood;
L. 27.6 cm, W. 3.6 cm,
Th. 0.8. cm; Cairo, Egyptian Museum, JE
32745.
Painter's palette
New Kingdom, Eighteenth Dynasty; limestone; L. 21 cm, W. 3.6 cm, Th. 2.2 cm; Cleveland, The Cleveland Museum of Art, Gift of
John Huntington Art and Polytechnic Trust,
1914.680.
The scribe's palette (left) has two very
shallow wells at the lower end to hold black
and red ink. They show clear signs of use. In
the central compartment with its sliding lid,
numerous rushes for writing have been
preserved. Palettes with several wells containing color were used to illustrate papyri with
colored images (vignettes). The Cleveland
example (right) contains five large slices of
pigment and is also inscribed. From this
inscription we learn that the owner of the
palette was a high-ranking official during the
reign of Amenophis II.

*40 Column (right) and page layout (left) on a
papyrus roll (schematic illustration)*

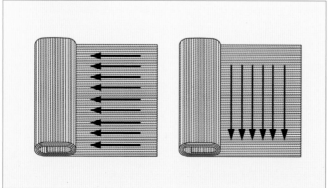

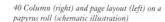

of writing; it persists today in languages such as Hebrew and Arabic.
Of course the lines were not continued over the entire length of the
papyrus roll each time, but were organized in blocks of text whereby
each new block was begun to the left of the preceeding one. If the end
of the roll was reached, it could be flipped horizontally and the writing
continued on the reverse side. After it was written on or read, a scroll
had to be rolled together again so that the beginning of the text would
appear first for the next person to read, similar to the manner in which
a cassette tape must be rewound after being played to the end.

Scribes, Archives, and Libraries

How many Egyptians could read and write? This question cannot be
answered with certainty. Surely the rather long training period was the
privilege of only a very small percentage of the population. Other than
professional scribes and, to a limited degree, workers responsible for
the decoration of temple and tomb walls, those who learned to write
were most likely priests, officials, and possibly also high-ranking military personnel. It is not surprising that the caste of scribes developed a
certain sense of self-assurance: "Become a scribe, take that to heart, so
that your name should become equally as (immortal)! A scroll is more
useful than a painted stela, than a solid wall. They (books) erect
temples and pyramids in the heart of him who speaks of their name…"
(from: Papyrus Chester Beatty IV).

In the scribal schools, one learned by copying prescribed texts,
among others the literary works regarded as classics. Thus, picture words
were memorized as entire units, rather than analytically composed sign
by sign. Individual characters were not learned – a method that anticipated the latest concepts in language teaching. It is not known how the
pharaonic libraries were organized. Institutions entrusted with the
production, transmission, and storage of scientific and religious works

41 Thoth as a baboon
Early Ptolemaic Period, ca. 300 BC; faience, silver, and gold; H. 15 cm; Paris, Musée du Louvre, E 17496.
Along with the ibis bird, the baboon was considered an attribute and apparition of Thoth. The god of writing and the sciences was also responsible for chronology. Thus this holy animal carries both a crescent and a full moon on his head; since time immemorial, the phases of the moon have been the most obvious basis for structuring time.

42 Statue of a scribe
Saqqara; Old Kingdom, Fourth/Fifth Dynasty, ca. 2500 BC; painted limestone; H. 53 cm, W. 43 cm; Paris, Musée du Louvre, E 3023.
With his left hand, the scribe holds the papyrus roll on his tightly stretched kilt; his right hand once held a writing implement (now lost). The facial expression as well as the folds of flesh around the stomach are demonstrative examples for the self-confidence and prosperity of the caste of scribes.

43 A seated scribe protected by Thoth
New Kingdom, Eighteenth Dynasty, ca. 1360 BC; graywacke; H. 19.5 cm, L. 20.5 cm; Paris, Musée du Louvre, E 11154.
Here the god of wisdom Thoth is represented by his sacred animal, the baboon. The inscription describes him as "lord of the divine words (= hieroglyphs)." The scribe Nebmertuf sits working at his feet. With his left hand he holds a papyrus roll open on his tightly stretched kilt.

44 Papyrus of Hunefer: the god Thoth at the last judgment scene (detail)
Thebes; New Kingdom, Nineteenth Dynasty, ca. 1285 BC; painted papyrus; H. 39 cm; London, The British Museum, EA 9901/3.
The vignette for the famous Spell 125 from the Book of the Dead shows the deceased before the court of the dead. Hunefer is led to the tribunal by the jackal-headed god Anubis, where his heart is weighed against a feather, the symbol of truth (Maat). If the feather on the scale has the same weight as the heart of the deceased, this proves that the man led a life in accordance with ancient Egyptian ethics. Directly beside the scales stands Thoth, the ibis-headed god of wisdom. Holding a palette and a rush for writing, he notes the result of the weighing. The accompanying inscription names Thoth as "lord of the divine words" while a wide sash across his upper body marks him additionally as a divine lector priest. Finally the deceased, whose justification was confirmed before the court, is led before the supreme judge of the dead and ruler of the netherworld, Osiris.

46/47 Scarabs

The dung beetle, scarabaeus, rolls animal dung into balls out of which its young emerge. The Egyptians saw the ball as the sun that travels across the sky, and the beetle as the symbol for "come into being, become, be created." Innumerable small scarabs, most of stone, served as seals and amulets.

Scarab (top right)
Steatite, glazed; H. 0.7 cm, L. 1.4 cm, W. 1 cm; Jerusalem, Israel-Museum, 76.31.2954. Amulet scarab with the phrase: "Amun-Re loves him who loves him!"

Scarab (right)
Steatite; H. 0.6 cm, L. 1.5 cm, W. 1 cm; Jerusalem, Israel-Museum, 76.31.4429. "Amun-Re is strength for the individual!"

45 Seal plaque of an official

New Kingdom, Nineteenth Dynasty, ca. 1250 BC; steatite; L. 1.9 cm, W. 1.4 cm; Munich, private collection.
Similar to scarabs, small, rectangular plates could also serve as stamp seals for official use. They usually have a hole bored through them lengthwise so that the seal could be worn hung around the neck. On one side, the lieutenant of the cavalry Ka-nakht is shown with his hands raised in worship before a cartouche bearing the name of his king Ramesses II. Here the name – that is, the writing – represents the king and serves by itself as the object of devotion. On the reverse, the name and title of the official are shown. Ka-nakht means "strong bull;" a bull can be made out in the right-hand column. The horse at the left is especially beautiful with an ostrich plume as a head decoration. It determines the word for cavalry. The function of these nameplates which appear in increased numbers during the Ramesside period remains unknown, but they could perhaps have been a form of visiting card or identity document.

48 Commemorative scarab of Amenophis III

New Kingdom, Eighteenth Dynasty, ca. 1385 BC; steatite with blue-green glaze; L. 8.8 cm, W. 5.8 cm; Leiden, Rijksmuseum van Oudheden, AS4.
Five different versions of large-size scarabs were commissioned by Amenophis III during the early years of his reign; today they are grouped under the heading "commemorative scarabs." The texts on the underside relate important events that the ruler wanted to publicize throughout the country via the easily distributed medium of the scarab.

The Leiden specimen belongs to the corpus of so-called wedding scarabs, somewhat confusingly defined since, after the full titulary of Amenophis III and the naming of his principal wife Tiye, the text proceeds: "The name of her father is Yuya, the name of her mother is Tuya, she is the wife of a powerful king whose southern border reaches as far as Karoi (Nubia) and whose northern border reaches as far as Naharin (the empire of Mitanni at the upper Euphrates)."

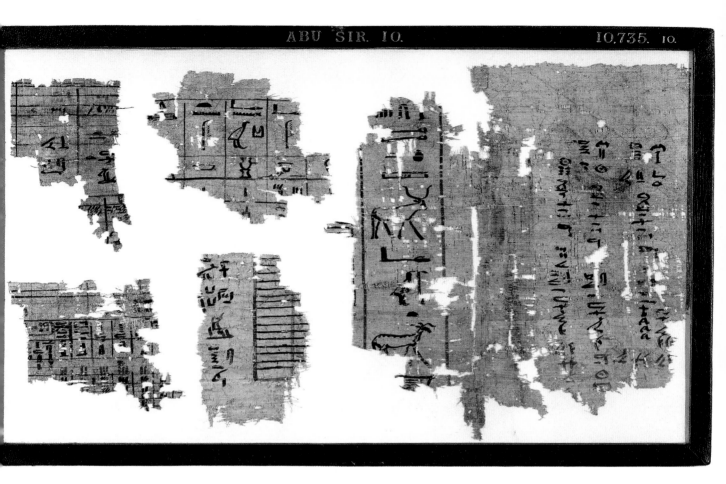

were associated with the temples. That they were called "house of life" gives some clue as to how highly the art of writing was valued. In individual cases we know of private individuals who collected books out of the sheer pleasure in literature. Such personal libraries could be passed down and expanded by the family over the course of generations.

The famous library at Alexandria belongs completely to the realm of the Hellenistic world, no longer to pharaonic culture. Even so, the flames that destroyed the library during Julius Caesar's occupation of Alexandria surely also have reduced innumerable intellectual treasures from the pharaonic millennia to smoke and ashes, never to be replaced. The Greeks took the material papyrus from the Egyptians, and in fact one can hardly imagine what would have become of antiquity had books (= papyrus scrolls) not existed. It is not for nothing that the Greek word for book, "biblos", is named after the Phoenician town Byblos, the major port for the export for papyrus rolls.

From the Book of the Dead to the "Jotted Sherd"

Egyptian literature, which, after all, encompasses a period of three thousand years, is of a richness and depth that can only be hinted at

49 Abusir papyri (fragments): list of goods
Abusir, funerary temple of Neferirkare; Old Kingdom, Fifth Dynasty, ca. 2470 BC; papyrus with hieratic script; fragment on the right (Palimpsest): 21 x 21 cm; London, The British Museum, EA 10735 (frame 10).
The oldest surviving documents in hieratic script are termed the Abusir papyri after the place of their discovery. The numerous fragments of various sizes originally belonged to the pyramid administration's archive and register, among other things, monthly deliveries of goods (here corn) destined for the daily offerings in the royal funerary temple.

here. The textual artifacts accessible to us today are vast in number, and yet they must represent only a comparatively tiny fraction of all of the writing that did not withstand the ravages of time. Even if, due to the importance of the "mortuary and temple culture" of ancient Egypt, mostly religious texts are discussed, we can by no means conclude that the literary production of that age was limited to this subject area. It would hardly be an exaggeration to conjecture that Egyptian texts comprised almost all subjects that we still – or rather once more – know today: fiction in lyric poetry and prose, ethical literature, scientific treatises, documents dealing with law, economics, and trade, official testimonials of royal power, the miscellaneous items of state bureaucracy as well as essays of a private nature, letters, and – of course – graffiti.

50 Papyrus Chester Beatty I
New Kingdom, Twentieth Dynasty, ca. 1150
BC; papyrus with hieratic script; H. 21.5 cm,
L. 5.02 m (unrolled); London, The British
Museum, EA 10682.
A papyrus roll in its original condition. The
book written in hieratic script contains a
mythological story, many economic notes,
and love songs.

52 Letter
Gebelein; Ptolemaic Period, 110 BC; papyrus
with demotic script; L. 22.5 cm, W. 7.5 cm;
Heidelberg, Sammlung des Instituts für
Papyrologie der Universität Heidelberg, P.
Heid. Inv. Dem. 781b.
This text contains a letter from several
soldiers to their comrades. The single line at
the bottom notes the date; "written in year 8,
month 4 of the inundation season, day 12
(= October 1, 110 BC)."

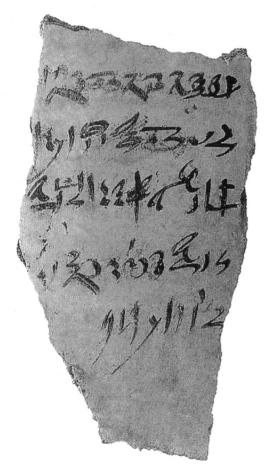

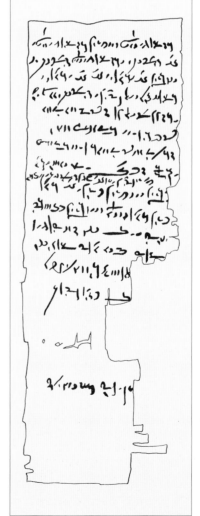

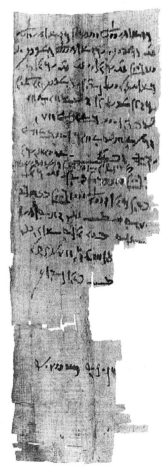

51 Ostracon
Western Thebes; New Kingdom, late
Nineteenth Dynasty, ca. 1200 BC; pottery;
L. 12 cm, W. 7 cm; Luxor, Egyptian
antiquities authority, Q 656/3.
The ceramic sherd from Deir el-Medineh

contains a short message in the hieratic
script. The recipient of the message is
reproached for passing his time "dancing
in the desert" (instead of working). The
sign for the dancing man can be made out
in the third line.

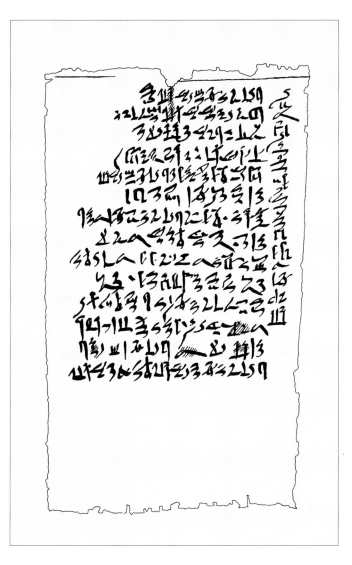

53–55 Letter on papyrus
Middle Kingdom, Twelfth Dynasty, ca. 1800 BC; papyrus, black ink; L. 30 cm, W. 19 cm; Möller, *Hieratische Lesestücke* I,19B.
This is a reminder notice from a man named Neni to his superior with reference to an affair concerning property – two previous letters had been left unanswered. The letter is written in hieratic script on papyrus. The modern reconstruction (see photograph) shows how the completed letter was folded, addressed, and sealed.

Texts from Everyday Life

It is precisely texts from everyday life that are especially suitable to grant us a direct glimpse into the joys and sorrows experienced by the ancient dwellers of the Nile Valley. In this context, the settlement at Deir el-Medineh on the west bank of Thebes occupies a unique position. According to the archaeological record, for many generations it was the home of the craftsmen and artists and their families who constructed the royal tombs in the nearby Valley of the Kings and in the Valley of the Queens.

Due to their professions, the number of people who could read and write was particularly high in that very special village, and in fact excavations there have unearthed many thousands of texts. Only a small number of them are written on papyrus. As elsewhere in Egypt, in Deir el-Medineh fragments of text were written on so-called ostraca, meant to be used for short periods of time. Ostraca are fragments of stone, available in unlimited quantity at the edge of the desert, and the clay sherds of broken vessels. This free writing material was used for school exercises as well as for protocols written in court, for invoices, lists of all types, letters, and simple notes.

It is interesting that, as of the second half of the New Kingdom, texts of a non-literary nature such as these were written in a language style whose grammar differed considerably from that of official, fictional, and religious texts. The extent of this gap could be likened to the difference between local dialects in comparison with the standard, "high" forms of modern languages. The everyday texts were written just as the language was spoken, while official and literary texts were written down in the classical, "high" language.

56 The vizier Ramose
Western Thebes, tomb of the vizier Ramose (TT 55); reign of Amenophis III, ca. 1350 BC. Even without the inscription providing us with names and titles, it is clear from the garment he wears that the person here depicted receiving a ritual purification is a vizier. This official uniform was the only badge of office known for civil state officials in Egypt. It consisted of a calf-length apron that reached up over the breast and was held by a strap around the neck. The staff and scepter held in the hands show the high social station of the vizier and the authority of his position. Ramose was vizier under Amenophis III and at the beginning of the reign of Amenophis IV, later Akhenaten. His tomb remained un-completed, work on it being abruptly term-inated. It can be assumed that he either died soon after the new king assumed power or that he fell into disfavor. However, as this relief indicates, there was no intentional destruction of the images in his tomb.

The Royal Administration and Its Organization

Eva Pardey

The King

Royal dogma stated that the king held a divine office. His role as the earthly representative of the royal god Horus – expressed in his Horus name, the oldest known royal title and dating from the Archaic Period – as well as his divine origins, which were a matter of dogma, qualified him to carry out this task. From the Fourth Dynasty on, the title "Son of the sun god" asserted his divine origins, which were depicted from the time of Hatshepsut's reign in a cycle of images, the so-called birth legend. During the New Kingdom the royal father was the imperial god, Amun-Re.

The Egyptian state was an absolute monarchy. At least in the legal sense, all activity in the land could be traced to the king. By virtue of his office he held sole legislative power, proclaimed laws and decrees, and commanded officials and priests who, as his representatives, performed their duties on his behalf throughout the country. Both legislative and executive branches of government were combined in the person of the king.

The Egyptians did not develop their own term for the state. "State" must be paraphrased with expressions meaning "king" or "kingdom." This, too, shows the king's key position: he was the state.

Ancient Egyptian sources describe the king as the individual who personally made all decisions affecting his empire. In official sources, such as the texts of the so-called royal novel, a staff of advisers appeared whose objections and suggestions the king ultimately disregarded. What the king said, went – and he was always right! In fact, these texts do not describe a real situation but rather they serve to document the greatness, the omnipotence, the wisdom and superiority of the king. They also underscore his unassailable hold on power.

The king was supreme commander of the armed forces. His personal presence during military campaigns can be proven in many cases. Moreover, he personally decided whether to pursue war or peace and it was his prerogative to dispatch the army.

The king was not only leader of the Egyptian homeland whose traditional borders were formed in the north by the Mediterranean and in the south by the cataracts at Aswan. During the eras of Egyptian expansionism he also commanded the conquered territories in both Nubia and the Near East. He maintained diplomatic relations with foreign states. The best-known evidence for foreign relations is provided by the clay tablet archive discovered at Amarna that recorded the correspondence between Egypt and the states of the Near East. The king was also responsible for foreign trade ventures of which the best

known were the expeditions to Punt; these were clearly royal and state undertakings. A military invasion or conquest of Punt never took place. From the time of Thutmosis IV peace treaties were usually sealed by the marriage of the king to a princess of the foreign land in question. Princesses from Mitanni came as royal brides to Egypt in the Eighteenth Dynasty for this reason and later, during the reign of Ramesses II, daughters of the Hittite kings as well. Peaceful relations between these states were therefore symbolized in the person of the king through such marriages.

The Vizierate

Supervision of executive power lay in the hands of the vizier. The term "vizier" derives from the Arabic and has entered the language of Egyptology as a description of the state's highest official, literally the prime minister. In the Old and Middle Kingdoms there was only one vizier responsible for the entire country, but the vizierate was divided in the New Kingdom. Besides the Lower Egyptian vizier with his headquarters in Memphis – or, for a short time during the Nineteenth Dynasty, in the capital of the Ramesside pharaohs, Pi-Ramesse – there was also an Upper Egyptian vizier at Thebes. It is still not clear today when this division occurred. It can, however, be shown to have existed at the time of Thutmosis III (Eighteenth Dynasty). Both viziers exercised their offices independently as colleagues of equal rank; each was responsible for his own area. In the Old Kingdom, Egypt was subject to the vizier's authority within its traditional borders as far as Aswan. In the Middle Kingdom the area under his control extended to Lower Nubia, which had by that time been conquered and annexed. After the reconquest of Lower Nubia and the additional annexation of Upper Nubia during the New Kingdom, Nubia received its own independent administration under the Egyptian Viceroy of Kush.

In the late Ramesside Period, part of the vizier's tasks were transferred to the administration of the temple of Karnak; the vizierate thus lost some of its importance, at least in southern Egypt.

The vizier's responsibilities are described in great detail in a text known as the "Instructions for the Vizier" recorded in various tombs of the New Kingdom. Although it can be proved that this detailed description of the vizierate originally dates to the Middle Kingdom, the tasks they document are nevertheless generally valid for later periods.

As head of the executive branch of government, the vizier functioned as the king's representative. He controlled and coordinated Egypt's internal administration and also had certain legal responsibilities. When the vizier is described as responsible for dispensing *maat* (law, or order), this meant not simply that he was a judge but that he was also accountable for the smooth operation of law and justice within the State. He had no legislative functions per se, for these were the sole prerogative of the king.

The vizier directed the administration of the country with its various national and regional authorities. The officials working in these organizations were accountable to him for any failures. In addition, the maintenance of the archives that held documents on the entire country and its people formed part of his responsibilities. The validity and accuracy of these surveys, which formed the basis for all obligations imposed by the state upon its citizens, were ultimately guaranteed by the vizier. According to his service instructions it was incumbent upon him, for example, to supervise the opening of the canal locks. As this task was of national importance, it could only be controlled centrally. The storehouses and the treasuries that administered the national income likewise fell under his jurisdiction.

As befitted the importance of the task, the vizier was also responsible for the construction of the royal tomb. The workforce of Deir el-Medineh, which built the tombs in the Valley of the Kings, was directly under his control. From time to time the vizier inspected the progress of these projects. He was responsible for the workers' wages and the delivery of required materials. In the Twentieth Dynasty, working conditions deteriorated badly, because wages, paid in kind, were long overdue. The artisans were compelled to strike and blamed the vizier for their misery.

The Judicial System

The separation of the executive from the judiciary branches of government so familiar to us was alien to the Egyptians. Administration and justice formed a single entity; there were no professional judges. It is therefore scarcely surprising that there is no official word for "judge" in Egyptian. In the New Kingdom there were only councils of judges known as a *kenbet*. In the reign of King Horemheb, as we know from the Horemheb Decree, many regional *kenbets* were reorganized. They were composed of the local governor and priests whose official rank in civil or temple administration entitled them to jurisprudence. We do not know, however, in what type of legal disputes these courts had jurisdiction.

The so-called "Great *kenbet*," chaired by the vizier, was made up of high-ranking officials. To describe the vizier therefore as the highest judge in the land is only partially correct. Generally he acted only as *primus inter pares*. Cases regarding property claims were, for instance, heard by the Great *kenbet*, as they were matters that affected the state; property was the source of the state's taxes. Moreover, because central office files were stored in the royal residence to which the vizier had constant unlimited access, such cases could only be resolved at the highest levels of state.

The trials of tomb robbers held at Thebes during the late Ramesside era were also heard by the Great *kenbet*. The high priest of Karnak played a leading role, as befitted the great importance this office had attained in affairs of states. These trials clearly show that the court had assumed the role of prosecutor. It also conducted the examinations and passed judgment. No distinction was made between judges and state attorneys. During interrogations in criminal cases, for example, suspects were often tortured with blows from a stick. As tomb robbing was considered the most heinous of crimes in Egypt, those found guilty were sentenced to death. For other offenses, such as those committed by officials, the court ordered confiscation of property, beatings, and sometimes forced labor. In the New Kingdom, it became common for the guilty to be mutilated by having their lips, nose or ears cut off.

After the assassination of Ramesses III by members of the harem a special court was established that, because of the severity of the crime, called for the death penalty. Some of those involved in the assassination, as well as the women of the harem, were conceded the right to commit suicide. How capital punishment was otherwise administered is not known.

The workers' settlement at Deir al-Medineh provides the greatest number of sources on the administration of justice and the judicial system. Workers living there not only administered themselves, they had their own jurisdiction in legal matters. Their college of judges, also known as a *kenbet*, was composed of foremen, scribes, and other well-regarded members of the community.

Apart from property crimes such as theft, unpaid work or unfulfilled claims to recourse, adultery and wife-beating were also matters for the court. The plaintiff was always a resident, and women were also granted the right to seek redress in the courts. The case was examined by the court and a judgment made based on the law of precedence. Legal rulings only affected the administration with respect to disciplinary procedures or the relationship between the administration and residents. However, the power of the local court of Deir el-Medineh to pursue the penalties it had imposed was rather limited: often, a case had to be taken up several times because the guilty party had not discharged the obligations place on him by the court. For example, litigation regarding payment for a pot of fat concerned the court over a period of more than a decade. Serious crimes such as murder were referred to the vizierate.

At Deir el-Medineh, some cases were decided by divine oracle. Because the deified king Amenophis I was particularly venerated by the workers, Amenophis, or rather his cult image, was "asked" to reach a decision on a matter of litigation between two parties in the course of a festival procession. In such cases priests were, of course, consulted; they were essentially the same individuals represented in the civil *kenbet*.

57 Hall of the Vizier
Western Thebes, tomb of Rekhmire (TT 100); reign of Thutmosis III, ca. 1430 BC.
The office of the vizier is shown in the central portion of this detail view. Originally the vizier Rekhmire sat to the right (now chiseled out), supervising the events in his office. Rekhmire held the highest state office under the kings Thutmosis III and Amenophis II.

The image is one of the few representations of a state department and the only known illustration of a vizier's office. The vertical lines of inscription just visible at the left edge are the beginning of the so-called "Instructions for the Vizier." The text dates from the Twelfth Dynasty and describes contemporary conditions. Its contents, however, also reflect the state of affairs in later ages. In front of the vizier's hall are five members of his administration receiving officials and others who prostrate themselves; also depicted is the messenger who distributed the vizier's orders throughout the land. Inside the hall, officials can be seen in two rows of ten; between them two men are introduced before the vizier. These officials are probably the so-called "Ten of Upper Egypt" who worked with the vizier in the Middle Kingdom and had to be present at meetings held in his office.

Elkab, tomb of Paheri; reign of Thutmosis III, ca. 1450 BC.

Paheri had a leading position in the regional administration. According to information contained in his title and recorded in several places in his tomb, he officiated in an area south of Thebes that included the nomes of Elkab and Esna. In his tomb, several of the duties of his office are depicted. Among these were supervision of agricultural work and especially the obligations of tax gathering such as calculating cattle tax (below) and delivering grain to the provincial storehouses under his authority (top). Although numerous such scenes have also been recorded in other tombs, they belong in those cases to the general theme of providing for the dead. Only in a few cases, as here in the tomb of Paheri, are they clearly depictions of official duties as the inscriptions show. Thus the inspection of agricultural labor is described as "all official duties which he, Paheri, completed." The depiction is an excellent example of one of the passages in the vizier's service instructions: "He (the vizier) is to send the nomarchs hence (that is, he commands them) to tend to the cultivation of the fields and the harvest (tax)."

The Central Administration

The various regional administrations were directly controlled by the most senior representative of the central administration of the vizier and worked directly with the central documents office. The taxes they raised were forwarded to granaries and treasuries that were among the most important administrative institutions. They administered the state income necessary for financing state ventures, which included foreign trade whereby imports had to be paid for with Egyptian products, and the maintenance and equipment of the armies as well as workers involved in large projects. Even the king's provisions had to be guaranteed. While the granaries were the administrative institutions responsible for grain, other products were submitted to the treasury: gold, silver, (semi) precious stones, as well as linen, cattle, wood, and so forth. Workshops adjoined the treasuries and processed the raw materials. Storehouses and treasuries also had their own ships for use in the transportation of goods. Armies of scribes dealt with the registration of revenues and expenditures.

In addition to granary and treasury directors, the chief domain director was one of the most important state officials working at a national level. He was required to exercise overall control of royal domains. In the second half of the New Kingdom, further to these firmly institutionalized offices, the so-called chamberlains assumed an important political role. They performed state tasks on the basis of special royal authority and owed their position to their personal relationship with the king.

Regional Administration

Egypt had already been divided into administrative districts commonly known as "nomes" at an early period. The hieroglyph for "nome" shows a

piece of land divided up into various parcels. With few exceptions, the names of nomes were derived from the names of the deities who were venerated in that area. These old nomes ceased being administrative units during the First Intermediate Period, a development that is well-documented for the southern part of Upper Egypt. In their stead, new administrative districts in the Middle Kingdom were named after the capital of their respective regions. This new administrative division survived into the administrative structure of Egypt in Greco-Roman times. The traditional forty-two nomes seen in temple lists of the Late Period do not reflect any administrative reality.

The most important tasks of the regional administration were raising taxes and drafting compulsory labor from the regional population for state projects. This was based on a regional survey of the country similar to a land register that was the responsibility of the district administrator. The importance of this task was reflected in the nome hieroglyph mentioned above: it portrayed in schematic form the

estates of a region that had been surveyed. The resulting documents were then sent to the central records office which was answerable to the vizier. The central office then calculated the taxes to be raised as well as the labor requirements for large state ventures. The actual business of collecting or recruiting then proceeded according to orders given by the vizier. The district governors were directly responsible to the vizier or, as was the case in the south in the late Old Kingdom and Middle Kingdom, to his immediate deputy, the overseer of Upper Egypt and to the so-called speaker, who took over the duties in the Middle Kingdom.

At a local level within the districts there were temples that each had their own administration and which, by royal assent, often operated outside the jurisdiction of the civil administration; they were thus freed from taxation and the obligations of providing labor. In the late Old Kingdom and Middle Kingdom the district governors were also the high priests of the local temples, so there was an overlap of personnel between two essentially separate levels of administration.

60 Grain transport
Elkab, tomb of Paheri; reign of Thutmosis
III, ca. 1450 BC.
In the upper register is a row of cargo ships
onto which grain is carried on board in sacks.
The transport of grain between various state
institutions is well documented from the time
of the New Kingdom. A number of texts from
the Twentieth Dynasty, the late Ramesside
Period, indicate large-scale thefts by the
captains of such transport ships. The vessels
in the lower register are for passengers, as is
clear from the arrangement of cabins. These
ships are in the service of Paheri.

This centuries-old practice was abandoned in the New Kingdom. Governors had to provide for law and order in their districts, for which reason they commanded troops of police. We know very little, however, about their authority as judges.

Officialdom

Apart from the king, his family, court, and personal servants, Egyptian society can be divided up into those who administered and those who were administered. The ranks of officials were faced by the bulk of the population. Officialdom represented – along with the military for limited periods – that stratum of society that was the very pillar of the state. As Egypt knew no separation of "church and state," temples were also state institutions. They were not just cult sites but also economic institutions that had at their disposal part of the means of production of the country, agricultural land, labor, and the means of processing raw materials. In the New Kingdom for example, the administration of the temple at Karnak had a structure similar to the state administration with its own treasury, domain manager, and storehouse.

All large-scale economic ventures were commissioned and financed by the state, and directed by state officials. The processing of raw materials took place in workshops adjoined to state institutions: amongst these, the treasuries were particularly important. Artists and tradesmen were in the service of the state and even science was controlled by officials.

Apart from the so-called "Satire on the Trades" from the Middle Kingdom, numerous texts from the Ramesside era sought to portray the advantages of the life of an official compared with the hard lot of the normal population. In reality, however, the officials did not possess one of the privileges described in the texts: as many other sources prove, they were not in fact exempt from taxation.

Praise for the life of an official can be found in texts that were directed at students in order to motivate the new generation of officials to greater diligence. Knowledge of reading, writing, and arithmetic were basic prerequisites for officials; this is why they liked to portray themselves as scribes. Scribe statues can be found dating from the end of the Old Kingdom onward. From the Middle Kingdom on, the term "scribe" entered the language as a general term for officials irrespective of whether it referred to a simple scribe at the bottom of the official hierarchy or one of the high state offices.

New scribes were educated at court or in the various branches of the administration to which the civil institutions, temples, and the military belonged. The demands and expectations placed on an official were essentially the same across the board, so that a change from one branch of administration to another was possible at any time and was often practiced.

The state paid officials for their services in kind. They received estates whose produce served to keep them economically prosperous, and they were the beneficiaries of the economic successes of their state institutions. Whatever was earned in the temple went to members of the temple; the relative position within the hierarchy was decisive in determining an individual's proportion of the share. In addition there were supplementary payments from the king on special occasions.

"Careers" of Officials

We know that many Egyptian officials followed their fathers into their professions. The desire of many Egyptians for their sons to take over their positions was expressed at an early stage in the so-called "wisdom literature." For example, in the first half of the Eighteenth Dynasty the council of viziers was in the hands of a family whose best-known representative was Rekhmire. In Middle Egypt during the Middle Kingdom, nomarchs inherited their office from their fathers. This, however, was not strictly a process of inherited succession, as the new incumbent was officially named by the king who had to sanction the family's claim to the office.

One can assume that only children of officials had access to education and training, a prerequisite for state office. Nevertheless, officials repeatedly emphasized in their biographies that they owed their career and advancement to high office to their personal achievements, diligence, and reliability.

On the other hand, during the reign of Akhenaten officials stressed above all else the fact that they owed their career progress to their submission and loyalty to the king. Akhenaten, who had broken with many traditions, required reliable men for his state apparatus, men who were not burdened by their positions in the older structures of traditional officialdom or priesthood. He preferred to rely on a new crop of individuals, from whom absolute loyalty was required. Amongst these were foreigners (something utterly new for Egypt) who are recognizable by their non-Egyptian names.

Different factors were, of course, important at different times. For example, numerous high state offices in the first half of the Eighteenth Dynasty were held by men from the administration of the Amun temple at Karnak; this temple thus featured prominently in the composition of the state. Personal ties from the king's youth could also be a significant factor in the allocation of State offices: Thutmosis IV appointed to high office several men who had grown up with him at the court.

In the New Kingdom the military became an important power broker, and members of the military and military administration were charged with important state tasks. Those members of the military who could rely on the economic power as well as the political and religious influence of the temple of Karnak assumed power in Upper Egypt at the end of the Ramesside Period.

At the close of their careers deserving officials often received, as a sinecure, well-remunerated positions as priests in large temples; these were intended as additional sources of income or provision for old age.

The Military

Manfred Gutgesell

Most of our information about Egyptian military affairs comes from the time of the New Kingdom when pharaohs like Thutmosis III or Ramesses II transformed Egypt into a dominant world power – or claimed to have done so on their monuments. The Egyptian military's equipment and organization underwent a considerable evolution.

We know little about the military in the time before the New Kingdom. There was no standing army in the Predynastic Period nor in the Old Kingdom. If necessary, men were levied, armed, and placed under the command of officials, who were also their superiors in civic life. They were armed with clubs, battle-axes, and daggers. Long-distance weaponry included lances, slings, and, of course, the bow and arrow. The technique for constructing bows was particularly sophisticated; long-range composite bows capable of deep penetration were used. These bows were made from different woods and pieces of horn that were glued together and bound with animal sinews. There were also simple wooden bows that were used by ordinary soldiers. Shields were made from animal skins stretched over wooden frames.

After the Old Kingdom the military changed significantly through the introduction of mercenaries. Professional soldiers were paid in gold and received land for their own use. Fighting units consisted of small groups divided into subunits. Ten men formed a group under a leader. A unit of 100 men was divided into two halves each of five groups. The entire unit was commanded by the leader of the first group of the first half whereas the second half was under the command of the leader of the first group of the second half. This system of organization was also used in the workforce.

Weaponry was also revolutionized at the beginning of the New Kingdom. The Hyksos, who ruled over most of Egypt for more than a century, brought horses and chariots into the country from their Asian homelands. The pharaohs began to breed horses and formed their own chariot units right after the end of Hyksos rule. They preferred light chariots drawn by two horses and carrying two men only, a charioteer and a soldier. The soldiers were equipped with superb composite bows

and long, metal-tipped arrows stored in leather quivers in the chariot. Mercenaries were hired ever more frequently – Nubians usually as archers and Libyans as light foot soldiers. These contingents fought for money under the command of their own officers. The Egyptian troops were commanded by "colonels," larger units by generals – so-called overseers of soldiers.

The armory of Egyptian troops was much improved during this time. Shields were now made of solid wood with a bronze shield buckle, the lances had long bronze tips, and the soldiers themselves were partly protected by helmets and leather armor set with bronze plates. The scimitar, adopted from Asian soldiers, became the preferred weapon for close combat. The king was supreme commander, while individual armies could be led by his sons or viziers.

61/62 Two companies of soldiers
Asiut; tomb of Mesehti; Middle Kingdom, Eleventh Dynasty, ca. 2000 BC; painted wood;
a) Cairo, Egyptian Museum, JE 30986 (CG 258); Egyptian troops: L. 169.8 cm, W. 62 cm,

H. 5.9 cm.
b) Cairo, Egyptian Museum JE 30969 (CG 257); Nubian troops: L. 190.2 cm, W. 72.3 cm, H. 5.5 cm.
The company of Egyptian soldiers comprises forty men, marching in ten rows. They are

armed with pikes and large shields. As the painted surfaces of the shields clearly show, they are fashioned from a solid wood frame on which animals skins are streched. The pikes have a broad bronze tip. The forty troops were discovered together with forty

Nubian archers, each equipped with bow and arrow, in the tomb of the powerful nomarch Mesehti at the Middle Egyptian site of Asiut. Mesehti most likely reproduced his personal guard for his tomb in model form for his own protection during times of upheaval.

Through the Desert by Donkey – Equipment and Provisions

The Egyptians had no war ships during the time of the pharaohs. Reinforcements were presumably transported using Nile ships protected by an armed guard. The construction of fortresses, however, was more advanced. A fully developed fortress at Elephantine, at that time a southern frontier town, was already known in the Predynastic Period. During the Old Kingdom, the Egyptians tried to protect themselves from Asian attacks by a long wall, the "Wall of the Ruler." It was later replaced by a dense system of fortresses along the eastern frontier. The most important base and starting point for Egyptian attacks on Syria was the fortress of Sile, lying in the easternmost part of the Delta. This fortress was military base, commercial center, and customs town all in one. It was the most important reinforcement base for Egyptian troops in Asia and was headed by its own fortress commander who held a very high rank in the Egyptian hierarchy.

Two deputies and an entire army of scribes and administrative officials supervised the provisioning of the troops. Transporting provisions was very difficult when they had to cross the eastern desert – which was, due to the political situation in the New Kingdom, quite often the case – because the Egyptians had no transport wagons and could hardly have used them in any case in the desert. Provisions were therefore transported on the backs of donkeys and, later, mules. Because of the scarity of oases and animal feed everything had to be carried by the animals; this meant that the longer the distance, the smaller the load that reached its destination. The Egyptians therefore tried to transport as many provisions as possible by sea and unload it at or at least near the battle site. These operations, however, had to be heavily guarded, as we know from the Ramesside Period. Nevertheless, the risk of losing equipment and provisions, or of receiving them too late for the troops, was still very high. The army was therefore forced to live off the land as much as possible. This consequently forced the Egyptians' attempt to maintain bases in Syria itself – that is, east of the actual border – at which they were quite successful. Controlling the port towns in Palestine and Syria was particularly important.

Because of logistical difficulties and the prevailing geography, there was virtually no alternative to marching east. They therefore set out from Egypt either in forced marches through the desert along the route of the few existing oases or along the easier but longer coast road. The sea route was ideal, but the Egyptians' seafaring abilities were rather poor. Their enemies, of course, knew these routes and could undertake appropriate countermeasures.

63 Chariot of Tutankhamun
Western Thebes, Valley of the Kings, tomb of Tutankhamun (KV 62); New Kingdom, Eighteenth Dynasty, ca. 1325 BC; gilded wood; L. 290 cm; Cairo, Egyptian Museum, JE 61989.
Chariots were introduced to Egypt by the Hyksos. This weapon was decisive in giving the Asiatics supremacy over the Egyptians; hence the pharaohs immediately adopted it. Success came during the reigns of the first rulers of the Eighteenth Dynasty, during which Egypt already had a powerful chariotry that was constantly expanded. The Egyptian chariots were lighter than those of the Asiatics and carried only a charioteer and a shield-bearer each. This unit was fast, extremely manoeuverable, and tactically superior in rough terrain to the clumsy Asiatic chariot with its crew of four.

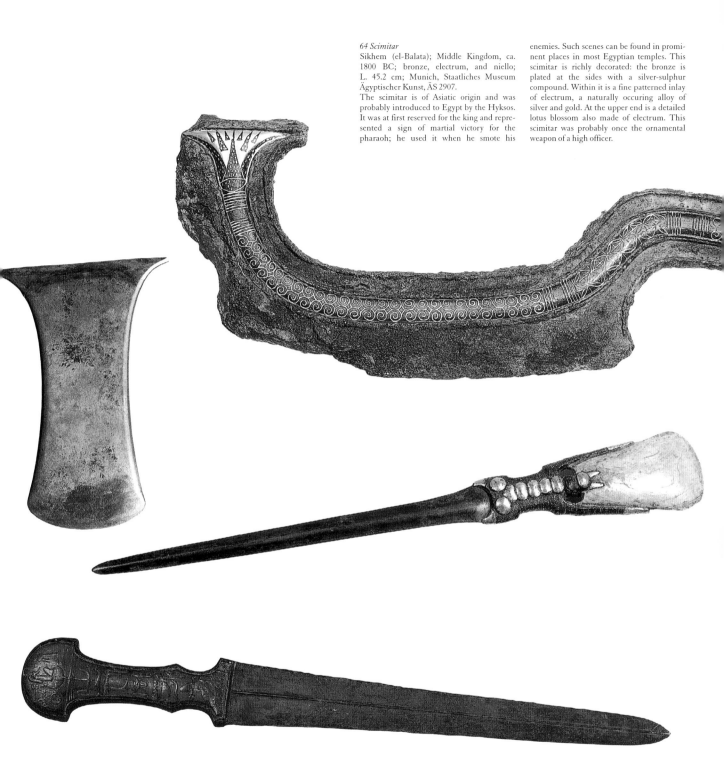

64 Scimitar
Sikhem (el-Balata); Middle Kingdom, ca. 1800 BC; bronze, electrum, and niello; L. 45.2 cm; Munich, Staatliches Museum Ägyptischer Kunst, ÄS 2907.
The scimitar is of Asiatic origin and was probably introduced to Egypt by the Hyksos. It was at first reserved for the king and represented a sign of martial victory for the pharaoh; he used it when he smote his enemies. Such scenes can be found in prominent places in most Egyptian temples. This scimitar is richly decorated: the bronze is plated at the sides with a silver-sulphur compound. Within it is a fine patterned inlay of electrum, a naturally occuring alloy of silver and gold. At the upper end is a detailed lotus blossom also made of electrum. This scimitar was probably once the ornamental weapon of a high officer.

65–67 Weapons of war (from top to bottom)
Blade of a battle-axe
Thebes; New Kingdom, Eighteenth Dynasty, ca. 1500 BC; bronze with gilt remains; Berlin, SMPK, Ägyptisches Museum, 2769.
Dagger
Western Thebes; ca. 1700–1450 BC; bronze, horn, ivory, gold; L. 40.5 cm; Berlin, SMPK, Ägyptisches Museum, 2053.
Dagger of Djehuti
Presumably Saqqara; New Kingdom, Eighteenth Dynasty, ca. 1450 BC; bronze, wood; L. 35.5 cm; Darmstadt, Hessisches Landesmuseum, Ae: I,6.
The Egyptians' weaponry was not very extensive. Axes and clubs were the preferred weapons for close combat of the infantry; swords were added in the New Kingdom. Bows and arrows served as long-distance weapons while spears were used for intermediate distances. Daggers were used for hand-to-hand combat. Many of the preserved weapons are highly decorated and only suitable for ceremonial or ornamental purposes. They were replaced by simple and rather plain weapons in actual combat. The elegant blade of the battle-axe was gilded and certainly never used in battle. The magnificent dagger of Djehuti, a general under Thutmosis III, must have been likewise an ornamental weapon.

The Battle of Kadesh – a Tactical Failure

Little is known about Egyptian strategy and tactics. The strategy was usually adapted according to the natural conditions and situations they encountered. Because there were no staff officers or similar ranks during the time of the pharaohs, there was apparently no thorough planning.

Only in one instance are we able to analyze a military action more closely, because we have not only Egyptian sources but also those of the enemy, the Hittites. In the fifth year of his reign (1274 BC), Pharaoh Ramesses II decided to go to war against the king of the Hittites, Muwatallis, and his many allies.

Ramesses II divided his army into four corps that were to move across the desert toward the Dead Sea. They were then to attack the town and fortress of Kadesh in the upper reaches of the Orontes where they believed the Hittite army was stationed. A second, much smaller army was to travel by boat, land north of Byblos, and then advance inland toward Kadesh. This second army was intended primarily to secure the baggage for the main army, which included the king and his bodyguard. The strategy was obvious: Ramesses II wanted to destroy the Hittites in a pincer movement.

But the king made some critical mistakes. The four corps of his army marched 10 km apart, which was almost a day's march in the trackless desert. It was virtually impossible for the corps to support each other. To make matters worse, the corps all crossed the Orontes at different times. Sure of his impending victory, the king did not bother to reconnoitre properly, something for which he was to pay dearly. Just before Kadesh a confusing situation developed. Ramesses II had crossed the Orontes with the first corps; the second corps had also crossed while the two other corps still remained on the right bank.

At this point the Egyptians captured two bedouins who reported that the Hittites had retreated in fear, a story Ramesses must have believed only too willingly. That the two bedouins were in fact Hittite spies he found out later to his regret. The Egyptians forged onward, as if they were on a day's outing. Disaster broke on the second Egyptian corps in the form of 1,000 heavy Hittite chariots, each manned by four or five warriors. Totally unprepared, they were attacked on their flank at a ford and, within a short time, completely routed. There was now a gap of over 20 km between the first corps and the two remaining armies and, in addition, the mighty Orontes lay between the two halves of the king's forces.

Ramesses II fled with his personal guard and the troops of the first corps to a hill and erected a fortified camp. The Hittites pursued and their vastly superior troops (their main force against a single Egyptian corps) almost completely captured the camp. Only the bravery of the king and his guard prevented an utter fiasco.

Messengers were sent to warn the remaining two corps and to stop them, probably to give them time to pick up survivors from the second corps. And then, from the Egyptian perspective, a miracle happened: the small army that had traveled by boat arrived at the camp – now almost completely under the control of the Hittites – and attacked the disorganized and plundering Hittite units. The Hittites retreated in the direction of Kadesh, Ramesses II reached his own troops in forced marches and immediately returned to Egypt where he celebrated the war as a great Egyptian victory. Scenes of the battle of Kadesh adorn the walls of almost every important temple erected during the king's long reign.

As a commander, Ramesses II had failed miserably because he had ignored the most basic military concepts. His units had been too far apart to support each other. Furthermore, his troops had crossed the Orontes one after the other, so that at the moment the King was attacked, the river lay between him and his supporting troops. But the biggest mistake was certainly the lack of common sense and his almost arrogant carelessness while moving through enemy territory; this is what made the Hittite ambush so successful. Only the perfect but accidental cooperation of the two Egyptian armies enabled the nearly defeated king to retreat and saved himself from utter destruction.

70 War camp at Kadesh
Luxor temple, first pylon of Ramesses II; New Kingdom, Nineteenth Dynasty, ca. 1265 BC. The relief shows the camp of the Egyptian army near Kadesh. The large tent belongs to the pharaoh and bears his name. These picture cycles also show the typical life of an army camp: horses are cared for, chariots are drawn up into rows and repaired, and soldiers eat peacefully at the back of the camp. On the right, however, the images show the Hittite attack and heavy fighting around the camp, which is protected by pallisades or shields. The camp has two roads that meet at Ramesses II's tent. Its construction resembles the much later camps of the Roman legions.

71 The battle of Kadesh (detail)
Abu Simbel, great temple of Ramesses II; north wall of the entrance hall; New Kingdom, Nineteenth Dynasty, ca. 1265 BC. Ancient Egyptian battle scenes are strictly structured. Enemies are principally shown in disorder, close to defeat, whereas the Egyptian troops are represented in perfect fighting order on the road to victory. The actual course of battle is of no importance. As this scene shows, this is particularly true for the depiction of the battle of Kadesh. Fortunately, we have a battle report by the Hittites that, contrary to the Egyptian representation, relates the course of events more truthfully.

STATE AND SOCIETY   369

Economy and Trade

Manfred Gutgesell

Of all the periods of pharaonic history, only the New Kingdom provides sufficient material for a reasonably certain interpretation of economic conditions. The discovery of an ancient well near the workers' settlement of Deir el-Medineh in Western Thebes, which had already run dry in ancient times, has been a real boon for our economic research. Up to 120 families lived and worked at Deir el-Medineh building the royal tombs of the Valley of the Kings and many private tombs as well. They also erected small tombs for themselves, some of which number among the finest in Egypt.

The lives of these people were played out almost entirely at their place of work or in their village isolated from the Nile Valley. They fought, loved, traded, and celebrated their festivals together. Of interest to us are their commercial activities, which they recorded on so-called ostraca, small flakes of limestone or potsherds: the prices of goods were listed, payment installments were fixed, credit guaranteed, donkeys rented, and much more. When the texts were no longer required they were simply thrown into the old well where archaeologists discovered them early in the twentieth century. The find consisted of several tens of thousands of ostraca written in hieratic; they provide us with an illuminating insight into the economy of ancient Egypt.

The ancient Egyptian economy was a strictly organized system that was administered centrally by the state and allowed for few personal freedoms. The state distribution system provided people with everything necessary for their personal maintenance as well as a fixed wage that served to provide for families and, to a limited degree, satisfy those needs that the state could not meet. In particular this meant the accumulation of appropriate tomb furnishings.

A free choice of career was only rarely possible. Generally, sons followed their fathers into their professions and became their apprentices. The children of officials were sent to the few state schools that existed in order to learn to read and write and eventually become officials themselves. There was no such thing as an entrepreneurial class. All this goes to show that the ancient Egyptian economy was not a free market system but rather a type of centrally administered economy such as is familiar to us from the modern world's recent history.

The most interesting items contained in the texts from Deir el-Medineh are prices and wages. Workers' wages and prices were constant over the course of centuries – another characteristic of a planned economy. Money in our modern sense still did not yet exist. Although coins first appeared in Greece in the eighth and seventh centuries BC, they were only introduced into Egypt in the middle of the fourth century BC to pay Greek mercenaries. But money was known in other forms. For instance, standard-sized sacks filled with grain (barley or emmer) were used as a means of exchange, or precious metals in standard sizes were used as money. Wages were paid in grain and could be converted into copper or silver at a fixed rate. Both foremen and the scribe of Deir el-Medineh received two sacks of barley per month and five and a half sacks of emmer. Simple laborers received one and a half sacks of emmer and four sacks of barley, apprentices only half and one and a half respectively, other assistants even less. One sack contained approximately 77 lb of grain. Copper was calculated according to so-called *deben,* each of 91 g. More valuable silver was measured in *shenati* (7.6 g.) or *ḳite* (9.1 g.). The value of metal to grain and therefore the size of the wage was sometimes subject to considerable fluctuations. It can be said, however, that an average worker received grain to the value of seven *deben,* a foreman 9.5 *deben.*

Work performance was subject to stringent controls by officials. If someone was sick or absent they had to make up the lost time. Work performance and absenteeism were registered in long lists and compared with a plan. The most diligent individual was a high administrative official who, in a particularly good year, had managed to double his performance quota and record this effort prominently on a large stela.

How was a sale conducted at Deir el-Medineh? One ostracon from the Twentieth Dynasty records: "What was given to Paidehu as payment for a copper vessel: ten *deben* of copper; sesame oil, five *hin* (= 2.5 l) at one *deben* per *hin*; one shirt of smooth cloth, making five *deben*; two leather sacks, making four *deben*; four mats, making two

73 *Metalworking*
Saqqara, tomb of Mereruka; Old Kingdom, Sixth Dynasty, ca. 2330 BC.
Intensive specialization of trades began in the Old Kingdom. This division of labor in the production process is an important indicator of the level of social development. Only the labor division made possible a considerable increase in productivity without far-reaching technical improvements. Smithing was one of the most important professions in many early cultures. We see here six metalworkers blowing air through long tubes into a crucible in order to increase the temperature. The molten metal is then cast in molds and worked by smiths into a variety of objects. Tools and weapons, containers and jewelry, household items of all sorts were produced in this way in great numbers. A few finished metal vessels are depicted in the register above the workers.

deben; four *hin* of salve, making two *deben*. Sum: 28 copper *deben*, amount owing: nine *deben*."

The text also tells us the prices of various oils, leather sacks, mats, and shirts. We know it is a credit transaction as nine *deben* are still outstanding. Moreover, the purchaser is paying partly in kind; for better comparison the barter goods are converted into copper. Such texts enable us to put together quite a comprehensive list of prices for the time around 1200 BC.

Several examples demonstrate the value placed on particular products. The cheapest was food: a chicken cost one-quarter of a *deben*, a piece of cake one-fortieth. Half a liter of fat was valued at half a *deben*; baskets, workers' aprons, and simple amulets each cost one *deben*. Furniture required higher expenditure: clothes chests up to five *deben*, a footstool two *deben*, a chair up to eight *deben*, and beds up to twenty *deben*. The price of a pig amounted to seven *deben*, while a cow was 140 *deben* and donkeys were available for thirty *deben*. Plain shirts cost five *deben*, fine cloaks up to sixty *deben*, and so on. One can see that certain items were unaffordable for workers or had to be purchased in installments.

Egyptians parted with large sums to furnish their tombs. Decorated coffins, as used by the foremen of Deir el-Medineh, cost up to 200 *deben*, and even those belonging to the workers cost around twenty-five. A mummy mask could be purchased for forty *deben*; sarcophagi were of course considerably more expensive. Tomb furnishings consisted of clothing, furniture, food, vessels, statues, and much more. One can assume that even simple laborers had around 200 *deben* to spend on their burial – in other words, around thirty months' pay. Because of higher expectations a scribe or a lowly official had to spend around 1,000 *deben* on tomb furnishings. And the king? The gold coffin of Tutankhamun, which weighed 100 kg, was alone worth the equivalent of 35,000 months' wages for a laborer! The value of many other objects found in the tomb of the young king is beyond our imagination even today.

The economy did not always operate flawlessly. There were often shortages and the payment of wages was deferred. People then went hungry; they were unable to fulfill their obligations and ended up in great financial difficulties. Around 1150 BC this led to the workers of Deir el-Medineh grouping together and striking for a short time to demand their wages, which hadn't been paid for months. The vizier, as the highest official in the land, came to them personally and promised them assistance. When this was not forthcoming, the workers struck again and even occupied the mortuary temples of the kings in Western Thebes. Not until the mayor of Thebes personally appeared with grain and copper did they return to work. The first recorded strikes in world history had a successful outcome for the strikers, the state refrained from applying sanctions and delivered what the workers were owed by law.

Tomb robberies in which the tombs of kings and officials were methodically plundered were an enormous problem for the economy of the country. These thefts could turn the best-laid plans of the various divisions of state administration awry, because tremendous quantities of gold suddenly came into circulation. At constant prices, for example, the entire workforce of Deir el-Medineh could have given up working and led a life of the greatest luxury from the tomb furnishings of a single king. But the state reaction was severe in the extreme. If the thieves were caught they were tortured and sent to the quarries. The proceeds of their theft were confiscated and so in part were not able to enter the economic cycle. And what did those people do who managed to evade capture? They used their booty to furnish their own tombs, perhaps bought themselves a cow on feast days and drank wine with honey, the luxury drink of Egypt. However, even the great tomb robberies at the end of the Twentieth Dynasty were not able to scuttle the Egyptian economy.

74 Weighing of gold and silver

Western Thebes, tomb of Ipuki (TT 181); New Kingdom, Eighteenth Dynasty, ca. 1380 BC.
The inspection of the performance of the workplace on the one hand and the distribution of materials on the other were some of the most important tasks of the ancient Egyptian administration. In this scene, taking place in the pharaoh treasury, a scribe monitors the weighing of silver and gold rings and records it on papyrus. On the scale are gold rings and weights. Not only precious metals but all other materials and items stored in the treasury were recorded with the utmost accuracy. One scribe was responsible for the distribution of materials to the workers, another supervised the work itself, yet another recorded the deliveries of finished products, and still others were charged with apportioning and issuing commodities for exchange or trade. Surprisingly, this incredibly inflated bureaucracy did not seem to have greatly affected economic performance.

75 The treasury of pharaoh
Western Thebes, tomb of Neferrenpet (TT 178); New Kingdom, Nineteenth Dynasty, ca. 1250 BC.

Neferrenpet, a high treasury official under Ramesses II, depicted his workplace on one of his tomb walls. We can see an administrative official in a huge hall overseeing the deposit of goods in the treasury. At the top and to the left are individual storerooms crammed full of valuables. Egypt's wealth was stored to a great extent in the royal treasuries. These institutions were the centers of the distributive economy. It is known, for example, that the wages of the Deir el-Medineh workers came from the treasury depicted here. Not only valuables of precious metals and stones were stored in the treasuries; clothes too, costly oils, cosmetics, and similar goods were present as the scene clearly indicates.

76 Model of a granary

Gebelein; Middle Kingdom; Eleventh Dynasty, ca. 2000 BC; clay and straw; W. 21 cm; Turin, Museo Egizio, 15802.

The storage of food was an absolute prerequisite for the birth of a state. Not until food producers have the means to produce more than they need themselves are the means available for feeding people who are themselves not directly involved in its production. These individuals included tradesmen and, of course, priests, officials, and the king himself.

Whoever succeeded in gaining control of the storehouse administration gained control of society as a whole. He could then decide on the quantity of grain to be distributed and even who lived and who died during times of famine. The administration of surpluses formed the power basis of the king and his followers. This was already the case in prehistoric Egypt; granaries and warehouses are always found surrounding temples and royal complexes.

The situation in the New Kingdom described here may also be considered to apply to Egypt's earlier eras. A few older commodity prices are known and they are comparable with those known from the New Kingdom. It is also known that wages were already paid in the Old Kingdom, but the size of the payment was never stated. One presumes that the economic system developed parallel to the state. It was based on the surpluses from agriculture which constituted Egypt's wealth. The economy of the storehouse and the introduction of the division of labor both mark the beginnings of Egyptian history. In the Old Kingdom, many new professions were "invented" that enabled the specialization of labor in production processes and even the construction of pyramids and huge temple complexes throughout Egypt. The tasks of agricultural production are among the oldest depictions in tombs and their enormous importance is indicated by the fact that scenes of rural labor occur in almost every tomb. Properly functioning agriculture was ultimately the foundation of the Egyptian state.

It is scarcely surprising then that the king owned the entire country. He endowed deserving officials and their families with agricultural land to be put to economic use; if they behaved disloyally, however, they were stripped of their possessions and expelled from the ranks of the property-owning classes. The people who lived on the land were part and parcel of it and so the king became owner of the means of production, or labor. He also had a monopoly on quarries and mines; in this way capital as a means of production was also in his possession. Not until toward the end of the Old Kingdom did a larger number of officials' families succeed in becoming landowners. This development continued into the New Kingdom; at that time the king controlled only small parts of Egypt but he was still able to make use of the considerable resources of temple property with its various levies. The dominating role played by the land's great temples in the economic life of the epoch cannot be overstated. Institutions such as the temple of Amun in Karnak had an enormous number of fields, herds of cattle, flocks of poultry, and craftsmen's businesses at their disposal. Tens of thousands of farmers and employees worked for the temples, whether directly or indirectly. The temples developed into the land's largest owners of cultivated land during the Ramesside period.

Perhaps the ancient Egyptian economy functioned for several thousands of years because, in spite of its planned nature, it still had a considerable degree of flexibility. It flourished because its legal system secured everyone's means of existence and people were able to aspire to a modest prosperity. On the other hand, perhaps it also survived so long because the populace was subject to strict control and mistakes were brutally punished.

77 Grain harvest

Western Thebes, tomb of Menena (TT 69); New Kingdom, Eighteenth Dynasty, ca. 395 BC.

Agriculture was the basis of the Egyptian economy. The fertility of the Nile Valley allowed several harvests a year. The work of farmers was subject to strict regimentation; almost the entire surplus had to be delivered to central storehouses from which, however, farmers received seed for planting. The production process was organized according to a division of labor and controlled by state administrators and their staff.

The tomb painting shows the key scene in the upper register to the left, that is, the delivery of the harvest to the property owner. The fact that agriculture was largely man's work is also interesting as it shows a division of labor between the sexes that can also be observed in other cultures.

Gifts of the Nile –
The Agriculture of a River Oasis

Christine Strauss-Seeber

The Nile and Agrarian Economy

The Nile is Egypt's lifeblood; the country owes its existence and its fertility to the river's annual floods. The cultural and economic development of no other civilization in the world has been influenced by its own river as much as Egypt has by the Nile.

Today the Aswan Dam controls the Nile floods, but in antiquity the seasons were characterized by the river's changing levels. Monsoon rains in the Ethiopian highlands and the southern Sudan caused the Nile to swell into a mighty torrent; the Egyptians then retreated with their livestock to their settlements on the slightly higher land of the desert fringe. Eventually, enormous floods inundated the fertile land. They reached their highest point at the start of September and the water then became placid. The fertile sediments carried along by the flood sank to the bottom. The waters only subsided in October – at first quickly and then gradually more slowly. Time and again the Nile carved out a new course for itself.

By this point the land was covered with black mud, an optimal fertilizer that made luxurious vegetation possible. The three types of fields were surveyed anew and allocated to farmers: the highlands – an older floodplain already covered with bushes, low-lying land, and the islands that had recently formed as freshly deposited land in the river's watercourse.

The fertile floods of prehistoric times gradually abated during the Old Kingdom. Texts from the First Intermediate Period tell of terrible famines. In order to use floodwater more effectively, canals were built

in arable land and the waters stored in broad reservoirs formed from earthen walls. When the floodwaters subsided again, these reservoirs were gradually opened. The local nomarch supervised the irrigation process, which was regulated according to the river level readings of the Nilometer. This intensification of agriculture meant new arable land could be won, resulting in an increase in agricultural yields.

---

78 (opposite) Agricultural work
Western Thebes; tomb of Menena (TT 69); New Kingdom; Eighteenth Dynasty, ca. 1395 BC.
Everyday agricultural life is comprehensively portrayed on the tomb walls of high officials. When the grain had ripened, land surveyors came (top register) to measure the exact size of the fields. Scribes record the readings from which the size of the levies or taxes were determined. As a badge of his office, the land surveyor carried on his shoulder a rope wound about several times, the measuring string knotted at regular intervals to form a strict unit of measure; the knots are clearly identifiable in this picture.
The harvest and transport of the grain are depicted in the lower register. The grain harvests also had to be recorded exactly.
In the middle register grain is measured in bushels and the result recorded. The image of the deceased in a pavilion indicates the omniscience of his supervision.

79 Nilometer
Elephantine; oldest scale from Roman times, first century AD.
In order to assess the height of the inundation in figures, Nilometers were built in the centers of ancient Egypt. They were stone structures either in the form of wells or a series of ascending steps whose walls were carved with measuring marks. Taxes and levies were calculated from these heights. An accurate a prognosis as possible of the annual Nile floods were of extreme importance for all aspects of public and economic life. Of all the water level markers, those in Nubia and those placed on the land's southern borders served as an early warning system, for only a flood with the ideal volume of water for the land and agricultural settlements along the Nile could be celebrated as a gift, full of blessings, from the god of the Nile, Hapi.

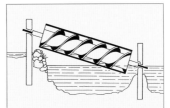

The moisture that remained in the ground was sufficient to nourish crops for their entire growth cycle. Using a system of basin irrigation, only one harvest per year was possible. Not until Ptolemaic times could a second harvest be achieved by converting to canal irrigation. Devices for raising water were used for irrigating large areas.

To regulate the forces of nature great projects of hydraulic engineering were undertaken. In the Third Dynasty a gigantic barrage was constructed in the Wadi Garawi south of Memphis to store the water that poured into the Nile from wadi flashfloods after torrential downpours.

In the Middle Kingdom canals were built to circumvent the first cataract or as transport routes from the Nile Valley to the Red Sea. The Faiyum

84 Modern saqiya, ca. 1960
The waterwheel, the *saqiya*, was invented in the Hellenistic era; instead of being turned by hand it was powered by animals. A horizontally rotating wheel was driven by cattle (today by water buffalo) and, by means of gearing, turned a wheel that moved vertically. This in turn drove in parallel another wheel fitted with buckets that scooped up water and raised it to fields up to a height of 10 m. Today, this laborious work has generally been replaced by automatic pumps.

marshes were drained by huge barricading dams and drainage canals and transformed into a fertile oasis. In the valley of el-Mala'a a reservoir was created known in Ptolemaic times as Lake Moeris. It had a capacity of 275 million cubic meters and a surface area of 114 square kilometers. From August until September it was filled by the Bahr Yussuf and then emptied from March until May so that from April the lakebed provided an area of 15,000 hectares on which summer crops could be grown.

The Nile was Egypt's most important transportation route. People, animals and all heavy loads were transported by river. Harbors as a rule were not necessary because ships could tie up on the river banks. Only Amenophis III built a harbor for his palace complex in Malqata with an area of 1 km by 2.4 km. The "Great Hymn to the Nile" praised the life-giving force of the river – but also warned of its destructive power.

Agriculture

The Nile Valley offered such favorable climatic conditions that nomadic peoples settled there as farmers and cattle breeders during the Neolithic era; they cultivated cereals, planted flax, and domesticated cattle, donkeys, sheep, and goats. Egypt soon achieved prosperity. A well-organized economy of supply also provided protection against lean years. Even in the post-Christian era, Egypt was considered the bread basket of the Roman Empire. The main phases of agricultural life determined the "civil calendar" and divided the year into three main seasons: inundation, growth, and summer.

After the floodwaters had subsided, it was time for planting between the middle of October and the beginning of November. The main crop was the two-eared cereal emmer, but six-eared barley was

86 *Corn-Osiris*
Late Period, sixth/fifth century BC; clay; L. 24 cm; Hildesheim, Pelizaeus-Museum, 4550.
Nature's life-giving force was venerated in cults throughout Egyptian history. The god Hapi was seen in the floodwaters; the snake-headed Renenutet was the goddess of the harvest, and Osiris, the god of vegetation, was seen in the fertile Egyptian earth. His body is often shown colored black as the fertile Nile mud. But Osiris also embodied the grain that germinates in the soil. The so-called corn-Osiris symbolizes rejuvenated nature. A figure of Osiris was hollowed out in the middle of a tile and filled with earth. When seed was placed in the earth, the grain would then seem to spring from the god himself.

87 Grape harvest
Western Thebes, painting from the tomb of Nakht (TT 52); New Kingdom, Eighteenth Dynasty, ca. 1390 BC.
Two men stand under a winding vine. The one in front picks the grapes, the one behind carries a full basket and grape clusters. Later, the juice was pressed out in a large vat. In order not to slip, the men have to hang on to straps suspended from the ceiling. The juice is then poured into vessels and placed to one side until offering bearers present it to the deceased.

also grown and used especially for making beer. Wheat played a less important role in the agriculture of ancient Eygpt. In April and May the harvest was gathered in and stored in granaries.

Scribes kept books on the harvest yields. The figures entered for barley were recorded in black ink, those for emmer in red ink. Documents also listed how much grain was dispensed to laborers and their families and how much was delivered to state bakeries.

Gardening was an important area of production. Egyptian gardens were surrounded by walls and divided into grids by canals. Around their pools stood shrubs, date and dom palms, Christ's thorn, carob-trees, tamarisks, willows, persimmon, and particularly fruit trees with figs, pomegranates or mandrakes. These gardens were liable to a special tax. Onions, leeks, garlic, lettuce, beans, lentils, pumpkins, and melons were also planted as were medicinal plants and herbs, spices such as caraway, coriander, and juniper berries, and oleiferous plants such as castor beans, sesame, or safflower.

Red grapes did particularly well in the Delta and the oases and were grown in specially constructed vineyards. The vines were set into hollows that were then filled with fertile mud and surrounded by a raised edge to keep in the water. They were regularly watered and fertilized with the droppings of pigeons kept in dovecotes in the vineyard. The wine of Ramesses II (Nineteenth Dynasty) from Pi-Ramesse, his residence in the eastern Delta, was fertilized with horse urine from the great royal stables!

An important branch of industry lay in the production of timber, which provided the materials for products such as coffins, furniture, and a wide variety of other items. Lumber was required in building for roofs and for supporting vast rooms, for ship-building, and also for scaffolding used in temple construction. Wood was burnt in the production of endless quantities of ceramics as well as in metallurgy. Clearly, a much greater quantity of trees must have existed then than is visible in Egypt today. In Neolithic times there were still great stands of forest on the banks of the Nile that were cut down over the centuries. The most important species were the sycamore, Nile acacia, tamarisk, date palm, and mulberry. Only the vizier could grant permission to fell large trees. Hard woods like cedar and ebony were imported from Nubia and Lebanon.

The often swampy soil suited the large-scale planting of flax for the production of the linen garments so popular on festival days. Cotton was not planted in Egypt until the Late Period. Agricultural

success was the subject of religious festivals, processions, and rituals. Min, Renenutet or Neper embodied the fertility of the land. But the very essence of rejuvenated nature was the god Osiris.

Livestock

The most important aspect of raising livestock was the production of meat and milk; after this came the extraction of skins, pelts, wool, horn, eggs, and fats. Domesticated animals also performed valuable work in the fields and in the transport of heavy loads. From ancient times, herds were increased by marauding raids, especially into Syria, Libya, and Nubia. Ramesses II boasted that he had captured 3,609 cattle, 184 horses, 864 donkeys and 9,136 goats and driven them to Egypt.

The most valuable domestic animal was the cow, the primary support of people involved in agriculture. The animals lived in great herds and when the floodwaters subsided they were driven to vast pastures in the marshes of the western Delta where feed crops had been planted. In the early summer the animals returned to their home pastures and were counted for tax purposes. Short-legged oxen were kept in stalls for fattening and used as sacrificial offerings in the mortuary cult and worship of the gods.

Cows' milk was a valuable product. For purposes of milking the animals were secured to a stake and their legs tied together. They were slaughtered by slitting their throats. Before use their general state and even odor were examined by an animal inspector. The famous Twelfth Dynasty "veterinary papyrus" from El-Lahun dealt specifically with the treatment of bovine diseases.

Sheep and goats were also kept. A hairy breed of sheep with screw-shaped horns was replaced in the course of the Middle Kingdom by a breed of fine-limbed woolly sheep whose wool and fat were highly prized. The skins of the screw-horned goat provided waterskins, an important transport medium for the arid desert regions of Egypt. Pigs were kept both in the open and in stalls but were not particularly prized. The middens of settlements show that pork was a popular dish. In agriculture, the animals were used to trample seed as well as for threshing on the barn-floor. Antelopes and gazelles were also bred and fattened primarily as sacrificial animals and as the source of horn. The same was true for ibexes and even hyenas, whose domestication was never entirely successful.

The most commonly used animal for transporting both people and goods was the donkey. If one did not possess one's own a donkey could be leased or loaned for three times the price of a female slave. The horse came to Egypt with the Hyksos but was not used in agriculture. The Arabian camel was already familiar in Egypt at the time of the New Kingdom but was used only as a beast of burden and for desert transport in the Late Period.

88–90 Three agricultural devices
Probably from the New Kingdom, ca. 1200 BC.; London, The British Museum
a) Plow, wood; L. 93 cm; EA 50705
b) Sickle; wood with flint; L. 27 cm; EA 52861
c) Winnowing device; wood; L. 40.5 cm; EA 18206.
Tools used in cultivation were simple but designed for optimum efficiency. Even the fellahin of today use similar picks, sickles, and plows. Because the Egyptian soil offers conditions well-suited to preservation, ancient wood, and on many occasions even the rope used with it, often survive undamaged. The cutting edge of the sickle is set with flint chips.

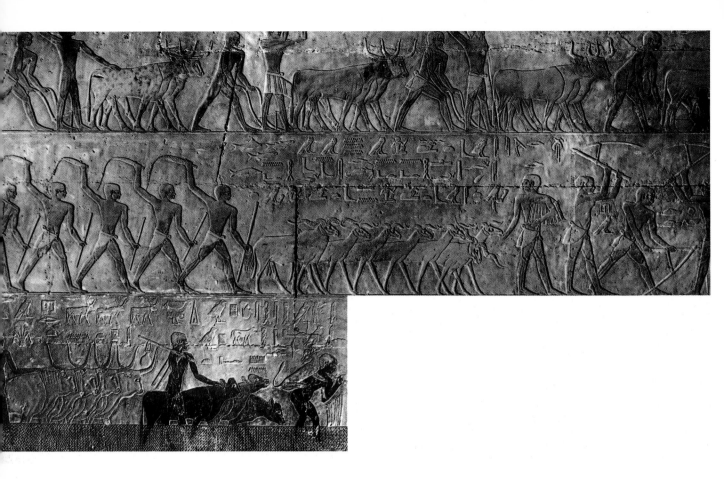

91 Agricultural scenes
Saqqara, tomb of Ti; Old Kingdom, Fifth Dynasty, ca. 2450 BC.
In the lowest register, cattle are driven through a ford. When the animals were driven to different pastures in autumn and early summer their route through the Nile Valley meant they had to cross difficult fords. A herdsman at the front carries a calf, followed by the mother and the rest of the herd. In the middle register to the right men till the earth swinging their picks with force. Finally, at the left, a herdsman drives the animals forward so they walk over the tilled soil and trample the seed deep into the earth with their hooves. In the center, one can see herdsmen driving sheep into the fields with whips; at the rear stands a man with a stick and bag of seed. In the top register at the right a cow with legs tied together is milked, while at the left cattle drag a plow. In the topmost and bottom-most register the most important Egyptian cattle breeds are depicted – the long-horned, short-horned, and hornless.

One essential branch of agriculture was poultry-keeping. Ducks, geese, quail, and pigeons were all eaten. Egypt had rich hunting grounds as it lay on the route of migratory birds; these were caught with folding or casting nets in the papyrus thicket, in the rushes or on the water. Alternatively, they were trapped with fine-meshed nets in bushes and trees. Ducks, geese, turtle doves, cranes, and even swans were kept on large poultry farms and fattened on noodles and moistened clumps of dough. The chicken, which "gives birth daily," was mentioned for the first time in the New Kingdom. As a domestic animal it did not assume any importance until the Late Period. Another staple of the Egyptian diet was fish, which were caught with hooks or in nets and baskets. Apart from the Nile, Lake Mansala in the eastern Delta and the Birket Qarun (Lake Moeris) in the Faiyum provided rich fishing grounds.

Valuable animals had to be taxed. From the time of the Second Dynasty, the assessment of cattle and other animals marked a watershed in the Egyptian calendar. At the time of the Ramesside pharaohs, a cow was worth two *aruras*, that is a good half hectare of arable land. From the Middle Kingdom, state and temple herds were under the direction of the mayor of the local city. In the course of the New Kingdom the administration of cattle was placed in the hands of

92 Beekeeping
Western Thebes, Pabasa (TT 279), portico in the tomb of Pabasa; Late Period, Twenty-sixth Dynasty, ca. 610 BC.
The Egyptians constructed hives from large numbers of clay pipes piled on top of one another in which the bees made their honeycombs. To get at the honey; smoke was blown into the pipes, forcing the bees out. As sugar was still unknown, food was sweetened with honey.

the king's cattle overseer. The herds often had their own names and the animals were identified by brands.

Agricultural Administration

The distribution of nature's bounty was the responsibility of a disciplined, centralized administration. According to ancient Egyptian royal dogma, land belonged to the king alone. As sole property owner he controlled the means of production: the field hands, animals and plants, seeds, the grain harvests, fruit and vegetables, as well as canals, ponds, or shadufs. Levies were imposed if land or other assets were used.

Land was divided into administrative units. These so-called estates or domains were villages with fields and ancillary buildings for processing, and were controlled by the king, the pyramid administration, or large temples. Supreme supervision was exercised by the domain overseer. Provincial officials administered the estates that covered on average an area of 23–54 *aruras* (ten *aruras* corresponded to 2.75 hectares).

From the Third Dynasty on, the king began to bestow land on deserving state officials; this gradually developed into private property. Later, in the New Kingdom, veterans or members of other professions received fields to cultivate in order to guarantee their livelihood. The standard size of these allocated parcels was between three and five *aruras*, according to social status. Equipment or working animals could be leased from the state. Independent farmers, in our modern sense – those who cultivated their land and were responsible only to themselves – came into being only during interregnum when the central state administration broke down.

Agricultural work was organized along the lines of a planned economy. Most Egyptians were "bondsmen" and worked on state or temple domains. According to decree these people could be bound to serve as plowmen, herdsmen, or laborers on the construction of dikes and canals. They were not allowed to refuse work and were bound to their domains.

A certain percentage of the estates' harvest was claimed by the state granaries. The quota that the estate manager had to provide was determined by the highest level recorded by the Nilometer during the last inundation. Afterward, every individual field was resurveyed. Tribute outstanding was submitted as sacks of grain, as cattle, or as wine or honey. During the Ramesside Period, leased land, given, for example, to veterans, had to provide five sacks of grain for every ten sacks, gross harvested. There were fixed quotas in other areas of production. It was reported, for instance, that a fisherman had to provide 5,000 fish per year. He who did not fulfill his quota was punished with a beating.

The total area in agricultural use in the Ramesside Period was around six million *aruras* and the population was 4.5 million. At the

93 Poultry enclosure
Saqqara, tomb of Ti; Old Kingdom, Fifth Dynasty, ca. 2450 BC.
Flocks of birds were kept in coops for breeding and fattening. The animals were fed mostly on barley and fattened on spindle-shaped noodles; the keeper grabbed the animal by the neck, opened its beak, and stuffed the noodles or balls of dough into its gullet. In the bottom register cranes are force-fed; above, two men cook the poultry feed. In the topmost register geese are fattened.

94 Procession of domains
Saqqara, tomb of Ti, cult chamber; Old Kingdom, Fifth Dynasty, ca. 450 BC; limestone. Female representatives from the domains bring the harvests of their estates to the deceased. They carry large, broad baskets with fruit, vegetables, and bread on their heads; some carry papyrus bundles. A calf and young goat are also led on leashes.

time of the Ptolemies some two-thirds to three-quarters of arable land was planted in cereals. According to the principles of the distribution economy, harvests stored in the granaries had to provide for the population for the whole year – agricultural laborers as well as tradesmen, officials, soldiers, and all those employed as specialists in their own occupations. During hard times it was common for wages not to be paid. Court documents record the suppression of grain payments that led to damaging strikes. The annual production of grain cannot be determined from ancient sources. Grain as a means of payment was subject to fluctuations of value that depended on the season or the success of the inundation. Barley was often twice as expensive as emmer. Work on the land was not something to strive for. Field workers were often contrasted with the more dignified officials by depicting them with stringy, white hair and bald spots. The dead transferred their arduous labors to their *shabtis* in the afterlife.

95 Fishing scene
Saqqara, tomb of Niankhkhnum and Khnumhotep; Old Kingdom, Fifth Dynasty, ca. 2380 BC; painted limestone.
Fishing was of great importance in everyday life. In the top register fish are caught in long nets from the riverbank. The men put all their effort into hauling their catch from the water. The diversity of species portrayed symbolizes the wealth of fish. A plump foreman gives the order to pull hard on the rope that is already coiling up on the ground.
In the bottom register, men are fishing from boats. Those in the papyrus boat are lowering the bottom end of a long basket into the water after securing the other end to stakes on both river banks. Further to the left, smaller baskets have already been placed in the water. To the right of the scene a man fishes with a large hand net.

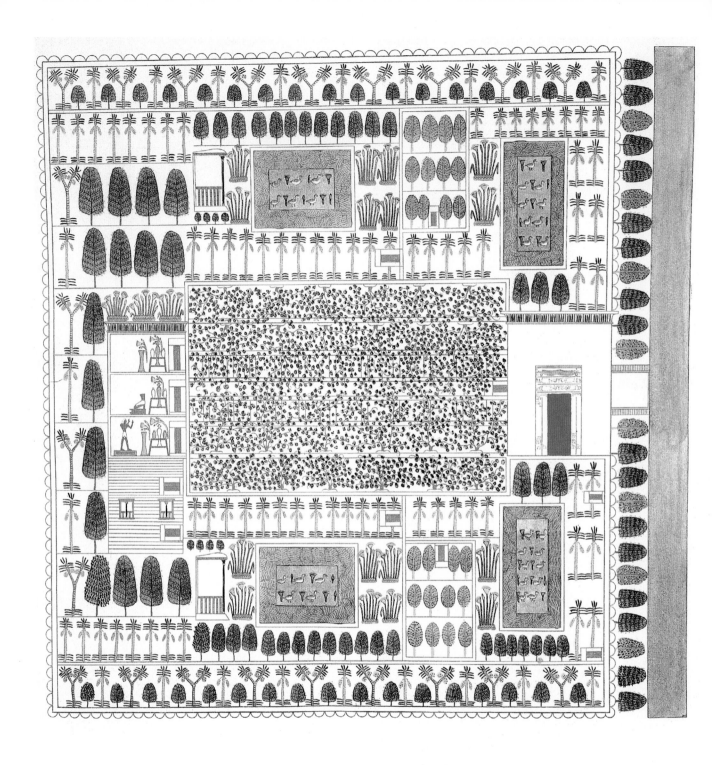

96 Garden in the tomb of Sennefer
Western Thebes, tomb of Sennefer (TT 96); New Kingdom, Eighteenth Dynasty, reign of Amenophis II, ca. 1410 BC.
The painting shows an extensive garden lying directly on the Nile or a canal (right), surrounded by a wall and entered through a main gate that has been turned to face the viewer. In the center is an area planted with vines. The single-story house (left) shows the brickwork of the exterior walls, two entry doors and two windows with center supports and balustrades. The upper part allows a view into the house; the three rooms lying one on top of another and connected by doors lie in fact directly behind each other. The furnishings are reduced to sacrificial platforms so that the dwelling function of the house remains discreet – hardly surprising in view of the funereal context of the depiction. Around the garden are four artificial ponds with ducks, lotus blossoms, swamps, and papyrus bushes. The whole arrangement is subject to a strict axial system right down to the finest detail and should therefore be seen as an idealized garden. Apart from its practical significance, the garden also had a symbolic one: it is a form of idealized nature and as such the preferred place for the edification so often emphasized in Egyptian literature.

Houses, Cities, and Palaces – Ancient Egyptian Lifestyles

Albrecht Endruweit

The popular image of pharaonic Egyptian architecture is essentially characterized by temples and tombs. They belong to those archaeological relics constructed of stone, a material endowed with durability, eternal permanence, and protection from tomb robbers. Yet one ought to be aware that this is only one side – albeit the side still visible today – of Egyptian architecture.

The other side, that of everyday architecture, is hidden from our view; its remains, for the most part, no longer exist or have been buried under modern building sites. This is due to the fact that houses were built of the material to which the country owed its wealth: the fertile mud deposited every year after the Nile inundation. Up until recent times it was made into bricks, which, if only dried in the sun, as was the case in Egypt, possess a much more limited durability than fired brick or stone. From the archaeological perspective this has had dire consequences. From antiquity down to the twentieth century the remains of villages and cities were plowed up and systematically plundered by local inhabitants in their search for fertile soil. This is how entire cityscapes have been lost. Nevertheless, remains from all three great periods of Egyptian history have been found, and these enable us to answer the essential questions concerning domestic architecture. It must be emphasized, however, that since mudbrick architecture is difficult to preserve, the buildings described here, sometimes brought to light by excavations decades ago, have for the most part now completely vanished.

Administrative texts from the Old Kingdom tell of the existence of so-called pyramid towns. These developed out of administrative centers for the construction of pharaonic tombs and later continued as institutions for performing the royal mortuary cult in the pyramid temples. On the Giza plateau, on the eastern side of the tomb of Queen Khentkaus, lie eleven priests' houses that date to the Fourth Dynasty. Their proximity to a royal tomb, and especially their high degree of uniformity, suggest that they were planned by the administration of the pyramid plateau. The houses presumably each had a flat roof and each roughly square plot comprised a gross area of about 170 square meters. Their interiors were subdivided into often irregular rooms of greatly varying size. Areas (see p. 389, no. 99) at the back of the house or which were difficult of access probably served as sleeping quarters (A), the large central areas as living quarters (B), and the rooms on the southern side, where ash was found, were most likely kitchens. These dwellings, intended to accommodate priests and other high officials for the mortuary cult of Queen Khentkaus, are exceptions and represent particularly luxurious living conditions in the pyramid age. They were

97 *Priests' houses at "Khentkaus's Ascension"* Giza; Old Kingdom, Fourth Dynasty, ca. 2500 BC.
The eleven houses in strict serialized order possibly represent one of the earliest examples of Eastern Mediterranean/Near Eastern town planning. The massive exterior and interior walls, up to 1.8 m thick, were whitewashed and thus well suited to the climate. The flat roofs – still awaiting reconstruction – were accessible and provided additional living space.

0   10 m

reserved for an exclusive social class and therefore should not be regarded as a universal standard.

The same may be said for the remains of living quarters and priests' villas excavated in the pyramid town near the tomb of Sesostris II in el-Lahun at the entrance to the Faiyum. These comprise, together with a great number of workmen's houses in the immediate vicinity, the main body of domestic architecture preserved from the Middle

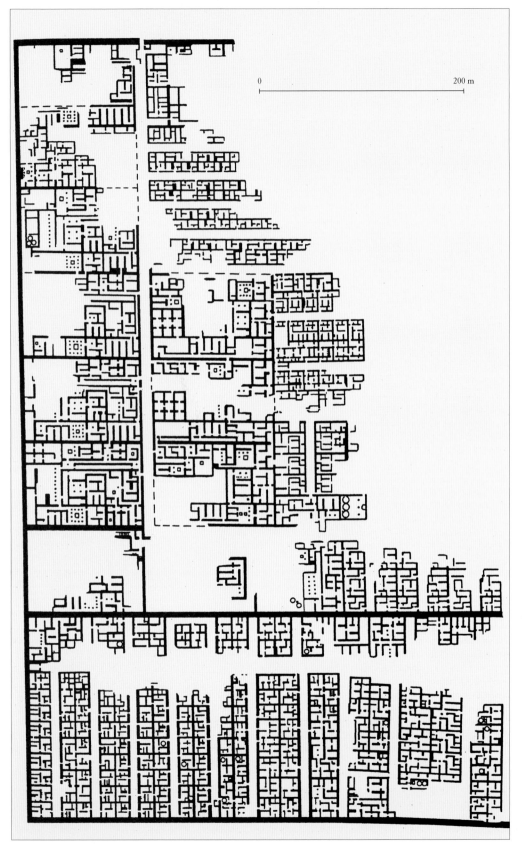

98 Workers' and priests' settlement at the pyramid of Sesostris II
El-Lahun; Middle Kingdom, Twelfth Dynasty, reign of Sesostris II, ca. 1875 BC.
The area covered by the town, the southern part of which has not yet been excavated, tilts slightly upward to the west and – being oriented to the edge of the pyramid lying approximately 800 m to the west – is aligned to the north. The building material for the houses consisted primarily of Nile mud mixed with sand; the roof beams and pillars were of wood.

99 (opposite, left) Priest's villa
El-Lahun; Middle Kingdom, Twelfth Dynasty, reign of Sesostris II, ca. 1880 BC.
The entrances to this vast complex lie to the south. The central house is indicated on the plan in cross-hatching; in the north and south, branching off from the courts E and F, lie separate, self-contained groups of rooms that can be regarded as "built-in" houses.

0 ⊢———————————————⊣ 200 m

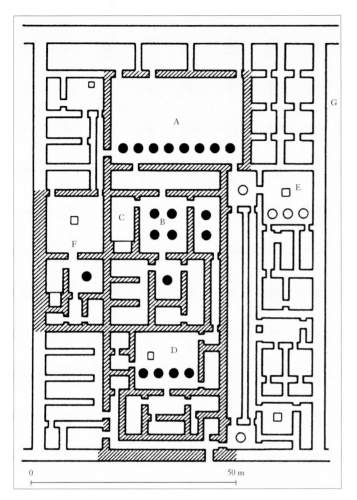

100 Model house of Meketre
Western Thebes, tomb of Meketre (TT 280); Middle Kingdom, Eleventh Dynasty, reign of Mentuhotep III, ca. 1990 BC; painted coniferous wood; L. 84 cm, W. 42.5 cm; New York, The Metropolitan Museum of Art, Rogers Fund and Edward S. Harkness Gift, 1920, 20.3.13.

This model does not show interior rooms but is rather reduced to the representative parts of a luxurious house: the artistically styled front (not seen here), the columned hall (two groups of four papyrus columns each), and a garden with a pool surrounded by trees (sycamores). Three gutter pipes extend from the roof into the garden.

Kingdom, that is the Twelfth Dynasty. This settlement, like its counterpart at Giza, was designed according to a rigidly followed orthogonal plan. The city – still not completely excavated – represents a walled rectangle of about 390 x 420 m and is subdivided into an eastern and southern complex. This basic plan dictates the entire road network and also the distribution of the residential areas. To the north lie primarily rows of large houses. Their main characteristic, apart from a generous area of up to 2,400 square meters, is an open court to the north to which the actual living quarters on the south side were joined. They lie between two rows of ancillary servants' and service rooms; their primary facade to the north is accentuated by a row of columns (A). The room with four columns (B) can, because of its central position, be regarded as a living and presentation room. To the west, recognizable through a niche at the rear, was a bedroom (C). The entire complex was covered by a flat roof and the remains of some stairs suggest that this was accessible. One characteristic detail of construction, unique to these and the adjacent larger buildings compared to most surviving domestic architecture, is the partly roofed inner court. The columned halls on the south side, open to the northerly wind provided, at least in the summer, a degree of comfort (A, D, E). A room with columns on all four sides and a central water basin situated on the west side (F) can be regarded as anticipating the Roman atrium. These configurations at el-Lahun of differently configured open courtyards are confirmed by miniature models of wood or earthenware that appear as burial offerings in tombs of the Eleventh Dynasty. The

best example is one of the two models from the tomb of Meketre at Thebes in which the courtyard with columned hall, trees, and a pond makes up the majority of the entire complex – an indication of how highly these architectural features were valued.

The "ordinary" population of the pyramid town, however, had to be content with the other approximately 400 living units, whose size of around 40–70 square meters gives us an idea of the enormous difference in social standing between their inhabitants and those of the villas. The elite furthermore had special granaries with a capacity of more than 300 cubic meters (G). These are capacities that suggest that they were used as a center to provide either the entire population or at least a significant part of it with food. It seems then that the function of these houses was not only to provide living space but also to accommodate some administrative branch of the pyramid town with its own supply centers; this might explain their huge size.

Comparatively speaking the architecture of the New Kingdom is best represented because of the number of settlements excavated from this era. The housing finds at Thebes are primarily limited to the workers' settlement of Deir el-Medineh. The arrangement of the approximately seventy houses shows that they, like the examples above, were planned by a supervisory body. This resulted from the fact that the residents were taking part in a state undertaking of the highest priority – the construction of a royal tomb – and that the state therefore wanted to optimize its control of the work force. The ground plans are

usually standardized and show the tripartite divisions characteristic of
the New Kingdom: the entrance or hallway led onto the main living
room, sometimes with a low, brick-built sleeping area. The rear served
as kitchen and pantry. A stairway led from the kitchen to the roof
where firewood was stored and which provided extra space for
domestic duties. The total area of the dwellings without the roof was
approximately seventy square meters.

A type of house or settlement otherwise rarely found in Egypt is
the conglomeration of seventy-eight single, compact, adjoining rooms
of irregular size that served as sleeping quarters for the workers in the
Valley of the Kings. This derived from the need for the most practical
use of the limited space and to provide shelter from the wind and cold
at night by skillfully incorporating the features of the landscape (a
mountain saddle). This is the principle difference from the layout of
those settlements built on a level plain and mentioned above.

The peak of Egyptian domestic architecture can be seen in the
finds from Amarna. The structural principle and basis of the city was a
dense accumulation of luxurious country villas of up to 400 square
meters mixed with medium-sized and small buildings through to the
smallest dwellings of 25 square meters. There was apparently no social
differentiation between city districts.

The residence of a high administrative official of the Aten temple
serves as a good example here (see p. 391, no. 104). Like all other larger
residences, it was situated on a generously proportioned property and
surrounded by ancillary complexes such as yards, workshops, gardens,
barns, ovens, and storage rooms. Sometimes such houses also included
living quarters for servants. High enclosure walls ensured that the

*101 (top) Workers' settlement of Deir el-
Medineh*
Western Thebes; New Kingdom, Eighteenth
to Twentieth Dynasty, 1525–1070 BC.
The solid interior structures at the rear of the
houses (kitchens, stairs) can be clearly seen as
well as the remains of lighter colored stone
bases (mostly in the main living areas) that
originally supported the wood columns for
the flat roof. In the background the remains
of tomb complexes built into the surrounding
slopes by the inhabitants of the settlement are
visible.

102 (above) Worker's house at Deir el-Medineh
Western Thebes; New Kingdom, Eighteenth
Dynasty, 1550–1305 BC.
The illustration shows the view into the front
room with a built-in domestic altar; the
passageway into the main room can be seen to
the right. The altars – like the houses built of
rough stones and mudbricks – were for
privately organized cults of gods and ancestors.
They were originally decorated with paintings,
stelae, and sacrificial plaques.

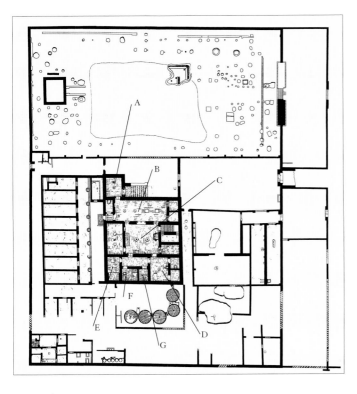

neighboring population was kept strictly at a distance. The 340 square meters area of the actual residence, which stood slightly elevated on a platform, was entered through the anteroom (A) and divided into three successive sections. The front section was dominated by a wide entrance hall supported by four wooden columns (B) with adjacent side rooms – it might be termed the reception hall. South of that lay the middle section with the main hall in the center of the house (C), which was very likely used for ceremonial purposes. All other rooms as well as the roof could be accessed from here. The rear section of the property comprised a living room (D), which had a solely domestic character, a bedroom (E), recognizable by its sleeping niche at the back, and sanitary facilities (F, G) with a built-in stone basin.

Above the entrance hall at the front of the house (C) was a kind of loggia that was used as a cool sleeping place during summer and which overlooked the large garden on the northern side. Inscriptions and reliefs in Theban private tombs often speak, not without pride, of the existence of such luxurious residences. Ineni (early Eighteenth Dynasty) meticulously records, for example, all the 540 trees that he had planted at great expense in a desert area.

The flat roof of the house, constructed of wooden beams and mud, was higher over the central hall than the adjacent rooms. Clerestories brought air and light into the hall, drew attention to the painted wooden columns and walls, and emphasized the special nature of the room. The impressive number of sparsely furnished rooms, as well as the fact that the roof could be used, enabled the occupants to alleviate greatly the rigors of a desert climate by choosing their living space according to the season.

105 House of an official
Tell el-Amarna, P47.17, inner stairs; New Kingdom, Eighteenth Dynasty, reign of Akhenaten, ca. 1345 BC.
The photograph from a 1914 excavation shows a detail of the 2 m-high mudbrick walls of a large villa situated in the central city of Amarna. As in all other houses, the stairs lead off from a central hall and still show ten massively supported steps each 18 cm in height. They originally led up to a flat roof. The illustration shows remains of the original plaster work on the left- and right-hand sides. The water trough, made of limestone, has unfortunately been pushed to the front of the stairs. It is highly likely that it does not stand in its original place, as is indicated by the remains of a relief on its rear side. The hall had a mudbrick floor and the walls were originally whitewashed.

106 Villa of Panehsi
Tell el-Amarna, New Kingdom, Eighteenth Dynasty, reign of Akhenaten, ca. 1345 B.C.
The raised house in the middle of the illustration covered approximately 450 square meters and lay on an extensive property whose outer walls are still visible. To the north (left) and therefore at the front of the house are the remains of a chapel that was probably surrounded by a garden with an artificial lake to the east. The organization of the inner rooms along a tripartite scheme is clearly visible, as is the "anteroom" at the front of the north side of the villa. The house has been relatively well preserved because of the thickness of the walls; at the time of excavation (1923/24) they were approximately 2 m thick.

107 Vignette of the Book of the Dead of Nakht
Thebes; New Kingdom, Eighteenth Dynasty, ca. 1300 BC; painted papyrus; original total L. 14.32 m; London, The British Museum, EA 10471/72.
The deceased appears with his wife Tjuiu before Osiris and the goddess Maat in a scene of worship; the backdrop is formed by Nakht's estate. The center of the illustration shows a pond surrounded by trees. To the right is a depiction of a house with two interesting features: the building's exterior is characterized by small clerestories designed to block the view into the house and to protect it from the sun's rays. The surface of the whitewashed outer wall of the one-story building is interrupted by the entrance door (right). There is a profile view of two triangular, wooden superstructures on the roof that have lockable openings on their left-hand sides. They were meant to channel the predominantly northern winds into the living area below.

This tower-like house type was predominant in
the later period of Egyptian history, as
American excavations in the 1920s at El
Faiyum (Karanis) have shown. In addition, the
Greek traveler Herodotus reported in the fifth
century BC that the Egyptians slept on the
roofs of houses resembling towers in order not
to be plagued by "immense swarms of
mosquitoes" that were unable to fly so high in
the wind (Histories, II, 95). This model shows
that – at least in the upper part – the building
was layered in a concave fashion so that it
tapered toward the top. The explanation for
this feature lay in the structural problems
associated with tall buildings: because of the
considerable forces pushing and pulling at the
structure the architect was forced to provide a
large base and locate the center of gravity
approximately in the middle of the house's
lower section.

Representations of houses in tomb reliefs and paintings confirm
these archaeological findings. Typically for Egyptian art, several
perspectives are combined into one in these scenes, so that the views
partly obscure each other. Seen in this light the house of Djehuty-nefer
represents only a one-story building. The three frames of the illustration refer to sections that lay not above but directly behind each other.
It is thus an exact representation of the tripartite ground pattern that, as
described above, constituted the fundamental pattern of New
Kingdom domestic architecture.

The positioning of the windows, the ventilation, arrangement of
chambers, and the solid walls all would have provided the occupants of
at least the larger residences with a comfortable, climatically adjusted
environment. Aesthetic considerations such as lighting, the arrangement of color, and the proportions of the rooms probably also influenced the architecture of large villas. One can see, for example, that the
doors and columns of certain rooms are symmetrically positioned in
the Amarna villa. Furthermore, it is striking that the passageway to the
stairs as well as the large double-doored main entrance are matched
only by niches on the opposite walls; this was done solely to maintain
the aesthetic and visual balance of these rooms. Thus an interior was
created that was designed down to the smallest detail; the Amarna
house type consequently became the archetype of pharaonic domestic
architecture; it ultimately joined the ranks of the "great designs" of
ancient Near Eastern and Mediterranean domestic culture.

The Palace

The palaces of the Egyptian kings were as impressive as the large
country villas. They were, however, mainly built for cult and ritual
purposes. The pharaohs did not reside there but used them for
performing their official duties. Nonetheless, we may rightly view
them as copies of the true residential palaces, of which few remains
have been preserved (see p. 395, no. 114).

It must be assumed that the palaces of the pharaohs at Memphis
and Thebes were powerful architectural symbols and thus permanently attested to pharaonic "presence" and "power" in the state's
administrative centers. There was a network of similar buildings
throughout Egypt in which the pharaoh could be comfortably accommodated during his travels. These palaces were independent in their
organizational and economic entities and can be compared with the
royal or imperial palaces of the Middle Ages in Europe. One can even
speculate as to whether a pharaoh had multiple administrative seats
within a single town. The preserved blocks from Hatshepsut's Red
Chapel in Karnak bear inscriptions documenting at least three palaces;
this number can be explained by the difference in their functions –
administrative, cultic, and residential.

With the exception of individual finds, such as at the Middle
Kingdom site of Tell ed-Dab'a in the eastern Delta, the Egyptian

The pictorial representation of this house is
divided into three rows and depicts rooms
that actually lie behind each other. In the
lower part domestic tasks are shown such as
weaving (left) and grinding flour (right). The
main hall of the actual house, in which the
deceased receives finished products, can be
distinguished from the rest of the rooms by its
height, its clerestory windows, and by the
double-winged doors that are also provided
with a high window; it almost completely
dominates the central part of the picture. The
upper section again represents the deceased;
the other individuals are offering bearers.
The roof can be reached by a staircase on
which five granaries and two ovens are safely
situated.

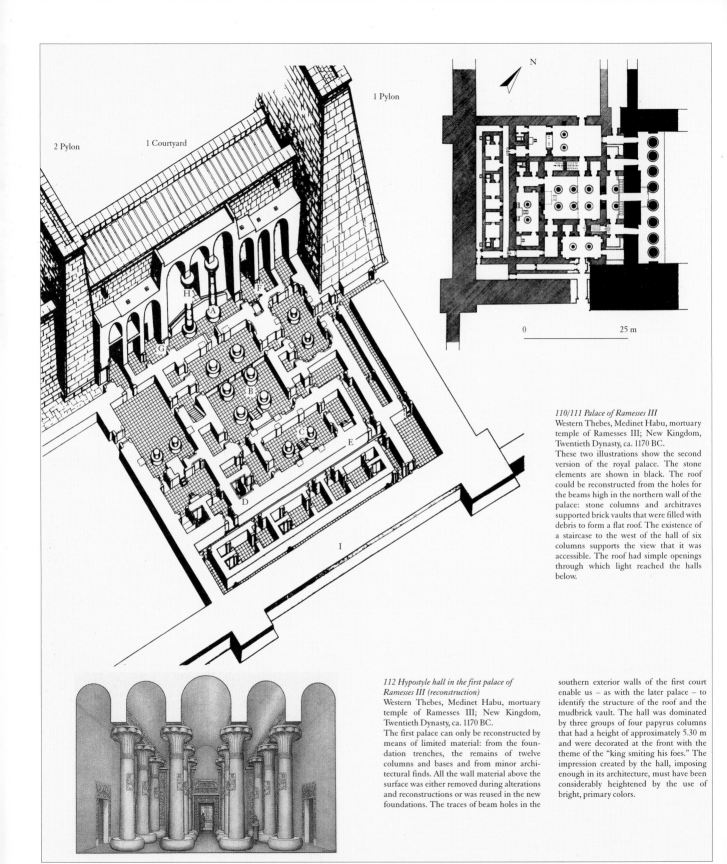

2 Pylon

1 Courtyard

1 Pylon

H

A

G

B

C

E

D

I

N

0   25 m

110/111 Palace of Ramesses III
Western Thebes, Medinet Habu, mortuary
temple of Ramesses III; New Kingdom,
Twentieth Dynasty, ca. 1170 BC.
These two illustrations show the second
version of the royal palace. The stone
elements are shown in black. The roof
could be reconstructed from the holes for
the beams high in the northern wall of the
palace: stone columns and architraves
supported brick vaults that were filled with
debris to form a flat roof. The existence of
a staircase to the west of the hall of six
columns supports the view that it was
accessible. The roof had simple openings
through which light reached the halls
below.

*112 Hypostyle hall in the first palace of
Ramesses III (reconstruction)*
Western Thebes, Medinet Habu, mortuary
temple of Ramesses III; New Kingdom,
Twentieth Dynasty, ca. 1170 BC.
The first palace can only be reconstructed by
means of limited material: from the foundation trenches, the remains of twelve
columns and bases and from minor architectural finds. All the wall material above the
surface was either removed during alterations
and reconstructions or was reused in the new
foundations. The traces of beam holes in the
southern exterior walls of the first court
enable us – as with the later palace – to
identify the structure of the roof and the
mudbrick vault. The hall was dominated
by three groups of four papyrus columns
that had a height of approximately 5.30 m
and were decorated at the front with the
theme of the "king smiting his foes." The
impression created by the hall, imposing
enough in its architecture, must have been
considerably heightened by the use of
bright, primary colors.

palace is best known from the New Kingdom onward. Apart from the complexes of Merenptah and Apries at Memphis, the following sites in Western Thebes have been shown to contain palatial remains of archaeological significance: the "Houses of Millions of Years" of Hatshepsut and Merenptah as well as that of Ramesses II, the Ramesseum. The most prominent example of all is Medinet Habu, the "House of Millions of Years" of Ramesses III (see opposite, no. 110/111), which was partially restored by American archaeologists in the 1920s (see essay by Regine Schulz and Hourig Sourouzian).

The palace is situated at the southern end of the first temple court and was connected with it by doors and windows. The columns, door frames and other exposed architectural elements were made of sandstone while the rest of the complex, including the massive barrel vaulting, consisted of mudbrick. The main chambers, encircled by ancillary and service rooms, can be distinguished by their sandstone columns reaching up to 7.5 m in height. The front was dominated by a central, double-columned hall that backed onto the center of the entire palace, a hall of six columns; it was probably used as an audience hall and contained a stone base for a throne against its rear wall. A side entrance led to the third, and "private" section of the palace at the rear, which was connected to a second throne room (C) on whose sides were situated sanitary facilities (D) and a bedroom (E). It thus becomes apparent that the palace ground plan is comparable to that of an Amarna villa, including the three servants' houses lying directly behind the palace, and that all were designed according to the same clear tripartite principle. This only seems odd at first glance: ultimately all buildings were intended simply to provide a person – be it the pharaoh or a servant – with dwelling space, regardless of what functions he or she might have performed there. In this respect, the palace can be seen as a house magnified to monumental proportions. Apart from providing a dais for formal audiences and serving as the ritual starting point for Theban festival processions, the central function of the palace was to provide the pharaoh with a stage from which to reward deserving officials. The Window of Appearances situated in the center of the palace facade indicates that this can be understood quite literally. The officials assembled in the first temple court in front of this window, and attended the ritual of "distributing the gold of honor." It was performed by the king on a wooden balcony in front of the window, thus transforming the entire palatial facade into a backdrop for a state spectacle.

Below both the Window of Appearances and the reliefs to the side, which show the king smiting his foes, are stone consoles featuring sculptures symbolizing Egypt's enemies. If these stone reliefs were to justify Egypt's rule over the world, and to preserve that rule for eternity, then this image briefly became tangible reality when the king appeared in person at the Window of Appearances and literally trampled his enemies underfoot.

A palace with a purely domestic function can be found in a complex lying at the southern end of Western Thebes and part of a city built by Amenophis III: Malqata (see p. 396, no. 116). The residence was entered through two adjoining courts, each with a throne pedestal (A, B). The entrance to the actual living quarters and therefore the border between the semi-official and private sectors was marked by a hall at right angles that led to a long corridor (D). At the rear of this section were the king's actual private apartments: a four-columned hall with an elevated seat (E) with three rooms behind it, one of these – recognizable by its niche – being the king's bedroom. The two groups of four rooms flanking the central hall (D) on both sides probably belonged to officials of the king's innermost circle. Fragments of wall and ceiling paintings in bright colors have been found distributed over the entire palace complex. The appearance of some rooms – for example, the central hall – was enhanced by floor paintings. Other wall paintings have been found in the northern palace in Amarna, which

113 Palace of Ramesses III
Western Thebes, Medinet Habu, mortuary temple of Ramesses III; New Kingdom, Twentieth Dynasty, ca. 1170 BC.
The illustration shows the view from the southern exterior wall of the first court into the palace precincts; in the right foreground can be seen the corners of the facing surrounding the second pylon. The walls were raised to a unified height (one and two meters) during reconstruction work by the Oriental Institute of the University of Chicago. Only the door frames, column bases, and throne pedestals could be recreated as the original building material, unbaked mudbrick, was no longer present. The plan of the building could only be reconstructed from the remains of the foundations and column bases.

114 The Window of Appearances in the palace of Ramesses III
Western Thebes, Medinet Habu, mortuary temple of Ramesses III; New Kingdom, Twentieth Dynasty, ca. 1170 BC.
The window is crowned with a row of uraeus cobras continued in relief on both sides. Together with the winged sun disk above and the vulture goddesses to the left and right they serve as protective symbols, part of the standard repertoire of Egyptian temple decoration. Their placement here was intended to bestow on the king divine assistance in the fulfillment of his duties; the king himself is pictured on both sides of the window in relief.

115 Tile inlays: the enemies of Egypt
Western Thebes, Medinet Habu, mortuary
temple of Ramesses III, palace entrance; New
Kingdom, Twentieth Dynasty, ca. 1170 BC;
polychrome glazed faience; H. 25 to 26 cm,
W. 7 cm, Cairo, Egyptian Museum, JE 36457
a, b, d, h; RT 12.3.24.13.
The palace entrances were decorated at the
bottom on both sides with representations of
Egypt's enemies. The five preserved tiles
show from left to right: a tattooed Libyan, a
Nubian, a bearded Syrian, a Shasu-bedouin
with a yellow headcloth, and a Hittite with a
round cap. They are all depicted with their
own characteristic clothing and hairstyles.
Since they are bound or handcuffed, they
pose no further threat to Egypt's continued
existence.

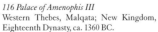

116 Palace of Amenophis III
Western Thebes, Malqata; New Kingdom,
Eighteenth Dynasty, ca. 1360 BC.
The central part of the complex is grouped
around the hall (D); its regular structure
indicates a tightly organized plan. The
residence of the "great royal wife Tiye" was
located at the southern end (G); the adjacent
buildings around the three courts (H)
probably housed the kitchen and other
facilities for servicing the palace.

probably served as the residence for the daughters of Akhenaten. Paintings of animals and plants, which seem almost impressionistic in their handling of color and theme, have been preserved in the so-called Green Room. In the center of Amarna was an enormous complex of two buildings connected by a bridge: the "Great Palace" and the "House of the King." The structure consisted of a succession of rooms of a more private nature in which Akhenaten probably resided. The rear of the building was occupied by storerooms. A Window of Appearances opened onto a courtyard in front of the house The ritual of rewarding deserving officials of the king took place here in the manner described above for the first courtyard of Medinet Habu.

The grandeur of the towering columned halls at the southern end of the palace provided an appropriate setting in which to receive foreign delegations and impress them with the majesty of the king and therefore of Egypt in general. This was the primary purpose of these buildings. Their rows of halls, elevated thrones, Windows of Appearances, sculpted heads of enemies, and reliefs showing the smiting of the foes can all be viewed as prototypes for an architecture of power.

117 Throne room in the palace of Ramesses III
Western Thebes, Medinet Habu, mortuary temple of Ramesses III; New Kingdom, Twentieth Dynasty, ca. 1170 BC.
The column bases are large in relation to the small diameter of the columns; this was characteristic of Ramesside architecture. There was probably a double false door situated behind the throne in which the deceased king was present in symbolic form to accept the homage of his officials and the representatives of foreign lands; such a feature highlights the cult function of the palace. In the background is the excellently preserved brick enclosure wall of the shrine.

Daily Life in the Home – The House as Living Area

Gabriele Wenzel

Even today the tombs of officials and tradesmen testify to the great care with which the Egyptians prepared themselves for life after death. Because they did not wish to lack for comfort in the hereafter, they provided their tombs with furniture, clothing, and tools and adorned the walls with scenes from everyday life. Details about their diet can be found in these tomb paintings, which document food production from cultivation and horticulture through to the actual preparation of meals. Lists of offerings depicted in reliefs or paintings also name those things believed to be essential for a secure existence in the hereafter. One can even find in these tombs numerous undisturbed offerings in the form of provisions still preserved by the dry Egyptian climate.

The Staples: Bread and Beer

The staple food items were primarily grain products, bread, and beer. They were used, for example, to pay workers in the quarries and on large construction sites. It has been proved that two types of grain, barley (Ancient Egyptian: *it*) and emmer (*bedet*) were cultivated. The addition of various fruits and the use of wholemeal or white flour provided the numerous baked goods with a variety of tastes. A painting in the tomb of vizier Rekhmire shows the preparation of a cake made of pounded "almonds of the earth," the tuber of a bush native to Cyprus with a nutty flavor, which was sweetened with honey and baked in oil.

Pulses, like lentils, beans, peas, and chick-peas as well as fenugreek played an important part in the Egyptian diet, particularly of the lower classes. The diet of the elite was considerably more varied. It comprised an assortment of vegetables: cress, portulaca, lettuce, onions, garlic, and pumpkins as well as the tubers and seeds of the lotus plant and parts of the papyrus; texts and pictures, however, do not tell us anything about their preparation. Favorite fruits were grapes, figs and sycamore figs, dates and dom palm nuts, and from the New Kingdom pomegranates. This plant was originally imported from the Near East and was soon thereafter cultivated in Egyptian gardens.

119 Shelf with food from a Theban tomb
New Kingdom, Eighteenth Dynasty, ca. 1550–1292 BC; London, The British Museum, EA 5340.
The deceased was provided with everything he needed for life after death. Food was included: different kinds of poultry and meat lie on a small rack; in the woven basket and earthenware dishes are bread, figs and dried fish.

118 Table of offerings piled high with food
Western Thebes, tomb of Rekhmire (TT 100); New Kingdom, Eighteenth Dynasty, ca. 1450 BC.
On the table lies a selection of food that might have appeared on the dining table of a high official: at the top is a lettuce and a bunch of leeks; below, a bowl of figs, grapes, several cucumber-shaped pumpkins, two geese – one already plucked and gutted – and the head, shank and ribs of a cow as well as several cakes and loaves of bread.

120 Breadmaking
Saqqara, tomb of Niankhkhnum and Khnumhotep (relief); Old Kingdom, Fifth Dynasty, ca. 2450 BC.
The most important method of baking bread did not require a stove or oven; instead thick-walled earthenware molds were used. These molds were stacked carefully over an open fire (left). When they were sufficiently hot they were taken down, placed upright and filled with liquid dough (center), which was then baked by the residual heat of the molds. Larger molds that needed an additional source of heat were covered with a second mold with its opening facing downward. A thin stick was used to check whether the bread was ready (right). The conical loaf was placed on top of the molds to cool. Walled ovens were invented in the Old Kingdom that allowed a great number of loaves to be baked simultaneously.

Delicacies: Meat, Wine, Spices

Part of the diet of the greater portion of the Egyptian population certainly included bread and beer, pulses and vegetables and probably also cheap fish and poultry (mainly pigeons, geese, and ducks) or goats' meat, mutton, and pork. There were, however, certain delicacies only affordable by the upper classes. Information on prices can be found on the so-called ostraca, potsherds and flakes of limestone found in great numbers on which letters and bills were written. The billing unit often consisted of an amount of copper, one *deben*. Basic food items were obviously not expensive: a 75-l sack of barley cost two *deben,* a sack of emmer one *deben,* and 5 l of beer could be had for two *deben.* For better types of food and drink one had to spend considerably more; meat in particular was quite expensive. A fully grown cow cost fifty *deben,* a 10-l amphora with salted meat was ten *deben.* These were considerable sums for a state-employed craftsman in the New Kingdom who earned, on top of his basic provisions, only seven *deben* a month.

Simple houses – including those in artisans' settlements – did not have the space to keep cattle. Only the farmsteads and estates of high officials had barns and other buildings with workshops for slaughtering and processing cattle.

Fattening was an important part of cattle raising. Tomb paintings also show game such as antelopes, gazelles, and ibexes, whose meat was apparently prized. The meat was processed for consumption immediately after slaughtering. It was cooked in cauldrons or grilled on an open fire fed with wood and dung, and sometimes also with charcoal. If the meat was preserved for later use it was either dried or salted. Little is known of the spices used to refine food. Small cloth

121 Brewery
Saqqara, tomb of Niankhkhnum and Khnumhotep (relief); Old Kingdom, Fifth Dynasty, ca. 2420 BC.
Breweries were always constructed close to bakeries because the most important ingredient in the production of Egyptian beer were round flat loafs called *pesen*. The second important ingredient were dates, which provided the necessary yeast cultures. The scene from the tomb of Niankhkhnum shows all the important stages in brewing from the baking of bread to the filling of vessels with beer. Chopped bread, water, and dates were mashed to a porridge in a large vat (left), which was left for some time to ferment. Later the mixture was pressed through a woven sieve into a large container with an outlet and the brewing process was concluded. The beer was then poured into special vessels coated on the inside with a thin layer of clay to act as a clearing agent for the beer (top center). Immediately afterward they were closed with a thick mud stopper – this had to be done quickly to prevent any carbon dioxide from escaping. Egyptian beer could only be kept for a short time; it had to be consumed quickly and therefore only small vessels were used.

sacks, some still containing coriander seeds, have been found in the worker's settlement of Amarna, but most of the spices – dill, coriander, cumin, caraway, juniper berries, and mustard seeds – seem to have been used only for medical purposes.

The consumption of wine was – except for special celebrations – restricted to the households of high officials and the royal palace. Some wines were imported from the Near East, particularly from Syria, while others were produced in Egypt. The vines needed particular care and were planted in hollows filled with Nile mud.

The best Egyptian wine-growing properties lay in the Nile Delta and in the oases. They often belonged to the state but it seems that – according to the inscriptions on amphorae – private wine-growing estates also existed. In the palace ruins of Amenophis III at Malqata near Thebes were found countless sherds of ceramic wine amphorae inscriptions in ink noting the time and place of production: "Wine from the southern oasis" or "Wine from the estates of the keeper of the seal…." In addition to details of the wine's origin, the name of the respective wine grower could also be noted on the delivered Amphorae.

The Kitchen

The kitchen usually lay toward the rear of the house or, on larger estates, in ancillary buildings. Because cooking was mainly done over an open fire it had no fixed roof. In one corner of the "kitchen yard" was the millstone for the production of flour and whole wheat, a small oven for baking bread, and a walled fireplace for cooking or grilling.

122 Preparation of beef
Western Thebes, tomb of Antefoqer (TT 60);
Middle Kingdom, Twelfth Dynasty, ca. 1900
BC.
Several butchers remove the intestines of the
slaughtered animal while assistants hang
single pieces on long lines. At the far right a
cook stands in front of a cauldron in which
meat is being cooked.

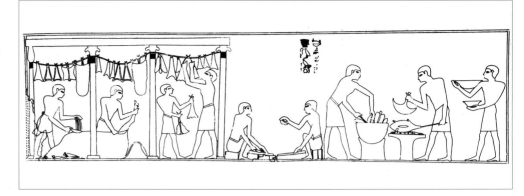

123 Figure of a female miller
Giza (Mastaba D 29); Old Kingdom, Fifth
Dynasty, ca. 2400 BC; limestone; H. 26 cm;
Leipzig, Ägyptisches Museum, 2767.
Grain was only milled by hand – usually by
women – and then sieved to remove the
remaining spelt. Fine stone particles remained,
however, which meant that the teeth of even
young Egyptians were badly worn. This was
especially true of the ordinary people, as a
skeleton found at the most recent excavation
of a workers' cemetery at Gisa demonstrates.

124 The wine press
Saqqara, tomb of Ptahhotep and Akhethotep
(relief); Old Kingdom, Fifth Dynasty, ca.
2420 BC.
After the harvest the grapes were placed in a
large basin and trampled by several men. The
juice ran out of a spout at the side and into a
container. The must was then forced through
a sack. To make better use of their strength
long poles were contra-rotated by several men
while another worker pushed them apart.
The first "still" fermentation took place in the
trampling vat; the second "turbulent"
fermentation only after the wine amphorae
had been filled. The vessels were then closed
with a mud stopper; several small holes let
into the stopper enabled the carbon dioxide to
escape.

fats or oils, and conserved meat, as seen from their inscriptions:
"Mutton from the estate of Aakheperure," "waterfowl for the jubilee,"
or "prepared meat from the estate of Amenophis." The house had a
small, low cellar for storing perishable goods that could be reached by a
few steps from the kitchen.

Furniture

Remains of moveable furniture have virtually never been found in
living quarters, but numerous finds in tombs give us an impression of
Egyptian furnishings. The walls were covered with dyed hangings
made of linen. Mats of woven plant fibers covered the floor, and sometimes served also as mattresses.

The oldest preserved pieces of furniture – legs and fixtures of
chairs and beds – are preserved from the Archaic Period, the First and
Second Dynasties. The designs used continued with only minor variations and modernizations throughout pharaonic times. Chairs seem to
have been the most common furniture of the civil service during the
New Kingdom. The price of a plain chair was four to eight *deben* –
easily affordable for an official. All types can be found, from the plain
low stool to the folding chair and on up to armchairs with backrests. A
soft cushion was often added to the seat for greater comfort.

Tables and storage receptacles complete the furnishings. These
were often made of wood but some articles consisted of sturdy inter-
woven materials. Judging from wall paintings of feasts there were no
large tables for the family and their guests to sit around for communal
meals. Instead, each person sat in front of his or her own little table or
slab of calcite alabaster or earthenware supported by a light wooden
frame. The dimensions of the tables found during the excavations
support this conclusion.

Great value was placed on hygiene in all households. The omnipresent vermin were combated by a variety of methods matched only by
the types of insects. Some can be found in medical papyri: "Beginning
of a remedy prepared to rid the houses of fleas. Sprinkle the house with
natron water that they might disappear." or "Another prescription.
Bebet (apparently fleabane) should be ground on charcoal, the house
should be rubbed with (it), that they might disappear." Other preparations were used to perfume the home.

The bed stood on a raised base to protect it from creeping animals.
Clothing and other personal items were stored in wall niches. Well-
equipped households also owned several boxes and chests of wood or
woven material.

127 Four-posted stool
New Kingdom, Eighteenth Dynasty, ca. 1550–1292 BC; wood, stuccoed canvas; H. 24 cm, W. 40 cm; Turin, Museo Egizio, cat. 6404. Chairs and stools had a much lower seat than modern furniture. The seat on this stool is made of canvas coated with stucco that was then painted with plant designs and geometrical patterns.

128 Table from the tomb of Kha
Western Thebes, Deir-el-Medineh; tomb of Kha (TT 8); New Kingdom, Eighteenth Dynasty, ca. 1400 BC; wood, 48 x 26 cm, H. 32 cm; Turin, Museo Egizio, Suppl. 8432. This table was used as a stand for a senet board game.

129 Chair with backrest from the tomb of Kha
Western Thebes, Deir el-Medineh, tomb of Kha (TT 8); New Kingdom, Eighteenth Dynasty, ca. 1400 BC; painted wood; H. 91 cm, W. 56 cm; Turin, Museo Egizio, Suppl. 8333. Costly chairs were often ornamented with ivory, ebony or glass paste inlays. If the owner could not afford such work the carpenter imitated their effects with paint. The inscription here, a sacrificial prayer, indicates that the chair was used in a funerary context; it was in fact found in a tomb.

130 Bedroom furniture
New Kingdom, Nineteenth Dynasty, ca. 1300 BC; London, The British Museum, EA 2470, 6526, 6639, 18196, 14708.
Some of the most coveted articles of furniture were beds, the legs of which often took the form of lions' paws or the legs of bulls. The mattress lay on a tightly woven system of halfa grass or other plant fibers tied between the beams of the frame. At the upper end was a headrest, which, like the lower end of the bed, was ornamented with the carved or painted image of the dwarf god Bes. He was considered to be a protector during the night, the destroyer of evil creatures – particularly snakes – and therefore had an established place in bedrooms.

Hygiene, Cosmetics, and Clothing

Most of the Egyptian population bathed in the Nile, in canals or ponds. Only the upper classes could afford a bathroom in which one could take a shower. The toilet was either in the same or in a separate room.

Natron or special washing pastes, thought to have a beneficial effect on the skin and made of animal or vegetable fats mixed with limestone or chalk, were used as soap. A prescription from the Ebers medical papyrus describes "Another medicine for beautifying the skin. One part ground (calcite) alabaster, one part red natron, one part salt from Lower Egypt, one part honey; to be mixed to a mass with this honey; the skin to be painted with it." Other medicines were used to prevent body odor; they mainly contained aromatic substances such as incense, styptic, and myrrh and were rubbed into the skin. Substances rolled into pills to prevent bad breath were also known. The best known were the "kyphi-pastilles" made of crushed fenugreek seeds mixed with incense, myrrh, juniper berries, rubbery resin mixtures, raisins, and honey.

The Egyptians preferred linen for their clothes; they also had a coarse cloth made of bark and, less commonly, wool. Particularly popular were completely white and extremely thin linen fabrics folded into fine pleats. Texts confirm that fabrics were bleached to obtain the purest white possible; after washing, they were simply put out in the sun. Dyeing of textiles was also known. Besides the mineral ochre the Egyptians used vegetable dyes: madder, safflower, and alkanet for red, woad for blue, and the bark of the pomegranate tree for yellow. Some modes of coloring needed a preparatory lye bath; they mainly used alum, an aluminum sulfate that is still used today.

131 Clothes chest
Western Thebes; New Kingdom, Eighteenth Dynasty, ca. 1390 BC; painted wood; 30 x 55.5 x 31 cm; Turin, Museo Egizio, Suppl. 13968.
Larger chests were used for storing clothes or wigs. Their interiors were fashioned according to the wishes of the respective owners.

133 Cosmetic case of Queen Mentu-hotep

Second Intermediate Period, Seventeenth Dynasty, ca. 1600 BC; palm fiber, reed, and papyrus; H. 42.7 cm, Berlin, SMPK, Ägyptisches Museum, 1176–77.
The case is divided into six compartments to hold small and fragile cosmetic utensils; the containers for ointments and eye make-up were only partly made of stone, more often of glass, faience, and even reed.

Statues of both kings and private individuals convey a vivid picture of changing fashions. During the Old and Middle Kingdoms, women wore plain, close-fitting dresses with shoulder straps, while men sported wrap-around kilts down to their knees or calves. During the New Kingdom, however, a preference developed for baggy tunics. During this period women wore wrap-around dresses made of a large rectangular piece of fabric wound around the body in various ways and held together with a folded sash. The official dress of men and women invariably included wigs of different lengths and styles.

The most important footwear were sandals made of plant fibers such as palm leaves, grasses, rushes or papyri. These were probably not made in workshops but in the home by women. Leather sandals were also manufactured; they were considerably more expensive but also more durable than woven sandals.

The Family

The "typical" Egyptian household consisted of members of the nuclear family, that is, the parents and only the children who had not yet attained their maturity. A loose relationship was maintained with more distant relatives. It is revealing that the Egyptian language had words only for relatives of the first order, that is, for father, mother, brother and sister as well as son and daughter, but no words for aunt, uncle, cousin, and so forth. To express more complicated relationships, one had to seek refuge in constructions such as "sister of the mother of her mother." On tomb stelae, however, representations sometimes included not only the immediate family of the deceased but also distant relatives.

More prosperous households also had one or more servants to do the bulk of the work. According to written sources the household of the engraver Qeni from Deir el-Medineh was home to some ten people who did not belong to his family. The household of one mid-ranking official comprised seventy-nine servants, most of them slaves of Egyptian or Asiatic origin.

Matrimony was the common living style. When a man reached the appropriate age – when he could support a family – he founded his household. The woman normally moved into the man's home, only very rarely did the married couple live in the home of the woman. There are no sources referring to regulations pertaining to a legally valid marriage; marriage contracts were made only from the Twenty-second Dynasty on. They provided the woman with financial security in case of divorce or the death of her husband. The man was primarily responsible for securing the family income. He was obliged to provide for his wife and children according to his means. Marriages were usually monoga-

134 Horizontal loom

Beni Hasan, tomb of Khnumhotep II (BH 13); Twelfth Dynasty, ca. 1880 BC.

Textile production was mainly a task for women. They spun linen thread and also wove the fabrics. The professional skills of textile workers from the Near East was highly prized. The innovation of the vertical loom at the beginning of the Eighteenth Dynasty was also presumably of Near Eastern origin. It was only used in larger weaving workshops, whereas the smaller horizontal loom was used in private homes to produce fabrics for household purposes. Its simple construction was a great advantage: the two crossbeams (so-called weaving posts) were not connected with each other. One could therefore weave a piece of cloth of any size, even in a restricted space.

135 Linen fabric with a fabric mark

Thebes, Deir el-Bahari, tomb of a soldier of Mentuhotep II; First Intermediate Period, Eleventh Dynasty, ca. 2050 BC; New York, The Metropolitan Museum of Art, Rogers Fund 1927, 27.3105/197/108.

Complete tomb equipment included fabrics, sometimes with clothes or fabric markings. Most examples come from a Theban tomb in which sixty soldiers, killed in confrontations during the First Intermediate Period, were interred. Well-preserved fabrics have proved that the Egyptians had different weaving techniques, used several types of linen weave and – for elaborate patterns – even used the Gobelin technique. Records of fabrics from tombs prove that there were a great number of textiles of different qualities. Unfortunately, only a few have been identified. The finest fabric was *sesheru nisut*, the "royal linen."

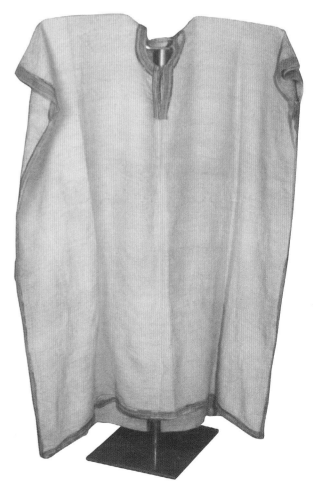

136 Woman's wig

New Kingdom, Eighteenth/Nineteenth Dynasty, ca 1550–1185 BC; human hair; L. 50.5 cm; London, The British Museum, EA 2560.

Several women's wigs have been preserved, dating from the New Kingdom. Research has shown that they were almost exclusively made of human hair that was knotted into a linen cap. Beeswax was used to set the often elaborate hairstyles. Such elaborate wigs would only be worn on ceremonial or official occasions, while both men and women preferred short hair styles or shaved heads for private life.

137 Tunic

Western Thebes, Deir el-Medineh, tomb of Kha (TT 8); New Kingdom, Eighteenth Dynasty, ca. 1400 BC; linen; 128 x 109 cm; Turin, Museo Egizio, Suppl. 8530.

The tunic was worn like a shirt. The most common version was made of a plain piece of white linen, while more lavish tunics had a braid trimming around the neck and the hem. The more fashionable dress of the New Kingdom was pleated at the side; a long, broad sash was worn on top, which held the baggy tunic together at the waist.

138 Funerary stela of the high court recorder Horhernakht
Middle Kingdom, Twelfth Dynasty, ca. 1900 BC; painted limestone; H. 68.5 cm; Turin, Museo Egizio, cat. 1613.
Horhernakht is shown together with a large part of his family: His parents, Sekhemsobek and Kheti, sit in front of him; behind them are his siblings Horemusekhet and It. The last three people in the second row are also his siblings. The first two, however, are uncles from his mother's and father's sides. The third and fourth persons in the third row are most likely his father- and mother-in-law, who both bear the name Sehetepib; they are also referred to as his mother and father.

139 Statue of a seated couple
New Kingdom, Nineteenth Dynasty, ca. 1290 BC; serpentine; H. 12.7 cm., W. 7.2 cm; Paris, Musée du Louvre, E 3416.
Even after death one tried to maintain family ties. Tomb statues therefore very often show a husband with his wife, in rare cases also his mother. During the New Kingdom, they were shown to be of equal height, a reference to the equality of men and women, at least in private life.

140 Woman with child
Predynastic, ca. 3000 BC; ivory; H. 6.5 cm; Berlin, SMPK, Ägyptisches Museum, 17600. From prehistoric times small statuettes of women with children have been found, primarily in temples. They were probably intended for a god as a votive in gratitude for an easy birth or to express the desire for a child.

141 Seated figure of a nursing woman
Middle Kingdom, Twelfth Dynasty, ca. 1900 BC; copper, H. 13 cm; Berlin, SMPK, Ägyptisches Museum, 14078.
Children were nursed up to their third year. Statues of mothers breast-feeding their children are seldom found in a profane context. High-ranking women and queens delegated this task to wet nurses who were considered part of the family. The husbands and sons of royal wet nurses often achieved high office because of their connections.

mous; only if it was childless was the man allowed to take another wife, normally a slave, into his household. Children resulting from these relationships had the same legal status as that of their mother.

In many respects, the woman was legally the man's equal. It was possible for her to make contracts, to be a plaintiff or witness in the courts, to be a child's guardian, and to bequeath her own property. She could only mediate the property of her husband to her children, however, because the law of inheritance was apparently restricted to blood relations.

The aim of every marriage was to produce children. Offspring had to provide for their parents in old age and were also responsible for performing the mortuary cult at the parental tomb. The birth rate was high, quite often a family had five to ten children, but infant mortality was equally high. Childlessness was felt to be a great tragedy but contraceptives were also known. However, a much larger collection of

folk remedies was available for pregnant women or women in childbirth. One tried, for example, to ease the act of giving birth with magic spells and by invoking the gods Bes and Thoeris. Women gave birth at home in a light chamber erected in the garden or on top of the house in which they spent the following two weeks. This time was meant for purification. As with many other cultures, women were seen as impure during menstruation and pregnancy.

The upbringing of the children in the formative years was essentially the task of the mother. From a certain age sons were brought up by their fathers, who trained them to be their assistants and successors. If children were intended to pursue a profession different from that of their father, they were sent to schools that were often affiliated to a temple. There, they were taught to read, write, and do arithmetic. Personal development according to the ideals expressed in the so-called Wisdom Literature was also emphasized in the education of children.

Stone and Quarries

Rosemarie Klemm

The material legacy of Egyptian culture impresses us not least because of its relatively good state of preservation over the course of thousands of years; this holds true particularly for architecture and sculpture. This durability is a striking reflection of an important aspect of the ancient Egyptian world view, the idea of a continued existence in the hereafter. A crucial requirement for achieving an afterlife, apart from conserving the remains of the dead by mummification, was the use of permanent materials for erecting tombs and temples and furnishing them with sarcophagi, statues, and obelisks.

The Egyptians found the ideal material in the great varieties of stone available the entire length of the Nile Valley from Cairo to far beyond Aswan, as well as in the Eastern Desert. They used about forty different types of stone – including several varieties of a single type – in their art and architecture. This colorful assortment of stone is at its most impressive in the compact space of an Egyptian museum, where ancient Egypt appears almost as a "state out of stone" (G. Evers).

Important Stone Types and their Geological Environment

1. The primary characteristics of the Quaternary Period in Egypt are the Nile deposits that form the Nile Valley itself and, in the north, the Delta. They consist of Nile mud of sand and clay forming the fertile soils of the country and constituting the oldest and most important building material for secular structures; indeed, it is still in use today.

In the north, the Pleistocene reefs along the Mediterranean coast are composed of oolite – a limestone formed from small round grains of fossil aggregates. It was used, particularly during the Greco-Roman Period, for building the town of Alexandria. In fact, the town itself is built on such a reef.

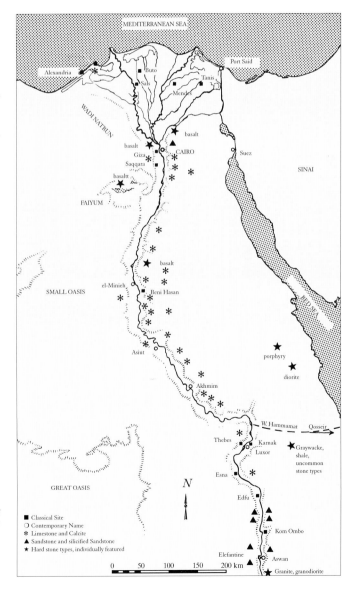

142 (opposite) Limestone quarry near el-Bersha
The gallery quarries, bound to the rock strata and shored up with supporting walls, penetrate about 20 to 30 m into the mountain. They were continuously exploited from the Middle Kingdom right down to the Late Period. In the early Christian era they were used by hermits or Christian sects because of their remote and protected location.

143 Map of Egypt with the most important rock types and quarries
The symbols indicate the larger quarries of antiquity, which consisted of numerous individual quarries.

144 *Basalt pavement*
Pyramid temple of Cheops; Old Kingdom, Fourth Dynasty, ca. 2590 BC.
According to scientific analysis these basalt blocks of different sizes came from the quarries in the Faiyum. They were fitted tightly together on site by sawing smooth edges on their adjoining sides.

145 *Red granite from Aswan*
This unique rock consists of conspicuously large, pink to deep red potassic feldspar crystals alongside porcelain – white plagioclases and gray shiny quartz. The dark component, which makes up to 30 per cent of the volume, consists primarily of black-brown biotite and green hornblende and lends the stone an attractive speckled look.

2. The Tertiary Period produced predominantly Pliocene deposits of sandy limestones, sometimes rich in fossil detritus, which were used, along with other types, in the cores of the Giza Pyramids.

3. The Oligocene Period furnished the basalts and quartzites (silicified sandstone) widely used in architecture and sculpture. In pharaonic times basalt was quarried in great quantities north of Giza near Abu Roash as well as along the northern edge of the Faiyum near Gebel Qatrani. Bright reddish quartzite was mainly quarried east of Cairo at Gebel el-Ahmas.

4. Eocene limestones of various types – from the extremely fine-grained to the coarse and fossilized – flank the Nile Valley in thick bands from Cairo to Luxor. These limestones proved to be the most commonly used material in all the regions and epochs of ancient Egypt, from the pyramids of the great necropolises of the Old Kingdom at Saqqara and Giza through to the temples of the Middle and New Kingdoms. The quarries were distributed right throughout the limestone deposits of the Nile and were most often situated near a particular building project.

Deposited within this series of limestone are passages or veins of Egyptian alabaster, or calcite alabaster, a transparent banded rock that was variously used in art and architecture and was always associated with the exceptional. Another local variant was red lime-breccia. This was the preferred material for vessels and small sculptures during the early dynastic era.

5. Cretaceous sandstone covering the area south of Luxor and up into Nubia was not only used for all later Egyptian temples but also for various types of sculpture and reliefs. The greatest quarries for this stone – also called Nubian sandstone – lie at Gebel es-Silsila north of Kom Ombo. Sandstone was quarried there from the Middle Kingdom down to Roman times.

6. The Precambrian rocks found along the Red Sea and locally in deposits near Aswan and in the Western Desert provided a rich variety of crystalline rocks used continuously in art and architecture from the beginning of Egyptian history. These include the numerous varieties of granite and granodiorite of Aswan, which range from dark to light red granite (pink granite) and from dark gray granodiorite to light gray quartz diorite.

Metamorphic graywacke and fine siltstone were systematically quarried in the Eastern Desert. They were highly prized for sculpture, small artworks, sarcophagi, building components, and the well-known cosmetic palettes from the Predynastic Period. The quarries for this material, marked with numerous inscriptions, lie in the Wadi Hammamat, halfway between the old and new roads connecting Quft with Qosseir.

Apart from serpentnite, steatite, diorite, and gabbro, the Eastern Desert yielded a rich variety of porphyry, which was, however, not quarried but hauled to the Nile Valley as individual boulders. Porphyry was primarily used to produce vessels in the Predynastic and early dynastic eras.

At Mons Porphyrites (red porphyry) and neighboring Mons Claudianus (light quartz diorite), extensive quarries existed during the time of the Roman emperors to produce magnificent baths, basins for springs, columns, building components, and sculptures for decorating the imperial buildings of Rome.

White marble with fine veins of the green mineral brucite can be found at Gebel Rokham in the southern part of the Eastern Desert. Comparative analysis of marble objects from the time of Thutmosis III has revealed that their stone was quarried there. The previous assumption, that marble used in Egypt was generally imported from the Aegean, has therefore been corrected.

In the Western Desert west of Toshka a formation of gray-green banded anorthosite gneiss was exploited since the days of the Old Kingdom. In the earlier scholarly literature, this stone has been given the incorrect petrographic name "Chephren diorite," presumably because the famous statue of Chephren with a falcon was carved from this material. It was highly prized because it occurs only as a flat stratum in desert sand, but especially because it had to be transported over a long and difficult route. It was for this reason that it was reserved for royal use during the Old and Middle Kingdoms. The later use of anorthosite gneiss can be attributed to the reuse of older fragments, a fact that testifies to the consistently high value of this exceptional stone.

The Quarries

Due to their sedimentary origin, limestone and sandstone mountains are layered, and thus contain rock strata of greatly varying quality. The Egyptians used only the best and therefore the most durable stratum in any geological profile; this meant they had to construct tunnels and galleries into the mountain. They chose such an efficient method not least to reduce the wear and tear on their precious metal tools. Only where the selected stratum was simply too massive or was the topmost stratum in a profile did they adopt an open cast technique.

Sandstone and limestone were at first quarried in blocks that could, depending on their use, be either rectangular (that is pyramid blocks) or square (that is construction blocks for larger temples). The stone was generally quarried from top to bottom. The blocks were separated by means of seams and then broken from their base.

From the beginning, the Egyptians used wooden hammers and metal tools to quarry sandstone and limestone. The tools were at first copper chisels, but from the end of the Old Kingdom they were replaced by ever harder bronze tools. In later periods iron chisels were also used. Traces of this tool development can be found even today on the quarry walls: from the short, mostly curving strokes of the Old and Middle Kingdoms the marks become increasingly longer and straighter. In the Late Period they reach lengths of up to 50 cm long and are conspicuously parallel, which can only be explained by the use of long, hard iron chisels. Contrary to popular opinion the ancient Egyptians did not use wooden wedges moistened to make them expand and split the blocks from their base in either the sandstone/limestone or crystalline rock quarries. The wedge holes along the separating planes found in the granite quarries of Aswan date from the Ptolemaic era at the earliest. These are holes in which iron chisels were fitted and which were then propped up with wedges to take the pressure of the rock – a method used from Roman times and still in use today, in modified form.

Work in the hard stone quarries of pharaonic times, however, varied greatly. Due to the exceptional hardness of these rocks they could not be worked with copper or bronze chisels. The Egyptians were therefore forced to attack it with tools of dolorite, an extremely hard and tough igneous rock. The unfinished pieces found *in situ* in the granite quarries of Aswan, as well as the dolorite tools found there and worn to varying extents, enable us to reconstruct Egyptian working methods quite clearly. At first they looked for a raw boulder suitable for the intended object; usually this was found in a form typical for the weathering of granite – a loose, roundish granite block called a "wool sack." This rock was worked with sharp-edged dolerite fragments until they obtained the desired rough shape.

146 Sandstone quarry in Gebel es-Silsila
This massive and mostly homogenous sandstone was quarried in this open cast mine. The chisel marks in the quarry walls (which can be up to 20 m high) reveal the era in which it was quarried (Ptolemaic) as well as the height of the blocks.

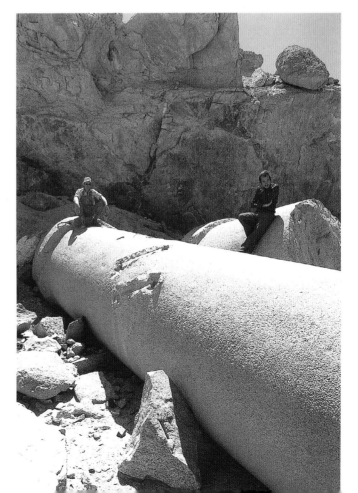

147 Colossal column at Mons Claudianus
The Roman quarries at Mons Claudianus primarily produced columns and basins for springs. This broken, and therefore abandoned, column is 21 m long. An attempt to mend the column with lead anchors apparently failed. Columns of 16 m in length from Mons Claudianus were used for building the Pantheon. The original construction plan still visible on the gable, however, clearly shows longer columns. It was possibly the mishap shown here that forced the architects to reduce the height of the columns.

148 Block quarrying in a limestone quarry near Tehna in Middle Egypt
The lowest stratum clearly shows the Egyptian method of quarrying. The blocks were separated with seams and then broken from their base using levers. Lever holes can be found on all the large blocks used in the necropolises of Giza and Saqqara. Blocks of smaller size were also chiseled free as can be seen from the unfinished blocks there.

150 Statue of Osiris
Aswan, quarry; New Kingdom, probably Nineteenth Dynasty, ca. 1200–1300 BC; red granite; L. ca. 450 cm.
Many unfinished monuments have been left in the vast quarries around Aswan, among others this monumental Osiris statue made of red granite. It was possibly a defect in the material that rendered the transport of this temple statue pointless. Although the essential anthropomorphic features of the statue are already clearly visible in the crown, its stylistic details are not so developed that we can date the figure within the period of the New Kingdom.

149 Unfinished obelisk near Aswan
Probably New Kingdom, Eighteenth Dynasty, ca. 1450 BC.
This obelisk of red granite is 41 m long and already excavated on three sides. The reason for its abadonment in the quarry was probably not the crack visible at the top but its magnitude. Its length and weight (ca. 1,000 tons) had attained proportions that presumably could not be managed during transport and erection. The wave-like marks of stone hammers are visible on all sides of the obelisk.

The stone hammers gradually became rounded during this process and were thrown away as useless blunt stone balls. Only in the final stages, such as the modeling of finer surface patterns or the engraving of an inscription, did they use metal chisels. To polish the surface of the stone Egyptian stonemasons used finely ground quartz with hand-held polishing stones.

The Quarry as Workshop

We know from inscriptions that not only laborers but specially trained stonemasons, sculptors, and scribes also belonged to the quarry team. The quarries were in this sense then also sculptors' studios in which the objects were artistically refined down to the details of their inscriptions and therefore largely completed. This was generally true, however, only for larger objects and is borne out by the large number of various pieces, mostly unfinished or broken, which still litter these quarries. Because of the often considerable distances between the quarries and the building sites, particular care had to be taken during transportation. For this purpose, special ramps made of rocks were built and covered by a slippery mixture of sand and mud; many are still

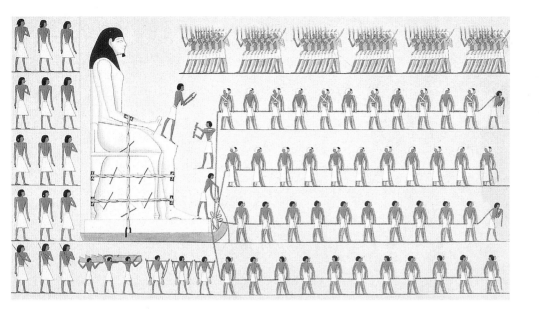

151 *Transport of a statue*
Depiction in the tomb of Djehutyhetep, el-Bersha; early Middle Kingdom, probably Eleventh Dynasty, ca. 2119–1976 BC.
The picture shows the transport of a statue from the quarries of Hatnub. The figure, made of calcite alabaster, is approximately 6 m high and mounted on a wooden sled drawn by four teams of men. Particular care was given to the edges when securing the statue. The ramp was moistened in front of the runners to make it more slippery; it was presumably covered with mud from the Nile.

152 *(right) Quarry ramp in central Egypt*
The clearly recognizable ramp led from the limestone quarry near Zawiyet Sultan in central Egypt to the loading bay on the Nile. The part of the ramp that runs through agricultural land can now no longer be seen.

visible today. One of the longest ramps led from the basalt quarries at Gebel Qatrani to the former banks of Lake Faiyum – a distance of 10 km. At this site, near the temple of Qasr es-Sagha, an installation for loading the basalt blocks onto ships bound for the Nile Valley is still recognizable. Basalt blocks were used, amongst other things, as paving stones in the funerary temples of the pyramids of the Old Kingdom; the great volumes of transport that would have justified such a prodigious ramp must then have taken place during this period. The objects for transportation were mounted on wooden sleds drawn either by oxen or men. There is pictorial evidence for both methods.

A Different World – Religious Conceptions

Ulrich Luft

When the Egyptians emerged from the darkness of prehistory they already manifested characteristics of the advanced civilization they were yet to develop. Very little is known of the Egyptian faith of the Neolithic Period. The idols and different types of burials indicate a religious conception that appears to be characteristic of all prehistoric cultures. The community, that is, the nucleus of human societal structure, accepted and desired divine supremacy. The role of mediator between the people and the gods was fulfilled by the chief and later by the king. The burial objects indicate a belief in life after death.

It appears that Egyptian gods had no names but were regarded as powers, according to the terminology of modern religious studies. But recent examinations have revealed that the most ancient gods of the Egyptian pantheon carried names that could be traced back to the roots of Afro-Asiatic languages. It follows that the gods were not exclusively called upon as "powers," even though the goddess Sakhmet (the "Almighty") can be traced to dynastic periods. In Egypt, naming the gods allowed the believer spiritual access to them: the gods became a comprehensible "substance" and a cult object. An unnamed "power" therefore seems, from an Egyptian perspective, highly unlikely even during very early periods.

The origin of the general term "god" (ancient Egyptian: *Netjer*) is still used today in Coptic liturgical language as *Nûti*, and the evaluation of its script character is still hotly disputed. The hieroglyphic symbol ⌐ has been recognized as a temple standard, as a divine symbol of power (axe?) and as a wrapped cult object. None of these interpretations withstands thorough criticism.

The Egyptian pantheon was structured partly on a regional, partly on a pan regional level; it always comprised the gods of Egypt's principal places. Well-known gods of this kind are Horus of Nekhen, Seth of Ombos, Sobek of Gebelein, Min of Coptos, Thoth of Hermopolis, Ptah of Memphis, Atum of Heliopolis, and Neith of Sais. It cannot be fully determined whether all of these deities were linked to conceptions of the creation of the world and the gods during the Predynastic Period. Min has obviously always disposed of potential creative power; in the case of Ptah and Atum creative power can only be reconstructed using later texts. Other gods possessed creative power only on a secondary level.

Since the earliest periods some gods are experienced in particular situations. This has fundamentally shaped their image as well as the oral tradition that has evolved around them. In the course of Egyptian history Seth's reputation, for example, fluctuated between positive and negative on an irregular basis. Until the beginning of the Late

Period, Seth is regarded as the powerful protector of the sun god and, at the same time, as Osiris's murderer. He is subsequently identified as an enemy of the sun god, which eventually led to his ostracization. Other gods completely retreated into oblivion, for example the hare goddess Wemut. In the early dynastic period the "god of light and the world" Horus appears to have played a unifying role, although this role is

1 The "Great White" god
Archaic Period, Dynasty 0, ca. 3050 BC; calcite-alabaster; H. 52 cm; Berlin, SMPK, Ägyptisches Museum, 22607.
A series of small baboon figures made of faience, found in the temples of Abydos and Hierakonpolis, were the precursors of the earliest Egyptian monumental animal sculpture pictured here. This god was later no longer worshipped, although its appearance was linked to the god Thoth.

2 Comb of King Wadj
Archaic Period, First Dynasty, ca. 2950 BC; ivory; Cairo, Egyptian Museum, JE 47176.
The comb of the pharaoh Wadj from the First Dynasty is a fine pictorial example of the link between heaven and earth. Horus is depicted above in his celestial barque and again atop the rectangle with the palace facade, where the pharaoh's name is inscribed in the top half. The celestial and the earthly Horus represent two separate worlds, unified by the king, who is himself identified with Horus.

3 *Figure of a man in fetal position inside a frog*
Naqada I; fourth millennium BC; fired clay; H. 8.8 cm, W. 25.3 cm, D. 11.3 cm; Leiden (NL), Rijksmuseum van Oudheden, F 1962/12.1.
The interpretation of this piece is still unresolved. The man lies in fetal position in a bowl, which has been identified as a frog due to the images on the handle-like long sides. In analyzing the bowl, scholars considered it to be a ship in the form of a frog, to be understood as a means of transformation of the deceased. The deceased is apparently lying inside the frog in anticipation of resurrection, since the frog goddess was later considered to assist with childbirth.

4 *Ceremonial mace head of Narmer*
Hierakonpolis; Archaic Period, Dynasty 0, ca. 3035 BC; limestone; H. 19.8 cm; Oxford, Ashmolean Museum, E3631.

The mace head depicts a scene from the ritual of the pharaoh's rejuvenation ceremony (*sed*). Narmer sits on a dais within a booth that is typically associated with this celebration.

assumed by Re in the Old Kingdom. According to later examinations, hierarchical structures already begin to form in the pantheon during the Predynastic Period.

Generally, the humanization of the gods is regarded as a prerequisite for the Egyptians' "theological" thinking toward the end of prehistory, although no proof exists for this process. In subsequent periods, both anthropomorphic and theriomorphic gods were worshipped. In this context, a particular god's image has no bearing on his importance. It is more likely that changes in the pantheon's hierarchy were the determining factors. Theriomorphic and anthropomorphic gods probably also existed in prehistoric times; good examples are the "bearded men" of the Naqada II period and numerous animal depictions of the Predynastic and Archaic Periods. The appearance of partly theriomorphic gods can be traced to the Dynastic Period. A link could possibly exist between these gods and the ambition to systemize the newly unified country. The few visual images that bear witness to those times do not really allow any further conclusions. In this polytheistic system, the gods presumably enjoyed equal status and their presence was experienced in a variety of forms.

During the Early Dynastic Period the site of ritual worship usually consists of a simple enclosed structure. This demarcation underscores the separation of the sacral from the profane. At this site, which the gods could claim as their "home," as it were, the divine world comes into contact with the human world. Early pictorial evidence shows only the appearance of these structures; they do not depict any ritual activity.

5 Slab stela of Nefertiabet
Old Kingdom, Fourth Dynasty, ca. 2580 BC;
painted limestone; H. 38 cm, W. 58 cm; Paris,
Musée du Louvre, E 15591
Nefertiabet, a daughter of King Cheops, sits
on a stool with animal legs before an offering
table full of bread loaves, which she receives
with outstretched arm. She wears a long
striated wig and a leopard skin, underlining
her high status. Around the offering table are
inscribed all the items the deceased required
for the existence in the hereafter. Above, two
sections depict offerings intended to make
her stay as comfortable as possible: unguents
and fruit, wine and dates. To the right is a list
of linen materials that are almost certainly
associated with the cult of mummification.
The fine preservation provides a glimpse
of the unparalleled excellence of two-dimensional illustration during the highpoint of the
Old Kingdom, which became the model for
Saite artists in the seventh century BC.

To find out more about ritual activity the objects of the royal cult
may prove more illuminating. Two cermonial mace heads from Hierakonpolis have been preserved, one of which, belonging to Narmer,
unifier of the kingdom, depicts the ritual procession during the "thirty
year festival." These celebrations serve to rejuvenate ritually the aging
king after thirty years of continuous reign.

During the Predynastic Period the chief, and later the king,
fulfilled the role of mediator between the gods and the people. It can be
assumed that over time the falcon god Horus, the "distant one," master
of the light and the world, is embodied by the mediator. The bearer of
this charisma ensures the world is functioning properly and is responsible for re-forming it annually. He is also in charge of performing the
necessary rituals, since the gods will withdraw charity from the suppli-
cant if no sacrifices are offered. The ritual performed for a god can be
considered as worship, as motivation to act or as appeasement of the
god's wrath, depending on the character. During the subsequent system-
ization of the pantheon, the Horus king is made the youngest member
in the dynasty of the gods.

When the Horus king appears in the context of a celebration he is
accompanied by deities on divine standards. These gods may be identified with local gods who accompany the Horus king in servitude, the
Horus entourage or "followers of Horus." By serving the Horus king in
this way, the gods provide him with the necessary power while he, in
turn, provides them with the required protection.

The deceased Horus can hardly be incorporated into the conceptions surrounding the Horus king. The question of where the deceased
Horus king has gone remains unresolved. It is unlikely that the
conception of the deceased god Osiris was developed during the Predynastic Period. On the other hand, excavated skeletal remains
of young people in the royal tombs of the First Dynasty, whose conditions indicated a violent death, allow the conclusion that these people
were interred alive. The deceased king probably took his household
with him into the hereafter. The transition from life to death was considered a departure: "You have not departed dead, you have departed
alive," the priest assures the king in the Pyramid Texts of a slightly later
date.

The Systematization of the Divine World during the Old Kingdom

Almost all gods that appear in later periods have been attested earlier in the Old Kingdom. Large religious centers developed in Memphis, one of the royal capitals, alongside principal cult sites around the country. The formation of religious systems placed the gods in a hierarchical structure and the various theologies came into competition with each other. Typical examples of this development are the systems around Ptah in Memphis and Atum in Heliopolis, city of the sun.

Although Memphis is the principal administrative center it is dominated, in the context of religious competition, by Heliopolis. A late copy of a presumably very old text on the Ptah theology conveys a creation myth quite similar to the Book of Genesis in the Old Testament. The Book of Genesis adapts well to Egyptian conceptions of naming objects to render them accessible.

Yet the Heliopolis creation myth later triumphed. Atum, the "accomplished," who later becomes the evening sun god, engenders the first divine couple, Shu and Tefnut, in an act of self-fertilization.

Other creation myths presumably existed apart from this one, but they were generally excluded from royal tradition and could therefore only have had local significance. There was, for instance, the doctrine of the ogdoad in Hermopolis, which, once later assimilated with Amun, was torn from the darkness and lost all common ground with the local god Thoth. The four divine couples are Nun (primordial water) and Naunet, Heh (infinity) and Hehet, Kek (primordial darkness) and Keket, Amun (obscurity) and Amaunet; the latter could be replaced with other divine couples. All four couples represent the primordial state before creation, yet in Hermopolis the god of creation remains intangible and he possesses, if named at all, attributes of the god of light.

The cult before the gods takes the form of a conversation amongst the gods, related by priests in the name of the Horus king. The divine status of the king ensures that offerings are accepted by the gods who, like the king, are obliged to act according to *maat*. *Maat* is the fundamental concept of Egyptian culture, which endorses all that exists, from the act of creation to the proper and just action of the people. The gods must ensure that *maat* is adhered to while the people must maintain it. The king as mediator must guarantee *maat*, which is, in fact, very close to the sun god and which, in the New Kingdom, is sometimes personified by the daughter of the sun god. Anyone who contrives to act against *maat*, be it a god or an ordinary mortal, is considered an enemy of the gods.

The cult site is the temple, the demarcated earthly residence of the god, where a cult image of the god, one of its forms, is placed. Only remnants of divine temples are preserved from the Old Kingdom.

Changes in divine theology are manifested most clearly in the changing royal theology. While the competition between Horus and Seth had played an important part in royal theology in the Early Dynastic Period (indicated by the queen's title "She who sees Horus and Seth"), the contest for domination within royal theory in the Old Kingdom seems to have shifted toward the sun god Re and the god of cities Ptah (indicated by the king's title "Son of Re" from the Fourth Dynasty onward).

6 Statue of Hetepdief
Memphis; Old Kingdom, late Third Dynasty, ca. 2650 BC; rose granite; H. 39 cm; Cairo, Egyptian Museum, CG 1.
The deceased official is depicted in prayer. The names of the three pharaohs of the Second Dynasty, alongside that of a phoenix on a pyramidion, are engraved on the right shoulder blade. It is probable that the deceased served the three named pharaohs in funerary rituals; the prayerful pose would, in that case, be associated with his former employment. The phoenix probably symbolizes ascension of the dead.

Despite all reservations the king's title indicates the subordination of the king in relation to the sun god. The mental link between these two conceptions is presumably the sky god, whose eyes are embodied by the moon and the sun.

The sun god represents the perpetually evolving part of the universe. It is indeed possible to identify this part with the sphere of the living. Solar theology and its pendant, Osirian theology (Osiris representing the silent part of the universe, tangible in death) develop and advance at about the same time. Both theologies together form the theology of the living and the dead king. Through Horus, the living king reaches Re and advances as Horus to the position of the son who protects and avenges his father Osiris, the deceased king, murdered by his brother, Seth. Yet Egyptian texts never mention the living Osiris, only his death. So, in royal theology two strands converge and form a not entirely homogenous theology.

Thanks to the ritual records, magical texts, and hymns found in the pyramids, the so-called Pyramid Texts, we get a much clearer picture of how the king's afterlife was conceived in the Old Kingdom. Again, two theological circles take shape that are influenced by changing royal theology: the solar circle and the Osirian circle. The collection of spells is found in the Old Kingdom's royal pyramids from the Fifth Dynasty onward. But the spells have not been inscribed for the kings on an ad hoc basis; their linguistic form indicates that they may date back as far as the Pre- and Protodynastic Periods.

The collection of spells served to ensure the deceased king's well-being and protection and was obviously written because the execution of the funerary cult, where the spells had to be read, was no longer guaranteed. The fact that the spells were fixed in written form signifies their magical availability. As opposed to earlier assumptions, a strict order of the spells according to the funerary ritual most probably did not exist.

The spells reveal three destinations. The first destination is the continuation of earthly life, a conception taken from the Archaic Period. The second destination is heaven, corresponding to the description of the king as the sky god Horus. This could be a reference to the nocturnal sky, where union with the never-setting circumpolar stars promises eternity, or to the diurnal sky, through which the king intends to travel in his solar barques. The hereafter, desired by all, represents the third possibility. Here, the Osirian faith, which proclaims continuation of life in the mummy, *ba* soul and cosmic double (*ka*), intersects with the solar theology. The enormous pyramids of the Fourth Dynasty, built as a backdrop to the living Horus's transformation into the dead Osiris, are archaeological monitors for this development. Huge ships were buried next to the pyramids, which can be linked to either the solar or the Osirian circle. Re rides on the celestial Nile in his boat and Osiris crosses the earthly Nile in his. During the Fifth Dynasty, the kings built smaller pyramids and, next to them, small solar shrines, featuring an obelisk with a pyramidal top placed in an atrium at the center of the shrine; this represents the architectural link between the solar and the Osirian circles.

In the desire for eternal life in the hereafter everyone was dependent on the king's continued existence. The choice of burial site was, therefore, a means of seeking proximity to the king.

7 The Unification of the Two Lands
Lisht, mortuary temple of Sesostris I; Middle Kingdom, Twelfth Dynasty, ca. 1950 BC; limestone; H. 200 cm; Cairo, Egyptian Museum, CG 414.
This relief originates from the throne side panel of one of the pharaoh's ten statues from his mortuary temple. The two gods Horus and Seth tie the two heraldic plants of Upper and Lower Egypt together into the hieroglyph for "unification", above which the name of the pharaoh Sesostris I is written in a cartouche. The gods are described by their aliases: "The great one, the one with colorful plumage" for Horus and "He of Ombos, lord of Upper Egypt" for Seth.

8 Depiction of the Temple of Sobek
Abusir, sun temple of Niuserre, chamber of seasons; Old Kingdom, Fifth Dynasty, ca. 2430 BC; painted limestone; Berlin, SMPK, Ägyptisches Museum.
A cult building is shown between the water and the rows of hieroglyphs in the Egyptian practice of perspective that is often confusing to the modern eye. The temple consists of three forecourts and the tripartite sanctuary with domed roof. The religious image of the god, normally invisible from the outside, has been placed in the forecourts in this scene.

9 *Cult image of the crocodile god Sobek*
Middle Kingdom, Twelfth Dynasty, ca. 1880 BC; bronze, niello, electrum; L. 22.4 cm; Munich, Staatliches Museum Ägyptischer Kunst, ÄS 6080.
This cult image is one of the very few preserved temple images of ancient Egypt. The ferocity of the animal, and of the god appearing in it, is depicted in perfect technical detail. The diversity of Egyptian gods could not have been illustrated more accurately than in this figure.

Amun's Entry into the Pantheon during the Middle Kingdom

Only a small number of gods were included or excluded from the pantheon in the periods following the Old Kingdom, when the pantheon was first formed. In the Middle Kingdom it was in fact Amun who, himself of unknown provenance, came to play an important role in the second millennium after having assimilated with the sun god Re. The new kings from the Theban area initially depended on the falcon-headed god Montu, attracted by the fact that his appearance was very similar to that of Horus. The new god Amun appears in a variety of forms, amongst others as an ithyphallic god, a typical form of the old god Min of Coptos.

Since the Middle Kingdom, Osiris, god of the dead, appears increasingly as master of the underworld. Now ordinary Egyptians also felt that they could, after death, transform into Osiris, just like the king, but the belief remains illusory that the god and the deceased transformed into Osiris are identical. In order to participate in Osiris's festival rituals, kings and officials built cenotaph chapels or stelae on the "god's terrace" at Abydos. This was the Osiris cult site, which had been a preferred memorial cemetery since the Predynastic and Archaic Periods.

Osiris's festival ceremonies formed part of the annual rejuvenation ritual, which was of fundamental significance for the re-establishment and the continuation of *maat*. In the Abydene cult performance the potential enemy of the god was repeatedly and successfully beaten.

In Egypt, the king's divine status was questioned in the dark periods of political fragmentation. Literary works from royal circles emphasize his human qualities: the king as state servant, the erroneous king, the king as sinner against *maat*. God's impact (here, god is called upon as a singular god or as a particular creation god), on the other hand, becomes less clear. He has ordered *maat* and abides by it himself, but reality amongst ordinary people looks different. God's impartiality is thrown into question and he is required to justify

10 *Sarcophagus of Sepi III (detail)*
el-Bersha, tomb of Sepi III; Middle Kingdom, Twelfth Dynasty, ca. 1920 BC; painted wood; H. 70 cm, W. 65 cm; Cairo, Egyptian Museum, CG 28083, JE 32868.
The representation of the netherworld on this "map" is limited to concentric circles around an island on which Osiris, ruler of the dead, can be seen wearing the typical atef crown. The fire canals that surround the Elysian fields are represented by the red concentric circles.

himself: it is the people who succumb to injustice. It is not quite clear whether this thinking developed during the Middle Kingdom only or whether it had a precursor in the Old Kingdom. The literary form of the Middle Kingdom could very well be the end of a reflective process that has Old Kingdom roots.

The educated elite among the population now believed that the king was no longer god, indeed that he was no longer god-like. Yet images of the king as sphinx or as bearer of offerings confirm that the king remained the mediator between the divine and the human spheres. As Horus, son of Re, the king continues to form part of the divine world and without his impact the divine element would disappear altogether from Egypt. He is the builder of temples, the master of offerings and the guarantor of life according to *maat*.

Conceptions of the Afterlife

Very little is known about the conceptions of the royal afterlife in the Middle Kingdom. The kings were buried in pyramids that stretch southward from the old metropolis of Memphis into the Faiyum. Sesostris II of the Twelfth Dynasty seems to have introduced a significant novelty when he moved his pyramid's entrance from the north to the south side. But this is not, in fact, as significant as the formation of the system of corridors and chambers within the pyramid's core. It was compared to an Osirian tomb, which served to emphasize the identity of the king with Osiris, god of the dead. During celebrations in the king's mortuary temple, however, the god mentioned by name was not Osiris but Sokar, the god of the dead of the necropolis of Saqqara. The "great procession" and the *wagi* ceremony are performed between celebrations, both of which are fundamental Abydene festivals. The destination of the deceased king in the New Kingdom is the perpetual renewal of the world of the sun god. Because Re and Osiris, attested since the Middle Kingdom, are regarded as two halves of the same ball, the king's double orientation toward the sun god and the god of the dead is also comprehensible in the nature of the living and the deceased ruler. The Egyptians appear to have merely added new variants to this way of thinking that dates to the Old Kingdom without ever retracting any of the old conceptions.

Ordinary individuals increasingly express the desire to take over the role of Horus, the "loving son" who looks after his father Osiris and avenges him. This development is generally seen as the democratization of the realm of the dead, although this is true only in a limited sense: the officials, whom the king promises to maintain in the afterlife, play a crucial part in this development. After death, they are given the epithet "justified," an honor usually only granted Horus. This epithet is apparently the mental link to Horus, the son, avenger of his father.

In the next world, the non-royal deceased faces a jury that considers his earthly deeds in relation to *maat*. After having passed this test the deceased joins the blessed who live on the "island of fire." The deceased requires a map, however, in order to find his way around all the canals and fire lakes. This is why the map of the Elysian fields is sometimes painted onto the floor of the coffin, the walls of which are adorned with magical spells (coffin texts) and images of burial objects.

11 Tutankhamun making an offering
Probably Karnak; New Kingdom, Eighteenth Dynasty, ca. 1325 BC; granite; H. 178 cm; London, The British Museum, EA 75.
This figure – created under Tutankhamun and later usurped by Horemhab – belongs to a rare New Kingdom type of royal sculpture. All known examples stem from the Eighteenth Dynasty and depict the king presenting an abundant offering. The portrayal of lotus plants and pomegranates, as well as ears of corn and poultry, are representative of the fertility of the Nile, personified by the figure of the Nile god Hapi. The ruling Pharaoh was the earthly guarantor of this perpetual abundance.

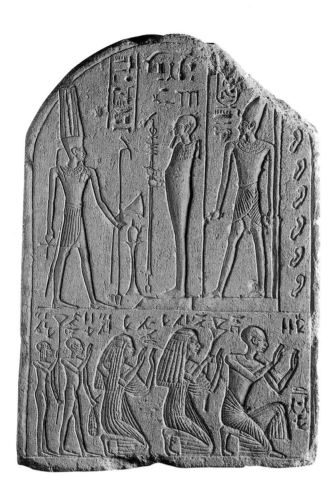

12 Stela of Setierneheh
Qantir; New Kingdom, Nineteenth Dynasty,
ca. 1250 BC; limestone; H. 34.5 cm; Hildesheim, Pelizaeus-Museum, 375.
This stela illustrates the difficulty inherent in
New Kingdom's theology. Amun-Re, king of
gods, ruler of heaven, presents offerings
before Ptah, the beautiful-faced father of the
gods, as well as before Ramesses, the god
Montu (religious statue of Ramessess I in Pi-
Ramesse). Amun-Re, therefore, assumes the
role of the pharaoh. The ears behind the
statue indicate that the prayers are heard.

14 Votive offering by the sculptor Ken
Probably from Western Thebes; New Kingdom, Nineteenth Dynasty, ca. 1250 BC;
painted limestone; Hildesheim, Pelizaeus-
Museum, 4544.
These nine Nile geese embody the divine
ennead of Heliopolis and Hermopolis, to
which Amun also belongs, and to whom Ken
has dedicated this offering. The Nile goose, as
ka image, is a manifestation of Amun and, as
ba soul, the god's representative on
earth.

*13 Akhenaten and Nefertiti beneath the god
Aten*
Tell el-Amarna; New Kingdom, Eighteenth
Dynasty, ca. 1340 BC; painted limestone;
H. 12 cm; Berlin, SMPK, Ägyptisches
Museum, 14511.
Nefertiti affixes a broad collar around the
neck of her spouse. The theme of this image is
the clothing of the god, here represented by
Akhenaten. The role of high priest, usually
fulfilled by the king, is fulfilled here by Nefer-
titi. Aten's blessing hands envelop the earthly
scene.

Empire Gods and the Sun God in the New Kingdom

The Eighteenth Dynasty sees the exemplary rise of the god Amun and the sun god Re. Amun-Re's dominance culminated in the Twenty-first Dynasty, when Amun's high priests assumed earthly rule after Amun had already been spiritual ruler for some time. The earliest signs of this development can be seen in oracles that served as the legitimization of Queen Hatshepsut's ascension to the throne.

The crucial shift in the understanding of god is manifested in the fact that almost all deities now participate in the sun cult. Even the crocodile-headed god Sobek takes on similar features in the Middle Kingdom. The participation of the gods in the solar theology further confuses the original character of each individual cult, making evaluation more difficult. In Amun-Re the two gods are so close, however, that a distinction no longer appears possible.

In the course of the New Kingdom the sun god Re has lost a large part of his elementary creative power. The Book of the Heavenly Cow, a myth inscribed on the walls of royal tombs since the end of the Amarna Period, records the retreat of the aging sun god to his celestial resting place because his rule over the rebellious people on earth has become too much of a burden. This shows very clearly the distance between the god and the people.

With the increasing hold of the cult of Amun, this god expressed a claim of exclusivity that began to overshadow the sun god Re's creator characteristics, previously assumed by Atum. The conceptions of the afterlife are based on the union of the deceased god Osiris and the living god Re. The theologists around Amun-Re did not maintain this concept, and thus Re was abandoned in the afterlife.

Amun-Re, however, became the current god of creation in the sense of the living political deity who, like the god of the Israelites, stood above earthly affairs, ruling them in realization of his divine will. Of course, *maat* also forms the basis for his actions; decisions are taken in the oracles that turn out to be the implementation of *maat*. But *maat* thus becomes less available to the earthly population, forming a strong link with the god and increasingly regarded as the god's will.

Parallel to these paramount theological developments, numerous smaller divine cults blossom as subsidiary cults in the larger centers of the country and in the principal cult sites of the relevant gods. The appearance of these divinities changes as well. During the Eighteenth Dynasty, theriomorphic gods increasingly appear. The animals were regarded as the living image of a particular god, that is as his *ba* soul, although this development obscures a much more complicated theological thinking, which probably links the god with the kings on the same level as in the Protodynastic Period with Horus's entourage.

The development of the solar theology reached its climax in the theological episode of Amarna. Akhenaten rigorously separated the sun god, now named Aten, from Amun and rejected all traditional creation gods in favor of the god of his choice. Aten is neither anthropomorphic nor theriomorphic – the sun disk and its rays are themselves the sun god. Akhenaten established a religion for the living, leaving little space for the dead, which is why Osiris continues to live in Amarna. The solitary status of the new god Aten is implemented by order of the king with the physical destruction of other divine names. It appears, however, that the population did not follow their ruler completely, and the attempt to propagate this particular monotheism in Egypt failed soon after Akhenaten 's death.

The duality of divine conceptions, that is of the political god of creation (known as Amun) and the prehistoric god of creation (known

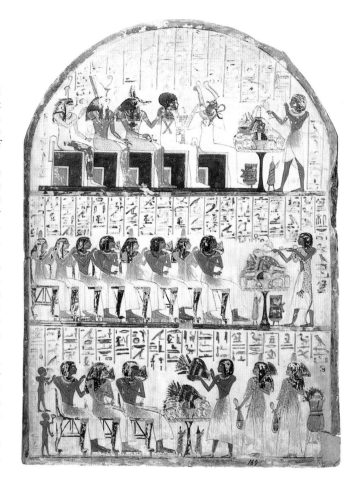

15 Stela of Kar
Western Thebes, Deir el-Medineh; New Kingdom, Nineteenth Dynasty, ca. 1280 BC; painted limestone; H. 81.5 cm; Turin, Museo Egizio, 50012.
The deceased worships five deities in the top register who were of significance to him in his afterlife: Osiris, ruler of the realm of the dead, Ptah, ruler of Memphis and the Lower Egyptian necropolis, Anubis, god of the embalmers, Horus, the ruler and, finally, the goddess of the west, female ruler of the realm of the dead. In the next register, Kar sacrifices before his ancestors and relatives. In the lower register, he receives the successor's offerings. The funerary cult in ancient Egypt was, in fact, divided into these three levels.

as Re) was emphasized once more during the Ramesside Period. All other cults were observed during this period as well. The gods were now also experienced in a historical dimension, which resulted in the systematization of the divine world into a dynasty. The political component of the divine figure eventually allowed the assumption of political rule through Amun-Re in parts of the country.

The king initially remained as the mediator between the divine and the human sphere in the New Kingdom. He was granted particular significance as god's son. God himself (Amun-Re) created the king and, in the divine council, decides on his fate. Under Akhenaten, the son of the sun god theologically became the junior partner of the first Egyptian theocracy. Together they commemorate the celebrations of rejuvenation, a spiritual privilege until now granted only to the king.

But although the kings made every effort to appease the gods with offerings, they were not able to uphold their own leading position within the cult; toward the end of the Ramesside Period Amun's high

16 Sphinx of Shepenupet
Late Period, Twenty-fifth Dynasty, ca. 720 BC; granite; L. 82 cm; Berlin, SMPK, Ägyptisches Museum, 7972.
The "god's wife of Amun," Shepenupet, daughter of King Piye, is depicted as a sphinx, the symbol of the ruler. She offers Amun a cult vessel with a ram's head, one of Amun's cult animals. Shepenupet's "Hathor wig" underscores her claim of royalty and divinity.

priests put severe political pressure on the monarchy. This is the manifestation for the inclusion of the gods, in particular of Amun-Re, king of all gods, into the historic sphere.

The duality of the conception of the afterlife continues in the New Kingdom. On the one hand, kings and ordinary citizens followed the solar theology, which offered the security of a perpetually renewed afterlife; on the other hand, the transformation into Osiris guaranteed physical eternity. Both were necessary for a successfully overcoming the threshold of death. This thought initially culminates in the Amduat, a funerary text that initiates the king's participation in the solar circulation. Other texts reserved exclusively for the king, such as the Book of Gates and the Book of Caverns, followed during the Ramesside Period. The Amduat describes the sun god's dangerous nocturnal voyage during which he mystically unites his body temporarily with Osiris. As the mobile part of this combination the sun god becomes the *ba* soul of Osiris. The merger of both circles is particularly evident here. The king has allowed his officials to inscribe this book in their tombs as well. For ordinary people, however, the more significant text was the Book of the Dead, a sort of basic version of the special books written for pharaohs. Since the Eighteenth Dynasty, ordinary persons begin to address god directly without going through a mediator.

The Divine World after the New Kingdom

The political powers having moved north, the cults of that region enjoyed increasing significance. While the primacy of Amun-Re appears to remain undisputed during the Twenty-first Dynasty, the following period of Libyan rule saw it gradually limited to the Theban area. The Libyan rulers worshipped the city god Harsaphes of Herakleopolis, where a Libyan central necropolis was located. In order to secure control of the Thebans, the Libyan rulers used a priestly office, for which evidence exists tracing it to the Eighteenth Dynasty: the "god's wife of Amun." By choosing female family members to fulfil this office the rulers in the north increased their influence in the south. But contemporary inscriptions prove that the Libyan rulers were excluded from Amun's mercy.

As there was no longer a mediator between the gods and the people, ordinary mortals were now forced to address the gods directly or to address a lesser-known god. Although only one god is mentioned and represented by religious images this hardly means that monotheism was practiced – either on a mental or a practical level; it signifies rather the god's omnipresent power, many aspects of which remained incomprehensible to ordinary people. The teachings of

17 Seated figure of the goddess Neith
Late Period, Twenty-sixth Dynasty, ca. 600 BC; bronze with gold inlays; H. 16 cm; Berlin, SMPK, Ägyptisches Museum, 15446. This fine, expertly crafted bronze is one of the most beautiful examples of its kind from the Late Period. The detailed workmanship is in complete harmony with the Saites' efforts to revitalize spiritually the grand classic epochs of the past. The small divine images may have been votive offerings for Neith's temple in Sais. As goddess of the city that produced the kings of the Twenty-sixth Dynasty, she wears the Lower Egyptian crown and once held a scepter in her left hand. In earlier times, Neith was worshipped as a warrior goddess, as indicated by her cult symbol, crossed arrows on a shield. Yet she was also regarded as a primeval goddess and she plays a maternal role in association with the crocodile god Sobek.

Amenemope have much in common with the teachings of the Old Testament, indicating a shared spiritual point of departure.

The further the god's distance from the official cult, the closer the proximity for the common believer. The god behind the religious images is the object of the ordinary person's attention. The pharaoh or the ordinary person offers the cult image to the deity in a shrine or at an altar, thus establishing a "residence" for the chosen god and ensuring his benevolence. The question of the separation of the gods from cult images was an on-going concern for Egyptian theologians that was now put into practice with vigor. But, as in the case of all innovations in ancient Egypt, it merely added a new facet to the established conceptions that remained.

The believer's introversion was boosted by his aversion of a cult driven by a foreign dynasty. This process was temporarily halted with the increasing intensity of the cult of Amun-Re and other gods in the Twenty-fifth Dynasty. The rulers of Upper Nubia, on whose territory one of the Amun cult's most significant sub-centers was located at Gebel Barkal, moved to Egypt in the eighth century BC in order to help re-establish the honor of Amun's cult. According to their own records, however, they also worshipped other traditional gods. Their inscriptions also show quite clearly that religion had become a political instrument.

The following Saite Dynasty, assisted to power by the Assyrians, encouraged the revitalization of ancient traditions with such intensity that this period was regarded as an Egyptian renaissance that even included the divine world. Despite this process, the so-called national gods lost their disproportionate influence in favor of smaller cults.

The new gods, advancing to levels of increasing importance since the Ramesside Period, are often regarded as gods of the people, although there are precious few indicators as to the validity of this title. It is also inaccurate to assume that the gods only now began to be responsible for specific domains. A deity could function as a patron god for a particular group of people; examples include Thoth for the scribes, or Ptah for the craftsmen. The new gods sometimes emerged from minor cults and insignificant gods advanced to new importance. This can only be ascertained from the failure of the large cults whose gods had become inaccessible.

A complicated conception of the cult image also forms a part of these religious changes. Animals are now generally kept at the temples, regarded simultaneously as cult image and the living divine element. The cult image is conceived as the god's *ka*, the animal as a living being is identified as the mobile *ba* soul, on whose relationship with the deceased corpse the Egyptians have reflected since the Middle Kingdom. The sacred animal is the *ka* figure, which can be inhabited by a god and, at the same time, the deity's living soul. The large variety of sacred animals can be explained with the large number of divine appearances; Egyptians obviously saw no contradiction in the combination of the two aspects.

The political power struggle between representatives of the Amun cult and the monarchy extends back as far as the Armana Period. With

the assumption of political rule by the high priests of the Amun cult during the Twenty-first Dynasty, one of the pillars of royal theology, the mediator between the celestial and the earthly sphere, is fundamentally thrown into question. The maintenance of the titles cannot conceal their exclusively political significance.

Of course, the kings attempted to keep traditions alive: the construction of new temples was encouraged. But preserved inscriptions tell us that the god, not the king, takes care of deceased officials. Amun-Re's intensified political activity, on the rise since the Eighteenth Dynasty, and the spatial separation of Amun's theocratic state in the south and the royal state in the north explains the irreversible departure from established conceptions of a kingdom. Even the temporary reestablishment of divine order (*maat*) under the kings of the Twenty-fifth Dynasty cannot reverse the separation. The monarchy has become a political institution, required to concentrate fully on maintaining power.

Entry into the sacred kingdom of Osiris is governed by the gods; the power over the fate of the deceased now lies in the hands of divinities and no longer with the king. This constitutes a shift of power away from pharaoh toward the gods, whose representatives strip the king of an increasing number of rights. The Osirian realm continues to flourish and remains the desired destination of the deceased. In order to reach this destination all sorts of magic is employed. All required items for the afterlife are brought ever closer to the deceased; burials are limited to the coffin and very little funerary equipment. But the Osirian funerary faith still maintains strong links with the cult of the sun. The kings seek new ways to ensure their well-being in the next world. The most interesting attempt to depart from the norm is probably the change in appearance of the mummiform coffin. For a short time, kings were buried in silver coffins decorated with the head of a falcon. Since the falcon-headed god could be linked to every deity who appeared as falcon or falcon-like, the significance of this new type of coffin is difficult to evaluate.

18 Horus and Nectanebo II
Late Period, Thirtieth Dynasty, ca. 350 BC; graywacke; H. 72 cm; New York, The Metropolitan Museum of Art, 34.2.1.
The god Horus with the Double Crown protects Pharaoh Nectanebo II. Horus's sovereignty over the pharaoh is thus clearly emphasized. This statue shows a development of an Old Kingdom statue type in reverse dimension.

The Systematization of Theology in the Ptolemaic-Roman Period

The fruitful encounter of the Greek spirit with Egyptian culture had a profound impact on the divine world. The new Macedonian rulers maintained traditional Greek cults within their circles, but were soon forced to show more respect for Egyptian religious tradition. In order to merge the Greeks with the Egyptians in the early Ptolemaic Period with the Egyptian tradition focusing on Osiris-Apis, a new god was created whose appearance completely corresponded to Hellenistic conceptions: Serapis.

The new god enjoyed considerable respect in the new capital "Alexandria of Egypt," but was not very popular in the rest of the country. Some deities, such as Osiris, Isis, and Anubis, were given a decidedly Hellenisitic appearance. While Osiris was still strongly associated with Egyptian traditions, Isis had been completely absorbed into a Hellenistic deity. Over time, the Isis cult was transformed into a myth to which only those believers who had participated in particular

19 Sacral garment (rear detail)
Late Ptolemaic – early Roman Period, ca. 30 BC; linen, red illustration; 73.5 x 105 cm; Cairo, Egyptian Museum, JE 59117.
In the midst of dense rushes, the young Horus's hiding place, Isis kneels on the hieroglyph for "gold," symbol for Seth, and holds a serpent (Osiris). The winged sun disk hovers above, as it does over Egypt. To the right, Isis-Uto with the Lower Egyptian crown worships the phoenix and to the left the same Isis-Nekhbet with Upper Egyptian crown worships a hybrid creature of scarab, crocodile, and snake; sun and moon hover above; the scene is to be understood in the context of time.

20 *Interior of the sarcophagus lid of Imeneminet*
Third Intermediate Period, ca. 1000 BC; wood, cloth with stucco, drawing; L. 187.5 cm; Paris, Musée du Louvre, E 5334.
The Osirian expectations of the deceased are depicted in compressed form in the various registers. The Osiris fetish of Abydos, protected by divine standards and by Isis and Nephthys, endangered by demons, is the symbol of Osiris' divine rule. This scene is a variant of the vignette of Chapter 138 of the Book of the Dead. The god is depicted in the barque of Sokar, the god of the Memphite Necropolis, in the following register. The final register shows Osiris having woken up, being delivered the sign of life by the vulture goddess, indicating the conception of the son.

initiation rites had access. The attraction of Egyptian gods was probably due to the fact that they had apparent power over fate.

Meanwhile, the traditional Egyptian cults, such as those of Horus of Edfu, Hathor of Dendara and other deities, flourished. The Greek colonists had given Greek names to the Egyptian gods; Amun was now called Zeus, Horus was Apollo and Bastet was Aphrodite. This Greek interpretation has sometimes helped us to recognize the character of the respective god in the Late Period. The god's principal seats were thus called Apollinopolis, Diospolis, Aphroditopolis, and so forth after the Greek fashion.

The temples became a safe haven for Egyptian thinking. The temple was a god's cosmos where he completed his creation. The Egyptians carved everything there is to know about the relevant god, his rituals, his cult myths, and the corresponding scrolls on the temple walls. The Ptolemaic and Roman temples therefore provide a tremendous amount of information on a particular deity that is only slowly coming to light. In some cases, traditions can be traced to earlier periods.

An increasingly apparent aspect of the Egyptian divine world is now the amalgamation of divine images. This sort of identification had been prevalent in hymns for some time, but images of deities – at times most bizarre – begin to appear only in the Late Period.

When Christianity came to full bloom in the form of the Coptic church in Egypt at the end of the second century AD, the country was soon profoundly influenced by a Christian elite who desired to impose their religious conception of monophysitism, which is based on the exclusively divine nature of Christ. The Copt's misunderstanding of the pharaonic monuments was immense. Coptic monks demolished most Egyptian visual art work when the Eremite movement began in the early third century and the monks retreated into abandoned caves (mostly old tombs). In the fourth century, Pachomius founded the monastic movement that was extended and completed by Shenute. All place names with the prefix "Deir" indicate many Coptic monasteries.

The Coptic god is the god of the Christians and shows no parallels to the Egyptian deities, although certain visual motifs such as the suckling divine mother may possibly have derived from the trinity of Osiris, Isis, and Horus. The new faith possessed two components lacking in Egyptian religion: ecstasy as the external form and mysticism as the internal form. In contrast to contemporary Egyptian religion, Coptic religion attracted a large proportion of the population. Egyptian cults were accessible only for the educated, yet they did not possess the characteristics of mythical faiths, for Egyptian religion was based on *maat*, the world order defined by god by which the gods themselves were also bound.

Although the Macedonian commander Ptolemy was surely no follower of Egyptian cults, he nonetheless crowned himself king of Egypt in the ancient city of Memphis. Without the consecration and anointing in Memphis his kingdom would not have been accepted by the Egyptians.

The early Ptolemies assimilated increasingly with the kings whose heritage they had assumed. The ancient practice of delegating

22 Horus as warrior
Probably first century AD; bronze; H. 46 cm;
London, The British Museum, EA 36062.
The divine court awards Horus, son of Osiris and Isis, his father's throne, but Seth also has designs on that position. During this period, Seth is no longer mentioned; Horus, on the other hand, the divine child on the throne of Egypt, continues to take his place as part of fundamental religious conceptions. In Hellenistic times, the old gods sometimes appear in new garments, as in this statue, which shows Horus in the dress of a Roman officer (imperator).

the royal role of priest was highly effective for the maintenance of the cult. They were able to secure the financial upkeep of the temples; taking care of the dead, however, had not formed part of the king's duties since the tenth century BC.

The Ptolemaic rulers began to practice a religious aspect that had only reluctantly been applied in earlier periods in Egypt – the apotheosis during life. Since Hellenistic rulers achieve divine status in areas outside the Egyptian cultural sphere, it remains to be clarified whether this conception can be derived from Egyptian faith or whether a general Hellenistic conception initiated these apotheoses.

In the final centuries of pharaonic culture the general principle applied that each individual was responsible for his or her own well-being. The Ptolemaic funerary rituals were of Greco-Macedonian origin and differed substantially from the Egyptian ones. In Upper Egypt, those who could afford it continued to have costly funerals, a tradition held over from previous centuries. The preservation of the body in the coffin was crucial, which explains the continued use of mummiform coffins, first developed in the Middle Kingdom.

The Greek population of the Faiyum used tomb sites very similar to those of the Egyptians; they changed the appearance of the actual mummy, however, by placing a portrait of the deceased within the bandages on the face. This mummy portrait, albeit used by Greeks and Hellenized Egyptians, may have had the same function as the reserve or replacement head in the Old Kingdom, which was used to help orient the free-floating soul. The portraits and mummification bear witness to the fact that the immigrants had absorbed the external aspects of the Egyptian funerary cult; it is, however, far from evident whether they also endorsed the corresponding theology.

21 (opposite) Mummy mask of a noblewoman
First century AD; linen, gilded stucco, glass, faience; H. 57.5 cm; New York, The Brooklyn Museum, 69.35.
The idea of the mummy-shaped sarcophagus is assimilated into the Hellenistic culture and becomes a symbol of the mixed culture of Ptolemaic–Roman Egypt. With reference to Egyptian tradition, the detail of the robe, arm and neck jewelry as well as treatment of the hair are especially strong indicators for a late production date for the masks.

Gods and Deities

Manfred Görg

Gods featured substantially in the lives of ordinary people in ancient Egypt. Their view of the world was not based on lifeless and abstract conceptions of distant spheres and inconceivable ages; they believed in powerful beings whose action was comprehensible and fathomable, and who moved around one another on a created stage, a sort of colossal world theater: the natural cosmos. For the people of ancient Egypt these beings, whatever their function, embodied the real world and the real form of living. Even where modern man might suspect chaos and death to dominate, the ancient Egyptian encounters a vital dynamic that stands in necessary and active contrast to the desired world. There is movement and drama, enacted by numerous gods in a sensual and visual world that the ordinary person is able to experience.

It is the diversity of the Egyptian divine world, which manifests itself in a conflict of binding uniformity and a diversity of forms, that simultaneously fascinates and vexes the ancient Egyptians as well as current observers. The bizarre form of appearance of the gods abandons all human aspects and begins to take on floral or animal features; the gods also begin to be present in attributes or symbols. Human gods, animal gods, floral gods – the natural state of living things mixes and elevates itself into the visual image of real powers that stand outside the strictly human. Here, aspects of the divine function attain significance within the chosen form. Fundamentally, however, it must be noted that the deity's actual character cannot be sensually experienced, even though its relevant forms of appearance do exist.

Three dimensions have become known to define comprehensively the reality of the divine world: every god presents himself by name, by his appearance within cosmic time, and by his image in the cult. This three-part manifestation does not, however, stand in the way of the conception of the unity of god but simply describes a universal significance that surpasses human comprehension. The conception of unity in diversity, that is the fundamental divine element in its various forms of appearance, accompanies us on our journey through the divine world of Egypt.

The Important Creator Gods

Let us begin with Atum, a god from very early times, based in Heliopolis, whose name means "completed" but also endorses the "not-yet-existing" and, therefore, bears a contradictory dimension: in the Middle Kingdom, for example, he is referred to as "the un-accomplished who has become accomplished" (coffin text). In the New Kingdom he is "Master of the universe, who existed before all others' and at the same time "Creator of primeval gods, who created Re so that he would be accomplished as Atum." As "father of the gods" he stands at the beginning of creation, the realization of which is told in the myth.

The myth continues from the point of the Egyptian's encounter with his real environment: here, the sun's daily voyage across the sky, from the beginning in the east, via the zenith at noon where its rays develop maximum power, to its setting in the west, where the cycle is completed. The three stages, evident in name through the embodiment of the morning sun in Khepri, the noonday sun in Re and the evening sun in Atum, culminate in the all-overpowering review of the evening god, out of whose accumulated potency creation is perpetually renewed.

The rarity of anthropomorphic depictions corresponds to the primary and universal role fulfilled by the god. The recently discovered statue cache in Luxor Temple features such a depiction. Inscriptions, headdress, and insignia identify the deity. More often it is a theriomorphic depiction that is linked to Atum's functions as hermaphroditic primeval god (amongst others as a lion or snake) or as sun god (amongst others as ram, beetle or ichneumon). Name, appearance, and depiction act together. They determine the deity's character and emphasize specific features. The link between theriomorphic appearance or depiction and the divine characteristic is not always evident for the modern observer. While analogies such as lion = strength and ram = fertility may seem perfectly obvious, the conceptions of the primeval god's features represented by the snake or of the beetle's power of regeneration can be examined in a number of religious texts.

23 Stela of Tanetperet
Thebes; Third Intermediate Period, Twenty-second Dynasty, ca. 850 BC; painted and stuccoed wood; H. 31 cm; Paris, Musée du Louvre, N 3663.

This small-format stela shows the falcon-headed figure of the sun god Re-Harakhty with the characteristic sun disk above his head. From the disk he emits life-giving rays in the form of rows of blossoms toward the female offerer, who worships him with upraised arms and presents a richly laden offering table. The cosmic framework of this scene is made up of a domed hieroglyph for heaven, which is supported on each side by two heraldic plants representing the two halves of the country (left: papyrus = Lower Egypt; right: lotus = Upper Egypt). Both plants emerge from human heads on the ground, representing humankind in general.

24 The god Atum; seated figure from a group statue with King Horemheb
Luxor; New Kingdom, late Eighteenth Dynasty, ca. 1300 BC; diorite; H. 190.7 cm, D. 151.5 cm, W. 83.5 cm; Luxor, The Luxor Museum of Ancient Egyptian Art, J. 837.
In 1989, an important cachette with buried statues of a number of gods was unearthed in Luxor Temple during routine conservation work. One of the first items found was a group statue with the pharaoh Horemheb kneeling in an offering pose before Atum. The seemingly rigid posture of the god underscores his dignity; he is depicted here with the Double Crown and holding the sign of life in his right hand.

25 The king offers before Amun
Western Thebes, Deir el-Bahari, temple of Thutmosis III, Hathor chapel; New Kingdom, Eighteenth Dynasty, ca. 1440 BC; painted limestone; H. 225 cm, W. 157 cm; Cairo, Egyptian Museum, JE 38574–5.
Thutmosis III built a rock-cut chapel in the valley of Deir el-Bahari (Western Thebes) for the statue of the Hathor cow. Today, both chapel and statue can be seen in the Egyptian Museum, Cairo. The rear wall shown here depicts Thutmosis III offering water and incense to the national and universal god Amun-Re. The tall, delicate feathers on his crown associate Amun-Re with the tangible yet invisible effect of moving air, and simultaneously identify him as the highest god of the New Kingdom.

The cosmic appearance of the primeval god, manifested by the three phases Khepri, Re, and Atum, comes to full effect through the emphasis of natural order and powers as expressed in the myth. The myth also reveals a conception of the world that does without abstractions and formulae but which defines the world as a living environment. Atum creates the Heliopolitan view (see p. 448, no. 43) by spewing out the air deity Shu and the humidity deity Tefnut, out of whom, in turn, the divine pair Nut (sky goddess) and Geb (earth god) are created. With the gods of the underworld the divine world has been transformed into an ennead (or group of nine), which is, from then on, defined as a mythical, non-numerical approximation for the wealth of divine truth.

The hardly less drastic or less intense conception of Ptah of neighboring Memphis competes with the cosmic (but not supra-natural) state of the primeval god Atum. Ptah's name defines him as the "maker" and "opener," that is also as a primeval and creator deity. According to the "Memphite theology," which only achieved the state of development we are familiar with in the royal residence of the New Kingdom, his "tongue" creates what his "heart" has designed, for example the diversity of the divine world as it was revered in Heliopolis. Ptah presides over the ennead in his very own style, his name defines the "maker," the divine craftsman, comparable to the Greek Hephaistos. Ptah's common epithets describe him as a deity "with an accessible face." The numerous depictions of Ptah usually show him anthropomorphic and in rigid pose, standing in a sort of chapel, with blue cap and tassel, holding the scepter with both hands. Here, his capacity as ruler of *maat* is manifest. Ptah has a special relationship with the kingdom and embodies the basic principle of the incarnation of the divine.

As in the central cult sites of ancient Egypt, Ptah also holds a divine triad's top position. Triads, which usually appear as divine families in the constellation father–mother–child, form the mytho-logical basis of actual cult events. In Memphis, the goddess Sakhmet and the divine child Nefertem stand by Ptah's side. The goddess Sakhmet, whose name means the "powerful," carries her name as the embodiment of vital dynamism, which manifests itself initially as protection, though, later, increasingly, as militant defence. In the myth she appears as an aggressive goddess who, according to the Book of the Heavenly Cow, is even prepared to annihilate mankind. She symbolizes in the most exemplary manner the healing and aggressive deity and thus endorses the apotropean (evil-preventing) concept that resides in all saints. The lion-headed figure, which often appears in sculptures in the round, emphasizes this double-aspect, which has a pendant in the depictions of the Theban mother deity Mut.

The Universal God Amun

In the triad of significant cosmogonies (notions of the creation of the world) first to consider is that of Hermopolis, which sees the mysterious primeval god Amun, "the hidden one," at the very beginning of the world. Initially belonging to the primeval gods of chaotic prehistory, he enters a process of transformation that leads him to the top of the Egyptian pantheon. Here, he combines with the sun god Re and finally creates an "composite deity" with the character of a world god.

Amun embodies the elementary life force, which remains obscure, which creates itself (Kamutef) and the expression of which takes place in space and time. As a god with pneumatic qualities his impact is felt everywhere, his breath is felt, but his provenance and destination remain unknown. As an air deity he is related to Shu. As the principal god of Thebes, the metropolis of the New Kingdom, he presides over the triad with the goddess Mut, comparable to Sakhmet, and the divine child Khonsu, the sky-traveler (moon god) and "maker of plans." As national and universal god Amun-Re is "father of all gods." The majority of Egyptian poetry is dedicated to Amun; he is the god who "has made himself into millions." In cult-related iconography, he often appears as a god on a throne, with a human face and bearing the so-called feather crown, which points to his celestial function. The name of the famous king Tutankhamun signals the relationship between the king and Amun in a most exquisite manner. The pharaoh's god-like image is a result of the unique relationship between Amun and the ruler.

In times of growing convergence of the southern and northern parts of the country (Upper and Lower Egypt respectively), the conception of the national triad, consisting of the high gods Re, Ptah, and Amun, emerges from the regional triad of figures of a stylized divine family.

One of the most revealing religious images of the national triad can be seen in the inner sanctum of the famous rock-cut temple of Abu Simbel (see p. 215, no. 128). The presence of the temple's builder and most powerful pharaoh of all times, Ramesses II, to the right of the Heliopolitan sun god Re may be confusing; but what we see is the manifestation of a self-conscious yet honest choice that elevates the king, in surpassing his title as "the son of god" onto the divine platform and, in this particular and extraordinary case, allows him to "take his place to the right of the almighty father." The position of the divine figures Re, Ptah, and Amun in conjunction with the pharaoh as god amongst gods recalls the cosmological pattern, which, finally, forms the basis for all central conceptions of creation. The primeval god, initially at home on the level of divine manifestation of chaos, elevates himself from the night in order to illuminate and rectify the world with his powerful beam, to perpetually re-create space that is linked with Ptah (Tatenen) and, finally, to attain absolute rule of the day and the cycle of time in the embodiment of Re. Only this elevation enables the implementation of the divine partner on earth, the king, who coope-rates with the sun god to ensure the well-being of cosmic events.

26 Statue of Ptah
Western Thebes, tomb of Tutankhamun; New Kingdom, Eighteenth Dynasty, ca. 1325 BC; gilded wood, faience, bronze, glass; figure: H. 52.8 cm; pedestal: H. 7.4 cm, D. 26 cm, W. 11.6 cm; Cairo, Egyptian Museum, JE 60739. Ptah is depicted here as the lord of world order. He is the god "with accessible face" whose word created the world. The deity stands on a pedestal whose exterior is based on the hieroglyph for truth, justice, and the righteous world order (*maat*). This partic-ularly beautiful and highly detailed statue was found in the tomb of Tutankhamun.

27 Seated statue of the goddess Sakhmet
Karnak; New Kingdom, Eighteenth Dynasty, ca. 1380 BC;
granite; H. 205 cm, D. 97 cm, W. 54 cm; Cairo, Egyptian
Museum, CG 39063.
The inscriptions on the seat of the goddess date the statue to
the time of Amenophis III, who had erected 800 stone statues
of this deity in the Mut temple of Karnak. This unique
construction project involving so many statues may be
accounted for by the belief that Sakhmet had been granted
magical healing powers which were to be employed in the care
of the chronically ill pharaoh.
The image of the deity with a lion's head, Sakhmet, characterized in inscription as "the ruler of fear," exemplifies more
than words ever could do the perpetual fascination of experi-
encing divine truth.

28 Statue of Horus
New Kingdom, Nineteenth Dynasty, ca. 1250 BC; syenite;
H. 163 cm; Munich, Staatliche Sammlung Ägyptischer Kunst,
GI.WAF 22.
The sky and royal god Horus is depicted here as human with a
falcon's head. This kind of image must not be misinterpreted
as an attempt to describe the appearance of a god. The animal
head is used to emphasize non-human characteristics the god
might possess. The long hair is a clever solution to ease the
transition from animal to human appearance in this statue. It
was found in Rome, in the former sector of the Temple of Isis
and Serapis, where it had been brought in antiquity.

29 Seated statue of the goddess Hathor
Luxor; New Kingdom, Eighteenth Dynasty, ca. 1370 BC;
diorite; H. 154 cm, L. 77 cm, W. 40.5 cm; Luxor, The Luxor
Museum of Ancient Egyptian Art, J 835.
Hathor, protectress of Western Thebes, goddess of heaven and
of love, is depicted here on a throne with a sign of life in her
left hand. In the inscription on her throne Amenophis III
declares himself beloved by her; he thus identifies himself as
the donor of this masterpiece in Luxor Temple, where it was
found in 1989, along with many other statues.

Heavenly Gods and Royal Gods

The notion of the "almighty father," which is also expressed in the kingdom triad, combines with the conception of the transformation of the primeval god in a process (that is the cyclical transformation of the sun god) to a divine figure of some magnitude called Re-Harakhty, "Horus of the horizon/the land of light." This figure indicates the mythological dimension of celestial power. In Re-Harakhty, the cosmic and universal role of the supreme god, who strides through the diurnal cycle, is presented; this god not only stands above heaven and the pantheon but is characterized by a mythical accessibility. The falcon-like appearance elevates the notion of distance, omnipresence, and insight, associated with the high-flying and visually acute falcon, to the highest level at which this deity can be experienced in distance and in proximity like no other.

One of the most important deities in the Egyptian pantheon is Horus, who is included in the name Harakhty, and whose name signifies "the distant one," that is the messenger and mediator of divine mystery. Horus is linked with the supreme in such a manner that in the divine world he is referred to as the "son of the sun god." This title has comprehensive significance in religious and historical terms as it forms the basis for every "son of god" theology. On earth, his position corresponds to that of the king, classified as the "son of Re" since the Third Dynasty, who maintains this title into Greco-Roman times. The falcon-headed Horus is embodied in the king who thus has a share of Horus's diverse presence in mythology. In the narrative myth, as his father's avenger, Horus comes into conflict with Seth, who has gradually been established as the embodiment of evil in Egypt. Horus is victorious and thus becomes the protagonist in the victory over death and the powers of chaos.

In the religious world of the Mediterranean, Horus, who embodies the symbolic figure of the eternal battle of light against darkness, enjoys exceptionally widespread significance in the form of the Horus child (Greek: *Harpokrates*). The Horus myth, for instance, recounts that Horus was borne out of the encounter of his divine mother Isis and his dying father Osiris who has been slain by Seth, and that he was initially kept hidden only to emerge finally and defeat his persecutor. The amulet depicting the divine child above the dangerous animal forces of chaos is one of the most famous and popular Egyptian "export products;" hardly surprising, since it magically ensured everyone protection from life-threatening violence and disease.

Mother and Love Goddesses

The maternal deity Hathor, whose name "house of Horus" implies clearly that she carries and enables the incarnation of the most supreme god, is strongly linked to the conceptions of Creation. As all-encompassing "ruler," her eyes are cast east, west, north, and south; she encompasses all aspects of life, from the joy of everyday existence to the exoticism of the attractive but unattainable distance of the Realm of the Dead. As a distant goddess who has left Egypt she must be brought back into the myth in order to secure the stability of earthly and celestial life. She is guarantor of creative love and of perpetually renewing vitality. Her iconography depicts her with a human face, crowned with ox-horns framing a sun disk: attributes of creative and regenerative power. She also appears in the form of a cow, providing the king with life force. As a savior, regardless of the circumstances, she is revered by large portions of the population.

Like Hathor, Isis is also to be understood as a mother of god. Since the New Kingdom, but particularly in the first century BC, she increas-

30 Stela of Horus
Early Ptolemaic Period, ca. 300 BC; slate; H. 44 cm, D. 12 cm, W. 26 cm; Cairo, Egyptian Museum, CG 9401
Horus the child ("Harpokrates"), in the nude and featuring the Egyptian sidelock of youth, effortlessly defeats all sorts of dangerous animals with his hands and feet. The divine child is depicted here as the one who triumphs over all manner of evil and fearsome creatures. The addition of the head of the god Bes, above Horus, is meant to increase the stela's effectiveness against any disease or disaster.

ingly assumes positions and functions formerly associated with Hathor, so that far beyond Egypt's boundaries she eventually becomes the "goddess of all goddesses." While the significance of her name is still disputed, she can nonetheless appear as Osiris's spouse and mother of Horus from the earliest times. The mythical mating makes her the figure of ultimate conception, a "virgin" and "divine spouse," ruler of magic and of heaven; the care and protection she extends to the Horus child makes her appear as an exemplary protector deity. As an attribute and unmistakable symbol the throne appears on her head. Apparently, this symbol does not represent the object but is a hieroglyph that phonetically represents the name of the goddess. It is hardly surprising then that Isis in particular should become the classic mother of god beyond Egypt, in the Mediterranean and in Europe, since her constellation with Horus as "nourishing Isis" could serve later religious images as a model.

Gods and People

The myth surrounding Horus, Isis, and Seth relates to a deity without which the human hope for an afterlife, indeed the belief in the ascension of the dead that had evolved in ancient Near Eastern religious history, would be unthinkable. We are, of course, referring to Osiris, whose name remains as enigmatic as that of his spouse. Osiris is originally a deity of vegetation and harvest from the Delta area. At Abydos, he becomes the "foremost of the westerners," that is he is representative and guarantor of eternal life, the resurrection of the dead and of ultimate vindication. The myth, after all, shows his metamorphosis from the physical, which depends on the victory of the avenging Horus. Re shares the supervision of the cycle of cosmic life with Osiris and delegates the supervision of the night and the Realm of

31 Isis with the Horus-child, Osiris, and Harpokrates
Late Period, Twenty-sixth Dynasty, ca. 600 BC; bronze, gold leaf, glass; Isis: H. 28 cm, Osiris: H. 24.5 cm, Harpokrates: H. 22.1 cm; Vienna, Ägyptisch-Orientalische Sammlung, 8564, 6622, 4162.
The figure of Isis (right) is seated on a lion throne with the Horus-child on her lap, an image later to become a model for Mary with baby Jesus. Isis is crowned with cow's horns and sun disk on a diadem base surrounded by cobras.

The mummiform figure of Osiris is equipped with the crook and flail, emblems of power. He wears the Atef crown featuring side feathers and a cobra above his brow.
The statuette of the adolescent Horus, Harpokrates, shows him in the nude and equipped only with a royal headdress, the sidelock of youth and an impressive *hemhem* crown (made of feathers, bundles of plants, sun disk, and cobras on a ram's horns). He holds an index finger to his mouth: a child's gesture.

32 Osiris, ruler of the realm of the dead, with the insignia of power
Deir Durunka (near Asiut), Cult chamber of Amenophis' rock tomb, right long wall; New Kingdom, Nineteenth Dynasty, ca. 1280 BC; limestone; chamber: H. 260 cm, W. 150 cm, D. 230 cm; relief block on average: H. 110 cm; Berlin, SMPK, Ägyptisches Museum, 2/63-3/63, 1/64-2/64.

In his capacity as judge in the celestial court, Osiris embodies ascension and eternal life for the just. He sits on a throne in his shrine; Nephthys and Isis stand behind him and raise their arms protectively. In front of the shrine, Horus and Thoth report the evaluation process that determines whether or not the deceased has lived righteously.

33 Statuette of mourning Isis
Late Period, Twenty-sixth Dynasty, ca. 600
BC; wood, painted stucco layer; H. 40.5 cm,
W. 10.4 cm, D. 28.3 cm; Hildesheim,
Pelizaeus-Museum, 1584.
Isis, kneeling on the ground, holds her right
hand flat to her mouth: she contemplates her
dead brother and spouse Osiris in bewildered
silence. She symbolically wears the hieroglyph for "throne" on her head; the same sign
is used to spell her name.

the Dead to him. He serves as judge who assists in accessing the sun
god after the council of the dead has passed a favorable verdict.

Egyptian gods are not alien to passion or emotion, even if they are
characterized by eminence and aloofness. The myth allows them to
attain human features from time to time. Particularly when facing
death, and despite all efforts to achieve eternal life, the Egyptian is left
with fear and sorrow, as manifested by the silently mourning Isis. Yet
mourning, along with lamentation, represent the "entry" into the way
out of desperation. Isis is not only a guiding light at birth but also a
patron for the transition from this life to the next. In Egyptian religious
history, every deceased individual is transformed in a mythical process
of unification into the god Osiris in order to share in Isis's life-
enhancing care. Life and death are bound within a system that
permeates the universe and that determines the relationships between
mortals and the gods. This concept, almost impossible to translate into
our language, is the fundamental order Maat, worshipped by the
Egyptians in the form of a female deity and even the daughter of
the sun god. Despite its extraordinary significance Maat hardly makes
its presence felt in iconography, not even where it is placed opposite
a deity as an explanatory attribute. The constellation of the small
figure of Maat next to the large Ibis, the visualization of the god
Thoth, clearly demonstrates by what form of authority even failed
gods must abide. Because Thoth is the wisest of all gods he is the
"master" of science and art, of mathematics and medicine. He is
the divine messenger, comparable to the Greek god Hermes, and
he possesses an esoteric aura. Thoth, the "threefold largest"
(Trismegistos), must be regarded as the religious-historical ancestor of
the Egyptian gnosis.

If Maat is already able to challenge the patriarchal claim on the
Egyptian philosophy of life and the world, further proof that the notion
of a maternal deity is of increasing significance can be found in the
seemingly less representative goddess Neith. This goddess, whose
name is probably linked to the conception of primeval water, was
initially understood as a warrior goddess, equipped with bow and
arrow. In the Late Period, she became the ultimate creator goddess,
possessing male and female qualities. Her descriptive epithets are
"father of fathers" and "mother of mothers." In her position as ruler of
the Lower Egyptian city of Sais with the religious-political weight of
the Twenty-sixth Dynasty, her attraction also increased within the
Greek conceptions of divinity so that she was on a par with the Greek
goddess Athena.

Maternal goddess and primeval goddess permeate the
conceptions of ordinary people, even outside the official cults that are
maintained by the country's prominent citizens. The goddesses
Meretseger and Thoeris were characteristic for the savior deities in the
everyday life of ordinary people. The former, whose name means "she
who loves silence," rules over life and death and usually appears with a

34 Statuette of Thoth and his spouse Maat
Late Period, Twenty-sixth Dynasty, ca. 600
BC; wood, bronze, gold leaf, glass; H. 19.5 cm,
L. 20 cm; Hanover, Kestner-Museum,
1957.83.
Thoth is represented by his sacred animal, the
ibis. As god of knowledge and script, who
determines and describes the world's events,
Thoth is joined by the "righteous world
order," Maat, goddess of truth and justice
with her common attribute, the ostrich
feather, on her head.

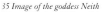

35 Image of the goddess Neith
Western Thebes, Valley of the Kings, tomb of Seti I (KV 17); New Kingdom, Nineteenth Dynasty, ca. 1280 BC.
In the eleventh hour of the Amduat, Neith appears in several forms; the examples shown here wear the crown of Lower Egypt charac-teristic for this goddess. Initially patron god-dess of the Delta city Sais, she attained sub-stantial prominence during the Twenty-sixth Dynasty when that city became capital of Egypt, and enjoyed renewed cultural and political importance.

36 Stela of Hay
Western Thebes; New Kingdom, Twentieth Dynasty, ca.1150 BC; limestone; H. 43 cm; Turin, Museo Egizio, Cat. 1606.
Workers on the Theban royal tombs offered this small stela to two goddesses: Thoeris, the hippopotamus patron goddess of pregnant women, responsible for the continuity of families, and Meretseger, a snake goddess, who resided in the valley where the royal tombs were located. The usually deadly cobra is reduced to the head of a slim female figure who holds the sign of life ankh in the center of the stela, in front of Thoeris's stomach. An enormous wig surrounds the snake's head and hood, which is crowned by cow's horns and a sun disk.

cobra face, indicating a spiritual kinship with the wise Maat. Meretseger comes from the tradition of life-creating goddesses, as do the cobra goddess of the harvest Renenutet, and Isis. She is also closely related to Hathor, and her effective companion is the patron goddess of pregnant women, Thoeris, "the great one." Equipped with the headdress of Hathor, they represent the creation of life on earth and in the hereafter. Appearing as a hippopotamus, and sometimes decorated with a crocodile's shell, Thoeris is the powerful, pregnant savior figure, represented in large-scale sculpture in the round as well as in miniature art, such as decorative amulets.

The kindness of the feline goddess Bastet is hard to ignore, even if this is only one of Bastet's many fascinating features. She is at home in Bubastis, a city in the Nile Delta that owes its name to her. Bastet is, like the unpredictable animal that is her symbol, a strong-willed goddess, related to Hathor (who originates in the distance) and supportive of women in their prayers for fertility and the safe delivery of children.

The most popular deity, though, is Bes; grotesque and dwarfish, loved by all as a dancer and musician, he is also the "little devil." The

37 Figure of Bastet
Saqqara, Serapeum; Late Period, sixth century BC; bronze, gold inlays; H. 14 cm; Cairo, Egyptian Museum, CG 38991.
The cat goddess Bastet is depicted here in an almost comical, even "cute" fashion as a woman with a cat's head carrying a basket on her left arm. She can, however, also appear as a wild lion goddess.

mythical dimension links him to the exotic Hathor whom he retrieves from far away in order to soothe her. Images of Bes adorn temple walls and votive offerings as well as everyday utensils and instruments. It is hardly surprising, then, that the Greeks had considered assimilating Bes with Pan, the disrupter of "mischief."

Outside the Pantheon

To conclude our journey through the pantheon we will look at two gods who, although by no means related to one another, both have particularly alien characteristics.

Serapis is a deity whose combined name consists of Osiris and Apis and thus reveals the nature of his composition. The artificial birth of Serapis in Alexandria was supposed to have helped Greeks and Egyptians to find a common orientation. Osiris and the Apis bull remind the Egyptian of vital renewal while the image of Zeus illustrates the inclusion in Greek religion. Serapis is worshipped as the savior in life and death, as the revealer in the oracle, as the redeemer in sickness and as the seafarer's companion. He is known in the entire Mediterranean and his reputation stretches as far as the Occident. His iconography contributes to the representation of the creator god in early Chrisian art. For the Egyptians, however, he remains an alien divinity.

Aten, the god named after the "sun disk," was supposed to have attained the position of "the One and Only" under Akhenaten (Amenophis IV). The principle of duality of Egyptian religion, that is of the One next to the Many, was temporarily suspended in this monotheistic model. Aten, a type of creator deity, formed as an alternative to the increasingly spiritual Amun and accessible only through the royal family, remained sufficiently attractive even after the fall of Amarna religion. Subsequently, the notion of "one who has become millions" applied even more than before to the Ramesside world god Amun-Re.

39 Cameo with Serapis and Isis
Late Ptolemaic Period; ca. 100 BC; multi-colored sardonyx, gold (setting from sixteenth century AD); 3.5 cm x 2.8 cm; Vienna, Kunsthistorisches Museum, inv. IX A 8.
The stepped busts of the gods Serapis and Isis display the brilliant achievements of the stone cutter's art. The Ptolemies combined in their new god Serapis the external appearance of the Greek father of the gods, Zeus, with the essential nature of the Egyptian god Apis-Osiris of Memphis.

40 Domestic altar with a scene of the Amarna royal family
New Kingdom, Eighteenth Dynasty, ca. 1340 BC; limestone; H. 44 cm, W. 39 cm; Cairo, Egyptian Museum, JE 44865.
Small domestic altars with the image of the royal family beneath the life-giving rays of the sun god Aten were installed by priests and officials of Amarna, city of the heretic king Akhenaten. Here he and Nefertiti play with their daughters, thus transmitting the sun's power to the person praying before the altar.

Conceptions of the Cosmos – The Universe

Günter Burkard

Our view of the cosmos today is based on scientific achievements: the earth is round and forms part of a planetary system that rotates around the sun, which is, in turn, part of a gigantic galactic system, the Milky Way. The Milky Way forms part of a universe, the unfathomable and infinite extent of which we have yet to explore fully.

Many questions still remain to be answered: where does the cosmos come from? Did it really originate in the Big Bang? For how long will it continue to expand? And what will happen at the end? Will it, in the distant future, contract and disappear? Only one thing is certain: after millions of years, a timescale we can hardly fathom, the sun will die and, subsequently, so will our planet earth.

Until just a few hundred years ago, the view of the world was characterized by geocentricity: the earth was the center around which the sun, the moon, and other stars rotated. One of the first people to challenge this predominantly theologically inspired conception, Galileo Galilei, was accused of heresy by the church and only recently officially rehabilitated.

Let us go back several millennia and examine the world view of the Egyptians, their conception of the cosmos: it was, as one soon learns, also characterized by geocentricity or, to be more precise, "Egyptocentricity." But more importantly, we find that the Egyptians were fundamentally asking the same questions that we struggle with today: where does the universe come from, how is it maintained, and how will it end? Prior to the modern study of the natural sciences, theological speculations had, of course, an important bearing on these matters, but there were other perspectives; the observation of nature, the solar cycle or the annual cycle, with the regular occurrence of the Nile flood, played a vital part in the deliberations.

But we also soon discover that an Egyptian view of the world *per se* did not exist. A variety of conceptions were nurtured in the different religious centers, such as Hermopolis in Middle Egypt, or in the ancient capital of Memphis, and later also in Upper Egypt, as Esna or Edfu. The priesthood of the temple of Heliopolis, where the theology of the sun god Re was formed, undoubtedly played a crucial role in this matter.

Despite all the differences, certain features common to all systems are discernible. The Egyptian conception of the cosmos contained three regions: the underworld, earth, and heaven. The underworld was the realm of the dead and of the gods of the hereafter, in particular Osiris, the god of the dead. Earth was the kingdom of the living, of the people, and of Creation. Heaven, finally, was the kingdom of the cosmic deities, in particular the sun god, and the moon and stars.

The Egyptians did not yet conceive of earth as a ball; this discovery was made by Greek natural philosophers. But it was in Egypt that the Greek Eratosthenes calculated the earth's circumference for the first time, in the third century BC.

According to the Egyptians, the earth was conceived as a disk surrounded by primeval waters, *nun*. Egypt formed the center, which is why we speak of Egyptocentricity. The *nun* also surrounded the remaining two regions, heaven and underworld, so that the entire cosmos was firmly lodged within an immeasurably huge primeval ocean. The Nile was nourished by the nun, particularly during the annual flood, and the land, in turn, was nourished by the Nile. One creation myth states that first a "primeval hill" was raised from the *nun* and that from that hill all life was created.

Heaven was conceived as a sort of dome, a stage on which the sun god Re traveled in his barque every day, descending in the evening at the "western horizon" into the underworld. He traveled eastbound through the underworld and reappeared in the morning on the "eastern horizon." During the night, moon and star gods resided in heaven. Four pillars, erected at the boundaries of earth, supported this "world building," the universe.

Let us take a closer look at these three regions. The deceased reach the underworld, the realm of Osiris, the god of the dead. Here, they stand before the celestial court, presided over by Osiris as senior judge, their contented existence in the afterlife, after being declared "true of voice" or "justified" by the court. Aside from this conception of the hereafter as a mirror image of life on earth, there were darker notions; the hereafter was also regarded as a world full of dangers and horrors, surmountable only by the initiated.

The sun god Re descended into this dangerous world every night, and traveled through it for twelve nocturnal hours from the west to the east. He stood in his barque, which was pulled by several deities and protected by yet others, in particular by Seth, the mighty and violent god usually associated with the role of divine enemy. This protection was quite necessary, as Re was threatened by a number of demonic creatures, amongst others his worst enemy, the Apophis snake. On his nocturnal crusade through the individual regions of the underworld, Re temporarily offered the resident creatures and beings light and, therefore, life.

People had different but very precise conceptions of the underworld's geography that were extensively documented in pictorial maps, using both text and images. These all served the purpose of helping the deceased find his or her way in the underworld, providing protection from the dangers that loomed there. Many of these guides, known as "Book of Two Ways," "Book of Gates," Book of Caverns," "Book of the Earth God" and so on have been preserved, particularly on the walls of royal tombs of the New Kingdom but also in papyrus

41 The sky goddess Nut
Dendara, Temple of Hathor, ceiling of the New Year Chapel, Greco-Roman Period, first century BC.

In front of the goddess's mouth is the evening sun that she swallows; on her lap is the morning sun that she will bear. The latter is depicted here as it sends its rays onto the

temple of Hathor at Dendara. The temple is symbolized by a pillared capital with the head of Hathor, located between two tree-covered desert mountains.

42 Nocturnal voyage of the sun god in his barque
Mythological papyrus of the Herubes (detail); Third Intermediate Period, Twenty-first Dynasty, ca. 900 BC; painted papyrus; H. 23.5 cm; Cairo, Egyptian Museum, no index number.
The barque is pulled by four jackals; below, four cobra deities are shown, arms raised in prayer. In the boat we see the sun god, behind him Horus and Thoth, in front of him Seth, striking the Apophis snake with his spear as the snake aggressively winds itself around the boat and rises before him. Behind the boat is a lion deity cutting up Apophis. Several knives are already stuck into the snake's body.

manuscripts or, in the case of the Book of Two Ways, on the floor of sarcophagi. The most common guide, apart from the Amduat, the "Book of that which is in the Underworld," is the Book of the Dead, which was placed in the deceased's tomb in a papyrus scroll; a great number of Books of the Dead have been preserved.

Earth, by contrast, was the place of the living, with Egypt, as noted previously, at its center. The Nile constituted the north–south axis of this world, and the solar cycle the east–west axis. Egypt's boundaries were the first Nile cataract to the south, the Mediterranean coast to the north and the desert mountains to the east and west, behind which the sun rose and set. Beyond these boundaries stretched the regions of chaos, of alien lands, the kingdom of enemies, in short, everything that was non-Egyptian. Egyptians were inclined to southern orientation: the terms for "right" and "west" are identical, as are the words for "left" and "east."

The celestial dome was more like a baldachin, supported by the four pillars erected at the world's end points. In another conception, the sky goddess Nut was perceived as bending over earth, hands and feet on earthly ground representing the four pillars, her torso representing the sky dome. This was the sun god's travel route, where the moon rose and set and where the stars appeared. Nut swallowed the sun at night, only to bear it the following day after it had traveled through her body. The stars traveled in much the same way through the sky goddess's body during the day. Rain was occasionally explained as an overflow of the primeval waters, *nun*, which, of course, also surrounded heaven. The Egyptians also had a clear conception of the different celestial regions, which are described in some detail, particularly in the royal pyramid texts of the Old Kingdom.

But how was this world created, how is it maintained, and how will it end? Several creation myths tell the story. Let us look at the creator god Atum, characterized by the Heliopolitan theology. His testimony, scripted in the first person, is preserved on a papyrus scroll from the fourth century BC.

In the beginning there is the primeval ocean, *nun*, in which the creator god floats lethargically and inactively. This primeval state, the

chaotic world without order, was not the result of a conscious act of creation – it was simply already there, pre-existent. Finally, after a long but undefined period, the creator god rises from the *nun* after he had found a place "where I could stand," as he puts it. This place eventually rises as the primeval hill out of the *nun*. Then, he reports, "I aroused myself with my fist, copulated with my hand and spew out (the seed) from my mouth: I spew out Shu and I spew out Tefnut." Thus the first divine couple was created, Shu, god of life, air, and light and Tefnut, goddess of moisture. The primeval god was, therefore, still hermaphroditic, he was father and mother of the gods. From Shu and Tefnut, Geb, the earth god and Nut, the sky goddess were born under circumstances not further explained. Now Shu raised Nut over the reclining Geb: thus heaven and earth were created. From the physical [sexual] union of Geb and Nut the deities Osiris, Isis, Seth, and Nephthys are created. The divine ennead of Heliopolis was thus completed and creation was able to continue.

Other conceptions of the creation of the world were similar, and still others were fundamentally different. At Heliopolis were conceived a group of eight primeval gods in pairs. In Memphis it is the creator god Ptah "in whose heart," that is in whose imagination, the will to create was formed and subsequently transformed into words. Here, as in Christianity, creation through the word is realized.

It is noteworthy that the creation of man is usually only mentioned in passing and with few words. In Atum's testimony of Creation, for instance, he says: "When I cried, man was created in the form of tears flowing from my eyes." Such an image was possible because puns played an integral part in Egyptian mythological thinking. The terms for "tear" and "human" are very similar.

The cosmos was not static but engaged in a dynamic, or rather cyclic stream of events. It was not a world created only once but constituted a process of perpetual repetition, comprehensible most sensibly in the daily solar cycle. That is why one referred to Creation as "the First Time", which was followed by several more "times." Surely, the observation of natural events played a crucial part in this conception. Nature's cycle manifested itself in the daily solar cycle, the lunar phases, the seasonal cycle and, last but not least, in the phenomenon of the annual Nile floods. The conception of the periodic repetition of what had previously taken place once developed from there. When a king ascended the throne, for example, he was obliged to reform the world order, eliminate chaos, and unify the "Two Lands," that is Egypt.

This cycle, however, was in constant danger of being disrupted. The sun god, for example, was prone to much danger during his nocturnal voyage through the underworld. A disruption would mean

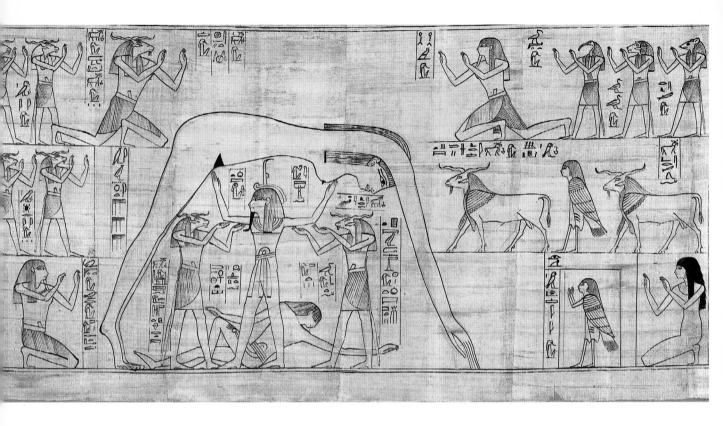

43 The creation of heaven and earth
Greenfield papyrus (sheet 87): Book of the Dead of Nesitanebtasheru (detail); Third Intermediate Period, Twenty-first Dynasty, reign of Psusennes I, ca. 1025 BC; inscribed papyrus; H. 47 cm; The British Museum, EA 10554.
The god Shu, supported by two ram deities, raises Nut, the goddess of heaven, over the reclining earth god Geb, symbolizing the creation of heaven and earth. Nut is depicted as the "celestial dome" and her hands and feet touch the ground on the earth.

44 The celestial cow
Western Thebes, Valley of the Kings, tomb of Seti I; New Kingdom, Nineteenth Dynasty, ca. 1280 BC; British Library (watercolor by Robert Hay).
Since the New Kingdom, heaven also appears in Egyptian conceptions as a cow. Among the gods who assist the cow in this illustration, the god Shu, supporting the cow's body, is the dominant figure. He manifests the same position as in the conception with Nut. The nocturnal stars are painted into the cow's body.

45 Pillared hall of Ptolemy VIII, Euergetes II
Philae, Temple of Isis; Ptolemaic Period, ca. 150 BC; (color engraving by Lepère for the *Déscription de l'Égypte* I, pl. 18, 1809).
The temple as microcosm: plant-like pillars rise from the primeval swamp, their capitals support the temple roof, that is heaven. Above the gate in the center we see the sun god in his barque, greeted in prayer by several deities. The top right margin of the ceiling is depicted as the night sky, with images of the goddess of heaven Nut and a star-studded night sky. On the walls and pillars there are numerous depictions of the king, performing the ritual before a variety of deities.

the end of the world. An enormous effort had to be made, particularly in the daily temple rituals, in order to meet this challenge and maintain the order and the course of the world. Keeping disruption of the world cycle at bay was the central duty of the king as executor of the rituals. The walls of all Egyptian temples contained images of such rituals, and it was always the king who executed them. Despite their conception of a world cycle the Egyptians were nonetheless aware of the linear course of time; a person is born and dies, one generation, one king follows upon the previous one. This thinking is particularly evident in so-called lists of kings, which record the names of the pharaohs right back to mythological prehistory, providing evidence of a long, uninterrupted line of rulers. It was most probably the linear conception of the world that provided the pendant to the notion of the beginning: the notion of the end, the end of the world. Let us return to the creator god himself. It is again Atum, this time in the Book of the Dead, who says: "But I will destroy everything I have created. This world will return to the primeval waters, the primeval flood whence it came. Only I will remain, with Osiris." The end of the world will not, then, take place in the form of a breakdown, but will be the conscious reversal of creation, albeit, as noted in the same text, only "after millions of years."

To gain an even clearer picture of the Egyptian conception of the cosmos one must visit an Egyptian temple, particularly one from the Late Period. The Egyptian conception of the world is represented there, chiseled in stone: the Egyptian temple as a miniature cosmos. This becomes evident as one approaches the walls surrounding a temple site: they are not constructed in straight layers of stones or tiles but in wave-like layers, rising and falling perpetually. According to a particularly vivid assumption these walls symbolize the waves of the primeval ocean surrounding the cosmos. The temple itself is usually located on an elevation (sometimes an artificial one); the floor leading up to the innermost sanctuary in the rear of the temple always rises slightly. Thus, the primeval hill rose from the *nun*.

The two imposing pylon towers, through which one enters the temple, are the horizon, the two hills between which the sun rises and sets. From floor level, that is from the ground, one descends into the subterranean crypts, the underworld. Papyrus- and lotus-shaped pillars rise from the floor like papyrus and lotus plants from the primeval swamp. They also serve as symbols for the celestial pillars; they support the temple roof, that is the sky. If one looks up, the architectural and visual interpretation of this notion becomes evident: one sees images of sky gods, particularly falcon and vulture gods, of the starry night sky, or of the sky goddess Nut herself.

Royal and Divine Festivals

by Joachim Willeitner

In contrast to the way we celebrate certain events today, regular celebrations appear to have played a less significant role in the life of ancient Egyptians. In the cultural setup of the day, birthdays, name days, wedding anniversaries, etc. were not considered to be special events worth celebrating. In ancient Egypt, neither an official act of naming a newborn similar to the Christian act of baptism, nor a relevant registration procedure existed. The act of circumcision, widely practiced in ancient Egypt, was not related to the event of birth, since it was apparently only executed at a much later stage. Patron deities, and a corresponding calendar of saints, did not feature in ancient Egyptian religious notion, of the world, even though particularly prominent characters such as Imhotep, Heqaib, or Amenhotep, son of Hapu, were transformed into popular saints after their death, and even Imhotep's day, of birth, death, and funeral were celebrated.

Furthermore, a wedding was not an official act. The bridal pair announced their will to become husband and wife and then took up residence in a shared domicile, without any ceremony requiring a priest or a registry official (although every citizen must have been known to the authorities for tax-raising purposes). The birth of a child surely constituted a major event in a family's life, not least because a large number of offspring provided security in old age, and when a child was born (as, indeed, in the event of a death) people did not go to work. But there is hardly any evidence that one's own birthday was in any way celebrated or commemorated. The only indication that people did somehow observe their birthdays are entries of absence in the worker's lists of Deir el-Medineh ("…was absent on account of his celebration").

The birth of the "god-king," the future pharaoh, however, constituted a major state event of such importance that everything, from the child's conception by the national god Amun to his delivery and nursing by divine wet-nurses, was incorporated into the visual program of the temple reliefs. But even for this important event we have no evidence of any public official celebrations. There are vague indications as to national victory celebrations after military triumphs (such as Thutmosis III's conquest of Megiddo) and to nationwide mourning in the event of a king's death.

We know much more, however, about an event celebrated by every king who had completed a thirty-year reign (and celebrated

46 Hatshepsut participating in the cult race
Karnak, temple of Amun, "Red Chapel"; New Kingdom, Eighteenth Dynasty, ca. 1460 BC; sandstone; H. ca. 60 cm; Karnak, open air museum, no number.
The *sed* festival (*hebsed*) was the most significant of royal celebrations, marking thirty years of rule and subsequently repeated approximately every three years. Since most pharaohs did not live long enough to celebrate this royal anniversary, it was rarely staged. Occasionally – perhaps when the last *sed* festival had been long overdue – it was brought forward. The cultic procedure required the ruler, among other tasks, to take part in a cult race, similar to the one Hatshepsut and the Apis bull participate in on this block relief from the Red Chapel of the central barque santuary in the temple of Amun at Karnak.

47 Amenophis III and Tiye celebrating the sed festival
Soleb, temple of Amenophis III, second court (detail); New Kingdom, Eighteenth Dynasty, ca. 1360 BC; sandstone.
Since the New Kingdom, the royal spouse played an increasingly important role in the *sed* festival, for example Amenophis III's wife Tiye, characterized by her high double-plumed headdress. In this detail of an elaborate depiction of the ceremonies in the temple of Soleb, Nubia, she stands behind her husband, who wears the Lower Egyptian crown, as they both take part in several cult ceremonies. The same later applies to Osorkon II and his wife Karomama (see p. 277, no. 7).

48 Lintel of Sesostris III
Medamud, jubilee building; Middle Kingdom, Twelfth Dynasty, ca. 1860 BC; limestone; H. 157 cm; Cairo, Egyptian Museum, JE 56497 A.
During the *sed* festival the king partook in several rejuvenation and birth rituals, all the while wearing a special cape, the *hebsed* coat. The scene shows the king symbolically accepting a long period of rule through personified emblems of each part of the country. During the procedure of these cultic events the king – in this case Sesostris III appearing as a pair (once with Upper Egyptian, once with Lower Egyptian crown) – sat enthroned under a ceremonial baldachin with characteristically domed roof. The gods gave the king the *sed* hieroglyph, designed in the form of a twin chapel with just such a domed roof, on temple reliefs as a symbol of a long reign.

49 The divine shrines of Osorkon II
Bubastis, temple of Bastet, block from the entrance gate; Third Intermediate Period, Twenty-second Dynasty, ca. 850 BC; red granite.
One of the most essential cultic procedures a king had to perform during the *sed* festival was the presentation of offerings to the gods in the appropriate shrines. This relief, depicting the course of the celebrations, is part of the entrance gate to the temple of Bastet of Bubastis, in the reign of Osorkon II; the gate is now completely destroyed. Like most representations it shows divine chapels with the cult images (here, those of Horus, Neith and an additional male god) in close proximity; they were probably brought to the event from all over the country. Osorkon depicted himself – today weathered almost beyond recognition – kneeling before the deity in the lower left-hand corner of each of the shrines.

50 *General Horemheb with honorary gold collar*
Saqqara, tomb of Horemheb; New Kingdom, Eighteenth Dynasty, reign of Tutankhamun, ca. 1325 BC; Leiden (NL), Rijksmuseum van Oudheden, H. III. QQQ.
The king's personally honoring meritorious

citizens constituted a particular cause for celebrations. There are many records, particularly from the times of Akhenaten, of "gold of honor awards," a popular event for such purposes. During this event the king, if we are to believe the reliefs from his then capital at Amarna, tossed the golden collars, each

weighing more than 15 lbs., out of a "window of appearances" in his palace into the cheering crowds below. Decorated with several such collars, which he probably received from Tutankhamun, the general, and later pharaoh, Horemheb presents himself in his Saqqara tomb.

somewhat prematurely by some kings who knew they would not live to see that day): the *sed* festival. These celebrations served to confirm the monarch's physical ability to continue ruling the country and featured a cultic race to be run by the sovereign, as well as regeneration and rejuvenation rituals. Once the *sed* festival had been celebrated after thirty years of rule it was usually repeated every three years. During his long reign, Ramesses II celebrated the *sed* in great style, often inviting foreign dignitaries and leaving the elaborate organization of the spectacle to the crown prince, his son Khaemwese.

In the earliest royal monumental tomb, the step pyramid of Djoser at Saqqara, several elaborate installations among the buildings surrounding the tomb were exclusively designed for performing the *sed* festival which Djoser, who did not live to reign for thirty years, was thus at least able to celebrate in the hereafter. The same more or less applies to Niuserre, who adorned the walls of his solar shrine in Abu Gurab with scenes of the *sed* celebrations. The reliefs of the temple of Amenophis III at Soleb illustrate the procedure of the rituals in most vivid detail. The depictions on blocks from a gate of the temple of Osorkon II at Bubastis, parts of which can be found in museums around the world, provide additional clues. Furthermore, the crowning ritual depicted in the so-called "dramatic Ramesseum papyrus" must have been used in the context of these rejuvenation ceremonies as well.

Large public festivities were also performed when the king personally honored meritorious citizens, usually by decorating them

with "golden collars of honor" made of pure gold and weighing more than fifteen lbs.

Most of the state festivities were repeated in an annual rhythm and were thus bound by the ancient Egyptian calendar with its three seasons flood (*akhet*), seed (*peret*) and harvest (*shemu*), each lasting four months. The year's first national annual event that merited celebrations was held at the beginning of the year in mid-summer; it marked the on-set of the Nile floods and the reappearance of Sirius – which the Egyptians regarded as a female deity called Sothis.

Most of the subsequent annual festivities only had regional significance and were always linked to specific deities. The festival calendars, carved on temple walls, reveal the relevant festival dates and are therefore an important source of information. Often, priests took the divine images from the temple shrines, placed them on large barques equipped with poles and carried them through the village in a resplendent procession that included music and dance. The cult statues were placed in portable shrines in order to protect them from the illicit stares of the public lining the procession route. But the public were able to address them with prayers and requests, to which the cult statue responded by way of specific movements – manipulated by the priests – of the barque. A number of prospective kings, whose claim to the throne was disputed, used these divine oracles as a means to legitimize their way into attaining pharaonic status.

Edfu, court side of the pylon; Ptolemaic Period, reign of Ptolemy XII. Neos Dionysos, ca. 70 BC; sandstone.

The climax of every temple celebration was the "excursion" of the gods in portable barques carried by priests in a celebratory procession. The destination of these processions was usually the temple of a deity of the opposite sex, so that the divine couples could be led to one another for a short while for a "holy wedding" in the sanctuaries at the

climax of the celebration. The best known of these processions was the annual voyage of Horus of Edfu to Hathor of Dendara, traveling on the Nile on a magnificent barque decorated with the Horus falcon head at bow and stern. Going downstream, the current was used for moving forward with additional acceleration achieved with oars; on the return journey, the sails were set, so that the permanent southern wind might push the boats upstream.

51 Festival calendar
Kom Ombo, second antechamber; Ptolemaic Period, reign of Ptolemy VI Philopator, ca. 170 BC; sandstone.

The ceremonial calendars on temple walls bear information on numerous annual temple celebrations which always occurred on the same day. The calendar depicted here is from the Sobek and Haroëris temple: the column on the right lists the dates of celebrations, the circular hieroglyphs indicating the month, the linear ones the single digits and

the curved ones the decimal digits of the date (for example: 2 curves and 5 lines = the 25th day). The corresponding names of the festivals are listed to the left of the column in the relevant row. There are no details of procedures or the amount of sacrifices to be offered. National festivals could be so important that the month in which they occurred was named after them. Ordinary citizens called the second month after the flood season, for instance, after the *opet* celebrations: *paopi* ("he of *opet*").

The movable barques were often loaded onto so-called divine boats to be transported on the water. This occurred when the divine image had to be ferried across the Nile, as in the case of Amun's cult image traveling every ten days from the temple of Luxor on the east bank to the shrine of Medinet Habu on the west bank. The river route was also chosen when the gods went to visit each other across long distances, as in the case of Hathor and Horus traveling between Dendara and Edfu on an annual basis. Edfu was also the place of public "cult games," as it were, based on the contest between Horus and Seth; temple reliefs in Edfu indicate that a hippopotamus made of bread was used to re-enact the falcon god's killing of Seth in revenge for the murder of his father Osiris.

The most famous barque festivals were held at Thebes: ever since the New Kingdom, the *opet* festival has been held during the "second month of flood," and since the Middle Kingdom the "beautiful feast of the valley" was held at new moon in the second harvest month. In the former event, the national god Amun, at home in the temple of Karnak, took his spouse Mut and their son and moon god Khonsu to visit Luxor Temple, which in this context is referred to as his harem (*opet*). Luxor Temple's lower rank in cultic terms is evident in the fact that its axis is not, as might be expected, perpendicular to the Nile but runs parallel to the river, pointing towards the national temple further north, to which it was linked by a magnificent alley lined with sphinxes. The divine barques did not, however, follow this elegant road but covered most of the three-kilometer trip on the river. Reliefs from the reigns of Tutankhamun, Horemheb and Ramesses II show detailed illustrations of the celebratory processions, in which ordinary citizens as well as musicians, dancers and the kingdom's entire nobility participated; there is a long row of decorated and fattened oxen intended for sacrifice at the end of which are the divine barques, having

53 *Decorated sacrificial bulls for the* opet festival
Luxor, court of Ramesses II; New Kingdom, Nineteenth Dynasty, reign of Ramesses II, ca. 1250 BC; sandstone.
The destination of the divine barques during the *opet* celebrations were the altars, laden with offerings, in the sanctuary of Luxor Temple. The fattened and decorated bulls used in the procession, to be slaughtered later in honor of the gods, had obviously been kept so immobile to retain all body fat during fattening that their claws would not wear off and thus developed horn-shaped growths towards the front.

54 *Musicians and acrobats*
Karnak, temple of Amun, "Red Chapel;" New Kingdom, Eighteenth Dynasty, ca. 1460 BC; sandstone; H. ca. 60 cm; Luxor, The Luxor Museum of Ancient Egyptian Art, J.151.

At the conclusion of the procession acrobatic dancers as well as a harpist awaited the barque bearing the cult image, as depicted in this block from the "Red Chapel" of Queen Hatshepsut in the temple of Amun at Karnak. Almost identical scenes can be found on the walls of Luxor Temple as well as in the rubble of the recently discovered terrace temple of Deir el-Bahari, also built by Queen Hatshepsut.

55 Banquet scene
Western Thebes, Dra Abu el-Naga, tomb of Nebamun (TT 146); New Kingdom, Eighteenth Dynasty, ca. 1380 BC; painting on plaster; H. 61 cm; London, The British Museum, EA 37984.
Although it is never explicitly stated that the banquet scenes in Theban tombs show the funerary festival of the "beautiful feast of the valley," it can safely be assumed that this is almost always the case. It is noteworthy that the depictions of scenes of the funerary meal are limited to the tombs of the Eighteenth Dynasty. The figures increasingly become more vivid as style is developed, and the initially strict gender differentiation of revellers also becomes increasingly diffuse, as in this depiction in the tomb of Nebamun, until it eventually disappears completely.

56 Group of musicians
Western Thebes, Sheik Abd-el-Qurna, tomb of Nakht (TT 52); New Kingdom, Eighteenth Dynasty, ca. 1390 BC; painting on plaster.
The "beautiful feast of the valley," held annually in the presence of the king, was also an occasion for the visit of a god for the purpose of conceiving a divine child: Amun of Karnak came to the «desert valley», now called Deir el-Bahari to visit the goddess

Hathor who resided there. For the deceased to benefit from the vast amount of cult offerings in this procession, Thebans would go into their relatives' tombs and celebrate with the deceased accompanied by music, as depicted here in Nakht's tomb, and seen to by servants. While these private celebrations are often depicted on the tomb walls, images of the official processions with the divine barque are very rare indeed.

finally arrived at their destination, richly laden offering tables awaiting them. The duration of the feast increased from eleven days initially to twenty-seven days.

The "beautiful feast of the valley" lasted several days. It soon enjoyed widespread popularity even beyond Thebes. In this feast Amun's barque traveled from his temple at Karnak to Deir el-Bahari, the desert valley providing the name, across the Nile and from there to all royal funerary temples on the Theban west bank where worship continued. According to Egyptian faith, the deceased rulers, whose funerary temples Amun would visit during this procession, benefited from the offerings made to him; ordinary Egyptians therefore expected that their deceased relatives might also benefit in the same way. There is evidence, particularly from the Late Period, that high officials were very keen to place their tombs as near as possible to the processional route of the divine barques, ensuring that their tomb entrance would face the route as well.

In the large area of the Theban necropolis, the relatives of deceased Egyptians buried far from the festival activities knew how to take advantage of the event: elaborately decorated and clothed, they visited their relatives' tombs and celebrated with them there. The experience of consuming excessive amounts of alcohol, thereby freeing oneself from earthly realities and thus supposedly achieving closer proximity to the deceased, played a significant part in these celebrations. It is understandable, then, that a principal endeavor during the funerary celebrations was maximum intoxication. Theban funerary illustrations and reliefs therefore not only show the agreeable side of these celebrations, where servants spoil the guests with food, drink, and aromatic essences and musicians provide entertainment – "to make holiday" was, after all, the Egyptians' interpretation of this feast – but also the disagreeable consequences of the attempt to enter the realm of the dead while still among the living: inebriated visitors to the tomb are sometimes shown vomiting.

Excessive alcohol consumption appears to have played an essential part in other festivities as well: one of the first national

57 "Climbing for Min"
Luxor, court of Ramesses II, inner side of the pylon; New Kingdom, Nineteenth Dynasty, reign of Ramesses II, ca. 1250 BC; sandstone. The celebrations for the god of fertility Min included the ritual depicted on the inner side of the pylon, "climbing for Min," a misleading term coined by Egyptologists insofar as it does not actually describe an athletic ritual but the erection of a con- struction for a very large festival tent. This cultic ritual was so characteristic for the entire event that it was often depicted on temple walls in lieu of the complete celebrations. In fact, the complete ritual has only been recorded once, on a barque kiosk erected under Sesostris I in Karnak, the so-called "White Chapel" (see p. 137, no. 61).

58 Seti I erecting the Djed pole
Abydos, temple of Seti I, hall of Osiris; New Kingdom, Nineteenth Dynasty, ca. 1285 BC; sandstone, painted polychrome.
During the second half of choiak, the fourth month of the flood season, the main event was the celebration of Sokar, a traditional Memphite god. The procession, lasting several days, included the events "breaking up the soil" and "wrapping onions," and culminated in the ritual of "pulling the barque of Sokar" with the subsequent procession of barques called "procession around the walls." The celebrations concluded with the erection of the Djed pole (probably made of woven wheat sheaf) as depicted in a similar fashion in this relief in the temple of Seti I in Abydos.

celebrations, held shortly after a new year had begun, was simply called "drunkenness" (*tekhi*). It was preceded by the Thoth festival, where, as Plutarch reports, honey and figs are devoured.

Most of the celebrations were more or less directly linked to the annual reappearance of vegetation and, correspondingly, with the cycle of death and renewal. This is visible most clearly in the various harvest celebrations, such as the festivals in honor of the goddess of nourish- ment Renenutet, which introduced the *shemu* season, or those of the god of fertility Min, which lasted several days, commencing at new moon in the first month of *shemu*. During this festival, the king released, for example, a flock of birds to the east, west, north, and south to symbolize the repossession of the entire world; he also sacrificed grain that had been harvested with a special ceremonial sickle. The act of feather-clad performers erecting a huge cone-shaped construction of

timber poles, apparently for building a cult tent, had for a long time been misinterpreted as the act of "climbing for Min" and formed an integral part of this harvest festival.

The annual cycle of festivals came to a conclusion on the final day of the fourth month of harvest, when a special evening meal called *mesit* took place and lights were lit in the context of the festival of light in order to achieve protection from the ominous epagomena, the last five leap days outside the mensual count, which had to be included to bring the number of days in the year to 365.

24,4

Mummification

Renate Germer

The embalming of the dead was a special feature of ancient Egyptian culture, and it had the aim of preserving bodies for eternity. The origins of mummification in Egypt lie in the climatic and geographical conditions of the region. In prehistoric times the dead were buried in the desert sands, wrapped in animal skins or matting. In this hot and dry environment, water was drawn out of the body tissues, preserving them, and thus a natural mummification took place.

At the beginning of the historical period, however, as people began to build tombs for the dead and place them in coffins, these conditions for preservation described above no longer applied, and bodies decayed. But ancient Egyptian religious beliefs required the preservation of the body for the desired afterlife, and they therefore began to experiment with ways of preventing the body's natural decomposition following death.

The first attempts to do this involved tightly wrapping the body in linen bandages. The Egyptians realized that without the removal of the organs from the chest and abdomen the processes of decay were inevitable. This fact could easily have been observed with creatures such as birds or fish caught for food, which would only keep fresh once their innards had been removed. In the Old Kingdom the embalmers thus began to open the abdominal cavities of the dead and take out the organs. Possibly the use of dehydrating salts was also taken over from the preservation of meat and fish to the mummification of humans using natron.

In the Old Kingdom techniques were not sufficiently advanced to preserve bodies that would survive even into our era, despite removal of the organs. Underneath the linen wrappings the only objects that survive today are bones and tissue fragments, which disintegrate easily if disturbed. On the other hand the linen wrapping is often in very good condition indeed, and this demonstrates clearly the Egyptian determination to preserve the body as much as possible in a lifelike and furthermore functional state after death. Frequently organs such as the genitals, the breasts of women, ears, eyes, mouth, and nose were modeled in linen, or at the very least a face was painted on the bandages. The outermost layers of the linen wrapping were made to resemble pieces of clothing, for women in the shape of a long narrow shift, and a loincloth for the men.

In the Middle Kingdom there was a new development in mummification techniques, consisting of the removal of the brain from the skull. At first this procedure was done only occasionally and judging from the remains it was associated exclusively with the higher social classes, those nearest to the royal family. From the New Kingdom onward it became customary when embalming to remove the brain as well as the internal organs from the body. Thus it finally became possible to preserve flesh too, and it has remained preserved for over three and a half millennia down to the present day.

At the close of the pharaonic era the Egyptians continued to embalm their dead, although this was generally done with less care. Even Coptic monks were buried in this way despite the Christian church's insistence on terminating this heathen practice. Embalming seems finally to have disappeared from Egypt altogether in the seventh century AD.

The Process of Mummification

There are two sources for our knowledge regarding the procedure for mummifying a body, and the technical changes that came about over the passing centuries. Besides examination of actual ancient Egyptian mummified corpses, we have the account of Herodotus, the Greek historian and traveler from the fifth century BC, and some passages in Diodorus that refer to this subject.

By contrast, the surviving Egyptian sources, papyri and the many texts and images on tomb and temple walls, make no mention of how embalming was done. Only two papyri from Roman times mention what we know as the embalming ceremony, but these concentrate on instructions of a ritual kind: how separate parts of the body were to be anointed, wrapped, and given magical protection by means of amulets and spells. Unfortunately, the actual technical process of preserving the body is not described.

Herodotus's account is astonishingly accurate when compared with recent analyses of mummies. His sources of information must have been very good. He must either have witnessed embalming himself in Egypt or have heard a precise account of it. Archaeological

59 Cartonnage mummy mask
Probably from Thebes; Middle Kingdom, Eleventh Dynasty, ca. 1990 BC; stuccoed and painted linen; H. 71 cm; Cairo, Egyptian Museum, RT 24.4.26.1.

Mummy masks were included in burials from the Old Kingdom onward. The earliest examples were made of plaster, but in the Middle Kingdom they consisted of several layers of linen with a thick coating of stucco that were then painted. This mask shows the face of a man with a long bipartite wig, a short stylized beard on the cheeks, and an artificial beard on the chin. The mask also covers the upper part of the body, and it is fitted with a multi-layered collar, which atypically reaches up as far as the base of the chin and ears.

finds of the last few years and more recent examination of mummies finally permit us to make a fully accurate translation of Herodotus's text and even to improve upon it in one or two places: "After the lamentation for the dead ... they bring the deceased to be embalmed. There are people who dedicate themselves to this art and who hand down the practices from generation to generation."

The embalmers worked at the edges of villages on the Nile, or on irrigation canals leading from the river, since plenty of water was needed for washing the bodies. The discovery of plant material adhering by chance to mummies shows furthermore that embalming took place in the open. The body would have lain on a wooden or stone table, the sides of which were decorated with a stylized lion figure. For the embalming of a king the tables used would certainly have been costly, like the alabaster examples that were used for the mummification of the Apis bulls. Small alabaster tables of this type, which may have served for the handling of the internal organs, were found in the Old Kingdom pyramid complex of King Djoser at Saqqara.

According to Herodotus, the embalmers began their work on the head of the deceased, by removing the brain from the skull: "First they

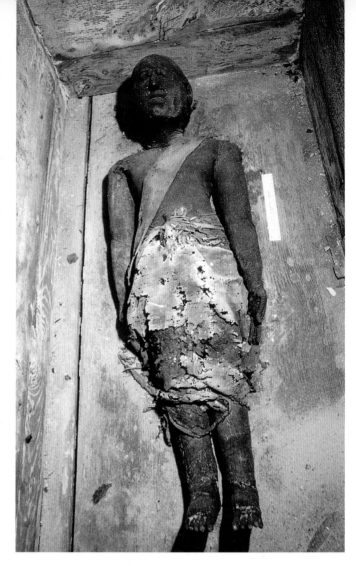

60 Mummy of a priest
Saqqara, shaft grave next to the causeway to the Pyramid of King Unas; Old Kingdom, Fifth Dynasty, ca. 2350 BC; excavation by the Egyptian Antiquities Service, 1986.
The mummy of an unknown man belongs to the group known as linen mummies, meaning that the deceased's body has not survived, but that the form of the body is reflected in the skillful manner of the linen wrapping, and in this case particular care has been taken with the making of the face. The man is clothed with a short loincloth and a red sash over the chest, possibly an indication that during life he had been a priest.

61 Mummy of a woman
Giza, West cemetery (G 2220 B); Old Kingdom, late Fourth Dynasty, ca. 2510 BC; L. ca. 150 cm; Boston, Harvard University–Museum of Fine Arts Expedition, 1933, 33.1017, now Museum of Fine Arts, 33.4–22a.
The mummy of this woman was found in a large wooden coffin 240 cm long, which was actually much too big for her. The body of the deceased was given an extremely elaborate treatment, the fingers and toes being wrapped individually, the breasts modeled with bandages and even indicating the nipples. There are as many as thirty-seven successive layers of bandages one on top of the other, the individual strips of linen being about 10 cm wide. The outermost layer of the wrapping is composed of a single sheet of linen, which was cut to the shape of a long narrow dress. Two of the linen packets used for modeling the body carried an ink inscription saying: *shemat nefret,* "good royal linen."

62 Ritual table
Saqqara, tomb complex of Djoser; Old Kingdom, early Third Dynasty, ca. 2700 BC; calcite alabaster; H. 38 cm, W. 42 cm, L. 89 cm; Cairo, Egyptian Museum, CG 1321.
This small ritual table was found together with another in a tomb corridor that was later covered over by the extension of the mortuary cult complex of Djoser. It therefore likely dates from the period before Djoser. Its form is reminiscent of the large and small embalming tables of the Late Period that are likewise decorated with figures of lions and show a drainage channel. The small size of these two tables from the Old Kingdom has so far been taken to suggest their use as embalming tables for the internal organs. This interpretation, however, is problematical because we are not at all sure if the removal and embalming of the viscera was yet practiced in this early period. Since biers in the form of animals later become an inseparable element of the mummification rituals, there is also a relevance to the burial rites here. The motif of the lion suggests that its use had a royal context.

take out the brain through the nostrils with a hooked steel spike, and when they have removed it, they dribble in a resinous liquid."

Many Egyptian museums today possess these hooks that were once used in embalming. They have survived because in some cases all the tools and materials used in the mummification were ritually placed in a pit in front of the tomb. The hooks are in any case not made of steel, as Herodotus states, but bronze, and they are up to 40 cm long. The tip of this tool could be given a variety of shapes: needle-like, hooked or even in a spiral like a snail.

An embalmer would probably have worked with a whole set of different hooks, since not only did he have to break through the ethmoid bone to enter the skull from the nostril, but also had to remove the brain matter and the meninges. Examination of mummies shows, however, that the embalmers did not always remove the brain through the nose, but that this procedure was frequently done through the occipital foramen of the skull.

According to Herodotus a resinous liquid was then poured into the empty skull. We know from chemical analyses made of this substance in recent years that it consisted of a mixture of various resins from coniferous trees, bee's wax and aromatic plant oils. Coniferous

63 Bronze hooks
Late Period, ca. 600 BC; bronze; L. 28 cm, 28.5 cm, 33.5 cm; Leiden, Rijksmuseum van Oudheden, AB 140 b-d.
Long-handled bronze tools with hook-shaped ends, or ends twisted into a spiral, were used by the embalmers to remove the brain from the skull. This was done either, as Herodotus describes, through the nose, or through the occipital foramen, the natural opening in the skull at the back where the cervical spine connects with it. Sometimes these tools and materials that had been used in the mummification were "buried" in a pit near the tomb, which has provided us with a number of examples.

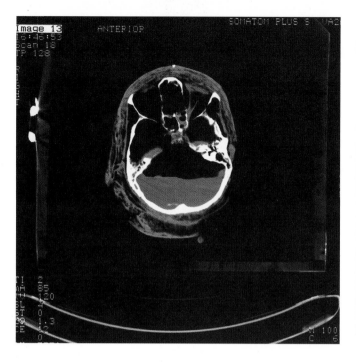

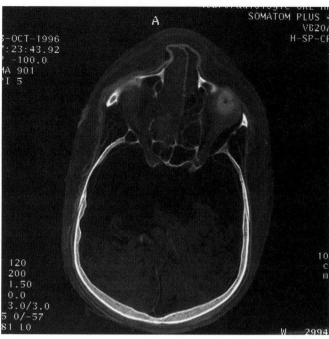

64 Computer tomography scan of a mummy skull of the Late Period (CT scan; Medical University, Lübeck).
In this cross-section the mass of resinous oil can be clearly seen in the rear portion of the head, poured in after the removal of the brain. This mass was originally fluid, and as it solidi- fied it was left with a flat surface. The bone damage in the area of the ethmoid bone shows that in this case the embalmers removed the brain through the nose. The head is still wrapped in its many layers of linen bandages.

65 Computer tomography scan of a mummy skull from ca. 900 BC (CT scan: Eppendorf University Hospital, Hamburg)
With this mummy the empty skull was filled with linen packing, a procedure that was used only occasionally.

resins must have been imported from Palestine, as was the bitumen that was sometimes added; these would have been unobtainable for ordinary Egyptians unless they were employed by the state or in a temple.

The different substances were heated up and made liquid so that they could be poured into the skull where they solidified. They can be clearly seen today in x-ray photographs of the mummy, or best of all in a computer tomography scan. In recent years numerous mummies have been scanned by computer tomography and this has revealed that the embalmers did not work according to an absolutely fixed technique of mummification. In some cases, in place of resinous ointment, they packed the empty skull with linen.

After treating the head the embalmers moved on to the trunk of the body and opened up the abdomen: "Next with a sharp Ethiopian stone they cut the body upwards from the groin and take out all of the entrails. But once they have cleaned it and rinsed it with palm wine, they then treat it again with powder and ointment." The cut in the abdomen wall was always made in the upper half of the pelvic crest on the left side. The embalmers removed and separately preserved the viscera: the lungs, liver, stomach, and intestines, wrapped them in linen bandages and placed each organ in one of the four so-called canopic jars, special vessels that were placed in the tomb beside the mummy. Canopic jars were included in burials as early as the Old Kingdom. Originally they were simple jars with a flat lid, but later their lids were modeled in the shape of a human head.

Four gods, known as the Sons of Horus, were responsible for the magical protection of the internal organs. "Amset" had the form of a man, "Hapi" of a baboon, "Qebehsenuf" was a falcon, and "Duamutef" a jackal. To display this protective function, canopic jars from the Nineteenth Dynasty onward show lids in the form of heads of these deities, and each was assigned one of the four organs removed from the body.

When the embalmers removed the internal organs they took care either to leave the heart inside the body or to replace it afterward. For the Egyptians the heart was the seat of the intellect and emotions and thus responsible for the individual's nature; it therefore had to remain in the body. Religious thinking of that period also allowed it to be replaced by a heart scarab, a magic symbolic heart that could stand before Osiris at the funeral tribunal and give an account of its owner's life in place of the actual heart.

The next and final stage in the embalming process was treatment with natron. This is a very hygroscopic substance, which means that it extracts the water contained in the body tissues, drying it out and thus conserving it. Until recently scholars were convinced that the Egyptians used a solution of natron, but recent research has shown that they filled the body with natron solids and piled them up around it. This treatment with natron lasted about thirty-five to forty days, after which the body was dry and decay arrested.

In order to give the body an appearance as lifelike as possible, the chest and abdominal cavities that had been emptied of their organs had to be filled up again. This was mostly done with linen packing or sawdust, occasionally with Nile mud or aromatically perfumed cloth packing. The mummy of a woman from Giza, dating to the Fourth Dynasty (see p. 460, no. 61), provides a particularly clear example of linen packing and modeling. Herodotus writes that after the body had been packed out in this way, the incision made in the abdomen to facilitate mummification was sown up again. In fact this happened only very rarely. Generally the embalmers closed the cut with linen, a layer of wax or, for members of royalty, by means of a thin gold sheet.

Mummification and Ancient Egyptian Medicine

One might imagine from all this that the intensive work on the body during the embalming process would have given ancient Egyptian physicians a good knowledge of human anatomy, but this was not the case. Both professions, physicians and embalmers, worked in complete isolation from one another. Doctors were not present during the mummification and therefore learned nothing from it about the inside of the body. This fact emerges from the many medical texts that have survived. These papyri show that the doctors of that time had an extensive empirical knowledge that told them how to treat certain illnesses. For this they used a variety of different cures, mainly extracted from plants. Their anatomical practice reflects knowledge gained from cattle breeding and the dissection of sacrificial animals. This is clear from the example of hieroglyphs for the external parts of the body, which are based on human examples, whereas parts of animals provided the models for hieroglyphs representing internal organs.

Herodotus also tells us about the advanced state of Egyptian healing, and this is confirmed by letters that have been found in Egypt and in Asia Minor from foreign rulers of the middle of the second millennium BC. These request the sending of Egyptian physicians to their courts, since the Egyptians had more extensive knowledge and achieved better results than their own physicians.

Medical papyri from Egypt describe many different diseases that affected the population of the Nile Valley. Up to the present day it has only been possible to identify a few of the diseases named in the texts. However, research by specialists in this area, known as paleopathology, using modern biological research techniques, has resulted in a series of new insights.

Modern Diagnoses in Mummies

There are presently three different routes by which diseases can be diagnosed in mummies. The first is the examination of a pathological change in the body caused by a illness. A well-known example of this kind is the crippled foot of the pharaoh Siptah. The cause of this abnormality is unknown, but it may have resulted from a childhood illness causing lameness, an example of which is illustrated on the stela of Rama. Other illnesses with pathological changes that are easily recognizable in mummies are arthritis and calcification of the arteries.

The second route to a diagnosis of illnesses is through the identification of the agent or of the actual cause. This could be a matter of, for example, parasites or of inhaled sand or soot particles, which cause serious damage to lung tissue. Examination of mummies has shown that worms were a particularly widespread cause of illnesses, and not just in the lower social classes. Tapeworms, ringworms, liver fluke, and trichinae have been identified. Then, as now, bilharzia was a common disease. It is transmitted by schistosomatid worms that develop in water snails in the Nile water. Infection therefore follows principally from swimming, or from working in stagnant water.

The identification of DNA, or the genetic information preserved in the mummy's cells, is quite a new method of finding agents of infection. In this way it has already been possible to diagnose tuberculosis in ancient American mummies, and preparation is being made for research of this kind on mummies from ancient Egypt.

In the last few years a third method of identifying disease in mummies has been found, by means of the detection of antibodies still present in the body. If foreign albumen, for instance in the form of a parasite, penetrates into a person's body, then the body makes antibodies to fight it, and these can be recognized even after thousands

66 Set of canopic jars
New Kingdom, Nineteenth Dynasty, ca. 1210 BC; glazed faience; H. 30 cm, Diam. 16.2 cm; Boston, Museum of Fine Arts, Gift of Mrs. J.D. Cameron Bradley 1948, 48.1286–89.
From the Ramesside Period the jar lids containing the viscera tended to show the heads of the Four Sons of Horus, the gods who gave protection to the internal organs. The form of the jars was therefore directly identified with the deities. Amset (with human head), Duamutef (with jackal's head) and Qebehsenuf (falcon-headed) are each shown here with a wig, whereas Hapi (with baboon's head) wears only his cloak-like fur. On the shoulder of the jar shown is a sort of collar of lotus blossom leaves as a symbol of regeneration, and on the body is a panel with an image of the deceased in prayer before the enthroned figure of Osiris, god of the dead.

of years by special sampling of serum. This method has the advantage that only a very small quantity of mummy tissue is needed. So far, in ancient Egyptian mummies, bilharzia and malaria have been diagnosed by antibody testing.

Modern laboratory techniques such as blood group testing and DNA analysis can also provide information about family relationships between mummies. This field of research, which can be used to examine relationships between the individuals in the royal families, is of interest both to scientists and historians.

Innovations in radiology and medical techniques now permit the making of a model and facial reconstruction from the skull of a mummy still in its wrappings. This procedure allows us to reconstruct the appearance of a person who died thousands of years ago, and whose mummy can be left undisturbed, still wrapped inside its coffin.

However, there are limits to the data that can be provided by scientific research. This was demonstrated by the example of work on the royal mummies. Establishing the age at death of individual kings on the basis of x-ray photographs is a problem that remains to be

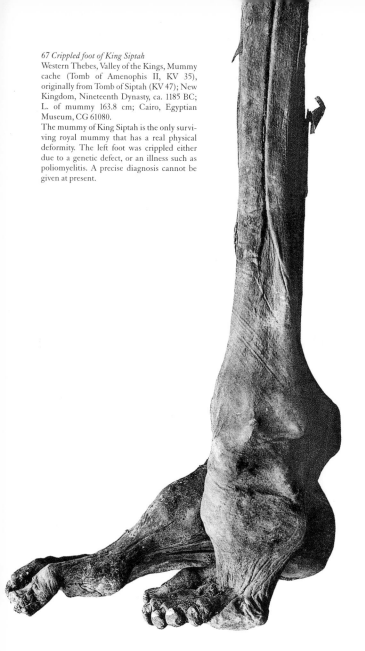

67 Crippled foot of King Siptah
Western Thebes, Valley of the Kings, Mummy cache (Tomb of Amenophis II, KV 35), originally from Tomb of Siptah (KV 47); New Kingdom, Nineteenth Dynasty, ca. 1185 BC; L. of mummy 163.8 cm; Cairo, Egyptian Museum, CG 61080.
The mummy of King Siptah is the only surviving royal mummy that has a real physical deformity. The left foot was crippled either due to a genetic defect, or an illness such as poliomyelitis. A precise diagnosis cannot be given at present.

68 Stela of Rama
New Kingdom, Eighteenth Dynasty, ca. 1380 BC; painted limestone; H. 27 cm, W. 18 cm; Copenhagen, Ny Carlsberg Glyptothek; Æ.I.N. 134.
The stela of Rama the doorkeeper is dedicated to the goddess Astarte. Rama is shown with his wife and son, making an offering to the goddess. His crippled leg is a remarkable feature. It can be clearly seen that the musculature is underdeveloped and that Rama could not stand normally on his foot. Physical deformities like this are not otherwise represented in Egyptian art.

solved. The data found by this means do not generally agree with historical sources. Besides, for none of the kings could the cause of death be established, not even for Tutankhamun. His early death remains a puzzle.

The Wrapping of the Mummified Body and the Preparations for Burial

The embalmers needed a large quantity of linen cloths and bandages with which to wrap the mummified body. For this they used strips torn to size from worn-out materials, both from clothing and from furnishings. In order to give the body more support it was sometimes placed on a board, which was wrapped up along with it, or a shaft was inserted between skull and thorax following the cervical spine, which kept the head and chest firmly together.

The embalmers placed many different amulets on the mummy as the wrapping was nearly finished, especially in the Late Period. All of these had a special protective function, and were to ensure the regeneration of the person after death. The amulets, however, could not be seen from the outside since they were covered by the last layers of the linen wrapping. Sometimes a beautifully worked net made up of faience beads was placed over the final layer of linen.

The head of the mummy was covered with a mask made of painted linen cartonnage; masks of gold were reserved for royalty. The face of the mummy mask presents the deceased as a deified being with an idealized face that is ageless and without individual characteristics. This form of representation came to an end in the first century AD under Roman influence. In Middle Egypt this development led to

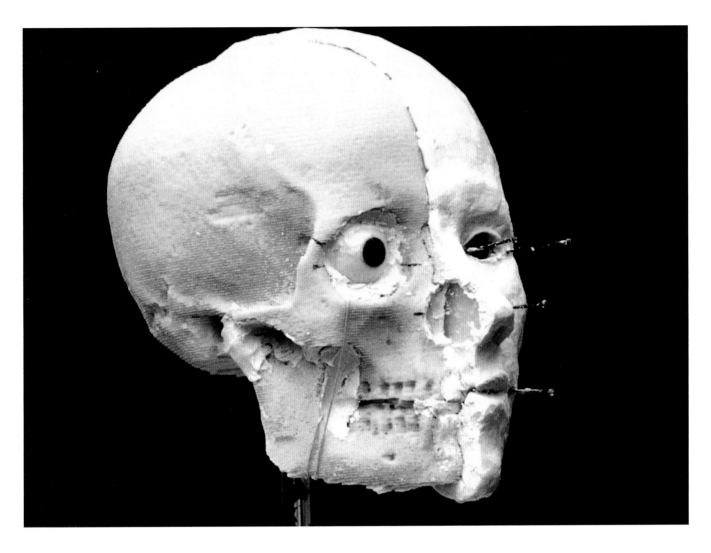

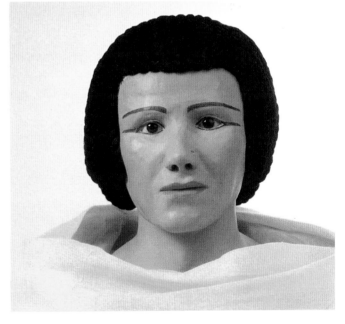

69,70 Facial reconstruction of a female mummy Akhmim; Ptolemaic Period, ca. 300 BC; Hanover, Kestner-Museum, LMH 7849 (formerly Provinzialmuseum). Reconstructed and modeled by R. Helmer and F. Möhr. Based on the data obtained from computer tomography it was possible to make a model of the skull of a mummy that is still in its wrappings.

Forensic scientist Professor R. Helmer has made a reconstruction of the face, which gives an impression of the appearance of this woman who died when she was between twenty and thirty years old.

mummies with stucco masks, and in the Faiyum to the manufacture of mummy portraits.

After the great expense of the preparation of the mummy, one or more coffins were provided that nested one inside one another. In the Old Kingdom and the beginning of the Middle Kingdom these were shaped like a rectangular coffin, but they later took anthropoid form resembling the shape of the mummy. The funeral took place about seventy days after the person's death, although there were also cases in which the actual burial did not happen until very much later. This may have been because the tomb or the tomb provisions were not completely ready.

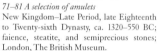

71–81 A selection of amulets
New Kingdom–Late Period, late Eighteenth to Twenty-sixth Dynasty, ca. 1320–550 BC; faience, steatite, and semiprecious stones; London, The British Museum.

From the earliest times amulets played a prominent role in the lives of ancient Egyptians as protective or lucky charms. They were worn by the living and taken by the dead into the tomb. The use of various amulets in combination could strengthen their magical power, or modify and broaden their influence. Because of their power they were frequently placed between the layers of deceased's bandages, to ensure their regeneration and and ward off all the dangers of this life and of the next.

From top left to bottom right:

Udjat eye; Twenty-second to Twenty-fifth Dynasty; faience, polychrome glaze; L.6.7 cm; BM EA 29222.

Heart amulet; Eighteenth/Nineteenth Dynasty; black steatite with inlay; H. 6.4 cm; BM EA 50742

Heart amulet; late Eighteenth Dynasty; faience, polychrome glaze; H. 6 cm; BM EA 29440

Tjt-loop ("Blood of Isis"); Eighteenth /Nineteenth Dynasty; red jasper, H. 6.5 cm; BM EA 7865

Pectoral with heart scarab; Nineteenth Dynasty; faience, polychrome glaze; H. 9.7 cm; BM EA 7865

Djed pillar; Twenty-sixth Dynasty; faience, blue glaze; H. 11.3 cm; BM EA 12235

Miniature headrest; Twenty-sixth Dynasty; haematite; W. 3.9 cm; BM EA 200647

Four Sons of Horus; Twenty-sixth/Twenty-seventh Dynasty; faience, blue glaze; H. 6.6-6.8 cm; BM EA 52244-47

82, 83 Mummy and coffin ensemble of Nesmutaatneru

Western Thebes, Deir el-Bahari, tomb of Djedesiuefanch, lower part of Hathor chapel; Late Period, Twenty-fifth Dynasty, ca. 700 BC; Boston, Museum of Fine Arts, Gift of Egypt Exploration Fund 1895, 95.1407 a–d. Outer coffin (post coffin): painted wood; L. 204 cm; outer anthropoid coffin: painted wood; L. 186 cm; inner anthropoid coffin: painted and stuccoed wood; L. 169 cm; mummy: L. 151 cm; mummy wrappings: linen; mummy net: faience, polychrome glaze.

Nesmutaatneru was the consort of Djedesiuefanch, who was priest of Montu, and belonged to one of the more influential families in Thebes. Her coffin ensemble consisted of one shrine-like post coffin with a vaulted lid, and two inner anthropoid coffins nested inside one another. The decoration of the outer one is poorly preserved. On the lid, beneath the impressive collar, the only representation is of a winged sun disk, a simple scene of offerings to the sun god and two central columns with inscriptions. On the inside of the coffin case is a picture of the Goddess of the West, personification of the kingdom of the dead. The innermost coffin is richly decorated. Above the breast is a ram-headed falcon crowned with a sun disk, with outstretched wings in a protective gesture. In the panels below various deities and symbols are shown, along with a representation of the mummy on the bier. The mummy itself is wrapped in a cloth; two colored mummy bandages cross over the upper body. A mummy net made of faience beads covers the body from the shoulders to where the feet emerge. Above the breast is a winged scarab, and images of the Four Sons of Horus, the deities who protect the internal organs.

85 Clay mask of a man
Diospolis Parva; Roman Period, ca. AD 100;
painted clay; H. 25.4 cm; London, The
British Museum, EA 30845.
In Egypt mummy masks made of plaster were
often included in burials from the earliest
times onward. In the Roman Period the
variety of physiognomical types was considerably broadened and an identifiable tradition
of mummy mask manufacture arose, distinguished from the Ptolemaic period by a much
more heterogeneous range of types, both in
terms of age and expression. Most of the
masks were made by casting, and they were
given a painted finish. This mask is quite
unusual in being freely modeled from clay.
The strong realism that characterizes it is
certainly markedly influenced by the Roman
portrait tradition.

84 Mummy portrait of Artemidorus (the younger)
Hawara; Roman Period, ca. AD 100; painted
wood (encaustic) and gilded; L. of mummy
167 cm; London, The British Museum,
EA 21810.
The mummy of Artemidorus (the younger)
was found toward the end of the nineteenth
century in a tomb at Hawara. It has been
examined by radiography, from which it
appears that Artemidorus was about twenty
years old and that he had a large fracture of
the skull, which may have caused his death.
The embalmers filled his body cavities with
large quantities of resin-soaked material,
probably sand, which made it extremely
heavy. The mummy portrait is painted onto a
stuccoed canvas decorated with gold leaf and
covering the entire mummy. On the lower
part of the collar are three panels in which
images of mummification by Anubis appear,
the adoration of the symbol of Abydos by
Horus and Thoth as provincial deities, and
the resurrection of the mummified Osiris by
Isis in the form of a hawk.

86 Plaster mask of a woman
Probably from Hermupolis; Roman Period, first half of second century AD; painted plaster; H. 34 cm; Hildesheim, Pelizaeus-Museum, 573.
This plaster mask shows a portrait of a young woman. Her fashionable coiffure consists of three rows of small corkscrew curls above her forehead, and to the sides are similar long hanging curls. Her necklace consists of a simple band with a lozenge motif and a wreath made of lotus blossoms. Masks of this type were originally constructed on a wooden frame fastened to the upper part of the mummy's body by means of linen bandages.

Mummies of Animals

For the Egyptians the art of mummification was not restricted to humans but was also practiced on animals. Here it is important to distinguish between different reasons for the burial. If a person's favorite pet died, perhaps a dog or cat, monkey or gazelle, this might be mummified. Sometimes pet animals like this were given a special coffin and occasionally even their own stelae. On the other hand the burial of a monkey that was the favorite of Princess Maatkare of the Twenty-first Dynasty was quite exceptional. He was embalmed and placed in the coffin with his mistress.

In some animals the Egyptians also saw the embodiment of a deity. So for example the god Ptah might be manifested in a bull, or Sobek in a crocodile; while living these animals would have been worshipped. When they died they received an appropriate burial with embalming of the body, coffins, and costly jewelry.

In the Greco-Roman Period, in addition to those few individual animals that were seen as the embodiment of gods, the entire species was regarded as sacred, and in certain areas quite different animals were worshipped. The number of animals that were subject to a cult was large, and ranged from the bull, ram, dog, ibis, falcon, fish, crocodile, and the cat to small rodents and even insects, to name only the most important. The pious Egyptian could dedicate a votive offering to the divinity, either in the form of a bronze statuette or an elaborately wrapped mummy of the corresponding deity. This practice appeared very strange to Greeks and Romans, but was very popular and led to the construction of huge animal cemeteries, mainly underground.

88 Cat mummy
Abydos; Greco-Roman Period; second/first century BC; H. 45.7 cm; London, The British Museum, EA 37348.
Egyptians often worshipped the goddess Bastet in the form of the cat. Bastet was responsible for protection of the house and the family. In the Greco-Roman Period especially, many cats were mummified, elaborately wrapped or even placed in a small coffin and dedicated to the Goddess Bastet.

87 Mummy shroud
Probably Saqqara; Roman Period, second century AD; stuccoed and painted linen (tempera); H. 185 cm; W. 125 cm; Moscow, Pushkin Museum, I 1a 5749.
From the New Kingdom onward painted shrouds were certainly in use. Most surviving examples, however, come from the Greek and Roman Periods. In the Ptolemaic Period these often bore an image of the mummified figure of the deceased in the center of the shroud together with the god of the underworld Osiris, or – in the case of a woman – her figure alongside the goddess Hathor. This mummy shroud shows the deceased in the center of the scene next to the mummified form of Osiris. On his other side stands Anubis, the jackal-headed god of the necropolis and of embalming, with his arm placed round the man's shoulders.

The Burial

Wafaa el-Saddik

"Death was the original mystery. It set man on the track of further mysteries. He raised his thinking above the visible to the invisible, from the transitory to the eternal, from the mortal to the divine."

Fustel de Coulanges: La Cité Antique

Body and Soul

Death – or more accurately preparation for the afterlife – played an extremely important role in Egyptian culture. Every Egyptian's dream was the mummification of his body as a means of preventing the decay of his mortal frame, and ensuring a life after death. Therefore the preservation of the body was one of the most important components of Egyptian funeral rites. Because of Egypt's desert climate, people from as early as Predynastic times must have noticed that the bodies of the dead remained preserved more or less completely when buried in the hot desert sands. It is therefore not surprising that every Egyptian who could possibly afford it placed great value on his burial, or more specifically his mummification, the equipping of his tomb, and the provision of offerings. His *ka* would only be able to return in a "body" that was well preserved. A damaged body could not be recognized by his *ka* and this destroyed his chance for a life in the hereafter. The fear of this second "death" took on a dimension for the populace of ancient Egypt that we can hardly imagine, and which led them to go to quite extraordinary lengths to preserve their corpses.

Egyptians believed that man was made up of six parts. Three of these were linked to substance: the body, *khet*, the name, *ren*, and the shadow, *shut*. Three were linked to the undying essence of life, the spiritual or otherworldly, and which are conveniently but hardly satisfactorily described as parts of the soul; these were the *ka*, the *ba* and the *akh*. The *ka* ensured the continuation of the individual's eternal life; it resembled him as a brother, and it was immortal. It was thought that at the moment of a person's birth the *ka* was permanently joined to the individual; this double aspect was often recorded in images. The creator god Khnum made man and his *ka* in the same moment on his potter's wheel. The *ka* can also care for a man after his death, as it alone

89 Anubis, god of death
Middle Egypt; early Ptolemaic Period, ca. 300 BC; painted wood; H. 72 cm, W. 10.2 cm, D. 20.7 cm; Hildesheim, Pelizaeus-Museum, 1582.

The jackal-headed Anubis is one of the principal funerary gods. He watched over the embalming and is also represented as an active participant in the procedure. This function is carried out by a priest representative wearing a mask of Anubis.

90 A "natural mummy" from the Predynastic Period
Gebelein; Naqada II culture, middle of the fourth millennium BC; length of outstretched figure 163 cm; London, The British Museum, EA 32751.

The mummy, known today as "Ginger," was dried out in the hot desert sands that preserved him quite naturally. The experience gained by prehistoric Egyptians from witnessing this kind of desiccation later led to the custom of embalming the dead.

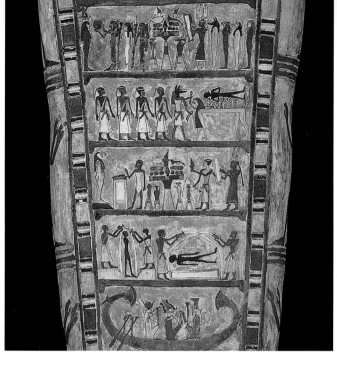

91 Mummy bandages of Princess Nesittanebasheru
Western Thebes, Deir el-Bahari, royal mummy cache; Third Intermediate Period, Twenty-first Dynasty, ca. 1000 BC; linen; max. L. 480 cm, max. W. 30 cm; Leiden,

Rijksmuseum van Oudheden, AMM 8.
Mummy bandages of varying length and breadth were used. The material shows a particularly fine weave. Some have ends finished with fringes.

92 Coffin of Mutirdis
el-Hibe; Greco-Roman Period, second–first century BC; painted wood; L. 170 cm, W. 46 cm; Hildesheim, Pelizaeus-Museum, 1953.
This coffin is decorated with eight panels, one

above the other, the fifth and seventh of which are rare illustrations of the embalming ritual: the body, represented as a black silhouette, is prepared for embalming by priests. They recite magical spells and are pouring purifying liquids.

could come and go between the actual tomb and the chamber lying in front with provisions. The *ka* receives the spiritual equivalents of the food offerings placed there. It is represented in the form of a man's up-raised arms, or as a human figure with these arms on its head.

The *ba*, the second element of the soul, on the other hand, is closely linked with the human heart; it leaves the body at the moment of death and is therefore represented as a bird with human head. It could assume any form and wander about, but it always returns to its appointed place, the tomb. The *ba* was an innate part of the individual, which enabled him to transform himself, in life as in death. Through this "bird spirit" it enabled the deceased to return to the land of the living by day, on condition that the body agreed to return at night unscathed to its resting place in the realm of the dead. A damaged body condemned the *ba* to everlasting homelessness, and thus eradicated the person's personality forever.

The third "spiritual essence" of an individual is the *akh*. It is also immortal and it can most accurately be described by the term "eternal soul." The *akh* belongs in the world of the gods, as emerges from the Pyramid Texts. Its iconographic representation takes the form of an Ibis with a crown.

It is almost a paradox that the ancient Egyptians regarded *ka*, *ba*, and *akh* as immortal, yet retained the principle of preserving the mortal body undamaged as far as possible, in the belief that only then could the three spiritual essences survive.

In prehistoric times, the dead were interred directly in the ground in a fetal position, either naked or covered with linen cloths. As long as the body did not come into contact with ground water, it would dry out completely in the hot desert sand. Furthermore, it would be sterilized by the natural salt content and protected from putrefaction. Often even the contents of the intestines have been preserved, so that in a few

cases the ingredients of the last meal can be determined. Possibly these contracted burial positions were later decisive in forming the belief that the deceased awaited rebirth in the land of the immortals, curled up like a fetus in the body of the earth. But if knowledge was lacking of the physical and chemical processes involved in "natural mummification" of this kind, then it might have been precisely this glimpse of the apparently undamaged bodies of Egyptians long dead that began a train of events leading eventually to artificial mummification. We can still partially reconstruct the exact procedure of mummification and the precise quantification of materials. There are clues contained in the etymological origins of the terms "mummy" and "embalming." The word "mummy" is of ancient Persian derivation and originally it denoted bitumen or pitch, which was much used in medicine. "Embalming" goes back to the Latin term meaning to rub the body with aromatic oils and ointments. Details of the actual procedure of mummification have not come down to us, or at least not from the highpoints of ancient Egyptian civilization. The topic is treated on one or two coffins of the second and first centuries BC, but they lack the kind of detail that would give us a more accurate view of pharaonic mummification than that provided by Herodotus (see pp. 459 ff.).

The Mummification Ritual

Two papyri from the end of the first century AD give an account of the ritual embalming of various parts of the body. They concentrate on describing the spells to be spoken, which guaranteed that the part of the body "being treated" would eventually reawaken for a new life. These texts undoubtedly reflect an actual "handbook" for embalmers compiled earlier, which gave a precise description of every

93 Wrapping the mummy and preparing the coffin
Western Thebes, Tomb of Tjai (TT 23); New Kingdom, Nineteenth Dynasty, ca. 1250 BC.

These scenes of the embalming ritual show in detail the wrapping of the mummy by the priests (left). Both scenes to the right show the preparation of the coffin.

detail: the movements appropriate when approaching the body, the materials to use, how to apply them, and which ritual formulas to recite. The application of the mummy bandages lasted for fifteen days. Every aspect was described, vast numbers of resin-soaked linen bandages of various thicknesses and widths had to be prepared, sometimes reaching a total length of 4,800 m. Some bandages were decorated with fringes; royal mummies such as those of Amenophis II and Thutmosis III have bandages with these fringes and hieroglyphic texts on them taken from the Book of the Dead. In general we can say that techniques of wrapping mummies were constantly improved upon in the course of the New Kingdom, up until the Twenty-first Dynasty.

Before the actual wrapping, all the bandages (in Egyptian, *wet*) were sorted out according to the use, length, width, and thickness, and the start of each course was marked. The body lay on a specially prepared couch, which enabled the embalmers to work unhindered all round the body. Normally, rough linen was applied to the body first, while the finer bandages were used to finish the wrapping. Large linen cloths were also used; these were attached to the head and to the feet. The material would either be bought specially for the burial or, as archaeological evidence has shown, linen was sometimes taken from the house of the deceased.

There were special kinds of cloth in which the image of a deity had previously been wrapped; these were treated as sacred and were very highly prized. The papyri mentioned above inform us of the "master of secrets," a priest who wore a mask of the god Anubis. He directed the embalming and placed his hand on the head of the deceased. Besides the heart, the head was the most important part of the body. It was thought to be the center of life; the features of the face allowed the soul of the deceased to recognize his body, to return to it again, and so bring it back to life. Next, the hands were embalmed and

wrapped, beginning with the left and then the right. After this came the feet. From the few scenes in which a mummification is shown, we know that a different priest accompanied every stage of the work with recitation of magical formulas that he recited from a papyrus roll.

After the head followed the embalming of the trunk of the body. In the papyrus text describing this task there are comments about the nature of the oil and the materials. The oil was considered to be of "divine origin;" in it were the body fluids of the four divine creators.

The prayers spoken by the priests are especially concerned with the "application" of the amulets and the talismen with magical powers placed between the bandages. The materials used for the amulets gives them special symbolic powers; gold is connected with the daytime, silver with night, turquoise with the daytime sky, and lapis lazuli with the night sky.

By far the most important amulet was the scarab, which corresponded to the heart and was laid on the chest. On its underside was a brief exhortation to the heart not to speak out against its owner at the underworld tribunal in the Hall of Osiris.

When the wrapping was complete, the outermost bandages were also decorated with amulets, for example with figures of the gods: the Four Sons of Horus, the protective goddesses Isis, Nephthys, Neith, and Selket, a figure of Anubis, and the winged scarab. The end of the embalming and wrapping with bandages were compared to sunrise and sunset. Finally the mummy mask was put over the head and shoulders. These were made of plaster-covered linen or metal – pure gold for some of the pharaohs – and they reproduced the features of the deceased.

Humans were not the only beings to be mummified; animals were too. Thousands of animal mummies have been discovered, especially from the Ptolemaic and Roman Periods. These discoveries allow us to drawn conclusions about animal mummification earlier, in the pharaonic period.

From Saqqara alone four million embalmed ibises are known. One reason for this mummification of animals was the burial of favorite pets along with the deceased, although more often it was an animal worshipped as a god that was being included. Frequently these

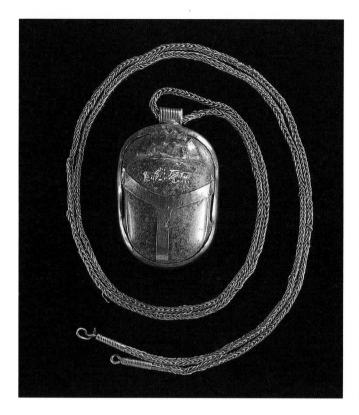

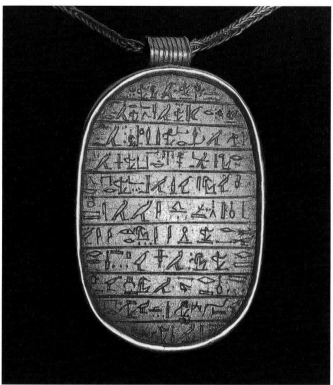

had their own coffins and tomb stelae. A good example of the extent of the honors accorded to sacred animals in Egypt is the Apis bull. These animals were provided with tombs and lavish burials in huge stone sarcophagi that can still be seen at the Serapeum at Saqqara. The embalming ritual was similar to that developed for humans. The mummies of the Apis bulls were covered with costly amulets and jewels just like the royal mummies. This is undoubtedly the reason why they were destroyed by tomb robbers, with the result that none has survived.

The Coffin

The mummification of the body is simply an attempt to equip the dead for eternity. The body was physically protected by embalming and wrapping in linen; then magical and spiritual protection was given by means of the amulets; after this followed the additional physical protection of a coffin, and where possible this was sealed inside yet another enclosure, the sarcophagus.

The coffin was generally painted on the inside. Doors and eyes played an important role in the imagery used. The deceased, who lived in his coffin as if in a house, also needed to be able to leave this home if he, or rather his *ka*, wished to visit the outside world. The udjat eyes helped him to recognize the tomb offerings, to see the rising sun, or to sense other events. Similarly a "map of the underworld" was sometimes included on the coffin, which helped him to choose the right way. There were magical spells to prevent him suffering a second death among the dangers of the netherworld.

Mummiform or anthropoid coffins were first developed during the Middle Kingdom when it became customary to fit a death mask over the head and shoulders of the body. This mask was probably also intended to compensate for the gradual alteration of the mummified body that could occur with the passage of time, so that the deceased could always be recognized again by his *ba*. At the same time this made the coffin resemble the funerary god Osiris who was usually represented as a mummified king.

The coffins were originally made of cartonnage, as well as linen or papyrus strengthened with plaster. Later, toward the end of the Second Intermediate Period, wooden coffins become much more common. These had plain decoration with bands of inscriptions identifying the deceased, and images of gods. We know from the discovery of the tomb of Tutankhamun that New Kingdom kings were buried in several coffins fitted one inside another. This practice of protecting the

94, 95 Heart scarab of General Djehuti
Saqqara; New Kingdom, Eighteenth Dynasty, ca. 1450 BC; slate, with gold clasp and long gold chain; L. of scarab 8.3 cm, W. 5.3 cm, H. 2.7 cm, L. of chain 133 cm; Leiden, Rijksmuseum van Oudheden, AO 1a. Heart scarabs played a particularly important role for the deceased. The text on the under-side derives from the Book of the Dead (Spell 30B), meant to ensure that the deceased's heart will say nothing derogatory about its owner at the judgment before the tribunal of the dead. (According to ancient Egyptian beliefs the heart was the seat of the intellect and of the conscience.) The scarab of Djehuti is one of the finest pieces of its kind.

98 (opposite, bottom) The "Book of Two Ways" – decoration on the inside of the coffin of Gua
el-Bersha, Middle Kingdom, Twelfth Dynasty, ca. 1910 BC; stuccoed and painted wood; L. of coffin 260 cm; London, The British Museum, EA 30839.
The painting on the inside of the coffin depicts a map of the underworld, with two different routes; the deceased uses the map like a travel guide.
The "Book of Two Ways" represents the Egyptians' earliest attempt to transfer their idea of the underworld into a cartographic representation. Since all examples of coffins originate from el-Bersha, this underworld book would have been created there.

96 Coffin of a cat
Roman, first century AD; wood, partly gilded;
L. 37.7 cm, H. 19 cm, W. 13.3 cm; Paris,
Musée du Louvre, E 2562.
Sacred cats, which belonged to Bastet,
goddess of kings and of fertility, played an
unusual and prominent role both in the Late
Period and in the Greco-Roman Period. The
animals were sometimes mummified and
buried in their own cat-shaped coffins in the
extensive cat cemetery.

97 Lid of the inner coffin of Henutmehit
Western Thebes; New Kingdom, Nineteenth
Dynasty, ca. 1250 BC; stuccoed, gilded, and
painted wood; L. 188 cm; London, The
British Museum, EA 48001.
Even people who were not of royal blood
were placed in several coffins made of varying
materials and fitted one inside the other.
Pictures, inscriptions, and amulets protected
the deceased, and ensured a safe passage into
the afterlife.

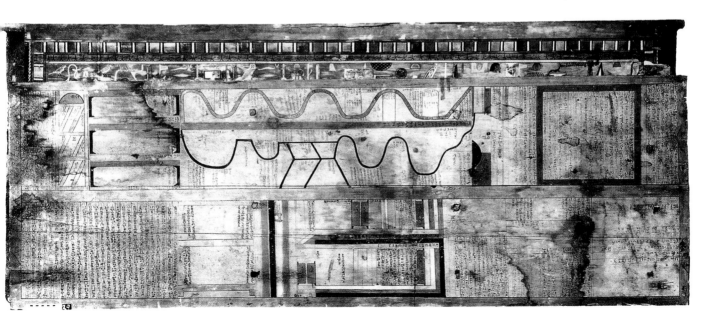

coffins fitted one inside another. This practice of protecting the mummy in a series of nested mummiform coffins became so popular during the Nineteenth to the Twenty-first Dynasty that even non-royal Egyptians were buried in this way. At that time people began decorating coffins even more lavishly both inside and out. All interior surfaces were painted with scenes of the underworld, protective gods, and images of amulets. The exteriors show scenes familiar from tomb decoration: the deceased worshipping the gods, the journey of the sun god in his barque through the underworld, the tribunal hall with Osiris and the Four Sons of Horus. The winged sun disk and the winged scarab afforded additional protection, reflecting the desire of the deceased to participate in the eternal cycle of the sun god.

In addition to these colorful and often overelaborate coffins were also the plainer but equally expensive sarcophagi made of the hardest stones, generally basalt or granite. On the upper surfaces are inscriptions containing the biography of the deceased as well as texts and beautifully carved figures from the Books of the Dead.

These comments about the rites surrounding the coffin as well as the form and decoration of coffins and sarcophagi apply principally to the funerals of kings, high-ranking officials of the state, and the wealthy elite classes. For the majority of the poor in Egypt there was little but wooden boards, matting, and earthen vessels to protect the body for its rebirth in the afterlife. For many, the costs of mummification simply could not be met, although paradoxically the bodies of many poor people have been better preserved in the hot, dry desert sands than some of the most elaborately embalmed mummies in coffins.

The Offerings

The canopic jars were placed close to the sarcophagus, usually protected in a canopic box. These contained the internal organs of the deceased, which were removed for mummification and thus formed a part of the burial as crucial as the coffin bearing the actual body. Around this ensemble was arranged a great number of offerings – some of them specially produced for the burial, others taken from the belongings of the deceased – to make life in the hereafter as pleasant as possible.

Yet this life of eternal serenity was complicated by the duties that the deceased had to perform in cultivating crops in the afterlife. His efforts were needed for food production in the fields. This was achieved by taking into the tomb as many servant figurines as possible, known as *shabtis*, who would undertake the roughest tasks. A magical text inscribed or painted onto the figures helped to bring this about. Up to 365 *shabtis*, that is one for every day of the year, have been found among some tomb offerings, while thirty-six well-dressed *shabti* overseers, equipped with whips, saw to it that the work was done without hindrance.

99–102 Coffin ensemble of an unknown person Western Thebes, Deir el-Bahari, second "cache" (Bab el-Gasus); Twenty-first Dynasty; stuccoed and painted wood; L. of outer coffin 194 cm; of inner coffin 197 cm; Bern, Bernisches Historisches Museum, Æ 10.
This mummy of an unknown woman comes from the second cache at Deir el-Bahari, known as Bab el-Gasus. A great number of mummies of priests of Amun and their relatives were taken there to keep them safe from robbers. Both of this anonymous woman's coffins are richly decorated with a variety of religious scenes. This is a clear example, so typical of the Twenty-first Dynasty, both of a preference for images with special power in as many variants as possible, and the attempt to place them as close as possible to the body of the deceased. Furthermore, temporal prosperity was demonstrated by precious jewelry, most prominent in the decoration of the wig and collar, also thought to guarantee prosperity for the afterlife.

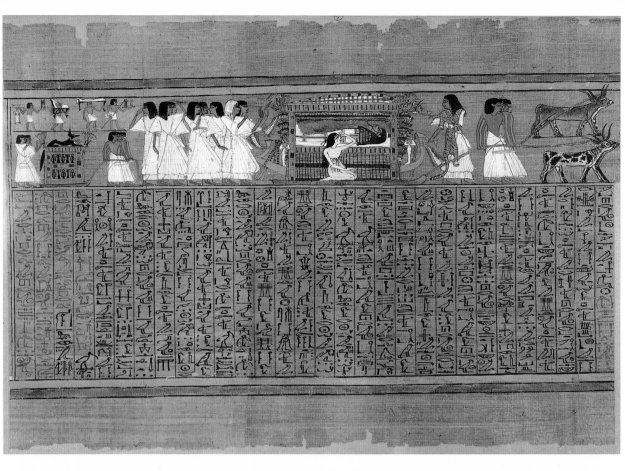

The Funeral Rites – Resurrection and Immortality

Ideally, before the body and tomb offerings were taken on the ceremonial procession to the prepared tomb accompanied by the laments of professional mourners, a journey to Abydos would first be undertaken.

The cult journey to Abydos was a voyage to the holy center of the god of resurrection, Osiris, and was inseparable from belief in this god. Yet in reality this journey would have taken place for most Egyptians only symbolically, as the funeral procession crossed the Nile toward the west and was led through the necropolis.

But people did wish to participate in the sacred beneficence of Abydos and in the mysteries that were performed there in honor of Osiris. The cult journey to Abydos is frequently represented on the walls of tomb chambers, indicating that this rite was of foremost importance to the Egyptians, an essential part of every burial.

After the body was embalmed, the funeral procession took place and is represented both inside tombs and on papyri of the Book of the Dead. The mummy was accompanied by its tomb furnishings. The deceased was taken to the necropolis in his coffin, followed by the canopic shrine, cult implements, burial equipment, and provisions. With the coffin also went an item called the Tekenu; this was a sack-like object with a human head, which may have contained human remains from the mummification.

Servants, priests, and mourners followed the procession to the tomb, where the mummy underwent the ritual "opening of its mouth" ceremony. This meant that the mummy or the statue was magically "revived" by the sem priest on behalf of the deceased's eldest son. Rites of purification were performed, incense was burnt, and ointment was put onto the face and various parts of the body in as many as seventy-five separate rites. These show clearly how firmly it was believed that the deceased would come back to life both physically and spiritually.

In summary one can say that the burial rites were intended to procure as secure a new life in eternity as possible for the deceased Egyptian.

The belief that life really begins only after death, and no effort should be spared in striving for it, gave the mortuary cult a more prominent place in the lives of Egyptians that in any other ancient civilization. For the living, this belief necessitated a series of extremely expensive preparations and obligations. As mentioned above, not everyone could afford every procedure required; this leaves us with the impression that only the wealthy longed for another "rich life" after death. However there are some texts that explain that attaining the afterlife did not depend on the fitting out of the tomb, but on the moral actions and thoughts of the person during his earthly existence.

105 Shabtis and shabti box of Henutmehit
Western Thebes; New Kingdom, Nineteenth Dynasty, ca. 1250 BC; cabinet: stuccoed and painted wood; H. 34 cm; London, The British Museum, EA 41549.
From the late Eighteenth Dynasty onward the number of mummiform servant figures known as *shabtis* or *Ushebtis* and used as funerary gifts for the dead rose drastically, and continued to be used up until the early Ptolemaic Period. Whereas the size, quality, and material of these funerary statuettes could vary widely according to the financial outlay of the grave's owner, their inscription with the sixth chapter of the Book of the Dead (the shabti magical text) was almost obligatory, although numerous variations and exceptions exist. Equally typical was the use of painted wooden boxes in chapel form to store away the shabtis .

103, 104 Papyrus with the Book of the Dead of Ani; funeral procession
Probably Western Thebes; New Kingdom, Nineteenth Dynasty, ca. 1250 BC; painted papyrus: H. 38 cm; London, The British Museum, EA 10470.
The papyrus of Ani is among the most famous and best-preserved Books of the Dead from the New Kingdom. The text is adorned with many colored vignettes. The image of the funeral procession is extremely detailed. In this vignette the sledge with the mummy and coffin ensemble is pulled by multi-colored bulls, accompanied by a priest who is burning incense and pouring libations. The smaller, richly decorated canopic shrine, is also pulled on a sledge. The procession includes priests and relatives, porters bringing the tomb furnishings, and a large group of mourners. In front of the tomb, Anubis is summoned to receive the mummy by the prayers and offerings of the priests. One of the priests holds an instrument for "opening the mouth," in order to perform the ritual reviving the deceased.

106 Stele of Heny with his children
Middle Kingdom, early Twelfth Dynasty, ca. 1920 BC; painted limestone; H. 30 cm, W. 35 cm; Copenhagen, Ny Carlsberg Glyptothek, Æin 1018

To the left stands the deceased Heny, son of Hetep, with a long staff in one hand – which characterizes him as an important man – and holding a scepter in the other. His clothing consists of no more than collar and loincloth; his head is adorned with a short wig, a moustache, and a beard. In front of him stands his son Rehu, whose nakedness symbolizes his youth, and who grasps his father's staff. To the right stands "It, born of Sat-Sobek." In the spaces between the figures are painted two offering ensembles, a smaller one on a mat above the son, a larger one on a low table in front of the daughter. The orientation of the figures relative to one another and their attributes reveal an image of son and daughter carrying out the mortuary cult for their deceased father.

The Mortuary Cult

Ursula Verhoeven

The words Ancient Egypt most readily conjure up associations with the pyramids, mummies, and golden tomb treasures. These are elements of the Egyptian mortuary cult that exemplify the fascination for and peculiarity of Egyptian culture. But the magnificent tomb buildings of the kings and their high officials are only part of something larger, and it must not be forgotten that there was a much greater number of burials of poorer people, about whose cult practices very little is known.

The cult performed for the dead is divided – in Egypt as practically everywhere else in the world – into two phases of different duration:

1. A limited period for the operations on the body, from the moment of death until the close of the burial ceremonies (for this see the essays on mummification, tomb layout, and burial). Particular equipment was included in the tomb to provide permanently for the needs of the dead: some were real objects, others were symbolic ones. There were written mortuary texts to supply the deceased with information about the realm of the afterlife, as well as ensuring his prosperity, keeping him well-provided, transfiguring him among the gods, and also ensuring his protection against malicious powers.

2. After the burial the offering ceremonies and festive rituals at the tomb begin. These were to be performed regularly, and were regarded from their inception as continuing without limit.

3. The general attitude of the living toward the dead can be counted as a third area, which was written down in the form of instructions and ideal biographies, all anchored in the practices of society. In Egypt an entirely personal approach can be seen in the letters written to the dead, analogous to the ancestor cult for respected villagers of the past.

Offerings for the Dead

In prehistoric times it was already the practice to place food in clay vases in the tomb at the time of burial, along with ornaments and weapons. There were other things that served to make the life in the underworld as safe and normal as possible: figurines of women (as tokens of sexuality, fertility, and regeneration) as well as a variety of amulets. We do not know how the cult that was later performed at the tomb at regular intervals looked, or even if there was one at all.

There is clear evidence that from the First Dynasty onward the tomb was conceived as a home for the deceased in which he would be

107 Magical offering plate
Middle Kingdom, ca. 2100–1900 BC; clay with red slip; H. 4 cm, L. 27 cm, W. 25 cm; Heidelberg, Collection of the Ägyptologisches Institut der Universität, 976.
Various foods are modeled on the plate: a trussed bull, two round loaves or cakes, a leg of beef, and ox horns. Two crossed channels and a third groove running around the edge allowed water poured over the plate to be collected and run off through the opening at the bottom. As the water moistened the symbolic dishes it produced a kind of magical "soup" for the dead.

able to live on in the afterlife. The splendor of the burial equipment corresponded to the varying living standards enjoyed in life. The offering cult took place mainly on the east side of the tomb, and it was marked by architectural features. The offering consisted primarily of provisions; the thigh of an ox can be seen as the archetypal offering to the dead. The same function could be magically substituted by food offerings modeled in clay or carved in stone, if these were regularly renewed by a ritual cleansing with water. Model versions of property such as stone vases, figures of servants, houses and boats were placed in

108 Model boat
Predynastic Period, ca. 3300 BC; painted ceramic with slip; L. 55 cm; Berlin, SMPK, Ägyptisches Museum, 13834.
Boats like this were provided as tomb furnishings in pre- and early dynastic times. They were to provide transport for the dead in the afterlife. This model reproduces a boat made of rushes, with a cabin in the middle and human figures in the bow and stern.

109 Nefernisut, mortuary priest at the funerary repast
Giza, West cemetery; Old Kingdom, early Sixth Dynasty, ca. 2340 BC; limestone; H. 45.5 cm, W. 47.6 cm, D. 14.4 cm; Hildesheim, Pelizaeus-Museum, 414.
This block comes from the false door of a professional mortuary priest ("servant of the *ka*"). His tomb was situated near the Great Pyramids and thus close to the dead kings. He sits with his wife Senet at the offering table with tall loaves, and above it are other offerings described in hieroglyphs: "incense, green and black eye paint, and a rinsing bowl." Beneath the table are listed: "1000 loaves, clothing and alabaster vessels." The offering formula in the horizontal bands above and below states that "on each day and on each feast day" an offering to the dead (*peret-kheru*) should be held, which is contingent upon the royal mortuary cult.

the tomb for the use of the deceased to stand in for his temporal conveniences.

The eldest son was normally responsible for the burial and the regular schedule of offerings that followed it. In this early period we know that there were already professional mortuary priests. Over time these became known as "spirit finder" (for the King) "servant of the *ka*" (life force of the deceased), "caretaker," "purification priest," or "libation provider." These individuals performed the offering rituals at the tomb, while a lector priest recited the magical spells.

In the bipartite tomb structure of the Old Kingdom, the body was placed in a burial chamber hidden underground, and in order to receive offerings it had to be summoned to the accessible part above ground. The offering place was marked with a cult niche, which developed into the false door, and in the New Kingdom a statue niche was placed here. It was the mortuary priest's responsibility to summon the deceased to emerge out of the false doorway or into the statue, and strengthen his *ka* with the fresh food placed on the offering mat or table. From this the mortuary offerings came to be known as *peret-kheru*, which means "coming forth at the call." The meal of fresh loaves became the earliest version of the funerary repast or table scene as is found on stelae, tablets, and tomb walls, showing the deceased dining at the offering table. Beside this is often a detailed list of offerings, with as many as ninety ingredients with their quantities given, including staple foodstuffs, oils, vessels, equipment, and victuals of all kinds. In one tomb from the Second Dynasty an actual meal was found, laid out next to the coffin on assorted ceramic and stone plates. The menu (reconstructed in order of courses) consisted of wheat bread, barley porridge, cooked fish, pigeon stew, roast quail, kidneys, ribs, fig compote, berries, cakes, cheese, and wine. The skeleton of the female tomb owner turned out to be that of a woman approximately sixty years old; she had only been able to chew on one side of her mouth for several decades.

The produce for the regular "feeding" of the dead was brought in an "offering procession." Civil servants who were allowed to build their tombs near the royal tomb complexes, and had the necessary means, were especially privileged because their needs were provided for by the royal mortuary cult. The dead pharaoh received goods from the royal domains. The surrounding tombs of courtiers and officials, who were provided for during the king's lifetime, then also benefited from these offerings, and finally the provisions were distributed for the use of the mortuary priests and their families.

The Mortuary Texts

The mortuary texts provide a glimpse into another way in which ordinary people could share in the privileges of royalty. From the Fifth Dynasty on, spells that conjured up the king's ascent into heaven to join the gods, known as the "Pyramid Texts," were carved on to the walls of the royal tomb chambers. These provide the earliest detailed information about Egyptian religious beliefs; they imply a pantheon that already had its particular character. Their function was originally as part of the mortuary cult, and they consist mainly of spells recited by priests at the burial and perhaps also on particular festivals. The act of carving them in stone "stored" them for ever for the king (and, fortunately, for us).

In the Middle Kingdom something of a democratization of funerary beliefs took place, and even the ordinary Egyptian could draw upon these and other texts (reworked to some extent) for his or her own burial. They were in any case not applied to the walls of the tombs – which in private burials were always reserved for scenes taken from everyday life and from offering rituals – but were placed close to the deceased on the walls of the rectangular wooden coffins. These "coffin texts" were also combined – as with tomb furnishings – with pictures of food and implements.

In the New Kingdom the number of these spells grew to such an extent (over 190), that the Egyptians began to write them on papyrus rolls, up to 25 m long. These could be placed inside the coffin to save space, sometimes fitted just underneath or above the mummy's head. In the nineteenth century this collection of spells was described using the slightly confusing term "Book of the Dead;" the Egyptian title states: "Beginning of the spells for going forth by day, for elevations and transfigurations, for entering and leaving the realm of the dead, to be spoken with justified voice on the day of the burial of " – the name of the deceased is to be filled in here – "who enters (again), after he has gone forth."

The compilation of the spells and their order varied for some time, until in the Twenty-sixth Dynasty a canonical list of 165 spells was established, in a sequence that we still use today to number them. Among them, for example, can be found the "Spell to prevent a man from being bitten by a snake in the underworld" (BD 34), and the "Spell to prevent rot in the underworld" (BD 45), and the "Spell to have air to breathe and water to drink in the underworld" (BD 59), a wish that takes on a special meaning in the oppressive tomb complexes in the desert. In these Spells the "Sycamore of Nut" is invoked as a tree

110 False door of Nikaure and of his wife Ihat Saqqara, tomb of Nikaure; Old Kingdom, Fifth Dynasty, ca. 2470 BC; painted limestone; H. 227 cm, W. 235 cm; Cairo, Egyptian Museum, CG 1414.
The false door was originally placed together with another one in the tomb chamber of Nikaure, who was "chief officer of the messengers and privy counsellor." It was prob-

ably intended mainly for his consort Ihat, the "priestess of Hathor," who is also represented on the door's central niche. In the upper part of the door the couple is seen in front of the list of offerings and at the offering table; in the lower part their children accompany them. On the base stones appear priests charged with maintaining the cult for the deceased, as well as a harpist and a woman singer.

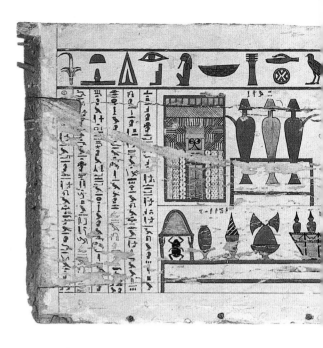

111 Offering table of Imhotep
Early Ptolemaic Period; third century BC; limestone; London, The British Museum, EA 1688.
The T-shaped offering table was like the simple clay plate used for a water libation, which can be seen in the streams running from the water vases in the center. Various divine figures feature in the panels promising food and drink to the deceased. In the triangles above are shown Isis and Nephthys, sisters of Osiris, who tend the *ba* bird of the deceased: "May your *ba* live from water." In the central sections, on either side of the water vases, are two Nile figures with the plant emblems of the Two Lands on their heads. This image uses fat men as personifications to represent a heavy inundation from the Nile, and the fertility of the fields that follows. Below, the deceased himself appears twice, once standing and the second time sitting before a tree goddess. To the left she grows out of the tree as a woman, to the right only her two arms reveal the divine nature of the "sycamore, mistress of the offerings." This is the name by which she is summoned in the spell from the Book of the Dead: "To drink water in the necropolis."

goddess who provides shade and food, and who is also frequently represented on stelae and tomb walls.

A central part of the Book of the Dead concerns the trial of the deceased before the tribunal of the afterlife, which is presided over by the "great god" Osiris (BD 125). Also of considerable interest is Spell 175 ("not to die a second time in the underworld"), which contains a dialogue between the gods Atum and Osiris about the end of the world and about the realm of the dead as a place of privation. The second part of Spell 136 A points out what people hoped to achieve by possession of these spells, explaining at the same time why they were so keen to acquire for themselves or for a relative a Book of the Dead containing many colored illustrations, for what must have been an enormous price:

> *"The spirit for whom you do this will not perish for ever.*
> *He will exist in the glory of a god.*
> *Nothing evil can befall him.*
> *He will exist as a spirit in the west with all his faculties.*
> *He will not die again.*
> *He will eat and drink with Osiris each day.*
> *He will be hauled with the Kings of Upper and*
>   *Lower Egypt.*
> *He will drink water from the drinking place at the river.*
> *He will enjoy sexual acts,*
> *and he will go forth and descend by day like Horus.*
> *He will be alive and will exist like a god.*
> *He will be worshipped by the living like Re."*

113 Stela of Niay, priest of Sakhmet, and of his wife
Saqqara; New Kingdom, beginning of the Nineteenth Dynasty, ca. 1290 BC; limestone; H. 56 cm, W. 59.5 cm; Hanover, Kestner-Museum, 2933.
A shaven-headed priest from Memphis and his wife, who wears a splendid wig and a cone of myrrh on her head, crouch by a sycamore. The tree has a woman's breast and arms, and is addressed in the text as the goddess Isis: it promises shade and water as well as food in the afterlife. The deceased wished that as "souls" free to move about – embodied as *ba* birds – they would be able to flutter over an idyllic scene such as this one, and feast on food and drink. Here, two *ba* birds with heads of the two addressees perform just this activity under the tree, by a small lake with lotus flowers.

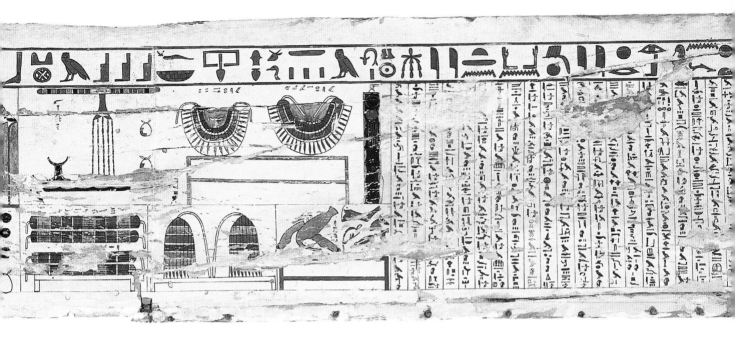

themes as the reunion with the king whose
privileges continue into the afterlife, with the
sun god, and with the scribe of the creator
god. The sections show: left, a magnificent
false door through which contact with the
outside world should be possible; next to it
are three water vessels in a rack and, underneath, various jars some containing wine. To

the right is a large offering table with narrow
half-loaves of bread; above is a leg of beef, and
below it packets and balls of incense. In the
middle is shown a small headrest next to a
belt, two collars, and a scribe's palette, and
under that appear ornamental accessories,
and a plate with a variety of meat. This way
the deceased had "within his reach" a variety

of necessities for the next world in addition to
the religious spells: food, drink, ornaments,
utensils, and even cult incense.

Some of the Books of the Dead were individually reproduced from
master copies by professional scribes working on commission for the
buyer, whose name and title would be worked directly into the text.
Others were compiled by the scribes for sale, and the name of the
subsequent owner had to be entered in the numerous spaces left empty
for this purpose.

In the region of Memphis during the Thirtieth Dynasty a variant
form of the mortuary texts became popular: these were written out on
long narrow mummy bandages that were wound right onto the body.

Beside the ever-popular "Book of the Dead," other funerary texts
came into use in the Ptolemaic Period, which were described as books
of the scribal god Thoth (Greek Hermes), for example, the "Books
(literally "letters") of Breathing." The "Book of Traversing in Eternity,"
which became widespread in Roman times, is a hymn to the dead
person that was supposed to transfer the deceased to numerous cult
centers and festivals in the world of the living and was probably recited
at the burial as well as at festivals for the dead.

The Obligations of the Living

The numerous objects that furnished the tomb, the scenes of daily life
and of offerings on tomb walls, the mortuary literature that
accompanies them, the mummification of the body, the power of the
amulets – not even all of this was sufficient to ensure one of future life
and prosperity in the hereafter. In ancient Egypt much was deemed
desirable in order for a person to live on in divine form in the afterlife:

a continual supply of fresh food, water to drink, the presence and
furthermore the voice by the tombside of the living, and the
remembrance of the name of a deceased; these were all regarded
as indispensable.

The obligations of the living to tend the tomb, remember the
dead, and carry on the mortuary cult were promoted by the existence of
precepts that cited these as characteristic of exemplary people. In the
teaching of Ani in the New Kingdom this included self-interest:
"Provide water for your father and mother who rest in the desert valley
… Let the people know that you are doing it and then your son will do
the same for you." The so-called ideal biographies extolled the virtue of
honoring of the dead, alongside the theme of caring for widows,
orphans, and the hungry or naked: "I did not forget to call all my
ancestors by name, each of them individually."

Djefaihapi, overseer of priests and provincial governor from Asiut
(Twelfth Dynasty), drew up ten contracts in his lifetime with various
priests (including one with himself as high priest of the God
Wepwawet) to make sure that the material means would be available
from which the offerings could be diverted. He engaged the priests to
carry out particular offerings on individual festivals "under the control
of his mortuary priest," effectively providing the funds from his own
resources in return for the services of the priests, and so founding the
local temple cult.

In times and places where the royal mortuary foundation
functioned unreliably, and with it the care for ordinary people, texts
were often carved onto the more accessible exterior walls of tombs that
were known as an "address to the living." The passersby – often the

114 Last judgment tribunal in the Book of the Dead of Iahtesnakht
Herakleopolis Magna; Late Period, Twenty-sixth Dynasty, ca. 600 BC; painted papyrus; H. 23 cm, W. 65 cm; Cologne, Seminar für Ägyptologie, Pap. Colon. 10207, column 58. This scene from the Book of the Dead, a later development of the Coffin Texts, illustrates Spell 125, which describes the entry into "the hall of the ultimate Truth" and the trial of the deceased before Osiris, supreme judge of the

dead. To the right, this example of the text shows the figure of a deceased man in a gesture of greeting, for the papyrus was painted for sale at a later date. It was, however, preserved with a woman called Iahtesnakht ("The moon is her strength"). In this important scene a small picture of her and her name have been subsequently inserted, as it was in nearly 400 other special places for the name throughout the text. Her heart (left) is weighed on the scales against

the seated figure of order, *maat* (truth). The balance is held by the small baboon of the officiating god Thoth, whose standing ibis-headed figure notes the result on his scribe's palette in the middle of the scene and shares it with the enthroned Osiris, judge of the dead. In cases of failure the "great devourer," a hybrid of various wild animals, destroys the heart of the deceased. Above, the deceased can just be seen (right edge) before a committee of forty-one small figures of

judges, in front of whom he utters what is called the "negative confession," saying: "I have not stolen, nor killed any man; I have not lied nor eavesdropped, not made any rash decisions, nor had sexual relations with (another) man's wife, I have not insulted the king or any god, and have not raised myself above my station."

literate professionals in question were named – were called upon to pour the water, place the offerings or – "if nothing was available" – at least to recite the offering formula and the name of the tomb's owner. This request was strengthened by reference to self-interest ("If you wish the king to praise you"), with allusions to their own lifespan ("If you love life and would hate to pass away") or with threats if the plea were not heeded (which were especially drastic in Asiut: "that person shall be boiled along with the criminals who have blasphemed against the god"). A stela of the Late Period in Berlin that was destroyed in the Second World War carried the following warnings: "The living, who will pass by the necropolis and who will come by this my tomb, who will see what lies in it and not obey the inscriptions or respect the statue: their god will not receive white bread, but they will belong to

the enemies of the presiding god. You may say (perhaps): 'What happens… happens. The sun is (yet) shining here, and the offering that is to be given is the business of him to whom it should be given. (But) you should not set your back against those who lie in your tombs! The punishment for that is in heaven… (At least) mourn for the one who is in darkness, without light!'

From the period following the New Kingdom, after the tomb robbing and destruction at the end of the Ramesside Period, many small-scale wooden stelae survive, especially in Thebes, which often show deceased women as well as men in an attitude of prayer before a god. The function and size of these mortuary stelae provide evidence that tomb complexes that were accessible above ground had now become quite unsafe and that a regular mortuary cult was often

Middle Kingdom, Twelfth Dynasty, twelfth year of the reign of Amenemhat II, ca. 1902 BC; limestone; H. 69.5 cm, W. 39 cm; Hanover, Kestner-Museum, 2927.
The owner of this stela had the same name as the contempoary ruling king, Amenemhat II (1914–1879/76 BC), whose throne name is written in a cartouche in the first line of text. The deceased is seated with his wife on a chair before a low table piled with various offerings. In the text he describes his exemplary life: "I was (like) a father to the orphans, (like) a spouse for the widows, I kept the wind from the cold, gave bread to the hungry, clothes to the naked, intervened with a man's superior without him being aware of it." Next he pleads: "O living people who pass by this stela! You should say: offer a thousand loaves and beers on the altar of the god Khontamenti, lord of Abydos, for the worthy Amenemhat, overseer of the cattle, justified, a master of veneration, and offer them also for Kem his beloved wife." Space became a problem for the last line and a half of the text as it approached the figures, and this was solved by reducing the size of the signs and also by inscribing them on the actual picture surface.

impossible. While kings and senior officials were buried within the safety of temple complex walls, less influential people made do with modest burials inside the shafts of older tombs. After the coffin, the stela was the most important tomb furnishing and took on the role of preserving the name of the deceased and of placing him or her directly in the protection of a god. An elaborately painted offering table now served to invite the divinity to make himself responsible for the prosperity of the deceased in the afterlife.

Letters to the Dead

The personal attitude of the living toward death and toward their deceased relatives is an area that, as one would expect, does not receive much attention in Egyptian sources. However, the few comments written about it reveal some interesting facets of the mortuary cult. Letters written by the living to a dead member of the family have survived from as early as the Old Kingdom. These are mainly addressed by widows and orphaned children to the former head of the family and concern such things as disputes over an inheritance. Alternatively, they were written because the writer was troubled by childlessness, illness or nightmares. They needed to communicate with the *akh* of the deceased, a term that recent research tells us should be interpreted as "active being with hidden origin;" one could also say "invisible being that can have influence," or more concretely "active spirit of the dead."

These messages were often written on small clay dishes on which a delicacy was placed. After the deceased had enjoyed the food, he would read the letter written underneath it and was expected to provide a service in return. The text reminded the *akh* of earlier promises. The crisis and the wrongdoer were actually named, and an urgent appeal to the dead was made: "Wake up your father! Rouse yourself against them (the wrongdoers) with your fathers, brothers and friends, and defeat them!" Then additional offerings were promised to the dead if he used his powers to help the sender. Even down to the Coptic Period the dead were called upon as mediators for help from God. For example, the Egyptians often placed a papyrus onto the mummy inscribed to "call out for all time what is written on this papyrus until God hearkens, and hurries to bring us justice, Amen."

116 Letter to the dead on a jar stand
First Intermediate Period, ca. 2050 BC; clay with red slip, inscribed in black ink; H. 23 cm; Chicago, University of Chicago, Oriental Institute Museum, 13945.
In this letter written in a total of eight columns, a man pleads with his deceased father to keep the promise made during his lifetime, and to intercede for him. In his capacity as "excellent spirit" he was supposed to keep two malicious servant women away from the writer's spouse and to help both him and his sister give birth to a healthy boy. In return he was promised: "The Great God will honor you and give you pure bread." On top of the jar stand there must have been a special bowl, which the writer mentions: "I bring you this bowl which your mother made. Be the judge of it!"

118 Ancestor cult stela
Tell el-Amarna; New Kingdom, end of the Eighteenth Dynasty, reign of Akhenaten, ca. 1340 BC; limestone; H. 14.8 cm, W. 10.7 cm, D. 0.25 cm; Amsterdam, Allard Pierson Museum, 3733.
Small stelae such as this one found opposite house number 4 in the main street of the workers' community of Tell el-Amarna stood in niches in front of the family's house and were used for the ancestor cult. The name of the deceased is not preserved here. He sits on an elegant chair, wearing a long white loincloth, with his feet on a footrest. On his head, above a wig, he wears an ointment cone, and he smells at a lotus flower, both symbols for the happy life that is wished for the deceased. In front of him stands an offering table with three loaves and a string of onions, which were used in Egypt both as a vegetable and as an antibiotic. It also played a special cult role in the mortuary festival of Sokar.

117 Letter to a dead woman named Ankhiry, along with her statuette
Saqqara; New Kingdom, Nineteenth Dynasty, ca. 1250 BC; papyrus inscribed on both sides; H. 35.5 cm, W. 19.5 cm; painted wooden figure: H. 23 cm; Leiden, Rijksmuseum van Oudheden, papyrus Leiden I 375 = AMS 64, figure AH 115.
The text written in hieratic script contains a letter "to the lovely, active spirit of Ankhiry" from her spouse, who wrote it three years after her death as he seemed unable to find peace from her. He asks several times: "What have I done to you ?" and accuses her: "See, you do not allow my heart any peace." At the time of her death he was away on business for the pharaoh. He now describes for her his irreproachable life, perhaps to free himself of conscious or unconscious guilt. The papyrus was glued to the statuette that he placed in the tomb as an image of his spouse.

Sometimes the spirits of the dead were actually regarded as bringers of illness or of disaster, and this was attributed to a reaction to untoward behavior by the living. Thus we read in the teachings of Ani: "Give satisfaction to the spirit of the deceased; do what he wishes. Keep yourself from offending his tabu, so that you protect yourself from the effects of his many harmful powers." Occasionally it seems to have been necessary to inform spirits of their mistakes, or misunderstandings. So, for example, a widower from the New Kingdom wrote a long letter to his deceased wife in which he reminded her of how well he had always treated her and that she had no reason for being angry with him.

Similarly, at least 1,000 years earlier, another man had made a request on the back of a stela to a deceased woman to rid him of his illness since he had always maintained her mortuary cult conscientiously. She was asked to appear to him in a dream to demonstrate that she was working for him: "Then when the sun has gone up I will lay out all the good things for you and perform an offering ceremony." The implication is that he spent that night in the tomb chapel in order to be as near as possible to her spirit.

The Ancestor Cult

Exemplary Egyptians who had enjoyed a high social position in their lifetime were honored as ancestors. On the island of Elephantine, a distinctive cult arose in the Middle Kingdom around a dead official named Heqaib, who was worshipped and invoked as a saint by people from all social classes, calling him "mediator god" and "patron in the afterlife." In the New Kingdom we know from the workmen's communities of Amarna and Deir el-Medineh of a widespread ancestor cult. Inside their homes people set up small stelae to dead people thought to have had a particularly close relationship with the sun god. Offerings were made at these shrines and prayers addressed to them. The ancestors were considered able to grant these prayers from beyond the grave because of their godlike powers.

In the cemeteries various mortuary festivals were celebrated that incorporated a particular gathering of the living and the dead. In the "Beautiful Festival of the Valley" the god Amun of Karnak went on a procession, first visiting his temple at Luxor, and then the necropolis across the river in the western hills of Thebes. Relatives marched with flowers and provisions while making music to their dead. They held extended celebrations in the tomb entrances, so that life went down to the spirits of the deceased in the dark chambers in the form of singing, chatter, and the flavor of food: "Celebrate the day, put perfume and ointment to your nose, put lotus and garlands on your chest while your beloved, who fills your heart, sits by your side" (tomb of Neferhotep). The texts of these songs were inscribed with the banquet scenes on the tomb walls, and it sometimes seems that the festivals for the dead were devised to make the living aware of their own mortality: "Celebrate the beautiful day, do not tire of it! Look,

nobody is granted to take his possessions with him. Look, no one who has left has returned." (Song of Antef).

Although we encounter many different ways of preparing for a life after death in Egypt, a fear of the beyond and doubts about the effectiveness of the mortuary cult were no doubt always present and went with a love of life on earth. The following words were inscribed by a widow called Nesmut on the statue for her deceased spouse Nakhtefmut in the Twenty-second Dynasty. Her formulation is hitherto unparalleled: "Do not let us enter this land of eternity, so that our names will always be remembered. One moment in the face of the sun's rays is more enduring than in the everlasting role of the lord of the underworld."

119 Chapel for the ancestor cult of Ani
Western Thebes, Deir el-Medineh; New Kingdom, Nineteenth Dynasty, ca. 1250 BC; limestone with remains of paint; H. 36 cm; W. 21 cm; Hanover, Kestner-Museum, 2936.
The deceased again sits at an offering table with loaves, a fig, a pumpkin, and a leek, while he sniffs a lotus flower. A tomb-like chapel has been set up around the scene. On the lintel the barque of the sun is worshipped by two baboons. In the pyramidion, often added above the tombs at Deir el-Medineh, the divine sisters Isis and Nephthys mourn the hieroglyphic sign for "west," which stands for the realm of the dead and therefore also symbolizes their dead brother Osiris. The inscriptions describe the deceased Ani as *akh iker en Ra,* which means "excellent spirit of the sun god." Particularly distinguished and deserving villagers were honored after their death both by their families and by the whole community because they were thought to play a role as intermediaries between living mortals and the gods. Their memory was preserved and small offerings were made in a cult niche in their house, which in emergencies could be used for general appeals to the dead.

120 Stela of Djedamuniu(es)ankh
Western Thebes, Deir el-Bahari; Third Intermediate Period, Twenty-second Dynasty, ca. 900 BC; stuccoed and painted wood; H. 27.6 cm, W. 23 cm, D. 2.7 cm; Cairo, Egyptian Museum, R.T. 25.12.24.20.
This stela of a deceased woman whose name means "Amun has spoken, she should live," is divided into two sections. The lower part shows a rare representation of a cemetery in the western hills, with tomb superstructures, one crowned with a pyramidion as was normal at Deir el-Medineh, and the other with cavetto cornices and cupolas. On the border between farmland and desert a woman crouches on the ground making two signs of mourning: she tears at her hair, and she has bared her breast. Behind her are a sycamore and two date palms hung with ripe fruit, and an offering table with loaves and a water vessel stands between them. This lush garden paradise stands in contrast to the hot and dry desert region of the tombs.

8924

Travelers, Correspondents, and Scholars – Images of Egypt through the Millennia

Regine Schulz

Egypt and Classical Antiquity

Interest in and enthusiasm for the civilization of ancient Egypt is not a modern phenomenon, but existed already in classical antiquity. Greek and Roman writers traveled through the country and left detailed accounts of ancient customs and practices, of Egyptian religious beliefs, and the organization of their cults. These writers included famous personalities such as the historian Herodotus (who visited Egypt in about 450/440 BC), Diodorus (60–56 BC), Strabo (25–19 BC) and the polymath Plutarch (end of the first century AD). They had direct experience of the country and so created a picture of the Egypt of their own times. Despite the fascination that the land doubtless exerted on visitors, misinterpretations arose repeatedly on all fronts. On the one hand, the Egyptian pantheon was used as the foundation for other systems of belief, and Egypt was understood as the original fount of wisdom; yet numerous aspects of cult practices seemed rather disturbing. Divine animals and living statues were not to be found in Greek or Roman religion, and it was difficult for them to assimilate the context of such traditions. This accounts for the mixture of fable and historic account, of analysis and prejudice. The real fashion for things Egyptian dates from the time of the Roman Empire. Egyptian monuments, even entire obelisks, were transported to Rome; at the center of the religious interest stood the goddess Isis who was worshipped throughout the Mediterranean region. In Rome even a national temple was constructed to her. She became the universal oriental goddess to such an extent that Isidorus of Narmuthis (first century AD) wrote a hymn to her: "... the Egyptians (call you) the only goddess, since you (are) the only one, (that is to say you are) all other goddesses, which the people call by their own names." The Roman armies took the cult of Isis into the farthest corners of the empire, until the rise of Christianity drove her out, and with her disappeared a passion for Egypt that had encompassed the entire Mediterranean.

The Battle against the "Heathen" – Early Christians and Muslims

In the battle for the "true faith," early Christians and later Muslims fought vigorously against all pagan tendencies. One of the favorite targets of this animosity was pharaonic civilization and all its surviving traditions and artifacts. Temples were torn down, and stelae and statues destroyed. Shenute of Atripe (AD 348–466) was one of the most devoted attackers of heathen monuments; he was Abbot of the White Monastery

of Sohag, and was said to have lived to the age of 118 years. In his sermons he repeatedly called for the destruction of idols and for a battle against the devil. Ancient knowledge was now regarded as witchcraft, and had to be suppressed, while script and symbol were no longer understood. Even the Egyptian language changed. In the early phases of Christianity Egyptian was at least still spoken (even if riddled with Greek terms and written in Greek characters), but the old language was almost completely displaced by the Arabic of Islam. After no more than a few hundred years, a linguistic culture that had survived for thousands of years became meaningless and forgotten. It belonged to the period before "enlightenment" and was therefore not regarded as worthy of enquiry. Isolated images of ancient Egypt did survive, as it was represented in the Koran and in the Bible stories of Joseph and Moses. But otherwise it was dominated by fantastic tales of occult magical practices, reflecting the antiquated image of the pharaohs with great wisdom and unimaginable wealth.

1 Scene from the cult of Isis
Herculaneum; first century AD; wall painting; H. 82 cm, W. 81 cm; Naples, Museo Nazionale, 8924.
Evidence for the cult of Isis at Herculaneum can be found in wall paintings such as this one, and another that forms a pendant to it.

A priest stands in front of the temple doorway, and with veiled hands he offers up a cult vase to the worshippers assembled there. Below, a servant lights a fire on the altar. The Egyptian context for this cult ceremony is underlined by the presence of sphinxes, palm trees, and ibises.

2 Mosaic with scene from the story of Joseph
Venice, San Marco; ca. 1240.
This image from the roof vault of the narthex shows Joseph (left) letting his brothers collect sheaves of grain from the pyramids, which were then thought to be pharaoh's granaries.

4 The necropolises of Western Thebes
From: Richard Pococke, *Observations on Egypt*, London 1743.
The British clergyman Richard Pockocke (1704–1765) undertook two journeys to Egypt. Each lasted several months and took him up the Nile as far as Philae. His view of Western Thebes shows the private tombs of Sheikh Abd el-Gurna (right), with the Ramesseum in the foreground (D); to the left is Medinet Habu (K), and in the near foreground can be seen the colossal statues of Memnon (M, N).

In Search of Wisdom – The Image of Egypt in the Middle Ages

Despite the fact that disapproval of the pharaohs' megalomania and the associated heathen traditions was firmly rooted in the Bible and the Koran, there was a series of interested observers and scholars who tried to recover the secrets of the ancient Egyptians. Their interest centered mainly on the Great Sphinx of Giza and the pyramids. Attempts to explain them were supported partly by reference to the Bible and the Koran and partly by direct observation of the facts, provided the two positions were not mutually exclusive. A typical example of this interest is the attempt to discover the function of the great pyramids. On this subject Bishop Cosmas of Jerusalem (middle of the eighth century) let it be known that the pyramids were the granaries of Joseph, whereas the pagans believed that they were tombs. Dionysius of Tell Mahré (ninth century), the Patriarch of Antioch, rejected out of hand the interpretation as granaries, stating firmly that they were the tombs of ancient kings, for he himself had proceeded as far as 25 m deep inside one of the pyramids. In the early thirteenth century an envoy of the Hohenstaufer King Friedrich II must have stayed in Cairo and visited the pyramids with the great Arab scholar al-Idrisi (1173–1251). Al-Idrisi later writes about this visit in his "Book of the lights of the heavenly bodies: concerning the unveiling of the secrets of the pyramids" and refers to the fact that this envoy had discovered Latin inscriptions, which he copied down and translated into Arabic. Al-Idrisi and a series of other Arab scholars diligently tried to integrate the monuments from the pharaonic period into their own Islamic world view. In so doing they took into account both the archaeological facts and the associated historical evidence available to them. To some the pyramids were seen as places of admonition and promise, to others as symbols of overbearing power that would be destroyed at the end of the world. One of the fundamental questions asked by Islamic scholars (for example al-Makrizi, 1364–1442) was whether the pyramids had been built before or after the great flood. In addition to theological considerations, Islamic and Christian researchers were also always driven by the quest for the secrets and the proverbial wealth of the pharaohs, which was guarded by spirits. This was why in the year 820 the Caliph al-Mamun attempted to break into the Pyramid of Cheops. Nonetheless it was not only treasure-hunters, alchemists, and the learned who sought after secrets, but there were travelers searching in more rational ways for information (such as Wilhelm von Bodensele, who traveled to Egypt in about 1335; Felix Fabri, a dominican monk from Ulm, who stayed in Egypt in about 1480 and again in 1483/84; or Baron d'Anglure from Champagne who was there in about 1395).

3 (opposite) The Pyramid of Cheops
From: Athanasius Kircher, *Turris Babel*, 1679.
Athanasius Kircher, a German Jesuit and polymath (1602–1680), aroused more interest in ancient Egypt than almost anyone else of his time. Kircher worked on various books on the language and civilization, among them an (ultimately failed) attempt to decipher hieroglyphs proceeding from a purely symbolical interpretation. Kircher represents the Great Pyramid at Giza as a stepped construction with monumental entrance portals and stairways descending to underground crypts.

5 Luxor Temple
From: Frederik L. Norden, *Travels in Egypt and Nubia*, 1757.
Frederik L. Norden (1708–1742), a Danish sea captain, was sent in 1738 by King Christian VI to explore Egypt. His account of the journey was very popular, and several editions were published beginning in 1751, which included translations into other languages. Norden represents the entrance pylon to Luxor Temple with twin obelisks and seated colossal figures of Ramesses II. He shows the scene as it was then, still largely buried.

6 Fallen colossal figure at Memphis
From: Richard Lepsius, *Denkmaeler aus Aegypten und Aethiopien*, Berlin 1859.
The final great investigative expedition of the nineteenth century was conducted by Richard Lepsius (1810–1884) who traveled to Egypt and the Sudan in the service of the King of Prussia in the years 1842–1845. This print from his lavish twelve-volume folio publication shows a colossal statue of Ramesses II among the palm-studded ruins on the plain of Memphis.

7 (opposite) From Alexandria to Philae
From: *Description de l'Egypte*, Paris 1825. This frontispiece is from the less expensive second edition of the original of 1809, and depicts temple sites in a virtual landscape with individual monuments in the foreground. Among them lies the famous "Zodiac of Dendera" relief (bottom right), which today hangs in the Louvre.

Hieroglyphs, Pyramids, and Mummies – The Search for the Key to the Puzzle

In the late Middle Ages and into the Renaissance the number of merchants and pilgrims visiting Alexandria increased constantly, and they began to expand their interests to include pharaonic monuments. In addition, a number of important finds further stimulated the general enthusiasm for Egypt. Research into hieroglyphs and the pyramids were at the center of this fascination. The discovery of the *Hieroglyphica* of Horapollon, a work probably stemming from the third century AD and which offers allegorical clues to the interpretation of some hieroglyphic signs, stimulated a series of new attempts at interpretation during the fifteenth and sixteenth centuries (for example the *Hieroglyphica* of Piero Veleriano, ca. 1556). The interpretation offered by these people claimed that the secret to hieroglyphs lay in a revelation to initiates. Isis, Osiris, and Horus were the protagonists in a pre-Christian experience of God that would lead to a mystical understanding of Christianity.

The function of the pyramids is a question that was heatedly debated from astronomical standpoints, something which is best illustrated by a book called *Pyramidographia* published in 1646 by John Greaves, Professor of Astronomy at Oxford. His sources were clearly the writers of classical antiquity as well as of the Arab world. The third center of interest focused on Egyptian mummies, which were not merely regarded as collectable objects, but were themselves of real value. Thomas Brown, who wrote *Hydriotaphia, or Urn Burial* in 1658, gave precise instructions on the use of *mummiya* as a universal remedy.

Egyptian objects were now extremely valuable and they formed the centerpieces of many cabinets of curiosities. Travelers were dispatched to Egypt with the specific task of acquiring manuscripts, coins, and artifacts. Among them was the Dominican Johann Michael von Wansleben, who was sent to Egypt in 1672 by Jean Baptiste Colbert, Minister under the French King Louis XIV, and who traveled as far as Middle Egypt. At the beginning of the eighteenth century a French Jesuit father, Claude Sicard, finally managed to reach Aswan and Philae. His account includes descriptions of no fewer than twenty pyramids, twenty-four temple complexes and more than fifty tombs. The picture of Egypt was further enhanced by the many accounts of mid-eighteenth century travelers such as Richard Pockocke or Frederick Ludwig Norden, which led to a gradual demystification of the country.

Explorers and Treasure-hunters in the Nineteenth Century

In 1798 a large team of scientists accompanied Napoleon's army to Egypt. Their task was to produce a thorough description of the country, and this was achieved in the space of a mere two years despite extremely difficult conditions. The results were published in Paris between 1809 and 1822 in nine folio volumes of text and eleven volumes of illustrations under the title *Description de l'Egypte*. D. Vivant Denon (1747–1825), leader of the expedition, and who later became General Director of Museums, wrote his own extensive account in another book called *With Napoleon in Egypt*. Together with the *Description,* this work and the atlas of the author's prints that accompanied it caused an outbreak of Egyptomania. From this point on a great many Europeans busied themselves with uncovering increasing numbers of monuments, drawing and recording them. A few buildings are known to us today only through these drawings and descriptions, since they were later demolished and their blocks consumed in the lime ovens. In addition, there were major outbreaks of plundering that resulted in incalculable damage. In Europe the desire to own Egyptian antiquities increased in proportion to the activities of the explorers: an interest in building large collections had been awakened and therefore many native Egyptians and foreigners began to specialize as antiquities dealers. The antiquities business expanded rapidly, and for many foreign envoys it became a favorite source of income. Of these the most prominent were Giovanni Anastasi (1780–1860), Bernadino Drovetti (1776–1852), and Henry Salt (1780–1827). These men assembled thousands of objects, conducted their own excavations, and bought everything that seemed to be of interest. They sold off their collections to the museums of Europe, and these objects formed the basis of the great collections in London, Paris, Turin, Berlin, and Leiden. For more difficult undertakings and more intensive excavations the diplomats hired adventurers such as Jean Jacques Rifaud (1786–1852) or Giovanni Battista Belzoni (1778–1823). Belzoni even managed to transport the upper section of a colossal statue of Ramesses II ("Younger Memnon") from his mortuary temple in Western Thebes to London. A veritable competition developed to see who could collect the fastest and transport the largest objects and the greatest quantities.

The First Egyptologists – A Discipline is Founded

Besides a longing for antiquities, the times also stimulated a serious desire to learn more about the ancient civilization. One reason for this interest was people's desire for confirmation of passages in the Bible. This is how the first real scholars began their work. The foremost was undoubtedly the Frenchman Jean-François Champollion (1790–1832) who, after many failed attempts by others, found the key to deciphering

hieroglyphs with the help of a trilingual decree of Ptolemy V from the year AD 196 (known as the Rosetta Stone). Within a short space of time the stone facilitated the reconstruction of a long-forgotten world. One of the most important achievements of this brilliant scientist was his discovery of the Turin museum's Royal Papyrus that had fallen apart into numerous fragments. He describes this in a letter of 1824 to his brother: "However, the most interesting papyrus, a real treasure trove for history whose almost complete destruction I shall forever regret, is a chronological table, an authentic list of kings in hieratic script including at least four times as many dynasties as the tables of Abydos in their original state. Amidst the dust I was able to collect approximately twenty hardly thumb-sized fragments that held the more or less mutilated names of seventy-seven pharaohs. In this case as well I am convinced that these belong to earlier dynasties …". In 1828, with Ippolito Rossellini (1800–1843), Champollion traveled the length of Egypt as far as Abu Simbel. Everywhere he went he copied surviving texts and busied himself with translating them. The publication of these results by Rossellini followed between 1832 and 1844 under the title *I Monumenti dell'Egitto e della Nubia*. Besides the *Description* this publication became one of the great standard works of the new academic discipline of Egyptology. A third monumental publication needs to be mentioned: Karl Richard Lepsius (1810–1884) was commissioned by the King of Prussia to record all the Egyptian and

8 The pronaos of the temple of Hathor at Dendara
From: David Roberts, *Egypt and Nubia*, London 1846–1850.
The British artist David Roberts (1796–1864) returned from an extended journey to Egypt with an extraordinary number of drawings and oil paintings. Many of his scenes of the ancient sites were turned into colored lithographs that still have a very broad appeal. Roberts had a particular liking for the great temple complexes of Upper Egypt, as can be seen in this view of the massive Hathor columns in the sanctuary at Dendera.

9 (opposite) Statues of the goddess Sakhmet in the temple of Mut at Karnak
From: C. Werner, *Nilbilder*, 1862–1864.
The dramatic effects of Carl Werner's drawings and watercolors made his pictures of Egypt ideal illustrations for popular works by Georg Ebers (1837–1989), especially his *Aegypten in Wort und Bild*. In addition to his work as professor of Egyptology at Leipzig, Ebers wrote several novels that contributed to the contemporary image of ancient Egypt.

Nubian monuments as completely as possible. His journey through the country between 1842 and 1845 resulted in the twelve-volume edition called *Denkmaeler aus Aegypten und Aethiopien*, published in 1859 and containing no less than 894 color plates.

The first major excavations were undertaken parallel to the work of documentation. The Frenchman Auguste Mariette (1821–1881) came to Egypt in 1850 with the aim of acquiring Coptic manuscripts. Various misfortunes prevented him from entering the monasteries and he was unable to carry out his task. So instead he started work on the first excavations at Saqqara. Despite difficulties between the French and Egyptian governments he eventually received official authorization for his work. His results were sensational. He uncovered the subterranean burial places of the sacred bulls of Apis, the Serapeum, with its catacomb-like complex and gigantic sarcophagi. After obtaining approval for further excavations in 1857, he went on to dig at other rewarding sites such as Abydos, Thebes, and Elephantine. The following year he was finally named director of the Egyptian Antiquities Service. Altogether he led seventeen major digs throughout the country employing a total of 7,200 workers. His aim was not just to make new discoveries, but also to be the first to take measures to protect the finds. He fenced off some of the sites to protect them from intruders, and he took many of the more easily transportable objects to the Egyptian Museum in Cairo to protect them from theft. It is thanks to Mariette's policies in running the Egyptian Antiquities Service, and to those of his successor Gaston Maspero (1846–1916), that a part at least of the legacy of the pharaohs could be saved for Egypt.

The English archaeologist and Egyptologist Sir William Matthew Flinders Petrie (1853–1942) was the first systematic excavator who sought not merely valuable treasures, but who endeavored to record the context of his excavations. His methodical working systems influenced all subsequent excavations in Egypt. He wrote on individual groups of objects and made precise records of each complex of finds. His career as an excavator lasted over forty-two years, during which time he studied more than forty different sites and published over 1,000 books, articles, and notes.

In the area of linguistic research Germans Adolf Erman (1854–1937) and Hermann Grapow (1885–1967) made magnificent achievements. With the help of numerous colleagues they established a headquarters for the analysis of ancient texts, still in existence today, which was responsible for the *Wörterbuch der ägyptischen Sprache* ("Dictionary of the Egyptian Language"). Other great philologists followed, men such as Kurt Sethe (1869–1934), Walter Ewing Crum (1865–1944), and Sir Alan H. Gardiner (1879–1963).

The Business Factor: Ancient Egypt

If scholars and the general public thought at the beginning of the twentieth century that all the questions about ancient Egyptian

civilization had been answered and that the most important sites had been excavated, then they were in for a surprise. Discoveries such as the capital city of Akhenaten, the "heretic king" at Tell el-Amarna with the famous busts of Queen Nefertiti (found by Ludwig Borchardt, 1913/14), the magnificent statues of Queen Hatshepsut at Deir el-Bahari (Herbert Winlock, between 1927 and 1931), the tomb treasures of Tuthankhamun in the Valley of the Kings (Howard Carter, 1922) or the tomb sites of the rulers of the Twenty-first and Twenty-second Dynasties at Tanis (Pierre Montet, 1939) showed just how much remained to be studied.

With each new discovery came an intensification of public interest. Increasing numbers of people could now afford the journey to Egypt where they found inspiration in ancient art and civilization. This enthusiasm for all things Egyptian also influenced modern design, which has successfully accommodated a number of ancient symbols. Since the second half of the twentieth century innumerable hordes of tourists have poured into Egypt, bringing with them a second wave of destruction to the monuments. This time the problems stem not only from antiquities theft, but it has been and continues to be primarily the sheer numbers of visitors that have done the most damage, particularly to the decorated tombs. A solution for this problem remains to be found, since ancient Egypt, through its timeless and ongoing appeal to tourists, has become the most important and consequently an indispensable source of income for the modern state.

Despite studies conducted in recent decades that have contributed to a better understanding of the ancient civilization, Egypt remains for many a land of concealed wisdom. People today often wilfully project their image of an "ideal world" onto the ancient state, regardless of whether they seek factual truth or evidence of contact from another planet. Pyramidologists and self-styled "reincarnations" of ancient rulers persist in their search for hidden information, fantastic myths debunked long ago by professionals or which never had any particular significance to begin with. Objectively speaking, ancient Egypt was no "ideal or sacred world," but many proceed in their wishful thinking anyway. Thus in many ways the modern passion for Egypt hardly differs from that of earlier centuries – the primary difference is that the "secrets" are now accessible to a much larger public and can therefore be more effectively marketed. However, due to this continuing popularity of almost all themes to do with Ancient Egypt, reports of new discoveries or findings are often presented in a way that cannot be regarded as serious. Even in our present Media Age priority should be given to respecting the achievements of an ancient high culture over the desire for ever more sensational headlines.

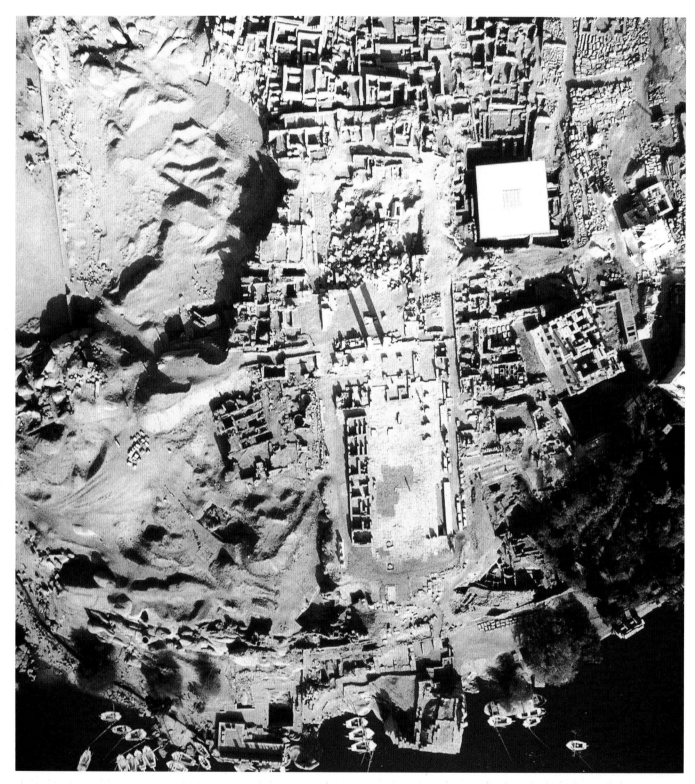

10 Aerial photograph of the excavations at Elephantine

This is an aerial view of the southeastern part of the Nile island of Elephantine. Approximately in the center of the photograph one can recognize the court of the Ptolemaic Period Khnum temple in the shape of a large rectangle. The white square above it is the contemporary protective roof of the Heqaib sanctuary from the Middle Kingdom. The smaller, right-angled building at right below this temple is the reconstructed temple of Satet from the Eighteenth Dynasty. At left and above the Heqaib sanctuary, extensive structures of housing from the Second Intermediate Period and early New Kingdom are visible. The abrupt steep ledge to the left of the group of houses (recognizable due to the distinct shadow line) is the so-called Kom ledge that came into being when the local populace removed the fertile domestic rubble during the middle of the nineteenth century.

The Responsibilities of Archaeology – Recent Excavations

Daniel Polz

Excavations have been conducted more intensively in Egypt than in any other country in the world – and they still are. Two main reasons account for this: the first lies in the unique geopolitical situation of the country and its principal artery, the Nile. Egypt is surrounded by desert, and agriculture and habitation are only possible close to the Nile. It was only along the last section of Africa's longest river, the last 1,000 km or so, from the first cataract at Aswan as far as the mouth into the Mediterranean, that settlements, cities, metropolises, and finally a nation state could arise. This geopolitical position has not altered significantly since ancient times, and the same area now houses a population that has increased disproportionately to about thirty times what it was. Many of the ancient settlements are largely identical with modern villages and towns, and they are often covered by later buildings. Frequently, the ancient necropolises have been reused since the beginning of the Islamic Period. Therefore these antiquities are and always have been part of the scene. Since Egypt returned to the European field of interest with the Napoleonic invasion in the years 1798 to 1799 and was visited more regularly, travelers have constantly encountered remains from the ancient civilization at stops along their route. These were visible above ground and were for the most part well preserved.

The second reason lies naturally enough in the Egyptian climate, which was ideal for the long-term preservation of both organic and inorganic materials. Early travelers such as the French poet and scholar Vivant Denon, who led the Napoleonic expedition, were overwhelmed by the almost perfect preservation of the colors used in the decoration of the reliefs in the temples of Upper Egypt, some of which had been open to the air for nearly two millennia.

Thanks to the environmental conditions that exist in Egypt an incomparable wealth of pharaonic monuments and objects have been preserved. Even today, after nearly 200 years of intensive interest in excavation – not all of it scientific – there are still blank areas on the archaeologist's maps. These areas include parts of Middle Egypt, the oases, and the southern part of Upper Egypt.

In Egypt today there are about 100 different annual foreign excavations in progress, and at least as many under Egyptian leadership. This archaeological activity ranges over the entire timescale of the development of the ancient civilization, and it includes prehistoric digs in the desert regions, such as at Gilf Kebir, the intersection of three countries, predynastic digs in the Nile Delta, the excavation of towns and settlements in the ancient centers of Memphis, Thebes, Avaris, Pi-Ramesse, Tanis as well the less accessible areas of Middle Egypt and the oases, and the "classical" digs in and around the pyramids in the north of the country. Many of the foreign excavations are organized or supported by archaeological institutes that have their permanent headquarters in Cairo. The most important of these are the German Deutsches Archäologisches Institut, Cairo (DAI), the Institut des Fouilles Archéologuiques Orientales (IFAO), the American Research Center in Egypt (ARCE), the British Egypt Exploration Society (EES), and the Austrian Österreichisches Archäologisches Institut (ÖAI). These institutions are partly financed by their respective governments, and in addition a number of European, American, and more recently also Australian and Japanese universities supervise short- and medium-term projects in Egypt. Many expeditions are financed by state and private charities, the most important ones in Germany being the Deutsche Forschungsgemeinschaft (DFG), the Volkswagen Foundation, and the Theodor-Wiegand-Gesellschaft (TWG).

As in other areas of "classical" excavation, Egyptian archaeology has changed substantially in recent years in technical respects: the deployment of electronic hardware and software has become routine in dealing with the enormous quantities of data encountered. There are other methods and techniques used specifically for archaeological inquiry, such as satellite imagery, the Global Positioning System, laser and infra-red instruments for measuring and recording site layouts, as well as innumerable laboratory procedures where materials or dating are concerned.

In the 1960s a general development also occurred in the actual premises underlying the discipline: that is, archaeology in Egypt is a subsidiary part of Egyptology, which has become a largely philological discipline since its inception with the deciphering of hieroglyphs by Champollion in 1822. For this reason Egyptian archaeology has always been dominated by interest in a particular type of objects and monuments: that is objects that were decorated and/or inscribed with hieroglyphic texts, whose appeal lay in the relative ease with which information can be gathered from them. This has in turn restricted interest to a particular group of monuments, namely those tombs and temples that are also easily accessible.

However, this specialization has led inevitably to an overemphasis on the mortuary aspects of ancient life – the everyday aspects of housing and urban life have largely lain, and in many cases still lie, in obscurity. Many monuments, settlements, and entire towns were known only from inscriptions, and their position could only be conjectured. Since the 1960s this picture has begun to change. To mention just one or two examples, the DAI has undertaken extensive

11 The "City of Ramesses"
Qantir Pi-Ramesse: general view over the burial area; Nineteenth/Twentieth Dynasty, ca. 1290–1180 BC.
In the eastern Nile Delta, near the town of Faqus, are the ruins of the former capital of the Ramesside kings of the Nineteenth and Twentieth Dynasties. The illustration shows eight square excavation sectors, which are separated by raised balks. The broad mudbrick wall that runs underneath the balks in the right half of the picture forms the south wall of an extensive royal stable complex from Pi-Ramesse, which has been under excavation for several years by a team from the Pelizaeus-Museum at Hildesheim.

12 Tomb complex of King Aha from the Archaic Period
Abydos, Umm el-Gaab, underground tomb chambers made of unbaked mudbricks; Archaic Period, First Dynasty, ca. 3100 BC.
The funerary sepulchers of the Archaic Period kings in the necropolis at Abydos consist mostly of several simple chambers dug into the ground and lined with unbaked mudbricks. This picture shows the three distinctly larger principal chambers of the tomb complex of King Aha, which once contained his burial and tomb furnishings. Aha's tomb complex had an additional thirty smaller chambers, in which possibly part of the royal household was buried with him.

13 Tomb superstructure, with chapel
Western Thebes, Dra Abu el-Naga; New
Kingdom, early Eighteenth Dynasty, ca. 1550
BC; wall made of unbaked mudbricks, coated
with lime mortar.

The recently uncovered tomb superstructures
in the necropolis of Dra Abu el-Naga in
Western Thebes can be considered a good
example of free-standing private mortuary
cult architecture. They consist of an entrance
portico angled toward the east (pylon) with
gently sloping walls leading to an open court
enclosed by lower walls. Approximately in the
center of the court lies the main shaft of the
tomb complex (not visible here), which leads
to the actual tomb chamber. Opposite the
pylon is a small chapel that once had a
podium for an offering table in front of its
west wall, and a stela decorated with an
image and texts relating to the tomb's owner.

excavations of settlements that have led to the identification in the east
Delta of the capital city of the Hyksos kings of the Fifteenth Dynasty.
A German project run by the DFG has been digging for some years in
"the city of Ramesses" (Pi-Ramesse), which is probably the Egyptian
capital of the Nineteenth and Twentieth Dynasties mentioned in the
Bible. The British EES is systematically researching large areas of the
ancient capital of Memphis. Further excavations by the DAI at
Elephantine near Aswan, an ancient border town on an island in the
Nile, which was previously known only as a large rubbish dump, have
contributed substantially to our knowledge of a city's development over
a period of more than 2,000 years.

The changing premises of the discipline, and the improved
technical and methodological procedures have also changed the
"classical" goals of Egyptian archaeology. The investigation of individual
tombs in necropolises is today part of a broader historical, sociological
or anthropological approach. The primary archaeological interest is no
longer the description of individual phenomena so much as linking
them in a cultural-historical analysis. One undertaking of the DAI in
the ancient, "sacred" necropolis of Abydos, the legendary burial place
of the god Osiris, focuses on the royal tombs of the earliest kings of
Egypt, of the First and Second Dynasties. Despite the fact that some of
these tombs have been examined by archaeologists at least twice before,
the recent re-excavation still yielded a wealth of new material, for
example the names of several unknown kings found in brief
inscriptions on ceramic vessels. This led to the establishment of a
Dynasty 0, something that has far-reaching consequences for early
chronology and has produced new information about the rise of the
Egyptian state.

Archaeologists from a joint project of the DAI and the University
of California, Los Angeles, are digging in Dra Abu el-Naga, the
northern part of the Theban necropolis. This is an extensive cemetery
dating from the long-obscured Second Intermediate Period and from
the early Eighteenth Dynasty. One of the aims of the dig is to study the
tombs and burials of members of the lower and middle classes. These
people probably made up about 85–95 per cent of the population, but
until now they have been almost completely excluded from the picture,
especially in the region of the ancient capital of Thebes. The
excavations have so far uncovered a new kind of tomb architecture as
well as considerable new information about the burial and cult
practices characteristic of this section of society.

This changing outlook has also ushered in a new sense of
responsibility for the effects of excavation: not even the use of state-of-
the-art technical procedures can defeat an old truism: archaeology is
destruction. All archaeological activity alters a find irretrievably;
each layer that is removed brings its ultimate destruction. It is the
responsibility of archaeologists to ensure with all the means at their

disposal that proper documentation is made of a site before digging commences and that it is continued during every stage of the process. Then, theoretically speaking, the site can be reconstructed – at the drawing board – using computer-aided design programs, based on the precise descriptions recorded. Only then can the destruction be justified.

Even when this minimum condition is met, archaeologists often find themselves in an ethical dilemma over the dig: it is in the nature of archaeological processes that older things are covered by later, often in adjoining layers. This layering of finds occurs particularly frequently in Egypt because of the geopolitical situation mentioned earlier: the same places have been in use for centuries, sometimes even for millennia, and they have been altered, built over, and recycled. For example, in the Theban necropolis, the second court of the best-preserved royal mortuary temple, that of Medinet Habu, was found by archaeologists almost completely intact beneath a Coptic church built over 1,500 years later. The church was completely removed to provide access to the architecture of the temple court and its decoration. Taking into account the archaeological principles that apply to the excavation of a temple such as this from the reign of Ramesses, the procedure is justifiable. The problem is that, although the church could theoretically be reconstructed in the form of a model, it could never be done in any practical way since it made use of the walls and columns of the pharaonic building.

Another aspect of responsible archaeology in Egypt that is becoming ever more important is the long-term care of ancient monuments. Although it has only recently become an issue, there are three vital areas that need separate consideration: conservation, restoration, and reconstruction.

Once objects have been uncovered they must first be conserved; this means that care needs to be taken that they do not decay. Today there are a number of physical and chemical procedures available that can be used to treat at least the most recently uncovered objects. In many cases these are procedures of which we have no long-term experience. It therefore cannot be known how a particular chemical, for example, may change in the short and long term under extreme climatic conditions or the applicable environmental influences, or even what side effects there may be. This applies particularly to the treatment of pigments used for temple and tomb decoration, which in many cases can no longer withstand the growing masses of tourists.

Another problem that so far remains unsolved is the task of conserving buildings and walls made of unbaked mudbricks, the building material that was used most frequently in ancient times. To date, two processes have been used to deal with this problem. Either the walls and buildings are buried again with the material that protected them before excavation, or several courses of new bricks of a different color and/or size are placed on top of the remains of ancient wall. This provides considerable protection for the short term, and the upper layer of new wall can if necessary be replaced.

When an excavation is taking place, the first priority is consolidation of objects on the spot, especially those made of organic materials, before they can be stored. This applies particularly to strata lying close to the water table in the case of a settlement mound, and to the contents of low-lying tomb chambers in necropolises. The procedures do not differ much in detail from those of conservation proper; the main difference being that conditions in the field are poorer. Once the objects or bones have been carefully uncovered, they are sprayed or drizzled with thinned resins (for example Mowilith) one

14 Temple of Seti I
Western Thebes, Qurna; New Kingdom, Nineteenth Dynasty, reign of Seti I/Ramesses II, ca. 1280 BC.

The massive enclosure walls and magazine structures in the court of the mortuary temple were the target of various restoration and consolidation projects in recent years. The modern walls that are visible today sit on top of the old mudbrick walls, but are different in form, color, and composition. The modern enclosure wall gives the temple area a permanent protection from modern development. In the right half of the picture can be seen the walls of the extensive temple magazines that have been reconstructed to just half their former height.

15–18 Wall paintings in the tomb of Nefertari
Western Thebes, Valley of the Queens (QV 66); New Kingdom, Nineteenth Dynasty, ca. 1250 BC; painting on stucco.

In 1995, the re-opening of the tomb of Nefertari, one of the principal consorts of Ramesses II, closed a spectacular restoration project by the Getty Conservation Institute. Over many years the tomb's wall paintings, which had been threatened by total deterioration, were consolidated and restored. The illustration top left shows the face and upper body of the death god Osiris-Khontamenti; small strips of tape that were used to prevent sections of the plaster from falling away can be clearly seen. The illustration top right shows the condition of the scene after restoration was completed, with the modelling replaced, done cautiously but in a way that is clearly recognizable.

The images below show the face and upper body of the tomb's owner Nefertari and they illustrate one of the principal reasons for the increasing danger to Egyptian monuments, namely the decoration. Salts that bloom on the porous limestone push between the rock surface and the layer of plaster on top or carry on through this too. In the section reproduced these blooms have already destroyed large areas of the collar and the right upper arm in the picture, although the face and the crown of Nefertari could be completely restored.

layer at a time – if necessary in many layers – until they are completely saturated and have solidified; then they can be stored.

Restoration has become increasingly important in recent years. Accessible monuments that have been open for a long time are showing signs of rapid deterioration that are only in part caused by the constant mass of visitors. Another unknown factor is the precise extent of the added effects from the Nasser Dam, which became operational in 1969, on fluctuations in the water table. There may be a connection between the dam and the discernible increase in the salt content of the soil. The micro-climate has also noticeably changed, especially in the southern part of Upper Egypt (and possibly that of the whole region from Luxor to Aswan).

The best-known example of the successful restoration of a monument that had fallen into decay is the tomb of Nefertari, consort of Ramesses II, in the Valley of the Queens. This tomb is in various respects one of the most important tombs of the New Kingdom, and its contents and the quality of its decoration are probably unique. The tomb was found in 1904 by the Italian archaeologist Ernesto Schiaparelli, and was recently restored in a seven-year joint project by the Supreme Council of Egyptian Antiquities and specialists from the Getty Conservation Institute at a cost of millions of dollars. Part of the tomb was reopened to visitors in the autumn of 1995. Although exemplary, this restoration project will unfortunately remain an exception. Similar expenditure on the restoration of most other endangered monuments, even if only in the initial stages, is not possible either technically or financially. In the region of the ancient capital Thebes alone there are known to be about 500 decorated tombs, in addition to the many temple buildings on the west bank and in Luxor and Karnak on the east bank.

The Theban tombs of officials, mentioned earlier, have been the goal of archaeologists and Egyptologists since systematic work began in Egypt, primarily because of the tremendous amount of information contained in their decoration and inscriptions. Two projects of the DAI with Heidelberg University, supported by the DFG, have been working here since the early 1970s and 1980s, methodically recording and publishing these tombs. In the course of this work extensive restoration measures were taken in conjunction with the Supreme Council of Antiquities, often at the same time as the recording of decoration and inscriptions. Many of the tombs had been used for centuries as dwellings and stables, and their decoration has deteriorated accordingly. The walls are often covered with layers of soot, which needs to be removed in an painstaking and time-consuming procedure centimeter by square centimeter.

The restoration of buildings can also bear special relevance for the history of stone architecture in Egypt. It often happened in pharaonic times that new buildings were constructed using the blocks of earlier complexes that had served as ready-made stone quarries. A very clear example is the magnificent mortuary temple of Amenophis III on the west bank in Thebes, with two giant seated statues, the world-famous colossi of Memnon that once flanked the entrance to the temple building. Above the level of its foundations, the building itself has disappeared, since it was "gutted" as long ago as the late New Kingdom, quarried for stone needed for other mortuary temples on the west bank and for a new temple building at Karnak. This recycling of older buildings can be observed at Karnak itself: the great pylons to the temple buildings are mainly constructed with masonry shells enclosing a solid core. This means that the decorated exteriors that we see today are just the outer layer, and the space inside is filled partly with rubble, but also with reused blocks from earlier buildings, some of which are decorated. Some time ago the French and Egyptian archaeologists and architects of the Centre Franco-Egyptien involved in excavating and

recording the temple at Karnak began to dismantle some of the pylons block by block to examine the reverse side of the facing blocks and the blocks of the core, and afterwards to rebuild them. This brought to light thousands of blocks from other buildings that had vanished long ago. In a few cases these buildings can be reconstructed and rebuilt – as was done for the "White Chapel," a small processional shrine of Sesostris I that is now one of the earliest buildings known at Karnak.

A similar procedure was used to reconstruct buildings long destroyed on the island of Elephantine at Aswan. The excavations here, the major project of the DAI, continued for more than twenty-five years, and they turned up, among other things, the architectural remains of several temples to the goddess Satet, built one over the other. These provide a more or less complete picture of the temple from the Old to the New Kingdom. Some of the temple buildings found among the blocks have been reconstructed in recent years and rebuilt close to their original positions. This site was planned as an "archaeological park" on the island, and gives the visitor a unique opportunity to follow the history of a temple over a period of more than 1,000 years, not just on paper, but in reality.

Despite or possibly even because of this changing approach and the demonstrable change in attitudes toward ancient monuments, there has been much debate in recent years whether in our "advanced" state of knowledge of ancient culture it is really necessary "to turn over every stone in Egypt." Bearing in mind the development of "less destructive" archaeological techniques, it would perhaps make better sense to leave the excavation of particular objects or sites to future

19, 20 Pillar decoration in the tomb of Meri
Western Thebes, Sheikh Abd el-Qurna (TT 95); New Kingdom, Eighteenth Dynasty, ca. 1390 BC; painting on stucco.
Both illustrations show a section of decorated pillar in the tomb of Meri, High Priest of Amun, before and after restoration of the pillar by the Commission for Egyptian

Antiquities. The image has survived in parts to show the High Priest Meri standing, with arms raised in a gesture of worship. Above the image is an important ritual described in seven vertical lines of text. It is quite clear that before restoration neither the picture nor the text could be made out.

generations of archaeologists. Turning again to the situation of modern Egypt described at the beginning of the chapter, and to our sometimes rather one-sided view of the ancient civilization, this question is not to be taken seriously. The requirements of today's inhabitants of the Nile Valley are far more important than any of the needs of archaeology and ancient history. The rapidly increasing need for space for the living and for business activity in contemporary Egypt will inevitably lead to more and rapid building over ancient towns that will thereby be lost to archaeology, or will at least become inaccessible. In today's Egypt, archaeology is no more than a question of salvage.

The Threatened Monuments – Reflections and Perspectives

Another controversial issue in this context is the fate of monuments already excavated, some of which have long been freely accessible at many of the older sites, and that of objects in Egyptian museums that came from the excavations. A large number of monuments have already been severely damaged by environmental conditions, altered micro-climates and not least the mass tourism of recent decades. A first step toward the salvage of damaged monuments was created by the planned flooding during the construction of the Aswan High Dam in the 1960s. In an international action unparalleled in the history of modern archaeology, innumerable surveys and emergency excavations were carried out between the first and third Nile cataracts before and partly during the flooding of an area about 500 km long affected by the dam. The Nubian Campaign, organized and partly financed by UNESCO, united scholars, architects, and engineers of virtually every country with Egyptological or archaeological institutes. Together with the Egyptian Antiquities Organization, whole settlements, necropolises and temple complexes that have now been flooded forever beneath the waters of the Aswan Dam were mapped and partially excavated. The Herculean task stretching over many years yielded a vast quantity of information and data about many Nubian sites in the Nile Valley that had previously been largely unknown. During the UNESCO campaign, in a unique undertaking, a number of temples were removed block by block and rebuilt on higher ground. A few smaller buildings ended up as gifts from the Egyptian government to European and American museums (for example the Kalabsha gateway in the Ägyptischen Museum, SMPK, Berlin, and the Temple of Dendur in The Metropolitan Museum of Art, New York). The most famous of the monumental buildings moved in this way are the Ptolemaic temple of Isis from Philae, and the twin temples of Ramesses II from Abu Simbel, which are now on the itinerary of every tourist group.

Today the question of long-term or even the short-term preservation of monuments is perhaps more urgent than ever before. From the ranks of sites and monuments under immediate threat let us consider the best-known group, the Valley of the Kings to the west of the ancient capital, Thebes. Some of these colorful and beautifully decorated final resting places of the New Kingdom kings are visited in high season by up to 2,000 visitors per day, yet scarcely a single tomb has proper climate control. Probably the most dangerous side effect of this mass of tourists is the constant high humidity inside the tombs, which has already led to several cases of fungus attacking organic pigments used in the decoration. There are other natural external influences too, for instance the unusually high and at times devastating rainfall in the years 1994 and 1995. The very real and constant deterioration could in fact now only be prevented by the immediate and complete closure of the tombs, unless a satisfactory method of conservation is developed and implemented.

Among the many measures that have been discussed to protect and preserve the tombs, some of which have not been fully published, is a project that deserves particular attention: Erik Hornung, an Egyptologist from Basel, has suggested that some of the best-preserved tombs with more or less complete decoration (such as that of Seti I) should be copied as replicas accurate to the smallest detail outside the Valley of the Kings. This procedure has already been successfully completed with the subterranean portion of the private tomb of Sennefer and with the famous caves at Lascaux. The criticism leveled at this "replica method," that visitors would not be satisfied with imitations, is not applicable in this case. It certainly lies in the interests of tourist to protect these unique cultural monuments for the foreseeable future.

Nonetheless, certain individual tombs in the Valley of the Kings have been preserved for the longer term, although the financial and material cost was tremendous. Yet other monuments look unlikely to be benefit from lasting conservation. The decoration of the temple buildings in Karnak has been endangered by the increasing salt content in the soil. Given the enormous extent of the complex it seems virtually impossible to try, for example, to create a water-resistant ground barrier beneath the temple.

Another level at which changes can be detected concerns the situation with Egyptian objects in collections and museums outside Egypt. Most of the great European collections of Egyptian art owe their foundation to the acquisition of "antiquities" for this purpose in the first half of the nineteenth century. In each period there were usually

"legal" agreements between the Egyptian government and the contemporary European diplomatic representatives, which permitted the large-scale removal to Europe of some of the objects brought to light by the excavations. Nevertheless, questions continue to arise over the "legality" of the original acquisition, and the appropriateness of the present location, especially with important masterpieces of Egyptian art. In some Egyptian circles the demand for the return of key pieces continues; example include the bust of Nefertiti in Berlin, or the beard fragments from the Sphinx of Giza, now in London. The recent decision of an Egyptian court to prohibit the temporary loan of exhibits from the Egyptian Museum in Cairo to a museum in the USA should probably be seen as part of this movement.

The great majority of museums and public collections are extremely careful today when purchasing "new" objects. Pieces lacking a full "history," that is without proof that they have been outside Egypt for a long time, are rightly ignored as possible acquisitions by the great museums and collections. Only a documented provenance ensures that they have not come from recent illegal excavations.In the last few years

illegal trading in Ancient Egyptian artifacts has been made a lot
more difficult thanks to pressure from international experts and a
new offensive, both at home and abroad, by the Egyptian antiquities
authority. Several large auction houses have expressed their willingness
to cooperate more closely with the authorities. In addition a preceden-
tial legal battle in London and New York against several art dealers has
resulted in fines and prison sentences, which must had made it clear
to all that the traditional greed for profit and collecting Egyptian
antiquities must become a thing of the past.

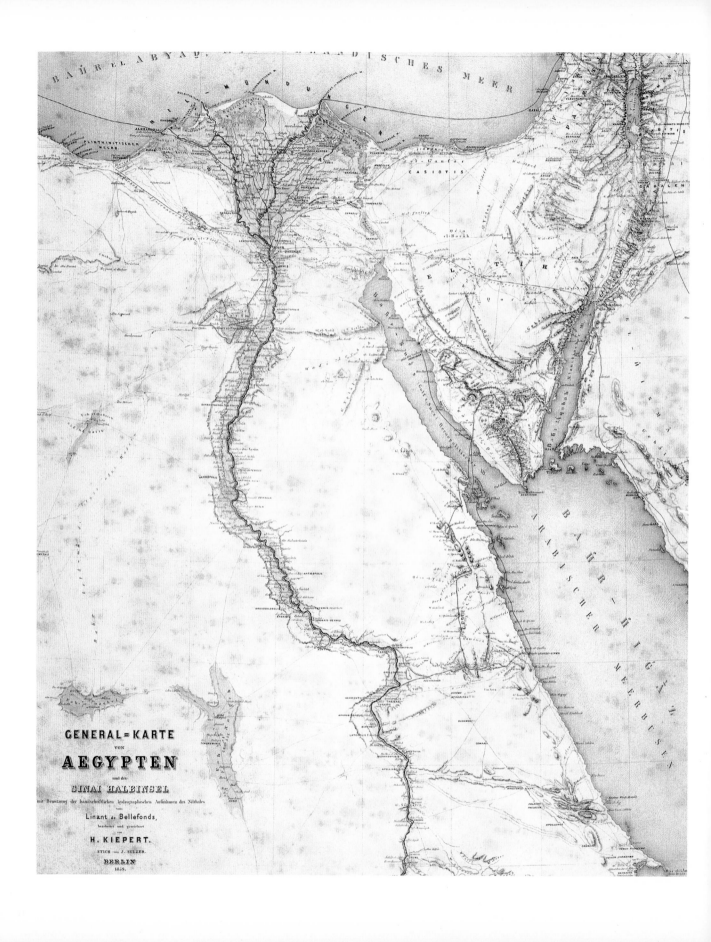

GENERAL = KARTE
VON
AEGYPTEN
und der
SINAI HALBINSEL
mit Benutzung der handschriftlichen hydrographischen Aufnahmen des Nilthales
von
Linant de Bellefonds,
bearbeitet und gezeichnet von
H. KIEPERT.
STICH von J. SULZER.
BERLIN
1858.

Appendix

General map of Egypt
From: Richard Lepsius, *Denkmaeler aus Aegypten und Aethiopien* (Monuments of Egypt and Ethiopia), Berlin 1859.

Glossary

Martina Ullmann

Abacus. Upper member of the capital that serves as a support for the *architrave*. Used in Egyptian architecture on columns and pillars and often inscribed with royal *cartouches*.

Achaemenian Dynasty (or Achaemenid Dynasty). Persian royal house, named after its founder Achaemenes. The Persian king Cambyses conquered Egypt in 525 BC and he and his successors ruled as the Twenty-seventh Dynasty until 402 BC. In 342 BC Artaxerxes III succeeded in imposing the so-called second Persian reign in Egypt. The last Achaemenid ruler, Darius III, was forced to cede control of Egypt to Alexander the Great in 332 BC.

Aegis. The semicircular ornamental plaques on the bow and stern of barques in which the statues of gods and kings were transported during large festivals. The aegis was usually made of metal and richly decorated with emblems of the gods.

Akh. (Egyptian "Spirit of Light," "Transfigured One") The spirit of the dead invested with magical powers. Every deceased person – king and citizen – wanted to live on in the heavenly afterlife in the divine form of the *akh* (see also *ba* and *ka*.

Akhet. Egyptian word for the season of the *Nile inundation*. See also *calendar*.

Ambulatory. Roofed aisles of pillars or columns around three or four external walls of a temple. Temples with this feature are generally called "ambulatory temples." Architectural structures of this kind were very popular from the Middle Kingdom on and were used for temples with quite distinct functions. These include, for example, an ambulatory chapel used as a *way station* for resting a cult barque during great festival processions.

Amduat. (Egyptian "[the book about] what is in the underworld") Term for the *Guidebooks to the Netherworld*. Today it has come to mean one of the books that presents the Egyptian view of the underworld in both word and image. Its central story recounts the nocturnal journey of the *sun-god* through the underworld in his barque. Every night, the sun-god is rejuvenated during the twelve hours of darkness by his encounter with the primal forces of creation in the depths of the underworld in order to climb to the horizon again as the *sun disk*. Originally written on papyrus, the Amduat became – from Thutmosis I on – an important part of the wall paintings of royal tombs in the Valley of the Kings. Through knowledge of the Amduat the dead king aimed to join in the everlasting journey of the sun in order to regain new life himself.

Anchorites. (Greek "withdrawn") In Egyptology, the term is principally applied to those who, in the early centuries of Christianity in Egypt, left their own societies to live a reclusive life of devotion to God in the desert regions bordering the Nile Valley. The widespread religious anchoritism of the men known as the Holy Fathers (and a smaller number of women) in Egypt during the third to the fifth and sixth centuries AD is closely associated with the rise of monastic life in the country in the fourth century.

Annals. List of the most important events during the rule of a king, ordered according to the consecutive years of his reign and originally used to name the years.

Aramaic. Language belonging to the Semitic family of languages. Widely used in the first century BC throughout the Near East. In the Persian Empire it was an officially recognized administrative language. Numerous Aramaic texts have been found in Egypt, largely dating from the sixth to the third centuries BC, and representing important historical sources. The archives of the Jewish community of Elephantine, written in Aramaic in the sixth and fifth centuries BC, are especially significant.

Architrave. Beam of stone or wood lying horizontally on the *abacus* of a column or pillar. Connects the columns or pillars with one another, as well as with the walls of the building, and bears the weight of the roof.

Atrium. Central courtyard often surrounded by columns; important part of Roman domestic architecture.

Ba. An Egyptian term, difficult to translate, that covers various levels of meaning. In modern literature it is often misleadingly translated "soul." Like both *ka* and *akh*, *ba* denotes a form of being common to both men and gods. Gods and kings possess a number of *bas* in which their power is manifest and through which their influence becomes perceptible to the outside world. The *ba* is the personification of all the vital forces of the deceased, and, in contrast to the mummy, it forms the active and unfettered element of the dead person. It is therefore often represented as a bird with a human head, especially in the private tombs of the New Kingdom. The *ba* of the dead resides in heaven but regularly returns to "its" tomb on earth in order to receive offerings.

Badarian. One of the earliest known Neolithic cultures in Upper Egypt (around 4500 BC). It precedes the Naqada Culture and is named after the site of el-Badari that lies just south of Asiut and where the first finds of this culture were made last century.

Bag wig. Wigs, usually made of human hair, were worn by Egyptian men and women as a status symbol. Their many different designs depended on the fashion of the time and reflected natural hairstyles. A kind of wig often depicted in freestanding sculptures of male figures in the Middle Kingdom, shows a shoulder-length hairstyle held together in a net, and is described as a "bag wig" because of its appearance.

Barque sanctuary. Important room in most of the larger Egyptian temples in which the portable cult barque of a god (and, to a certain extent, those of kings) were stored and provided for. These barques were painstakingly constructed from highly prized materials. During large festival processions, a small-scale statue of a god or king was placed in a shrine in the middle of the barque and then carried out of the temple to visit other cult sites. Normally the barque and other ritual scenes were depicted on the walls of the sanctuary. As a rule, the sanctuary lay on the main axis of the temple and had a stone pedestal in the middle upon which to place the barque.

Benben Stone. Sacred stone in Heliopolis in the form of an irregular, conical pillar. Venerated since ancient times by the sun cult there as a stylized *Primeval Mound* and therefore as the manifestation of the primeval god Atum. The *obelisk* form developed out of it during the Old Kingdom.

Birth house. See *mammisi*.

Birth legend. Traditional myth of the divine origin of the Egyptian king. The god Amun-Re came to earth in the form of the king in order to take to himself the queen, to whom he revealed his divine nature. Together they conceived the successor to the throne. After the child's birth he was cared for by divine wet nurses and recognized by his father Amun-Re as his son. This dual nature of the Egyptian king – both divine and human – is represented in several temples of the New Kingdom.

Birth name. See *royal titulary*.

Blue Crown. See *khepresh*.

Book of Caverns. Modern term for a *Guidebook to the Netherworld* from the Nineteenth Dynasty, that like most of the other "guidebooks," deals with the Egyptian idea of the afterlife in the underworld. In contrast to the older books of the netherworld (*Amduat*, *Book of Gates*) it contains many addresses of the sun-god to the beings of the underworld emphasizing, in particular, those gods most closely related to earthly matters. The oldest surviving text is found in the cenotaph of Seti I in Abydos. It was part of the standard decoration of royal graves in the late Nineteenth and in the Twentieth Dynasties.

Book of the Dead. Modern term for a large collection of texts and illustrations concerning Egyptian beliefs on death and intended to secure a continued life in the hereafter. Different types of Books of the Dead were interred with the deceased from the New Kingdom onwards. In contrast to the *Guidebooks to the Netherworld* they were available to non-royal persons from the very start. They are often written on long papyrus scrolls, while individual sayings or depictions are found on tomb walls, coffins, statues, etc. The body of thought they express derives from a variety of sources, from the *Coffin Texts* of the Middle Kingdom back to the *Pyramid Texts* of the Old Kingdom.

Book of the Divine Cow. Modern term for a literary work that probably first appeared in the Amarna Period and is often depicted in royal tombs of the New Kingdom. It tells the myth of the planned destruction of a rebellious mankind by the aging sun-god Re. After a small part of mankind had been saved, Re withdrew from earthly rule to heaven on the back of the Divine Cow. The text provides a mythological explanation for the separation of heaven and earth and the mortal and immortal spheres.

Book of Gates. Modern term for one of the Egyptian *Guidebooks to the Netherworld* portrayed on the walls of royal tombs of the New Kingdom from the time of Horemheb. It was based on the *Amduat* and similarly showed the barque journey of the *sun-god* through the underworld during the twelve hours of night. The individual night hours, representing the various regions of the afterlife, lay behind a locked gate guarded by subterranean creatures, in front of which the dead person had to demonstrate his knowledge of the underworld.

Book of Two Ways. Modern name for the oldest of the Egyptian *Guides to the Netherworld*, evidence for which is found in the *Coffin Texts* of the Middle Kingdom. It was generally written on the bottom of the coffin. It consisted of a map of the netherworld, showing the underworld and heaven, as well as magical spells, and was meant as a guide for the dead in the afterlife. The texts of the New Kingdom like the *Amduat*, the *Book of Gates* and the *Book of Caverns*, on the other hand, dealt only with the underworld.

Books of the Underworld. See *Guidebooks to the Netherworld* as well as *Amduat, Book of Caverns, Book of Gates*.

Bucheum. Grave complex of the sacred Buchis bulls of Armant on the west bank of the Nile, several kilometers south of Thebes. They were interred in great stone sarcophagi in catacombs similar to those in the Serapeum at Saqqara from the Thirtieth Dynasty to Roman times.

Cache. (French "cachette") A series of hiding places for mummies in the valley of Deir el-Bahari in Western Thebes as well as for statues in the temples of Karnak and Luxor. The most famous is the cache in tomb DB 320 in Western Thebes, where about forty coffins containing many royal mummies of the New Kingdom were discovered towards, the end of the nineteenth century. They had been placed there in the Twenty-first Dynasty after the Valley of the Kings had been plundered.

Calendar. The solar year was the basis of the "official" calendar. Historic inscriptions were dated from it and it was used by the state's administrative apparatus. The year was divided into three seasons: *Akhet* "inundation", *Peret* "emergence" (of seed) and *Shemu* "heat," which were each four months long, and each month had thirty days. In addition, five *epagomenal days* were added so that the year had 365 days and only diverged from the solar year by one-quarter of a day. From the beginning there was also a natural year oriented to the phases of the moon. It began with the annual rise of the Nile (see also *Nile inundation* and *Sothis*).

Calendar of Feasts and Offerings. List of the daily, monthly, and yearly sacrifices in a temple that were recorded on the walls as part of the temple decoration. Attested from the Old Kingdom onward. Regular sacrifices were offered every day and additional sacrifices were made every month at the new moon. Other special sacrifices took place throughout the year on festival days.

Canopic jars. Vessels in which the embalmed entrails of the corpse were placed. Often of calcite-alabaster or limestone, they have the form of a tall vase, originally with a slightly vaulted lid, and were generally grouped in fours in the tomb. The organs were wrapped in bandages and guarded by the *Sons of Horus*. The lids came to be shaped like human heads, and later also in the shape of baboon, jackal, and falcon heads.

Canopus Decree. Decree of the Egyptian priesthood that gathered at the court in the ninth year of Ptolemy III's reign (238 BC) in order to reach agreement on issues of religion, temple organization, etc. Several examples of this decree exist. Named after one of their meeting places in Canopus, near Alexandria. Decisions made here about cult ceremonies for the royal house were recorded in three languages – hieroglyphs, *Demotic,* and Greek – and made public on great stelae in the outer courts of temples.

Cartouche. (French) The oval frame around the nomen and prenomen of the king

(see *royal titulary*). Originally it was a rope whose tied ends extended slightly beyond the knot and which were generally represented by a horizontal stroke at the end of the oval. The circular or oval form symbolized eternity and placed the person named under the magical protection of the gods (see also *shen ring*).

Cataracts. Greek term for the rapids in the southern, Nubian part of the Nile Valley. At six places between Aswan and Khartoum the hard rock stratum of the eastern desert appears through the sandstone of the Nile floor and forms rocky barriers several kilometers long in the course of the river. The first cataract at Aswan had always formed a natural border between Egypt and Nubia.

Cenotaph. (Greek "empty grave") A funeral monument not used for the purposes of burial. Not only used for such "false tombs" but in the wider sense for any monument dedicated to the memory of a deceased person. Numerous examples of cenotaphs as "false tombs" are found in Abydos. In the Middle Kingdom, private citizens – mostly high *officials* – from throughout Egypt had chapels with stelae built to them in order to participate in the Festival of Osiris which took place there every year (see also *Journey to Abydos*). Royal cenotaphs from the Middle and New Kingdoms were also erected in Abydos, the best known of which is the great complex of Seti I located behind his temple (often called Osireion or *Tomb of Osiris*).

Chamberlain. Translation of an Egyptian title which, in the Eighteenth Dynasty, referred to persons in the intimate circle around the king who waited on him at table and tended to his personal needs. Soon, however, chamberlains were granted influential state offices; by the time of the Nineteenth and Twentieth Dynasties they had attained the status of special ministers and could achieve great political prominence.

Chiton. (Greek) Important part of dress in Greek culture: shirtlike garment worn down to the knee or calf, with or without sleeves and generally worn tied at the waist.

Coffin Text(s). Comprehensive body of religious texts consisting of many individual spells that, in varying combinations, were written on coffins, particularly in the first Intermediate Period and Middle Kingdom. They developed from the *Pyramid Texts* of the Old Kingdom, were available to nonroyal citizens, and became the basis for the *Book of the Dead* and *Guidebooks to the Netherworld* of the New Kingdom. By means of magical incantations they were meant to help resurrect the dead and described the afterlife that awaited him or her(see also *Book of Two Ways*).

Commemorative scarabs. A series of unusually large scarabs (up to 11 cm) with an engraved hieroglyphic text of several lines on their base. Historical events, sometimes events with religious connotations, are related. In the time of Amenhotep III

Statuette of Sesostris I with the White Crown
el-Lisht; Middle Kingdom, Twelfth Dynasty, ca. 1950 BC; painted and stuccoed cedar; H. 56 cm; Cairo, Egyptian Museum, JE 44951.

several series of commemorative scarabs were produced in large numbers.

Corn Mummy. Figure of the mummy-shaped god Osiris formed from earth in which grain was made to germinate. The sprouting of the grain symbolized the fertile powers of the resurrected Osiris through which he raised the dead and caused the periodic renewal of vegetation.

Cosmogony. Egyptian ideas about the creation of the world, the functioning of cosmic processes, and the possible end of the world can be reconstructed from a variety of literary and artistic sources. Common to Egyptian creation myths is the coming into existence of the world out of a state of chaos as the conscious act of a god (see *Primeval Mound*). After increasing refinement, this unformed primeval matter became the ordered world. In order to guarantee the continuity of the cosmos, the potentially destructive forces that were always present in it had to be defeated daily. This was achieved by the ritual acts of the king. This explains the dynamic character of the Egyptian world, which was conceived as cyclical and recurring.

Cubit. Egyptian unit of length. The most important measure in architecture; around 52.5 cm divided into seven hands of four fingers each.

Cuboid statue or Block statue. Egyptian statue in which the figure has its legs drawn up, its arms crossed on its knees, and is shown squatting either on the ground or on a cushion. The body is often covered by a cloth, which gives the statue a cubelike appearance. Produced in great numbers from the beginning of the Middle King-

dom to Roman times and used exclusively by private persons.

Cuneiform. Script developed in Mesopotamia at the turn of the fourth to the third millennia BC. The individual signs were in the shape of wedges formed by pressing a stylus into soft clay. Used for a variety of languages from the early third to the first millennia BC, for example Sumerian, Hittite, Hurrian, Ugaritic. The most widespread form was Akkadian, which was used as a diplomatic language in the second millennium BC throughout the Near East. The most important cuneiform find in Egypt were the clay tablets of the Tell el-Amarna archive. They represent records of diplomatic correspondence between the Egyptian royal house and the various states of the Near East (fourteenth century BC).

Cycle of offerings. The redistribution of an offering (food, clothing, ointments, flowers, etc.) first brought to a god, then to other recipients. At first these recipients were the statues of kings and then later, those of individuals in temples or private graves. This cycle of sacrificial offerings was governed by individual sets of rules; ultimately, they were used to pay the priest of the very last sacrificial recipient (see *mortuary cult*).

Cylinder seal. Form of seal in widespread use in the Near East and Egypt, particularly in the third millennium BC. Pictures and inscriptions carved on the seal were rolled onto the sealing material, which was usually of clay.

Dancing dwarves. There is literary and artistic evidence since the Old Kingdom of ritual dance performances by dwarves. These dances were not intended as profane entertainment but were part of religious devotions in worship and burial rites. It is open to debate whether the dwarf imported for such dances by Pepi II in the sixth Dynasty from central Africa was a pygmy.

Deben. Egyptian unit of weight in the form of stones. In the Old Kingdom a deben weighed around 13.6 g. The Middle Kingdom had a gold deben of 13.6 g and a copper deben of double that weight. In the New Kingdom, a deben weighed 91 g, divided into ten smaller units (see *kite*).

Demotic. (From Greek "demotika grammata" or "people's script") Egyptian language from the seventh century BC to the fifth century AD. Demotic developed from *hieratic* during the Twenty-sixth Dynasty and represents a strongly cursive form of script that was at first largely used for secular purposes. Not until Ptolemaic and Roman times were literary and religious texts written in Demotic. It was mainly written on papyrus. Linguistically, Demotic is a further development of *Late Egyptian*.

Divine cow. See *Book of the Divine Cow*.

Divine pronouncement. See *oracle*.

Divine standards. Composed of an upright pole with a crosspiece that bore a divine figure generally in the form of an animal or an object otherwise associated with the divinity. The divine standards were considered sacrosanct objects and symbolized the gods represented. They were carried at the head of festival processions.

Djed pillar. A pole wound around with bundles of plants in several stages and worshipped as a fetish from earliest times. It became a symbol for permanence and constancy and, as such, was very popular as an amulet. The ceremony of the "raising of the Djed pillar" comprised an important part of the Festivals of Osiris during the month of Khoiak.

Djeme. Coptic name for the settlement around Medinet Habu in the southern part of Western Thebes. Refers to an older Egyptian name for the *Primeval Mound* site of Medinet Habu, which is well-known for the great neighboring funerary temple of Ramesses III. Perhaps the origin of the Greek word Thebai (= Thebes).

Domain. In Egyptological usage, properties of greatly varying size mostly used for agriculture. As a rule, such domains or estates were established at the initiative of the state and administered by *officials*. They might belong to the king or various state institutions. They could also be transferred to a temple or a deserving official, who then disposed of their revenue but was obliged to pay taxes to the state. Fixed tributes to the royal and private *mortuary cults*, were drawn from domains selected specifically for this purpose (see *endowments to the dead*).

Double Crown. Combination of the White Crown representing Upper Egypt and the Red Crown symbolizing Lower Egypt. Portrayed from the early Old Kingdom onward. It could be worn by the king and the gods and demonstrated dominion over both parts of the country.

Dyad. (Greek and Latin "duality") A term often used for a pair of statues. The depiction of two people in the same freestanding sculpture was very popular in Egyptian art, and led to the development of different types of statues. The figures are most frequently shown standing or seated side by side. Various kinds of relationships between the people depicted could be illustrated in this way: for instance a close personal link in family groups of husband and wife, or a particular theological concept when the king is shown beside a god.

Electrum. Alloy of gold and silver that occurs naturally in the desert areas bordering Egypt but which can also be made artificially. Used in jewelry since the early Old Kingdom and later in large quantities as an inlay or an embellishment for temple walls and doors.

Endowments to the dead. Royal, and later private, foundations were established to supply offerings to graves on the basis of legally binding tributes from certain *domains*. In this way one could, during one's own life, ensure the later provision of

offerings for one's *mortuary cult*. These endowments were often organized as a *cycle of offerings*.

The Ennead. The gods grouped around the main divinity of a particular area. The number nine represented a multiplying of the number three, which the Egyptians believed was an indefinite quantity; it therefore stood for a vast number. The groups of gods described in this manner do not necessarily have to number nine and the composition of the groups may also change. The best known are the enneads of Heliopolis, Memphis, Abydos, and Thebes, the latter having generally fifteen members ("Great Ennead").

Epagomenal days. Greek term for the last five days of the year. In the Egyptian calendar they were added to twelve months of thirty days each so that the year consisted of 365 days. The epagomenal days were considered festival days and the birthdays of the gods Osiris, Horus, Seth, Isis, and Nephthys.

Eye of Horus. Eye of the falcon god Horus that, according to myth, was stolen and damaged but always brought back and healed. A complex cycle of myths developed around the Eyes of Horus, which were equated with the sun and moon – the so-called Mythologies of the Osirian Horus. The eternally recurring injury to the eye reflected the setting of the constellations or the changing phases of the moon. Because the Eye of Horus, like the sun and moon, always returned whole it became one of the most popular symbols of regeneration and, as such, was often depicted or worn as an amulet (Udjat eye).

False door. Stone, sometimes wooden, imitation of a door with a closed-off entrance. The required elements of doorframe, lintel, and recessed center section could be designed in different ways so that a variety of false doors developed. False doors are an important decorative element in the private tombs of the Old Kingdom but less common in royal buildings, temples, and later tombs. They mark the division between this world and the next, that is the divine. In the Old Kingdom, they represent the central cultic site of the tomb where offerings to the deceased were to be placed.

Festival of the Valley. Besides the *Opet festival*, the most important annual processional festival held in Thebes. Probably dates from the time of the early Middle Kingdom. The barque of Amun, accompanied by gods and statues of the kings (both living and dead), was taken out of his temple in Karnak and over the Nile to the West Bank on great river boats to visit the royal *funerary temples*. This festival was of great importance for the royal cult and a large proportion of the population actively participated in it; deceased family members were visited at their tombs in Western Thebes and a feast was celebrated in the imaginary company of the dead.

Flag poles. Flag poles, sometimes over 30 m high, flanked the entrances to tem-

Shrine for a cult statue of Tutankhamen
Western Thebes, Valley of the Kings, tomb of Tutankhamen (KV 62); gilded wood; H. 50.5 cm; Cairo, Egyptian Museum, JE 61481.

ples. They consisted of a smooth tree trunk and were lowered into niches in the facade of pylons. The crown was partly plated with electrum and decorated at the very top with bright banners. They probably derive from *divine standards*, which were set up in sacred sites since the very beginning of Egyptian culture.

Flail. See *royal insignia*.

Flint. Also known as silex; a particularly hard kind of stone used from the Old Stone Age onward to make many kinds of implements, such as tools and weapons. In Egypt flint is plentiful in the terraces of the banks of the Nile, and consequently it was frequently made into flint tools of many different kinds. In the later prehistoric and the Early Dynastic periods, highly sophisticated flintworking methods produced technically outstanding tools, including knives.

Followers of Horus. In the early era the king – who was considered Horus living on earth – and his court proceeded through the land to collect tribute and dispense justice. Also the name given to a certain group of *divine standards,* which accompanied the king during certain ceremonies, for example the *sed festival.*

Foreign ruler. See *Hyksos.*

Foreigners. Every country outside the Nile Valley and Delta was considered by the Egyptians to be "foreign." In their view these countries lay beyond the ordered world (that is Egypt). These chaotic forces had to be conquered in order to integrate them into the divine (that is Egyptian) world order. This is why the king was often portrayed holding an Asiatic, a Nubian, and a Libyan (as typical representatives of foreigners) by the hair and symbolically smiting them.

Funerary repast. Refers to portrayals of the deceased that show him or her seated at a table of offerings. Frequently occurring motif, showing the material provision of the dead, and seen from the beginnings of Egyptian culture. In the tombs of the Old Kingdom often related to the *false door.* In

the broader sense also used for depictions of gods or kings seated before a meal.

Funerary stele. Gravestone and place where offerings to the dead were made since the beginning of Egyptian culture. Funerary stelae bear the names and titles of the dead and indicate the place of burial. They were mostly made of stone and later developed from a wide rectangular into a tall rectangular form with a rounded top. They could be erected on their own or incorporated into funerary architecture. In the Middle and New Kingdoms it was common for the deceased and his family to be represented with an accompanying text containing a sacrificial prayer and biographical details on the deceased.

Funerary temple. Refers to two main types of complex temple: 1. Temples attached to the pyramids of the kings of the Old and Middle Kingdoms in which rituals relating to the perpetual renewal of power (see *sed festival*) and the *mortuary cult* were performed for the king; also known as the pyramid temple. 2. Religious sites of the New Kingdom in Western Thebes (which differ from 1. in their architecture and religion) where a royal statue cult was practiced, closely related to that of Amun in Karnak (see *House of Millions of Years*).

Gods of the dead. All Egyptian gods connected in one way or another with the *mortuary cult* or beliefs regarding death. The god who epitomized these beliefs was Osiris, whose resurrection after death became the mythical model to which every Egyptian aspired in order to achieve immortality.

Gods of the empire. In the context of state and *royal ideology* some of the gods in the Egyptian pantheon possessed a significance that raised them above the plethora of other gods. This was particularly true for the *sun-god*, Re, from at least the Fifth Dynasty on. In the New Kingdom, especially in the Nineteenth and Twentieth Dynasties, the gods Amun of Thebes, Re of Heliopolis and Ptah of Memphis together formed the trinity that embodied the entire Egyptian pantheon.

God's Wife of Amun. Generally used as the title of the high priestess of the temple of Amun in Thebes; during the New Kingdom it was borne by the wives and daughters of the kings. The office-holder was considered the bride of the god Amun and her person guaranteed the eternally recurring creation of the world through the life-giving primeval powers of the god. In the Third Intermediate Period the title-holder was the religious head of the Theban theocracy of Amun and the office was exercised by unmarried daughters of the royal house. Heirs to the office were adopted. In the Twenty-sixth Dynasty it declined in importance and ultimately ceased to be occupied.

Golden Horus. See *royal titulary.*

Gold of honor. The Egyptian custom of rewarding deserving officials with gold is recorded in Egypt from the Old Kingdom onward. In the New Kingdom the public award of such distinctions is often pictured in private tombs. The king stands at the "Window of Appearances" giving the gold of honor to the official standing below. Usually the gold takes the form of various kinds of jewelry, such as gold bracelets and collars of lentiform gold beads. These decorative items were often shown in depictions of the person thus distinguished, for instance on his statues.

Gold stater. In Greek numismatics the gold stater is the "norm" or "unit coin." A gold stater weighed 11 g, later 8.1 g. In addition, there were mintings in electrum and silver. The first Egyptian gold staters with the inscription "Nub-nefer" ("perfect gold") were minted in the Thirtieth Dynasty under Teos and Neltanebos.

Graffito. (Greek in origin; pl. graffiti) This term is used in Egyptology for carved or painted inscriptions found on stone walls, statues, potsherds, and many other materials bearing text. The script (usually hieratic or Demotic) and the content (administrative or economic notes, religious texts, etc.) may be of many different kinds. Inscriptions relating to a particular building project are classified as construction graffiti. They are usually brief remarks on the transport and assembly of stone for building, and were recorded on the stones themselves.

Guidebooks to the Netherworld. A series of illustrated didactic "books" that describe the Egyptian vision of the hereafter. The systematic description of what awaited the deceased in the afterlife was intended to enable him to join the cycle of life – described in terms of the course of the sun – and therefore achieve immortality. Initially, the Books of the Dead were almost always the exclusive preserve of the King. They form the most important part of the wall decorations of the royal tombs of the New Kingdom. Later, they were increasingly used by private citizens on coffins and papyri. For individual Guidebooks to the Netherworld, see *Amduat*, *Book of Caverns*, *Book of Gates* and *Book of Two Paths*.

Hadra vase. Type of ceramic vase produced in Alexandria probably from the late fourth century BC on. Named after the main find at Hadra, a modern suburb in the east of Alexandria. This pot-bellied and painted vase with one vertical and two horizontal handles was used as a cinerary urn in the funeral rites of Ptolemaic Egypt.

Hat-Mehit. (Egyptian "the first of the fishes") Name of the nome goddess of Mendes, in Lower Egypt; mostly represented as a woman with her sacred animal, a fish, on her head.

Hathor column. Column in Egyptian architecture whose capital shows, on either two or four sides, a sculpted face of the goddess Hathor (or Bat) with cow's ears. Used especially from the Middle Kingdom on in temples of female divinities.

Heka scepter. (Egyptian "ruler" or "government" scepter) As part of the king's ceremonial costume this scepter was an important component of the royal insignia. It was a staff ending in a crook, and the king usually held it in his right hand as a sign of his regal power.

Herakleopolitans. The kings of the Ninth and Tenth Dynasties who resided in the central Egyptian city of Herakleopolis after the end of the Old Kingdom. Only a few of these kings, who generally ruled only for a short time, are known by name.

Herm. (Greek) In cultural areas of Greek origin, a sacred monument consisting of a four-sided stone shaft, originally surmounted by a head of the god Hermes. Later, the heads of other deities might be shown. This form of statue, set up in temples, beside tombs and roads and in public places, and probably connected with ideas of protection, was also found in Egypt in the Ptolemaic and Roman Periods.

Hieratic. (From the Greek "*grammata hieratica*" or "sacred script") Cursive form of Egyptian script whose development ran parallel to that of the monumental hieroglyphic script. In hieratic, the individual signs or hieroglyphs became so simplified that their pictorial content was no longer recognizable. Written primarily with reeds on papyrus and fragments of limestone or pottery, it was the script most commonly used for administrative and economic purposes but also for works of literature. From the seventh century on, this function was taken over by *Demotic* and hieratic was then mainly used for religious texts – hence the derivation of the Greek term.

High priest. Head of the priesthood of a temple; corresponds to the title "first servant of God." The high priests represented the king and managed the personnel, administration, and finances of their temples. These sometimes possessed great wealth and large estates.

Hin. Egyptian term for a hollow measure holding around 0.48 l; mostly used for grain but in the New Kingdom also for myrrh and gold.

Hittites. Indo-European people who, expanding from their fortified settlement of (modern Bogazkay), established what was at first a short-lived empire in the seventeenth century BC in Northern Anatolia. In the fourteenth century the Hittite state developed into a great power ruling Anatolia and Syria and soon controlling the empire of *Mitanni*. The Hittites therefore became the fiercest competitors of the Egyptians in the struggle for domination of Asia Minor in the fourteenth and thirteenth centuries BC. After heavy fighting, a peace treaty was finally secured under Ramesses II. In the twelfth century BC the Hittite Empire collapsed.

Horemheb decree. Decree of King Horemheb around 1330 BC detailing the new structure of part of the state administration and courts. Special emphasis was placed on the elimination of corruption. It is preserved as a duplicate on a stele ereted in front of the tenth pylon of the Amun temple at Karnak.

House of Millions of Years. Traces its origin to an Egyptian term for temple complexes, especially those of the New Kingdom, in which the veneration of royal statues in close association with the cult of the gods was particularly important. The cult aimed to preserve the reign of the king and confer eternal life on him, thus making him king of Upper and Lower Egypt for millions of years. The *funerary temples* of the New Kingdom in Western Thebes were a special type of "House of Millions of Years."

Hurrians. Peoples who spread out from Transcaucasia on a broad front through the north and southeast of Turkey, northern Syria and Iraq toward the end of the third millennium BC. The evidence for this migration is largely derived from linguistic evidence. Their greatest power and influence was wielded by the empire of *Mitanni* from the sixteenth to the fourteenth centuries BC.

Hyksos. (Greek form of the Egyptian *heqa khasut*, "foreign rulers") Asiatic kings who established a 100-year reign in the Fifteenth Dynasty in Egypt (ca. 1650–1542 BC). From their base in their capital in Avaris in the eastern Nile Delta, long home to Syro-Palestinian tribes, they ruled Egypt as a group of vassal states. After a long struggle the Theban Seventeenth Dynasty drove the Hyksos out of Egypt and established the New Kingdom.

Hypogeum. (Greco-Latin) Subterranean vault; in Egypt, the terms refers to multi-chambered underground tomb sites used for multiple burials. Several examples are known from the necropolises of Alexandria.

Hypostyle Hall. (Greek) Hall whose roof is borne by columns or pillars and which therefore has several naves. In Egyptian architecture it generally refers to halls of columns, sometimes very large, with a raised central nave. Particularly well-known from the temple complexes of the New Kingdom. The most famous example is the great hall at Karnak with 134 columns and covering an area of around 5500 square meters.

Imhotep. High *official* under King Djoser in the Third Dynasty. Known to be high priest of Heliopolis and the architect of Djoser's Step Pyramid complex. In later times he was credited with the invention of building in dressed stone and, as a wise man and cultural hero, he was accorded divine honors. As son of the god Ptah he was also worshipped in his own temples in the area around Memphis.

Incense cones. Small cones of ointment worn on the head on festive occasions. The cones were made of animal fat mixed with aromatic substances, probably various kinds of myrrh and perhaps resin as well. Depictions of banqueting scenes in the tombs of the New Kingdom regularly show them on the heads of the participants. During the banquet the cone would melt, anointing the hair and upper body of the person wearing it.

Inlay work. A favorite method of ornamenting surfaces in metalwork, particularly in the making of bronze figures and tools. Depressions left unfilled during the casting process, or grooves cut with a chisel after casting, had thin sheets or wires of precious metal – gold, electrum or silver – hammered into them, and finally the surface was filed smooth.

Instructions. Egyptian literary genre that enjoyed great popularity, as can be seen from the countless copies made at scribes' schools. At least sixteen individual works have been preserved completely or in part. They attempt to teach the new generation of *officials* the basic rules of Egyptian society and to educate them in the fundamental ethics of the state. They are, therefore, important sources for the Egyptian conception of mankind and the world. Their influence extended beyond Egypt, evidence for which can be found, for example, in the Bible.

Instructions in Wisdom See *Instructions*.

Isfet. (Egyptian "chaos," "wrong," "sin," "evil") The opposite of *maat*, that is, the rules laid down by the gods according to which the world, the state, and the life of man should be ordered. Whoever infringed the rules of this "divine world order" committed *isfet*.

Ished tree. A sacred tree in the precincts of the temple of the sun-god at Heliopolis, probably to be identified with the persea tree. Many depictions in temples from the Eighteenth Dynasty onward record a religious ceremony in which the king's royal titulary was inscribed on leaves of the ished tree, thus placing his names and his reign under the protection of the sun-god and ensuring that his power would last for ever.

Israel Stele. Stele from the fifth year of the reign of King Merenptah (around 1210 BC), found in his funerary temple in Western Thebes; today in the Egyptian Museum in Cairo. This enormous granite stele of almost 3.2 m in height and inscribed on its front by Amenhotep III was covered by a long poetic text on its reverse side by Merenptah, which glorified the king's victory over the Libyans. At the end, several areas and cities in Syria and Palestine are mentioned that were also vanquished by Merenptah – including the only mention of the name Israel in Egyptian texts.

Journey to Abydos. Representation of a boat trip of the mummy or a statue of the deceased in private tombs of the Middle Kingdom. In the course of a burial a ritual journey to Abydos was performed so that the dead person could partake in the

Festivals of Osiris held there. Every year in Abydos the death and resurrection in the afterlife of the god Osiris was observed, in which every deceased person wished to join as a guarantee for his own eternal life in the hereafter. By depicting this journey to or from Abydos in the tomb, the participation of the dead in the so-called Osiris mysteries was documented and thus perpetuated for all eternity.

Ka. Difficult Egyptian concept pertaining to an aspect of the personality of gods and men. See also *akh* and *ba*. *Ka* was considered bearer of the generating and life-giving forces, a symbol of uninterrupted vital strength passed on from generation to generation. It came into existence at the birth of a person and continued to exist after his death. Like the *ba* it also accepted offerings and guaranteed eternal life after death.

Ka statue. Statue embodying the *ka* of a person that, according to the rites of the mortuary cult, was erected in a tomb. Royal *ka* statues, moreover, were worshipped during the lifetime of the kings in specially built cult complexes – so-called *ka* houses – adjoined to large temples at various places throughout the country.

Kassites. People who migrated from Iran to Babylon, documented from the eighteenth century BC. After the collapse of the native dynasty in Babylon in 1595 BC., brought about by the *Hittites*, the Kassites took control and ruled Babylon until the middle of the twelfth century BC. From the late fifteenth century BC regular diplomatic contacts were made with Egypt and trade flourished. Amenhotep III married the sister of the Kassite king.

Kenbet. Egyptian name for a committee composed of high-ranking *officials* in the New Kingdom that was responsible for matters of local justice. There was also a "Great *Kenbet*" under the *vizier*, which met in his residence and formed the highest court in the land with sole responsibility for appeals.

Khepresh. Egyptian term for the Blue Crown. Distinguished by a high bonnet-like shape with wing-like projections at the sides and often depicted being worn by the king from the time of the early New Kingdom. It is generally represented as blue and covered with small yellow rings. Probably made of leather with a metal overlay.

Khoiak. Coptic form of the old Egyptian name for the fourth month of the season of the Nile inundation. During this month great festivals in honor of Osiris were held throughout the country. The main focus of these were the ritual resurrection celebrations of Osiris in temples dedicated to him.

King List. Written inventory of kings' names in chronological order with a note on the length of their reign. Used for purposes of dating in administration and historiography. The most famous example is the Turin Royal Canon, which has only survived in fragmentary form. The Egyptian King Lists

are one of the most important sources for reconstructing Egyptian chronology.

Kiosk. Light open-sided pavilion. In Egyptian architecture often made of stone with partition walls of medium height between outer columns or pillars and which had a wooden or canvas roof. Such kiosks were often found in the entrances to great temple complexes or along processional routes where they offered protection and temporary resting places to cult images during festival processions (see also *way stations*).

Kite. Unit of weight corresponding to 9.1 g. Ten kite make a *deben* of 91 g.

Kouros. (Greek pl. kouroi) In ancient Greek sculpture a term for the figure of a naked youth.

Kumidi. Kamid el-Loz in Lebanon; a city state in the Near East that Thutmosis III put at the head of the list of places conquered on his first Syrian campaign, after which it belonged to the Egyptian sphere of influence.

Kushite cap. Flat, close-fitting headgear of the Nubian kings ("Kushites" after the Egyptian word "Kush" for Nubia, or a part thereof) who ruled over Egypt and Nubia as the Twenty-fifth Dynasty. At the front were affixed two uraeus serpents (see *uraeus*), while at the rear long ribbons hung down to the wearer's back.

Kyphi pastille. From the Egyptian word for "incense." Term for various mixtures of up to sixteen ingredients (resins, woods, grasses, spices, animal parts, and, sometimes, dung), which were burnt in temples for purification purposes and as air fresheners. They were also used a cure for different illnesses, and could be used as a mouthwash, or added to wine.

Labyrinth. The description used by Greek and Roman travel writers for the temple precinct of Amenemhat III's pyramid at Hawara, at the edge of the Faiyum. The complex cannot be reconstructed today but it encompassed a huge area (158 by 385 m) and was probably composed of various courtyards and rooms of cult images with shrines for statues of the gods and king.

Late Egyptian. Stage of development of the Egyptian language lasting from the late Eighteenth Dynasty into the Third Intermediate Period. A large number of texts dealing with administrative, trade, and economic matters as well as literary works have been found in Late Egyptian. It was written in the cursive *hieratic* script on papyri and ostraca (see *papyrus* and *ostracon*) as well as in hieroglyphs on stelae and temple walls.

Libu. See *Libyan.*

Libyan. From the Egyptian Rebu/Reby describing a people who lived just west of the Nile Delta. In modern usage it means a variety of peoples who lived in the west and southwest of the Nile Valley. They often appear in Egyptian representations of

foreigners and were obviously a serious danger in the Nineteenth and Twentieth Dynasties with their constant incursions into the Nile Valley. Because more and more Libyan tribes were settling in the western Nile Delta at this same time, local Libyan princedoms arose. These succeeded in seizing power in Egypt in the Third Intermediate Period temporarily establishing the Twenty-second Dynasty.

Loculus. (Latin pl. loculi.) Term for an individual burial site in Greco-Roman funeral practices. In Egypt it usually refers to the location of a sarcophagus in a walled niche of a tomb and, especially, for the corresponding niches in the Roman burial grounds of Alexandria.

Mammisi. Expression borrowed from the Egyptian-Coptic meaning "birth-house;" refers to small temples that stood within the outer ramparts of a larger main temple; mostly situated at right angles to these on processional roads and often fitted with an *ambulatory*. On particular ceremonial days, the processions of the gods entered the *mammisi* in order to celebrate the birth of the god-child of the locally honored divine trinity (father, mother, and child) with whom the king was identified. The rituals of the *mammisi* were therefore part of the royal *birth legend*.

Mastaba. (Arabic "bank", "bench") Royal and private tomb complexes whose upper structure consisted of a solid, rectangular area of mudbricks or stones with sloping sides. The actual burial usually occupied a subterranean chamber that could be surrounded by storerooms. Common in the predynastic era and in the Old Kingdom.

Menat. A necklace consisting of several rows of beads joined at the ends and clasped with a metal plate that lay on the wearer's back like a kind of counterpoise. The *menat* could also be carried in the hand, so that the beads would make a sound when shaken. There is evidence that it was used as a musical instrument in this way, particularly in the cult of the goddess Hathor.

Min festival. One of the most important religious festivals all over Egypt was the festival of the primeval fertility god Min. It is recorded in inscriptions from the Archaic Period onward and is portrayed on many temple walls, particularly in the New Kingdom. The festival, associated with the making of offerings and many ritual acts, took the form of a solemn procession in which the cult image of the god was carried from his temple. The statue, accompanied by divine standards and the statues of former kings, was carried by priests to reside temporarily in other cult buildings. This "procession of Min" was closely connected with rites of thanksgiving for harvest and was intended to impregnate nature, "wounded" by the harvest, with new fertility. At the same time the ceremony renewed the king's authority.

Mitanni. Kingdom established in the sixteenth century BC in western Mesopota-

mia between the upper Tigris and the Euphrates. Most important of the *Hurrian* states. In the fifteenth century BC Mitanni and Egypt were rivals for control of Syria. War was ended with a peace treaty under Amenhotep II. Thutmosis IV as well as Amenhotep III married daughters of the Mitanni kings. The power of Mitanni gradually declined in the fourteenth century BC due to the constant expansion of the *Hittite* Empire.

Mortuary cult. Acts carried out for the dead, intended to secure their continued existence after death, date from the prehistoric period. The mortuary cult of the king, however, was different from that of private individuals because of his dual human-divine nature. The notions of preserving the body (through mummification and biographical texts in the tomb) and providing for it (equipment and offerings placed in the tomb) were central to the mortuary cult. Having one's own tomb built was necessary for the private individual to establish a mortuary cult. When the rites had been completed after embalming and interring, the mortuary cult was set in motion by daily offerings performed by the eldest son or a priest employed for this purpose (see *endowments to the dead*). During certain festivals the tombs received set contributions (see *Festival of the Valley*) from the temples and mortuary establishments to which they belonged in the *cycle of offerings*.

Mummy. Derived from the Arabic, meaning "asphalt," and indicating a corpse protected from decay by artificial means or natural desiccation. Early forms of embalming took place in Egypt from the very beginnings of its culture. Later, the embalming process lasted seventy days, after which the mummified corpse was buried. According to Egyptian beliefs, the preservation of the corpse was absolutely necessary for ensuring life after death (see also *ba*).

Naophorus. (Greek "naos bearer") Type of statue generally showing a kneeling man holding a *naos* with a figure or emblem of the gods; seen in temples from the time of the Eighteenth Dynasty. In later periods, standing or seated naophori occur frequently.

Naos. (Greek "temple," "house of the gods") Lockable shrine for storing religious images; generally made of wood or hard stone and placed in temples or tombs. Also used for the sanctum of the inner temple in which the statue of the god was stored and serviced.

Natron. Used for drying the corpse during mummification and for purification and incensing in cult ceremonies. Occurs naturally as the compounds sodium carbonate and sodium bicarbonate and was mined in Lower Egypt in Wadi Natrun.

Nebty name. See *royal titulary*.

Nemes headcloth. Headgear of the king depicted from the time of the early Old Kingdom. Consisted of a rectangular piece of cloth folded and laid over the head so that the ears remained uncovered. The two ends were draped as lappets over the shoulders and chest and the back was arranged into a type of plait.

Nile inundation. Caused by the summer monsoon rains in the upper reaches of the Nile in Ethiopia and southern Sudan. Up until it was dammed in recent decades, the Egyptian Nile rose by several meters every year in late summer. Through an elaborate system of canals and dams, flood water was channeled to fields where it seeped into the soil for several weeks, leaving behind fresh soil enriched with nutrients.

Nile level. See *Nile inundation*.

Nilometer. A narrow canal or well shaft connected to the Nile whose walls had a scale marked on them, by means of which the height of the Nile could be read. The systematic observation of the level of the Nile was carried out from the beginnings of Egyptian culture. It was important for monitoring the *Nile inundation*, for distributing water for irrigation correctly and for determining the annual taxes on agricultural production.

Nimmuria. Cuneiform version of the throne-name "Nebmaatra" of Amenhotep III (see also *cuneiform*).

Nomarch. (Greek) 1. Ruler of a *nome*, or province. 2. In the Ptolemaic era the nomarch was at first the title of a civil administrative *official* responsible for agricultural production in a particular district. Later it became the title of a low-level financial official in a nome.

Nome. Usual term for the administrative units into which Egypt had been divided since the Third Dynasty. Ideally, there were twenty-two Upper Egyptian and twenty Lower Egyptian nomes. Each was headed by a *nomarch*. This administrative division was also reflected on the religious level as gods or goddesses were specifically allocated to nomes as their divinities. In the course of time the religious character of the nomes came to eclipse their secular function to such an extent that separate administrative entities began to emerge.

Nome hieroglyphs. In order to identify them, a symbol was allocated to most nomes that was directly related to the local divinity worshipped there. As a rule this symbol – such as a crocodile, a scepter or a harpoon and rope – was set on a standard and considered to represent the divinity. This combination of symbol and standard is what is called today the nome hieroglyph.

Nub-Nefer. See *gold stater*.

Nubians. Generally used for the inhabitants of the Nile Valley south of the first cataract who were ethnically and linguistically distinct from the Egyptians. From the Egyptian point of view Nubians were *foreigners* and, as a potential threat to Egypt, had to be politically and militarily

subdued. Contacts with Nubians had been made from earliest times and were partly military, partly peaceful (trade). It has been shown that many Nubians were present in Egypt – for economic reasons, amongst others. In Egyptian art, Nubians are usually depicted as dark-skinned with curly hair.

Oasis Road. Up to the modern era a much-traveled caravan route from Coptos in Upper Egypt through several oases of the western desert and into the Sudan. Described as a trade route in Egyptian texts from the Old Kingdom onward.

Obelisk. Tall stone pillar tapering toward the top, whose end often formed a *pyramidion* coated with electrum. Probably developed in the early Old Kingdom from the *Benben Stone*, a stylized recreation of the *Primeval Mound*. Obelisks sometimes attained a height of over 30 m and were generally hewn from a single piece of hard stone (often red granite) and erected in pairs at the entrance to a temple. They were considered symbols of the *sun-god*.

Offering table. A stone slab on which offerings for the dead were laid, associated with the false door as the main cult area of the tomb, and also with the cult of the dead. It usually had hollows to hold food and drink. Such typical offerings as different kinds of loaves were carved on the upper surface of the offering table.

Official. A person who "officially" worked for the Egyptian state apparatus in an administrative position. However, the term says nothing about the actual tasks he or she carried out. Officials had to be literate and were provided for by the state for which reason they often, but not always, had a high social station. At their head was the *vizier*.

Opening of the mouth ritual. This ceremony, for which there is evidence from the Old Kingdom onward, was seen as giving life to cult objects that were lifeless in themselves. Recorded in texts and depictions on papyri and on the walls of temples and tombs until the Roman Period, the ritual, involving many very complex actions, was most frequently performed on statues, into which it was supposed to "breathe life." They would then take part in the ritual acts and would be capable of accepting the offerings made to them. In this way the mummies of the dead and of sacred animals were "awakened" to life in the next world. A key episode in the rite, often shown in d epictions, was the opening of the mouth with a tool shaped rather like the body of an adze or chisel.

Opet festival. The Opet festival, considered one of the most important of all festivals, was held annually for up to twenty-seven days in Thebes. Its high point was the procession, attended by great pomp and circumstance, of the barque of Amun of Karnak to the temple of Luxor 2.5 km away. There, the statue of the god stayed for several days before the procession

Statue of the vizier Nespekashati as a scribe
Karnak, temple of Amun-Re, "cachette," ca. 650 BC; H. 80 cm; W. 47 cm; Cairo, Egyptian Museum, JE 36662.

returned. Detailed depictions of this festival procession can be found on the walls of the Temple of Luxor ("Great Colonnade"). The rituals carried out during the visit to Luxor were thought to renew the royal claim to rule, vouchsafed by Amun.

Oracle. The custom of petitioning the gods for advice, information or a decision was practiced from the time of the early New Kingdom onward. Requests were given by priests to the gods (that is their statues) in either written or oral form. The gods would then make their decision known by certain movements (for example made by the statue during a public procession) or by manifesting their divine will in the priest. The requests may have concerned matters of state, legal judgments, official appointments or personal affairs.

Osiride pillar. A statue of the king resting with its back engaged to a wall or pillar. Because they were often in the shape of a bandaged mummy and were similar to depictions of the god Osiris, this somewhat misleading term has found its way into the language. Osirid pillars date from the early Middle Kingdom and are found above all in the facades and courtyards of the great royal temples of the New Kingdom.

Ostracon. (Greek "potsherd") Sherd of pottery or flake of limestone that bore an inscription. Thousands of ostraca have been found from the New Kingdom when they were used for a variety of texts in daily life (letters, bills, notes, school exercises) since they were much cheaper than *papyrus*. They were also used by artists for trial sketches.

Palermo Stone. The main fragment of an inscribed stone slab, today in the Palermo Museum. It lists the names and years of the earliest kings up to the Fifth Dynasty as well as details on endowments made to the gods. The Palermo Stone is the most important source for annals of the Old Kingdom and is crucial for the reconstruction of Egyptian chronology.

Palm column. Popular type of column in Egyptian architecture in which palm fronds were tied to the column shaft to imitate a palm tree. From the Fifth Dynasty they were made in stone and had capitals that curved gently outward in imitation of palm leaves.

Paopi. Coptic name for the second month of the *Nile inundation* (see *Calendar*). Can be traced back to an Egyptian term – "the month of the Opet festival" – from the late New Kingdom. From the early Eighteenth Dynasty onward, the Theban Opet festival began in this month.

Papyrus. (From the Greek *papyros*, probably from an Egyptian word meaning "that of the pharaoh"). The great numbers of papyrus plants that once grew in the swamps of the Nile Delta were used for a variety of practical purposes (mats, baskets, architecture, boots, sandals and the like) as well as religious ones (offerings). Their great symbolic value (freshness, fertility, regeneration) meant they became the pattern for architectural forms and religious objects. They were most important, however, for the pith of their stems, which provided the writing material "papyrus." Its use dates from the First Dynasty.

Papyrus column. Type of column, widespread in Egyptian architecture, imitating one or several papyrus plants. Different variants were developed. The shaft of the column could imitate a bundle of papyrus plants or just one stem, and the capital might have an open or closed flower spray. Made in stone from the time of the Old Kingdom.

Peoples of the Sea. Modern term for a number of different peoples, most of whom probably lived on the west coast of Asia Minor and in the Aegean. In the twelfth and thirteenth centuries BC they migrated in several waves through Asia Minor and as far as Egypt in search of land in which to settle. They caused enormous political and ethnic upheavals, especially in Syria-Palestine. Several Egyptian kings led campaigns against them in order to prevent them from settling on the Egyptian coast. Battles against the Sea Peoples can be seen in the decoration of various Theban temples of Ramesses II, Merenptah, and Ramesses III.

Per-aa. See *pharaoh*.

Peret. Egyptian term for the season when new plant growth emerges. See *calendar*.

Peristyle. (Greek and Latin) An inner courtyard surrounded by columns; see also *atrium*.

Pharaoh. From the Egyptian *Per-aa*, meaning "Great House." From the beginnings of Egyptian culture it meant the royal palace and its occupants, that is the court. Used from the Eighteenth Dynasty on for the person of the king and later as the title of the ruler.

Phyle. Greek. The most important unit in the Egyptian workforce. Workers (for example in construction and transport) as well as various trades and temple priests were strictly organized into phyles or gangs with a specific number of staff and a rotating work schedule.

Portcullis. (Latin) Stone slabs lowered into position from above and used to block the entrance to tombs after burial. Often, several slabs were placed tightly behind one another. Seen in royal and private tombs from the First Dynasty onward.

Portico. (Latin "porch") A hall of columns, similar to the *pronaos,* positioned on the entrance side of a building. The term "portico" is, however, used more extensively and often means a single or multiple group of columns or pillars before the entrance to temples, graves or secular buildings. Sometimes used for the rows of columns on the sides of large courtyards ("colonnades").

Primeval Mound. The Primeval Mound was of paramount importance in Egyptian cosmogony. From the Primeval Waters, which represented chaotic forces, arose the first piece of land, the Primeval Mound, on which the primeval god created the world. In Egyptian architecture, literature, and art the Primeval Mound is an important motif and a symbol for the eternally recurring process of creation (see also *Cosmogony* and *Benben Stone*).

Primeval Waters. See *Primeval Mound.*

Pronaos. (Greek) A hall of columns situated in front of a temple. Its front is either open, or – more frequently – closed by medium-high walls between the columns in the foremost row. The architectural form of the pronaos was developed during the Eighteenth and early Nineteenth dynasties before ultimately becoming a magnificently designed element of Egyptian temples in Ptolemaic and Roman times.

Prophet (Priest). Usual modern term for the Egyptian title "servant of the God", which, from earliest times, was used to describe one of the most common temple offices. Usually suffixed by details of the god, king or even religious site where or for whom the priest was employed (for example "servant of the god Amun"). The position of prophet could either be held as an office in itself or occupied by *officials* who performed their priestly duties in addition to their main functions. From the New Kingdom on there was a more diverse hierarchy at whose head stood the *high priest* as the "first servant of god", followed by the second, third, and fourth servants of a temple.

Punt. Egyptian term for a region farther to the southeast in Africa with which Egypt traded since the days of the Old Kingdom. Egyptian trade expeditions to Punt sailed down the Red Sea and then turned inland from about the latitude of northern Ethiopia/northern Eritrea. The best-known of these expeditions was dispatched by Hatshepsut and is recorded in her *funerary temple* in Western Thebes. The most important products from Punt were myrrh, incense, ebony, ivory, and animal skins.

Columns with composite capitals
Esna, pronaos of the temple of Khum; Roman Period, first to second centuries AD; sandstone; H. of columns 6.12 m.

Pylon. (Greek "large portal," gatehouse) In Egyptological usage, a monumental gateway to a temple flanked by two towers. The passage through the middle was filled by two large double-winged wooden doors, often with a metal covering. The towers had steps within that led up to a roof and were usually decorated on the outside with scenes of the annihilation of an enemy (see *foreigners*). In front of the pylon often stood *flag poles*, *obelisks* and colossal statues of the king.

Pyramid town. Settlement planned and financed by the state and situated in the vicinity of the royal pyramid(s). The first was constructed next to Sneferu's pyramids in Maidum and Dahshur. Inhabitants of these towns belonged to the royal *endowment to the dead* and were therefore priests, tradesmen and *officials*. The latter administered the endowment, together with its agricultural production, and were responsible for carrying out sacred rites in the pyramid complex.

Pyramid Text(s). Modern name for the religious texts found in the pyramids of the kings and queens of the Old Kingdom. The oldest known example is in the burial chambers of the pyramid of Unas at Saqqara. The Pyramid Texts are not a unified body of work but rather a collection of individual texts consisting of hymns, litanies, incantations, etc., which had as their theme the eternal life of the king in the hereafter.

Pyramidion. Term derived from the Greek for the apex of pyramids and obelisks; in the case of pyramids it was made separately, usually from stone, and decorated with pictures and texts related to the course of the sun. On obelisks it formed the pyramidlike peak on top of the monolithic shaft and was often coated with *electrum*.

Red Crown. Royal crown dating from late prehistoric times. Consisted of a conical base surmounted at the back by a high rectangular piece from the bottom of which a long strip protruded, spiraling inwards at the end. It was colored red and symbolized Lower Egypt (see also *Double Crown*).

Regions of the world. According to Egyptian state and *royal ideology*, the *pharaoh* was not only king of Egypt but ruler of the entire world, which had to be subordinated to the divine, that is Egyptian, world order. When assuming power therefore, and during the regularly executed rituals of its renewal (see *Sed festival*), symbolic claim was laid to all four regions of the world. This might be done, for example, by having birds fly off to the four cardinal points.

Rhomboid wrapping. Particular method of wrapping the mummified corpse. Fine linen bandages several meters long were wrapped around the mummy in such a way that an elaborately graduated geometric pattern resulted. Common in the late dynastic era.

Rosetta Stone. A stele discovered in 1799 by a French officer in Rosette, near the Egyptian Mediterranean coast; today in The British Museum in London. The trilingual text of this decree – in hieroglyphic, *Demotic* and Greek – was the basis for Jean-François Champollion's deciphering of hieroglyphs in 1822. The decree recounts the decisions of a meeting of Egyptian priests regarding honors for Ptolemy V and Cleopatra I in 196 BC (see also *Canopus Decree*).

Royal beard. Part of the royal ceremonial costume. It was an artificial beard, slightly splayed at the bottom and held in place with straps hooking around the ears. Depicted in most representations of the king.

Royal ideology. All the concepts and beliefs associated with the Egyptian kings. According to the Egyptians the king represented the gods on earth and in his person he embodied the Egyptian state. He was the representative of the people of Egypt in the world of the gods and was responsible for maintaining the divine world order (Egyptian: *maat*). This was guaranteed by his historical deeds, ritually exaggerated countless times in depictions on temple walls. By virtue of his office, granted him by the gods, he was also attributed with godly qualities. For this reason he was not only the highest priest of the land but was himself worshipped during his lifetime.

Royal insignia. Those parts of the king's ceremonial costume that were bestowed on him by the gods at his coronation as symbols of his power. These included, besides various scepters and staffs (see *was scepter*), the so-called flail, which he held in his left hand, and the crook, held in his right. The crook was said to originate from a shepherd's crook. Both objects were also carried by Osiris.

Royal novel. Popular literary form dating from the early Middle Kingdom, the focus of which was an historically important undertaking of the king for example the decision to go to war, or to build a new temple. This sort of literary history served to glorify the king whose wisdom was shown by the successful outcome to his decisions.

Royal titulary. The official titles of the Egyptian king consisted of five names that – with the exception of his fifth name given him at birth – were conferred on him at his coronation. They were composed of a Horus name, a Nebty name, a Golden Horus name, a prenomen (birth name) and a nomen (throne name). The last two were written in *cartouches*. The choice of names showed clearly the interrelationship of the king with the most important gods of the country and consituted a sort of religious and political program for a particular ruler.

Rubric. (Latin in origin) Sections of text or single characters written in red ink and thus standing out from an otherwise black text. Used as a method of dividing up particularly long texts and emphasizing certain passages. For instance, the titles of separate sections in large papyrus collections of texts are often rubricized.

Saff tomb. (Arabic "row") Type of cliff tomb popular in the early Eleven Dynasty in the northern part of the Theban necropolis. The grave facade was fronted by a courtyard and generally had one, if not two, rows of pillars hewn from the rock face. Behind the pillars an entrance opened into the actual rooms of the grave within the cliff.

Safflower. Plant, *Carthamus tinctorius*. A water-soluble yellow dye and an alkaline-soluble red dye could be obtained from the dried petals that were used for coloring textiles. Cooking oil could be made from the seeds and the petals woven into sacrificial garlands.

Saqiya. Device for raising water first used during Greco-Roman times. By means of two intermeshed wheels, water was lifted in a chain of buckets to a height of several meters. It allowed for a more efficient irrigation of larger fields. Today the saqiya is usually powered by water buffalo. Earlier, this was done by cattle or donkeys.

Sanctuary. (Latin "holy place") The term can be used for an entire cult building devoted to a deity, but is generally applied only to the room in the god's temple where his or her statue was worshipped daily. As a rule this room, also called the cult image chamber, lies at the very back of the temple, on the central axis of the building. Its walls are ornamented with scenes from the daily ritual, in which the statue deputizing for the god (see *opening of the mouth ritual*) was dressed in its robes every morning, anointed, decked with its insignia, and worshipped with offerings and the singing of hymns (see also *barque sanctuary*).

Satire on the Trades. Modern term for the teachings of the sage Khety. In this literary work of the Middle Kingdom, later widely read and copied in scribal schools, a father describes to his son a number of mostly tradesmen's occupations in a rather mocking fashion in order to emphasize their negative aspects. An apprenticeship as a scribe and subsequent career as an *official* is portrayed as the only worthwhile profession.

Satrap. (Old Persian "country-protector") From the time of Cyrus, the Persian Empire was divided into administrative units called satrapies. These were under the leadership of a satrap who had civil and military authority. At the time of Persian control of Egypt the country was a satrapy of the Persian Empire (see also *Achaemenides*). After the death of Alexander the Great, the Macedonian general Ptolemy ruled Egypt as a satrap from 323 BC until he had himself declared king in 306 BC.

Scarab. The beetle *Scarabaeus sacer* was considered by the Egyptians to symbolize the young *sun-god* and to embody the life that continually arose anew from the depths of the underworld. They believed that the young beetles were hatched from the dung balls that the scarabs rolled with their hind legs. They saw this as an analogy (the dung balls representing the earth) to the path of the sun, which was born again each morning. The scarab image was the most popular amulet seal and was made in huge numbers from the most diverse materials.

Scribe. Learning the Egyptian script was a precondition for becoming an *official* and embarking on a career that could possibly lead to the highest state offices. The profession of scribe was therefore well-regarded (see *Satire on the Trades*). Scribes formed the backbone of the bureaucratically organized Egyptian state. Writing, along with other specialized knowledge, was taught in state schools generally connected to temples.

Sed festival (Egyptian *heb-sed*: "royal jubilee") Royal festival that is documented from the beginnings of Egyptian culture up to the Greco-Roman epoch through depictions on temple walls and frequent textual references. By means of complex rituals lasting several days the physical and magical powers of the king were renewed in order to effect a continuation of his reign. The influence of *sed* festival celebrations was thought to carry over to the hereafter so that the rule of the king could be perpetuated for all eternity.

Sem priests. There is documentary evidence from the Archaic Period of the use of the word "*sem*" as the title of the king's eldest son, who could deputize for his father, particularly in worshipping the gods. The *sem* played a leading part in the opening of the mouth ritual and at funeral ceremonies. Increasingly, the word became a purely priestly title. The office of the sem priest was particularly significant in the cults of Ptah, Sokar, and Osiris, and is also represented in the royal funerary temples of the New Kingdom. In depictions on the walls of temples and tombs, the *sem* priest can be recognized by his leopard-skin cloak.

Senet game. An ancient board game for two people and extremely popular throughout Egyptian history. It could be interpreted religiously: moving the pieces over the board was considered the equivalent of the journey of the dead through the afterlife and winning a game guaranteed one's re-birth.

Serdab. (Arabic "cellar") The *serdab*, first found in the funerary precincts of King Djoser of the Third Dynasty, was a completely enclosed chamber containing one or several statues of a person. In the private tombs of high officials of the later Old Kingdom in particular, statues of the dead man and his family were placed in one or sometimes more *serdabs* above the ground After the statues had been placed in these rooms no one might enter them, and there were usually slits at eye level through which offerings laid in the offering chamber of the tomb, directly in front of the *serdab*, could be accepted by the people represented by their statues. Architecturally, the false door of the tomb often had close connections with the serdab (see also *mortuary cult*).

Shaduf. Simple device for obtaining water used from the Eighteenth Dynasty. At one end of a long levered pole was a bucket and, at the other, a lump of clay as a counterpoise. Water raised in this manner from wells or canals was used for irrigating small gardens.

Shemu. Egyptian term for the hot season, see also *calendar.*

Shen ring. Ring formed from a tied rope whose ends extend slightly past each other. Its magical meaning of "permanence, regeneration, protection" led to its being depicted on stelae and grave and temple walls and to its use in modified form as a *cartouche.*

Shenati. (Egyptian) Measure of value corresponding in the New Kingdom to one-twelfth *deben* of silver.

Shoinos. (Greek) Measure of length that, according to Herodotus, derived from an Egyptian unit. Probably corresponded to a distance of about 10.5 km.

Sirius. See *Sothis.*

Sistrum. A musical instrument resembling a rattle, especially important in the worship of goddesses. It consisted of a handle with a metal hoop containing holes through which metal rods were passed; the ends of the rods were then bent. Shaking the instrument produced a rattling sound used to mark the rhythm of liturgical ceremonies in temples.

Smiting of the foes. See *foreigners.*

Sokar festival. The festival of Sokar, god of the dead and the underworld, is recorded from the early Old Kingdom. Later, the god was closely associated with Osiris and Ptah. In the New Kingdom the Sokar festival is very often shown on temple walls, for instance in the temple of Ramesses III in Medinet Habu. The procession of the barque of Sokar around the sanctuary featured prominently. It can be identified by its high bows, ornamented with antelope and cattle heads, by a series of transverse braces and by the long steering oars at the stern.

Solar barque. The course that the sun seemed to take every day around the earth was interpreted in Egyptian myth and religion as the journey of the *sun-god* in his barque. With his escort, he crossed the underworld at night unseen in the Night Barque before emerging in the Morning Barque to cross the sky in the opposite direction.

Son of Re. Title of the birth-name of the king. See *royal titulary*

Sons of Horus. The four tutelary gods Hapi, Amset, Duamutef, and Qebehsenuf were considered the children of Horus. They participated in the ritual resurrection of Osiris and therefore every deceased person transmuted into Osiris. In particular, they protected the inner organs of the dead as lords of the *canopic jars* in which the embalmed innards were stored.

Sothis. Greek term for the star Sirius, from the Egyptian Sopdet. Often personified as a goddess. Because Sirius appears again in northern Egypt in mid July, and the level of the Nile rose annually at the same time, Sothis was considered the bringer of the *Nile inundation*. Together they marked the beginning of the year of which Sothis was considered the embodiment (see *calendar*).

Sphinx. (Greek) A hybrid of lion's body and human head. Sphinxes were frequently depicted in a variety of forms – sculpted, painted, and in relief – from the early Old Kingdom on. In most instances they represent the king for which reason the feminine Greek word "sphinx" is often used in masculine form in Egyptology. The best-known example is the great sphinx of Giza from the Fourth Dynasty. In the New Kingdom sphinxes were erected in large numbers on both sides of processional routes ("sphinx alleys"). In Thebes, sphinxes of the god Amun can be seen with a ram's head on a lion's body.

Staff of flowers. An elaborate flower arrangement in which many kinds of flowers and leaves were tied to papyrus stems. When fully assembled it could be of considerable height. In the worship of the gods and the cult of the dead, staffs of flowers were used as offerings to procure fertility and life. Specimens buried with the dead as grave goods have been found in New Kingdom tombs.

Statues Guérisseuses. (French "healing statues") Statues of the gods from which one could expect a magical cure for a variety of illnesses. They were covered with magical depictions and texts and were especially popular in the Ptolemaic era. Erected in temples, they were doused with water, the external or internal application of which was supposed to have a curative effect.

Stelophorus. (Greek "stele bearer") Statue of a kneeling person whose hands, raised in prayer, were laid on a stele-like slab. This slab was decorated with a hymn to the *sun-god* and related depictions. Attested from the Eighteenth Dynasty on. It is likely that stelophori were usually erected in small, private funerary pyramids of the New Kingdom.

Stela. (Greek.) Upright slabs of stone (and later often of wood), generally in the shape of a tall rectangle and often rounded at the top. Stelae frequently bore texts and pictures referring to a wide range of subjects; for instance, they could be erected in memory of the dead in or near a tomb (see *funerary stelae*), or as the public record of various events or political treaties. Such stelae are often of great size, and most of them stood at the gates or in the courtyards of temple complexes.

Strategist. (Greek) From the beginning of the Ptolemaic era, military authority was in the hands of the strategists in the individual districts of Egypt ("*nomes*"). In the reign of Ptolemy III they also took over civil administration and were therefore the highest ranking *officials* of a nome. Later on, their military authority was gradually lost.

Sun disk. In Egyptian art, depictions of the sun disk occur frequently as befits the importance the sun played in the Egyptian state and religion. The sun disk combined the earthly and godly realms and was portrayed, for example, on the lunettes of stelae or on *architraves*. Particularly popular was the combination of the sun disk with a pair of falcon wings and two uraeus serpents (see *uraeus*). This "winged disk" is often depicted floating over the king where it symbolizes his dominion over Upper and Lower Egypt sanctioned by divine authority.

Sun-god. As the most important heavenly body, and the one which determined the life of man, the sun was considered the expression of divine power by the Egyptians and personified as the sun-god Re from at least the beginning of the Old Kingdom. The path of the sun was interpreted in a complex theological way. The course of an individual's life and his rebirth in the hereafter, that is to say his immortality, were bound up with it, as were the maintenance and well-being of the Egyptian state as a whole. The king, as "son of Re" and embodiment of the sun-god on earth, was held accountable for this well-being. Special types of sun-god were worshipped under their own names and a series of gods were syncretistically related to Re, such as Amun-Re.

Sycamore fig. (*Ficus sycomorus*) The sycamore fig has been cultivated in Egypt since prehistoric times for practical purposes (fruit for food, wood for building or furniture, etc.) but it also had great religious significance. Several sycamore cults are known, the most important being that of Hathor who was Lady of the Southern Sycamore in Memphis.

Temple archive. As temples were frequently large institutions in terms of space, personnel and property, they possessed archives as storage and collection points for written matter significant to their operation. Temple archives could therefore hold texts for ritual or liturgical purposes as well as legal and economic documents on temple property and administration. The most well-known is the *funerary temple* of Neferirkare from the Fifth Dynasty at Abusir, which provides information on priestly organization and daily temple matters (the so-called Abusir Papyri).

Temple synod. (Greek/Latin) Meeting of priests of a temple to discuss and decide on all matters affecting their cult. During the Ptolemaic era there were national gatherings of high-ranking priests for a set period at the court each year in order to reach decisions on matters relating to religion or temple organization for the whole country (see also *Canopus Decree* and *Rosetta Stone*).

Tent pole column. Column in Egyptian architecture that imitates the wooden supports used in light tent or mat constructions. This type of column was depicted in illustrations and made of stone from the early Old Kingdom onward. Only one stone example is known, from a building in the Amun temple of Thutmosis III in Karnak (the so-called Akh-menu).

Terenuthis stelae. A large group of grave stelae in the necropolis of Terenuthis in the western Nile Delta dating from the Roman occupation of Egypt. They belong to the burial equipment of the Greek population of Terenuthis and are evidence for the acceptance of some Egyptian mortuary beliefs by the Greek inhabitants of Egypt.

Theophorus. (Greek "god bearer") Statue in which a standing, sitting or kneeling person holds a small figurine of a god; attested from the New Kingdom on and particularly popular in the late dynastic period. Such statues were erected within temples.

Thinites. Belonging to the Thinite era, that is the first two dynasties. The kings of the First Dynasty were said to have come from the city of Thinis near Abydos in Upper Egypt.

Throne name. See *royal titulary*.

Tomb of Osiris. According to the myth of Osiris, the tombs of the god's limbs were spread throughout the country. Osiris tombs were therefore erected in many places, a number of which can be traced from textual or archaeological evidence. The great *cenotaph* of Seti I in Abydos was also considered an Osiris grave and showed the shape typical of such structures – a tree-covered *Primeval Mound*, underneath which the sarcophagus rested in a hall of pillars.

Toreutic. Art of metal-working seen in Egypt in finds and representations from the prehistoric period on. Besides base metals such as copper, bronze, and iron, precious metals like gold, silver, and electrum were also worked.

Treasury. 1. Rooms found in archaeological excavations, particularly of temple buildings, and used to store implements used for cult purposes (vessels and jewelry) and made of valuable materials such as precious metals. 2. The institution administering the goods produced by the estate of, for instance, a large temple. The treasuries of the countrywide state administration were of particular importance, occupying a key position in the economy and financial administration of Egypt. They were collecting points for all products levied as tax – with the exception of grain – and controlled raw materials, as well as supervising the further processing and distribution of goods.

Trials of tomb robbers. Several legal documents in *hieratic* written on *papyrus* have been found dealing with large-scale thefts from tombs. These took place in the royal and private sepulchres of the Western Theban necropolis at the end of the New Kingdom under Ramesses IX and XI. The documents preserved are principally accounts of the interrogation of the accused before the court as well as reports on the associated investigations (for example examinations of the tombs).

Triglyphic frieze. (Greek) In Doric architecture the ornamentation lying between the *architrave* resting on top of the columns and the beams supporting the roof.

Tumulus. (Latin) A burial mound or earth heaped over the actual burial site; a type of grave particularly seen in the Prehistoric Period before the superstructure took on an architectural form.

Tunic. (Latin) Type of shirt from the Roman era of linen or wool, with or without sleeves, and usually worn as an undergarment with a belt. The male version usually reached to the knee while that of the female was somewhat longer.

Tyskiewicz statue. A magical statue with curative properties from the Ptolemaic era (see *statues guérisseuses*) today in the Louvre. From a collection of the Polish Count Tyskiewicz who conducted excavations in Egypt in the mid-nineteenth century.

Udjat eye. *See Eye of Horus.*

Unification of the Two Lands. Refers to the presumably long historical process during which the various areas of Egypt came to form a political whole. A unified state arose from the different regions and ethnic groups of Upper and Lower Egypt in the Fourth millennium BC. Later historical records condensed this to the deeds of one man – Menes, the first king of Egypt. An echo of these historical events can be found in the ritual of "the unification of the two lands" that was performed at the coronation of every king and was often referred to in art and literature.

Uraeus. (Greek) Term for the cobra depicted rearing up and worn on the brow of the king or gods. An important part of royal ornamentation from the Old Kingdom on, its threat of poison was said to ward off danger and served also as a symbol of royal power.

Viceroy of Kush. Title of the highest royally appointed *official* in Nubia in the New Kingdom. He acted as the king's Nubian representative between the early Eighteenth and late Twentieth Dynasties, at a time when Egypt ruled its southern neighbor from the first cataract in the north by Aswan to well beyond the fourth cataract in the south. His capital was the fortified city of Aniba in Lower Nubia.

Vizier. (Arabic) Usual word for an Egyptian title for the highest *official* of the land. The vizier was at the head of the Egyptian bureaucracy. As a representative of the king, who appointed him, all areas of administration, justice, public works, etc. were accountable to him. The office existed from the early days of the Old Kingdom. In the Eighteenth Dynasty it was divided into an Upper Egyptian and a Lower Egyptian vizier's council with headquarters in Memphis and Thebes.

Votive offering. In the narrower sense, an offering dedicated to a deity in its sanctuary as the result of a vow. In Egyptology, however, the term is often used for any kind of object donated to a temple. Usually these offerings were rather small figures of gods, symbols connected with the deity, or stelae.

Wab Priests. (Egyptian "the pure") Numerically the largest group in a temple. They had their origins in the Old Kingdom and were later organized into phyles. In the temple hierarchy they were ranked below the servants of god (see *prophets*). They performed a large part of the daily sacrifices in the temple. Besides the office of priest they were generally also *officials* or held another position in the state or temple.

Wadi. Arabic "desert valley."

Walls of the Ruler. Refers to the military defenses along the northeastern border in Egyptian literature of the Middle Kingdom. In the eastern delta, on the border to Syria and Palestine, there were presumably watchtowers and fortifications linked in a chain for protection against Asiatic invasion.

Was scepter. Staff with a forked lower end and a stylized animal's head at the upper end. Attested since the early dynastic period and carried as a symbol of power by the gods who bestowed it on the king (see *royal insignia*).

Waset. Egyptian term for the *nome* of Thebes. Can also be used for the city of Thebes.

Way stations. Refers to small cult structures along a processional route in which the statue of a god or king carried in his barque could be temporarily placed. Many such structures have been preserved in the Theban area. They assumed various architectural forms, such as three adjoining rooms, as a *kiosk* or as an *ambulatory*.

White Crown. Crown of the Egyptian king with a tall, tapering shape and a knob at the top. Attested from the Early Dynastic Period onward. It was white and symbolized Upper Egypt (see also *Double Crown*).

Window of Appearances. Balcony with a low balustrade in the royal palace, overhung by a baldachin, where the king appeared to the public, usually in order to commend deserving *officials*. The scene is often represented in the tomb of someone so honored. A smaller variant of the Window of Appearances with a religious function is found in the temples of the New Kingdom in Western Thebes.

Woad. The plant *Isatis tinctoria*. A blue dye can be extracted from the crushed and fermented plant. In Egypt its cultivation can be traced back only to the Hellenistic era.

(opposite)
Karnak, temple of Amun-Re
Noctual view of the rear part of the temple complex with the obelisk of Hatshepsut.

Gods of Ancient Egypt

Regine Schulz

Amaunet. Female counterpart of the god Amun; their names mean "the hidden ones." First mentioned in the Pyramid Texts, she and her partner Amun were worshipped in Karnak in the New Kingdom period. She was also associated with Amun in the creation myth of Hermopolis, and was thus one of the primeval deities.

Amun, Amun-Re. From the Middle Kingdom onward this god, depicted in human form and wearing a tall plumed crown, was regarded as the local deity of Thebes. His principal cult center was at Karnak, where he was worshipped with Mut and Khonsu. As god of the whole kingdom, embodying the abstract idea of multifunctional divinity, Amun was the product of New Kingdom theological thinking. By association with the fertility god Min, as Amun-Min-Kamutef, he was the primeval creation god who had engendered himself. As Amun-Re he guaranteed the constant regeneration of the world, and he ruled the spheres of earth and heaven as king of the gods. In the Twenty-first Dynasty a theocracy of his own was set up for him in Thebes, securing his character as the supreme deity until the conquest of Egypt by Alexander the Great, who had himself confirmed as the son of the god by the oracle of Amun at Siwa Oasis.

Anubis. From the Early Period onward, Anubis was the protecting deity of necropolises, and was portrayed as a jackal or depicted with a human body and a jackal's head. He was the god of embalming, the guardian of secrets and judge of the dead, and made up a divine family with his mother the cow goddess Hesat and the bull god Mnevis. In later texts, however, he was also regarded as the son of Osiris. The records show that he was worshipped in many parts of Egypt, but his place of origin may probably be located in the seventeenth nome of Upper Egypt.

Anuqet. Goddess of the annual inundation of the Nile, as her tall crown of reeds indicates. She, Khnum, and Satet made up the divine family protecting the Nile cataract region, and she was also regarded as mistress of the southern border areas.

Apis. The Apis bull was worshipped from the Early Period onward in Memphis, and may be regarded as a god of royalty and fertility. A blaze on his forehead and other special features marked out the animal chosen as the divine bull of its time. After death the Apis bulls were mummified, and from the New Kingdom period they were buried in the Serapeum at Saqqara. In the Ptolemaic period the association of Osiris with Apis gave rise to the new Egypto-Hellenistic deity Serapis.

Aten. The sun god of Akhenaten's Amarna theology was represented as a solar disk with long rays ending in the shape of human hands. Aten is the most abstract form of deity ever devised in pharaonic Egypt. He represented daylight bringing life to humans and animals. In this theological scheme Akhenaten and the royal family assumed the role of a divine family ensuring that offerings were made to the god, and therefore that he would reappear daily. The figure of Akhenaten also represented the king in his capacity as a creator god. Although Amarna theology was later banned, the prohibition did not affect the concept of the divine Aten himself but only the idea that Akhenaten was his earthly representative.

Atum. The name of the primeval god in Heliopolitan theology can mean both "not to be" and "to be complete." This ambiguity was no doubt consciously intended, and indicates the original creation concept made manifest in Atum. He formed as a singularity in the Primeval Waters that existed before the earth appeared, and out of himself he engendered the elements of creation and all the many different forms of being. In the process he created space (air and moisture, the sky and the earth), set in motion first cyclical time and then, through the creation of this world and the next, linear time. Mankind and the gods were made from his tears and sweat. At his main cult center in Heliopolis the figure of Atum in human form, wearing the royal Double Crown, was also regarded as the evening manifestation of the sun-god.

Bastet. The main center of worship of this royal goddess, originally portrayed as a lion and later as a cat, was Bubastis in the east of the Delta. From the Old Kingdom onward, however, she was also worshipped in Memphis, where she was associated with the local goddess Sakhmet. The records show that she had further links with Hathor and Mut, and in Heliopolis she was regarded as daughter of the creator god Atum. During the Late Period and in the Greco-Roman era, innumerable bronzes of cats were dedicated to her in her capacity as a protector goddess endowed with magical skills.

Bes. This protective deity, first referred to in Old Kingdom records, was shown as small in stature, with a grotesque, alarming face, and a beard. He was closely connected with the warrior god Aha. With Hathor, he watched over sexuality and birth, and used his magical powers to combat disease and danger. He was also regarded as the god of joy and the dance. Small stelae and amulets bearing the god's image were thought to bestow his protection.

Geb. The earth god Geb, created by Atum, was shown in human form. He was part of the Heliopolitan creation myth. With Nut (the sky), Shu (the air), and Tefnut (moisture), he created the space in which the sun-god could set cyclical time in motion. As first ruler of the earth he also stood for the divine legitimacy of the kingship.

Hapi. The god of the Nile personified the fertility of the country through the regular inundation of the arable land. He was shown as a well-nourished man with women's breasts and a crown of papyrus reeds. Instead of Horus and Seth, two figures of Hapi could represent the symbolic unification of Upper and Lower Egypt on the king's behalf, and similarly a number of Nile deities, rather than the personifications of the nomes, could be regarded as maintaining the country.

Hathor. As her name, meaning "house of Horus," indicates, this goddess, depicted either in human form or as a cow, was linked from a very early period with Horus, god of the sky and of kingship. Her solar aspect was indicated by the disk of the sun borne between her cow's horns. She was part of many different mythological systems, and had a number of cult centers all over Egypt. She was therefore regarded not only a royal goddess but as the goddess of love and maternity, the protecting deity of birth and regeneration, and the eye of the sun or the moon. Her heterogeneous qualities meant that she could be associated with almost any other goddess or appear in several guises. At her main cult center of Dendara she was associated with the god of the sky, the Horus of Edfu.

Heket. A frog-headed goddess, one of the female deites who presided over pregnancy and childbirth. In association with Khnum and Osiris she stood for the creation and regeneration of life.

Horus. The name of Horus ("the distant one") was used to designate a number of very different sky gods and gods of kingship who took the form of a hawk. The first kings themselves were regarded as the divine Horus and thereby became part of the cosmic process. In Osirian theology, where Horus was the son of Isis and Osiris, the royal part of his nature took on an additional mythical dimension principally concerned with the opposition of the structured and chaotic elements of creation. As the rightful successor of Osiris, Horus stood for world order, while Seth represented wild and disordered tendencies. In the Greco-Roman period, finally, Horus assumed all the mythical and magical aspects of the kingship, superseding the actual ruler in that capacity.

Ihy. The god of music, shown with a sistrum and a *menit*, was worshipped in Dendara as the son of Hathor and Horus. As god of childhood he had links with the primeval beginning of creation, and could also be regarded as the son of the sun-god.

Isis. The goddess Isis was depicted in human form with her head surmounted by an emblem showing the hieroglyph of her name – the throne – or by cow's horns and the solar disk. She represented the royal power that she had assumed as wife of Osiris and had borne again as mother of Horus. Consequently she linked this world and the next, and was both the mother goddess and goddess of the dead. Although she probably had no special cult center of her own at first, with the rise of the cult of Osiris she was worshipped throughout the country. A significant feature making Isis increasingly popular from the New Kingdom onward was her possession of special magic powers in her capacity as a protecting goddess. She was the most important of the deities in the Greco-Roman period, when she was worshipped throughout the Roman empire. There is evidence that her cult survived on the island of Philae into the sixth century AD.

Khepri. The god of cyclical renewal and of the daily rising and variable aspects of the sun was depicted in the shape of a scarab beetle. In the course of the sun across the sky, he represented morning sunrise, while Ra personified the hours of the day and Atum the evening.

Khnum. This creator god, shown in the form of a ram or as a man with a ram's head, was very closely associated with the origin of living beings. He was thought to have made their bodies and their *ka* forces on a potter's wheel. With Satet and Anuqet, he protected the sources of the Nile at the first cataract and thus ensured the fertility of the land. As he was also worshipped in many other parts of Egypt, however, his person split into several different aspects. His main cult centers were at Elephantine and Esna.

Khonsu. The youthful god who was the son in the Theban triad or divine family was usually shown as a mummiform figure, with the sidelock of youth and the symbol of the moon on his head. Originally he was regarded as both a bringer of misfortune and a protective deity, probably in connection with the changing shape of the moon. Later he was regarded as the lord of life and an oracular and healing god.

Maat. The concept of *maat* stood for the principle of the structured world. that is, for order and equilibrium, ethical values and justice, culture and creativity. *Maat* was thus the opposite pole to all that was disordered, chaotic, destructive and unjust but powerful. It was the main task of every king to guarantee *maat*, order, and thus maintain not only the Egyptian state but the world itself. The goddess Maat was the personification of this principle. She was regarded as the companion or daughter of the sun-god and was shown in human form with a plume on her head. She does not seem to have had a cult of her own until the New Kingdom, when she was worshipped with the gods of the kingdom at Karnak and Memphis.

Meretseger. The snake-headed or serpent-shaped goddess of the western mountains of Thebes was the protector of the dead and the patroness of necropolis workers in Deir el-Medineh. In association with Renentutet she was also seen as a nurturing goddess.

Min. The god of fertility is one of the earliest of Egyptian deities to have had his name preserved in the records. Huge statues of Min were already being erected in Coptos at the end of the fourth century BC. In pharaonic times he was shown as a mummiform body with an erect phallus, one arm raised and holding a flail, and with a plumed crown on his head. As Kamutef, "bull of his mother," he was regarded as a creator god.

Mnevis. The sun bull of Heliopolis was portrayed as a black bull with the solar disk between his horns. His strikingly large genitals refer to his great procreative power. In his solar aspect, he had particularly strong links with Re and Atum.

Montu. This god, whose name is recorded in the Old Kingdom, was shown with the head of a falcon, a plumed crown, and the solar disk and two *uraeus* serpents over his forehead. He was originally a royal god, and had his major cult centers at Armant, Tod, Medamud, and Thebes. As god of war he fought against the enemies of the gods and stood at the king's side in battle. In the Middle Kingdom a bull cult was devoted to him, probably in order to emphasize his warlike qualities yet further.

Mut. The worship of this goddess in human form, shown wearing a vulture headdress and the Double Crown, was directly dependent on the worship of Amun. From the New Kingdom onward she, Amun, and their son Khonsu formed the Theban divine triad, and her maternal role is indicated by her name, written with the vulture hieroglyph and meaning "mother." Amun and Mut were also regarded as the king's parents from the Eighteenth Dynasty onward. As lady of Asheru she had a cult center of her own at Karnak with a crescent-shaped sacred lake, and was depicted there in the form of a lion. She was closely associated with other vulture or lion goddesses such as Nekhbet, Uto, Sakhmet, and Bastet.

Nefertem. Nefertem, worshipped in the form of a lotus blossom, was linked particularly closely with the sun-god, and could be seen as one with him. He was described as "the lotus flower before the nose of Re" or the "great lotus flower appearing from the primeval ocean," and also as a youthful child of the sun. Nefertem was generally depicted in human form with a headdress consisting of the lotus flower symbol crowned with plumes. In Memphis he was venerated as part of a divine triad with Ptah and Sakhmet.

Neith. An ancient goddess of hunting and war, Neith was worshipped in the Memphite area during the Old Kingdom as a protector of the kings. However, her main cult center was at Sais in the Delta, where she was particularly popular during the Twenty-sixth Dynasty, since the kings of that period came from Sais. At a later date she was even promoted to the status of a creator goddess in Esna. Neith wore the crown of Lower Egypt; her emblem was a shield with crossed arrows.

Nekhbet. A goddess who appeared in the shape of a vulture or as a woman wearing a vulture headdress. As goddess of the crown of Upper Egypt she usually wore the White Crown of that part of the country. She was closely associated with the snake goddess Uto, her Lower Egyptian counterpart, and with the goddesses Mut and Tefnut. In addition Nekhbet protected and suckled the royal child. Her main cult center was at Elkab in the third nome of Upper Egypt.

Nephthys. In the famous Ennead of Heliopolis, Nephthys was the daughter of Geb and Nut and thus sister to the deities Osiris, Seth, and Isis. With Isis, she protected, mourned, and revived the dead. She also performed an important function as one of the four canopic goddesses. She was depicted with the hieroglyph of her name above her head, and often with wings on her arms.

Nun. As a personification of the primeval water from which the first land, the Primeval Mound, arose when the world was created, Nun was very seldom shown in pictorial form. He and Naunet were the first pair of primeval creation gods in the Ogdoad of Hermopolis, and were depicted in that context with frogs' heads.

Nut. Among the major concepts of the sky goddess Nut was the image of a naked woman with her body arching over the earth, feet and fingertips touching the ground, as she is shown in many tombs and temples. The heavenly bodies were seen as running their course through the body of the goddess, in particular the sun, which she bore again every morning and swallowed in the evening. The texts accompanying these depictions make such comments as: "Her backward part is in the east, her head is in the west," or: "The sun appears between the thighs of Nut."

Osiris. The mummiform god with the atef crown of plant stems and ostrich feathers was probably originally a god of harvest and fertility. As the opposite of the wild, desert god Seth he stood for cultivated land and a well-ordered world. The constant battle between these two adversaries was the basis for the Egyptian account of creation, and the death of Osiris as a result of the struggle was necessary before the world beyond the tomb could come into being. Osiris died, was revived in the next world by Isis and Nephthys, and engendered his successor Horus, who continued the battle against Seth in this world. As the principal god of the underworld and judge of the dead, he represented justice and order in the next world, and as its ruler he bore the insignia of royalty, the crook and the flail. One of his most important cult centers was Abydos, where his burial place was situated in the myth, and mystery plays in honor of the god were performed there.

Ptah. The god's main cult center was at Memphis, where he was associated with various other deities (as Ptah-Sokar-Osiris or as Ptah-Tatenen). In so-called Memphite Theology he was the creator god who led the Ennead. Under the Ramessides (the Nineteenth and Twentieth Dynasties), Ptah, Amum, and Re formed the great "Triad of the Kingdom." Ptah's importance is reflected in many associated cults; for instance, he had a separate building to himself in the temple precincts of Karnak. Ptah was recognized as the patron of artists and craftsmen, and the Greeks therefore equated him with Hephaistos. The canonical depiction of the god shows him in mummified form with a close-fitting cap, holding a composite scepter.

Re, Re-Harakhty. As early as the Old Kingdom the falcon-headed sun-god Re appeared in the form of Re-Harakhty, the morning aspect of the deity. As the supreme figure of the Egyptian pantheon, he pervaded many layers of cult and myth. For instance, the concept of the cyclical course of the sun as a diurnal and nocturnal journey of twelve hours each, taken by the god in the solar barque, is synonymous with the eternal repetition of creation and all regenerative powers. Re's most important cult center from the Old Kingdom onward was in Heliopolis, the city of the sun, while the Fifth Dynasty rulers had special buildings known as sun sanctuaries erected for his cult of Re at Abusir. The most impressive of the god's cult symbols are the obelisks; their gilded tips were defined as the seat of the sun-god. Probably the most famous temple of Re-Harakhty was built under Ramesses II (Nineteenth Dynasty) in Abu Simbel. From the middle of the Fourth Dynasty, every ruler was held to have a special relationship with the god, and it is regularly reflected in his titulary description as "Son of Re."

Renenutet. Names such as "lady of granaries" and "lady of the fertile land, she who nurtures with good things and brings plentiful food" indicate the nature of this serpent-shaped goddess of harvest and fertility. Her cult was prominent in the Faiyum at the time of the Twelfth Dynasty and in Thebes during the New Kingdom.

Sakhmet. The special cult center of the lion-headed goddess Sakhmet was at Memphis, where she formed a divine family with Ptah and their son Nefertem. She was also closely associated with the goddess Mut in Thebes. Amenophis III alone had several hundred granite statues of Sakhmet set up in Karnak. In the myths the goddess, whose name means "the mighty one," destroys the enemies of the sun-god Re or of Osiris. She also supports the king in fighting the country's enemies, and a text reads: "His arrows fly after enemies like the arrows of Sakhmet." Besides her warlike character, however, the goddess was also seen as patroness of the art of healing and of doctors, who were often also her priests.

Satet. Satet was probably worshipped on the island of Elephantine from the early Old Kingdom, and formed a divine triad with Khnum and Anuket. The temple dedicated to her was extended again and again over the millennia up to the Greco-Roman Period. As goddess of the cataracts Satet guarded the southern border of Egypt, and was seen as provider of "the cool water that comes from Elephantine." The goddess is portrayed wearing the crown of Upper Egypt, with gazelle horns rising erect at the sides.

Selket. A goddess worshipped in the form of a scorpion, and usually shown with a human body and a scorpion above her head. She was an important figure in the cult of the dead. Together with Isis, Nephthys, and Neith she guarded their entrails and mummified bodies.

Seshat. Such names as "lady of ground plans and writing" given to this goddess clearly indicate her nature. Seshat, who presided over the arts of writing and calculation, is depicted in coronation scenes listing the king's years of rule and his jubilees. She was also involved in the ritual of the foundation of temples from very early times, and was specifically associated with establishing a temple's ground plan.

Seth. Seth, god of storms and bad weather, is frequently described as "lord of deserts and of foreign lands." The zoological nature of the "Seth animal" is not clear; at an early period it must have undergone a process of stylization that cannot now be identified with any certainty. In the myth of Osiris, Seth represented the wild, chaotic element and was the murderer of his brother Osiris. He then fought Horus, the successor of Osiris, for dominion. On the other hand, he and Horus also functioned together on an equal footing as divine protectors of the king, who is shown receiving the crowns of the country from the hands of both gods. In the emblematic plants of Upper and Lower Egypt, the crowns symbolize the "Unification of the Two Lands".

Shu. In the creation myth the god of the air, Shu, was born with his sister Tefnut from the mouth of the primeval god Atum, and then divided the sky from the earth. Human beings, like gods, need air, and temple lofts open to the air were often described as "windows of Shu."

Sobek. This deity was shown either in purely animal shape, or in the classic hybrid form as a man with a crocodile's head. Among his principal cult centers was the old town of Shedyet in the Faiyum, later called Crocodilopolis, and Kom Ombo in Upper Egypt in the Greco-Roman Period. In accordance with the place where his sacred animal lived, Sobek was regarded as a fertility god and could even assume the nature of a primeval creator god.

Sokar. The god Sokar, depicted as a hawk or with the head of a hawk, was originally the death god of the Memphite necropolis. In close association with Osiris and Ptah, he was worshipped until the Late Period as Ptah-Sokar-Osiris. As an earthbound deity, he was also regarded as lord of the kingdom of the dead. The climax of the festival of Sokar was the carrying in procession of a divine cult barque, known as the henu barque.

Sons of Horus. Amset, Hapi, Duamutef, and Qebehsenuf, whose respective heads were those of a man, a baboon, a jackal, and a falcon, protected the internal organs of the dead. From the New Kingdom, the lids of canopic jars were made in the shapes of their heads, and as youthful gods they ensured the regeneration of the dead and defended them from danger. In their capacity as defenders they also joined the sun-god in battle against the enemy of creation, Apophis.

Tefnut. The lion-shaped goddess Tefnut and the air god Shu were the first divine couple in the Heliopolitan creation myth. Atum created them either by masturbation or by spitting. In various mythological cycles Tefnut acquired a cosmic character of her own.

Thoeris. The goddess Thoeris was usually depicted as a pregnant hippopotamus standing upright, with drooping breasts and the paws of a lion. Her character of mother goddess associated her closely with Hathor and Isis. She was particularly important as a protector of women in childbirth and mothers suckling babies.

Thoth. Thoth was one of the outstanding divine figures in the Egyptian pantheon, and was worshipped throughout the country from the Old Kingdom onward. His main cult center was at Hermopolis Magna in Central Egypt. He is portrayed as a man with the head of an ibis, or in purely animal form as an ibis or a baboon. As moon god, Thoth was responsible for the calendar, the measurement of time, and mathematics, and consequently he is depicted in coronation scenes as listing the years of the king's rule and writing royal names on the leaves of the sacred *ished* tree of Heliopolis. Thoth was the inventor of writing and language, guardian of divine order, of all rituals and of secret knowledge, and was therefore the patron of scribes. At the judgement of the dead, Thoth recorded the verdict of Osiris.

Uto (Wadjet). The serpent-shaped Uto was patron goddess of Lower Egypt; her home there was at Buto. She and Nekhbet, the vulture goddess of Elkab, are the "two ladies" thought to protect the king, embodied in the crowns of Upper and Lower Egypt that he wore.

Werethekau. Goddess of the crowns and of snakes, "the lady rich in magic", Werethekau is usually shown as a woman with a lion's head, and from the time of the New Kingdom is depicted as present at the coronation of the king, on whom she bestows her protection. She also nurtures the royal child.

List of Historic Sites

Susanne Wohlfarth

Abu Gurab. Best-preserved sun temple of the Old Kingdom from the reign of Niuserre; remains of the sun temple of Userkaf.

Abu Roash. Stone pyramid of Djedefre (Radjedef), son and successor of Cheops; to the east is an ancillary funerary temple. Remains of brick structures and a mastaba field from the Thinite Period.

Abu Simbel. Two rock-cut temples from the reign of Ramesses II. The so-called "Great Temple" is devoted to the gods Amun-Re and Re-Harakhty, amongst others, and to the deified Ramesses II. The "Small Temple" is devoted to the goddess Hathor and the wife of Ramesses II, Nefertari. Both sanctuaries were moved inland to a higher elevation to save them from being flooded by Lake Nasser.

Abusir. Pyramid complex of kings Sahure, Neferikare, Neferefre, and Niuserre from the Fifth Dynasty. The pyramid of Queen Khentkaus and mastabas from this era are also significant, amongst them the complex of Prince Ptahshepses.

Abydos. One of the oldest and most sacred sites in Egypt with tombs, temples, and city ruins from the First Dynasty to the New Kingdom. Royal cult complexes from the Twelfth to the Twenty-sixth Dynasties have been found. Two temples from the Ramesside Period, one built by Seti I (accompanied by a subterranean cenotaph of Seti I, the so-called "Osireion") the other by Ramesses II; prehistoric town ruins and some remains from an Osiris-Khontamenti temple.

Alexandria. Founded in 332 BC by Alexander the Great. Remains of the Serapis temple ("Serapeum"). Catacombs from Kom esh-Shuqafa: a Roman burial complex dating from the first and second centuries AD; necropolis of Anfushi: Greek rock-cut tombs from the second century BC.

Armant. Oldest temple complexes date from the Eleventh Dynasty, restored during the Thirtieth Dynasty and the Ptolemaic Period; a destination for cult pilgrimages until Roman times; birth house (*mammisi*) of Cleopatra; from the Twenty-ninth Dynasty the "Bucheum" or necropolis for the Buchis bull, the holy bull of Montu.

Asiut. Nomarchs' tombs from the First Intermediate Period and the early Middle Kingdom.

Beni Hasan. Thirty-nine rock-cut tombs of nomarchs dating from the First Intermediate Period and the Middle Kingdom. Important for their architecture and unusual reliefs.

el-Bersheh. Thirty-seven rock tombs, especially of nomarchs of the Twelfth Dynasty.

Dahshur. Important royal necropolis of King Snefru from the Fourth Dynasty (Red Pyramid and Bent Pyramid), and of the Twelfth Dynasty with pyramids from the reigns of Sesostris III, and Amenemhat II and III;

also, the greatly damaged mastabas of the royal families.

Dendara. Hathor temple built in 54 BC under Ptolemy XII Neos Dionysos (Auletes) on top of several structures dating between the Old Kingdom and the Thirtieth Dynasty. In the exterior walls there is a series of crypts reaching down into the temple foundations; on the temple roof, a kiosk and two Osiris sanctuaries. Alongside the main temple within the monumental outer walls are: the *ka* chapel of Mentuhotep II (now in the Egyptian Museum in Cairo); a sacred lake; a *mammisi* for Nectanebo I (extended in the reign of Augustus); a Roman *mammisi*; an Augustan Isis temple; a "sanatorium;" and an early Coptic church. City ruins of Tentyris.

Edfu. Horus temple begun in 237 BC under Ptolemy III Euergetes I and finished in 57 BC. Considered to be the best-preserved temple in Egypt. From the Old Kingdom, remains of settlements and tombs. In the sanctuary, a shrine of Nectanebo II (Thirtieth Dynasty). At right angles to the main temple a *mammisi* dedicated to the divine child Harsomtus.

Elephantine. Settlement from the Thinite Period to early Islamic times. Temple of Khnum from Nectanebo II and temple of Satet, which had its origins in an ancient sanctuary and was built on repeatedly down to the Ptolemaic Period (reconstructed today: building of the Eighteenth Dynasty). Sanctuary from the Middle Kingdom for the deified official Heqaib from the Sixth Dynasty.

Elkab. Main cult site of the goddess Nekhbet. Within the town's mudbrick enclosure wall were the main temple, a birth house, several smaller temples, a sacred lake, and cemeteries from the Predynastic Period. Outside the walls are rock-cut tombs from the Middle and New Kingdoms (early Eighteenth Dynasty). Deep in the desert is a small sanctuary of Thutmosis IV and Amenophis III.

Esna. Only the entrance hall (pronaos) has been preserved from the Ptolemaic-Roman Khnum temple. The previous building was from the Eighteenth Dynasty.

Gebelein. Remains of a prehistoric settlement. Traces of a now destroyed Hathor temple date from the Third Dynasty through the Middle Kingdom and down to Greco-Roman times. The tombs are mostly from the First Intermediate Period.

Giza. Necropolis of the Old Kingdom lying west of Cairo. Well known for the Sphinx and the three pyramids with their accompanying temples from the reigns of Cheops, Chephren, and Mycerinus from the Fourth Dynasty; mastaba tombs of family members and dignitaries were arranged in a regular layout around the pyramids (down to the Sixth Dynasty). A few monuments were erected in later eras.

Heliopolis. Originally one of the largest religious and intellectual centers in Egypt. Only blocks and fragments and an obelisk from the time of Sesostris I remain. His father, Amenemhat I, built a new temple for Re-Harakhty on an older sacred site. The remains of several temples are known from the New Kingdom. There was also a sanctuary for the god Atum and a tomb site for the Mnevis bull.

Herakleopolis. Royal residence of the Ninth and Tenth Dynasties; tombs of officials. The temple dedicated to the local god Herishef is from the Twelfth and Eighteenth Dynasties.

Hermopolis. Main cult center of Thoth (Greek: Hermes); remains of a temple for Amenemhat II; Amun temple of Ramesses II; Thoth temple from the reign of Nectanebo I; several baboon figures in granite endowed by Amenophis III; Christian basilica; remains of a Roman town.

Hierakonpolis. Prehistoric capital of Upper Egypt. Remains of a town wall with primal sanctuary of the Horus falcon; prehistoric settlement and cemetery with the painted tomb of a chieftain; tombs from the Middle and New Kingdoms. "Fortress" of mudbrick (Second Dynasty).

Kom Ombo. Greco-Roman twin sanctuary for the divinities Sobek and Haroeris; because of their proximity to the Nile, entrance gate and *mammisi* partly damaged and washed away; well structure.

el-Lahun/Kahun. Pyramid and temple of Sesostris II from the Middle Kingdom (Twelfth Dynasty); mastabas. The town of Kahun – built for the construction of the pyramid – lies to the north.

el-Lisht. Necropolis of the Twelfth Dynasty with pyramid complexes of Amenemhat I and Sesostris I as well as private tombs of the Middle Kingdom; tombs of high officials within the pyramid complex.

Medamud. Remains of a temple to the war god Montu and his sacred bull Buchis from the Greco-Roman Period; onlya few isolated blocks remain of a temple of the Eleventh/Twelfth Dynasty – which replaced a plain twin sanctuary dating from the Old Kingdom – and of a temple from the Eighteenth Dynasty.

Medum. Necropolis of the late Third and Fourth Dynasties; only the core of the pyramid of Snefru remains.

Meir. Numerous rock-cut tombs of nomarchs of the Old and Middle Kingdoms.

Memphis. First capital of historical Egypt around 3000 BC. Administrative center and garrison town. Statue temples and Hathor temple from the reign of Ramesses II. Only remnants of the palaces of Merenptah and Apries and of the main temple of Ptah

remain. The embalming tables date from the Late Period. The living quarters have not been examined in depth.

Mo'alla. Two rock-cut tombs from the First Intermediate Period with murals in the provincial style (tomb of Ankhtify).

Philae. Island south of Aswan. Most important place of pilgrimage to Isis in the Late Period; also sanctuaries for various other gods. After the construction of the Aswan High Dam it was dismantled and rebuilt on the neighboring island of Agilkia. It was the last temple of ancient Egypt, closed by the emperor Justinian between AD 535 and 537.

Qantir. Royal residential town of the Ramesside pharaohs; several palaces; houses of dignitaries; main temple for Amun-Re-Harakhty, additional temples to the gods Seth, Astarte, and Wadjet. Archaeological research has discovered, amongst other buildings, a chariot garrison, multi-functional workshops and stables. It was abandoned at the beginning of the Twenty-second Dynasty, the blocks carried away and reused in the construction of temples at Tanis, the Egyptian capital during the Twenty-second Dynasty.

Qubbet el-Hawa. Tombs of nomarchs and officials from the Old and Middle Kingdoms.

Rosetta. Town in the Nile Delta made famous by the discovery of the "Rosetta Stone" in 1799. This stone was crucial in the deciphering of hieroglyphs by the Frenchman J.F. Champollion in 1822. The trilingual text – in hieroglyphic (mostly destroyed), Demotic and Greek – is a decree of the synod of the Egyptian priesthood that met in Memphis to honor King Ptolemy V Ephiphanes, on 27 March, AD 196.

Saqqara. Necropolis of the capital of the Old Kingdom, Memphis; necropolis dating from the Archaic Period; burial complex of King Djoser with Step Pyramid and ancillary structures; tombs of high officials of the Old and New Kingdoms; pyramids of Unas, Userkaf, and Teti; monastery of St. Jeremiah from the end of the fourth century; Persian tombs; unfinished pyramid of Sekhemkhet; "Serapeum:" burial site of the sacred Apis bulls (Eighteenth Dynasty to Ptolemaic Period). In the south, additional pyramids of the Old Kingdom (Fifth and Sixth Dynasties).

Soleb. Amun temple south of the third cataract built by Amenophis III on the occasion of his coronation jubilee; necropolis dating from the New Kingdom.

Tanis. Royal residence and burial place for kings of the Twenty-first and Twenty-second Dynasties; mudbrick enclosure with several temples, among others the main temple of Amun; also, royal tombs ("temple tombs").

Tell el-Amarna. Capital during Akhenaten's reign with palaces, living and working quarters, and several sanctuaries; tombs of the

The Egyptian Museum in Cairo (built 1897–1902)

royal family in a wadi in the eastern desert; numerous tombs of officials.

Tell ed-Dab'a. The former capital "Avaris" during the Hyksos era (1650–1540 BC); remains of archaic settlements; several layers of remains of extensive urban settlements from the Middle Kingdom to the Second Intermediate Period; from the early Eighteenth Dynasty on, site of a new settlement and a temple of Seth; additional remains of construction from the Ramesside Period to the time of Psusennes I (Twenty-first Dynasty). Palace and temple complexes from the Middle Kingdom as well as tombs and settlements from this era and the Second Intermediate Period.

Thebes. Residence of the Egyptian kings during the Eighteenth Dynasty. Luxor Temple on the east bank and temple precinct of Karnak comprising several districts; on the west bank several thousand private tombs, over fifty royal tombs (some in the Valley of the Kings) from the Eleventh Dynasty to the end of the New Kingdom (though no evidence of continuous use); additionally, tombs of queens and royal children; mortuary temples belonging to royal tombs at the edge of the arable land. Remains of several settlements (Deir el-Medineh; palace complex of Amenophis III in Malqata) have been excavated.

el-Tod. Remains of a large Montu temple dating from the Ptolemaic era and the Roman Empire resting on the remains of a Middle Kingdom temple; ruins of a town.

Tuna el Gebel. Animal cemetery from the Ptolemaic era consisting of a system of subterranean galleries and cult chambers. Tombs of temple personnel from the Eighteenth Dynasty; in the Twenty-sixth Dynasty development of new burial zones; most important tomb is that of the deified high priest Petosiris (320 BC); from the Ptolemaic era, tombs in a Greco-Egyptian composite style; temple of the Late Period. Of the so-called "Great Temple" only the section built during the Roman Period is known.

Egyptian Collections

Edith Bernhauer

Austria

Vienna
Kunsthistorisches Museum
Ägyptisch-Orientalische Sammlung
Burgring 5
1010 Vienna

Belgium

Antwerp
Museum Vleeshuis
Vleeshouwer Str 38
2000 Antwerpen

Brussels
Musèes Royaux d'Art et d'Histoire
Collections égyptiennes
Parc du Cinquantenaire 10
1040 Brussels

Morlanwelz
Musée Royal de Mariemont
Chaussée de Mariemont
6510 Morlanwelz-Mariemont

Brazil

Rio de Janeiro
Museo Nacional
Universidade Federal de Rio de Janeiro
Departamento de Antropologia
Setor Arqueoligia
Qinta da Bona Vista São Cristovão
20000 Rio de Janeiro

Canada

Toronto
Royal Ontario Museum
Egyptian Department
100 Queen's Park
Toronto
Ontario M5S 2C6

Croatia

Zagreb
Archaeological Museum
Trg Nikole Zrinskog 19
41000 Zagreb

Czech Republic

Prague
National Museum
Section Náprstek Museum
Department of Prehistory and Antiquity of
Middle East and Africa
Betlémské nám. 1
11000 Prague 1

Denmark

Copenhagen
Ny Carlsberg Glyptothek
Egyptian Collection
Dantes Plads 7
1556 Copenhagen V

Nationalmuseet
Antikansamling
Department of Near Eastern and Classical
Antiquities
Ny Vestergade 10
1220 Copenhagen K

Egypt

Alexandria
Greco-Roman Museum
Museum Street
21521 Alexandria

Bibliotheca Alexandrina
The Archeology Museum
5005 Duke Street
Alexandria, UA 222304 - 2903

Aswan
Aswan Museum
Elephantine Island
Aswan

Nubian Museum
Aswan

Giza
Cheops' Boat Museum
The Pyramids
al-Giza

Cairo
The Egyptian Museum
11556 Midan el-Tahir
Misr al-Kahira

Coptic Museum
Masr Ateeka
Misr al-Kahira

Luxor
The Luxor Museum of Ancient Egyptian Art
Corniche Street
al-Uksur

France

Amiens
Musée de Picardie
48 Rue de la République
80000 Amiens

Avignon
Musée Calvet
65 Rue Joseph-Vernet
84000 Avignon

Lyons
Musée des Beaux-Arts
Palais St. Pierre
20 Place des Terreaux
69001 Lyons

Marseilles
Musée d'Archéologie Méditerranéenne
Collection Egyptienne
2, Rue de la Charité
13002 Marseilles

Paris
Musée National du Louvre
Département des Antiquites égyptiennes
Palais du Louvre
75058 Paris

Roanne
Musée Joseph Déchelette
22 Rue Anatole France
423000 Roanne

Strasbourg
Collection de l'Institut d'Égyptologie de l'Université
Palais de l'Université
67000 Strasbourg

Toulouse
Musée Georges Labit
43 Rue des Martyrs de la Libération
31400 Toulouse

Germany

Berlin
Staatliche Museen zu Berlin
Preußischer Kulturbesitz
Ägyptisches Museum und Papyrussammlung
Bodestr. 1–3
10178 Berlin and Schloßstraße 70
14059 Berlin

Bonn
Ägyptisches Museum
Ägyptologisches Seminar der Universität
Bonn
Regina-Pacis-Weg 7
53113 Bonn

Hannover
Kestner-Museum
Trammplatz 3
30159 Hannover

Heidelberg
Sammlung des Ägyptologischen Instituts der Universität
Marstallhof 4
69117 Heidelberg

Hildesheim
Pelizaeus-Museum
Am Steine 1–2
31134 Hildesheim

Frankfurt/Main
Liebighaus
Schaumainkai 71
60596 Frankfurt

Leipzig
Ägyptisches Museum der Universität Leipzig
Schillerstr. 6
04109 Leipzig

Munich
Staatliches Museum Ägyptischer Kunst
Hofgartenstraße (Residenz)
80539 Munich

Tübingen
Sammlung des Ägyptologischen Instituts der Universität
Hohentübingen Schloß
72070 Tübingen

Würzburg
Martin von Wagner-Museum der Universität
Residenzplatz 2
Tor A
97070 Würzburg

Great Britain

Birmingham
City Museum & Art Gallery
Department of Archaeology & Ethnography
Chamberlain Square
Birmingham
West Midlands B3 3DH

Bolton
Central Museum and Art Gallery
Le Mans Crescent
Bolton
Greater Manchester BL1 1SE

Cambridge
Fitzwilliam Museum
Department of Antiquities
Trumpington Street
Cambridge CB2 1RB

Edinburgh
The Royal Museum of Scotland
Department of History and Applied Arts
Chambers Street
Edinburgh EH1 1JF

Glasgow
The Hunterian Museum
Egyptian Department
University of Glasgow
Glasgow G12 8QQ

Liverpool
Liverpool Museum
Department of Antiquities
National Museums and Galleries on Merseyside
William Brown Street
Liverpool L3 8EN

London
The British Museum
Department of Egyptian Antiquities
Great Russell Street
London WC1B 3DG

University College London
Petrie Museum of Egyptian Archaeology
Gower Street
London WC1E 6BT

Oxford
The Ashmolean Museum
Department of Antiquities
Beaumont Street
Oxford OX1 2PH

Swansea
Wellcome Museum of Egypt and Greco-Roman Antiquities
University College of Swansea
Singleton Park
Swansea
Wales SA2 8PP

Hungary

Budapest
Szépművészeti Múzeum
Egyiptomi osztály
Dózsa György út 41
1146 Budapest XIV

Israel

Jerusalem
The Bible Lands Museum
25, Granot Street
Jerusalem 93704

The Israel Museum
Department of Egyptian Art
Hakiriya
Jerusalem

Italy

Bologna
Museo Civico Archeologico
Via dell' Archiginnasio 2
40124 Bologna

Como
Civico Museo Archeologico
Piazza Medaglie d'Oro 1
22100 Como

Florence
Museo Egizio
Soprintendenza Archeologica della Toscana
Via della Pergola 65
50122 Florence

Milan
Museo Archeologico
Raccolta Egizia
Castello Sforzesco
20121 Milan

Naples
Museo Archeologico Nazionale
Via Museo 19
80135 Naples

Pisa
Musei di Ateneo
Università di Pisa
Collezioni Egittologiche
Via San Frediano
56100 Pisa

Turin
Soprintendenza per le Antichità Egizie
Museo Egizio
Via Accademia delle Scienze 6
10123 Turin

Japan

Kyoto
Heian Museum of Ancient History
3rd Archaeological Section
8–1 Takeda Naasegawa
Fushimu-ku

Lebanon

Beirut
Archaeological Museum of the American University of Beirut
Bliss
Beirut

Netherlands

Amsterdam
Allard Pierson Museum
Archeologisch Museum van de Universiteit
Oude Turfmarkt 129
1012 GC Amsterdam

Leiden
Rijksmuseum van Oudheden
Egyptische Afdeling
Rapenburg 28
2311 EW Leiden

Poland

Warsaw
Muzeum Narodowe
Gallery of Ancient Art
Aleje Jerozolimskie 3
00-495 Warsaw

Portugal

Lisbon
Museu Calouste Gulbenkian
Ab. de Berna 45 A
1093 Lisbon

Russia

Moscow
Pushkin Museum of Fine Arts
Department of Ancient Orient
ul. Volkhonka 12
121019 Moscow

St. Petersburg
The Hermitage Museum
Department of Orient
Dvortsovaya Nabereznaya 34
191065 St. Petersburg

Spain

Barcelona
Museo Arqueológico de Barcelona
Instituto de Prehistória y Arqueología
Parc de Montjuic s/n.
08004 Barcelona

Madrid
Museo Arqueológico Nacional
Departamento de Antigüedades Egipcias y del Próximo Oriente
Calle de Serrano 13
28001 Madrid

Sudan

Khartoum
National Museum
El Neel Avenue
P.O. Box 178
Khartoum

Sweden

Stockholm
Medelhavsmuseet
Egyptiska advdelingen
Fredsgatan 2
11152 Stockholm

Uppsala
Uppsala Universitet
Institutionen för Egyptologi
Victoriamuseet för egyptiska Fornsaker
Gustavianum
75310 Uppsala

Switzerland

Geneva
Musée d'Art et d'Histoire
2, Rue Charles Galland
1211 Geneva 3

United States

Baltimore
Walters Art Museum
600 N. Charles Street
Baltimore, MD 21201

Berkeley
The Phoebe A. Hearst Museum of Anthropology
University of California
Berkeley, CA 94720

Boston
Museum of Fine Arts
Department of Ancient Egyptian, Nubian and Near Eastern Art
465 Huntington Avenue
Boston, MA 02115

Chicago
University of Chicago
Oriental Insitute Museum
1155 East 58th Street
Chicago, IL 60637-1569

Cleveland
Cleveland Museum of Art
Department of Ancient Art
11150 East Boulevard at University Circle
Cleveland, OH 44106

Detroit
The Detroit Institute of Arts
5200 Woodward Avenue
Detroit, MI 48202

Los Angeles
Los Angeles County Museum of Art
Department of Ancient and Islamic Art
5905 Wilshire Boulevard
Los Angeles, CA 90036

Memphis
Art Museum
3750 Norriswood Avenue
The University of Memphis Campus
Memphis, TN 38152

New York
The Metropolitan Museum of Art
Department of Egyptian Art
1000 Fifth Avenue
New York, NY 10028-1998

The Brooklyn Museum
The Department of Egyptian, Classical and Ancient Middle Eastern Art
2000 Eastern Parkway
Brooklyn, NY 11238-6052

Philadelphia
University Museum
University of Pennsylvania
33rd and Spruce Streets
Philadelphia, PA 19104-6324

Pittsburgh
Carnegie Museum of Natural History
4400 Forbes Avenue
Pittsburgh, PA 15213

Richmond
Virginia Museum of Fine Arts
Department of Ancient Art
2800 Grove Avenue
Richmond, VA 23221-2466

Seattle
Seattle Art Museum
100 University Street
Seattle, WA 98101

Vatican

Vatican City
Musei e Gallerie Pontificie
Museo Gregoriano Egizio
Viale Vaticano
00120 Vatican City

Rulers of Egypt

Regine Schulz (according to Jürgen von Beckerath)

Prehistory (Predynastic Period)

Dynasty 0	about 150 years

Archaic Period

First Dynasty

Aha (Menes)	ca. 3032–3000*
Atoti (Athotis I)	3000–2999
Djer	2999–2952
Wadji	2952–2939
Dewen	2939–2892
Adjib	2892–2886
Semerkhet	2886–2878
Qaa	2878–2853

Second Dynasty

Hetepsekhemui	2853–2825
Nebre	2825–2810
Ninetjer	2810–2767
Wenegnebti	2767–2760
Sekhemib	2760–2749
Neferkare	2749–2744
Neferkasokar	2744–2736
Hudjefa	2736–2734
Opposing king of the last three rulers	
Peribsen/Khasekhemui	2734–2707

Old Kingdom

Third Dynasty

Nebka	2707–2690
Djoser	2690–2670
Djoserti	2670–2663
Khaba	2663–2639
Mesokhris	2663–2639
Huni	2663–2639

Fourth Dynasty

Snefru	2639–2604
Cheops	ca. 2604–2581
Djedefre	2581–2572
Chephren	2572–2546
Bikheris	2546–2539
Mycerinus	2539–2511
Shepseskaf	2511–2506
Thamphthis	2506–2504

Fifth Dynasty

Userkaf	2504–2496
Sahure	2496–2483
Neferirkare	2483–2463
Shepseskare	2463–2456
Neferefre	2456–2445
Niuserre	2445–2414
Menkauhor	2414–2405
Djedkare	2405–2367
Unas	2367–2347

Sixth Dynasty

Teti	2347–2337
Userkare	2337–2335
Pepi I	2335–2285
Nemtiemsaf I	2285–2279
Pepi II	2279–2219
Nemtiemsaf II	2219–2218
Nitocris	2218–2216

Seventh Dynasty
("70 Days" according to Manetho)

Eighth Dynasty (17 kings)	ca. 2216–2170

First Intermediate Period

Ninth/Tenth Dynasties (in Herakleopolis, 18 kings)   ca. 2170–2020

Middle Kingdom

Eleventh Dynasty (at first only in Thebes, later in all of Egypt)

Mentuhotep I	2119–
Antef I	–2103
Antef II	2103–2054
Antef III	2054–2046
Mentuhotep II	2046–1995
Mentuhotep III	1995–1983
Mentuhotep IV	1983–1976

Twelfth Dynasty

Amenemhat I	1976–1947
Sesostris I	1956–1911/10
Amenemhat II	1914–1879/76
Sesostris II	1882–1972
Sesostris III	1872–1853/52
Amenemhat III	1853–1806/05
Amenemhat IV	1807/06–1798/97
Nefrusobek	1798/97–1794/93

Second Intermediate Period

Thirteenth Dynasty

(approx. 50 kings)	1794/93–1648

Fourteenth Dynasty

(petty kings in Nile Delta)	?–1648

Fifteenth Dynasty (Hyksos)   1648–1539

Salites	1648–1590
Beon	1648–1590
Apakhnas	1648–1590
Khaian	1648–1590
Apophis	1590–1549
Khamudi	1549–1539

Sixteenth Dynasty (Hyksos vassals, parallel to Fifteenth Dynasty)

Seventeenth Dynasty (only in Thebes, approx. 15 kings)   ca. 1645–1550)

New Kingdom

Eighteenth Dynasty

Ahmose I	1550–1525
Amenophis I	1525–1504
Thutmosis I	1504–1492
Thutmosis II	1492–1479
Hatshepsut	1479–1458/57
Thutmosis III	1479–1425
Amenophis II	1428–1397
Thutmosis IV	1397–1388
Amenophis III	1388–1351/50
Amenophis IV/Akhenaten	1351–1334
Smenkhkare	1337–1333
Tutankhamun	1333–1323
Ay	1323–1319
Horemheb	1319–1292

Nineteenth Dynasty

Ramesses I	1292–1290
Seti I	1290–1279/78
Ramesses II	1279–1213
Merenptah	1213–1203
Amenmesse	1203–1200/1199
Seti II	1199–1194/93
Siptah and Tausret	1194/93–1186/85

Twentieth Dynasty

Sethnakht	1186–1183/82
Ramesses III	1183/82–1152/51
Ramesses IV	1152/51–1145/44
Ramesses V	1145/44–1142/20
Ramesses VI	1142/40–1134
Ramesses VII	1134–1126
Ramesses VIII	1126–1125
Ramesses IX	1125–1107
Ramesses X	1107–1103
Ramesses XI	1103–1070/69

Third Intermediate Period

Twenty-first Dynasty

Smendes	1070/69–1044/43
Amenemnesut	1044/43–1040/39
Psusennes I	1044/43–994/993
Amenemope	996/95–985/84
Osochor	985/84–979/78
Siamun	979/78–960/59
Psusennes II	960/59–946/45

Twenty-second Dynasty

Sheshonq I		946/45–925/24
Osorkon I		925/24–ca.890
Takelot I	ca.	890–877
Sheshonq II	ca.	877–875
Osorkon II	ca.	875–837
Sheshonq III	ca.	837–798
Sheshonq IIIa	ca.	798–785
Pami	ca.	785–774
Shoshenq V	ca.	774–736

Upper Egyptian rulers

Harsiese	ca.	870–850
Takelot II	ca.	841–816
Pedubastis I	ca.	830–805
Iuput I	ca.	816–800
Sheshonq IV	ca.	800–790
Osorkon III	ca.	790–762
Takelot III	ca.	776–755
Rudamun	ca.	755–735
Ini	ca.	735–730

Twenty-third Dynasty (in the Delta)

Pedubastis II (*in Bubastis/Tanis*)	ca. 765–732/30
Iuput II (*in Leontopolis*)	ca. 756–725
Osorkon IV	ca. 732/30–722

Twenty-fourth Dynasty (in Sais)

Tefnakht	ca. 740–719
Bikharis	719–714

Late Period

Twenty-fifth Dynasty (Kushites)

Kashta	before 746
Piye	ca. 746–715
Shabako	715–700
Shebitku	700–690
Taharqa	690–664
Tanutamun (*successors reign in Nubia*)	664–ca. 655

Twenty-sixth Dynasty (Saite)

Psammetichus I	664–610
Necho I	610–595
Psammetichus II	595–589
Apries	589–570
Amasis	570–526
Psammetichus III	526–525

Twenty-seventh Dynasty (First Persian Domination)

Cambyses (*in Persia from 529*)	525–522
Darius I	522/21–486/85
Xerxes I	486/85–465/64
Artaxerxes I	465/64–424
Xerxes II	424/23
Darius II	423–405/04
Artxerxes II (*in Persia until 359/58*)	405/04–401

Twenty-eighth Dynasty

Amyrtaios	404/401–399

Twenty-ninth Dynasty

Nepherites I	399–393
Achoris	393–380
opposing king Psammuthis	393/92
Nepherites II	380

Thirtieth Dynasty

Nectanebo I	380–362
Teos	364/362–360
Nectanebo II	360–342

Thirty-first Dynasty (Second Persian Domination)

Artaxerxes III Ochos (*in Persia from 359/58*)	342–338
Arses	338–336
Darius III	336–332
Egyptian opposing king Khababash	338/37–336/35

Greek Rulers

Alexander the Great	332–323
Philip Arrhidaeus	323–317
Alexander IV	317–306

Ptolemaic Era

Ptolemy I Soter (*Satrap from 323*)	306/4–283/2
Ptolemy II Philadelphus (*co-regent from 285/4*)	282–246
Ptolemy III Euergetes I	246–222/1
Ptolemy IV Philopator	221–204
Ptolemy V Epiphanes	204–180
Anti-king Harwennefer	206–200
Ankhwennefer	200–186
Ptolemy VI Philometor	180–164
and	163–145
Ptolemy VII (*non-existent*)	
Ptolemy VIII Euergetes II	164
and	145–116
opposing king Harsiese	131/130
Ptolemy IX Soter II	116–107
and	88–81
Ptolemy X Alexander I	107–88
(Cleopatra) Berenice III	81–80
Ptolemy XI Alexander II	80
Ptolemy XII Neos Dionysos	80–58
and	55–51
(Cleopatra) Berenice IV	58–55
Cleopatra VII Philopator	51–30

Roman Emperors

30 BC–AD 313

* The dates for the First Dynasty to the First Intermediate Period may also be fixed some fifty years later. The chronological table is based on Jürgen von Beckerath, *Chronologie des pharaonischen Ägypten*, MÄS 46, Mainz 1997.

Chronological Synopsis

Marcel Schoch

Egyptian chronology is of great importance in dating the early cultures of antiquity. If Egyptian inscriptions and documents from all eras had not been handed down to us – containing information about the Egyptian calendar, astronomical events, and the lengths of the pharaohs' reigns – the chronologies of the ancient world would all be mere estimates. This information has enabled Egyptologists to work out a chronology, ordered according to pharaohs and dynasties, dating to about 3100 BC. By means of so-called synchronisms, it has enabled archaeologists to date even those cultures that have left few or no written documents. We speak of a synchronism if imported and local goods are found together in a site sealed off from external influences. If during an archaeological dig – for example in Crete – an Egyptian vessel is discovered together with Minoan ceramics, then we are able to make a statement about the age of the Minoan ceramics. Likewise, imported Minoan ceramics discovered in Egypt can help date artifacts from Crete. Research has shown repeatedly, however, that this method can often be unreliable. In many cases it is not known how long a chronologically significant item had been in use before it was finally deposited in a sealed site. This question sometimes arises where scarabs are concerned. These were made of stone or similarly durable material and thus could have been used by a family for generations. Chronological statements about items found with such scarabs necessarily lead to incorrect datings.

Unfortunately, the sources for the reigns of Near Eastern kings during the Archaic Period are also incomplete. For some short periods no data has been found. There were also periods when the royal succession was disputed and it must be assumed that two competing kings held power simultaneously. Despite the fact that some data can be pinpointed to a particular year through astrological events, a conclusive chronology of the Near East is still a matter of some controversy because of this degree of uncertainty. For these and other reasons, scientific methods such as radiocarbon dating – better known as the C14 method – or dendrochronology are used to work out an independent chronology of Egypt and the Near East or to improve the existing one. Because the C14 method also has considerable drawbacks many researchers reject these new dating methods as well.

The following chronological table, however, does take into account the new scientific dating methods. Because the debate about the correct dating method still continues, the data presented here should be seen as provisional. The dates for the Egyptian dynasties are based on the most recent results published by Jürgen von Beckerath (*Chronologie des pharaonischen Ägypten*, MÄS 46, Mainz 1997).

Minoan dignitaries bearing gifts
Western Thebes, tomb of Rechmire (TT 100), wall painting in the transept; New Kingdom, Eighteenth Dynasty, ca. 1450 BC. Among the delegations of foreign peoples depicted in the tomb of Rachmire, vizier under Thutmosis III, Minoans can be readily identified by the style of their hair, their clothing, and the types of vessels they are carrying.

Year	Egypt	Crete	Greek Mainland	Near East
		(C14 dates are in italics)	(C14 dates are in italics)	
ca. 7000 BC ca. 6000	Neolithic (after 7000)	Early, middle and late Neolithic (ca. *8000–3100*)		Hassuna culture (ca. 6000)
ca. 5000	Faiyum A culture (ca. 5000 BC)			Halaf culture (ca. 6000–5000) Samarra culture (ca. 5600–5300) Ubaid culture (ca. 4700–3500)
ca. 4000				
	Naqada I culture (ca. 3700)		*Neolithic (before 3600)*	Uruk (ca. 3500–3200)
	Naqada II culture (ca. 3300) Naqada III culture (ca. 3200)			Jemdet-Nasr Period (ca. 3200–2900)
	Archaic Period			

ca. 3000	Predynastic
	    (ca. or before 3150)
	Dynasty 0
	    (approx. 150 years)
	First Dynasty
	    (3032/2982–2853/2803)
		Sub-neolithic (3100–2800)	Sesklo stages I–III
			    (ca. or before 3000)	

		Pre-palatial Period		
ca. 2800	Second Dynasty (ca. 2853/2803–2707/2657)	EM I (2800–2500) *EM I–I B/II A (3100–2650)*		
ca. 2700	**Old Kingdom**			

ca. 2500	Third Dynasty
	    (ca. 2707/2657–2639/2589)
	Fourth Dynasty
	    (ca. 2639/2589–2504/2454)
	Fifth Dynasty
	    (ca. 2504/2454–2347/2297)
	Sixth Dynasty
	    (ca. 2347/2297–2216/2166)
	Eighth Dynasty
	    (ca. 2216/2166–2170/2120
		EM II (2500–2200)
		EM II A (2650–2450/2350)
		EM II B
		    (2450/2350–2200/2150)
		EM III (2200–2000)
		EM III
		    (2200/2150–2050/2000)
			Arapi and Dhimini stages
			    (before 2500)
			
			EH I (2500– ca. 2250)
			EH I (3600–2900)
			
			EH II (ca. 2250–2000)
			EH II (2900–2570/2410)
				Kings of Lagash
				    (ca. 2520– ca. 2355)
				Akkadian Dynasty
				    (ca. 2350–2200/2150)
				Third Dynasty of Ur/
				    New Sumerian Period
				    (ca. 2200/2150– 2100/2000)

	First Intermediate Period			

ca. 2000	Ninth/Tenth Dynasty
	    (in Herakleopolis, ca.
	    2170/2120–2025/2020)			

	Middle Kingdom	**Old Palaces**		

ca. 2000	Eleventh Dynasty
	    (in Thebes, later in all Egypt,
	    2119–1976)
		MM I (2000–1850)
		MM I A
		    (2050/2000–1925/1900)
		MM I B
		    (1925/1900–1900/1875)
			EH III (2000–1850)
			EH III
			    (2570/2410–2090/2050)
				Old Babylonian Period
				Larsa Dynasty
				    (2025–1763)
				Isin Dynasty
				    (2017–1817)
				Hittite Empire
				    (ca. 2000– ca. 1200)

ca. 1750	Twelfth Dynasty (1976–1794/1793)	MM II (1850–1700) *MM II (1900/1875–1750/1720)*	MH (1850–1600) *MH (2090/2050–1600)*	
	Second Intermediate Period	**New Palaces (until 1450)**		

ca. 1750	Thirteenth Dynasty
	    (1794/1793–1648/1645)
	Fourteenth Dynasty (?–1648/1645)
		MM III (1700–1550)
		MM III A (-B)
		    (1750/1720–1700/1680)
				First Babylonian Dynasty
				    (1894–1594)
				Hammurabi (1792–1750)

Year	Egypt	Crete	Greek Mainland	Near East
	Fifteenth Dynasty (Hyksos, 1648/1645–1539/1536)	*MM III B/I A (1700/1680–1675/1650)*		
	Sixteenth Dynasty (Hyksos vassals, coeval with Dynasty 15)	**Santorini catastrophe? (ca. 1648)**		
ca. 1550	Seventeenth Dynasty (in Thebes, ca. 1645–1550)			

	New Kingdom		**Mycenae**	
ca. 1550		LM I (1550–1450)	LH I A and B (1600–1450)	Kassite Period (ca. 1570–1157)
	Eighteenth Dynasty (1550–1292)	*LM I A (1675/1650–1600/1550)*	*LH I (1600–1510/1500)*	
		LM I B (1600/1550–1490/1470)		
		LM II (1450–1400)	LH II (1450–1400)	
		LM II (1490/1470–1435/1405)	*LH II (1510/1500–1390)*	
		LM III (1400–1100)	LH III (1400– ca. 1190)	Middle Assyrian Period (1364–935)
	Nineteenth Dynasty (1292–1186/1185)	*LM III A: 1 (1435/1405–1390/1370)*	*LH III A (1390–1340/1330)*	
		LM III A: 2 (1390/1370–1360/1325)	*LH III B (1340/1330–1185/1180)*	
		LM III B (1360/1325–1200/1190)	*LH III C (1185/1180–1065)*	
	Twentieth Dynasty (1186/1185–1070/1069)	Sub-Minoan (from *1190* or 1100)	Sub-Mycenaean (1190/*1065–1015*)	
ca. 1100			**Hekla-3 Volcanic catastrophe? (ca. 1159)**	**Hekla-3 Volcanic catastrophe? (ca. 1159)**

	Third Intermediate Period			
ca. 1100	Twenty-first Dynasty (1070/1069–946/945)		Sub-Mycenaean and Proto-geometric ceramics (ca. 1100–900)	Beginnings of royal rule in Israel (ca. 1012)
	Twenty-second Dynasty (946/945– ca. 735)		Early, middle and late geometric ceramic (ca. 900–700)	New Assyrian Period (911–631)
	Upper Egyptian rulers (ca. 841–730)			
	Twenty-third Dynasty (in the Delta, ca. 756–714/712)		First Olympic Games (776)	
	Twenty-fourth Dynasty (in Sais, ca. 740–714/712)		Orientalizing and early archaic ceramics in Corinth (ca. 720–540)	
ca. 650	Twenty-fifth Dynasty (Kushites, ca. or before 746– ca. 655)			

	Late Period			
ca. 650	Twenty-sixth Dynasty (664–525)		Archaic (ca. 700–490)	Persian kings (559–330)
			Attic blackware (ca. 600–480)	
			Attic redware (530–300)	
	Twenty-seventh Dynasty (Persian kings, 525–401)		Classic (490–323)	
	Twenty-eighth Dynasty (404/401–399)			
	Twenty-ninth Dynasty (399–380)			
	Thirtieth Dynasty (380–342)			
	Thirty-first Dynasty (Persian kings, 342–332)		Alexander the Great (336–323)	
	Ptolemaic Period (304–30)		Hellenism (323–27)	Seleucids (311–65)
27 BC	Egypt becomes a Roman province (from 30)			

EM: Early Minoan   MM: Middle Minoan   LM: Late Minoan   EH: Early Helladic   MH: Middle Helladic   LH: Late Helladic

Selected Bibliography

Peter Der Manuelian and Martina Ullmann

W. Y. Adams, *Nubia, Corridor to Africa,* London 1977

Cyril Aldred, *Akhenaten, King of Egypt,* London 1988

Cyril Aldred, *Egyptian Art,* London 1980

Cyril Aldred, *Jewels of the Pharaohs,* London 1971

Carol Andrews, *Amulets of Ancient Egypt,* London 1994

Carol Andrews, *Ancient Egyptian Jewellry,* London 1990

Carol Andrews, *The Rosetta Stone,* London 1981

Dieter Arnold, *Building in Egypt: Pharaonic Stone Masonry,* Oxford 1991

Dieter Arnold, *Lexikon der ägyptischen Baukunst,* Zurich 1994

Dieter Arnold, *Die Tempel Ägyptens. Götterwohnungen, Kultstätten, Baudenkmäler,* Zurich 1992

Dorothea Arnold, *The Royal Women of Amarna,* New York 1996

Roger S. Bagnall, *Egypt in Late Antiquity,* Princeton 1993

John Baines and Jaromír Málek, *Atlas of Ancient Egypt,* New York 1993

Morris Bierbrier, *The Tomb Builders of the Pharaoh,* London 1982

M. Bietak, *Avaris: the Capital of the Hyksos,* London 1996

Alan K. Bowman, *Egypt after the Pharaohs, 332 BC–AD 642, from Alexander to the Arab Conquest,* Berkeley 1986

James H. Breasted, *Ancient Records of Egypt.* 5 vols., Chicago 1906

Brooklyn Museum, *Cleopatra's Egypt: Age of the Ptolemies,* Brooklyn 1988

Brooklyn Museum, *Egyptian Sculpture of the Late Period,* Brooklyn 1960

Betsy M. Bryan and Hornung (pub.), *The Quest for Immortality,* Washington 2002

K.W. Butzer, *Early Hydraulic Civilization in Egypt: A Study in Cultural Ecology,* Chicago and London 1984

Somers Clarke and R. Engelbach, *Ancient Egyptian Construction and Architecture.* New York 1990 (reprint of 1930 Oxford University Press ed: *Ancient Egyptian Masonry*)

Mark Collier and Bill Manley, *How to read Egyptian,* London 1998

W. V. Davies, *Reading the Past: Egyptian Hieroglyphs,* London 1987

Wolfgang Decker, *Sports and Games in Ancient Egypt,* New Haven 1992

Aidan Dodson, *Egyptian Rock-cut Tombs,* Princes Risborough 1991

I. E. S. Edwards, *The Pyramids of Egypt,* Harmondsworth 1995

Arne Eggebrecht, ed., *Das alte Ägypten. 3000 Jahre Geschichte und Kultur des Pharaonenreichs,* Munich 1984

Arne Eggebrecht, ed., *Pelizaeus-Museum Hildesheim: Die ägyptische Sammlung,* Mainz 1993

Walter B. Emery, *Archaic Egypt,* Harmondsworth 1961

Raymond O. Faulkner, *The Ancient Egyptian Coffin Texts.* 3 vols., Warminster 1973–78

Raymond O. Faulkner, *The Ancient Egyptian Pyramid Texts, translated into English,* Oxford 1969

Raymond O. Faulkner, Ogden Goelet, Carol Andrews and James Wasserman. *The Egyptian Book of the Dead,* San Francisco 1994

H. G. Fischer, *Ancient Egyptian Calligraphy,* New York 1979

H. G. Fischer, *Egyptian Women of the Old Kingdom and of the Heracleopolitan Period,* New York 1989

Werner Forman and Stephen Quirke, *Hieroglyphs and the Afterlife in Ancient Egypt,* Norman 1996

Sir Alan Gardiner, *Egypt of the Pharaohs,* Oxford 1961

Sir Alan Gardiner, *Egyptian Grammar.* 3rd edition, Oxford 1973

Nicolas Grimal, *A History of Ancient Egypt,* Translated by Ian Shaw. Oxford 1992

J. R. Harris, ed., *The Legacy of Egypt.* 2nd ed., Oxford 1971

Zahi A. Hawass, *The Pyramids of Ancient Egypt,* Pittsburgh 1990

Wolfgang Helck, *Die Beziehungen Ägyptens und Vorderasiens zur Ägäis bis ins 7. Jahrhundert v. Chr.,* Darmstadt 1995

M. A. Hoffman, *Egypt Before the Pharaohs: The Prehistoric Foundations of Egyptian Civilization,* New York 1979

Erik Hornung, *Conceptions of God in Ancient Egypt: The One and the Many.* Translated by John Baines, Ithaca 1982

Erik Hornung, *Idea into Image: Essays on Ancient Egyptian Thought.* Translated by Elizabeth Bredeck, New York 1992

Erik Hornung, *The Valley of the Kings.* Translated by David Warburton, New York 1990

T. G. H. James, *Ancient Egypt: The Land and its Legacy,* Austin 1988

T. G. H. James, *Pharaoh's People: Scenes from Life in Imperial Egypt,* Oxford 1985

R. M. Janssen and J. J. Janssen, *Getting Old in Ancient Egypt,* London 1996

R. M. Janssen and J. J. Janssen, *Growing Up in Ancient Egypt,* London 1990

Barry J. Kemp, *Ancient Egypt: Anatomy of a Civilization,* London and New York 1989

Geoffrey Killen, *Egyptian Woodworking and Furniture,* Princes Risborough 1994

K. A. Kitchen, *The Third Intermediate Period.* 2nd ed., Warminster 1986

Rosemarie Klemm and Dietrich D. Klemm, *Steine und Steinbrüche im Alten Ägypten,* Berlin 1992

Dieter Kurth, *Treffpunkt der Götter. Inschriften aus dem Tempel des Horus von Edfu,* Zürich/Munich 1994

Karl Lange and Max Hirmer, *Ägypten. Architektur-Plastic-Malerei in drei Jahrtausenden,* Munich 1967

J.-P. Lauer, *The Royal Cemetery of Memphis: Excavation and Discoveries since 1850,* London 1976

Jean Leclant ed., *Egypt, 3 vol.,* Munich 1979–1981

Miriam Lichtheim, *Ancient Egyptian Literature, a Book of Readings.* 3 vols., Berkeley 1980

Antonio Loperino, *Ancient Egyptian. A linguistic introduction,* Cambridge 1995

Geoffrey T. Martin, *The Hidden Tombs of Memphis. New Discoveries from the Time of Tutankhamun and Ramesses the Great,* London 1991

A. Mekhitarian, *Egyptian Painting,* New York 1979

William J. Murnane, *Texts from the Amarna Period in Egypt.* Society of Biblical Literature Writings from the Ancient World 5, Atlanta 1995

Museum of Fine Arts Boston, *Egypt's Golden Age: The Art of Living in the New Kingdom, 1558–1080 B.C.,* Boston 1981

John E. Nunn, *Ancient Egyptian Medicine,* London 1996

D B. O'Connor, *Ancient Nubia: Egypt's Rival in Africa,* Philadelphia 1993

R. B. Parkinson, *Voices from Ancient Egypt: An Anthology of Middle Kingdom Writings,* London 1991

R. B. Parkinson and Stephen Quirke. *Papyrus,* London 1995

Geraldine Pinch, *Magic in Ancient Egypt,* London 1994

Stephen Quirke, *The Administration of Egypt in the Late Middle Kingdom,* New Malden 1990

Stephen Quirke, *Ancient Egyptian Religion,* London 1992

Donald B. Redford, *Egypt, Canaan and Israel in Ancient Times,* Princeton 1992

G. A. Reisner, *A History of the Giza Necropolis* I, Cambridge, Mass. 1942

G. Robins, *The Art of Ancient Egypt,* Cambridge 1997

G. Robins, *Egyptian Painting and Relief,* Princes Risborough 1986

G. Robins, *Women in Ancient Egypt,* London 1993

G. Robins and Charles Shute, *The Rhind Mathematical Papyrus: An Ancient Egyptian Text,* London 1987

Edna R. Russmann (pub.), *Eternal Egypt,* London-New York 2001

Jack M. Sasson et al., eds., *Civilizations of the Ancient Near East.* 4 vols., London and New York 1995

H. Schäfer, *Pnnciples of Egyptian Art.* Translated by John Baines from the German *Von ägyptischer Kunst,* Oxford 1978

Bernd Scheel, *Egyptian Metalworking and Tools,* Princes Risborough 1989

Wilfried Seipel, ed., *Ägyptomanie. Ägypten in der europäischen Kunst 1730–1930,* Vienna 1994. French edition: *Egyptomamia. L'Égypte dans l'art occidental 1730–1930,* Paris 1994

Ian Shaw and Paul Nicholson, *The British Museum Dictionary of Ancient Egypt,* London 1995

Ian Shaw, *The Oxford History of Ancient Egypt,* Oxford 2000

Abdel Ghaffar Shedid, *Das Grab des Senned. Ein Künstlergrab der 19. Dynastie in Deir el-Medineh,* Mainz 1994

Abdel Ghaffar Shedid and Matthias Seidel, *Das Grab des Nacht. Kunst und Geschichte eines Beamtengrabes der 18. Dynastie in Theben-West,* Mainz 1991

David P. Silverman, general ed., *Ancient Egypt,* New York 1997

David P. Silverman, *Language and Writing in Ancient Egypt,* Pittsburgh 1990

William K. Simpson, ed., *The Literature of Ancient Egypt,* New Haven and 1973

W. Stevenson Smith, *The Art and Architecture of Ancient Egypt.* 2nd edition revised by W.K. Simpson, Harmondsworth 1981

A. J. Spencer, *Death in Ancient Egypt,* New York 1982

A.J. Spencer, *Early Egypt: The Rise of Civilization in the Nile Valley,* London 1993

Eugen Strouhal, *Life in Ancient Egypt,* Cambridge and Norman 1992

B. G. Trigger, B. J. Kemp, D. B. O'Connor and A. B. Lloyd, *Ancient Egypt: A Social History,* Cambridge 1983

E. Uphill, *Egyptian Towns and Cities,* Princes Risborough 1988

Miroslav Verner, *Forgotten Pharaohs, Lost Pyramids at Abusir,* Prague 1994

Philip J. Watson, *Egyptian Pyramids and Mastaba Tombs of the Old and Middle Kingdoms,* Princes Risborough 1987

Edward F. Wente, *Letters from Ancient Egypt.* Society of Biblical Literature Writings from the Ancient World 1, Atlanta 1990

Dietrich Wildung and Sylvia Schoske, *Kleopatra. Ägypten um die Zeitenwende,* Mainz 1989

Richard H. Wilkinson, *Reading Egyptian Art. A Hieroglyphic Guide to Ancient Egyptian Painting and Sculpture,* London 1992

K. T. Zauzich, *Hieroglyphs Without Mystery,* Austin 1992

Karl-Theodor Zauzich, *Hieroglyphen ohne geheimnis Eine Einfüfirung in die Altägyptische Schrift für Museumsbesucher und Ägyptentouristen,* Mainz 1980

Authors

Prof. Dr. Hartwig Altenmüller
Hamburg, Universität, Archäologisches Institut; Ordinarius.
Main research: Mortuary complexes of the Old and New Kingdom, excavation in the Valley of the Kings.

Dr. Dorothea Arnold
New York, Metropolitan Museum of Art, Department of Egyptian Antiquities; Curator in charge.
Main research: Art of the Middle Kingdom, Ancient Egyptian pottery.

Edith Bernhauer, M.A.
Munich, Staatliche Sammlung Ägyptische Kunst; Mitarbeiterin.
Main research: Ancient Egyptian architecture and sculpture.

Prof. Dr. Günter Burkard
Munich, Universität, Institut für Ägyptologie; Ordinarius.
Main research: Ancient Egyptian language and literature. DFG-Project on ostraca depicting non-literary motifs of Deir el-Medineh.

Dr. Albrecht Endruweit
Göttingen, Universität, Seminar für Ägyptologie und Koptologie; Lehrbeauftragter.
Main research: Architecture and architectural history in Ancient Egypt and the Near East.

Dr. Rita E. Freed
Boston, Museum of Fine Arts, Department of Ancient Egyptian, Nubian and Near Eastern Art; Curator. Chairperson of the International Committee for Egyptology (CIPEG) in ICOM.
Main research: Ancient Egyptian art, excavations in Saqqara.

Dr. Renate Germer
Hamburg, Universität, Archäologisches Institut; Wissenschaftliche Mitarbeiterin.
Main research: Interdisciplinary research of science and Egyptology, flora of pharaonic Egypt and contemporary mummy research.

Prof. Dr. Dr. Manfred Görg
Munich, Universität, Institut für Biblische Exegese; Ordinarius.
Main research: Theology of the Old Testament, history of Ancient Near Eastern religion, relationship between Egypt and Israel.

Dr. Manfred Gutgesell
Rethen; Freier Wissenschaftler, Ägyptologe.
Main research: Ancient Egyptian economic history and ancient numismatics.

Dr. Friederike Kampp-Seyfried
Heidelberg, Universität, Ägyptologisches Institut; Wissenschaftliche Mitarbeiterin.
Main research: Archaeology of the Theban necropolis, history of the New Kingdom, excavation in Qurna (Western Thebes).

Prof. Dr. Dieter Kessler
Munich, Universität, Institut für Ägyptologie; Professor für Ägyptologie.
Main research: Ancient Egyptian religion, animal cult, excavations in Tuna el-Gebel.

Rosemarie Klemm, M.A.
Munich, Universität, Institut für Ägyptologie; Lehrbeauftragte und wissenschaftliche Mitarbeiterin.
Main research: Archaeology, archaeometry, field research in Egypt and Sudan, DFG-Project on ancient gold and metal alloys in Northern Sudan.

Prof. Dr. Dieter Kurth
Hamburg, Universität, Archäologisches Institut; Professor für Ägyptologie.
Main research: Greco-Roman Period of Egyptian History, data collections at the temple of Edfu.

Prof. Dr. Ulrich Luft
Budapest, Universität, Seminar für Ägyptologie; Professor der Ägyptologie.
Main research: Ancient Egyptian literature, history of religion and papyrus study.

Dr. Eva Pardey
Hamburg, Universität, Archäologisches Institut; Lehrbeauftragte und wissenschaftliche Mitarbeiterin.
Main research: History of Ancient Egyptian administration and law.

Prof. Dr. Daniel Polz
Los Angeles, University of California, Department of Near Eastern Languages and Cultures; Professor of Egyptology.
Main research: Archaeology of the Theben necropolis during the New Kingdom, excavation in El-Chocha (Western Thebes).

Dr. Wafaa el Saddik
Cairo, Supreme Council of Antiquities; Mitarbeiterin.
Main research: History of the Late Period, Egyptian collections.

Prof. Dr. Helmut Satzinger
Vienna, Kunsthistorisches Museum, Ägyptisch-Orientalischen Sammlung; Direktor.
Main research: Ancient Egyptian grammar, art and epigraphy.

Dr. Thomas Schneider
Basle, Universität, Ägyptologisches Seminar; Assistent.
Main research: Ancient Egyptian history and linguistics, Egyptian–Near Eastern relations.

Dr. Marcel Schoch
Munich, Deutsches Museum, Wissenschaftlicher Mitarbeiter.
Main research: Archaeometry, scientific and conventional data basis, topography.

PD Dr. Regine Schulz
Munich, Universität, Institut für Ägyptologie; Privatdozentin. Pelizaeus-Museum Hildesheim; Freie Mitarbeiterin. Secretary of the International Committee for Egyptology (CIPEG) in ICOM.
Main research: Ancient Egypt history of art, religion, and coptology.

Dr. Matthias Seidel
Hildesheim, Pelizaeus-Museum; Wissenschaftlicher Mitarbeiter.
Main research: Ancient Egyptian archaeology and art.

Prof. Dr. Stephan Seidlmayer
Berlin, Freie Universität, Ägyptologisches Seminar; Privatdozent.
Main research: Ancient Egyptian archaeology, prehistory, social and cultural history.

Prof. Dr. Abdel Ghaffar Shedid
Cairo, Universität Helwan, Akademie der Bildenden Künste, Abteilung Kunstgeschichte; Professor. Munich, Institut für Ägyptologie; Lehrbeauftragter.
Main research: Egyptian painting, art history.

Elisabeth Siebert, M.A.
Munich; Freie Wissenschaftlerin.
Main research: Art of the Late Period.

Hourig Sourouzian
Docteur d'Etat des Lettres. Cairo, Deutsches Archäologisches Institut; Korrespondierendes Mitglied. Munich, Universität, Institut für Ägyptologie; Lehrbeauftragte.
Main research: Ancient Egyptian art history, Armenian monuments.

Prof. Dr. Rainer Stadelmann
Cairo, Deutsches Archäologisches Institut; Erster Direktor.
Main research: Ancient Egyptian archaeology, architectural history of the pyramid period, excavations, e.g. in Dashur.

Dr. Christine Strauß-Seeber
Munich, Universität, Institut für Ägyptologie; Freie Mitarbeiterin.
Main research: Ancient Egyptian art history, religion.

Martina Ullmann, M.A.
Munich, Universität, Institut für Ägyptologie; Lehrbeauftragte.
Main research: Ancient Egyptian language and religion.

Prof. Dr. Ursula Verhoeven
Mainz, Universität, Institut für Ägyptologie.
Main research: Ancient Egyptian writing, literature, language and religion.

Gabriele Wenzel, M.A.
Potsdam, Historisches Institut; Wissenschaftliche Mitarbeiterin.
Main research: Art history of the Old Kingdom.

Joachim Willeitner, M.A.
Munich, Freier Wissenschaftler.
Main research: Egyptian regional policy.

Dr. Stefan Wimmer
Munich, Universität, Institut für Ägyptologie; Lehrbeauftragter. München, Bayerisches Staatsbibliothek, Orientabteilung, wissenschaftlicher Angestellter.
Main research: Hieratic palaeography, Egyptian–Near Eastern relations.

Susanne Wohlfarth, M.A.
Munich, Universität, Institut für Ägyptologie; Freie Mitarbeiterin.
Main research: Ancient Egyptian wall painting.

Picture Credits

The publisher and the editors wish to thank the following museums, archives, and photographers for making available the illustrations and granting us the permission to print them. Our special thanks goes to the Scala photographic archive for its cooperation.

Egyptian Museum, Cairo: p.127/No. 45; p. 272/ No. 3

Ägyptisches Institut der Universität Heidelberg: p.249/No. 195; p.254/No. 205; p.256/No. 207, No. 210; p.259/No. 217; Sammlung des Instituts: p.481/No. 107

Nicole Alexanian, Berlin: p.38/No. 56

Fratelli Alinari, Florence: p.491/No. 2

Allard Pierson Museum, Amsterdam: p.488/No. 118

Reproduced by permission of Andromeda Oxford Ltd.:, Albingdon/UK ©: p.41/No. 2; p.105/No. 2; p.143/No. 2; p.271/No. 2; p.292/No. 2

Antikenmuseum und Sammlung Ludwig, Basel p.130/No.53

Archeophoto, Geneva: p.49/No. 12; p.50/No. 14; p.209/No. 116; p.214/No. 127; p.323/No. 2,p.415/Nr.151

Archiv White Star: p.113/No. 15

In: Arkell, A. J.: The Prehistory of the Nile Valley, Leiden 1975: p.11/No. 6

In: Arnold, D.: Die Tempel Ägyptens, Zürich 1992: p.175/No. 54; p.187/No. 76

In: Arnold, D.: Lexikon der Ägyptischen Baukunst, Zürich 1994: p.80/No. 71; p.113/No. 16

In: Arnold, D.: The Pyramid of Senwosret I. The South Cemeteric of Lisht: vol. 1, Metropolitan Museum of Art, Egyptian Expedition, vol. 22, New York 1988: p.111/No. 13

The Ashmolean Museum, Oxford: p.27/No. 34; p.30/No. 40; p.38/No. 58; p.278/No. 9; p.418/No. 4

In: Assmann, J.: Die Inschrift auf dem äußeren Sarkophagendeckel des Merenptah, in: MDAIK 28, 1972: p.228/No. 149

In: Ausst. Kat.: L'Egypte des millénaires obscures, Paris 1990: p.15/No. 13; p.16/ No. 16

In: Ausst. Kat.: Sethos – ein Pharaonengrab, Basel 1992: p.448/No. 44

In: Ausst. Kat.: Tanis – L'or des pharaons, Catalogue III, La nécropole royale de Tanis et ses trésor, Galeries Nationales du Grand Palais, Paris 1987: p.281/No. 15

© Spektrum/Bavaria: p.512/513

In: Baines J. /Málek, J.: Atlas of Ancient Egypt, Oxford 1980: p.155/No. 12

In: Baines, J. /Málek, J.: Weltatlas der alten Kulturen – Ägypten, München 1980: p.304/No. 26

Ch. Bayer, Coesfeld: p.378/No. 81, No. 83, No. 84

Bernisches Historisches Museum, Bern: Stefan Rebsamen p.477/No. 99–102

Bildarchiv Foto Marburg: p.382/No. 91; p.383/No. 93, p.385/No. 94

In: von Bissing, F. W.: Das Re-Heiligtum des Königs Ne-Woser-Re, Berlin, 1905: p.71/No. 52

In: Borchardt, L. /Ricke, H.: Die Wohnhäuser in Tell el-Amarna, Berlin 1980: p.391/No. 104; p.392/No. 105

bpk, Berlin: p.16/No. 17; p.18/No. 20, No. 21; p.80/No. 72; p.146/No. 6;

Jürgen Liepe: p.17/No. 19; p.143/No. 1; p.159/No. 20; p.286/No. 26; p.291/No. 1;

p.318/No. 57; p.367/No. 65, No. 66; p.409/No. 140; p.417/No. 1; p.421/No. 8; p.424/No. 13; p.427/No. 17; p.439/No. 32;

Margarete Büsing: p.76/No. 63; p.203/No. 102, No. 104; p.212/No. 124; p.321/No. 62; p.323/No. 1; p.338/No. 25; p.346/No. 34; p.406/No. 133; p.409/No. 141; p.435/ No. 26;

G. Murza: p.319/No. 60; p.320/No. 61, p.426/Nr.16

The British Library, London: p.195/No. 89

© The Trustees of the British Museum, London: p.9/No. 2; p.13/No. 10; p.14/No. 11; p.29/No. 37; p.34/No. 50; p.100/No. 103; p.150/No. 9; p.186/No. 74; p.189/No. 79; p.194/No. 87; p.212/No. 122; p.228/No. 148; p.249/No. 196; p.275/No. 6; p.276/No. 7; p.325/No. 4; p.329/No. 8; p.334/No. 14; p.351/No. 44; p.381/No. 88–90; p.392/No. 107; p.393/No. 108; p.399/No. 119; p.405/No. 130; p.407/No. 136; p.423/No. 11; p.431/No. 1; p.448/No. 43, No. 44; p.466/No. 71–81; p.468/No. 84, No. 85; p.469/No. 88; p.471/No. 90; p.475/No. 98; p.475/No. 97; p.479/No. 103–105; p.484/No. 111

Andreas Brodbeck, Basel: p.218/No. 133; p.220/No. 137; p.227/No. 146

Courtesy of The Brooklyn Museum of Art, New York: Charles Edwin Wilbour Fund: p.45/No. 7; p.48/No. 11; p.76/No. 64; p.134/No. 56; p.141/No. 67; p.165/No. 32; p.271/No. 1; p.283/No. 22; p.332/No. 10; p.338/No. 26; p.431/No. 21

In: Brunton, G.: Matmar, London 1948: p.13/No. 9

Günter Burkard, München: p.354/No. 51

In: Cerny, C.: A Late Ramesside Letter, Brussels 1939: p.348/No. 40

In: Champollion le Jeune: Grammaire égyptienne, Paris 1836: p.345/No. 33

In: Chassinat, E. / Daumas, F.: Le temple de Dendara I. 2, Cairo 1934: p.301/No. 16

Maurice et Pierre Chuzeville, Musée du Louvre, Paris: p.353/No. 49; p.429/No. 20

© The Cleveland Museum of Art, Cleveland, Ohio: Gift of the Huntington Art and Polytechnic Trust, 1914: p.348/No. 39

In: Daumas, F.: Dendara et le temple d'Hathor, RAPH 29, Cairo 1969: p.301/No. 17

In: Davies, N.: The Tomb of Antefoker, TTS 2, London 1920: p.402/No. 122

In: Davies, N.: Two Ramesside tombs, PMMA V, New York 1927: p.378/No. 80

In: Dawson, W. R. , in: JEA 13, 1927: p.473/No. 93

Deutsches Archäologisches Institut, Cairo: p.12/No. 7, p.39/No. 60; p.51/No. 17; p.503/No. 14; p.504/No. 19/20; Dieter Johannes: p.39/Nr.60

Deutsches Archäologisches Institut/von Pilgrim/DMT Jürgen Heckes: p.498/No. 10

Peter Der Manuelian, Boston: p.79/No. 68

G. Dreyer, Cairo: p.27/No. 33; p.31/No. 41; p.32/No. 45; p.500/No. 12

In: Dreyer, G.: Umm el-Qaab, Nachuntersuchungen im frühzeitlichen Königsfriedhof. 3. /4. Vorbericht, in: MDAIK, 46, 1990: p.32/No. 44, No. 45

Edition Flammarion, Paris: p.155/No. 13

Josef Eiwanger, Bonn: p.9/No. 3

Albrecht Endruweit, Göttingen: p.390/No. 101; p.391/No. 103; p.395/No. 113; p.397/No. 117

In: Emery, W. B.: The Great Tombs of the First Dynasty II, London 1954: p.33/No. 47;

p.34/No. 48

Eva Engel, Göttingen: p.390/No. 102

In: Engelbach, R. , in: JEA 20, London 1934: p.38/No. 57

Joachim Feist, Pliezhausen: p.443/No. 38, No. 39

In: Fox, P.: Der Schatz des Tut-Ench-Amun, Wiesbaden 1961: p.229/No. 152

In: Gardiner, A. H.: The Library of A. Chester Beatty, London 1931: p.354/ No. 50

Kai-Uwe Götz, Hamburg: p.382/No. 92

Grabung Quantir-Piramesse: P. Windszus: p.500/No. 11

© Zahi Hawass, Gisa: p.67/No. 41

In: Hassan, P.: Excavations at Giza, Vol IV (1932-1933) Cairo 1943: p.387/No. 97

Hessisches Landesmuseum, Darmstadt: p.367/No. 67

Friedrich W. Hinkel, Berlin: p.36/No. 53

© The J. Paul Getty Trust, The Getty Conservation Institute, Los Angeles: Guillermo Aldana: p.503/No. 15–18

The Griffith Institute, Ashmolean Museum, Oxford: p.229/No. 153; p.232/No. 158, No. 160, No. 161; p.236/No. 167, No. 168; p.237/No. 170

Hirmer Fotoarchiv, München: p.452/No. 48

In: Holmes, D. L.: Chipped Stone-Working, Hierankonpolis and the Rise of Civilization in Egypt, in: Friedmann, R. , Adams, R.: The Followers of Horus. Studies dedicated to Michael Allen Hofman, London 1992: p.22/No. 27, No. 28

In: Hölscher, U.: The Mortuary Temple of Ramses III, Part I, OIP 54, Chicago 1941: p.394/No. 110–112; p.395/No. 114

In: © Cleo Huggins, Dover/New Hampshire: p.344/No. 32; p.347/No. 36

Image Bank, München: Guido Alberto Rossi: p.47/No. 8

Institut für Ägyptologie, München: Sh. Shalchi: p.232/No. 159; p.449/No. 45; p.494/No. 7; Vorsatzpapier

Israel-Museum, Jerusalem: p.352/No. 46; p.352/No. 47

Leonhard Jehle, Ulm: p.208/No. 114

Andrea Jemolo, Rom: p.66/Nr.40; p.74/Nr.60; p.278/No.10; p.303/Nr.20, Nr.23; p.377/No. 89;

In: Jéquier, G.: Le monument funéraire de Pepi II, Bd. III, Cairo 1940: p.73/No. 58

Dieter Johannes, Istanbul: p.86/No. 81; p.89/No. 86

In: Junker, H.: Gisa I, Bericht über die Grabungen auf dem Friedhof des Alten Reichs, Vienna 1929: p.79/No. 69

© Justin Kerr, New York: p.238/No. 172–174

Friederike Kampp-Seyfried, Heidelberg: Originalgrafiken: p.250/No. 197, No. 198; p.251/No. 199

In: Kaplony Heckel, U.: Ein neuer demotischer Brief aus Gebelên, in: Staatliche Museen zu Berlin, Mitteilungen aus der Ägyptischen Sammlung VIII (Festschr. zum 150jährigen Bestehen des Äg. MuP.), Berlin 1974: p.354/No. 52

In: Kemp, B. J.: Ancient Egypt – Anatomy of a Civilization, London 1991: p.388/No. 99 reprinted by permission of Routledge Publishers, London

In: Kemp, B.: Amarna from the Air, in: Egyptian Archaeology. The Bulletin of the Egypt Exploration Society 2, 1992: p.392/No. 106

Kestner-Museum, Hannover: M. Lindner:

p.371/No. 72; p.440/No. 34; p.465/No. 69/70; p.484/No. 113; p.487/No. 115

O. Teßmer: p.489/No. 119

In: Klebs, L.: Die Reliefs und Malereien des mittleren Reiches, Heidelberg 1922: p.407/No. 134

In: Klemm, R. /Klemm, D.: Die Steine der Pharaonen, Staatliche Sammlung Ägyptischer Kunst München, München 1981: p.411/No. 143

Rosemarie Klemm, München: p.332/No. 11; p.411/No. 142; p.412/No. 144, No. 145; p.413/No. 146, No. 147; p.414/No. 148, No. 149, No. 150; p.415/No. 152;

Kodansha Ltd, Tokio: p.231/No. 155, No. 156;

© Könemann Verlagsgesellschaft mbH, Andrea Jemolo, Rom: p.52/No. 20; p.67/No. 44; p.72/No. 54; p.73/Nr.57; p.76/No. 62; p.77/No. 67; p.80/No. 70; p.82/No. 75; p.84/No. 77, No. 78; p.85/No. 79, No. 80; p.86/No. 82; p.87/No. 83; p.88/No. 84; p.89/No. 85; p.90/No. 87; p.91/No. 88, No. 89; p.93/No. 90; p.98/No. 99; p.100/No. 102; p.102/No. 105; p.110/No. 9; p.114/No. 14; p.114/No. 17-18; p.134/No. 57; p.135/No. 58, No. 59; p.136/No. 60, No. 61; p.156/No. 16; p.159/No. 21; p.161/No. 22, No. 25; p.162/No. 26, No. 27; p.164/No. 30; p.169/No. 38; p.173/No. 47; Nr.48; p.174/No. 51; p.176/No. 56; p.177/No. 59; p.178/No. 60; p.179/No. 61; p.180/No. 63, No. 64, No. 65; p.182/No. 66; p.198/No. 95; p.206/No. 109; p.217/No. 131; p.221/No. 138; p.222/No. 142, No. 143; p.224–225/No. 143; p.226/No. 144; p.227/No. 147; p.228/No. 150; p.231/No. 157; p.235/No. 164; p.237/No. 169; p.239/No. 178; p.240/No. 179; p.241/No. 180, No. 181; p.242/No. 186; p.258/No. 213, No. 214; p.259/No. 215; p.260/No. 219; p.261/No. 221; p. 224, 225/No. 143; p.262/No. 223; p.282/No. 18; p.285/No. 24, No. 25; p.287/No. 29; p.297/No. 7; p.298/No. 8, No. 10; p.300/No. 12; p.301/No. 14; p.305/No. 28, No. 29; p.306/No. 30, No. 31; p.308/No. 36; p.309/No. 39; p.310/No. 43, No. 44; p.327/No. 5; p.335/No. 16; p.348/No. 38; p.356/No. 56; p.358/No. 57; p.360/No. 58; p.361/No. 59; p.362/No. 60; p.368/No. 68/69; p.372/No. 73; p.379/No. 85; p.385/No. 95; p.399/No. 118; p.400/No. 120; p.401/No. 121; p.402/No. 124; p.417/No. 2; p.421/No. 7; p.428/No. 19; p.434/No. 25; p.446/No. 42; p.513-518; p.529; Umschlagvorderseite; Umschlagrückseite

In: Kozloff, A. P. /Bryan, B. M.: Egypt's Dazzling Son, Cleveland 1992: p.188/No. 78

Klaus-Peter Kuhlmann, Cairo: p.317/No. 55

Kunsthistorisches Museum, Vienna: p.96/No. 92; p.98/No. 98; p.99/No. 100; p.101/No. 104; p.141/No. 68; p.144/No. 3; p.252/No. 201; p.260/No. 218; p.279/No. 12; p.313/No. 45; p.439/No. 31; p.443/No. 39

In: Kuper, R.: Afrika – Geschichte zwischen Weide und Wüste. Die Kölner Forschungen zur prähistorischen Archäologie Afrikas, in: Archäologie in Deutschland, Heft 2, 1989: p.10/No. 4

Dieter Kurth, Bispingen: p.307/No. 34; p.308/No. 35

In: Leclant, J.: Ägypten, Band II–Das Großreich, München 1980: p.155/No. 14; p.157/No. 18; p.208/No. 115

In: Legrain, G. , in: ASAE 14, 1914; p.164/No. 28

Jürgen Liepe, Berlin: p.9/No. 1; p.15/No. 14; p.28/No. 35, No. 36; p.29/No. 38, No. 39; p.34/No. 49; p.35/No. 52; p.40/No. 1; p.51/No. 18; p.52/No. 20; p.70/No. 51; p.72/No. 55, No. 56; p.77/No. 65. ; p.107/No. 5; p.130/No. 52; p.131/No. 54; p.148/No. 7; p.149/No. 8; p.151/No. 10; p.164/No. 29; p.174/No. 52; p.185/No. 70; p.191/No. 80; p.196/No. 91; p.201/No. 101; p.233/No. 162, No. 163; p.236/No. 166; p.239/No. 177; p.242/No. 184; p.259/No. 216; p.274/No. 5; p.280/No. 13; p.316/No. 53; p.335/No. 17; p.365/No. 61, No. 62; p.398/No. 115; p.402/No. 123; p.420/No. 6; p.422/No. 10; p.426/No. 16; p.436/No. 27; p.437/No. 30; p.441/No. 37; p.442/No. 38; p.443/No. 40; p.459/No. 59; p.461/No. 62; p.483/No. 110; p.489/No. 120

J. E. Livet, Paris: p.247/No. 192/193

Lotos-Film, Kaufbeuren: p.18/No. 22; p.57/No. 22; p.63/No. 32, No. 34; p.68/No. 46; p.69/No. 48, No. 49; p.82/No. 76; p.95/No. 91; p.106/No. 4; p.122/No. 33; p.145/No. 4; p.153/No. 11; p.165/No. 32; p.166/No. 33; p.169/No. 39; p.172/No. 46; p.185/No. 72; p.186/No. 73; p.188/No. 77; p.206/No. 111; p.220/No. 136; p.235/No. 165; p.245/No. 188–190; p.253/No. 202, No. 203; p.254/No. 204; p.255/No. 206; p.257/No. 211, No. 212; p.262/No. 225; p.264/No. 227; p.266/No. 230, No. 231; p.280/No. 14; p.288, No. 31; p.343/No. 31; p.366/No. 63; p.369/No. 70; p.373/No. 74; p.374/No. 75; p.375/ No. 77; p.377/No. 78; p.404/No. 138

The Luxor Museum of Ancient Egyptian Art, Luxor: p.177/No. 58

Medizinische Universität, Lübeck: p.462/No. 64

© The Metropolitan Museum of Art, New York:

Theodore M. Davis Collection 1915: p.26/No. 32;

Bequest of Theodore M. Davis, 1915, The Theodore M. Davis Collection: p.337/No. 24;

Gift of Mr. and Mrs. V. Everit Macy 1923, New York: p.265/No. 229;

Gift of Egypt Exploration Fund 1907: p.110/No. 10;

Edward S. Harkness Gift – Bruce White, New York: p.201/No. 99;

Edward S. Harkness Gift 1917: p.138/No. 63;

Museum Excavations, 1927: p.337/No. 21;

Josef Pulitzer Bequest 1960: p.37/No. 55;

Rogers Fund 1908: p.111/No. 11;

Rogers Fund 1911: p.130/No. 53;

Rogers Fund 1918: p.45/Nr.6

Rogers Fund 1919: p.333/No. 12;

Rogers Fund 1921–1922: p.104/No. 1;

Rogers Fund 1922 (1979): p.211/No. 119;

Rogers Fund 1927, Photography by the Egyptian Expedition: p.407/No. 135;

Rogers Fund 1934, Photograph: Bruce White: p.428/No. 16;

Rogers Fund 1936: p.336/No. 20;

Rogers Fund and Contribution from E. F. Harkness Gift 1922: p.187/No. 75;

Rogers Fund and E. F. Harkness Gift, 1922: p.64/No. 37;

Rogers Fund and Edward S. Harkness Gift 1920: p.389/No. 100;

Rogers Fund and Henry Walters Gift 1916: p.116/No. 23;

Rogers Fund: p.96/No. 93 (photo: Lee Schecter);

Gift of Norbert Schimmel, 1985: p.201/No. 100;

© Ministero Beni culturali e ambientali, Museo Egizio, Turin: p.16/No. 15; p.17/No. 18; p.19/No. 24; p.39/No. 61; p.249/No. 196;

p.294/No. 4, No. 5; p.375/No. 76; p.403/No. 125; p.404/No. 127, No. 128, No. 129; p.405/No. 131; p.406/No. 132; p.407/No. 137; p.425/No. 11; p.441/No.36

H. W. Müller-Fotoarchiv, Universitätsbibliothek Heidelberg: p.43/No. 4; p.106/No. 3; p.107/No. 6; p.272/No. 3; p.288/No. 32

Musées Royaux d'Art et d'Histoire, Brussels: p.15/No. 12; p.19/No. 22; p.242/No. 182; p.321/No. 63/64

© Museum of Fine Arts, Boston:

Museum Expedition: p.42/No. 3, p.43/No. 5; p.68/ No. 47; p.103/No. 106; p.118/No.14; p.201/No. 98; p.331/No. 9;

Charles Amos Cummings Bequest: p.201/No. 98;

Gift of Theodore M. Davis: p.227/No. 145;

Harvard University, Expedition: p.335/ No. 18;

H. L. Pierce Fund: p.340/No. 29;

James Fund Purchase and Contribution: p.341/No. 30; p.460/No. 61;

Gift of Mrs. J. D. Cameron Bradley 1948: p.463/No. 66;

Gift of Egypt Exploration Fund 1895: p.467/No. 82, No. 83;

In: Museumskat.: Ägyptisches Museum Berlin, Berlin 1986, Bd. III: p.346/No. 35

National Museum, Athen: p.339/No. 22

The Nelson-Atkins Museum of Art, Kansas City: Purchase Nelson Trust p.336/Nr.19

In: Nelson, H.: Festival Scenes of Ramses III, Medinet Habu, OiP 51, Bd. 4, 1940: p.25/No. 30

In: Newberry, P. E.: Beni Hassan I, ASE 1, London 1893: p.121/No. 28

In: O'Conner, D.: The earliest royal boatgraves, in: Egyptian Archeology. The Bulletin of the Egypt Exploration Society, 6, 1995: p.32/No. 46

Courtesy of the Oriental Institute of the University of Chicago: p.487/No. 116

In: Pantalacci, L. /Traumecker, Cl.: Le temple d'el – Qal'a I – Relevés des scènes et des textes, Cairo 1990: p.304/No. 27

In: Parkinson, R. B.: Voices from Ancient Egypt, The British Museum, Department of Egyptian Antiquities, London 1991: p.355/No. 53-55

Pelizaeus Museum, Hildesheim: p.65/No. 39; p.81/No. 73; p.82/No. 74; p.97/No. 94;

Sh. Shalchi: p.167/No. 37; p.175/No. 53; p.183/No. 67, No. 68; p.207/No. 112; p.218/No. 134; p.318/No. 58; p.379/No. 86; p.386/No. 96; p.424/No. 12, No. 14; p.440/No. 33; p.449/No. 45, p.469/No. 86; p.471/No. 89; p.472/No. 92; p.482/No. 109; p.485/No. 112; p.493/No. 4, No. 5; p.494/No. 6, Nr.7; p.496/No. 8, No. 9; p.510/

J. Liepe: p.185/No. 71

In: Pendleburey, J. D. P.: The City of Akhenaten, Part III, Vol 2: Plates, EES, London 1951: p.200/No. 97

In: Petrie, W. M. F.: Illahan, Kahun, Gurob, London 1891: p.388/No. 98

In: Petrie, W. M. F.: The Royal Tomb of the Earliest Dynasties II, EEF 21, 1901: p.31/No. 42; p.38/No. 59

Courtesy of Petrie Museum of Egyptian Archeology, London: University College London: p.327/No. 6

In: Piankoff, A.: The Shrines of Tut-Ankh-Amon, Bollingen Series 40. 2, New York 1955: p.229/No. 154

© Photo Scala, Florence: p.275/No. 6 (The British Museum); p.286/No. 27 (The Vatican Museum); p.353/ No. 49 (The British Museum); Jacket front (Cairo, The Egyp-

tian Museum); p.469/No. 87; p.490/No. 1

Daniel Polz, Heidelberg: p.501/No. 13

In: Porter-Moss, Topographical Bibliography of Ancient Egypt. Hyrographic Texts, Reliefs, Paintings, Bd. 1 – The Theban Necropolis II. Royal Tombs and Smaller Cemeteries, Oxford 1975: p.247/No. 194

Privatsammlung Schweiz: p.140/No. 65

Hans Pusback, Ulm: p.157/No. 17

Ilka Pusback, Ulm: p.193/Nr.84

In: Quibell, J. E. /Green, F. W.: Hierakonpolis II., BSAE 5, London 1902, Tfn. 75–76: p.20f. /No. 25, No. 26

In: Reeves, N. /Wilkinson, R. H.: The Complete Valley of the Kings, 2. Aufl. , London 1997, drawn by Philip Winton, published by Thames and Hudson Ltd., London and Econ Verlag, Düsseldorf: p.219/No. 135

In: Reeves, N.: The Complete Tutankhamun, London 1990, drawn by Tracy Wellman, published by Thames and Hudson Ltd., London: p.229/No. 151

Rijksmuseum van Oudheden, Leiden: p.252/No. 200; p.260/No. 220; p.262/No. 224; p.267/No. 232, No. 233; p.268/No. 234, No. 235; p.269/No.236, Nr.237; p.339/No. 28; p.352/No. 48; p.418/No. 3; p.453/No. 50; p.460/No. 60; p.461/No. 63; p.472/No. 91; p.474/No. 94, No. 95; p.488/No. 117

© RMN, Paris: p.155/nr.13; p.171/No. 44; p.203/No. 103; Endvignette;

D. Arnaudet, G. Blot: p.133/No. 55; p.138/No. 62; Chuzeville: p.97/No. 95–97; p.128/No. 49; p.289/No. 34, No. 36; p.328/No. 7; p.349/No. 42; p.408/No. 139; p.419/No. 5; p.475/No. 96;

B. Hatala: p.99/No. 101;

Ch. Larrieu: p.146/No. 6;

H. Lewandowski: p.26/No. 31; p.77/No. 66; p.287/No. 28; p.349/No. 41, No. 43; p.433/No. 23;

R. G. Ojeda: p.275/No. 6;

Jean Schornmans: p.284/No. 23

Sammlung des Instituts für Papyrologie, Universität Heidelberg: p.354/No. 52

In: Sauneron, P/Stierlin, H.: Derniers temples d'Egypte – Edfou et Philae, Paris 1975: p.298/No. 9; p.303/No. 22

Matthias Seidel, Baltimore: p.116/No. 22; p.139/No. 64; p.158/No. 19; p.164/Nr.28; p.165/Nr.31; p.238/No. 175; p.239/No. 176; p.256/No.208; p.295/No. 6; p.324/No. 3; p.441/No. 35; p.445/No. 41; p.493/No. 3; p.507/No. 21; p.521

Ingrid Seipel, Vienna: p.176/No. 55

Seminar für Ägyptologie, Köln: p.486/No. 114 (photo: Gisela Dettloff)

Helmut Schulz, Berlin: p.171/No. 45; p. 256/No. 208; p.369/No. 71; p. 491/No. 2

Regine Schulz, Baltimore: p.161/Nr.24; p.176/Nr.57; p.184/No. 69; Endpaper

Abdel Ghaffar Shedid, München: p.119/No. 24; p.120/No. 25; No. 26, No. 27; p.121/No. 29, No. 30; p.122/No. 31; No. 32; p.123/No. 34; p.124/No. 35; p.125/No. 36, No. 37, No. 38, No. 39; p.126/No. 40, No. 41, No. 42, No. 43; p.127/No. 44; p.128/No. 46–47, No. 48; p.129/No. 50, No. 51; p.223/No. 141; p.256/No. 209; p.263/No. 226; p.283/No. 20; No. 21; p.337/No. 22; p.380/No. 87; p.393/No. 109; p.434/No. 24; p.436/No. 29

In: Smith, G. E.: The Royal Mummies, Cairo 1912: p.464/No. 67

In: Smith, W.: The Art and Architecture of Ancient Egypt, London 1958: p.396/ No. 116

Hourig Sourouzian, Cairo: p.166/Nr.35; p.167/Nr.36; p.169/No. 40, No. 41; p.170/No. 42; p.171/No. 45; p.173/No. 49–50; p.180/Nr.62; p.191/No. 81; p.192/No. 82, No. 83; p.193/No. 85, No. 86; p.195/Nr.88; p.196/No. 90; p.197/No. 92;

p.198/No. 93, No. 94; p.199/Nr.96; p.204/No. 105; p.205/Nr.106; p.206/No. 108, No. 110; p.207/No. 113; p.211/No. 120; p.213/No. 125, No. 126; p.525

Staatliches Museum Ägyptischer Kunst, München: p.261/No. 222; Leihgabe der Bayrischen Landesbank: p.289/No. 35; p.333/No. 13; p.347/No. 36; p.367/No. 64; p.422/No. 9; p.436/No. 28

In: Stadelmann, R.: Die Ägyptischen Pyramiden, Vom Ziegelbau zum Weltwunder, Mainz 1985: p.109/No. 8

In: Stadelmann, R.: Die Ägyptischen Pyramiden, Vom Ziegelbau zum Weltwunder, Mainz 1991: p.37/No. 54; p.48/Nr. 9; p.59/No. 25; p.63/No. 33, No. 36; p.68/ No. 45

Rainer Stadelmann, Cairo: Originalgrafik: p.69/No. 50

Rainer Stadelmann, Cairo: p.48/No. 10; p.50/No. 15; p.51/No. 16, No. 19; p.53/No. 21; p.54–55/No.20a; p.57/No. 23; p.58/No. 24; p.59/No. 26, No. 27; p.60/No. 28–30; p.61/No. 31; p.63/No. 35; p.64/No. 38; p.67/No. 43; p.71/No. 53; p.73/No. 59; p.75/No. 61; p.109/No. 7; p.111/No. 12; p.113/No. 15; p.114/No. 19; p.115/No. 21

Städtische Kunsthalle, Recklinghausen, Ikonen-Museum : p.115/No. 20;

In: Tausing, G.: Nefertari – Eine Dokumentation der Wandgemälde ihres Grabes, Graz 1971 (Taf. 6): p.244/No. 187

Frank Teichmann, Stuttgart: p.209/No. 117, No. 118; p.221/No. 139; p.222/No. 140; Frontispiz

Claude Traunecker, Straßburg: p.304/No. 25

Uni-Dia-Verlag, Großhesselohe: p.25/No. 29; p.31/No. 43; p.49/No. 13; p.115/No. 20; p.334/No. 15; p.482/No. 108;

Universitätskrankenhaus-Eppendorf, Hamburg: p.462/No. 65

A. A. Van Heyden, Naarden: p.314/No. 47;

Victoria and Albert Museum, London: p.403/No. 126

The Walters Art Museum, Baltimore: p.273/No.4; p.288/No. 32-33

In: Wendorf, F.: Prehistory of the Nile Valley, London 1976: p.11/No. 5

Joachim Willeitner, München: p.67/No. 42; p.156/Nr.15; p.166/No. 33; p.211/No. 121; p.212/No. 123; p.215/No. 128–130; p.218/No. 132; p.247/No. 191; p.265/No. 228; p.277/No. 8; p.278/No. 10; p.279/No. 11; p.281/No. 16, No. 17; p.282/No. 19; p.286/No. 27; p.287/No. 30; p.299/No. 11; p.300/No. 13; p.301/No. 15; p.302/No. 18, No. 19; p.303/No. 21; p.304/No. 24; p.307/No. 32; p.308/No. 37, No. 38; p.309/No. 40–42; p.313/No. 46; p.314/No. 48/49; p.315/No. 50; p.316/No. 51/52; p.317/No. 54; p.318/No. 59; p.337/No. 23; p.369/No. 71; p.451/No. 46, No. 47; p.452/No. 49; p.454/No. 51, No. 52; p.455/No. 53, No. 54; p.456/No. 55, No. 56; p.457/No. 57, No. 58

Stefan Wimmer, München: p.352/No. 45

Erich Winter, Trier: p.307/No. 33

M. Ziermann, Köln: Originalgrafik p.34/No. 51

FRONTISPIECE:
King Horemheb before Deities
Valley of the Kings, Horemheb's Tomb, New Kingdom,
Eighteenth Dynasty, ca. 1300 BC
The ruler is depicted between the goddess Isis (at left) and the
jackal-headed god Anubis, to whom he offers a sacrifice.

ENDPAPER:
The temple of Luxor
Much space in the monumental work *Description de l'Égypte* (copperplate engraving :
Paris 1809–1822) is devoted to the monuments of antique Thebes. This page shows the
large entrance pylons of the temple of Luxor with both obelisks and two colossal seated figures
of Ramesses II (New Kingdom, Nineteenth Dynasty, ca. 1260 BC).
Striking is also the dense post-antiquity building on the temple site.

Dust jacket, front:
Gold mask of Tutankhamun
(see pages 234/5, nos. 164/5)

The famous mask covering the mummy of the young pharaoh is of beaten, thick-sheet gold;
the details are inlaid with colored paste and various precious stones. "Gold is the flesh
of the gods": probably no other Egyptian work of art illustrates this concept better than the mask of Tutankhamun.

Dust jacket, spine:
Scarab pendant
(see page 239, no. 176)

Dust jacket, back:
The goddess Selket
(see page 236, no. 166)

This gilded figure of Selket stood with three other goddesses outside the canopic shrine
of Tutankhamun, arms outstretched to protect the vital organs of the king.

© 2004 Tandem Verlag GmbH
KÖNEMANN is a trademark and an imprint of Tandem Verlag GmbH

Idea and concept: Ludwig Könemann
Art director and design: Peter Feierabend
Project coordinator: Ute E. Hammer
Assistant: Jeanette Fentroß
Picture research: Barbara Linz

Original title: *Ägypten. Die Welt der Pharaonen*
ISBN-10: 3-8331-1037-6
ISBN-13: 978-3-8331-1037-5

© 2007 for this edition:
Tandem Verlag GmbH
h.f.ullmann is an imprint of Tandem Verlag GmbH
Special edition

Translation from German: Helen Atkins, Peter Barton, Anthea Bell,
Peter Black, Jacqueline Guigui-Stolberg, Pieter Hos,
Tobias Kommerell, Iain Macmillan
Editor: Dr. Peter Der Manuelian, Boston
Project manager: Bettina Kaufmann
Assistants: Jackie Dobbyne, Stephan Küffner
Cover design: Peter Feierabend

The usage rights for the images attributed to Könemann Verlagsgesellschaft mbH, Köln in the picture credits
lie with Tandem Verlag GmbH, Königswinter.

Printed in China
ISBN 978-3-8331-3271-1

10 9 8 7 6 5 4 3 2 1
X IX VIII VII VI V IV III II I

The publisher would like to thank all participating researchers and institutes
for their gracious cooperation, and above all both editors of the original edition,
Prof. Regine Schulz and Dr. Matthias Seidel for their untiring
and active advice and support.